To Alex , my muse

Transnational Crime, Crime Control and Security

Series editors:
Anastassia Tsoukala, University of Paris XI, France
James Sheptycki, York University, Canada

Editorial board:

Peter Andreas, Brown University, USA, **Vida Bajc**, Flagler College, USA, **Benjamin Bowling**, King's College London, UK, **Stanley Cohen**, London School of Economics and Political Science, UK, **Andrew Dawson**, University of Melbourne, Australia, **Benoît Dupont**, University of Montreal, Canada, **Nicholas Fyfe**, University of Dundee, UK, **Andrew Goldsmith**, University of Wollongong, Australia, **Kevin Haggerty**, University of Alberta, Canada, **Jef Huysmans**, Open University, UK, **Robert Latham**, York University, Canada, **Stéphane Leman-Langlois**, Laval University, Canada, **Michael Levi**, Cardiff University, UK, **Monique Marks**, University of KwaZulu-Natal, South Africa, **Valsamis Mitsilegas**, Queen Mary, University of London, UK, **Ethan Nadelmann**, Drug Policy Alliance, USA, **John Torpey**, CUNY Graduate Center, New York, USA, **Federico Varese**, University of Oxford, UK.

Titles include:

Jude McCulloch and Sharon Pickering (*editors*)
BORDERS AND TRANSNATIONAL CRIME
Pre-Crime, Mobility and Serious Harm in an Age of Globalization

Georgios Papanicolaou
TRASNATIONAL POLICING AND SEX TRAFFICKING IN SOUTHEAST EUROPE
Policing the Imperialist Chain

Leanne Weber and Sharon Pickering (*editors*)
GLOBALIZATION AND BORDERS
Death at the Global Frontier

Linda Zhao
FINANCING ILLEGAL MIGRATION
Chinese Underground Banks and Human Smuggling in New York City

Transnational Crime, Crime Control and Security
Series Standing Order ISBN 978–0–230–28945–1 hardback
978–0–230–28946–8 paperback
(outside North America only)

You can receive future titles in this series as they are published by placing a standing order. Please contact your bookseller or, in case of difficulty, write to us at the address below with your name and address, the title of the series and one of the ISBNs quoted above.

Customer Services Department, Macmillan Distribution Ltd, Houndmills, Basingstoke, Hampshire RG21 6XS, England

Surveilling and Securing the Olympics

From Tokyo 1964 to London 2012 and Beyond

Edited by

Vida Bajc
Flagler College, USA

First published 2016 by
PALGRAVE MACMILLAN

Palgrave Macmillan in the UK is an imprint of Macmillan Publishers Limited,
registered in England, company number 785998, of Houndmills, Basingstoke,
Hampshire RG21 6XS.

Palgrave Macmillan in the US is a division of St Martin's Press LLC,
175 Fifth Avenue, New York, NY 10010.

Palgrave Macmillan is the global academic imprint of the above companies
and has companies and representatives throughout the world.

Palgrave® and Macmillan® are registered trademarks in the United States,
the United Kingdom, Europe and other countries.

ISBN: 978–0–230–28955–0

This book is printed on paper suitable for recycling and made from fully
managed and sustained forest sources. Logging, pulping and manufacturing
processes are expected to conform to the environmental regulations of the
country of origin.

A catalogue record for this book is available from the British Library.

A catalog record for this book is available from the Library of Congress.

Contents

Part III Conclusion

List of Illustrations

Figures

Tables

Preface

This book is a team effort to articulate a coherent theoretical and empirical approach toward a historically and comparatively informed understanding of how surveillance and security have served as a means to cope with the increasing complexity of the Olympic Games. Security meta-ritual is outlined as a theoretical framework, while historical and comparative team ethnography is proposed as a research method. The book is divided into multiple sections.

The Prologue invites theorist and ethnographer of public events Don Handelman to reflect on this research agenda. His essay draws connections between an insistence on equality and competition for the Olympic athletes and a preoccupation with exactness of measurement and controlled outcomes through continuous and systematic surveillance of athletic performance. He points out that this surveillance of the athletes is based on that bureaucratic ethos on which the modern Olympics were founded. Surveillance helps to uphold the venerable Olympic values and their motto *Citius – Altius – Fortius* (Faster – Higher – Stronger) and provides a supporting structure to the quest for security against interruptions of the staging of the Games. In this way, surveillance is foundational to the Olympics, yet interestingly very much misunderstood. Surveillance for the purposes of exactness of measurement of outcomes in competitions is so accepted and taken for granted that it is not even seen as surveillance. In contrast, surveillance in the name of security is assumed to be an intrusion that is necessary to protect the Games from disruption but must not interfere with their festivities. Handelman offers insights into this confusion by drawing on the literary work of French novelist Georges Perec for inspiration.

Following the Prologue are two introductory essays. Vida Bajc, the book's editor, outlines historical and comparative team ethnography as a research method and explicates security meta-ritual as a new form of social control, which has morphed in the context of global planned events through the nexus between surveillance technologies and techniques and security concerns. The surveillance–security nexus emerges through efforts to reduce the complexity of such events in the hope of being able to tame their uncertainty. Complexity of the Olympics stems from two sources: the organizational structure of the Games; and their actual performance in a particular time period and geographical location. A set of variables is articulated to analyze how security meta-ritual of the Olympic Games has historically emerged as a form of control of uncertainty. When the public is made aware that preparations for the Olympics are underway, there is a shift of local and international attention to the host city and country, including through public protests and critical journalism, all of which tend to push security to the forefront. Official and public discourses draw on references to collective memories of violent disruptions in collective public life in the past. Institutions of public order have their own memories of such disruptions, using them as knowledge to envision protective measures. These memories support the push for making all possible resources available to ensure a safe Olympics. Everyone and everything related to the Games, including local legislation, is made to cooperate towards this common goal. At the heart of this activity is a purification of social and physical spaces through which the potentially dangerous is separated from what is deemed safe. These practices lead to the creation of sterile zones of safety within which the Olympics are to unfold as planned and without unwanted disruption.

Richard Pound offers insights into ways in which perceptions of surveillance and security have shaped the decision-making of the International Olympic Committee, of which he has been a longtime member, close observer, and decision-maker. The Committee is the sole arbiter in selection of the host city, inclusion of sports in each program, selection of athletes eligible to compete, accreditation of National Olympic Committees, and signing of broadcasting and promotional contracts. Among the numerous dilemmas, conflicts, and paradoxes that accompany this decision-making, one guiding principle takes center stage; namely, to ensure that the Olympics survive and thrive into the future.

The second section considers 15 Olympics as case studies spanning the period between the 1964 Tokyo Winter Games and the 2012 London Summer Games. Each Olympics is situated in its particular cultural, social, political, geographical, and historical circumstances. Detailed empirical evidence was compiled and analyzed for each case with the following in mind: What does security of the Olympics mean in this context? What constitutes its disruption? What kind of surveillance technologies and procedures are put in place to ensure security of the Games? The chapters are cross-referenced to suggest interconnections and show continuities but can also be read at random as each stands as an independent contribution. They are outlined in historical progression for practical reasons of clarity and ease of organization.

The earliest case we consider, the 1964 Tokyo Winter Games, highlights a preoccupation with self-image and its global media representation. Christian Tagsold finds little evidence for concerns with potential disruptions to the security of the Games. The organizers seemed to have been much more focused on how to portray Japanese culture to the world. For this they did not use the occasion to spotlight particularities of local and indigenous culture, as the Olympic values would encourage, but to demonstrate that Japan adhered to Western standards of development and sophistication. To this end, every effort was made to avoid what the West could have perceived as disorderly behavior. Traditional, spontaneous, exuberant elements of folk carnival were curtailed. In their place came the promotion of patriotism and sportsmanship. Participation of the military and police was acknowledged to be central to the success of the Games. As becomes evident in the subsequent chapters, preoccupation with Western perceptions of orderliness and the roles of the military and police toward achieving these standards during the Olympics have been central to concerns regarding security at the Games.

The 1968 Mexico City Games took place during a period of worldwide outbursts of popular discontent, collective mobilization, and public protest. Kevin Witherspoon shows that while the official post-event report makes no mention of security issues or surveillance measures, other empirical evidence suggests that the organizers made use of an extensive network of state institutions with a known history of repression. The push to organize the Games came from the highest-ranking military official in Mexico, who also happened to be the highest-ranking sports official in the country, a member of organizing committees of other high-profile sport events in the region, and an elected official of the International Olympic Committee. Reliance on hyper-powerful individuals for the organization of the Games is another defining feature of this event. The Mexican elites and their supporters were eager to showcase the country, and themselves, to the world, but they were out of touch with the general public and its grievances. Days before the Opening Ceremony, several hundred people died in the central public square in the government's attempt to squash any protest. Foreign reporters and film crews were in the city for the Games, and various media outlets reported on the killings. Yet, decades later, this disruption of the Olympics remains largely forgotten outside of Mexico.

In the history of the Olympics, it is the Munich Games that have come to be widely remembered in this regard. To understand surveillance and security in relation to such disruptions, however, the Winter as well as the Summer Games in 1972 are of interest. The Sapporo Olympics in February faced extensive public protests, yet Kiyoshi Abe found no empirical evidence to suggest that the organizers consulted Mexico City on matters of public dissent. It seems clear, however, that staff was sent for consultation to a number of other cities that had previously organized such global events. This kind of institutional knowledge accumulation later comes to be known as "best practices." Some form of public protest tends to accompany most Olympics. The Sapporo organizers took their own, culturally specific approach to dealing with it. They used mass media to discredit the protesters by accusing them of disrespect for the emperor, an issue of deep concern for the Japanese public. The police conducted raids in the red light district, arrested pickpockets, locked up drug dealers, and surveilled dissenting citizens. These undemocratic activities on the part of the state were faced with little public outrage or debate. Instead, the police was able to successfully claim that it was its pre-emptive surveillance tactics that ensured the safety of the Games.

The organizers of the Summer Games in Munich consulted previous Olympic cities, particularly Rome, Tokyo, and Mexico City, and took advice from organizers of similar events in Asia and South America. Jørn Hansen shows that this institutional memory was used in different ways. Special temporary regulation was put in place in the city of Munich to prohibit the right to demonstrate. Such legislation has become an element of the organization of the Olympics. For culturally specific reasons, however, a heavy military presence was not appealing to the organizers of the Munich Olympics of 1972. They wanted the Games to be open, audience friendly, and clearly disassociated from the militaristic Olympics organized under Hitler in Berlin in 1939. Several days into the Games, eight members of the Palestinian Black September Organization pushed their way into the quarters that housed the Israeli team, killing several and taking others hostage. The act and its failed rescue mission were televised live by a German station and followed by millions around the world. In this decisive moment in the history of the Olympics, the then president of the International Olympic Committee stepped in front of the television cameras and declared to the world that despite the tragic disruption the Games must continue.

Four years later, the same president made it clear to Canadians that ensuring security was their responsibility. The organizers of Montreal 1976, however, were not only concerned about what had happened in Munich. They were also focused on internal political issues, including labor strikes, the nationalism movement in Quebec, and the gay rights movement. Bruce Kidd details how surveillance featured prominently on all fronts. The most advanced military technology was employed in cooperation with special intelligence units, police, and border-crossing agents. Helicopters patrolled in the air, soldiers with automatic weapons and sharpshooters patrolled on the ground, and hidden surveillance cameras and listening devices patrolled the rest. In addition, the most advanced biomedical testing laboratory was set up to surveil athletes for banned substances. This show of force infamously put the city of Montreal into debt for decades.

In their own way, the 1980 Moscow Games, like those in Montreal, were also about security and order, but, as Carol Marmor-Drews shows, this case highlights what it meant to organize a global event of this scope in a society that saw itself as bearing the responsibility of representing to the world an alternative model of social organization. The Moscow organizers hoped that the country would be acknowledged by the Western world as like but different. There was anxiety about the boycott campaign spearheaded by the United States, internal subversive activities with support from outside the country, and the threat of crime, which would be seen to reflect badly on Soviet culture. The acute awareness that the world was watching for any mishap also created high sensitivity to negative representation and critical reporting on the part of the international media. Huge pressure exerted on the organizers through global news reporting becomes more evident in later Olympics. The Soviet state had a policy of tight control of state border crossing as well as restrictions on internal geographic mobility. The International Olympic Committee, however, demanded that the organizers enable free movement within the host cities. The task was enormous as the Games were staged in five cities separated by huge distances. To both meet Western expectations and be able to enforce a crime- and sabotage-free environment, the Moscow organizers resorted to tested and trusted strategies from the past: Stalin era residential policies and community-order policing.

The 1988 Seoul Olympics exposed another Cold War rift – this one between North and South Korea. The push by the military government of South Korea to host the Games in Seoul ignited, in multiple countries, fierce opposition and attempts to derail the plan. Gwang Ok and Kyoung Ho Park show how the Seoul Olympics became an opportunity for a wide-ranging cooperation in matters of surveillance and security between South Korea and its Western supporters, including France, Israel, Japan, the United Kingdom, the United States of America, and West Germany. The allies supplied intelligence, special forces, navy and air force support, and surveillance know-how. South Korea shared all its intelligence on North Korea in exchange for information on international terror suspects, a computer system identifying forged passports, and antiterrorism training with foreign special operations forces. The South Korean military was on full alert and was battle-ready. Personal information on participants at the Olympics was subjected to background checks, and individuals were monitored throughout their stay in South Korea. Thousands of volunteers were trained in surveillance and used to fill up space at competitions and ceremonies. Private computer and software-related companies were commissioned to develop central management systems to oversee all the surveillance activities. These systems are early examples of the search for capacity for a central command and control, which appears to have become one of the most highly priced surveillance technologies and strategies for the Games.

There was much diplomacy and publicity management at work in Spain for the 1992 Barcelona Games. As Stephen Essex argues, the goal was to show to the world and the emerging European Union that Spain had moved beyond its decades-long military-style rule. It was now able to democratically integrate the different interest groups vying for political autonomy and independence, and it was on its way to be prominently positioned as an economically vibrant and modernized state with favorable conditions for international investment. A number of political activists were jailed to prevent disruption, which nevertheless took place but was neglected by the global media and dismissed by the organizers as inconvenient but not threatening to the Games. Those responsible for security had learned from the successful implementation of surveillance in Los Angeles, Calgary, and Seoul and then designed their own model for the Barcelona Games. The Director of Security subsequently acted as adviser for the next four Olympics, demonstrating that experience in dealing with surveillance and security during the Olympics can be highly marketable, and showing an early example of consolidation of the role of security advisers as powerful players in the emerging field of private security expertise of the Olympics.

With little fear of internal political conflict, terrorism, or crime, security did not seem to be a prominent concern for the Norwegian organizers of the 1994 Lillehammer Games. Rather, Ingrid Rudie shows that the public took issue with the conflicting values between the egalitarian tendencies of Norwegian society and the elitist orientation of the Olympics. In response, the organizers opted for surveillance strategies that were to be sufficient but not overshadow the festive atmosphere of the Games. There was free pedestrian movement in the central area of Lillehammer and between the venues. Entry into competition venues and areas for athletes, as well as special guest quarters, were monitored through checkpoints. As a member of a research team, Rudie was accredited with "observer" status, which allowed her to enter only the sports venues directly relevant to her research agenda – and within those venues, only the zones designated for administration and the press. Adjusted to local needs, this accreditation system seems to have become a standardized surveillance strategy on the ground, regardless of where the Games are hosted.

In the United States, the ambition to centrally command and control surveillance procedures during the Olympics is faced with a number of challenges. The federal constitution limits the power of federal agencies over local districts, public sentiment tends to be strongly against federal involvement in municipal affairs, and events such as the Olympics are considered to be private enterprise and therefore not the government's responsibility. With hindsight from the disruption to the 1996 Atlanta Games, and on the heels of 9/11, Sean Varano, George Burruss, and Scott H. Decker show how a series of special legislation, aimed at bypassing constitutional restrictions, allowed the 2002 Salt Lake City Games to be designated as a "National Special Security Event." Through this classification, the United States President or head of the Department of Homeland Security can allocate extraordinary powers by designating certain events and their private infrastructure as nationally significant. This designation permits the use of the military for domestic security, allows for the allocation of federal tax money, and positions the United States Secret Service as the umbrella agency for the implementation of all technologies and techniques of surveillance. Such implementation of extraordinary legislation to enable surveillance at the Olympics has become an integral part of the preparation for the Games.

The case of the 2004 Athens Olympics exposes the workings of vast internationally networked political and economic power structures and their strategies of exerting pressure on a host country. Anastassia Tsoukala illuminates some of these tactics, including shaming Greece for inadequate policing capacities, threatening to boycott the Olympics in the absence of adequate antiterrorism efforts, media reporting strategically aimed at influencing Greek public perceptions of threat, and demands for foreign special forces agents to carry weapons in the state of Greece. These pressures successfully challenged the sovereignty of the Greek state when the host city was forced to purchase, from a consortium of corporations, a state-of-the-art surveillance technology, which was to remain in place after the Olympics to fight terrorism. The system, however, was not delivered by the agreed deadline and, in addition, turned out to be so complex that those parts which were delivered failed to be fully installed in time to be operational for the Games with proper training of personnel. This failure of super technology demonstrated, in fact, that conventional surveillance technologies and techniques were more than sufficient to prevent disruption of the Games.

The case of the 2006 Winter Games allows us to understand the spatial configuration of surveillance. As Alberto Vanolo details, the Olympic zone in Turin was divided into three sections: the urban area; and two mountain regions. Each of the three spaces was further divided into noncompetitive, competitive, and residential areas. Within each of these sub-areas, the space was divided by concentric circles leading toward the central "security ring" isolated by a high fence. Olympic Villages were self-contained spaces with their own daily newspapers, flower shops, convenience stores, hair salons, disco parties, prayer sessions for many faiths, recreation rooms, coffee houses, ballroom dance parties, shopping centers, Broadway shows, live concerts, and birthday celebrations to give the athletes little desire to leave the village. Every village and competitive venue also had a doping control station. Samples were collected daily from randomly selected athletes and delivered to the Olympic laboratory to be analyzed by accredited physicians, and the results were then reported directly to the International Olympic Committee.

The 2008 Beijing Games were conceived as an event of the people, showcasing the culture and heritage of the roughly 50 ethnic groups of the People's Republic of China, at home and in the diaspora. Gladys Pak Lei Chong, Jeroen de Kloet, and Guohua Zeng show, however, that this aim was disrupted by uprisings in Tibet, protests surrounding the Olympic Flame Relay as it traveled around the world, and demonstrations inside China to counter this international response. In the midst of these dynamics, the International Olympic Committee began to publicly pronounce that the Beijing Olympics would be safe and that safety of the Olympics was more important than the competitions, while the organizers turned to the domestic public for support. They began a huge media campaign, using television, radio, street billboards, and posters, asking people to help create a festive and safe Olympics by cooperating, following the rules, and acting as security guards in their own neighborhoods. A public television program aired a feature on the history of surveillance and security in the Olympics, explaining that disruptions such as in Munich 1972 and in the United States on 9/11 prompted a global trend in the use of surveillance technology and techniques to ensure safe Olympics. The public was to accept that a special visa regime was imposed requiring everyone in Beijing, both Chinese and foreign, who was not a resident of the city to register with the local police. Despite these efforts, it seems that in the eyes of the organizers, intentions and behavior of the general public could nevertheless not be unconditionally trusted so, in some venues, specific individuals were recruited as volunteers and trained as audience to replace the public.

Olympic hosts showcase their cities as idealized spaces that are secured and ordered to the liking of global economic, financial, and political elites. How this is achieved is locally specific. Jacqueline Kennelly details how various municipal guidelines tutored the residents of Vancouver for their 2010 Olympics on good manners, pride, and patriotism. Those who were deemed not suitable for such civility, particularly the homeless, the marginalized youth, and other vulnerable populations, were targeted for jaywalking, possession of drugs, loitering, or squatting, and promptly removed from the host city. Others were educated in good behavior. Frowning, for example, was said to convey anger, so the residents were asked to smile. They were informed, however, that exaggerated smiles could come across as artificial or even invite suspicion, so people were asked not to simply smile but to do so with sincerity. Such strategies aimed at purifying the host city of inhabitants whose ways of being are not in line with the image of a wealthy, prosperous, and technologically developed host country have become a part of the process of staging secure Olympics.

The scope and complexity of this ambition to stage secure and perfectly ordered Olympics were on full display in London for its 2012 Summer Olympics. So, too, were the role of the military, the importance of volunteers, and the shortcomings of a reliance on privatization of surveillance and security services. Joseph Bongiovi shows that the enormity of this undertaking was such that a corporate security behemoth, together with thousands of volunteers, a huge police force, a military force larger than that deployed in war zones, and military technology such as missiles positioned on residential rooftops of east Londoners, all struggled to deliver a safe Olympics. A major global security corporation was entrusted with putting together the labor force for the Games. Despite its extensive history of operations in areas as diverse as diplomatic missions, war zones, immigration detention centers, prisons, hospitals, asylum centers, and police stations, the Olympics proved to be a challenge the corporation could not handle. The day before the ceremonial opening of the Games, the company publicly admitted that some 9,000 volunteers were still waiting to be approved and trained for work in the Olympics. At the last hour, additional volunteers were asked to assist and the military was forced to make available several thousand more soldiers to help make safe Olympics happen.

There are local variations in how security meta-ritual, as a form of social control of the Olympic Games, transpires through intensive attention by the mass media and a public dissent directed toward the host country, the workings of collective and institutional memory, the push for mobilization of all possible resources, efforts to make participating institutions and individuals adhere to a centralized authority, purification of social and physical spaces, and the nature of the sterile zone of safety created through this process. The symbolic meaning of this activity seems nevertheless to have crystallized with the message: If there is the ambition to stage the Olympics, this is how it is done safely.

The secure social order which emerges through this process is a challenge to the values espoused by the Olympic Games and the democratic principles of social organization. This is a large-scale, maximally controlled social and physical environment in which social complexity, ambiguity, and uncertainty are controlled through hierarchy, exclusion, and authoritarian decision-making. The book concludes with an artistic rendering of these Olympic dilemmas by cartoonist Bruce Beattie. The editor, Vida Bajc, in turn, offers her reflection on ways in which this experience of delivering secure Olympics on the part of the host country may reverberate in everyday life well beyond the event itself with potentially lasting transformations in multiple domains of society.

Acknowledgments

The opportunity to begin to develop this idea of a historical and comparative analysis of surveillance and security in the Olympics into a book became possible during my Postdoctoral Fellowship at the Surveillance Studies Centre at Queen's University in Kingston, Canada. I am most indebted to the contributing authors for their endless patience in closely working with me on their chapters. As in my other writings, Don Handelman's contribution remains indispensable.

Assembling the team of contributors was a lesson in and of itself, as was the processing of the immense amount of information to which this project exposed me. John MacAloon's *Schnellkurs* in poetics and politics of the Olympic scholarship and its academic circles was invaluable to get the project started. Help to locate contributors, review chapter drafts, share insights about the topic, or provide encouragement along the way came across continents. This includes colleagues who are familiar with my work and others whom I met over e-mail and through phone conversations: Julia Adams, Elijah Anderson, Peter Andreas, Sarah Babb, Alan Bairner, Robert Barney, Didier Bigo, Michał Buchowski, Diana Crane, Eyal Ben-Ari, Philip Boyle, Susan Brownell, Elaine Carey, Jean-Loup Chappelet, Simon Coleman, Daniel Dayan, Robert Edelman, Volker Eich, Henning Eichberg, Tamar El-Or, Ivan Ermakoff, Jackie Feldman, Gary Alan Fine, Chiara Fonio, Andreas Glaeser, Judith Grant Long, Hugh Gusterson, Allen Guttmann, Kevin Haggerty, Lisa Hajjar, Douglas Hartmann, Harry Hiller, Richard Hobbs, Peter Horton, Marc Jacobs, Hochan Jang, Steven Kaplan, Elihu Katz, Barbara Keys, Eunha Koh, Vladimir Kudriavtsev, Charles Kurzman, James Larson, Yagil Levy, Wojciech Lipoński, Wolfram Manzenreiter, John Levi Martin, Martha McIntosh, Brian J. McVeigh, Juan Díez Medrano, Evelyn Mertin, Sirio Modugno, Andreas Niehaus, Pál Nyiri, Midori Ogasawara, Serguei Oushakine, Jenifer Parks, Andrew Perrin, Oriol Pi-Sunyer, Maurice Roche, Minas Samatas, Magali Sarfatti Larson, Saskia Sassen, Joseph Schafer, David Segal, Philip Smith, Ori Swed, Greg Swedberg, John Torpey, Robin Wagner-Pacifici, Christopher Young, and Leif Yttergren.

Illustrations are an important part of the way this book tries to communicate with the reader. Bruce Beattie, Steve Nease, and Terry Mosher have graciously agreed to have their cartoons reproduced, as Steve Nease put it in his e-mail, to "pay it forward ... do a favor for someone else someday." So it will be. In the same spirit, Andrey Krilov's cartoon is in the public domain because it was published in the Russian satirical magazine *Krokodil* prior to 1991. I am also grateful to the Herblock Foundation and Daniel Necas from the Immigration History Research Center and Archives at the University of Minnesota, for locating Edmund Valtman's cartoon, which, unfortunately, could not be reproduced in this book. Gregory Oliveri helped with the final version of the Olympics' table.

Scott H. Decker, Bruce Kidd, Richard Pound, and Ingrid Rudie enthusiastically embraced the idea for the front cover and shared images of their identity cards. Pound also facilitated communication with the International Olympic Committee for permission to reproduce. Purmina Swaharu gave advice on the early drafts. The final version of the front cover came to life with the help of J.R. Osborn.

A Fulbright Fellowship at the Institute of Ethnology and Cultural Anthropology at Adam Mickiewicz University in Poznan, Poland, made it possible to bring this project to completion. My introductory chapter benefited from multiple audiences at Adam Mickiewicz University, as well as Goethe University Frankfurt, Jagiellonian University, Heinrich Heine University Düsseldorf, Kazimierz Wielki University, Technical University Berlin, The Hebrew University of Jerusalem, and the University of Southern Denmark. An earlier version of the introduction was shared with colleagues at the University of North Carolina at Chapel Hill.

A project of this scope is best accomplished when course release and grant support are available to organize a conference where ideas can be collectively shared and developed. Short of such resources, some of us had an opportunity to meet in person at the sessions I organized on the topic at the American Anthropological Association meetings in Montreal in November 2011 and at the Eastern Sociological Society meetings in New York in February 2012. My undergraduate students at Methodist University in Fayetteville, North Carolina, many with first-hand experience from the United States Special Operations Forces, read the drafts with great interest and unique insight. Laurice Mitchell provided secretarial assistance. Series editors Anastassia Tsoukala and James Sheptycki and Palgrave Macmillan's editorial team helped to complete the process.

Notes on Contributors

Kiyoshi Abe is a professor at the Graduate School of Sociology at Kwansei Gakuin University, Nishinomiya, Japan. His works in English include "Everyday Policing in Japan: Surveillance, Media, Government and Public Opinion," *International Sociology*, 19(2) (2004); "The Myth of Media Interactivity: Technology, Communications and Surveillance in Japan," *Theory, Culture & Society*, 26(2–3) (2009); and "The Spectacle of Fear: Anxious Mega-events and Contradictions of Contemporary Japanese Governmentality" (with David Murakami Wood) in C. Bennett and K. Haggerty (Eds) *Security Games Surveillance and Control at Mega-Events* (2011). His research interest is in critical sociology of media and communication in relation to changing political conditions in postwar Japanese society. His focus is on how new information and communication technologies, including surveillance, shape social change. Currently, he is investigating the sociocultural conditions of globalized surveillance society in relation to the transformation of the public sphere (kiyabe922@gmail.com).

Vida Bajc is Visiting Associate Professor of Sociology at Flagler College, St. Augustine, Florida, United States, and a 2013/14 Fulbright Fellow at Adam Mickiewicz University, Poznan, Poland. Her empirical research is focused on global events; surveillance, security and privacy in collective public life; pilgrimage and holy cities; and Christians in Jerusalem. Her theoretical interests are focused on the relationship between ordering practices and uncertainty. She is the coeditor (with Willem de Lint) of *Security and Everyday Life* (2011). She is the editor of three journal special issues: "Watching Out: Surveillance, Security, and Mobility" (with John Torpey) for the *American Behavioral Scientist*, 50(12) (2007); "(Dis)Placing the Center: Pilgrimage in a Mobile World" (with Simon Coleman and John Eade) for *Mobilities*, 2(3) (2007); and "Collective Memory and Tourism" for *Journeys: The International Journal of Travel and Travel Writing*, 7(2) (2006). She is currently completing *Christian Pilgrimage in Jerusalem: Performing Social Realities*, based on years of ongoing ethnographic research in Jerusalem (vida.bajc@gmail.com).

Joseph R. Bongiovi is a PhD candidate in the Department of Sociology at the University of North Carolina, Chapel Hill, North Carolina, United States. He graduated from Cornell University with a Master's in Industrial and Labor Relations, and from the University of Notre Dame with a BA in Government and International Studies and Spanish. He is the Assistant Director of Undergraduate Studies and an adviser for the Management and Society major at the University of North Carolina at Chapel Hill, where he also teaches courses on organizations and work. His doctoral dissertation is a study of private military and security companies as the emergence of a new organizational population. He was a research assistant for the Mellon Foundation Sawyer Seminar on Precarious Work in Asia. He served in the US Army as an infantry officer and military historian from 1985 to 1989, and worked as a global human resources executive for a number of organizations. He is a fellow of the Inter-University Seminar on Armed Forces and Society (bongiovi@live.unc.edu).

George W. Burruss is an associate professor and Graduate Program Director in the Department of Criminology and Criminal Justice, Southern Illinois University Carbondale, Carbondale, Illinois, United States. He is the author of "The Questionable Advantage of Defense Counsel in Juvenile Court" (with Kimberly Kempf-Leonard), *Justice Quarterly* (2002), and "A Stone's Throw from the Metropolis: Re-examining Small-Agency Homeland Security Practices" (with Matthew Giblin and Joseph Schafer), *Justice Quarterly* (2012). His main research focus is on criminal justice organizations – recently on how US law enforcement agencies respond to homeland security matters. He also has research interests in cybercrime and white-collar crime (gburruss@siu.edu).

Gladys Pak Lei Chong is Assistant Professor of Liberal and Cultural Studies in the Department of Humanities and Creative Writing at Hong Kong Baptist University. Her doctoral research examines processes of subjectification and the interplay between technologies of domination and technologies of the self. She has written on Chinese governmentality, cultural governance, gender, placemaking, and Olympics security. Her research interests include Chinese youth, power relations, globalization, nationalism, gender, and the politics of identity (gladyschong@hkbu.edu.hk).

Scott H. Decker is Foundation Professor in the School of Criminology and Criminal Justice, Arizona State University, Phoenix, Arizona, United States. He is coauthor (with Margaret Townsend Chapman) of *Drug Smugglers on Drug Smuggling: Lessons from the Inside* (2008) and *Confronting Gangs: Crime and Community* (with G. David Curry and David C. Pyrooz, 2014). He is a fellow in the American Society of Criminology and the Academy of Criminal Justice Sciences. His main research interests are in the areas of gangs, criminal justice policy, and the offender's perspective with the focus on drug use, violence, and desistance. He is currently involved in a study of gang desistance and the use of technology, funded by Google Ideas. His study of gang member reentry is funded by the National Institute of Justice. He has worked with teams to study the provision of security at the 1996 Atlanta and 2002 Salt Lake City Olympic Games (Scott.Decker@asu.edu).

Stephen Essex is an associate professor (reader) in the School of Geography, Earth and Environmental Sciences at Plymouth University, UK. His research interests are in urban and rural planning, and tourism. His joint papers with Brian Chalkley, "Urban Development through Hosting International Events: A History of the Olympic Games," *Planning Perspectives*, 14(4) (1999); and "Mega-Sporting Events in Urban and Regional Policy: A History of the Winter Olympics," *Planning Perspectives*, 19(2) (2004), analyzed the infrastructural implications of staging the Summer and Winter Olympic Games respectively. Other research is focused on the importance of networks on the decision-making and outcomes of planning processes during post-Second World War reconstruction plans in the UK, particularly "Vision, Vested Interest and Pragmatism: Who Re-made Britain's Blitzed Cities?" *Planning Perspectives*, 22(4) (2007); and "Boldness Diminished? The Post War Battle to Replan a Bomb-Damaged Provincial City," *Urban History*, 35(3) (2008) (both with Mark Brayshay) (sessex@plymouth.ac.uk).

Don Handelman is Shaine Professor Emeritus of Anthropology at The Hebrew University, Jerusalem, and is a member of the Israel Academy of Sciences and Humanities. He has done fieldwork in Nevada, Newfoundland, South India, and Israel. His research interests include cosmology, ritual, play, nonlinearity, and bureaucratic logic. Among his published works are *Models and Mirrors: Towards an Anthropology of Public Events* (2nd ed., 1998); *Nationalism and the Israeli State: Bureaucratic Logic in Public Events* (2004); and *One God, Two Goddesses: Three Studies of South Indian Cosmology* (2014). With David Shulman, he coauthored *God Inside Out: Siva's Game of Dice* (1997); and *Siva in the Forest of Pines: An Essay on Sorcery and Self-Knowledge* (2004). With Galina Lindquist, he coedited *Ritual in Its Own Right: Exploring the Dynamics of Transformation* (2005); and *Religion, Politics, and Globalization: Anthropological Approaches* (2011), and with T.M.S. Evans, he coedited *The Manchester School: Practice and Ethnographic Praxis in Anthropology* (2005) (mshand@mscc.huji.ac.ili).

Jørn Hansen is a professor at the Institute of Sports Science and Clinical Biomechanics, University of Southern Denmark, Odense, Denmark. He was Head of the Institute (1993–2000) and a member of the Academic Council for the Faculty of Health (2001–2012). He is Head of Research Group: Movement, Culture and Society. His recent published works in English include "The 1912 Olympic Games in Stockholm – The First Meeting of the Highly Trusted Men and What Happened to Them Since," *International Journal of the History of Sport*, 31(5): 542–556 (2014); "Playing on the Same Side: Danish Sporting Collaboration and the Recognition of East Germany," *Revue D'Histoire Nordique/Nordic Historical Review*, 13: 109–126 (2012); "The Institutionalization of Team Denmark" in *Nordic Elite Sport: Same Ambitions – Different Tracks*, Svein, Andersen, Tore (Eds), Universitetsforlaget Oslo (2012); and "The Olympics in Beijing – Moral Arguments Defeated by the Market?" *International Journal of Eastern Sports & Physical Education*, 8(2) (2010). His research interests include history of health and social, historical and political

xxii *Notes on Contributors*

aspects of sports with the focus on Germany, Denmark, the Olympics, and soccer (jhansen@health.sdu.dk).

Jacqueline Kennelly is an associate professor in the Department of Sociology and Anthropology at Carleton University, Ottawa, Canada. She is the author of *Citizen Youth: Culture, Activism, and Agency in a Neoliberal Era* (Palgrave Macmillan, 2011) and coauthor (with Jo-Anne Dillabough) of *Lost Youth in the Global City: Class, Culture, and the Urban Imaginary* (2010). Her research interests encompass youth cultures, social movements, gentrification, homelessness, social exclusion, citizenship, and democracy. She is currently completing *These Games Are for You: Olympic Games, Social Legacies and Marginalized Youth*, which describes the experiences of homeless and marginally housed youth in two Olympic host cities, Vancouver (2010 Winter Games) and London (2012 Summer Games) (jacqueline_kennelly@carleton.ca).

Bruce Kidd is Vice President and Principal, University of Toronto Scarborough and a professor in the Faculty of Kinesiology and Physical Education. He teaches and writes about the history and political economy of Canadian and international sport and physical activity. He has authored numerous books, articles, lectures, plays, film and radio scripts. His *The Struggle for Canadian Sport* (1996) won the Book Prize of the North American Society for Sport History in 1997. His most recent book is *Critical Support for Sport* (2014), a collection of previously published essays and research reports. He has been involved in the Olympic Movement throughout his life, as an athlete (track and field, 1964), journalist (1976), contributor to the arts and culture programs (1976 and 1988) and accredited social scientist (1988 and 2000). He was founding chair of the Olympic Academy of Canada (1983–1993), lectures at the International Olympic Academy and is an honorary member of the Canadian Olympic Committee. He has served on many advisory and governing bodies in Canadian and international sport and currently chairs the Selection Committee of Canada's Sports Hall of Fame (bruce.kidd@utoronto.ca).

Jeroen de Kloet is Professor of Globalisation Studies and Director of the Amsterdam Centre for Globalisation Studies at the University of Amsterdam, the Netherlands. His work focuses on cultural globalization, particularly in the context of East Asia. He is the author of *China with a Cut – Globalisation, Urban Youth and Popular Music* (2010). With Yiu Fai Chow, he coauthored *Sonic Multiplicities: Hong Kong Pop and the Global Circulation of Sound and Image* (2013), and with Lena Scheen, he coedited *Spectacle and the City – Chinese Urbanities in Art and Popular Culture* (2013) (b.j.dekloet@uva.nl).

Carol Marmor-Drews is a research associate and a PhD student in the Department of Recent and Modern East European History at the University

Passau, Germany. She completed her MA in 2010 in the East European Studies Program at the Ludwig-Maximilian University Munich on the topic "Tallinn – Our Hometown: The Olympic Sailing Regatta as an Integrative Project of Late Socialism in the Estonian Soviet Socialist Republic." Her doctoral dissertation is titled "The Olympic Summer Games of Participation: Dependences and Affiliations in the Imperial Project 'Olimpiada-80.'" Her research interests are in the relationship between participation in Olympic sports, national/local identity, and state politics. She has a number of publications in German on culture, collective memory, nationality issues, and State Socialism in the Baltic States (carolmarmor@yahoo.co.uk).

Gwang Ok is an associate professor at Chungbuk National University, Director of External Affairs, Korean Society for the Study of Physical Education, regional board editor of the *International Journal of the History of Sport* and *Asia Pacific Journal of Sport and Social Science*. His articles have appeared in the *International Journal of the History of Sport, Korean Journal of Physical Education, Recreation and Dance,* and *Korean Journal of Physical Education*. His works in English include the monograph *The Transformation of Modern Korean Sport: Imperialism, Nationalism, Globalization* (2007) and chapters respectively in the *Olympics in East Asia: Nationalism, Regionalism, and Globalism on the Center Stage of World Sports* (W. W. Kelly and S. Brownell, Eds, 2011) and *Korean Leisure: From Tradition to Modernity* (E. Dong and J. Yi-Kook, Eds., 2010). He is coeditor, with J. A. Mangan and Sandra Collins, of *The Triple Asian Olympics: Asia Rising – The Pursuit of National Identity, International Recognition and Global Esteem* (2012) (gwangok@yahoo.com).

Kyoung Ho Park is a research professor at Jeju National University, Jeju, South Korea. His article on the 1988 Seoul Olympic Games appeared in the *International Journal of the History of Sport* in 2011. His articles have appeared in Korean journals. He serves as Secretary of Editing for both *Korean Journal of Golf Studies* and Korean Alliance of Martial Arts. He also serves as an advisor for the National Unification Advisory Council of Korea (kyongho1@hanmail.net).

Richard W. Pound, a lawyer and chartered professional accountant, was educated at McGill University and Sir George Williams (now Concordia) University, both in Montreal, Canada. He has served as Chair of the Board of Governors of McGill University and as Chancellor and is currently Chancellor Emeritus. He is the author of several books, including *Inside the Olympics, a Behind-the-Scenes Look at the Politics, the Scandals, and the Glory of the Games* (2004); and *Five Rings over Korea: The Secret Negotiations Behind the 1988 Olympic Games in Seoul* (1994). A former Olympic swimmer, he served as secretary (1968–1977) and president (1977–1982) of the Canadian Olympic Committee and has been a member of the International Olympic Committee since 1978. He served on the IOC Executive Board (1983–2001), including two terms as vice president. He was responsible for television negotiations for all Olympic Games from 1988 until the 2008 Olympic Games in Beijing and was Chair of the IOC Marketing Commission. He was the founding president of the World Anti-Doping Agency (1999–2007). He is Chairman of Olympic Broadcast Services, an executive member of the International Society of Olympic Historians, and serves on the International Council of Arbitration for Sport (RPound@stikeman.com).

Ingrid Rudie is Professor Emerita at the University of Oslo, Norway. She has been conducting fieldwork in Malaysia since the mid-1960s on local organization, gender, and personhood. She is the author of *Visible Women in East Coast Malay Society* (1994). An earlier article, "Household Organisation: Adaptive Process and Restrictive Form," *Folk*, 11–12: 185–200 (1969/70) was a seminal contribution to household and family studies. She also studies methodology, particularly how communication between the researchers themselves and with those whom they study is manifested in the published works by the researchers and in the life world of the research subjects. These interests are reflected in several works, including "A Hall of Mirrors: Translating Gender over Time in Malaysia" in *Gendered Fields* (Bell, Caplan and Karim, Eds, 1993) and a joint publication with a Malaysian colleague who conducted a new and differently focused research in the same locality: "Translating Gender through Time and Theories: A Case Study of Living, Thinking and Rethinking" in *Gendered Entanglements* (Lund, Doneys and Resurrección, Eds, NIAS Press, forthcoming). She was part of the team of ethnographic researchers who conducted group fieldwork on the 1994 Lillehammer Olympics (ingridr@ulrik.uio.no).

Christian Tagsold is Associate Professor of Modern Japanese Studies at the Heinrich Heine University, Düsseldorf, Germany. His research topics include sports mega-events, Japanese welfare and aging, Japanese diaspora communities in Europe, and Japanese gardens in the West. His doctoral dissertation, "The Staging of Cultural Identity in Japan: The Olympics Games Tôkyô 1964," received a special award at the 2nd Academic Competition of the National Olympic Committee of Germany in 2001 and was published by Iudicium (2002). His habilitation, "Spaces of Translation: Japanese Gardens in the West" (written in English), received the JaDe-award of the Foundation for the Promotion of Japanese-German Cultural and Scientific Relations in 2012. He was a member of the Local Organizing Committee for the FIFA World Cup Germany 2006 and the FIFA Women's World Cup Germany 2011, working as team liaison officer for the Japanese national football teams (tagsold@phil.hhu.de).

Anastassia Tsoukala is Professor of Criminology at the University Paris 11 and a senior researcher at the University Paris 5 (Sorbonne), Paris, France. She is assistant editor of French political science quarterly *Cultures &*

Conflicts and editor of the book series *Transnational Crime, Crime Control, and Security* for Palgrave Macmillan. She is involved in the design and implementation of European security policies in relation to football hooliganism, counterterrorism, immigration, and social construction of threat. She is the author of *Football Hooliganism in Europe: Security and Civil Liberties in the Balance* (Palgrave Macmillan, 2009) and coeditor (with Didier Bigo) of *Terror, Insecurity and Liberty: Illiberal Practices of Liberal Regimes after 9/11* (2008) (tsoukala.anastassia@gmail.com).

Alberto Vanolo is Associate Professor of Politico-economic Geography in the Department of Culture, Politics and Society at the University of Turin, Italy. He has authored a number of books in Italian on the topic of human economic geography. He is coauthor (with Ugo Rossi) of *Urban Political Geographies: A Global Perspective* (2012) and is currently writing a book on city branding and the politics of urban representations. His research is focused on urban geography with a particular interest in politics of the creative city, urban branding, representations, gender, and globalization (alberto.vanolo@unito.it).

Sean P. Varano is an associate professor in the School of Justice Studies at Roger Williams University, Bristol, Rhode Island, United States. His recent publications include "Fear of Crime, Incivilities, and Collective Efficacy in Four Miami Neighborhoods" (with Craig Uchida, Marc Swatt, and Shellie Solomon), "Street Outreach as an Intervention Modality for At-Risk and Gang-Involved Youth" (with Russell Wolff), and "Correlates and Consequences of Pre-incarceration Gang Involvement among Incarcerated Youthful Felons" (with Beth Huebner and Timothy Bynum). His research interests include juvenile justice policy, violent crime reduction strategies, gang violence, police technology, and program evaluation (svarano@rwu.edu).

Kevin B. Witherspoon is Associate Professor of History and Chair of the Department of History and Philosophy, Lander University, Greenwood, South Carolina, United States. His book *Before the Eyes of the World: Mexico and the 1968 Olympics* (2008) won the 2009 North American Society for Sport History annual Book Award. His current research is focused on the US–Soviet sports rivalry during the Cold War. He is particularly interested in sporting exchanges between the United States and the Soviet Union and has also written about men's and women's basketball in this era. He is currently working on a book provisionally titled *Sport in the Cold War: A Short History with Documents*. He runs courses on US and Latin American history. In 2009, he was awarded the Young Faculty Scholar award at Lander University, and in 2014 was recognized with Lander's Distinguished Faculty award. He recently served as Program Director for the Teaching American History in the Lakelands program, a four-year federal grant (kwitherspoon@lander.edu).

Guohua Zeng is an assistant researcher (assistant professor) at the Institute of Journalism and Communication, Chinese Academy of Social Sciences, Beijing, China. His research interests include political communication, popular culture, social class, new media, and China. His ongoing project focuses on the limits of ICT empowerment and their impacts on social change in China (zeng.guohua.01@gmail.com).

Part I
Introduction

Prologue: Olympic Surveillance as a Prelude to Securitization

Don Handelman

The modern Olympic Games were founded in the late 19th century with values of egalitarianism, brotherhood, and competition foremost in mind, in some ways close to those of the 18th-century French revolutionaries yet intended officially as utterly apolitical in their application. The Olympic authorities established regulations with which to govern the management of Olympic organization and the rules whereby athletes competed in the Games. In effect, the Olympic authorities began to shape a bureaucracy for Olympic sport and manned this assemblage with officials, just as other officials supervised and adjudicated the competitions themselves. Bureaucracies manage and control by receiving, creating, and modifying *classifications* by which to order, organize, and surveil realities. The Olympics are no exception. Though the values of the Olympics are given pride of place in discussions of the significance of the Games in the modern era, the bureaucratic ethos of *surveillance* is no less central to the existence of the Games, indeed is "native" to the Games, to their selections and competitions. I emphasize this point because surveillance is the closest of kin to securitization.

Securitization is perceived as an unwanted, extraneous, even alien form that threatens to engulf the Games, walling them off from their lived surrounds. Securitization is nonetheless perceived as warranted, given the threat "terrorism" (covering a munificence of potential disruptions) poses to the Games. On the other hand, the idea and practice of surveillance have been embedded within the modern Olympics from its beginnings and are integral to its operation. In this sense, the Olympic Games have never been that distant from securitization. Yet surveillance is so taken for granted *within* the Games that it is almost never if ever called by its name. To take this argument one step further, the potentials for surveillance and securitization are deeply embedded within the bureaucratic *zeitgeist*, and any organization that is constructed bureaucratically and that assembles people and things in terms of what I call "bureaucratic logic" (Handelman, 2004) will at some point actualize these potentials in varying degrees. The qualities of bureaucratic logic are raised further on.

In this Prologue I discuss surveillance as an unremarkable, common-sensical and ever-present phenomenon built into the very integrity of the Games (and certainly into competitive sport more generally), and as such an introduction to the phenomena of blatant securitization which embroil the Games at present and which are the subject of this volume. At the close of this Prologue, I ask again whether the ethos of the Games is that distant from surveillance and its bureaucracy by briefly discussing a novelist's projection of what would happen if a new statelet, organized and run by bureaucrats, was founded on the values of Olympic egalitarianism, brother-hood, and competition. The novel in question is the late Georges Perec's *W or the Memory of Childhood*.

Surveilling and Securing the Olympics: From Tokyo 1964 to London 2012 and Beyond is a milestone in the social-historical analysis of the Olympics, a mega-event that has grown in popularity and wealth with the advent of the information age. The information age, ironically, is also becoming the age of popular terrorism, or at least that of terror threats, from those aimed at individuals to those against public settings, public events, and indeed against entire populations. So much information about how to assemble deadly means of interpersonal and national assault has never been so easily available to so many, especially through cyberspace. The Olympic Games seems to be a soft target for disruption, given the vast crowds and multiple venues often spread over extensive areas, with each venue's loca-tion, shape, timing, and the nature of competitions therein presenting its own often complex security considerations. Protecting entry into a small, enclosed space is vastly different from protecting the route of the 42 km marathon. Many of these problems came to the fore during the massacre of Israeli team members at the 1972 Munich Olympics.[1] Yet the last thing that Olympic organizers and bureaucrats want is an intrusive security apparatus that will delay spectators reaching their places to see events that cannot be delayed, given the tremendously lucrative TV and other contracts that require adhering to a strict timetable for viewing commercials no less than competitive events.[2]

Nonetheless, in the months leading up to the 2012 London Games, one could well think that the police had rehearsed a multitude of crowd control strategies on Londoners in the streets; and that the security and intelligence forces were no less doing their surveillance and communications rehearsals in more surreptitious domains. The British government publicly committed 17,000 troops to Games security (more British troops than were serving in Afghanistan at the time), atop the thousands provided by a giant British-based security company, while MI5 and MI6 together considered the risk of a terrorist attack at three on a five-point scale.[3] The sense was of a huge security *exoskeleton* encompassing and enwrapping the London Olympics. Britain already had more Closed Circuit Television cameras – themselves a sort of endoskeleton – in public places than probably any other state in the world. Exoskeleton – endoskeleton, with the London Olympics security and surveillance, had arrived full front to put into blatant perspective the apparent contradiction between Olympic values of peaceful athletic competition through egalitarian coexistence and comradeship and, on the other hand, the militarization and securitization of anything and everything relating to the Games.[4] A near war footing of a kind in order to secure the Olympic city by force of arms during the 17 days of the Games.

The milestone of this book is that for the first time intensive scholarly attention is given to issues of surveillance and securitization in a series of Olympic Games during the 20th century and into the 21st, taking into account national, international, and commercial issues as well as relations between the International Olympic Committee and local organizing Olympic committees. As the scale of the Olympics becomes gigantic, the many interfaces between the world of the Games and the manifold complexities of the world beyond require delicate and lengthy negotiations that enable entry into this Olympic world yet try to control (with limited success) the degrees to which these externalities impact on the events within. In this gigantism, commercialization and securitization are the primary bludgeons, whacking at the claims of the Olympics to embody "true internationalism" based on "a common global humanity" (Archetti, 1999: 195). Referring to the 2012 Olympics, Boykoff and Tomlinson state, "The I.O.C. has turned the Olympics into a commercial bonanza. In London, more than 250 miles of V.I.P. traffic lanes are reserved not just for athletes and I.O.C. luminaries but also for corporate sponsors. Even the signature Olympic Flame Relay has been commercialized: the International Olympic Committee and its corporate sponsors snapped up 10% of the torchbearer slots for their stakeholders and members of the commercial sponsors' information technology and marketing staff." The Olympics also has been called "the world's longest commercial," through time.[5]

The exoskeleton of securitization embraces and protects the vulnerable competitions in which all eyes are turned to athletes who themselves are entirely engrossed in attempting to achieve maximum effort. Indeed, one might say that the certainty of security enables the certainty of the uncertainty of outcome in contest and competition. Yet the interiority of the Games is no less pervaded by surveillance; and, so, the surveillance *endoskeleton* in the modern Games, historically present from their very outset, resonates powerfully with the exoskeleton of securitization. Persons close to the Olympic Movement worry about the growth of the exoskeleton of securitization. In terms of international relations, the Olympic Movement was a peace movement from its outset and enshrined sport in the Olympic Charter as "at the service of the harmonious development of man ... [and] ... a peaceful society."[6] During the Games, the Olympic Movement calls for the Olympic City to be treated as neutral space, beyond national and international conflicts. Yet today this perhaps can be accomplished only by shaping Olympic venues as armed camps and by strengthening national and international security apparatuses. The contradiction between ideals of peaceful and dignified international competition that takes place deep within bastions of security continuously searching for hostiles likely is not lost on the Olympic Movement. In this regard, securitization may well be the elephant in the room for the Olympic Movement, an alien presence that together with the flourishing marketing of the Games to corporate interests are forces inimical to the well-being of the Movement.

Yet one wonders why this "elephantine" presence should be surprising given the intimate resonance between the exoskeleton of securitization and the endoskeleton of surveillance. Consider that the organization of the Games – if not from its outset, then not that long after – has been ruled by the bureaucratic imperative of *lineal* classification. Anthropologist Dorothy Lee (1950) distinguished between what she called lineal and non-lineal codifications of reality. Bureaucratic logic is one form of the lineal codification of reality, which creates and practices taxonomies whose categories are clearly and neatly defined and demarcated. In the case of organized sport, there are numerous taxonomies: of events included in the competitions; of the selection of athletes, of the rules of competition, of how an event begins and ends, of how winners and losers are decided, and so forth. Bureaucratic logic demands that the categories produced by classification be monitored carefully for any infractions. This, in essence, is the idea of surveillance; especially the surveillance of boundaries as hard-and-fast straight lines.

The Olympics and other venues for competitive sport have been allied with applied technology and science for a long time. Advances in the applied sciences are a hallmark of Western modernity. The bottom line for much of applied science has been an emphasis on greater effectiveness, reliability, speed, output, and productivity, achieved through increasing the efficiency of relating means to ends, of cause to effect or outcome. This has been no less so for the economic and the social. In the applied sciences, this relationship of cause and effect is predominantly a linear one, of various versions of the shortest distance between two points being a straight line. The Olympic motto of Higher, Faster, Stronger is an athletic version of linear cause-and-effect relationships, and the straight line as the shortest distance between two points is the basis of all timed athletic events. In striving to achieve the higher, the faster, the stronger, Sports Science has strong affinities to Taylorism, and is a burgeoning field, for record athletic performances go only forward and can only do so linearly.[7]

In the 1950s, cosmologist Gregory Bateson (1972) warned against turning complex relationships – especially ones that turned recursively on themselves, took roundabout routes, and thereby processed complex information – into straight lines that excluded information deemed irrelevant to increasing the efficiency of their relationships between means and ends.

Unlike recursive relationships that processed complex information, linear causal relationships cut out information necessary to a more holistic understanding of human beings (and of the world, more generally). Missing this information, linear relationships could only generate partial effects and partial knowledge. In a funny way, we also can understand Bateson's admonition as a warning against mistaking the athlete for a whole person, and so, too, the official, the bureaucrat. In these terms the athlete-as-athlete is a partial person, boxed by the classifications of bureaucratic logic to be trained for extreme causal relationships between athletic means and the goal of winning competitions defined with lineal exactness. Endoskeletal surveillance is designed to protect athletes as partial persons from becoming otherwise through athletics.

Without official, bureaucratic surveilling of the boundaries and contents of the relevant categories there is no competition that produces the unequivocal outcomes demanded by linear causality. From the perspective of competitive sport, linear classification, the crystal-clear boundaries between categories and the clear-cut differences between winners and losers is common-sensical, obvious, and essential. What other logics of classification could there be? What other outcomes could there be to competitions? Without surveilling the boundaries of categories to exclude unwanted influences and inputs, how else could the fairness of competition be assured? In comparative cultural terms there *are* other ways and they have had cosmic significance in other cultures. Moreover, they do not necessarily position individual achievement at the apex of accomplishment, nor do they place record-keeping at the forefront of unlimited progress in human endeavor, which, after all, is one of the mainstays of modernity's vision of open-ended futures.[8]

Therefore, on closer inspection the growth of the exoskeleton of securitization during the past 40-odd years actually complements the surveillance that, to reiterate, is *native* to the Games as the product of lineal classification, bureaucratic organization, and the *zeitgeist* of modernity. So, too, such surveillance is native to any competition that pits clearly distinct entities (say, individual competitors, teams of competitors) against one another in a quest for victory that distinguishes absolutely between distinct categories of winners and losers. In other words, the logic of securitization is not simply an unwanted appendage, an undesirable burden on the Games, one which grows by leaps and bounds given the force majeure of threats, instabilities, and uncertainties.[9] Security, not strangely at all, has powerful affinity with the endoskeletal surveillance native to the Games, which from the outset protected the competitions, their selections of competitors, their outcomes, and their rewards. This is what I raise here through themes that, during the history of the modern Olympics, converged, forming a constellation of surveillance and, I suggest, eventually becoming grounds for the relatively easy turn of the Games toward securitization.

Lineal classification and surveillance

Informing this argument is the recognition that organized sport – of which the Olympic Games is at the apex of prestige – exists only through the bureaucracies that enable, hold together, and manage their structures. This is no less so for the organization of surveillance and securitization. Yet there are two aspects here that should not be confuted. One is bureaucracy as an institution. This is the oeuvre of Weber, Crozier, Blau and numerous others. The other concerns the métier of every bureaucratic institution, whether to a greater or lesser degree. This métier is the invention and modification of taxonomies, of classifications and their categories, that are then applied to human beings and to other "things" in order to make order and relatedness among them, and, on this basis to allocate qualities to them and to dispose of them in terms of the purposes for which the classifications exist. This aspect, then, takes up the logic by which and through which classification and its categories are applied and operated. The study of this latter aspect receives an impetus from Foucault's *The Order of Things* (1973) and is developed by Bowker and Star's *Sorting Things Out: Classification and its Consequences* (1999) and Handelman's *Nationalism and the Israeli State: Bureaucratic Logic in Public Events* (2004: 19–42). Bowker and Star are concerned with lineal classification, which they call "monothetic." My concern has been with the logic that informs monothetic classification, which I call "bureaucratic logic." Vida Bajc's studies of "security meta-framing" (2011), which are the theoretical impetus for this book on the securitization of the Olympic Games, are strongly related to the idea of bureaucratic logic.

In the case of the Olympic Games, issues of classification, and consequently of endoskeletal surveillance, were related to what can be called an ethos of "purity," at times more implicit, at others more explicit. A tacit yet powerful premise of the Olympic Movement from its beginnings is that the Games must be different from everyday life and everyday values. The Games therefore must be set apart, insulated by their own values and their own organization. This insulation from the everyday had prominent utopian qualities, and these qualities centered on the body and its perfectibility. This desire for the perfection of the body, as an index of the wholeness of Human Being, may be likened to the purity of the body and its spirit, developed and honed through liberal values of individual hard work and effort. To put this in another way, from its outset issues of "purity" have been central to the Games. Coubertin, in my view, linked purity to character and character to the body, not to the mind. "After all, Gentlemen," he declaimed, "there are not two parts to a man, body and soul; there are three, body, mind, and character. Character is not formed by the mind, but primarily by the body. The men of antiquity knew this, and we are painfully relearning it" (quoted in MacAloon, 1981: 173). The honesty and integrity of the honed body exercised for its own sake knew no compromise or deceit, and therefore was the most valuable route to building character. The morality that knew no compromise or deceit came with character, formed through, honed through, shaped through the body and tested through sport competition (MacAloon, 1981: 166).

Nonetheless, in Olympic terms the body – the speculum of character – had to be kept pure of corruption, so that the processes that formed character could be nurtured and protected. Thus individuals who compromised these values were to be selected out, just as those who exemplified the highest degrees of physical capacity were to be selected in. The body of the athlete best developed character when it did sport for its own sake and not for ulterior or exterior motives. Coubertin's somatic project was a *moral* one, and with varying degrees and emphases this remains so today. Although "purity" was not part of the official discourse of the Olympic Games, there is no doubt that this overall quality of the athlete's body embodied and inlaid the quest for character and morality that could be developed through the somatic body. Character, we can say, existed in the natural potential of the somatic body, yet for character to emerge and blossom, the natural body had to be protected. Even, one might say, protected from the mind of the athlete himself or herself. From this perspective, it is more the mind of the athlete rather than the body that is likely to be corrupted by external factors.

"Pollution" often is paired with purity as its despoiler and destroyer.[10] In the case of the Olympic Games, a sense of pollution (even if the term is not used explicitly) indexes whatever exterior intrusion dirties and demeans the elite physical condition of the athlete striving to perfect the natural capacities of the somatic body through the highest levels of training and competition. The ideal of purity likely can be known as such only if it is contrasted with its nullity, pollution. Once more this is integral to the utopian qualities of the origins of the modern Games. Therefore the apartness of the Games and their athletes is enabled ideally by a non-permeable boundary between inside and outside, which needs to be protected and guarded against threats of pollution originating from the exterior. Put otherwise, there must always be (and, so, will always be) an exterior threat to purity in order to uphold the standards of the latter. Eventually the apparatus to surveil individual athletic bodies for signs of corruption also was developed. For the modern Games, the ethos of surveillance, if not its organization and means, existed from the beginning.

The anthropologist, Claude Levi-Strauss, has argued that games (in which he included sport) are a mechanism through which to create difference and hierarchy from sameness and equality. Coubertin, for example, emphasized that "social differences do not matter within sport participation" (Martinkova, 2012: 791). Ideally, cultural and social differences are held constant, as it were, to enable athletes equal to one another prior to the contest to be differentiated by the doing of the contest, thereby producing the ranking to one another that they achieve through the contest. As obvious as this is, that which follows is less so. Especially since these contests are processes of selection, their bureaucrats cum officials endeavor to ensure that the participants are not made unequal prior to the contest through something that is externally added to the "natural" capacities of the contestants. These additions are considered illegitimate by the authorities who organize the contest. We can say that the selection of athletes through contest "cleanses" their ranks, bringing together the very best of them (and, through competition after competition, altering their rankings over and again in relation to one another).

What is considered by the International Olympic Committee to be polluting to the purity of the athletic body and its character-building has changed radically over the years, even as the ethos of purity remains.[11] In the early Games, the greatest threat to the Olympics was perceived to be playing for money and therefore becoming professional. To accept payment was to introduce an external, instrumental incentive, which stained playing and competing for their own sake. Yet it is imperative to recognize that once the absolute difference between being interior to the athletic competition and being exterior was related to value, there always would exist the principled grounds for distinguishing between pure and impure, moral and immoral, regardless of, in practice, which particular content constituted the difference. In terms that Emile Durkheim would well have recognized, a positive value could be held to only if a parallel negative value existed. Then the aim of the International Olympic Committee was to keep the negative value at bay, preventing it from penetrating the Games bubble; and if the negative intruded, to exorcise and expel it forthwith.

Consider the following better-known examples of International Olympic Committee reactions to perceived violations of Olympic and athletic value. At the 1912 Stockholm Games, the Native American athlete Jim Thorpe was awarded gold in both the pentathlon and decathlon.[12] Yet Thorpe also played minor league baseball for money ($25 a week) under his own name (unlike the pseudonyms used by other athletes). He was exposed by a journalist and labeled a professional, his medals stripped in 1913 by the International Olympic Committee. In 1936, the defending Olympic gold medalist in the 100-meter backstroke, Eleanor Holm Jarrett, was booted unceremoniously off the United States team for her lack of decorum – for not going to bed on time and instead having a few drinks at an evening cocktail party onboard the ship taking the delegation to Germany. In 1968, gold and bronze medalists in the 200 meters, Tommie Smith and John Carlos, gave the Black Power salute from the awards podium during the playing of the American anthem. Accused of violating the political neutrality of the Olympics, the two were expelled from the Games and did not participate in the relay events. In every Olympics following the 1972 Munich Massacre of Israeli team members by the Palestinian Black September, the International

Olympic Committee has refused Israel's requests to hold an official Olympic memorial within the Games for the slain athletes and coaches (Handelman and Shamgar-Handelman, n.d.). One way to understand this is that, from the International Olympic Committee perspective, to hold a memorial within the rubric of the Games would be to acquiesce to the intrusion of politics into the Olympic bubble. In 1988, the 100-meter Olympic gold medalist and new record holder, Ben Johnson, was stripped of his award because traces of anabolic steroids were found in his drug test. In the view of the International Olympic Committee, steroids violate, "the naturalness of the sporting body" (MacAloon, 1990: 41).

In the 100 meters at the 2008 Games, whose winner (by a fraction of a second) is dubbed the fastest man in the world, Usain Bolt built a huge lead and, as he dashed full tilt to the finish line, he half-turned toward the other competitors and lightly pounded his chest, and still broke the world record. International Olympic Committee President Jacques Rogge ripped into Bolt for his lack of proper Olympic etiquette in mocking the other competitors and flaunting the extent of his own overwhelming victory. Bolt had transgressed the unspoken rule that Olympic athletics must be treated in dead earnest with the utmost seriousness. Bolt played with the play of the Games within the play defined as reverently serious. There is no place within the linear causality of a competition for the expression of fun and spontaneity.[13] Just about every detail must be calibrated and sanctioned by bureaucrats, by officialdom.[14] Flashing sheer joyous exuberance, Bolt looked ready to party before he crossed the finish line. In striving for ultimate victory, a more proper attitude was expressed by an Israeli judoka medalist at the 1992 Barcelona Games: "You have to be...I don't want to say a god, but close to a god, in order to win a medal. Only special people get to experience that moment when everything comes together."[15] Yet only so long as such attitudes exemplify (even immodest) modesty and self-effacement. In contrast to this tunnel vision in self-perception, in the split-second thrust of the 100 meters, Bolt suddenly experienced a playful moment, deviating with his bodily character from the utterly linear causality of the race, his head, arms, and fists pointing joyously to the very success of his body in motion, running to a new record.

Bolt did more than race to a new record time – he suddenly made running in that event a more complex phenomenon as he spontaneously and recursively commented on himself as he was running, thereby becoming momentarily a fuller person within the race itself. And this is quite that which Rogge and other Olympic officials railed against. Becoming a fuller person within the narrower confines of a classification intended to shape participation in events organized through linear cause and effect simply threatens the viability of the classification to properly domesticate the human being. The "character" that Coubertin extolled is Human Being domesticated into the bureaucratic logic of classification, embracing the categories of the classification as absolute and unquestioned, demanding the kind of discipline that would make a military machine proud. And this in order to excel and perhaps be the very best in an athletic event of extremely limited horizon.

Classification and surveillance of the miscreant athlete

The Western pedagogical attitude inlays the doing of athletics. Modern athletic and sport competitions are inherently pedagogic in their premises. The athletic competition is no less a pedagogical examination than that pertaining to knowledge acquisition and carried out in a classroom or lecture hall (or before a computer screen), except that the athletic contest selects and tests for physical capabilities and skills. Coubertin's vision of character developing through the trained, disciplined body modified the mind-body dichotomy of Cartesian dualism in terms of which the mind orders and the body obeys, a paradigm that continues to govern much of the Western conceptualization of the human being. Coubertin transferred to the body qualities of character usually attributed to the mind. This perspective strengthens the pedagogical premises of the modern athletic competition. In this regard, to paraphrase Clausewitz on war and politics, athletics are a continuation of scholastic pedagogy by other means; these other means are the shaping of the body set to strive for perfection in an endeavor of highly circumscribed bureaucratic classification.

Despite the venues of playing fields and stadia, modern athletic competitions are exams that rank performers in relation to one another according to their outcomes. Performers not only are ranked as ordinals but also are given a mark or grade, a means of objectively measuring the gap between each and every participant. The grade exists as an abstraction, apart from the ordinal, physical contiguity among participants in a competition. Thus a particular competitor can be evaluated individually over a number of competitions, or in relation to other competitors who are conceived of in this way. All results are inscribed as formal records that are chronological histories of events, performers, and performances.[16]

Athletics today are focused on the accomplishment and measurement of exact difference, with the exact repetition of movements; with the control of virtually each and all movement, large and small; with the analytic fragmentation of the body in motion into categories of form that are added up by sport science to constitute an utterly surveilled and totally determined performance. This is the aesthetics of the practice of rules, the aesthetics of the practice of the very ruledness of rules – an aesthetics of surveillance through bureaucratic logic – that saturates athletics today (Handelman, 1998: xl). Who among us can actually *see* the difference of one one-hundredth of a second between athletes racing the same course? The difference can only be represented through the use of technology, through clocked time that is a symbol of something that is said to have occurred. The difference itself is invisible, yet is said to be oh-so-significant, the difference between winner and loser (which is the true significance here). Therefore the exactness of measurement must itself be turned into a representation of difference in order to be communicated as different. Much difference in athletics has become detectable only through the use of technology that surveils, even as the bureaucrat-officials of sport increase their demands that the body of the athlete not take in any substance that is bureaucratically classified as performance-enhancing (and whose effects are *not* visible to the naked eye). Technology enhances the perception of bureaucrat-officials to detect difference even as the capacity of athletes to make difference is becoming narrower and narrower in many events. As technologies to detect difference (temporal, spatial, forms of body style) are improved, so are the capacities to make increasingly infinitesimal differences that finally will represent nothing more than the visible artificiality of the making of difference (and symbolically the critical distinction between winner and loser). This is the control of bureaucrat-officials over the invention and application of classification, and so their control over athletes domesticated to these parameters of classification and its endoskeletal surveillance.[17]

Though the contents of what the International Olympic Committee considers immoral, impure, and immodest behavior change, guarding and surveilling the borders of classification itself remain a constant. If, in 1913, in the case of Jim Thorpe, categorical surveillance was haphazard, and if, in 1936, the decision in the Eleanor Holm Jarrett case was straightforwardly authoritarian, by 1988 and onward, endoskeletal surveillance and policing had become fully professional, rigorous, and indeed scientific. That endoskeletal surveillance has found science and is treating its evidence as the non-impugnable gold standard for evidence of impurity in athletes seems foreordained, given the bureaucratic desire for increasing exactness in differentiating between categorical inclusion and exclusion and the science of sport's advances in improving athletic performance. During this same period, the commercialization of the Olympics and its athletes and the sale of the Games to corporate interests have been huge. Nonetheless the border between pure and impure, between moral and immoral remains in place and is surveilled constantly, as if such distinction and separation were the last bastion and refuge of the Olympic Movement from the corruption of commercial onslaught and its glitz. The onus of endoskeletal surveillance focuses on individual athletes (who as isolated individuates are also the most vulnerable yet nonetheless vital components of Olympic organization) and not on the buying of athletics (and sport, more generally) by corporations; for the former can be monitored, tracked, and tested by parameters of rigorous science, while the latter control sponsorship, monies, and influence that the Olympic Movement needs to survive in the globalized world.[18]

The pursuit of miscreant athletes who use so-called performance-enhancing drugs is becoming a moral crusade in sport generally (and perhaps, too, a moral panic). By now the naturalness of virtually *all* athletic bodies is considered to be despoiled by steroids, growth hormones, and the like, regardless of whether this actually influences the kind of performance practiced by the sport in question. The World Minigolf Sport Federation's rule book states that "Doping is fundamentally contrary to the spirit of sport," and here "spirit" encompasses much more than bodily reaction to a drug.[19] Shades of Coubertin's "character." Today any sport federation that dreams of its sport becoming an Olympic event subjects its competitors to official drug testing by, for example, the United States Anti-Doping Agency. Among these sports are ice fishing, darts, miniature golf, chess, and tug-of-war (and in 2011, two minigolfers, two bowlers, and one chess player tested positive for banned substances).[20]

The scientific search for ways of identifying miscreants more accurately and classifying them more precisely continues. A case in point is the Athlete Biological Passport, which tracks the athlete's body historically, biographically, indeed autobiographically, since the athlete will have great difficulty suppressing from the authorities information that the body surrenders about itself in routine times, routine tests. In the words of the World Anti-Doping Agency, "the Athlete Biological Passport is based on the monitoring of selected biological parameters over time that will indirectly reveal the effects of doping rather than attempting to detect the doping substance itself."[21] In other words, if the athlete's natural body is not true to itself through time, to *its* own rhythms, then suspicion is aroused. The use of the word "passport" is revealing, bureaucratically. The athlete is to be turned into a migrant seeking permission over and again from an endoskeletal passport control to enter the correct and legitimate category of a sport taxonomy. Perhaps the athlete-as-immigrant, continually surveilled and in danger of becoming stateless. The desire of the guardians of the naturalness of the sporting body – sport bureaucrats in the main – is categorical, to purge all sporting bodies of such impure alien intrusions. Especially because they control access to the most prestigious of theaters in the sport universe, the Olympic Games' authorities have had a major role in stimulating this enhanced surveillance.

As defined by sports bureaucracy, performance-enhancers are the great threat today to the purity of the God-given naturalness of the athlete's body. What is it that officially turns a performance-enhancer into a culprit? According to one commentator, "Additives are claimed as illegal when their names have been listed by a sports federation. That's about it."[22] A bureaucratic decision to add a substance to a proscribed category of substances is intended to have an immediate impact on the use of the substance for a given category of person, the competitive athlete whose event falls under the aegis of that sport federation. The effects are categorical. And the categorical defined in absolute terms is at the base of both surveillance and securitization. The bottom line of Olympic endoskeletal surveillance is *how* bureaucrats classify, *not* why they do so. This has been the case from the rudimentary beginnings of Olympic surveillance practices. To a significant degree, the logic of how lineal classification is done applies to both surveillance and securitization. At issue are the nature of the categories of surveillance that are invented and the way they are applied. First and foremost, monothetic classifications informed and shaped by bureaucratic logic are the province of bureaucrats and of those who enforce their promulgations. In today's world, this is true in so many ways for how official classification shapes the ongoing formation of social realities (Handelman, 2004).

The stated values of the Olympic Games are presented by the Olympic Movement as embodying the best of humankind through the verity of the athletically developed human body practicing its truth through competition. Every competition is egalitarian, open to showing, indeed proving, which competitor is the best; and every subsequent competition like every prior one begins with each competitor on an equal footing with all the others. Therefore outcomes are, in principle, arrived at in democratic fashion. Yet the parameters of egalitarian, democratic competition are established rigidly through the use of an authoritarian bureaucratic logic, and these parameters are set into the infrastructure of the Games organized bureaucratically. The directives of the infrastructure are to supervise unyieldingly the obedience of athletes to the parameters of egalitarian competition; hence, as noted, the ongoing emphasis on endoskeletal surveillance to guard the competitions.

Yet what of the relations between the governing and the governed, the bureaucrats and the athletes? An issue implicitly yet continually present is whether there is contradiction and conflict between the community of athletes and the bureaucratics of officialdom. Their relationships are highly authoritative, unequal and undemocratic (see, for example, Koss, Peel, and Orlando, 2011; Teetzel, 2011). Are these qualities of relationship built into the Olympic Movement, into the Games, indeed into the structures of modern athletics? And is endoskeletal surveillance one ground for the ongoing subordination of athletes in the Olympics?[23] To take this question a step further, it is worth noting a structural similarity between organized athletics and service industries that are said to exist first and foremost for the sake of and the benefit of their clients. But the clients turn over while the organization managers stay in place for lengthier periods, providing services, but at the same time becoming in practice indispensable to the organizations, which orientate primarily to their needs and desires. Does this speak to the relations between Olympic bureaucrats and athletes? To the increasingly comprehensive endoskeletal surveillance employed to monitor athletes?

Bureaucrats and athletes, surveillance and subordination

One response to the questions in the previous paragraph comes from an unexpected direction – from Georges Perec's novel *W or The Memory of Childhood* (1996), which juxtaposes two texts: one a fragmentary autobiography of a childhood during World War II and the other a fantasy of this selfsame teen about "a land in thrall to the Olympic ideal."[24] My interest here is in the idea of a statelet founded on Olympic ethos and to where Perec's keenly intelligent imagination takes this. I will not enter into any details of the book here, but encourage those interested in and concerned with the Olympic Movement to read the book...and let loose their own imaginations.

Just suppose that the stated values of the Olympic Games embodied the best of humankind. And that an isolated mini-state was founded based on the Olympic ideal of Higher, Faster, Stronger; a statelet in which men competed continually in athletics to embody, to generate, and to reproduce this ideal and to establish and reestablish their social statuses vis-à-vis one another.[25] In what direction might this seemingly utopian social order lead? In the adolescent Perec's fantasy, a group travels (probably during the interwar era) to an uninhabited island in the South Atlantic to establish their utopia based on the Olympic ethos of achievement through athletic competition. Yet a social order cannot be founded only on the basis of egalitarianism and competition between equals striving for the apex of modernity, the reach for perfection. Therefore, there are officials who organize and supervise the ongoing rounds of athletic competitions, which are the raison d'être of the statelet, in practice one run if not founded by bureaucrats.[26] Thus Perec's seemingly perfect society is established on the basis of (and confounded by) the deep, structural contradiction stated above, between egalitarian athletics and hieratic officialdom through which the latter comes to rule through the creation of classifications based on bureaucratic logic. And, so, endoskeletal surveillance is necessarily set in place.[27]

Most interestingly for the discussion here is that, in *W*, the bureaucratic rule that governs through the arbitrariness of lineal classification is not bound by the selfsame Olympic values in the name of which the statelet was established. Indeed, these values are corrupted in the name of upholding them – the bureaucrats who run the system of classifications are themselves outside the system of competition and fiddle with it. Perec writes that the running of a sports state requires Law, and an utter impartiality and implacable neutrality on the part of officials in deciding outcomes and their consequences. Yet *W* is ruled by Law that is "both absolutely powerful and absolutely unjust" (Spiro, 2001: 144). This policy of organized injustice by suddenly changing a classification or altering the rules is deliberate (and also is strictly implemented), and the stadium audience participates in this. The reason is that if the Law is unpredictable, then the events become more spectacular, the athletes more aggressive, and the competitions more inter-esting (and heaven help the competitor who finishes last...).

Perec's phantasmagoric vision of a statelet founded on Olympic values is that of a fascist universe (Spiro, 2001: 134), one resonating strongly with the war years he spent in occupied France.[28] Yet we must not overlook that his statelet is based on the Olympic ethos of (largely) individual achieve-ment, through which the sky should be the limit, and on the division between an officialdom with great power and athletes with little. And that officialdom is the ruling class, controlling to a high degree (and arbitrarily so) the means of classification – of practices, of events, of athletes, and of consequences. Perec's systemic organization of competitions for a place in the social order emphasizes the visual, the gaze, the spectacle, as does the Olympics for its audience. Of course the outré vision of the precocious Perec has nothing in common with the Olympic Games as we know it. And *W* after all is an isolated dot in the vast ocean somewhere near Tierra del Fuego, while the Olympics is embedded in complex assemblages and networks of the globalized world. Though one can argue that the Olympic Movement has tried hard to lock the Games into itself partly through endoskeletal surveillance, within a bubble that resists the corruption of Olympic values by rapacious corporate and other interests, yet nonetheless the Movement has had to surrender bit by bit in order to survive as a great mega-event. But certainly the Olympics has nothing whatsoever in common with Perec's vision, has it? I think again on Levi-Strauss' argument that competition turns equality (protected in the Olympics by endoskeletal surveillance) into status difference (again protected by endoskeletal surveillance), and how all of this is made systemic in the Olympics through the rule of a class of bureaucrats and officials (as is so in all modern, organized, competitive sport). Of how athletes come and go with the vagaries and time lines of their careers and how bureaucrats tend to stay in place or shuffle positions with one another. Of how, given the resonance between them, endoskeletal surveillance morphs quite easily into exoskeletal securitization, and that this may be due in no small part to great corporate interests magnifying the Olympic Games into a larger and larger mega-event bursting from within itself...And I wonder.

Notes

1. My own research at the Olympic Games was in Los Angeles, 1984. Lea Shamgar-Handelman and I were part of a loosely organized team of anthropologists assem-bled by John MacAloon to study aspects of the Games. Lea and I studied how the Israeli team was received in Los Angeles and, as we discovered, how the athletes of a third-rate team were welcomed as heroes.
2. Vida Bajc (2007) evocatively discusses this conflict between the scheduling of an event and the security procedures that process spectators waiting to see the event in her discussion of the second Bush inauguration.

3. See, "British military to further bolster Olympic security," *New York Times*, July 12, 2012.
4. At the ready were helicopters, strike aircraft, surface-to-air missiles…and sharpshooters. Boykoff and Tomlinson commented that, "Even the Olympic mascots look like two-legged surveillance cameras." See, Jules Boykoff and Alan Tomlinson, "Olympic arrogance," *New York Times*, July 4, 2012.
5. See, Jules Boykoff and Alan Tomlinson, Ibid. No less, the Olympic Torch Relay has become the world's longest commercial traveling through space. John MacAloon, an anthropologist who has been studying the Olympics since the 1970s, discusses how the organization of the Olympic Torch Relay was given to a private company (founded by security and intelligence types), which applied an Americanized model of managerial, technocratic "world's best practices" to the Relay, while sponsors like Coca-Cola and Samsung turned the Relay segments of solemnity and joyousness into halftime spectacles at an American football game combined with aggressive and tasteless marketing giveaways (MacAloon, 2006: 31–32; 2012: 586–588).
6. The International Olympic Committee's *Olympic Charter,* 2010, p. 11.
7. Categories of classification, created by bureaucratic logic, are also altered by this logic when deemed necessary. For example, in the javelin throw, the length of the throw was judged by where the point of the missile landed. However, the javelin would appear to float to the ground, landing flat, so that it was difficult to judge the precise length of the throw. In the 1980s the International Amateur Athletic Federation moved the center of mass of the missile 4 cm forward, which kept its nose down so that the point would land first. This change substantially reduced the length of javelin throws. The bureaucrats dealt with this shift by creating a new category of "new rules" world records (Haake, 2012: 28–29).
8. It would be fascinating to have a study of the ways in which running as a culturally embedded way of moving across country in Kenya and Ethiopia became a reservoir for the training of world-class athletes for long-distance competitions. How, for these athletes, the lineal classification of distance, time, outcome, and record-keeping replaced running as the way to cover distance effectively and likely with enjoyment.
9. In 2009 the IOC was granted permanent observer status at the United Nations, in recognition of its encouragement of building peaceful internationalism through sport as education (Bousefield and Montsion, 2012: 823).
10. Such contrasts are characteristic of Cartesian dualism (e.g., mind and body), which characterizes so much phenomenal perception and interpretation in the Western world; and which, I argue, enters deeply into numerous domains of social life including the political (Handelman, 2007).
11. Whether de Coubertin was influenced by the German cultural conception of *bildung* is unclear.
12. In 1912, he also led the Carlisle Indian School to claim the National Collegiate football championship and went on to play major league baseball for six years.
13. Spontaneity (and fun) should be kept away from venues in which the athletes publicly display themselves, as Hope Solo, the goalkeeper of the United States soccer team, has intimated. See, "Hope Solo on Olympic Village: 'There's a lot of sex going on,'" www.USmagazine.com (accessed October 21, 2012).
14. This includes surveillance by sport federations of technological changes that improve performances and ban some, for example, a javelin designed to improve

performance, and so, too, full-body women's swimsuits with polyurethane panels (Haake, 2012).

15. "Greater expectations," *Ha'aretz* (English edition), July 27, 2012.

16. Hoskin and Macve (1995) and Hoskin (1996) argue for the historical, pedagogical confluence of the formal examination, quantification, and inscription.

17. A case in point of extreme surveillance and control is American football, referred to today as America's game, the most popular team sport in the United States. American football is at one and the same time the most surveilled, controlled, and bureaucratic of team sports *and* the most violent. This is a game that must be played through legitimate interpersonal violence, yet one that must be continually and lawfully interrupted by bureaucrat-officials, often at peak moments of legitimized violence. Bureaucrat-officials then organize the field of play for the subsequent amplification of violence, and the next … and the next. This is the natural history of the game. There is an aesthetic here that predicates interpersonal violence on bureaucratic logic. American football is *the* game of the modern bureaucratic state, which ignites, amplifies, and turns off violence in accordance with the rules of classification it invents for itself in ongoing ways. There likely are more violent team sports (rugby, lacrosse, Australian-rules football, and water polo come to mind), yet none whose actual rhythm of play – of igniting and ceasing violent contact – is always set officially by bureaucrat-officials.

18. Nor, of course, on states, who operate their own surveillance and spying programs on the training regimens of prominent competing states (Greg Bishop, "Long before London Games, James Bond tactics," *New York Times*, July 23, 2012).

19. "Dope Tests in Ice Fishing? No, Beer Doesn't Count," *New York Times*, February 26, 2013.

20. Ibid.

21. World Anti-Doping Agency website, www.wada-ama.org (accessed March 10, 2013). The International Tennis Federation recently announced that it would adopt the Athlete Biological Passport ("Pressured, Tennis Moves to Strengthen Its Drug Testing," *International Herald Tribune*, March 8, 2013).

22. Matthias Heitmann, "Let Le Tour competitors take drugs," www.spiked-online.com/site/article/3423/ (accessed October 19, 2012). And the list of proscribed additives is lengthy and complex. See the World Anti-Doping Agency website, Note 21. The pervasiveness of the mood of categorically classifying and apprehending performance-enhancing miscreants was caught recently in a news report and a cartoon. The report is of a 12-year-old girl in Pennsylvania who wanted to play sports and join a scrapbooking club in her school. She came home with a permissions form for her parents, which informed that to take part in any school sport or to participate in any club, she would have to consent to drug testing. ("Civil Libertarians Go to Court over Drug Testing of Middle School Students," *International Herald Tribune*, September 24, 2012). A cartoon in the *Wizard of Id* series, shows two armies, that of Id and that of their enemy, the Goths, facing one another armed to the teeth, ready to do battle. Separating them is a desk behind which are seated two officials. One official announces, "Ok, before we begin, let's have everyone line up to be tested for performance-enhancing drugs," at which an Id soldier turns to another and quips, "The Geneva Convention is sure getting picky."

23. For a historical perspective on Olympic inequality, see Chatziefstathiou (2011).

24. The book is translated from the French original, and the *W* of the title is the French W, called *"double-ve"*, indexing the two tales together.

25. My thought is that Perec chose the ideal of Higher, Faster, Stronger as the basis for his utopian social order because this is a universal symbol of peaceful egalitarian striving for achievement through competition in modernity, and therefore seemingly worthy of emulation and practice.
26. The founding of a state by bureaucracy rather than by nationalism and nationhood is the case for the European Union, as Walby (1999) argues.
27. Since W is an isolated island, exoskeletal securitization would be irrelevant.
28. At the close of *W*, Perec explicitly links its sports state to totalitarianism, to the Nazi State, to the Pinochet military dictatorship in Chile.

1
The Olympic Games as Complex Planned Event: Between Uncertainty and Order Through Security Meta-ritual

Vida Bajc

The juxtaposition of older and recent Olympic Identity and Accreditation Cards on the front cover is an invitation to reflect on the subject of this book, namely, a historical and comparative look at how surveillance and security have been serving as means to cope with complexity and uncertainty of the Olympic Games. In the Olympic circles, these identity cards are associated with what is known as "accreditation." This is a surveillance procedure that makes it possible to manage membership by regularly updating databases on participants and, at the same time, control access to the Games by designing patterns of spatial mobility and social interaction within the Olympic space. Today, the Olympic space has become a maximally controlled enclosure, which separates insiders from outsiders – those who are allowed to enter the space and others who remain outside. Within the enclosure, these identity cards divide the insiders into two general categories: spectators who hold admission tickets for specific competitions or ceremonies and other participants who are "accredited" for entering other areas of the Olympic enclosure. To be "accredited" means to be subjected to precise identification and clear classification into categories of privilege. These correspond to segmentation of the enclosure into subareas that are themselves stratified on the basis of privilege of access. The various codes and designations on the cards are pictorial abstractions of how this procedure of hierarchy of classification of participants works. As such, they provide some insights into how its process may have evolved over time.

A "Radio Representative" at the 1952 Helsinki Games, much like an "Athlete" at the 1964 Tokyo Olympics, is identified by a photo, name, address, place and time of birth, nationality, and capacity in which they participated. While the document folds like a passport to fit neatly in the holder's pocket, a scholar of the University of Oslo at the 1994 Lillehammer

Games was expected to wear the card visibly around her neck for easy verification. The front of her card displays her participation status on a starkly
colored background with the code "O" for the category "Observer." The icons
show "Access Rights" and "Accreditation Zones" designating the privilege to
attend specific sports competitions and enter particular areas in which she,
a member of the category "O," is permitted during those specific Games.
Apart from the name and the photo, personal details are now encoded in a
barcode, which communicates to a checkpoint scanning machine whether
the individual should be allowed to enter and when the individual is
exiting. Someone attending the 2010 Vancouver Games in the capacity of
Member of the International Olympic Committee has access to "All Sports
Venues," "All Olympic Villages," "Main Media Center," "Whistler Media
Center," "Olympic Family Hotel," as well as "Village Dining," "Allocated
Vehicle and Driver," and a host of other areas and activities as specified
by white letters and numbers on a blue background. It still has a photo
with a name and membership designation ("IOC"), but all other personal
information is encoded not only in the barcode but also in the chip. For the
2014 Sochi Winter Games, a so-called fan passport was introduced, a kind
of counterpart to the identity card, which now also required from spectators wishing to attend specific competitions and ceremonies that they
provide their personal information for background check and show their
"fan passport" at checkpoints.[1] These procedures allow the organizers of the
Games to regulate how many people are participating, where and in what
capacity. In addition, every time such a card is scanned, information about
the time and place of entry or exit is recorded and stored in a database so
that a complete pattern of movement for each and every individual, for the
category of individuals, and for each specific Olympics can potentially be
mapped out at any given time. This type of surveillance, however, produces
data for operatives entrusted with security of the Games.

   This kind of surveillance is one of the many elements of what has
emerged as a new form of social control of global planned events such as
the Olympics, which I have named security meta-ritual. Social forms, Mary
Douglas (1966) and Georg Simmel (1971) remind us, are ways of organizing
the social world, means for social practice of ordering of collective life. The
dominant effect of this new social form of control of the Olympics seems
to be to encapsulate, encircle, and envelop such global planned events to
ensure control over their process. Social forms come in many shapes and
manifestations and with varying effects on social life. This particular
social form, which transpires through efforts to minimize uncertainty in
global planned events, resembles what anthropologists would identify as
ritual (Handelman, 1998).[2] As is the case with rituals, its effect is to enable
a particular kind of transformation. This is a process of change from routine
everyday life, which is considered by the surveillance and security apparatus
as dangerous and uncertain, into a different kind of social order, which is

considered by the apparatus to be secure and safe for the performance of the event. As such, the purpose of security meta-ritual seems to be primarily instrumental. It seeks to create a sterile zone of safety by transforming everyday social and physical spaces into maximally controlled environments in which events such as the Olympics can then unfold according to the plan. The strategy is to reduce complexity in order to minimize uncertainty. The prefix "meta" is meant to communicate that there is a relationship of domination and subordination between two sets of activities; on the one hand, the transformation of unsafe social spaces into sterile zones of safety and, on the other hand, the performance of a planned event such as the Games. In this meta relationship, the performance of such a planned event is subordinated to parameters and specifications of security. This conceptual framework for the study of surveillance and security in global planned events has analytical roots in ethnographic research of the United States presidential inauguration in Washington, DC (Bajc, 2007b) and the papal visits to Jerusalem (Bajc, 2011b). By analyzing surveillance and security in the Olympic Games, starting with Tokyo 1964 and through London 2012, this book is an effort to understand how this form of social control has emerged historically.

Uncertainty, complexity, and the surveillance-security nexus

In bureaucratic terms, surveillance is a process of identifying and classifying for the purposes of monitoring, tracking, blocking, managing, planning, and otherwise controlling mobility of people, objects, and information in space and through time. The aim is to reduce social complexity in order to minimize uncertainty by devising strategies to anticipate the future. This has become a multifaceted process. One aspect of this process involves surveillance as a bureaucratic and technocratic practice in the service of security. The use of surveillance in the service of security has recently been capturing public attention. In this context, surveillance is translated into a set of policies and strategies put in place in the service of the security agenda (Bajc, 2013, 2011a). There is, however, another use of surveillance, which is customarily not reflected on or even much publicly debated, yet is fundamental to the functioning of bureaucratically structured organizations and institutions of all kinds; namely, surveillance as a mode of governance (Bajc, 2010, 2007a). Security meta-ritual is one of the outcomes of this multi-layering of surveillance. A brief discussion of the differences between surveillance as a mode of governing and surveillance in the service of security provides a necessary foreground for an understanding of implications of the coupling of surveillance with security for the historical emergence of security meta-ritual as a new form of social control in the Olympics.

Surveillance is fundamental to ordering, organizing, and managing social activity in such bureaucratically structured social systems. No contemporary formal organization, be it state, bank, corporation, or elementary school, can function without collection and processing of information about its affiliates, not the least for the purposes of planning, forecasting, or otherwise controlling the future of the organization. So, too, in order to establish and maintain its success as a global event, the Olympics must continue to demonstrate perfection of planning and execution of the Games, insist on precision of measurement of athletes' performance, and claim the commitment to achievements and standards of purity – all of which are based on surveillance. This use of surveillance developed in relation to the modern state and its rationale to regulate, survey, and evaluate social life within the state for the purposes of planning for the future (Foucault, 2008). Such governing was achieved by treating human behavior as information and converting that information into data to be analyzed with the use of statistics (Hacking, 1990; Desrosières, 1998). This way of governing accompanied the development of what we know today as modern bureaucracy in which the work of officials fundamentally depends on the mastery of gathering and processing information for the purposes of planning (Weber, 1964).

Surveillance in the service of security of collective public life has different historical roots. The notion of security itself seems to have been a part of political thought and ideas of statesmanship since the time of Cicero (Rothschild, 1995). It's saliency as a meta-frame of social organization (Bajc, 2011a) has come to be articulated during what Bacevich (2007) calls "the Long War" between the superpowers of the 20th century. During this conflict, security took center stage as an issue of state defense. This notion of security has carried over into the 21st century as an existential issue not only of the state but also private enterprise and human well-being (Wæver, 1995). Today, security has come to encompass all kinds of domains of social activity, including planned global events such as the Olympics, as a perception of reality which has a particular understanding of what is safe and what is dangerous and a prescription of what constitutes ordered social life (Bajc, 2013). Surveillance is its primary tool.

One important reason why surveillance and security have found close affinities is because they share the same ambition; namely, to order and control social life, which is envisioned to be unfolding in some future time. Together, security and surveillance comprise a synergetic strategy to impose a particular vision of social order of the Olympics with the goal to be able to minimize uncertainty by controlling how the Games are to unfold. This surveillance-security nexus (Bajc, 2015) seems to have pushed surveillance and its effects to the level of the systemic. As David Lyon (2003) has argued, it would be a mistake to conclude, as it is frequently done, that it was the events of the type such as 9/11 that prompted the widespread implementation of surveillance. Quite the contrary, such events have simply provided an impetus for security to be accelerated to the top of collective priorities as the dominant ordering principle (Bajc, 2011a) so that legal basis could be established and public legitimacy provided for surveillance to be taken to a new level.

As a system, surveillance manifests itself as an effort to achieve security by interrelating all possible sources of information gathering, intertwining all potentially available databases, and centrally coordinating all available institutions in service of public order and state security, including the burgeoning private security sector. This is supported by data experts, from statisticians to applied mathematicians, who work with the assumption that more data and more complete data sets will generate more accurate patterns of human behavior and so more accurate predictions. Data can be used in a retrospective and prospective sense. Retrospectively, patterns of behavior of a particular individual or social group are reconstructed after-the-fact. This is how athletes can be stripped of their medals as technology for identifying unauthorized substances is perfected. Prospectively, future human behavior is envisioned down to the detail of scientific specifications for how to train athletes to enable their optimal performance during competitions.

In this dynamic, security dominates as a particular kind of logic that perceives indeterminacy as a threat to its understanding of planned order. To this end, the notion of security translates to efforts to minimize uncertainty through the use of surveillance. This means efforts to control how people will act when the time comes for the Games to be performed and to preempt the kinds of social behavior from transpiring that were not planned by the organizers. Potential disturbances to the Olympic Games tend to be treated by the organizers less as issues of safety and crime and more as problems of security, effectively blurring distinctions between issues of social order and disorder and matters of war and peace (see Graham, 2011). In these dynamics, security battles against other values associated with the Olympics such as equal access, open participation, inclusion, festivity, spontaneity, unstructured interpersonal bonding, cross-cultural friendship, or respect for individual privacy. In this battle, the imperative of security is positioned hierarchically in relation to all other values such that the public is made to understand that only if they follow the specifications of the template of the social order envisioned by the surveillance and security apparatus will they be able to have successful Olympics. Through these dynamics, security meta-ritual emerges as a new form of social control of the Games.

Security meta-ritual of the Olympic Games transpires at scales very different from other planned global events. By scale, I am referring to the space/time dimension of the Olympics; that is, their particular expanse in space throughout a specific duration in time. The expansion of the Olympics into 17 days of coordinated activity of millions of people spread within a geographical space of hundreds of square kilometers, encompassing water and land, valleys and mountains is necessarily also related to complexity. Complexity of the Olympics is related to the way the Games were originally conceived as a planned, performative, cyclical, and inclusive event.

Olympics were to become a sports competition that is to take place every so many years, include representative teams from as many nations as possible, and be staged at different locations around the world. Each of these aspects of the Olympics' design contributes to their complexity and therefore conditions for unexpected outcomes. The very nature of the Olympics as a performative type of event also means that potential for uncertainty is generated through the actual staging of the Olympics. If, as I suggest, uncertain outcomes are considered by the organizers as something undesirable unless they can be effectively controlled, and if, in turn, the purpose of security meta-ritual is to create a maximally controlled space within which the organizers hope to be able to minimize uncertainty, then it becomes necessary to think about the sources of uncertainty of the Olympic Games in relation to their complexity. The security meta-ritual of the Olympics reflects the complexity of the Games in relation to their design and in relation to their actual performance in a specific place in time. Its central role as a form of social control in space and through time transpires at the interface between the event and the host location.

To think in complexity terms does not mean to simply import concepts from physics, biology, cybernetics, and informatics where the theory originates and adopt them to the study of the Olympics. Rather, complexity theoretical thinking is more of a catalyst and a signpost to take the study of surveillance and security in the Olympics, and in global planned events more generally, in a new direction. In line with this, while the study of complex phenomena and processes tends to be approached through computational and modeling tools, we pursue this agenda ethnographically.

Historical and comparative team ethnography of the security meta-ritual of the Olympic Games

Of all methodologies available to social scientists, ethnography offers the highest empirical, analytical, and theoretical potential for the study of global planned events in ways that archival research, content analysis, focused interviews, or statistical analysis alone cannot. Indeed, ethnography has increasingly been advocated as the methodology of choice for the study of the Olympic Games (Klausen, 1999c; MacAloon, 2006, 1992). By being embedded with those who are participating in the event, an ethnographer is able to record in detail what is actually happening, engage in focused dialog with the people on the ground, and make on-the-spot decisions about which empirical observations can be most productive in illuminating some aspect of the event. In analytical terms, the ethnographer is then able to study the totality of these written and tape-recorded notes in ways that can generate novel insights and conceptual discoveries about some aspect of the event and the larger social process in which the event is embedded (Bajc, 2012b). Once a theoretical understanding is developed in this way, it can be turned into a process of focused construction of theory. These are some of the insights of the British social anthropologist Max Gluckman in his pioneering ethnographic approach to analysis of social mechanisms using a specific event as a starting point (Evens and Handelman, 2006). My attempt to develop security meta-ritual into a systematic theoretical framework for the study of surveillance and security in the Olympics resonates with his approach.

I began to be interested in surveillance and security while I was embedded as an ethnographer with Catholic pilgrims during the visit of Pope John Paul II in Jerusalem in March 2000. My empirical focus was drawn toward checkpoints, concrete barriers, metal detectors, operatives, and public discourse about security during the event. An intensive emersion into that data began to yield a pattern, which I discuss below, and three central theoretical insights: first, during this millennial pilgrimage to the Holy Land, surveillance and security took center stage; second, the organization of the event was subjected to the activity of the surveillance and security apparatus; and third, the activity of the apparatus was itself transformative (Bajc, 2011b). A central question followed from these insights; namely, whether this may have been a special case. I was able to answer this question by comparing the millennial pilgrimage in Jerusalem with the second presidential inauguration of George W. Bush in Washington, DC, in January 2005. The same ethnographic approach yielded a central conclusion that these were two very different types of global planned events and in two different countries, and yet, the surveillance and security dynamics followed a very similar pattern (Bajc, 2007b). This conclusion prompted a new question: was the pattern I had come to articulate as security meta-ritual of planned events, in fact, a global phenomenon?

The Olympic Games offered themselves as an ideal case study to try to understand how this phenomenon has emerged historically and how its empirical manifestations have varied cross-culturally. Ethnographers who have tried to understand how the past is related to the present have named their approaches historical ethnography (for example, Glaeser, 2011; Comaroff and Comaroff, 1992) and have used a variety of data to analyze how the past relates to what they were studying in the present. The Olympic Games can be studied in historical as well as cultural-comparative terms. They are cultural phenomena practiced in different states, which leave behind documentation that testifies to their practice through time. Such documentation includes minutes from committee meetings, official reports, press releases, memories of participants and those involved with the organization of the event, as well as mass mediated news, commentaries, and feeds. Official documentation can be found in the archives of the host cities and at the headquarters of the International Olympic Committee in Lausanne, Switzerland. Some of this research material has restricted access, but much of it is open to the public and in many cases also available through online databases.

Upon analytical reflection of some of this data, it became clear that a historical and comparative ethnographic approach to the study of the emergence of security meta-ritual through historical time can be utilized to its highest potential when individual Games are considered as events in their own particular cultural, social, political, geographic, and historical circumstances. In this way, it becomes possible to identify how surveillance and security dynamics, as they played themselves out in their specific contexts, through time, have come to shape the individual elements of the security meta-ritual. The more detailed the empirical reconstruction of the past Games, the more accessible an understanding of the historical trajectories may become. That is, to grasp these trajectories, I would need the past Olympics to be empirically reconstructed so that the data organized in this fashion can be used as ethnographic evidence for the analysis of security meta-ritual.

The next important methodological decision had to do with which Olympics can actually be considered in some ways as significant in the development of the security meta-ritual in historical terms. This dilemma was approached in analytical as well as practical terms. Fifteen Summer and Winter Olympiads between 1964 and 2012 were selected for analysis: 1964 Tokyo, 1968 Mexico City, 1972 Sapporo, 1972 Munich, 1976 Montreal, 1980 Moscow, 1988 Seoul, 1992 Barcelona, 1994 Lillehammer, 2002 Salt Lake City, 2004 Athens, 2006 Turin, 2008 Beijing, 2010 Vancouver, and 2012 London. This approach also made it clear that a project of this scope necessarily becomes a collective effort of scholars with empirically grounded knowledge of the specific Olympics and access to primary data regarding security and surveillance. Sources for these Olympiads are available in multiple languages, some are in English while others are only accessible in the languages in use in a given host country. The choice of the case studies required an assembly of a team with access to primary data in 13 countries and in 10 different languages. For many of the team members, English is their second or even third language. The contributors thus come from a wide spectrum of disciplinary focus, including history, anthropology, sociology, media and cultural studies, geography, sports studies, urban studies, and criminology.

Students of the Olympics often lament that Olympic scholarship tends to suffer from two major shortcomings: first, that most researchers who write about the Olympics have never themselves attended the event and, second, that a more comprehensive approach to the study of the Games requires a team effort. To this end, Arne Martin Klausen (1999c) assembled a team of anthropologists who were granted permission to study the Lillehammer 1994 Winter Games. One of their team members is contributing to this book. The team approach to the study of the Olympics was first tested out during the 1984 Los Angeles Games. Anthropologist Don Handelman was a part of that team. He evaluates this methodological experiment in the Prologue to the book. Several other contributors have also attended the Olympics in different capacities, such as spectators and advisers. Their experiences of the Olympics are reflected in the focus of their analyses. For others, however, data about the event they are describing is derived from sources other than participant observation.

The very topic of surveillance and security in the Olympics poses another set of challenges. Given that surveillance is shrouded in obscurity, security issues often legally protected as a secret, and writings by journalists and surveillance and security practitioners increasingly treated as scholarly contributions, how such documentation is to be evaluated by a scholar as empirical evidence is an urgent issue. To this end, chapters were sent to multiple reviewers for comments. In the final instance, each team member has made his or her own final decision for how the evidence they were able to assemble was to be evaluated. For these reasons, sources used as empirical evidence are detailed in footnotes in each chapter and in this way separated from the bibliography of scholarly references, which is compiled at the end of the book.

In this research agenda, my own contribution as a theoretical ethnographer of the security meta-ritual is to ground my theoretical explication of this model in the empirical evidence provided by the contributing authors. In line with this, I make use of their empirical evidence freely without repeated attribution while evidence from sources not presented by the authors is separately footnoted. This project is an effort to begin to systematically build a theory of surveillance and security in the Olympics through close and ongoing analysis of empirical evidence, taking the complexity of the event into account empirically and theoretically. The intension is that the theory explicated here can continue to be evaluated and adjusted beyond the scope of this book in dialog with new empirical materials and theoretical constructs.

There is an additional motivation in exploring complexity theoretical thinking for the study of security and surveillance in the Olympics; namely, to probe whether it may be possible to think in more interrelated terms about the vast and continuously growing empirical evidence of the various small- and large-scale processes involving the Olympics today and in the past. This may be despite (or perhaps because of) the fact that, as John Bale and Mette Krogh Christensen (2004) have emphasized, positions from which the Olympics are interpreted, described, criticized, analyzed, reflected on, and otherwise studied or experienced are so wildly divergent and involve such a huge spectrum of understandings. So, too, while the Olympics may well be, as in the words of John MacAloon (2006: 17) "literally unknowable in their full complexity," it would be nevertheless analytically useful to begin to take on the challenge to envision more holistic theoretical tools to help us make sense of these multiplicities of experiences and understandings about the Olympics. For if, as Maurice Roche (2000) and others have argued, the Olympic Games are, in fact, an example of a global collective happening with potentially wide-ranging consequences, as complexity theoretical thinking would also suggest, attempts to integrate this divergent and variegated knowledge, however challenging this may be, could potentially generate novel and useful insights much beyond the study of security and surveillance in the Olympics.

The Olympics as a complex event

The Olympic Games may well be the most complex global planned event in practice today. This is often acknowledged by scholars and lay people alike in more intuitive, common-sensical terms, suggesting that something very big and very complicated is going on. At a more analytical level, the Olympics do appear to be a phenomenon, which exemplifies what has come to be articulated in the social and natural sciences as complexity theory (Urry, 2003). Complexity theory tries to capture a state of affairs where what is happening through time acts like a highly dynamic system where whatever is involved in this happening is interrelated in such a way that it gravitates toward its own ordering. This would imply that the Olympic Games as an event have self-organizing features that have the potential to lead their performance to highly unpredictable outcomes. The notion of "system" in this context refers to a process through which the different elements that comprise a particular happening relate to each other in such a way that their interactions generate relationships that are causational, so that they can potentially lead to unexpected outcomes. We could well see the Olympic Games as such a dynamic system. Every time the Games are staged in a particular environment, the various actors involved come together to collectively (re)create through performance the event we have come to know as the Olympic Games, while, at the same time, as the history has shown perhaps most forcefully in Munich in 1972, this activity can take unexpected directions.

If what makes the Olympics complex is its nature as a highly dynamic system to gravitate toward unintended paths despite the fact that they are meticulously planned and the performance of this plan is tightly controlled, then we need to think about the sources of these dynamics, which make the event complex. The impetus for complexity of the modern Olympic Games seems to come from two directions: one emanates from the way the Olympics were designed by their creators, while the other transpires through the process of their performance. Three aspects of the design are of particular interest to our discussion here: competition, inclusiveness, and location. Competition is the central characteristic of the Olympics, which suggests that indeterminacy is a part of its performative practice in that the outcomes of the Games may not be known in advance, lest the event be reduced to a farce. Inclusiveness is the central motto of the Games. The implication is that there is a tendency for the Olympics to continue to expand, incorporating additional athletes, sports, sports federations, participating countries, venues, sponsors, television audiences, and entertainment-type events to accompany the competitions. As the number of elements in the Olympic system increases, so, too, does the number of possibilities in which these elements could interact with each other and the unintended effects such interactions can produce. The location of the Games is continuously changing. This means that the hosting of each subsequent event in a different geographic locale requires that the planning for the event be adapted to ever-changing physical environments and their cultural, social, and political contexts. We can think of these dynamics related to the way the Games are structured as complexity by design.

The dynamics of complexity by design help shape how the Olympic Games transpire through the process of their actual performance in a given place and through a specific period of time. An event of this type does not come to exist until it is actually performed as such. As everyone assembles with everything in place, the Opening Ceremony officially marks the beginning of the process through which the Olympics emerge as an event to then be officially drawn to a close through the Closing Ceremony. This process is highly particular and dependent on specific situations and their contingencies. This implies dynamics of a different kind, where each performance is staged under very specific historical, sociocultural, environmental, and political conditions that change with every performance. Here, complexity is related to the place/time performance of the Olympics, each of which must be fitted into a particular socio-physical environment, enacted in front of an audience, and able to generate some kind of collective experience. We can think of the dynamics generated through this process as complexity through performance.

To pay attention to the complexity in the Olympic Games is to consider: first, ways in which uncertainty is central to the nature of the Games and the kinds of dynamics that make the uncertainty explicit, and second, how such dynamics are controlled through security meta-ritual. Uncertainty here refers to sets of interrelated forces such that any specific outcome of the interaction of these forces is not predictable. It is important to emphasize that this is different from risk, which refers to situations in which negative consequences of interrelations of forces are predicted by using established statistical models. This conception of uncertainty becomes analytically important when we consider how the various features that make the Olympics a complex system generate dynamics through which conditions of uncertainty are created and how such conditions open up possibilities of highly unpredictable outcomes. By distinguishing between complexity by design and complexity through performance, it becomes possible to illuminate, on the one hand, attempts to reduce complexity in the hopes to tame uncertainty stemming from the organizational structure of the Games and, on the other hand, the tension generated through the interface between the planned structure of the Games and their performance in a specific geographical area.

Complexity by design

Global planned events, as Handelman (1998) analyzes them, have their own internal order, an inner organization that makes them stand apart from the routine everyday life and, at the same time, holds them together as events that we can see and experience as a happening, different from daily, routine life. In the case of events such as the Olympics, this internal order did not come to be practiced through tradition but was intentionally designed by their creators for specific purposes. Such events are, in terms of Eric Hobsbawm and Terrence Ranger (1983), invented traditions, made popular in 19th-century Europe, where the goal was to create rituals that would have the capacity to unite large numbers of people who were not related through kinship ties. In this spirit, the inventors of the Olympics envisioned that, through competition, inclusiveness, and continuously changing location, the Games would be able to unite people around the world through the virtue of physical education in the form of sports (MacAloon, 1981). Given that such events are not traditions organically embedded within close-knit cultural systems, their fate, Handelman (1998) suggests, can be very vulnerable. They tend to be subjected to, on the one hand, continuous critique, questioning, and reevaluation and, on the other hand, efforts and strategies of reassurance.

Competition

One of the most well-known early designers of the modern Olympics, Baron Pierre de Coubertin, is often quoted to have said that what was important about the Olympics was not to win but to participate (MacAloon, 1981; Guttman, 2002; Young, 1987). Yet, the Olympics were nevertheless envisioned as a contest. Every Olympiad must have winners, and therefore losers, and there seems to have been little tolerance for uncertainty regarding these results. Measurement technology, television, and the push for perfection have accompanied this competitive spirit. As professional athletes, who have now largely replaced the amateurs, continue to perfect their physical, mental, and emotional skills needed to win, rather than simply participate, the distinctions between winners and losers have become less and less perceptible to the naked human eye, and ever more sophisticated surveillance technology has taken the role of the arbiter.

Some examples from the survey of these developments, provided by the *Encyclopedia Britannica* (Abrahams and Young, 2013), will suffice to demonstrate how surveillance technology has been put in place to deal with uncertainty regarding results of competitions. Human timekeeping was already replaced by electronic timing devices during the 1912 Summer

Games in Stockholm. The photo-finish camera and uniform automatic timing were introduced in Antwerp in 1920. The 1936 Berlin Summer Games were televised for the first time, using telex to transmit results, closed circuit to transmit to the local theaters, and zeppelins to transport newsreel footage to various European cities. By 1960, the Rome Summer Games were brought to homes in Europe via television and the tapes of the footage later flown to New York to be broadcast on the CBS television network. The Tokyo Games of 1964 were already televised live via satellite and in color. Four summers later, the timing and scoring were perfected by the use of computers.

Today, cameras are directed at every aspect of the athletes' bodies and follow their every move in time, not only for the pleasure of global audiences but more importantly for the purposes of exactness in measurement. This technology now allows the information, that is, a slice of the performance in real time, to be replayed and replayed again until the decision is reached about the final result. Moreover, since the data for every athlete and every competition is stored indefinitely and technologies and techniques for surveilling athletes are continuously perfected, the results can be reexamined and reevaluated retrospectively at any moment. This has become a major source of uncertainty, as medals can be revoked and winners disqualified if impurity is detected in the data retrospectively. The policy of the World Anti-Doping Agency is perhaps most publicly visible in this regard. The race to perfection of mathematical algorithms and technological means to discern patterns in preexisting databases allows the agency to go back in time and reanalyze old blood samples collected from the athletes for traces of unauthorized substances, previously not detected, and to retrospectively strip athletes of their medals. Given that surveillance is also prospective in the sense that it is performed to preempt future activity from transpiring, it remains to be studied what strategies are used by the watchful, not only to classify substances in terms of permissibility but also to profile athletes in terms of categories of more and less likely to use such substances.

It is easy to see how this policy could be a great source of uncertainty not only for the athletes but also for the International Olympic Committee as the vigilant guard of its image. The stakes here are high as this surveillance technology supports the Olympic logo of five rings, expressing the Olympic ideals of purity, fair play, and friendship, which have become a major source of revenue for the International Olympic Committee and the Olympic Movement as a whole. The logo and the ideals it represents must be upheld in all its purity if television audiences and the corporate interests are to continue to want to be associated with them. Interestingly, these purity tests are not applied equally to all involved, in that it is the athletes, not the corporate sponsors, who are subjected to continuous panoptic surveillance where each one could be flagged out at any moment.

Inclusiveness

The ideals of global friendship imply that the Olympic Games must be as inclusive as possible, which in practical terms means adapting to the changing cultural and social sentiments as well as adjusting to the ever-shifting political climate. Without this capacity of the Olympics to adapt to the changing environment, the Olympic Games would have become a closed system, caught in entropy of reproducing itself without change and in this way probably eventually degenerate. Indeed, there was a real danger in the early years that the Games would fade into oblivion. This continuous internal (re)organization tends to produce additional components, thereby contributing to the growth of its own complexity and by implication the system's own internal dynamics, which means uncertainty and so more surveillance. Two obvious examples of cultural adaptation are the addition of women and winter sports. The decision to finally add women to what used to be an all-male happening has been contributing to the overall expansion in the number of competing athletes. As Chappelet and Kübler-Mabbott (2008) show, at the 1980 Moscow Games, there were 4092 male athletes and 1125 female athletes. By the time of the 2004 Athens Games, there were 6296 male and 4329 female athletes. The Beijing Games in 2008 had a combined participation of more than 11,000 athletes. Introducing winter sports in Chamonix in 1924 led to an official sanctioning by the International Olympic Committee as a new series, the Winter Games, which subsequently led to the Games being staged every two, rather than four, years and by implication contributed to the increase in the number of sports included in the Games.

Also interesting to note are consequences of the adaptation to the shifting geopolitics. The end of World War II and the demise of the colonial powers following the struggle for independence in Asia and Africa put the International Olympic Committee in a position to expand its membership. At the time of the 1980 Moscow Summer Games, there were 145 recognized member countries of which 81 participated in the Moscow Games. A decade later, following political changes in the central and eastern part of Europe, new countries were again invited to join so that by the time of 2004 Athens, there were 202 recognized members with 201 teams participating. Each country is represented through its own National Olympic Committee, which chooses its own athletes to compete at the Games, each of whom is accompanied by his or her own entourage. Meanwhile, the number of media representatives has been rising, as have audiences to the point that we may say that the Games are broadcast to more than half of the world's population. In line with these developments, there are efforts to sort out the growing complexity and uncertainty through hierarchies of decision-making, centralized mechanisms of coordination, formalization of expertize of judges and officials, standardization of rules defining particular sport, exactness of measurement of performance, and, therefore perfection of surveillance technologies to monitor and enforce all of these.

Location

The provision that each subsequent Olympiad be organized and staged in a different city is perhaps the most persistent source of uncertainty embedded in the design of the Olympics. While there have, historically, been various attempts to change this practice, it has been the position of the early inventors as much as of the International Olympic Committee today, that changing the location contributes to the internationalization and so inclusion of the Olympics.[3] The privilege to choose the next Olympic host, however, has contributed not only to the endurance of the Olympics as a global event, but also the political power of the International Olympic Committee. Indeed, on its part, there has historically been an active political thinking behind the process of selection of host cities. Following World War I, the 1920 Games were awarded to Antwerp because Belgium was on the right side of history, while Austria, Bulgaria, Germany, and Turkey were not invited to participate at these Games as a "punishment" for being the war's losers. This policy was repeated after World War II where for the London Games of 1948, neither of the defeated powers of the war, Japan and Germany, were invited to participate. South Africa was banned from participating at the 1964 Tokyo Games because of apartheid. The choice of Tokyo for the 1964 Olympics was to show that, in the eyes of the International Olympic Committee, Japan has been forgiven for its role in World War II, and it was time to see the Games in Asia. Similarly, the choice of Mexico City for the 1968 Games was to see the Games staged in Latin America, in a country that was able to demonstrate satisfactory economic growth. The 1976 Games went to Canada where Montreal was selected to avoid a diplomatic standoff between either of the other two contenders, Moscow and Los Angeles. The next time around, Moscow was judged to be going in the direction of disarmament and so deemed suitable for the 1980 Games, which meant that Los Angeles was next in line for the 1984 Olympics. The staging of the 1988 Games in Seoul required a lot of time and energy from the International Olympic Committee, as it struggled between the demands of the two superpowers of the Cold War and the two Koreas through which their powers were played. At the same time, it is hard to imagine that the International Olympic Committee could not foresee that such a power struggle might ensue when they made their decision. It took the Chinese several tries to play through the politics but by 2001, they had learned the ways and the biases of the predominantly Western International Olympic Committee and were finally able to lobby successfully for the 2008 Games. By 1990, the United States needed forgiveness for the trouble they stirred with the boycott of the 1980 Olympics because the other party that put in a bid for the 1996 Games, Athens, was deemed not ready for an event of this size; so Atlanta had to win. The following illustration (Figure 1.1) captures this power play within the time frame of 1964–2012, the period considered in this book.

Figure 1.1   Summer and Winter Olympic Games, 1964–2012

The difference in font size used to indicate the host cities is meant to highlight those Games that were selected for analysis in this book.

This politics behind selecting the host cities, however, continues to expose the Olympics to vulnerability beyond its turbulent years at the turn of the 20th century and around the time of the two World Wars. Ignoring the widespread popular discontent in Mexico turned the central part of the Olympic space in 1968 into a site where several hundred protesters perished at the hands of the state. There has also been commotion and reshuffling between the promised and the actual Olympic host cities. As the 1976 Montreal Summer Games left the city in financial difficulties, Denver reneged on its commitment for the 1976 Winter Games, throwing the International

Olympic Committee into a position to have to scramble for a different location, eventually persuading Innsbruck to take on the commitment even though the city had just hosted the Games in 1964. After Vancouver withdrew at the last minute, Lake Placid was the only remaining city interested in the 1980 Winter Games. For the 1984 Summer Games, the only city that showed interest was Los Angeles. It was not the first time, though, as for the 1932 Summer Games there was again only one bidder, and as it happened, it was again Los Angeles.

During recent decades, there has been an increasing interest in staging the Games. Nevertheless, this provision to continuously change the host city is likely to remain the most pressing source of uncertainty embedded in the Olympic design. There may be a number of reasons for the recent surge of interest to host the Olympics, not least the discovery that the Games could actually be a financial success for their investors, the trend among aspiring global cities to use such global planned events as means of global promotion, and changes in the process of selection of candidate cities put in place by the International Olympic Committee. This shift seems to have created new sources of uncertainty in that it opened up novel possibilities for corruption. The International Olympic Committee responded by gradually abandoning the more casual approach to selecting the host city and increasingly implementing surveillance procedures and other bureaucratic measures to impose control on potential complexities of the selection process.

Today, the cities aspiring to become candidates are expected to present an elaborate and costly pre-bidding dossier, following detailed specifications for preselection procedures. This allows the International Olympic Committee Executive Board to reject cities it does not see fit at the initial stage. The cities which make it to the next level must agree that the Evaluation Committee may visit the area for on-site inspection, specifically paying attention to possible corruption and rule breaking. A representative of the winning city signs a detailed contract with the International Olympic Committee and the National Olympic Committee to form an Organizing Committee of the Olympic Games. The Organizing Committee of the Olympic Games becomes responsible to organize the Olympics and must also allow the Coordination Commission to surveill the preparations and monitor the planning for the Games.

Through the cycle of host city selection, every two years, a new city is added to the list. Each victorious locale is faced with the fact that the event is to take place seven years into the future. This means that the winning cities necessarily become exposed to the vagaries of potential sudden cultural, social, economic, and political shifts beyond their control, which cannot be foreseen seven years in advance. At the same time, for the city and the country, this becomes an opportunity to promote its own sense of greatness as a global metropolitan player to the largest possible number of people around the world, and do so precisely by demonstrating that it is capable of not only organizing an event of this scope but also, in fact, carrying out its performance as it was planned in 17 days without disturbance..

Complexity through performance

The Olympic Games as a planned global event only come to exist as such when they are actually performed in real place and time. The athletes may have surpassed the world record at other competitions or during their own individual practice under the tutelage of their trainers. To be bestowed the title of the gold medal winner at the Olympics, however, carries a different kind of prestige. This prowess must be demonstrated at a very specific time in a particularly designated place, and in front of the officially sanctioned judges of the Olympics with the ever-present cameras that record the minutest detail of their performance for the entire world to see. If this were not the case and results were to be known in advance, there would be no reason for the Olympic Games. The years-long preparations are, therefore, tested in real time when all the numerous elements that comprise what we know as the Olympic Games, including the thousands of athletes and their supporting staff, world dignitaries with their security details, special guests, corporate personalities, various officials, thousands of newspaper, radio and television journalists and photographers, service sub-contractors, volunteers, millions of paying spectators, and untold others, all congregate together, each contributing their own part to perform the Olympic Games in some two weeks' time in a host city, where the organizers, architects and urban planners, construction crews, military, special forces, undercover and regular police, and a host of surveillance and security experts have been preparing the grounds for the event.

By the time they all gather in the Olympic space, venues are expected to have been completed and ready to be used to their intended capacity, amenities to function as expected, services available as promised, television cameras ready to start rolling as agreed, and the grand Olympic program to begin unfolding as planned. The performance is officially set into motion through the Opening Ceremony of the Olympic Games as the television, radio, social media, and front-page newspaper coverage connect this collective happening through live broadcasting with billions of people around the world, and then officially concludes as the Olympic Flame is put out during the Closing Ceremony only to be lit again in two years' time. This implies dynamics of a very different kind where uncertainty is integral to the performative practice of the event and no less central to its success in generating an emotionally intensive experience for its participants. Complexity of the Olympics through performance and the uncertainty this performance can potentially generate begins to reveal itself as the program is about to unfold. We can think of three general aspects of complexity through performance: emplacement, enactment, and experience. Emplacement has to do with how the performative activity is put in place, how it is laid into its actual socio-physical environment in the host location. Enactment refers to how closely to its planned version the program is carried out in actuality in front of the audience. Experience is about the extent to which the performance is able to generate the desired emotional outcomes.

Emplacement

Emplacement of the performative activity of the Olympics has particular characteristics. Apart from the Opening and the Closing Ceremonies, the Olympics do not have a single focal point around which the collective activity would be concentrated. Rather, the event is made up of numerous sub-events, which take place simultaneously and in widely divergent venues in hugely spread apart geographical areas. The Opening Ceremony on the eve of the Games is generally emplaced within a physical enclosure of some kind, likely an arena, of the kind in which surveillance, ordering, and imaginaries of interruption are built into its architectural design (Stoppani, 2012). Everyone is seated according to a prescribed order and any out-of-the-ordinary movement can be easily spotted and preempted by the surveillance apparatus. The following day, however, begins with competitions taking place down mountain slopes, through water streams, along city avenues and urban plazas, through wooded forests, and enclosed arenas, each connected through a network of walkways, roads, subway lines, and railways along which the performers and the audiences will travel to attend the sub-event and then return after the performance, back to their respective residential quarters. Each competition is a sub-event of its own, with its own venue, event design, performers, and engaged audience, and these repeat through the schedule of semi-final and final competitions, and their awards ceremonies, for over two weeks. Each requires its own adaptation to a particular physical environment and these vary from host city to host city. On the evening of the last day, everything culminates in the Closing Ceremony, again emplaced within a surveillance-friendly architecture of the performance arena. It is well known that Summer Olympic Games have many more sub-events scheduled on the same day as do Winter Olympic Games and so create more potential for uncertain outcomes. The distance between the specific geographic locations for the venues vary. For example, the 2012 London Summer Games were largely concentrated in the eastern part of London with some venues in its suburbs. The 2006 Winter Games in Turin were spread between seven different municipalities in multiple mountain valleys of the province of Torino. Emplacement of the 1980 Moscow Summer Games created potential for uncertain outcomes at a different scale in a geographical area stretched between five cities as much as 1200 km apart.

Enactment

Uncertainty is an integral part of every enactment, be it a sports competition or a ceremony, in that there can be no certainty of the anticipated outcome until the act is, in fact, completed. With the drive to perfection and ever more daring performance, athletes fail, sustain injuries and even die, as was the case with a luger in 2010 in Vancouver. With the Opening and the Closing Ceremonies becoming not only a visual but also a technological spectacle, accidents happen, some perhaps more embarrassing, while others potentially serious. There was much ridicule about ineptness and inability to perform at the highest of levels on the part of the Russian organizers when the world witnessed only four of the five Olympic rings light up across the winter sky in Sochi in 2014. In contrast, the barely averted disaster in 2000 in Sidney remained unreported but could have been potentially lethal. MacAloon (2009:42) describes how during the Opening Ceremony in Sydney, the torch bearer walked into a pool of water, lowered the torch toward the water, lighting up a ring of fire around her, at the moment of which a giant hidden cauldron circle was to rise out of the water. The fire circle was lit in the water as rehearsed, the athlete standing in the middle as planned, but the cauldron failed to rise according to the plan. Luckily, during those long minutes, the athlete was able to keep her composure and the potential for disaster seemed to have gone unnoticed by the audiences. MacAloon reveals that the failure turned out to be an act of intentional tempering with the electronic system backstage.

Extension of such an enactment to audiences around the world is particularly interesting in terms of how uncertainty dynamics relate to complexity through performance. The live broadcasting of the Games to some half of the world's population, Daniel Dayan and Elihu Katz (1992) have shown, is an important factor in the performative process because it makes it possible to connect the event on the ground with Olympic fans around the world. Which details are conveyed through these broadcasts varies widely from country to country and region to region. These variations are contributed to local mass media cultures, national politics in relation to the Olympic host city and country, and differences in broadcasting rights (de Moragas, Larson, and Rivenburgh, 1995). Though sharing photographs and videos from the inside of the Olympic space tends to be subordinated to the demands for protection of sponsors, the social media nevertheless offer new possibilities for how images, texts, and other expressions of the performance are transmitted to and received by the public worldwide. It is through these media that the amplification of effects becomes most pronounced to the general public. Mistakes and disruptions tend to be conveyed minute-by-minute and recycled over and over. As Karin Knorr-Cetina (2005) reminds us, it is precisely this capacity of complex systems to have effects disproportionately magnified that attracts those who may seek to intentionally disrupt the Olympics.

Experience

The ability for the Olympics to generate desired experiences, not only for those present in situ but also others around the world, is in many ways central to the Games. Uncertainty is a precondition to the potential to generate any such emotional state. The process of enactment of each of the sub-events and the Olympics as a whole is expected to generate emotional tension, excitement, anticipation, exuberance, some kind of positive collective sentiment that can be shared in some capacity between these individuals who find themselves geographically and socially together in the Olympic space and others who are following the sub-events on their computers and television screens. Given this immense diversity, the spectrum of these experiences must necessarily be incomprehensibly wide. Nevertheless, for the Olympics to be successful as a performative event, they must be able to organize these experiences in some collectively identifiable ways lest the Games be reduced to confusion, indifference, or mere bureaucratic procedures of determining winners and losers.

According to John MacAloon's (1984b, 1989, 1999, 2006, 2012) pioneering analysis of the organization of experience of the Olympics, the International Olympic Committee has been committed to articulating these through four different social forms: games, ritual, festival, and spectacle. Competitions are given shape through the form of games. These are expected to be fair play and resonate with the participants as symbols of discipline, ambition, self-sacrifice, effort, and sportsmanship. Victory ceremonies as well as the grand Opening and Closing Ceremonies are expected to articulate experiences through the form of ritual. Successful performance of such rituals fosters a sense of individual achievement, emotional transformation, and effect and, at the same time, generates feelings of collective sentiments such as national identity and shared humanity. Parades, street dances, and concerts in the Olympic Park are meant to show openness and broaden participation by providing a venue that is able to include those who may not be in a position to attend competitions so that a social environment can be created in which athletes, spectators, and others within the Olympic space could interact. This socializing experience is to be articulated through the form of festival, which is to encourage an atmosphere of excitement, joy, and festivity through less structured and more spontaneous celebrations. Reaching out to global audiences through televised sub-events takes the form of spectacle, which is to help foster sentiments of universal participation by enabling those not present in situ to be included in the Games by sharing some of the festivity through visual effects. Another social form of organizing experiences that is able to foster global connections between participants in situ and others around the world is the Olympic Flame Relay, which MacAloon (2012) articulates as a global ritual form.

As MacAloon (1984b) points out, various kinds of dynamics are threatening to undermine these forms of articulation of experience of the Olympics. Distinctions between winners and losers are measured by surveillance technology in hundredths of a second so that the extent to which the Games can continue to articulate collective experience of the values of sports competition may not be so clear. The insistence on the part of the organizers on inflexible ordering and surveillance of access to Games venues through entrance tickets and accreditation have the effect of preventing the fans from coming in contact with athletes. Reaching athletes seems to have become impossible even for a researcher with an accreditation. At the smaller Lillehammer 1994 Games, athletes were practically sealed from the spectators. The fans were, instead, directed to huge television screens where they were to wait patiently for live broadcasters to interview individual athletes. It has become increasingly challenging to create occasions for spontaneous intermingling and collective emotional transformation. Olympic Villages, which house athletes and their entourage, seem to have become more like what Erving Goffman (1961) calls total institutions, collectivities that discourage social interaction with the outside world. A newsletter from the 2006 Turin Games suggests that all kinds of social occasions are organized in the Village specifically for athletes and with the purpose to provide them with all desirable entertainment so that they would not feel the need to leave that venue in search for socializing experiences elsewhere. Opening and Closing Ceremonies are increasingly becoming occasions to showcase engineering, technology, and daring maneuvering by the performers. In the rush by the host countries to try to outdo each other, ceremonies now resemble less and less the form of ritual and its individual and collective transformative potentials and more and more the form of spectacle with its emphasis on the visual. There seems to be a tendency to give the televisual experience preference over face-to-face interpersonal interaction. In this dynamic, MacAloon (2012) demonstrates, the Olympic Flame Relay may well be the most unstructured of the Olympic forms in terms of accessibility and, in this way, also potentially the most ritually transformative.

Security meta-ritual has emerged as another form of organization of Olympic experience, the significance of which is to transform potentially dangerous social and physical spaces into a maximally controlled sterile zone of safety so that games, ritual, festival, and spectacle are able to transpire without disruption. In relation to other social activity, security meta-ritual is the dominant form. Its meta constitution has the effect of subsuming all other Olympic forms – games, ritual, festival, and spectacle – under its orbit. Security meta-ritual encircles, envelops, and encapsulates the entirety of social interaction at the Olympics and then, within its sterile Olympic enclosure, further protects, facilitates, manages, and secures human interaction in order to create safe physical and social conditions for the participants to experience the Olympics.

The security meta-ritual of the Olympic Games

These dynamics and their uncertainties related to complexity by design and through performance all come into focus within a larger, often global context of intensive political, cultural, social, religious, and economic conflicts, themselves now increasingly played out on the Olympic stage. All efforts are made to try to deal with uncertainties in the design and performance before the event. Because the Olympics are highly sensitive to a specific locale and its larger context within which they are practiced, however, the dynamics created at the interface between the event and its specific socio-physical locale make the outcome of the Olympics highly unpredictable. During the run-up to the Olympics and throughout the event, these dynamics have the potential to become a disruption, build up into crisis, or even turn to an affront to the event with potentially disastrous consequences. Security meta-ritual is a form of social activity that tries to deal with uncertainties that come to focus at the interface where the event and the locale meet. In this process, security meta-ritual emerges through juggling between these multitudes of forces, which are a part of the process of the Olympics and yet beyond direct control of the organizers, by developing various strategies. These strategies amount to attempts to control the future because they are based, first, on imaginaries of how dynamics will transpire as the Olympics are to unfold and, then, on inventions of procedures and technologies to preempt and prevent these envisioned scenarios from actually happening. We can think of these forces that transpire at the interface between the event and its specific locale as well as the efforts to control them as clusters of dynamics that can be analytically articulated. I have so far articulated the following : shift of attention, collective memory, institutional memory, mobilization of all resources, cooperation of all involved, purification, and sterile zones of safety.

Shift of attention refers to dynamics within the time span between the date when the decision is made about which city will host the Olympics and the dates during which the Olympics are performed. This time span allows for potentially endless uncertainties to come to the fore as public attention begins to be directed toward the city and the country that is preparing for the Games. During this period, security tends to rise to the top of collective priorities. This rise of security is related to collective memory, which has to do with references to violent disruptions in the past. Related to collective memory is institutional memory, which refers to how institutions use such disruptions from the past and attempts to prevent them to envision the so-called future scenarios and surveillance strategies and technologies to be put in place to preempt them. Institutional memories and their imaginaries of disruptions envisioned to happen in the future help to give impetus to mobilization of all resources. This refers to the urge to engage all institutions serving public order and to implement the latest surveillance technology. In this push for using all available resources, we see another cluster of dynamics emerge: cooperation of all involved. This has to do with an expectation that everyone taking part in the event, including individuals and institutions, will cooperate with rules and restrictions put in place for the Games. Participants are expected to either adjust their behavior to the specifications of the surveillance and security apparatus or be removed or remove themselves from the Olympic space. Institutions of order are pushed to be coordinated under an umbrella of a centralized command. These clusters of dynamics work toward purification, which is at the heart of these strategies. This is a process of sterilization of physical and social spaces where whatever is deemed potentially dangerous is "neutralized" or removed from the Olympic space. The ultimate goal is to create a sterile zone of safety. This is a maximally controlled social and physical space within which all sub-events on the Olympic program are made to unfold. This is done with the hopes that within this sterile enclosure, games, ritual, festival, and spectacle will be able to generate the kinds of collective sentiments and experiences participants expect from the Games. In this way, security meta-ritual tries to deal with complexities of the Games in a prospective sense. This means inventing ways to control human activity that is envisioned to transpire when the Olympics are scheduled for performance at some time in the future.

Shift of attention: all eyes on the Olympics

As the public is made aware that preparations are underway to organize a global event in a given metropolitan area, there is a shift of attention, locally and internationally, toward the upcoming event, the city in which the Olympics are to be organized, the country, and the region. We can think of this shift as a kind of trigger that sets in motion all kinds of dynamics that are not so much related to the organization and the performance of the Olympics but much more so to the social, cultural, economic, environmental, and especially political elements that comprise the context within which the Olympics are been organized. Once set in motion, these contextual dynamics build up through time to create uncertainties of various kinds. The time frame between the date when the International Olympic Committee votes on the host city and the actual date of the staging of the event has been expanding. The decision for the 1912 Games in Stockholm was made in May 1909, only three years before the Games; the news about the London 2012 Olympics was released in July 2005, giving London a period of seven years to prepare. For the organizers, this shift becomes a race against time to prepare the grounds and the program for the ever more elaborate and complex Olympics. During this race, anticipated and unforeseen dynamics can come to play, generating uncertainties with which the Olympics' organizers must engage, all of which tend to elevate security to the top of priorities and in this way set the stage for the activity of security meta-ritual.

One set of dynamics that can generate uncertainty is the international political context at the time of this shift. Uncertainties are generated through international political power struggles, playing themselves out on the Olympic stage. The choice of Seoul 1988 exacerbated the rift between North Korea and South Korea through their respective supporters, with the North under the influence of the Union of Soviet Socialist Republics and the South in the orbit of the United States of America. The North tried various strategies; it protested vehemently to the International Olympic Committee against awarding the Games to Seoul, it then lobbied for cohosting the event with the South, and finally it tried to push for forming a unified Olympic team for the 1984 Los Angeles Games. As all negotiations failed, North Korea seems to have resorted to other means, including boycott by Ethiopia, Cuba, and North Korea; bombing directed at high-ranking South Korean officials in 1983; and bombing of a South Korean passenger plane in 1987. Another well-known international brawl ensued around the 1980 Olympics in Moscow and the 1984 Games in Los Angeles where Jimmy Carter pushed for a boycott of the Russian Games and the Russians reciprocated four years later, under Konstantin Chernenko, to push for boycott of the American Games. The decision that Munich should host the 1972 Games was bitterly contested by the German Democratic Republic, which at the time of the bid was not yet a member of the International Olympic Committee, so the protest was carried out by what was then Czechoslovakia. The Nazi past was continuously brought up. Here, too, the Cold War was on stage in no uncertain terms, with East Germany belonging to the Warsaw Pact and West Germany to the North Atlantic Treaty Organization alliance. Other struggles seem more tangential where Egypt, Iraq, and Lebanon boycotted the 1956 Melbourne Games in protest of the invasion of the Sinai Peninsula by Israel in October of that year. Just a few weeks before the Games started, the Soviet Army marched into Hungary, prompting the Netherlands, Spain, and Switzerland to boycott in protest. The 2012 London Games were awarded a day before the 2005 London Tube bombing, an event which helped push security to the top of priorities while, had it happened earlier, it would likely have influenced the bidding politics. In the language of interstate politics, such activities tend to be viewed as threats to national security, which require involvement of agencies of state defense. While the International Olympic Committee often finds itself squeezed in the middle of such tensions, the process of host city selection is, as I discussed earlier, a political decision. Locally, at the level of the state, the aspiration to host the Olympics carries a strong political message, which is itself a source of uncertainties, recently increasingly turned into an issue of security. Interestingly, in historical terms, this message has remained to date remarkably consistent; namely, to be accepted into the ranks of the world's leading Western powers by showing that the country follows Western values and Western ways of life, that it is achieving Western economic standards and most recently also security and surveillance standards, and by these measures is worthy and ready for the international investors to elevate the country to the ranks of the global financial networks and stamp its logo on the global tourist map. To give but a few examples, for Tokyo 1964 it was important to show that the world had acknowledged that Japan's role in World War II was left behind. Mexico City 1968 was to demonstrate to the world the "miracle" of its economic developments in relation to its relatively poor southern neighbors. Munich 1972 wanted to leave behind the pervasive image of Hitler's Berlin Olympics. The Union of Soviet Socialist Republics bid for the 1980 Moscow Olympics to gain international approval. The 2014 Sochi Games have made little reference to the Russian Federation's past Olympic tradition, focusing instead on demonstrating the new global power it strives to be.

Countries have coped with these pressures in different ways. The organizers of the 1980 Moscow Games played a fine dance between, on the one hand, the hopes that the West would acknowledge that a socialist country can be quite "normal" and culturally "civilized" with a comfortable standard of living and, on the other hand, the confidence that the organizers were fully capable of staging the Games according to Western expectations and Western standards. The organizers of the 1964 Tokyo Games seem to have chosen a different path. They drew a sharp distinction between the customs and traditions of joyfulness and unruly spontaneity associated with Japanese public festivities that were actively discouraged and an international sports competition, promoting restraint, pride, and patriotism, which the public was instructed to follow. For the 2004 Summer Games, Athens seem to have had little choice as it found itself under intense pressure by the hegemonic global powers to follow "global standards." In turn, in the 2014 Sochi Games, we observe resistance to such pressures and determined attempts on the part of the Russian Federation to "do it our way."[4]

The political message communicated through the ability to host the Olympics not only sheds light on the country's potential membership into the elite club, it also communicates about prestige and power of specific individuals who themselves seek recognition or membership in the elite network of global powerbrokers. Their names come to be associated with success or failure of the Olympics. Judging from the English language news reports at least, the Sochi Olympics are remembered as "Putin's Games," and it would appear that the president of the Russian Federation did invest much of his time and energy to oversee the project; but in historical terms, his case is far from an exception and more like a rule. For the 1912 Stockholm Olympics, as discussed by Leif Yttergren and Hans Bolling (2012), it was the "father of Swedish sport" and an acquaintance of Pierre de Coubertin who did the bulk of efforts to bring the Olympics to Stockholm. It may well be that such a project requires a personal commitment of an individual in power. So, for the Olympics to be awarded to Mexico City, it took an effort from a military general, who was not only the highest-ranking military officer but also the highest-ranking sporting official in Mexico at the time. For the Munich Games, it was famously the city's mayor and the head of the West German sport. At the time of bidding for the 1992 Barcelona

Games, the President of the International Olympic Committee was himself a Barcelona native who then worked closely with the city's mayor to stage the Games. Two key players pushed for the 1988 Seoul Olympics, a major general who led the coup d'état in 1961 and imposed a military dictatorship and his colleague, who became Chief Officer of the Presidential Security of his regime. This dependency on key powerful and determined individuals is, at the same time, a weakness. With another political turmoil in Seoul's government, the push for the Games died out but was later salvaged as the project found a supporter in the leader of the 1979 coup who installed himself in power and pushed the project through. More recently and more famously, the role of Gianna Angelopoulos-Daskalaki in the bidding and the organization of the 2004 Olympics in Athens has been enshrined in a best-selling book about this process, which she herself has written. The book's descriptive title *My Greek Drama: Life, Love and One Woman's Effort to Bring Glory to Her Country*[5] is telling of how the individuals involved in the bidding and the organization of the Games are able to wield an enormous power to make things happen. Directing focus to security as the top concern is a useful means to this end.

These processes also have internal reverberations, building up uncertainty internally, which can spill out beyond the national boundary and reach international dimensions. Leading up to the 1964 Games in Tokyo, there were huge public protests against the United States military bases in the country. Interestingly, these protests were not seen as threats to security, as Tokyo at the time was primarily concerned about traffic jams and how to control overly joyous outbursts of local festivity that could offend Western sentiments. Before the 1988 Seoul Games, there were internal demonstrations against the military dictatorship and the staging of the Olympics as the source of ruin of the relationship between the two Koreas. In Mexico, years of strikes and uprisings against the government culminated in huge student demonstrations in the summer of 1968, just weeks before the Games, which resulted in the killing of hundreds of students just days before the Games began. The years leading up to the 1972 Sapporo Games saw students protesting against the military bases in Japan and poor learning conditions. In Montreal before the 1976 Games there were general labor strikes and separatist movements for Quebec to secede from Canada. The Barcelona Games of 1992 were staged in the midst of Catalan separatist movements from Spain. Before the 2006 Turin Games, people protested against planned high-speed railway, which was to become a part of the Olympic landscape, and against surveillance technology corporations supplying the Olympics because of their association with the war in Iraq. The people of Tibet rose against the minority politics by the Chinese in the wake of the 2008 Beijing Olympics and were supported by international protests against the Olympic Flame Relay as it traveled through London, Paris, Tokyo, and Seoul on its way to Beijing. The 2014 Games in Sochi were mired in scandals and controversies involving reports of corruption and huge overspending, protests by popular culture celebrities, the international outrage against legislation pertaining to the rights of gay, lesbian, bisexual, and transgendered individuals in the Russian Federation, and intensive international reporting about potential threats of terrorist activity during the Games.[6]

These tremendous pressures can and do create intensive dynamics and uncertainties. Interestingly, it would appear that despite this fact, the International Olympic Committee has grown increasingly more confident that the Olympics will transpire without interruption. In the midst of relentless international accusations about huge overspending in Sochi 2014, an official came in defense of the organizers with the famous reply to a journalist, "I don't recall an Olympics without corruption."[7] Such public demonstration of confidence on the part of the International Olympic Committee can be used in different ways. In the case of Sochi, London, and Beijing, its president has been asserting to the public his "full confidence" that these cities are sure to stage uninterrupted Olympics. In April 2014, two years before the scheduled 2016 Winter Games, after his monitoring visit to Rio de Janeiro, the vice-president of the International Olympic Committee bitterly and publicly complained that the city is so far behind the schedule in its infrastructure and venue construction that the delays cannot be compared to any other delays in the history of the Olympics – only to retract his own words a few days later with confidence that Rio 2016 can indeed deliver excellent Olympics.[8]

The last several Olympics have been performed under ongoing public discussion about two sets of issues: the effects of mass surveillance on democracy and the rise of the surveillance and security apparatus as an extra-state formation with a global scope. In the case of the former, people are concerned about the fundamentals of a democratic society, which are grounded in freedoms from state interference into individual private life and collective public life. In the case of the latter, at stake is state sovereignty, which is based on the ability of the state to act in the best interest of its citizenry and free from outside interference. Continuous innovation in surveillance technology has made it easy to penetrate personal spaces of the lives of individuals and collective spaces of the lives of social groups. Sharing of surveillance data and expertize, in turn, seems to have given impetus to the development of global formations of surveillance and security alliances between national secret agencies otherwise in the service of their respective state, and potentially also including global security corporations. The most frequently mentioned formation is the so-called "Five Eyes," involving surveillance and security operatives from the United States, the United Kingdom, Canada, Australia, and New Zealand. In relation to this discourse, the public is debating the essence of security; namely, what does security mean for the quality of life of the individual and the well-being of society, and what does security mean for the workings of the state? Against this backdrop, at least in relation to the Olympics to date, the surveillance and security apparatus has been able to rise in prominence in the eyes of the public and exert its power to impose its vision of order on the Olympics by setting the parameters and the conditions for the organization and performance of the Games. This activity of the surveillance and security apparatus is given shape through the form of security meta-ritual.

Collective memory

The ways of the surveillance and security apparatus do resonate with the public. How security meta-ritual transpires to deal with uncertainties in the Olympics resonates with the participants and the audiences alike. This is, to a large extent, because it draws on collective memories related to public discussions of what comes to be articulated as failures of the apparatus to preempt a disruption. These public discussions become a part of collective memory, which is a particular way of experiencing social life in the past. This is an experience that allows people who do not know each other to create a collective awareness about events in the past that they themselves may not have witnessed and to articulate this awareness through commonly identifiable narratives, symbols, and emotions. Mass media play a central role in the shaping of this kind of memory as the principle means of articulating and disseminating of images and narratives about tragic consequences of such disruptions to public life (Neiger et al., 2011). These memories of the past become a part of collective experience of the present and, as Daniel Levy and Natan Sznaider (2006) suggest, help orient social action in the present with the future in mind. In this way, referring to collective memories of such failures helps to strengthen the validity of security meta-ritual and works to legitimize its ways.

Failure to prevent the disruption to the performance of the 1972 Munich Olympics is often said to have been a catalyst in the process of articulation of security meta-ritual as an Olympic form of its own. As the Olympics were in full swing, a group from a Palestinian organization called Black September found its way into the Olympic Village and the Israeli team's quarters and took hostage Israeli athletes, demanding an exchange of the athletes for the Palestinian prisoners in Israel and an airplane to an Arab country. The International Olympic Committee was forced to suspend the Games as the television cameras shifted their focus from the competitions to the interruption, delivering live minute-by-minute interactions between the hijackers, their hostages, and the German security services to their fatal conclusions. It was the decision of the president of the International Olympic Committee at the time that, in his own famous words, "the Games must go on" because such disruptions cannot be allowed to destroy the international cooperation and goodwill that the Olympics represent.

Important to our understanding of the role of collective memory in this process are wide variations in what is remembered, and by whom, about specificities of interruptions of particular global planned events. Only four years earlier, just a few days before the Opening Ceremony officially marked the beginning of the 1968 Olympics in Mexico City, as thousands of people gathered in a public square in protest, army troops sealed off all exits from the square and began firing into the crowd, killing an estimated three to five hundred people and jailing more. There were many newspaper journalists and television commentators in the city as the Games had already been commercially broadcast since the 1960 Games in Rome.[9] Yet, there was nevertheless relatively limited media attention paid to what transpired in the plaza and so this disruption has been selectively collectively forgotten. The event is commemorated in Mexico but seldom discussed in relation to the Olympics.[10] A more often remembered interruption is the explosion at the Centennial Olympic Park during the 1996 Games in Atlanta, which killed one person and injured over a hundred, by a visitor who was caught five years later and found guilty of two other bombings: an abortion clinic and a gay bar.[11]

Collective memories of other such fatal disruptions to collective public life have shaped the security meta-ritual of the Olympics. For the 2014 Sochi Games, it was the bombings first of a trolleybus and two months later a railway station in a major urban transportation hub several hundred miles from Sochi just weeks before the Olympics, leaving dozens dead and injured.[12] For the 2012 London Olympics, it was a series of bomb explosions on three different subway lines and a commuter bus in 2005 that killed more than 50 and injured hundreds. These bombings reminded the public of similar acts in the past, particularly the bombings of a commuter train in Madrid in 2004, which killed almost 200 people and injured some 2000, the gassing of the Tokyo subway by a religious group in 1995, and also the strategies of the Irish Republican Army. In the case of the 1988 Seoul Olympics, it was a bombing in 1983, which killed high-ranking South Korean officials, and another in 1987 of a South Korean passenger plane, killing all on board. The Salt Lake City Games in 2002 had association with collective memories of four such events: the 2001 destruction of the World Trade Center Twin Towers in New York City and partial destruction of the Pentagon building in Washington, DC, took the lives of several thousand people; the 1996 explosion in Centennial Olympic Park was mentioned above; the bombing of the Murrah Federal Building in Oklahoma City in 1995 left more than 160 people dead; and the bombing of the World Trade Center in 1993 killed six.

Mass mediated reports of interruptions that result in this kind of destruction of human life tend to have a shocking effect for people in numerous locations around the world in that they are forceful reminders of uncertainty. They expose unpredictability and underscore vulnerability and, in this way, stand in sharp contrast to the efforts to showcase the power to organize and then stage in a controlled way a global planned event such as the Olympics (Bajc, 2012). Collective memories of such interruptions have the capacity to compete with the legacy, which both the hosts of the specific Games as much as the International Olympic Committee have been painstakingly constructing in hopes to be closely associated with it (Rowe, 2012). The interruptions themselves also have a potential to take charge of the actual planned event, as was the case in 1972 Munich.

Paying attention to more recent interruptions, however, gives us some sense of other twists and turns their capacity to take charge could potentially take. Millions of people followed on television screens and over the Internet the combing of the city of Boston by special weapons and tactics law enforcement units for more than four days as the city was locked down to find two suspects of two bomb explosions close to the finish line of the Boston Marathon in April 2013.[13] Their images were widely circulated through the mass and social media. Culling through thousands of hours of surveillance camera footage, photographs, and videos pouring in from businesses, residents, and tourists, allowed the surveillance and security apparatus to relate the two explosions to two backpacks left on the scene by two young men. Through tweeting, blogging, and commenting on newspaper reporting, the public actively participated in the confusion, misinformation, ensnaring of innocent individuals, urge for the manhunt, and demands for justice. For one of the two suspects, justice was served then and there. The other was taken to custody, plead not guilty, and awaited investigation and trial. Such situations can become exercises in confidence building that the strategies employed by the apparatus are effective and efficient, and that they are met with approval and support on the part of the public.[14]

Another telling example is the hunt for the disappeared Malaysian Airline Flight MH370 in March 2014, which was followed by millions of observers around the world, including family members of the flight crew and passengers waiting for details.[15] Family members were accusing the Malaysian government of misconduct. Observers were weighing in on their understanding of the whereabouts of the plane and offering their advice on aviation, terrorism, and satellite reconnaissance capacities. The Malaysian government was put under intense pressure to which it had not been accustomed and was exposed to accusations of mistreatment, withholding information, and incompetence. The intensive hunt across the Indian Ocean in the midst of accusations had failed to locate the plane. Over a year later, in July 2015, a piece of aircraft wing washed ashore on an island, encouraging renewed efforts to locate the other parts of the plane.[16] It appears that such situations also have a potential to be turned into opportunities for competing state intelligence and military agencies to uncover one another's state security secrets.[17]

No less instructive was the frantic attempt to save the people aboard the sinking South Korean ferry Sewol in April 2014. Throughout the mission to recover the bodies, family members and observers around the world directed their anger at the captain, who was accused of negligence and abandoning the ship.[18] There was little discussion about the potential structural problems of the vessel or its cargo, which may have contributed to the listing of the ferry. Rather, the government of South Korea promptly released a transcript of the conversation between the officers on the vessel and the traffic officials, which took place as the vessel was listing. Journalists accused the crew of indecision and hesitation, the public concluded that the crew was incompetent and negligent, while South Korea's president publicly accused the captain of murdering non-surviving passengers before the rescue mission was even finished. Such use of social and mass media to disseminate information about disruptions gives Walter Benjamin's (1968[1936]) concerns about the loss of the original through mass reproduction another layer of meaning, posing interesting questions about how these dynamics relate to the workings of the surveillance and security apparatus in such contexts.

Collective memory of the kinds of disruptions discussed in this book is kept alive through media reporting, mass mediated public commemorations, memorials, public speeches, and official documentation associated with the organization of global planned events. The aftermath of such disruptions also tend to generate public and policy discussions that events such as the Olympics may attract negative attention and desire on the part of their adversaries to interfere with the planned event. At the same time, as was the case with the 2002 Salt Lake City Games, they tend to cement the resolve that nothing will stand in the way of hosting the Olympics. Such collective memories appear to have also provided an impetus to the initiative of resilient urban centers where the public and its civic institutions cooperate with state institutions of power and economic organizations together to envision, anticipate, prepare, and respond to such dynamics. [19]

Institutional memory

In the eyes of the apparatus, each such fatal interruption to collective public life is a potential attempt to breach the maximally controlled enclosure of safety. In this way, each such interruption serves as a new vision of a possible future; another imaginary of what is possible. The 1972 Munich interruption created a new vision of how life in the Olympic Village can be disrupted. The bombing in Centennial Olympic Park made it possible to envision disruptions to exhibits by sponsors, art presentations and street entertainment. The bombing of the London Tube and the trains in Madrid, and the gassing of the Tokyo subway, created new imaginaries of disruption to public transportation systems during the Games. Given that the disruption in Atlanta was caused by a disgruntled person also expanded the visions of perpetrators beyond the individuals and organizations already on the list as enemies of the state.

What can be called institutional memory is the tendency on the part of the institutions involved with the organization of the Olympics to treat collective memory as knowledge and instruction about how to avoid such disruptions in the future. In their parlance, these are "best practices" to be followed and "lessons learned" about how to prevent such disruptions from transpiring in the future. Institutions such as the International Olympic Committee, Organizing Committees of the specific Olympic Games, various institutions of public order, the military, and, not least, private security and surveillance corporations accumulate knowledge about how social order for the Olympics was planned and carried out in the past and ways in which disruptions to such orders transpired. They establish procedures through which such knowledge is to be passed on to other organizers of the Olympics.

This compilation of institutional knowledge seems to have been long going. Officials responsible for the 1964 Tokyo Games looked back at the 1936 Games in Berlin to justify why there had to be a large involvement of the Japanese military in the Tokyo 1964. They argued that the 1936 Games, particularly the Opening Ceremony, were successful because the German military was able to enforce order and keep control over the participants. It appears that the organizers of the 1972 Sapporo Games did not consult Mexico City on how to maintain order in the face of public protests, but officials were sent to Grenoble and Tokyo and also to Osaka, which hosted a different kind of a global planned event years earlier. The organizers of the 1972 Olympics in Munich sent their officials to Rome (to consult with those organizing the 1960 Games), Tokyo, Sapporo (which had just organized a Winter Olympiad a few months earlier), and Mexico City (which staged the 1968 Games), as well as to Moscow, Glasgow, and Bangkok (which all staged various sports events of similar size). Interestingly, not all advice was equally useful to the Germans for the 1972 Games. This applied particularly to the extensive use of the military, which the Germans found unappealing.

The failed hostage rescue mission in 1972, which resulted in the killing of a part of the Israeli Olympic delegation and some of the Palestinian hijackers, has become what Paul Virilio (2007) calls an original event – a happening that becomes uncovered as something hidden and just waiting to happen. Any such original event, Virilio argues, is turned into a preventive as a means to control the future. The 1972 Olympics became the most studied and investigated Games in history for every subsequent Olympics. For the surveillance and security apparatus, the original event of 1972 exposed not only the inadequacy of the German police but also it prompted other countries to examine their own counter-terrorism units. In the United States, this original event prompted the Federal Bureau of Investigation to acknowledge that their own response would have been no better than that of the Germans, setting off the push to establish the Hostage Rescue Team, which was created in 1983, just before the Los Angeles Olympics.[20] Shortly after the 1972 Olympics, the Germans also established an antiterror group that was put into practice in 1977 in a hostage rescue operation in Mogadishu.

The 1976 Montreal Games scrapped the original plans for light Olympics and instead became, at the time, the largest military operation by Canada since World War II.

The International Olympic Committee has recently set up its own service of knowledge transfer, which has come to be called Olympic Games Knowledge Management. This is envisioned as assistance to future Olympics organizers in a wide variety of ways. It not only makes available technical manuals and archival documentation about the previous Games. It also offers hands-on learning experience through seminars with previous organizers and workshops with experts, and even makes arrangements for real-time observations of operations during the actual Games. This assistance is designed to ensure continuous learning about the past with the purpose to inform how the future is to be envisioned and organized.[21]

In recent years, we notice in the public sphere the appearance of security "experts" whose institutional knowledge of such original events seems to have become the measure of the past, the present, and the future. These "experts" have positioned themselves in a privileged role of access to security-related information about past events, prompting the organizers to feel compelled to consult them in preparations for the next event (see Richards et al., 2011). There is a history to this practice. Security experts for Barcelona 1992 also advised for the Games in 2000, 2002, 2004, and 2006, and they helped evaluate the soundness of security plan in the bid for the 2010 Winter Olympics that went to Vancouver. The expert adviser for what constituted a threat to security of the London Olympics was a subsidiary of Rand Corporation, a policy think tank known to conduct its own analysis on the basis of which it offers policy recommendations. Such recommendations are based on envisioned "scenarios" of what can be expected to potentially happen in the future for which the Olympic organizers are to prepare their responses. The corporation produced more than two dozen such scenarios, based on understandings that London has become an attractive target for the so-called lone wolf terrorists and extremists, who were said to reside in the various neighborhoods of London, waiting for the right moment to strike.

Such individuals and organizations with institutional knowledge used to work away from the public eye and have only recently come to be used by journalists as legitimate public sources for their reporting. Increasingly, they have been called on to give their "expert opinion" on the "situation" for the general public. So, for example, a Chief Executive Officer of a private corporation shared his assessment about Sochi 2014, saying, "you just don't have competitions in places like Sochi with any frequency." What makes the place different, he argued, was that "the Olympic venues are located in the shadow of a terrorist battleground." He did not provide any more information about who the terrorists might be and behind which shadow this battleground is hiding. He suggested that the location of the Sochi Games has "got the possibility for there to be some kind of event, though we don't expect there to be" and emphasized that his company offered "evacuation contingencies" for 200 passengers on an aircraft and, in this way, also implied that there was money to be made. The information provided by this Chief Executive Officer left the journalist to connect the dots and suggest that such arrangements "underscore growing concerns about Olympic security in the wake of two suicide bombings last week on transportation targets nearly 500 miles from Sochi."[22] Such mass mediated dissemination of institutional knowledge to the general public helps to add to the push for constant vigilance in identifying and envisioning threats (Boyle and Haggerty, 2012). So, too, it helps to endow these experts, their knowledge, and their role in the security meta-ritual with competency and legitimacy in the eyes of the public.

Mobilization of all resources

Collective memories about past disruptions and institutional scenarios and imaginaries about potential futures support the push for making all possible resources available to be mobilized for the purposes of creating a maximally controlled social space within which joyous and festive Olympics, as the Olympic Charter describes them, can unfold. This urgency for total mobilization appears to eventually gain wide support. Disruptions to the Olympics undermine the continuous claims on the part of the organizers, the International Olympic Committee, and the various surveillance and security agencies involved that "the Olympics will be safe." There also seems to be little tolerance for such disruptions among the general public, event participants, and event sponsors. While, as discussed above, the Olympics often are preceded by public demonstrations and there also tends to be a widespread discontent about many aspects of the Olympics, once the Games begin, people tend to conclude that it is best for everyone that everything be done for the event to pass without disruptions.

The most visible aspect of this push for total mobilization has perhaps become the ubiquitous presence of the military. This association between the military and the Olympics often reminds us of the 1936 Berlin Games, which have come to be remembered as an event that showcased Hitler's rise to power through ostentatious exhibitions of the military prowess of the German state. In historical and comparative terms, however, it appears that this relationship between the Games and the military has been quite intimate since its early beginnings. Aspects of this closeness have varied according to different host countries and historical periods. Yttergren and Bolling (2012) show, for example, that the Swedish Organizing Committee and its subcommittees of the 1912 Olympics were dominated by military men and, to a large extent, their athletes were drawn from the ranks of the Swedish military and police. Moreover, the person centrally responsible for organizing the Stockholm Games effectively combined his high-ranking military career with a high-ranking sports career and, in addition, was an original member of the International Olympic Committee with close contacts with Baron Pierre de Coubertin. The Swedish National Sport Federation was dominated by military officers together with people from business and politics. Similarly, in Mexico City, it was a military general, who became vice-president of the International Olympic Committee in 1966, who had an idea to establish the Olympia Battalion. These were special forces compiled from the ranks of the military, district and federal police, and a security and treasury agency. The Battalion nicely blended with the image of peace by wearing white gloves and white helmets to complement the message of the 1968 Mexico City Games. Meanwhile, some 10,000 armed soldiers stood around the venues with machine guns as student protests gained momentum and ended in tragedy. As mentioned above, military also shined as an institution of order in Tokyo. Before the 1964 Games, the Self-Defense Forces were very unpopular because of their connection to the Imperial Army during World War II. The Olympics changed all that as their involvement in the Games raised the image and esteem of the military in their own eyes and the eyes of the public. So, too, the military was asked at the very last hour to supply additional volunteers for the 2012 London Games when a private security corporation failed to deliver fully on the contract.

The involvement of the military in the Olympics is an opportunity on the part of the military to show how it can convert its expertize acquired through military training and battle experience in war zones into partaking in the collective public activity in the homeland. Historically, this participation on the part of the military in the civil sphere has served as an important means of legitimation of this institution in the eyes of the public. At the same time, and no less important, public approval of such military role in public life also provides the military with the capacity to potentially shape and mold the civil society to its own liking (see Janowitz, 1960).

Another trend in this urge to use all available resources to deliver safe Games is the pressure to purchase and put in place the latest surveillance technology and strategies, often provided by private corporations. There are a number of variations about the politics of acquiring such technology with regards to the different Olympic hosts. Some host countries seem to show preference to rely primarily on their own domestic resources, maybe reasoning that they are the most trusted and proven to deliver. This seems to have been the case with the former Soviet Union in relation to the 1980 Moscow Games, where the old and trusted strategies of management and control of internal migration and residency patterns were enforced for the purposes of control of mobility during the Olympics. In the case of Mexico City, it also appears that its own extensive network of surveillance and policing agencies, which developed through the long history of repression of domestic dissent, may have been largely sufficient for the purposes of the Olympics. In contrast, Seoul 1988 is an early example of exerted efforts on the part of South Korea to rely on its Cold War allies to supply intelligence and surveillance expertize. It remains to be studied what kinds of forces work to create dynamics of this decision-making. Some insights can nevertheless be offered at this point, particularly in terms of how importing surveillance technology and interstate sharing of intelligence data may potentially help create (co)dependencies between apparatuses of different states. It would appear that those who designed a computer program or technology likely also possess the most know-how not only on how such programs and gadgets can be used to their maximal potential but also how their purpose can potentially be abused. This would imply that the ambition to strive to gain complete control and oversight of all activity at the Olympics could potentially be much more within reach for those who designed, created, and installed the latest technologies than for the Olympic organizers who purchased them for use in the Games. Importing surveillance technology and intelligence information likely also means allowing international experts and advisers access to *the what* and *the how* of the domestic surveillance and security apparatus.

At the turn of the century, this push to use the latest surveillance technology and strategies was given a huge impetus by the so-called Global War on Terror through which the global hegemonic powers sought to push for standardization in the matters of surveillance and security at a global level and impose compliance on individual nation-states. In this context, Athens 2004 became perhaps the most notorious example of a host country that was said not to have sufficient surveillance technology of its own to comply with the latest demands. Greece became caught in the middle of fierce bidding wars over which cluster of corporations would supply this technology. The technology eventually purchased was a centralized system called Command and Control Center for the Olympic Games from Science Application International Corporation, involving seven companies from the United States, three from Greece, four from other members of the European Union, and two from Israel. As democracies go, it was apparently important that the Greek public understood the implication of security policies of its government in relation to the 2004 Olympics. The United States seemed to have invested much energy to this end, disseminating its own understanding of threats to security in hopes to be able to influence public opinion on the importance of purchasing this technology. Another epic failure in terms of relying on private security corporations was London 2012, where Group 4 Securicor was forced to acknowledge on the day before the Games were to begin that it had failed to deliver the needed workforce to make the Games happen.

Interestingly, in the case of Turin 2006, the Italian organizers seem to have been able to avoid such pressures. As the media reports suggest, this tendency to "do it our way" was also indicated in the case of Sochi 2014 by the Russian Federation. Indeed, Sochi was the only city among the five that officially applied to host the 2012 Games that did not mention the inclusion of private security corporations in the list of available surveillance and security services. This is not to imply, however, that the Sochi organizers relied only on their internal resources. Multiple Israeli outlets reported, for example, that the Russians purchased the highly desirable computer program and system of centralized control from an Israeli company called NICE. The company named its version of the program Safe City Solutions. It is worth mentioning just what the Israeli version of this highly priced and sought after computer program apparently promised to deliver. It was to enable surveillance data gathering in real time from all sources into a single location. It was to be able to oversee the workings of all entities involved in ordering the Games, all at the same time, and from that same central location. The ultimate bonus, however, seemed to have been a feature with not only advance warning of a potential disturbance but also a set of immediate suggestions to all the different institutions involved about how to respond to that potential disturbance.[23]

It should not come as a surprise that this push for implementation of the most sophisticated surveillance technology and training of operatives, in conjunction with newly built surveillance-friendly architecture and infrastructure, also has a tendency to add to the ever rising expenses associated with the organization and the performance of the Games. It took several decades to finally pay off the staggering debt incurred to the city of Montreal as a result of the 1976 Winter Games. The expense was so shocking that it threatened to wipe out the interest to host the Games, were it not for the Cold War rivalry in which the city of Los Angeles, the only bidder for the 1984 Games, took it as its mission to demonstrate the Olympics could, in fact, be profitable – at least for the investors. To mention but one more example, Athens 2004 spent double the original estimated expense and ended with billions of dollars of debt, all of which was exacerbated by the subsequent economic crisis. Here it must be noted that the centralized surveillance system Greece was pressured to purchase ended up malfunctioning altogether. In recent decades, every Olympics seems to have come to be associated with criticism that the costs involved with the event had increased exponentially so that we now have a new Olympic distinction tagged to the event: "the most expensive Games ever." Among the many pressing questions raised about this cost inflation, one should be given more attention, namely, how this push to buy the latest meets the pressures to adhere to the so-called austerity policies and budget cuts. A possible insight into ways in which some of these conflicting demands may be resolved could be found in mass media reports about gross abuse of workers who construct sporting facilities and the hazardous conditions in which they are made to work.[24]

Public complaints and accusative media reporting about expenditures for the Olympics are common and seem to accompany every Olympics. Yet, if there were to be a disruption, the question would always be asked: Could we not have done more to prevent this? Indeed, the tragic disruption of the 1972 Olympics in Munich was followed by extensive post factum examinations of decision-making and organization of the various components of the Olympics. There was much hindsight wisdom sharing of how these could have been done differently to prevent the tragedy, and intensive international diplomatic scuffles over which government should be blamed for the failure (Schiller and Young, 2010). Decades later, news reports and scholarly articles related to security and surveillance of the Olympics still hold the 1972 Munich Games as an example of how an event should never be organized. This tendency to blame the organizers for unwanted disruptions seems to have only increased, as suggested by the way the work of government commissions set up after such disturbances to investigate "what went wrong" are interpreted publicly. As Robin Wagner-Pacifici's (2010) detailed reading of the *9/11 Commission Report* shows, the narrative structure of the text tries to avoid definitive blame and assigning causality. Interestingly, public discussions of the report often have a different logic. They emphasize that information was available to suspect that a disturbance was being planned. They argue that had that information been shared between the different agencies on time, these tragedies could have been thwarted. This reasoning leads them to conclude that these were "missed opportunities" and "intelligence failures."[25] Pressures of these kinds can only contribute to the persuasion that no resources should be spared in the organization of the Olympics.

Each Olympics is, to a degree, a testing ground in a number of ways. We read about individuals, sometimes even the journalists themselves, who look to cause disruption to be able to "prove" that the system is not "tight enough" or not "secure enough," despite all that money invested in surveillance technology, architecture, and operatives or despite all the rhetoric that everything was done to ensure security. Then there are security and surveillance corporations and agencies that see the Olympics as an opportunity to test how their latest technological innovation and strategic ambition actually works or could potentially work in real time on the ground. Historians have demonstrated that using public social life as a testing ground for surveillance strategies may not be such a novel pursuit as the colonized peoples were often used for such experimental purposes (Bayly, 1996; Hevia, 2012; McCoy, 2009). Today, cities that aspire to be put on the global map through their ambitions to host global planned events may well have become new surveillance laboratories, not only for the latest strategies, operative training, and technologies but also for the changing perceptions of privacy and understandings of democracy. Indeed, the post-event city has become a test of political will – or lack thereof – to remove the surveillance technologies and services after they had served their purpose for the Olympics (Boyle and Haggerty, 2009). The trend seems to be that the surveillance know-how is becoming one of the Olympic legacies associated with the host city.

Cooperation of all involved

With the help of this push to make the host city into a laboratory for the latest surveillance technology and strategies, the Olympic organizers strive for the Games to be meticulously planned and repeatedly rehearsed in advance so as to leave as little as possible to chance. This is in the face of the fact that the Olympics are an exceedingly complex and therefore ultimately uncertain and unpredictable system. These contradictions seem to have found their expression in the conviction that the planned order of this highly complex event can be performed safely, efficiently, and smoothly if everyone cooperates toward this common goal. The scale of this intended cooperation can be understood in terms of modernity's inventions of tradition (Hobsbawm and Ranger, 1983). Much like nation-states, the Olympics were invented as occasions that bring together huge numbers of individuals who have no common kinship ties to orient them toward common goals. As Benedict Anderson (1991) understood, such individuals who are not connected through indigenous traditions must develop a collective identity, which is imagined to be common to all involved. In the absence of loyalties, which would be expected and enforced in the case of kinship ties, invented traditions such as the Olympics require an ideology that will voluntarily commit the minds but also the hearts of the people involved toward the common goal. As the scope of the Olympics has continued to grow, involving more and more people from across the globe with an ongoing struggle to attract commitment to the values of the Olympic Movement, the security meta-ritual has come to prominence with its common goal of "safe Olympics." With security as the top priority, commitment to safe Olympics must be continuously demonstrated and therefore continuously surveilled. Gilles Deleuze (1992) reminds us that to have evidence of commitment to collective values now requires power to control through mechanisms of a different kind and scope, because ordering through discipline, as Michel Foucault (2008) understands this, can no longer be trusted.

This push for cooperation toward the common goal of safe Olympics and control mechanisms that accompany this agenda are a multilayered process. On the part of the public, people are expected to agree to adjust their behavior in accordance with the parameters of the security imperative. This adjustment works in different ways. Residents of the host city are asked to abide by the new rules of movement in the city, which tend to be highly disruptive to their daily routine life. Those who do not wish to comply may temporarily take a leave for some other vacation spot. Others who refuse to comply or are deemed unsuitable for the event, including the city's poor and itinerant, are relocated to areas away from the Olympic zone. While many people may not agree with these parameters, once the event is on, most come to conclude that it is in everybody's interest to comply voluntarily so that the event can take place without disruption. Participants who obtain accreditation to attend the Olympics or those who are able to purchase a ticket to attend competitions or other events are given clear instructions how to comply with the specifications of the apparatus or else risk being excluded. To mention just some examples from the earlier Olympics, during the 1976 Montreal Games, a journalist entering an area designated for photographers rather than storytellers was promptly removed and deprived of his accreditation. A photographer who positioned himself in an unoccupied seat with a better view rather than the one to which he was assigned was violently handled by the police, handcuffed, and taken into custody.

In this push for cooperation of all involved, the Olympic athletes are in a particularly difficult position. They are seen to be the very embodiment not only of the Olympic ideals of peace, human dignity, rights, and equality for all but also of the official policy of the Olympic Games as sports festival in which political expression is said to have no place. The immortalized raising of the black fists by two African American athletes during the medals ceremony in 1968 Mexico City in support of the civil rights struggle in the United States is historically, perhaps, the most well-known challenge to the Olympic Charter, which instructs that "no kind of demonstration or political, religious or racial propaganda is permitted in any Olympic sites, venues or other areas."[26] For their support of human rights, the two African American medalists, members of the very minority whose rights were grossly violated, were punished not only by the International Olympic Committee but also by being publicly ostracized in their home country (see Bass, 2004). These stark contradictions came sharply into focus half a century later when people around the world, including many athletes, protested against human rights violations in China, which was hosting the 2008 Olympics. As Kidd (2010) documents, the International Olympic Committee assured that the athletes competing in Beijing had the right to their freedom of expression; at the same time, the Committee made it clear that the Olympic athletes were obliged to abide by the restrictions on political expression imposed by the organizers in China, of course, in full support of the International Olympic Committee. Those who refused to cooperate were told to stay home and found their visas revoked.

This quest for maximal control through cooperation is also applied to disparate types of institutions that were, historically, set up for very different purposes and with very different organizational policies. For example, the military, the police, undercover agents, special forces units, national intelligence agencies, and various corporations, all of which are often from multiple states, are made to work together. This attempt to include all kinds of different agencies has been criticized, often on the part of the International Olympic Committee, as lack of coordination between too many institutions. This criticism seems to have morphed into a challenge of how to centralize their coordination. This process has come to be articulated as an attempt to implement a "central command and control" structure, which seems to be a strategy developed by the military (see Sloan, 2012). Applied to the Olympics, as illustrated above, the system is designed to, at the same time, oversee the workings of all these institutions in a hierarchical way and also process surveillance and intelligence data as it is streamed into the center in real time and from various sources. Such a command is expected to coordinate forces at an enormous scale, control simultaneous events at dozens of venues spread geographically, and analyze in real-time information as it is being collected through all surveillance technologies.

How this attempt to centralize control of all institutions involved is achieved in each Olympics, and to what extent, remains an open empirical question. Each of these institutions has its own organizational culture and its own ways for how their tasks are accomplished. Given that institutions function on the basis of the ability to collect and process their own surveillance data, this attempt at centralization also likely includes a push to disclose surveillance data and expertize not only between different institutions but also between different countries. By implication, to be able to work together effectively there needs to develop some shared way of how things are done and how surveillance data is exchanged. The central command and control model appears to be a top-down authoritarian structure in which one of the institutions and its organizational culture takes charge. We learn from the Salt Lake City Games in 2002, for example, that in that case it was the United States Secret Service which became the umbrella institution to oversee the works of all other institutions and agencies of order. The 1988 Seoul Games is one of the early examples of such attempts at centralized control, which was particularly challenging given that the Games were under the spell of the Cold War and involved institutions from so many different countries, including the United States, Israel, South Korea, Japan, West Germany, and the United Kingdom. After the Cold War and with the Global War on Terror, the emerging global network of intelligence sharing, high-technology surveillance, and political alliances in relation to globalized counter-terrorism efforts has not only shaped the work of the police and the involvement of the military in domestic affairs. It also reflects the growing presence of private surveillance and security corporations, which support this global network with their surveillance technology innovations and on-the-ground policing services. The case of the 2004 Athens Olympics suggests that not only can the host city become an experimental laboratory for implementation of such exceedingly expensive venture but also the sovereignty of the host state can be seriously put into question, as Greece was made to cave under tremendous pressures to adhere to the demands for surveillance and security standards. A closer reading of media reports on Sochi 2014 provides a glimpse into what this power struggle may look like. Less than three weeks before the Games, the United States complained bitterly that the Sochi organizers did not sufficiently consult American surveillance and security expertize. They argued that with thousands of Americans planning to travel to Sochi, the Russian security apparatus should fully cooperate with the American counterpart. The Russian hosts, however, insisted that all the necessary surveillance technology and strategies had already been put in place and therefore no additional surveillance assistance was needed. If, however, their American guests wished to provide any other protection, it would all need to be coordinated with the Russian hosts.[27] Indeed, how host countries are able – or fail – to maintain their sovereignty in the face of such tremendous international pressures is an important empirical question. To a large extent, these dynamics appear to be playing themselves out through global mass media reporting.

Another important pattern in this push for cooperation is enactment of various kinds of legislation for the Olympic event to comply with the local, regional, national, and even international law. As Kim Scheppele (2010) shows, the push for states to implement anti-terrorism laws has been coordinated through the United Nations, which adopted a special resolution to push the governments of all member states to adopt their own national laws to the new legal template. How laws are able to be modified internally within each state to adapt to this global template varies. In this regard, the case of the United States is particularly instructive. Its federal structure gives each state a constitutionally protected right to determine its own safety legislation. This right is further decentralized within each state to the point that municipalities and counties determine their own specific policing legislation. For the 2002 Salt Lake City Games, a special unit, Utah Public Safety Command, was created by a statute of the state of Utah to bring under a central command local, state, federal, and private security apparatus, including agencies as varied as the police, medical emergency services, fire departments, public works, and the National Guard. The legalization of the involvement of the military in domestic law enforcement is also particularly interesting in that such activity is explicitly historically prohibited with the exception of natural disasters, in which case it would be through the act of Congress that the military would be asked to act – and this would be in response to a crisis, but not its prevention.

Such local municipal measures have morphed into a more comprehensive legislation to legalize all sorts of undemocratic measures in the context of global planned events. In some countries, this process has been legally sanctioned through classifications such as "National Special Security Event." In the United States, this is an official classification for which the explanation is available for the populace on the official Internet website of the Homeland Security Office. This classification was made official through an executive order by President Bill Clinton in 1998, an act that is not subject to public debate or legislative review. This order, accompanied by a series of other presidential directives, made it lawful for either the President of the United States or the Secretary of the newly established Homeland Security Office to declare any occasion they may deem under threat as an event that requires full control of the security forces of the federal government, including the military, and put the matters related to security of such events under control of the United States Secret Service. The thinking behind this designation seems to have begun to develop in the aftermath of the 1996 Atlanta Games. It may well be, however, that the highly secretive Delta Special Forces were deployed clandestinely already for that event. This legislation also makes it possible to streamline public resources for what, at least in the United States, is otherwise considered to be a private event. This allowed for the 2002 Salt Lake City Games to be funded by the federal government. Since litigation has become a major weapon in international politics and business alike, following the law, or else passing relevant legislation, seems to be a priority. In light of this, we see that in the case of the 2016 Rio de Janeiro Games, bitter complaints have been publicly expressed on the part of the International Olympic Committee, which surveills the progress of preparation and planning for the Olympics, claiming that it is lack of coordination between city, state, and national governments that has been delaying construction of the venues.[28]

Attempts to legalize this push for cooperation also extend to the right to public protest. A part of the contract between the host city and the International Olympic Committee stipulates that public demonstrations against any aspect of the Olympics must be confined to specially designated areas where they cannot disturb the event and special local legislation must be passed to make this possible. It was not always so. The 1968 Mexico City Games were surrounded by huge student protests. The response on the part of the Mexican government, however, was brutal suppression, which turned a protest into a massacre. This act demonstrated in no uncertain terms why and how it is that the military is trained to kill the enemy and may not be so well versed in ways of responding to civil disobedience. By 1972, the city of Munich expressed concerns about "Olympic peace" and simply passed a municipal ordinance, which prohibited marches and demonstrations inside the Olympic Park. Similar regulations were passed in Montreal, Seoul and other Olympic cities since. In the case of the United States, such provisions are included in the National Special Security Event classification discussed above. This becomes more complicated when public protests erupt in multiple places around the world, as was the case in relation to the Beijing Games of 2008, where the human rights movement in Tibet gained support all over the world and when anti-globalization movements disrupted the Olympic Flame Relay during the Turin, Beijing, and Sidney Games. Judging from the case of Beijing, as discussed by Kidd (2010), the future trend may well turn out to be that the countries involved and the International Olympic Committee will come to converge in their opposition to such protests. We have yet to see what kind of pressures will be exerted on local governments in the future to ensure that the Olympic Flame passes through countries uninterrupted.

Purification

At the heart of the security meta-ritual as a form of social control in the Olympics is the activity of purification. This is a process of separation of safe from potentially dangerous, that which belongs and the other which must be excluded or kept at a distance. It is a process of purifying not only individuals involved in the Olympics but also physical environments where the Games are staged. The concept of purification has been developed by scholars of comparative religion and theorists of ritual who seek to understand how different social groups establish criteria for who belongs to the group and who is to be excluded and what are the ways in which a social group seeks to separate itself from another with differing worldviews, cosmologies, and ways of life (see Douglas, 1966). This activity of separation is based on inventing classifications that specify criteria according to which individuals, objects, and environments are to be evaluated and subsequently categorized into acceptable or threatening to the group. Classifications enable the creation of boundaries, which serve as concrete and indicative barriers to physically separate members of one group from all others and to symbolically communicate to the people involved how to interpret these divisions. As I demonstrate elsewhere, at its core, surveillance in planned events is a practice of classification of individuals, objects, and information based on criteria of security and potential danger. These criteria are used by those responsible for the organization and the staging of such events as the basis for separation of what they deem secure from potentially disruptive (Bajc, 2011a, 2010, 2007a). Purification processes of the Olympics are manifested in a variety of ways.

The least visible and perhaps the most taken for granted of such purification activities is the process of accreditation, illustrated on the front cover of the book. Everyone who aspires to participate in the performance of the Olympics must undergo an evaluation procedure, which involves criteria set by the organizers about who is deemed acceptable to take part in the Games, in what capacity, and what, specifically, their participation may entail. Every single individual, from athletes, their entourage, journalists, special guests, officials, dignitaries, volunteers, members of state and private agencies of order, to merchants, cleaning personnel and everyone else who is considered to be a part of the performance of the Games, must obtain an identification card that enables entry and exit to designated Olympic subareas. Fans attending competitions as audiences must obtain an entry ticket, which allows them access to a specific competition venue within a specified period of time and according to specified rules. This procedure was already fully imposed for the 1976 Montreal Games. Everyone, including the Prime Minister of Canada, was required to undergo accreditation. So important was this purification procedure in Montreal that in the final report, which was submitted to the International Olympic Committee on the part of the organizers, the criteria of selection are described as a separate entry. These criteria have since become more detailed and the surveillance technology in place to enforce them increasingly sophisticated.

Purification of physical spaces also shows interesting patterns. Olympics are staged in designated municipal areas that are sometimes concentrated in urban centers and other times spread between multiple surrounding areas. These areas undergo construction of Olympic facilities, upgrading of the transportation and tourist infrastructure, and beautification of landscape and urban facades – all of which alter the existing landscape. The aestheticization of commercial and residential neighborhoods includes removal or alteration of structures that are seen as not compatible with the envisioned order. Areas of East London and old residential areas in Beijing were cleared of their existing infrastructure and rebuilt to match the new standards for the 2012 and 2008 Olympics, respectively. For 2006 Turin and 2010 Vancouver, squatter houses were evacuated and the disadvantaged urban populations relocated. Most recently, for the 2016 Rio de Janeiro Games, entire neighborhoods known as favelas were demolished and their residents displaced to make way for the event infrastructure.[29]

This trend was already present for the 1964 Tokyo Games when the people of Japan were told to adapt to the Western spirit of sporting competitions rather than succumb to indigenous-style festivities because the traditional culture of joy would tarnish the image of Japan as a modern Western nation. The Olympics, the public was told, was a pure sport festival, very different from the passionate and exuberant carnival practiced by the local cultures. To this end, an educational campaign sought to rid the locals of improper conduct and instruct how to show support for the Games that would be appreciated by foreign visitors and television audiences. A few years later, in 1972, the Japanese police combed through the red light districts of Sapporo to purify the areas of prostitutes, drug addicts and petty thieves. So, too, the policy of zero tolerance for crime rid the municipal areas in Moscow in 1980 of anyone who was not a documented resident or visitor. The 2008 Beijing Games were accompanied by aesthetically pleasing posters, cartoon characters, television programs, and advertisements on public transport, instructing residents how to legally lease out their property, visitors how to register at local police stations, and others how to report suspicious activities. Canadians had their own instruction on good behavior when the world was watching the 2010 Vancouver Games. The city devised a wide-ranging etiquette protocol, from how to ensure one's socks match pants, smile with sincerity, avoid a frown on one's face, and shake someone's hand, to how to share love for the city with visitors and offer them directions.

The beautification process includes expectations that local ways of life incompatible with the planned order of the Olympics be suppressed, at least for a time when the country is under global mass media scrutiny. In addition, as the time of the event nears, entire areas are expected to be sectioned off by an impermeable boundary and within these enclosures no stone is to remain unturned to ensure a purified zone of safety. As we learn from the 2006 Turin Games, these purified areas are at the center of concentric rings, each with increasing perimeter and a different set of surveillance procedures and checkpoints. They spread out and away from the purified zone so as to make access toward the center increasingly difficult by making people pass from one ring to the next.

Pressures to purify the Olympic space are tremendous. This is so not only on the part of the host city toward its citizens but also on the part of the International Olympic Committee toward the host city, as well as the international audience toward the organizers. These pressures often seem to be playing themselves out through the global mass media. International media mocked the lack of preparation for the 1980 Moscow Games, creating tension and anxieties on the part of the organizers who interpreted this news as threats not only to the safety of the Games but also to national security. In the case of the 2004 Athens Olympics, journalists mocked the organizers for claiming that their surveillance apparatus was trained on the site when the venues had not yet been completed and wondered how technologies could have been successfully installed on the infrastructure when walls of the buildings had not yet been completed. Most recently, a senior International Olympic Committee official complained that after six inspection visits, Rio de Janeiro was nowhere close to being ready for the 2016 Games. He revealed how such pressures might work by stating that while there were certainly talks about relocating the 2016 Olympics from Rio to Tokyo, a special task force was set up on the part of the International Olympic Committee to push the preparations forward in Rio at a higher speed.[30]

Sterile zones of safety

These sets of dynamics – that is, shift of attention, reliance on institutional and collective memories, push for total mobilization, expectations of cooperation, and strategies of purification – lead toward the creation of a maximally controlled social space within which the Olympics can take place as planned and without unwanted disruptions. As I have been emphasizing throughout these pages, security meta-ritual is a new form of social control that is transformative in its nature. This transformative process turns a social and physical space of everyday metropolitan living, considered by the organizers to be dangerous and unpredictable, into a sterile zone of safety, envisioned by the surveillance and security apparatus as a predictable and controllable space. This sterile zone of safety is a product of rehearsals, perfected performance, latest technologies, and meticulous planning. It is a social space within which complexity of social life has been reduced so that uncertainty can be minimized for the duration of the Olympics.

How such sterile zones of safety are configured has varied in terms of the specificities of the host location, particularly their geographical features and the scope of the Games, but also historically in terms of the local political culture, global political dynamics, understandings of which strategies have proven to be effective and what has been technologically possible at the time of each Olympics. Among these variations there nevertheless appear to be a number of convergences that give us some sense of the vision of social order inside a sterile zone of safety, particularly in terms of the norms of social interaction and culture of social relations, notions of cosmopolitanism and diversity, hierarchies of freedom of movement, cultural notions of the aesthetics of the environment, understandings of privacy, and structures of authority.

The sterile zones of safety seem to strive to be culturally and socially self-sustaining units in the sense that those who have been chosen to enter are introduced into a world within which there is little stimulation to intermingle with those who remained outside. The Olympic Village, accessible only to athletes and a small number of others may be the most perfected example of such a social and physical enclosure within which all forms of elite and popular entertainment, desires for culinary choices, spiritual and religious needs, idiosyncrasies of consumer practices, and other ways of individual and collective living are provided for every taste and lifestyle.

These zones are also impressively diverse and cosmopolitan. The design of the Olympic Games ensures that athletes from every country attend the competitions. The eagerness on the part of the International Olympic Committee to stay in pace with the changing popular cultures and sporting tastes of the young generations brings together people with interests in the widest possible array of sporting activities. This tendency to be inclusive has also contributed to increasing gender diversity, particularly among the athletes. The sterile zone of safety now includes people of all religious persuasions, genders, social classes, and ethnic backgrounds, those with and without disabilities.

Within the zone, this diversity is particularly ordered. Every individual is properly positioned in the assigned space for a period of time. Through ticket purchase, spectators are assigned specific seats within a specified time frame for a specific sporting competition in a particular competition venue so that, for example, ice skating fans from around the world are positioned in the same venue at the same time. The privileged hold an accreditation identity card, which allows them to enter areas in which spectators are not welcome. These accredited areas are hierarchically ordered in that access to these spaces is stratified according to prestige each cardholder commands within the Olympic social circles.

There is a tendency to make these zones aesthetically pleasing. Newly built tourism, sports, and transportation infrastructures add to the feeling of freshness and novelty. This landscape tends to be enriched with parks and various types of vegetation, adding to the sophistication of the environmental design. This new architecture is surveillance friendly. It is designed to be beautiful, harmonious with nature and social life and at the same time, to enable policing. This is consistent with the insistence on the part of the International Olympic Committee that surveillance technologies and techniques should be subdued so as not to interfere with the festive mood of the Games. Surveillance capacities are built into the façade of the buildings and the cultivation and design of the plant life. As Erin Despard (2012) details, urban spaces, designed through the prism of security threats and surveillance strategies, are comforting, the harmonies of which discourage their inhabitants from questioning who designed these psychologically pleasing spaces of control and for what purpose.

Participants are made aware that communications through electronic devices between all individuals within the zone and between the zone and the outside world are intercepted, monitored, and recorded for security assurance. The system also makes it possible to account for every single identity cardholder at any given moment, to locate their position in space and time, and to note patterns of movement within and between the subzones. Such information is stored to facilitate efficiency and effectiveness of the organization and the staging of the next Olympics.

Decisions about who may enter this sterile Olympic space of safety, how individuals are to be positioned within, and what kind of freedom of movement comes with the right to enter are made by the Olympic organizers. While some of the participants may have supported the campaign to host the Olympics in their city and some have even helped to sponsor the event, the vast majority had little input in the election of Olympic officials or the organization of the event. Everyone who has been granted permission to enter is expected to become part of this social order, adjust to its norms, and follow its rules. Extensive educational and informational efforts on the part of the organizers strive to help the participants understand why it must be so.

CODA

Going forward with the research agenda outlined here and empirically elaborated in the rest of the chapters that follow, perhaps the most pressing question may not be what kind of variations in the workings of the security meta-ritual may likely or potentially be observed during the future Olympics. Indeed, the 2014 Sochi Games and the 2016 Rio Games preparations suggest that the variations are more likely to be in terms of intensity of the components of the conceptual schemas already mentioned here and less so in the radical novelty of some other variables. More empirical details pertaining to the cases analyzed here as well as additional empirical studies of the Olympics not included in this book would further help to elucidate the various patterns in the working of the security meta-ritual. They would also provide empirical evidence of how variations in intensity of various components in the conceptual schemas so far identified may themselves potentially lead to change. At this point, however, the most pertinent question seems to be how enduring the transformation made possible through the security meta-ritual is and how lasting its effects may be. Some of these questions are pursued in the conclusion of the book.

Notes

1. "Sochi Olympics Beat Vancouver on Ticket Sales – Official," *Sputnik News,* April 7, 2014.
2. There is a vast amount of scholarship on human capacity to create and engage in ritual activity, and discussions on just what constitutes such an activity are ongoing. See Catherine Bell's (1997) *Ritual: Perspectives and Dimensions* for an authoritative summary of these efforts.
3. "Give the Olympics a Home," *New York Times,* March 1, 2014, by Charles Banks-Altekruse, Op-Ed Contributor.
4. "Distorting Russia: How the American Media Misrepresent Putin, Sochi and Ukraine," Stephen F. Cohen, *The Nation,* March 3, 2014.
5. The book, *My Greek Drama: Life, Love and One Woman's Olympic Effort to Bring Glory to Her Country,* was published in 2013 by Greenleaf Book Group Press. The author's name on the cover appears as Gianna Angelopoulos.
6. Ibid.
7. "The Ring and the Rings: Vladimir Putin's Mafia Olympics," Dave Zirin, *The Guardian,* June 18, 2013.
8. "Rio 2016 Olympic Preparations Damned as 'Worst Ever' by IOC," *The Guardian,* Owen Gibson, April 29, 2014. "IOC Vice-president Backtracks on 'Worst Ever' Olympics Comments," Australian Associated Press, *The Guardian,* May 1, 2014.
9. The Rome Olympics are described in a book by journalist David Maraniss titled *Rome 1960: The Olympics That Changed the World,* which was published in 2008 by Simon and Schuster.
10. Some of the declassified documents and commentary about this disruption are available to the general public through the National Security Archive, http://www2.gwu.edu/~nsarchiv/NSAEBB/NSAEBB10/intro.htm
11. "Olympic Bomb Suspect Rudolph Caught," *ABC News,* May 31, 2001.
12. "Volgograd Train Station Rocked by Suicide Bombing," Leonid Ragozin, *The Guardian,* December 29, 2013.
13. "102 Hours in Pursuit of Marathon Suspects," *Boston Globe,* April 28, 2013.
14. "Why Was Boston Strong? Lessons from the Boston Marathon Bombing," by Herman B. "Dutch" Leonard, Christine M. Cole, Arnold M. Howitt, and Philip B. Heymann. Kennedy School of Government, Harvard University, April 2014. http://www.hks.harvard.edu/content/download/67366/1242274/version/1/file/WhyWasBostonStrong.pdf. For a commentary on this report, see "Harvard University report endorses police state measures in Boston Marathon lockdown." *World Socialist Web Site.* By Nick Barrickman, April 7, 2014.
15. "MH370: Sub Searches for Plane, Again, as Families Fume," Calum MacLeod and John Bacon, *USA Today,* April 16, 2014. "Réunion debris is from Malaysia Airlines flight MH370, French prosecutor says." By Reuters in Paris. *The Guardian.* Thursday September 3, 2015.
16. "Réunion debris is from Malaysia Airlines flight MH370, French prosecutor says." Reuters in Paris, September 3, 2015.

17. "Disappearance of Malaysian Airlines Flight MH 370: The Trillion Dollar Question to the U.S. and Its Intelligence Services." *Global Research*. By Matthias Chang, July 20, 2014.
18. "South Korea Ferry: President Says Captain's Actions Were Like 'Murder'," Justin McCurry, *The Guardian*, April 21, 2014.
19. An example of such efforts is a book by the president of The Rockefeller Foundation, Judith Rodan, titled *The Resilience Dividend: Being Strong in a World Where Things Go Wrong*, published by Public Affairs in 2014.
20. "Inside the FBI's Secret Relationship with the Military's Special Operations," Adam Goldman and Julie Tate, *Washington Post*, April 10, 2014.
21. The International Olympic Committee Factsheet; Olympic Games Knowledge Management; February 20, 2014. http://www.olympic.org/Documents/Reference_documents_Factsheets/OGKM_UK.pdf
22. "Olympic Response Team: Security Firm Ready in Wings," Kevin Johnson, *USA Today*, January 7, 2014.
23. "Sterilizing Sochi for the 'Big Brother' Games," *Ha'aretz*, Anshel Pfeffer, January 31, 2014. On the description of the program see "Sochi Chooses NICE Systems Solution," Amy Rojkes Dombe, http://www.israeldefense.com, February 12, 2014.
24. "Brazilian World Cup Builders Call for National Strike as Construction Death Toll Rises," *Russia Today*, December 15, 2013. Another example is preparations for the 2022 Soccer World Cup in Qatar. See "Qatar's World Cup Will Cost 62 Dead Workers Per Game," Marina Hyde, *The Guardian*, May 20, 2015. It appears, however, that such hazardous and abusive working conditions may have long been in practice. Reports about death and injuries of workers building the Olympic facilities for the 2004 Athens Games point in this direction. See "Thirteen workers die as safety standards are ignored in race to build Olympic sites." Daniel Howden, Nikolaos Zirganos, and Nikolaos Leontopoulos. *The Independent*, April 3, 2004.
25. See, for example, "Losing the Plot," Richard Norton-Taylor, *The Guardian*, July 22, 2004.
26. See Rule 50 "Advertising, demonstrations, propaganda." Olympic Charter. International Olympic Committee. September 2015, pp. 93. http://www.olympic.org/Documents/olympic_charter_en.pdf
27. "Olympics Security Worries U.S. Officials," Brian Knowlton, *New York Times*, January 19, 2014.
28. "Rio 2016 Olympic Preparations Deemed as 'Worst Ever' by IOC."
29. "World Cup: Rio Favelas Being 'Socially Cleansed' in Runup to Sporting Events," Owen Gibson and Jonathan Watts, *The Guardian*, December 5, 2013.
30. "Rio 2016 Olympic Preparations Deemed as 'Worst Ever' by IOC."

2
On Security and Surveillance in the Olympics: A View from Inside the Tent

Richard W. Pound

The International Olympic Committee was established in 1894 as the principal outcome of an international Congress convened in Paris by a young French educator, Baron Pierre de Coubertin. One of its ambitious goals was to renovate the ancient Olympic Games and hold quadrennial celebrations of these Games, beginning in Athens in 1896. The event set in motion what has become an extraordinary international sport system, involving hundreds of millions of athletes and spectators, currently in 205 separately recognized countries or territories. The Olympic Games now include Winter, as well as Summer Games, are normally concentrated in a single location and into a 17-day time frame, and are watched by some four billion spectators. They attract huge television, media, sponsorship, licensing and ticketing revenues, on a scale unimaginable even half a century ago, much less than when Coubertin and his initial colleagues launched their initiative. The spin-off of such revenues plays a vital role in the maintenance of the international sport system, which has allowed the Olympic Movement to become, for all intents and purposes, universal. In addition to the visible sport component, the Games now transcend mere sport and exist as an event in their own right as a world symbol, characterizing international understanding, friendship and peace.

"Security," in its modern usage (and with its many possible meanings), was not a term known to or considered by the Committee when the Games were born. Europe, the location of all but one edition of the Games until the 1930s, was relatively calm until the outbreak of World War I, and other regional conflicts of the day were far enough away that they had no impact on sports events in Europe. In its early days, the International Olympic Committee was concerned mainly with trying to ensure the continuity of the quadrennial celebrations. According to the Olympic Charter, the Committee has the overall responsibility to ensure the regular celebration of the Games, selecting the sites of each Games, determining which sports will be on the program of the Games, recognizing national Olympic committees, promulgating eligibility rules, and determining who may compete in the Games.

In more recent years, however, the International Olympic Committee has been forced to consider increasingly complex risks. As the world has shrunk, travel between continents has become a matter of a few hours and worldwide communication a phenomenon of immediacy and breadth unthinkable in the 19th century. In some cases, the emerging concept of security has had an impact on decisions of the Committee, although, since the Committee is a small nongovernmental organization, even if security risks might be identified, responsibility for the security issues and execution of related strategies and tactics has typically rested with the authorities of the host country. These risks may constitute active or potential threats to the success, continuance or existence of the Games or may affect the contestants themselves. They must be evaluated across a broad spectrum of perspectives, including political, military, terrorist, economic, organizational, societal, demographic and reputational. In time, the International Olympic Committee has become more adept at such considerations and better at finding ways either to avoid such risks or to mitigate them.

The International Olympic Committee did not and, even today, does not characterize what it does in relation to any edition of the Olympic Games in terms that are as nuanced as those used in conceptual or academic analysis of security. Its actions are empirical and forward-looking, all focused on making sure that its showcase event takes place successfully and as planned. This naturally involves elements of surveillance, in the sense of observation of conditions and developments, and of intervention, when progress toward the goal is too slow or is misdirected. Such surveillance has become more pronounced in recent years as the importance and complexity of the Games have increased. The surveillance is prophylactic, in some respects, at the stage of selecting host cities: the selection process is divided into an application phase, in which all interested cities submit applications, which are reviewed on an in-house basis, and in which preliminary decisions are made regarding cities that can be considered sufficiently prepared to advance to the stage of a candidate city, while those that are judged unready do not progress beyond the stage of applicant. Recent evolution of this process has led to a far more informal and collaborative early communication between the prospective candidates and the International Olympic Committee. The candidacy phase involves more detailed bids, which address the security, economic, political, organizational and infrastructural aspects of the candidate cities. From a "surveillance" perspective, the Committee then establishes an Evaluation Commission, made up of Olympic Family representatives and independent experts, which visits each candidate city and reviews in detail the proposals submitted to the Committee against a detailed matrix of considerations. It then prepares a report to the Committee members (with a right of reply given to the candidate cities) who are called upon to determine the host city by a secret ballot.

Since the International Olympic Committee is composed of volunteer members, supported by a relatively modest professional staff, it cannot exercise a specific security action in its own right. It has no "territory" over which it has jurisdiction and its event, the Olympic Games, is always celebrated in someone else's territory. Security is, therefore, almost always the responsibility of third parties. The Committee itself can evaluate certain security risks and may avoid some of them when choosing host cities. It may also, when monitoring the progress toward the staging of the Games, identify new risks or an increase in known risks and encourage or order the organizing committees to adjust accordingly. Its ultimate authority rests not in its positive action to impose security measures, but in its legal ability to withdraw the Games or to cancel them.

Once selected, the host city is bound by a contract, drafted by the International Olympic Committee, setting out detailed requirements relating to the organization of the Games – perhaps a form of surveillance by anticipation. The Committee also establishes a Coordination Commission having representation similar to that of the Evaluation Commission, which follows closely all aspects of the Games preparations, making suggestions and ordering changes when necessary. Surveillance in the larger sense of the expression is an essential feature of today's Games, especially by the Committee as the sponsoring body of the Games. Such surveillance is not the only organizational surveillance, since host country governments often have major financial and other responsibilities and normally follow the proper application of state funds with considerable interest. All host governments have significant responsibilities of a more orthodox security nature, some of which are normal crowd control, but others of which are more sophisticated and require national and international coordination. International sports federations must approve all competition and training facilities, competition and training schedules, qualification standards, and the appointment of technical officials for the competitions. National Olympic committees must approve the accommodations for their athletes, ensure that their athletes are eligible competitors, and select their teams from among the qualified athletes who are nationals of the country or territory. This requires constant monitoring of activities and people, plus the rendering of decisions and, where applicable, imposition of sanctions.

Surveillance is, therefore, an essential component of any Olympic Games, stemming primarily from the franchise-like system of Olympic organization and a series of clearly established authorities within the international sport structures, which must be regularly exercised in order for the system to function properly. That said, the relatively predictable universe of sport is surrounded by a swirl of external considerations, some of which may be controllable, some partly controllable, and others that the sport world has no power whatsoever to control nor, possibly, even to influence. The alternatives are either an organizational paralysis or proceeding with an awareness of the vulnerabilities and taking whatever steps are feasible to minimize and mitigate the attendant risks. It is important to distinguish between security as a post mortem or after-the-fact analysis of an event or phenomenon and the real-time operational considerations of an organization concerned primarily with ensuring that a complicated international event occurs as planned and at the technical levels expected by participants and spectators alike. The former is, in effect, a dissection of the specimen, while the latter is proactive and inherently uncertain. The vocabularies of each reflect different perspectives and actions taken, but the membranes between them need to be permeable.

A brief look through history: "Events, dear boy, events!"

The section heading comes from a response by British Prime Minister Harold Macmillan, responding to a question of what he feared most about elections, to which he replied, "Events, dear boy, events!" In some cases, events to which the Prime Minister was referring might be foreseen, while in others they are completely unexpected. Some may be fixable, while others simply have to be accommodated and plans revised to cope with the new conditions. Whatever the case, effects on the Games can be profound.

The early Games were such a minor event that there was considerable doubt they would even survive, so that security in the traditional sense could not have been further from anyone's mind. The inaugural Games of 1896 were staged with the help of the Greek royal family and some private citizens. The 1900 Games were tacked onto and submerged in the Paris World Exposition and spread over several months so much so that some athletes did not even know they were participating in the Olympic Games. When St. Louis inherited the 1904 Games from Chicago, the Olympics were poorly attended and indifferently organized and were made an adjunct to another world's fair, this time the celebration of the Louisiana Purchase. The survival of the Games was in such sufficient doubt that, lest they disappear altogether, intermediate (now referred to as intercalated) Games were organized on an emergency basis in Athens once again, in 1906. Eruption of Mount Vesuvius led the Italian government to pass on the 1908 Games originally awarded to Rome, so the Games went to London instead. While much better than those in Paris or St. Louis, the London Games were far short of a model of superb organization. It would not be until 1912 in Stockholm that the International Olympic Committee could look forward with some degree of confidence to the continued existence of its quadrennial festival.

Two years after the Stockholm Games, war in Europe intervened and security in the classical sense was at issue when the decision was made to cancel the 1916 Berlin Olympics. The post–World War I Games of 1920 went to Antwerp, Belgium. It was a political decision on the part of the International Olympic Committee, repeated following World War II, to reward countries that suffered particularly severely as a result of the war or were considered the "winners" in the conflict and to impose sanctions on the "losers," including Germany, Austria, Bulgaria, Hungary, and Turkey, by excluding them from participation in the Games. The inclusion of ice hockey on the program of the Summer Games expanded the scope of the event and led to the creation of a separate series of Olympic Winter Games, the first of which were held in Chamonix, France, in 1924. After 1924 in Paris and 1928 in Amsterdam, the 1932 Summer Games made their way out of Europe to the only candidate, Los Angeles. The committee chose Tokyo as the host for the 1940 Summer Games and Sapporo for the 1940 Winter Games. To what extent the possible desire to have Games in Asia may have blinded the Committee to Japan's increasingly aggressive positions in the region is not clear. Either way, the two Japanese cities withdrew from hosting both Games, leaving the Committee with little choice but to find another site on short notice. The 1940 Games went back to Europe. As Helsinki began to prepare, World War II intervened, once again triggering classic security concerns throughout Europe. The same was true for the 1944 Games, which had been attributed to London only about three months before the war began.

The last Games before World War II were held in Berlin in 1936. The International Olympic Committee has been widely criticized for permitting the Berlin Games to proceed as a result of the discrimination against Jewish athletes and the overt political trimmings attached to them by Hitler's Third Reich. This event demonstrated how important the Games had become on the world stage, both athletic and political, and they ushered in a whole new spectrum of considerations to be evaluated by the Committee. By this time, the Olympic ceremonies and public perception of the Games had invested the Games with elements of what may be termed public ritual. It would be a mistake to say that the International Olympic Committee managed to avoid all of the inherent risks of the rapidly shrinking and interconnected world that followed World War II and the increased accessibility arising from air travel and almost instant communication. But it did become more aware of them and conscious of the need to take them into account when making decisions.

In March 1946, by mail vote, the Committee confirmed London as the host city for the 1948 Games. Discussion about holding the Games in 1948 had begun even before the war had been resolved. Losing countries were, again, excluded and, as was the case in Antwerp in 1920, the Games were very much a bare-bones effort, as Europe struggled with the after effects of six years of devastating war. Security, as such, was not an issue. Although the Iron Curtain had descended, and the Cold War was very much a fact of life, the Soviet Union was not then part of the Olympic Movement, and there was little concern within the Committee that it would be actively belligerent in any manner that might cause concern regarding the Games in London. Indeed, there were some early signs that the Soviets might be rethinking their voluntary exclusion from the bourgeois concepts of organized sport and the Olympic Movement following the 1917 revolution. This had not yet taken the form of creating a national Olympic committee and applying for International Olympic Committee recognition, but certain national federations had been established and were in the process of seeking recognition from the appropriate international federations.

At the International Olympic Committee Session held in Stockholm in June 1947, Helsinki was selected again, this time to host the 1952 Summer Games, while the 1952 Winter Games went to Oslo, Norway. The Committee was still wrestling with the matter of Germany and eventually allowed it to compete in the 1952 Games but would only accept a single team from the so-called two Germanys. The Committee members were primarily Western and most of the Western countries refused to recognize the separate existence of the German Democratic Republic, a position the Committee maintained until the 1972 Games in Munich. The combined team first appeared in Oslo, as did that of the Soviet Union National Olympic Committee, which was recognized by the Committee in 1951. With Soviet athletes involved in both Oslo and Helsinki, there proved to be no external security threat, although an interesting variation on security presented itself when the Soviets demanded a separate Olympic Village and training facilities for their athletes, on the grounds of "security." After 1952, the Committee refused to permit separate villages and required the Soviets to use the main Olympic Village.

Having awarded no Games outside Europe since 1932, by the time it was ready to choose a host city for the 1956 Games, in 1949, the Committee had candidates from Melbourne and eight cities from the Americas. Despite the Cold War and the polarized political groupings around either the Union of Socialist Soviet Republics or the United States of America, the only security issue that emerged in the 1956 Melbourne Games was the Australian concern regarding the importation of horses and the lengthy period of quarantine it insisted upon before it would allow foreign horses into Australia. This led the Committee to remove the equestrian events from Australia two years before the Games and to assign them to Stockholm. Although Australia had been active during the Korean conflict between 1950 and 1953, no Asian security issues arising from that participation were evident. As matters turned out, 1956 had its share of European security crises with the Soviet Union's military intervention in Hungary to crush an anti-Soviet revolution. This caused boycotts by Spain, the Netherlands, and Switzerland, and the Suez crisis in 1956 also led to boycotts by Egypt, Iraq, and Lebanon. Rounding out the political spectrum, China withdrew in protest over the Committee's continued recognition of a national Olympic committee in Taiwan, seat of the Chiang Kai-shek nationalist government, under the name of Republic of China Olympic Committee.

In June 1955, with many of the events that would have some impact on the 1956 Games still unknown, the Committee chose Rome as the host of the 1960 Games. It was a significant choice for the Committee to award the first Summer Games to a losing country in World War II. Nothing of a security nature was anticipated, despite an active Communist Party in Italy and a constant instability in the national postwar governments, a syndrome generally regarded as more hopeless than serious.

Continuing a loose policy of reintegrating the losing countries from World War II, in 1959 the International Olympic Committee awarded the 1964 Games to Tokyo. These were also the first Games to be held in Asia. The Korean armistice was holding, no doubt in good measure as a result of the presence of American forces south of the 38th parallel demilitarized zone, armed forces at Japanese bases and the deployment of significant United States naval forces in the area. While there might have been some initial concern about the ability of Japan to organize the Games, the event proved to be a "coming out" party for the new Japan, which had moved from relatively modest postwar manufacturing to high-quality and state-of-the-art production of everything from automobiles to electronics to equipment, foreshadowing the dominance it has now achieved.

The decision of the Committee to award the 1968 Games to Mexico City was a further departure from the norm of hosting the Games mainly in Europe and North America. Mexico was the closest of any host country to the economic category of developing country. In addition to its economic challenges, it had the additional handicap that most of the events would be held at 8000 feet above sea level. There was a degree of political instability that needed to be taken into account and, indeed, led to disturbances and the most unfortunate killing of hundreds of unarmed demonstrators at the hands of the authorities shortly before the Games began. There were calls for suspension of the Games, but the Committee refused to consider this. That decision was undoubtedly correct and the message was clearly received that no consideration would be given to canceling the Games, but the Committee was perceived in some quarters as unfeeling when it declared the matter to be an internal Mexican affair. The Games were also the occasion for a political statement, when two African American athletes used a medal presentation ceremony to demonstrate on behalf of Black Power. In response, the Committee made it clear that no political demonstrations should occur during the Games and ordered the two athletes out of the Olympic Village and the country.

Germany was finally considered ready to host the Games 36 years after the Berlin Olympics. Meeting in Rome in 1966, the Committee awarded the 1972 Games to Munich, which beat Montreal, Madrid and Detroit in the process. Denver fought long and hard to win the Committee decision to award it the 1976 Olympic Winter Games, only to renege three years later, leaving the Committee to scramble to find an alternate site. Fortunately, the 1964 host city of Innsbruck was able to step in to fill the gap. The practical matter is that there is little the International Olympic Committee can do should this occur: the original city cannot be compelled to honor its commitments, and there are no enforceable financial sanctions available to the Committee. Experiences of this nature have resulted in much more extensive evaluation of candidate cities.

The 1972 Munich Games would be the first postwar Games in which the Federal Republic of Germany and the German Democratic Republic were permitted to enter as separate teams. Notwithstanding the inherent tension arising from the division of Germany and the odious Berlin Wall, there were no specific security concerns anticipated in relation to the Games. Unfortunately, there was to be a paradigm shift in thinking about security, resulting from the actions of the Palestinian Black September against the Israeli delegation. A botched German rescue attempt at the Munich airport culminated in the death of the hostages and terrorists. Despite some calls for cancellation of the Games, the International Olympic Committee decided that they should nevertheless continue. Even during the balance of the Munich Games, security was dramatically increased and personal protection afforded to certain prominent Jewish athletes, such as Mark Spitz.

Before the Munich Games, security considerations were limited to keeping the Olympic Village free from the local population and tourists, so that athletes would not be distracted. The overlay on the normal security regulations was quite benign. The Black September episode introduced an entirely new level of surveillance and threats to security. The Olympics had become such an important event, with media coverage unprecedented in modern times, that the possibility of hijacking them for political agendas, whatever the level of violence involved, could no longer be discounted. The Munich episode created a new level of problem for the organizers of the Montreal Games in 1976, the first Summer Games following Munich. Montreal began its organization under the traditionally benign security climate that had marked earlier editions of the Games. Its problems were largely financial in nature, with some attendant domestic political difficulties. The Committee's biggest practical concern was whether the necessary facilities would be finished in time for the Games, and the Quebec government was obliged to step in to take over the construction projects from the city of Montreal for that purpose.

Following Munich, however, increased measures were required to deal with threats of a similar nature. In Quebec during this period, there were many violent actions taken by would-be separatists, including bombings, kidnappings and the murder of a Quebec government minister, which added an actual local threat to possible external threats. This was exacerbated by the fact that the Games were to be officially opened by Queen Elizabeth II, who is the Canadian Head of State and a symbol of the perceived domination of French-Canadians by the English. By the time of the Games in 1976, a sophisticated international intelligence network had been developed, with shared information regarding known or suspected terrorist groups. The Committee began to understand that the new challenge was to provide full security without destroying the festive atmosphere surrounding the Games. The more open the society, the more difficult this challenge, compounded as it often is by differing domestic jurisdictions in matters of police, security, intelligence and enforcement.

Part of the Committee's problem of choosing host cities is structural in nature. The Olympic Games have become such a large and complex event that they are awarded six or seven years in advance. No one's crystal ball is clear enough to predict what might happen between the time the Games are awarded and the time they are scheduled to occur. There was obviously some risk involved in awarding the 1980 Games to Moscow in 1974 (only six years' advance notice was given at the time), but the first steps in the direction of détente had occurred and the second invitation from the Soviet Union to a sports event of the size and scope of the Olympics was an intriguing possibility that the Iron Curtain might be pulled aside to permit a worldwide glimpse of the threatening and mysterious regime behind it. It was, indeed, a risk, but the potential reward was particularly huge.[1] The same considerations would apply to giving the Games one day to the People's Republic of China. During the organizational phases of the Moscow Games, the problems encountered were predictable, arising mainly from the rigidity of the Soviet bureaucracy and the general Soviet suspicion of anything coming from the West, but they were manageable with patience and persistence. No one anticipated the Soviet intervention in Afghanistan shortly after Christmas in 1979, nor the extreme reactionary response that would be led by the United States, as President Jimmy Carter, already in trouble in his efforts to be reelected and smarting from the ignominy of being unable to resolve the hostage situation in the United States Embassy in Teheran, desperately tried to give some semblance of being in control of the international agenda.

The International Olympic Committee, under the presidency of Lord Killanin, was much too slow to react to this crisis and even slower to understand the rapidity with which an anti-Soviet media, especially in the United States, could stir up public opinion. Seen from any reasonable perspective, the Soviet intervention to prop up an unstable pro-Soviet regime in Afghanistan was far removed from some of its more egregious actions in Europe and was never the threat to Middle East oil supply that was trumpeted by the United States. There was never a credible national interest issue for the United States, and certainly not a "national security" threat, which Carter was forced to declare in order to ensure that the United States Olympic Committee would support the Olympic boycott he called for in response to the intervention. Killanin, who was never impressed by the United States and who had no concept, both of what the media would do with the issue and the enormous pressure the United States would impose on other countries, failed to intervene with both the United States and the Soviet Union until well after the positions on each side had been carved in stone. In the end, all that remained for the International Olympic Committee was to ensure that the Games were celebrated in Moscow as planned, showing that the Committee had some remaining teeth in the face of political posturing. The Games were a technical success, but largely joyless, given the absence of a large number of countries that had succumbed to United States political pressures.

It took two further major boycott threats before the Committee learned how to deal with the problem, as well as to realize that it should not rely on governments to solve political issues on its behalf. The first boycott related to the 1984 Games in Los Angeles. While it might have been easy to predict that there would be a retaliatory Soviet-led boycott of the 1984 Games, the early indications were that this would not happen. Leonid Brezhnev, Soviet leader at the time of the Moscow Games, had died and was replaced by Yuri Andropov, former head of the Committee of State Security (KGB). His position had been in favor of Soviet participation in Los Angeles, but he died during the 1984 Sarajevo Olympic Winter Games and was replaced by Konstantin Chernenko. Almost immediately, the atmosphere changed and within two months, the Soviets announced that they would not be participating, on the pretext that their athletes would not be "secure" in Los Angeles. Their public position was that this was a Soviet decision and that no effort would be made to influence other countries to follow its example. Yet, behind the scenes, there was a desperate struggle to mount an effective boycott. This time, the Committee became active at once, under a new and far more politically sensitive and adept president, Juan Antonio Samaranch, who worked with the United States and the Soviet Union to try to find some accommodation, all without result, other than to demonstrate to the rest of the world that the "security" issue was not substantive but purely political. This made the Committee's subsequent efforts to convince the great majority of countries not to follow the Soviet lead all the more effective. In the end, the boycott was a political failure, limited essentially to most of the Warsaw Pact countries, Cuba and the Democratic People's Republic of Korea.

Los Angeles had bid for the third successive time and, despite some indications that Teheran, then ruled by the Shah, might also bid, ended up as the sole candidate and was duly elected as the host city for the 1984 Games. The fact that it was the only candidate gave it some additional leverage to use against the Committee. The Games were to be privately funded and no government guarantee regarding financial responsibility was available, normally a condition of the Games being awarded. The only guarantee provided was from the United States Olympic Committee, which was of cold comfort, since it had no significant financial resources, especially should there be a financial crisis affecting the Games. The boycott position of the Soviets, outlined above, came as a late issue and certainly had an impact on the quality of the competitions in several of the sports and the number of athletes attending the Games, but it never put the celebration of the Games in doubt. The latter problem was alleviated to some degree by other countries adding to their teams in response to requests from the Los Angeles organizers.

The Los Angeles boycott activity occurred against the background of the 1988 Games, which had been awarded to Seoul in 1981, itself a decision fraught with political uncertainty, not the least being the fact that the country had just undergone a military coup. It would not be healthy for the reputation of the Olympic Movement to be faced with a fourth successive major boycott of the Olympic Games. Athletes, sponsors, broadcasters and the public needed to be reassured that the Olympic Games would take place as planned and athletes from all countries would be able to participate. Governments, too, needed to know that their investments in sports infrastructure and the high-performance training of their athletes would be worthwhile. Following the Los Angeles Games, the Committee organized a special Session in Lausanne in December 1984 to consider a series of symbolic measures that might reduce the risks of future boycotts. Some initial thought had been given to suspending national Olympic committees that did not attend; however, more mature reflection led to avoiding such a sanction, recognizing that national Olympic committees were often powerless to combat government decisions and that the underlying purpose of the Committee should be to encourage participation rather than to find ways to exclude athletes for governmental actions beyond their ability to control.

Two of the principal decisions were deceptively simple yet effective: the invitations to participate in the Games would, henceforth, be issued by the Committee itself, not the host country, which would be inviting the Olympic Family to participate in its Games that would be celebrated in whatever was the host country, and the invitations would be sent a year prior to the Games, with a response to be provided several months before the Games. This would allow for competition schedules not to be disrupted at the last minute and also allow the Committee time to determine the real reasons for any non-participation. It became a part of the Olympic Charter that non-participating countries would not share in any Olympic revenues from the Games and accreditations would not be issued for their sports officials.

Samaranch's first official visit following the Los Angeles Games was to the Soviet Union. Despite his annoyance with the 1984 boycott, he was determined to begin at once to rebuild the bridges leading to the 1988 Games in Seoul, especially since no one was under the illusion that the Republic of Korea was anything more than a United States client state, in the same way that the Democratic People's Republic of Korea was a Soviet and Chinese client state. In addition, the two portions of the Korean Peninsula were technically still at war. There was a good deal of manufactured outrage from the Soviet and non-aligned *blocs* at the Committee's decision to give the Games to Seoul. There were many twists in the political road, including the sudden reversal of the Democratic People's Republic of Korea position that the Games should never have been awarded to Seoul to the remarkable view that the Games should be cohosted in both parts of the Korean Peninsula. As I discuss elsewhere (Pound, 1994, 2004), the Committee was much more proactive on this occasion and did not depend on the usual political mechanisms to find a solution. Instead, it took the public position that participation and the cohosting agendas were merely Olympic Family issues, which should be negotiated and settled within the family.

In fact, of course, these were desperately important political issues that had consumed the Koreans on both sides of the line of military demarcation for decades, as well as the diplomatic world in general. Samaranch persuaded the Republic of Korea to allow him to manage the whole affair and, to their great credit, the Koreans allowed it. A number of meetings were held at the Committee headquarters in Lausanne, all with the professed objective of finding a solution satisfactory to both sides, and none with the slightest likelihood of succeeding. Their main purpose was to demonstrate to the world, especially to the supporters of the Democratic People's Republic of Korea, that the Committee was making every effort to understand and accommodate the Democratic People's Republic of Korea position and to show, from the outcomes of the meetings, that the real problem lay with the unrealistic expectations of the Democratic People's Republic of Korea and its complete lack of flexibility. This gave its allies time and reason to avoid a boycott and, in the end, apart from the Democratic People's Republic of Korea, the only country of significance that did not participate was Cuba, which was dependent at the time on financial support from the Democratic People's Republic of Korea.

From the perspective of securing the Games, the Committee initiative of assuming control of its own destiny and the success of its efforts have effectively put an end to the tendency of states to seek Olympic boycotts. To this has been added the political conclusion that such boycotts are not only ineffective vis-à-vis the target country but also hurt only the boycotters and their athletes. It would overstate the case to say that the boycott threat has disappeared entirely, since it was raised in the spring of 2008 during the United States presidential campaign in relation to Beijing but later dissipated. The trigger for this suggestion had been disruptions of the international portion of the Olympic Flame Relay prior to the Games as part of protests regarding China's relationship with Tibet and human rights issues. With the minor exception of United Nations Security Council Resolution 757, targeting certain of the former Yugoslavian republics in relation to the 1992 Games in Barcelona, to which the Committee found a solution, there has been no recent attempt by governments to suggest a concerted boycott of any Games since 1988.

Barcelona and Spain won the Games for 1992. In addition to the challenges of the Olympic Games, Seville was the site of a World Exposition in 1992, an equally ambitious project, and the two concurrent events would tax the construction capacity of the country to its limits. The relationship between Catalunya and Madrid has been complicated, especially since the actions of the Franco regime to expunge the language and culture of Catalunya, and the Games were seen as a chance for Barcelona to assert itself at the expense (literally) of the federal government in Madrid. Domestically, there was a terrorist threat from the Basque separatist group Euzkadi Ta Askatasuna (ETA), which led, in addition to other subtler measures, to visible overkill, such as a tank with military personnel manning mounted machine guns, located outside the Committee hotel during the Games. Part of the spectator accommodation, since Barcelona was notoriously short of hotels, was to be on cruise ships in the Barcelona harbor, which exacerbated security issues. In the end, while there were organizational shortcomings, the joie de vivre of Barcelona overcame the lack of perfection, and the Games will go down in history as a great success.

With the decision to be made in 1990, only ten years after the United States had done its best to cripple the Olympic Movement and only six years after the Los Angeles Games, it was something of a long shot that the Committee would award another Summer Games to the United States and to Atlanta, in particular. The city was small, impecunious, and manifestly unable to organize anything on the scale of the Olympic Games. The largest event it had organized in recent years was a Democratic Party Congress. It was also in the state which produced Jimmy Carter, not a well-regarded leader among the Olympic Movement following his efforts to destroy the 1980 Games. After a well-organized campaign and several rounds of voting, however, it emerged as the consensus choice to confront Athens, which was bidding for the centennial Games and which had a significant block of support, although short of a majority, in the early rounds. Athens purported not to understand why anyone would bid against it for the centennial Games and effectively took the position that it had a right to host them. Yet the risks of awarding the Games to Athens at that time were monumental, to the point that it would have been reckless in the extreme to have done so.

Atlanta, no doubt to its own surprise, won the day. The strength of the United States economy was such that it was unthinkable that the job of organizing the Games could not be done. Nevertheless, the organizational problems were as acute as had been expected and were exacerbated by the city administration, which appeared intent on doing everything in its power to lower the reputation of the city in the eyes of the world. There was a security failure, which allowed a bomb to be placed and detonate, killing one person directly and another indirectly – the first Olympic-related deaths since Munich in 1972. The subsequent rush to produce an arrest (of an innocent person) and announce the solution to the bombing did nothing to improve the image of the responsible security forces.

The decision in 1993 to prefer Sydney to Beijing was an example of the Committee's hesitation to incur unnecessary risk. It was the first time that China had bid, following the "Olympic" political solution of 1981 that allowed both China and Taiwan to participate separately, and there was no doubt that the largest country in the world should, someday, host the Games. It was, however, only four years since the drama in Tiananmen Square, which had profoundly affected China and its reputation. Beijing's bid committee was inexperienced, inflexible and defensive, unable to deal with Western media. The risks of going to China for the Games were high, as would be the rewards, but by the narrowest of margins, the Committee opted for Sydney, where the risks were decidedly lower. Sydney produced, as expected, excellent Games.

Sooner or later, the Committee knew it would have to take the Games back to Greece and the only possible city was Athens. By 1997, Greece had achieved somewhat more stable government and entry into the European Community, with access to the funding required for badly needed infrastructure. The risks were considered low enough to justify a choice of Athens over Rome. Greek politics remained chaotic. Every decision took forever and was intensely political, construction was delayed, and there was a serious concern that Athens would not be ready. It proved to be a last-minute affair, which cost far more than it should had the construction been properly planned and executed. Over and above the huge organizational risks, the security threats were real and serious. Domestically, Greece had shown surprising reluctance to deal with terrorism. It had troubled relationships with Turkey, had a porous eastern border and was perilously close to the Middle East in the post-9/11-paradigm shift affecting international security. Athens had two harbors to secure: one commercial, in which there were thousands of containers whose contents were uninspected, and the other a port in which passenger ships would be used as accommodation for Olympic spectators. Greece took advantage of security expertise from around the world to assist with the Olympic project, and the outcome was a successful joint venture, which added to the experience of all contributors. Crowd control was breached during the men's marathon when a spectator interfered with one of the leading runners.

By 2001, enough time had passed since Tiananmen Square, China was emerging on the world stage, as opposed to regional only, and its bidding committee had come to understand that although Games in Beijing might have a distinct Chinese "flavor," the decision as to whether it would have the opportunity to stage the Games would be made by a predominantly Western Committee. The lobbying and presentations were far more adept than they had been eight years previously and there was little doubt as to the outcome. The Western concerns about human rights and Tibet persisted, but while they were serious, they were not at a level that put the Games at risk. Internal security expertise was more than sufficient to manage domestic threats, and the likelihood of external disruption was regarded as minimal.

Media access and content were significant concerns and required consistent pressure on the part of the Committee to ensure that satisfactory levels of comfort on both accounts could be achieved. It was only during the international portions of the Olympic Flame Relay that security failed. This was something that the Committee should have anticipated, and it provided ammunition for those who opposed the Games in Beijing, creating a minor crisis for the Committee. Olympic Flame Relays are high-cost, high-risk, low-reward events. On the other hand, Olympic Flame Relays are particularly effective within the host countries in the period immediately prior to the Games, as a communications exercise and enthusiasm booster. Security during the Games was highly visible, with the presence of enormous numbers of police and military personnel, almost all of whom were unarmed. There were certainly emergency response teams out of sight and nearby, but they did not impinge on the atmosphere of thorough but benign security.

London, Paris and Madrid had a vigorous competition in 2005 to host the 2012 Games, with London edging Paris in the final round of voting. London was perhaps fortunate (in relation to the timing of the Olympic decision) that the coordinated bombings in London the day following the Committee decision had not occurred a day earlier, but those events demonstrated yet another feature of challenges for the Olympic Games, where, as in the case of London, many of the potential terrorists are already embedded in the community. This calls for, in addition to the international security dimension, different and comprehensive domestic surveillance, in which Great Britain has already developed a certain degree of sophistication. It will, however, add to the costs of security, which have now become a fact of life. Organizationally, there was minimal concern about London, although the financial crisis beginning in 2007 and 2008 affected London, as a financial center, more acutely than many others.

Experience has shown that external comments regarding progress can have a salutary effect within the host country. The Committee had its fingers crossed in relation to the 2014 Olympic Winter Games in Sochi, where, again, despite the many hurdles that made construction and transportation extremely difficult, it was unthinkable that Russia would permit its international reputation to be severely damaged by an inability to deliver the Games.

The decision to award the 2016 Summer Games to the first South American city was made in October 2009, much too soon to have a good focus on the likely risks, other than to note that Brazil had never organized anything approaching the scale of the Olympic Games and that it would have the double challenge of organizing both the World Cup and the Olympic Games, the two most important sport events in the world, within two years of each other. The Brazilian economy has not performed to the levels predicted by its financial experts, with the result that financial risks have not been minimized. The prevalence of crime in Rio de Janeiro remains a significant concern, and the efforts to date by Brazilian authorities to find appropriate solutions have not been marked with much success.

A complex event which cannot fail

Apart from the concerns discussed so far, organizational aspects of the Olympic Games are particularly complex and time sensitive. In the Summer Games, there are 28 different sports, several of which have more than one discipline, all of which must fit within the tight timetable of 17 days and be coordinated with each of the other sports. Everything must work perfectly, the first time. The Games are scheduled, years in advance, to start at a particular time on a particular date. If the time to start the Games is scheduled at 8:00 p.m. on Friday, July 27, that is when the Games must start – that is, not at 8:05 p.m. and not on Saturday, July 28. Because of their international nature and their importance, many commitments, usually involving substantial financial implications, are made across a broad range of stakeholders, who incur their own Olympic-related risks, based upon certainty of schedules. These have the effect of further locking-in the Games period and include, for example, on the part of broadcasters, the reservation of satellite commitments and bookings, as well as their other significant programming and financial commitments on either side of the anticipated Olympic period. State-of-the-art facilities must be provided for the competitions and training venues. The finest athletes in the world will be competing and must be given every opportunity to do their best.

Hand in hand with this consideration is the desire to ensure that the Olympic hosting experience is regarded as positive within the host country. Good results on the playing field are helpful but fleeting. More important, however, is making certain (or at least as certain as possible) that the host country does not spend too much money on expensive facilities that will have no after-use or will be regarded as the classic White Elephant. The International Olympic Committee must be careful not to send a message to candidate or host cities that Bigger is Better. This entails being certain that the international sports federations, which have a natural interest in promoting their own sports, especially during the Games, do not make excessive demands, asking for facilities that may be filled to capacity for an Olympic final, but then never again. Maintaining such policies requires constant surveillance of all the parties involved. In 2002, the Committee created the Olympic Games Study Commission with a mandate to determine how to reduce the costs and complexity of organizing Olympic Games. This

Commission, which I chaired, reported in 2003, and its recommendations began to be applied immediately, even to host cities that had already been awarded the Games.

The modern Olympic Games attract hundreds of thousands of extra people to the host city, including athletes, support personnel, media, security, service personnel and spectators. It would be a rare city indeed that has existing sufficient excess capacity to handle this influx. It is always a major challenge to obtain or construct what is needed for the purpose. Issues can range from a concern that facilities for accommodation can be finished too soon, as was the case with the Moscow Games in 1980, where the Soviet officials, having been pressed by the Committee to finish the Olympic Village sooner, explained that the demand for public housing (for which the village would be used following the Games) was so great that there would be social and political difficulties were the village to be finished and remain unused months before the Games. In some places, it is simply not feasible for permanent accommodation to be constructed for which there will be no after-use following the Games. Examples are Barcelona and Athens, where cruise ships were chartered and docked at port facilities in the city. In Winter Games, physical conditions, primarily altitude, may require the construction of satellite villages for acclimatization purposes. Financing is almost always a question of importance, where the range may include government financing, to private, or public-private partnerships, or variations of the three. In each case the risks are different and it would be wrong to conclude that possible problems disappear with government funding.

Making certain that facilities and accommodation are available in time for the Games is an important part of risk assessment but far from a complete answer to securing the Games. It is one thing to plan a track meet, a swimming meet or a basketball tournament and quite another to deliver each of them flawlessly. At the Olympic Games, everything must work perfectly – you cannot ask the winner of the 100 meters to rerun the race because your timing system failed. Winter Games involve more than their share of execution risk due to the outdoor nature of many of the events and the impact of weather conditions. In Calgary, during the Olympic Winter Games in 1988, there were six days in a row when the temperature there was higher than it was in Miami. Many Olympic Winter hosts have had to manufacture or import snow for events, including cross-country and ski jumping.

For most Olympic cities and organizing committees, the Games being organized are the first they have ever attempted. It has been said, often in jest but with enough ring of truth to be relevant, that the only amateurs left in the Olympics are the organizers. The Committee, on the other hand, having followed the organization of many Games and other events, has the benefit of experience gained on every continent and every form of government and private sector. It has an obvious interest in making that experience available to the new generations of organizers and has institutionalized this in structures designed to assist the current organizers in the form of Transfer of Knowledge Services. As mentioned earlier, it also establishes a Coordination Commission, which follows the progress of each organizing committee, providing guidance, and, where necessary, direction as may be required. The first such Commission, of which I was the chair, was created with respect to the 1996 Olympic Games in Atlanta, when the International Olympic Committee concluded that effective delivery of the Games might be problematic. The Atlanta Games were the first time the Committee undertook a coordinated surveillance of the preparations of the Games. Coordination Commissions typically include International Olympic Committee members and senior staff, international federations, national Olympic committees and athlete representatives, as well as outside experts in matters such as transportation, environment and construction. None of this provides a guarantee of success, but it helps with the ongoing assessment of risk and the avoidance of problems that have been encountered on other occasions. It also helps reinforce the concept of a partnership between the Committee and the host city rather than the remote deus ex machina relationship, which existed in earlier days.

Requiring a ticket to enter the premises where events are held is standard surveillance measure. In the case of Olympic Games, the situation becomes more complicated than mere domestic events, due to the size and duration of the Games and the need to ensure that a meaningful level of foreign spectators have reasonable access to the events. A complex system of tickets as well as payment and distribution mechanisms must be established, sufficiently robust to deal with several million individual tickets and to resist counterfeiting attempts. Sophisticated monitoring systems are also used by Games organizers to ensure that tickets are not accumulated for commercial resale (perhaps to or by organizations that are not sponsors of the Games and that hope to "ambush" the official sponsors) or scalping.

Of those who experience the Games, 99.9% do so through the media, not through physical attendance, with the result that the Committee has an interest to ensure that optimal conditions exist to enable media to bring Games to the world, including the emerging New Media. Television, at the present time, is also the largest source of income for the Olympic Movement, which leads to a special interest in being sure the media are provided with working and other conditions that will lead to maximum exposure. There are huge technical and transmission risks involved, which include partial or total loss of the broadcast signal, inability to get a signal to an operating ground station, up to a satellite and down to reception in the home territory. Broadcasts, since television rights are sold on a territorial basis, may also be affected indirectly by missing sports, missing countries or nominal participation. A United States television audience has minimal interest in watching Olympic Games if there are no American athletes or if popular sports such as swimming, gymnastics, athletics and basketball are not included. One of the International Olympic Committee's objectives with the Games is to ensure that they may be hosted in many different countries. One of the risks inherent in this objective is that not all countries have the broadcast and media structures necessary to deliver high-quality audio and visual signals. The Committee has, therefore, undertaken the responsibility of producing the Games coverage through Olympic Broadcasting Services, rather than leaving that responsibility to the Games organizing committees. This initiative was launched in relation to the 2010 Olympic Winter Games in Vancouver and has continued ever since.

Someday, the Olympic Movement will be faced with a pandemic, such as SARS or avian flu. While this has never happened to date, it appears, statistically, to be inescapable. Surveillance of preparations for the mitigation of the risks and the impact on the Games must now be regarded as part of the assessment and organizational profiles of a modern Olympic Games.

Guarding the Olympic reputation

As the "owner" of the Games, the International Olympic Committee must have confidence in the choices it makes of the Olympic host cities. There may be many opinions as to which of several candidates is the "best" city, some of which may be personal bias, but the main objective of the Committee must be to avoid making a "mistake" and granting the Games to a city that proves to be incapable of organizing them at a level that meets the sport and media expectations for Olympic Games, or has a serious risk of being unacceptable for some reason. The process of awarding the Games must be transparent and free of perceived corruption. It must also demonstrate some degree of sensitivity to global and other issues, including geographic. And, finally, the competitions at the Games must be seen to be fair. The general public does not differentiate between the Games and the international federations responsible for the management of the competitions. Thus, when Canadians Jamie Salé and David Pelletier were cheated out of a gold medal in the pairs figure skating event at Salt Lake City in 2002, the public thought that the Olympics were crooked and did not distinguish the fact that the outcome had been caused by corrupt figure skating officials.

The host city and country take on their own share of risk, which can affect their own reputations, whether positively or negatively, ranging from organizational ability, the friendliness and accessibility of the country, the public support of the Games, the legacy impacts, the quality of the large-audience opening and closing ceremonies and, finally, the perception of the media, which, in many respects, determine whether the Games have been "successful" or not.

Even the media have their own reputational risks. Traditionally, the importance of the Olympic Games has been such that the media looked for new features to enhance their coverage of such a worldwide event, to attract even larger audiences. These range from new techniques, equipment, camera positions and unilateral coverage of events of interest to their broadcast audiences, to background features that bring audiences closer to the athletes, expert commentators, interviews, and historical materials to build a sense of continuity. Outcomes for media tend to be immediate and measurable. Audience sizes can be estimated with considerable accuracy. These ratings impact the amounts that can be charged for advertising and, therefore, the economic outcome of the Games for broadcasters. The search for new audiences and demographics is a constant feature of the media's approach to the Games. What was once restricted to the written press and radio has now expanded from standard television to interactive media, which can be accessed virtually anywhere and at any time, which changes the whole presentation of an Olympic Games.

A final audience, which must remain attracted to the Olympic Games if they are to be secure for the future, is the athletes of the world. Maintaining that interest is one of the principal challenges for the Committee in a world that, despite becoming more integrated through travel, business and communications, is nevertheless even more diffuse at the level of individuals and what they choose to do with their leisure time. The values formerly attached to hard work, self-discipline, competitiveness and measurable achievement are, today, neither self-evident nor necessarily motivating. One of the major appeals of the Olympic Games is the realization of a dream, of participating against the finest athletes in the world. If that aspirational dream is not maintained, tomorrow's athletes will not enter the competitive sports structures that provide the means to become high-performance athletes. If the only athletes who participate in the Games are a narrow class of professionals, there will be no future for the Games, and they will degenerate into sterile entertainment for fickle mobs, as they did in ancient Greece. With that outcome, there will be a collapse of government interest in constructing sports facilities and an even more rapid descent into a sedentary society, morbid obesity and dramatically increased costs of health care. Failure to maintain the interest of youth in the joy of effort is the greatest risk facing the Committee as the ultimate Olympic "insider."

The key with risk is to be sure that one factors it into all decisions and considerations. Risk will not go away and will be a constant, occasionally terrifying, companion. On the other hand, it should not become the cause of organizational or decisional paralysis. Risk is a fact of life. As with the case of medical and other conditions, it must be managed. Security considerations are a response to perceived risks. Constant and informed surveillance of the factors and the actors involved is a vital part of that process. Therefore, equally important as recognition is the mitigation of risk, both to reduce the likelihood that the apprehended "downside" does not occur as well as minimizing the adverse consequences should it occur.

Note

1. The decision followed the International Olympic Committee's adept avoidance of risk with the superpowers in its selection of Montreal as the 1976 host city, opting for neither country's candidates in Moscow and Los Angeles. Diplomatic niceties in that regard were observed by the subsequent choices of Moscow for 1980 and Los Angeles for 1984.

Part II
Case Studies

3
Modernity and the Carnivalesque (Tokyo 1964)

Christian Tagsold

When the Opening Ceremony of the Tokyo Olympics took place on October 10, 1964, audiences around the world were watching live on television. Only four years earlier, the 1960 Olympics in Rome were recorded on reels, and these tapes were sent around the world for broadcasting. For the Tokyo Olympics, however, the United States provided the necessary technical support for Japan to be able to broadcast the Games via satellite and in color (Tagsold, 2002: 105–107). The Tokyo Olympics were also the first Games to be staged in Asia. Tokyo had already won the bid to stage the Olympics in 1940 but due to war, the right to the Games was given back to the International Olympic Committee in 1938 (Collins, 2007).

The 1964 Games were highly important for Japan in that they were expected to prove to the world that the country had overcome the dark years of the 1930s and 1940s and was now a worthy member of the peaceful international community of nations symbolized by the Olympic Games. The global audience was to be convinced that the Japanese were peace-loving and calm people, able to celebrate the youth of the world. When commenting on the Opening Ceremony the next day, the *New York Times* put it this way: "The crushing defeat of 1945 was not only a physical, but also a psychological blow from which [the Japanese] are only now recovering. Warm-hearted and chivalrous by nature they have yearned to be accepted again by the nations they once had opposed."[1]

There were other considerations, however, which were discussed intensively within Japan. Would the organization of the event be efficient enough to deal with all the challenges associated with staging such a large-scale event? Japanese newspapers like the *Asahi Shimbun* or *Nikkei Shimbun* had been voicing such fears since Tokyo had won the right to host the Games in 1959. *Asahi Shimbun* ran a series of discussions among its journalists entitled "The Olympics are coming but...." For example in its second installment on May 29, 1959, the discussants asked where the incredible sum of 100 billion yen for the cost of the Games would come from and showed no confidence in their ability to provide an answer.[2] As can be seen from the commentary of East Asian scholar Ivan Morris, for example, voices from abroad had similar doubts.

> Looking at their newly-independent country in the clear light of day – small, deficient in investment capital, and lacking almost every natural resource except human population, dependent for her economic survival on finding markets in a world of fierce competition and rigid trade barriers, distrusted, even disliked by many of her Asian neighbors, faced with the overwhelming might of communist power on the near-by-continent, and unable to defend her territory without assistance from a country 6000 miles away – even most sanguine Japanese were hard to find grounds for national ebullience. (Morris, 1960: 150)

In the midst of these discussions, "security" as we know it today was at the time a very minor concern. Japanese terms for security were used very sparsely, not only in official documents but also in newspapers and in public discourse in general.[3] Three words were in use for security in the Japanese sources in 1964: *hōan* (保安), *anzen* (安全) and *antei* (安定). These three words, although used in 1964 as a literal translation for security, have different semantics, as described in more detail by Kiyoshi Abe in his chapter on the 1972 Sapporo Games. Briefly, for the purposes of this chapter, today the word "security" would be more often translated into Japanese as a borrowed word from English: *sekyuriti*.[4] At some point in the last four decades hōan, anzen and antei have in many cases been deemed semantically too different from the English word security to serve as translation.[5] In *Asahi Shimbun*, the word "sekyuriti" appears for the first time in 1969. It is used very infrequently – about 15 times – in the 1970s, then starts to appear more regularly in the 1980s, and is in common use today.[6] Hōan, anzen and antei all have the Chinese character "an" (安) as compound meanings of "relax," "quiet" and "peaceful." Hōan thus means the upkeep of public peace and quietness, anzen is mostly used in Japanese for a state of safety, and antei includes stability as a connotation. The fact that they start with the Chinese character "an" very well characterizes the official attitude about security during the Olympic Games in 1964. On the occasions when hōan, anzen and antei were actually used, they underlined the official wish to organize peaceful and dignified Games.

   To set the context for questions of hōan, anzen and antei during the Tokyo Games, I first provide a short overview of the dynamics in Japanese society in the 1960s. Crucially, these relate to friction and violence surrounding discussions about the extension of the Security Treaty between the United States and Japan, which led to public demonstrations in 1959 and 1960. Next, I analyze the general attitude concerning hōan, anzen and antei. This topic was not especially important in 1964, even though the historical context of the 1960s might suggest otherwise. As I show in the third part, opinion polls suggest that the major fear of the officials in terms of hōan, antei and anzen was that the Japanese would behave in ways thought by the officials as unruly and carnivalesque. However, the main approach to achieving orderly behavior by citizens was not policing and surveillance but rather an extensive educational preparation campaign. The last section analyzes the important role played by the Self-Defense Forces, that is, the Japanese army, in the organization and implementation of the Olympics. The case of the Self-Defense Forces shows very clearly that the official stakes in showing force during the Olympics were less founded in what is understood as "security" today in the context of such public events and much more founded in symbolic politics.

Japan between anpō crisis of 1960 and student protests of 1968

When the Olympics began on October 10, 1964, World War II was just 19 years past. Another occurrence in the more immediate past was also important for evaluating hōan as a potential problem for the Olympics. In 1959–1960, the country had lived through a major political crisis causing public unrest. Along with regaining sovereignty in 1952, Japan had signed the Security Treaty between the United States and Japan[7] in 1951. This allowed the United States Army to station forces in Japan even after the end of the occupational period following the capitulation of the county in 1945. Since Japan had not maintained an army of its own until 1954, the American forces were an important player in the defense of the country.

In 1959 the Security Treaty of 1951 was due for revision. Prime Minister Kishi Nobusuke,[8] imprisoned as a Class A war crime suspect in 1948 but never indicted, pushed for a more active role for Japan and proposed a new Treaty of Mutual Cooperation and Security. Under the stipulations of the new treaty, Japan would have been an equal partner with the United States in terms of military activity. Many Japanese objected strongly and organized national protests. They felt that Japan should refrain from an active role in military matters only 15 years after the end of World War II (Sasaki-Uemura, 2001; Avenell, 2010). Some of the demonstrations drew hundreds of thousands against the renewal of the treaty. These demonstrations lead to violent clashes between police and protesters, and many hundreds were injured (Takagi, 1985). This so-called anpō crisis ("anpō" being the abbreviation of the treaty, in Japanese), forced Kishi to resign his post in 1960. However, the new Treaty of Mutual Cooperation and Security between the United States and Japan[9] passed by default when the House of Councilors did not vote in time, shortly before Kishi's resignation.

The discussion on the renewal of the Security Treaty ten years later again caused huge protests. This time social unrest was connected to the worldwide students movement of 1968–1969 (Takagi, 1985). At the peak of confrontations, students occupied Tokyo University for almost a month. As in 1959–1960, the unrests were called anpō crisis.

The Tokyo Olympics were therefore conditioned by two anpō crises that nearly tore Japan apart. Discussions on the anpō treaty of 1959–1960 triggered the biggest political crisis of postwar Japan. Japan in the early 1960s was anything but "harmonious" and "peaceful" as sometimes stated (Leonardsen, 2006). In order to reconcile the fractions, new Prime Minister Ikeda Hayato who replaced Kishi in 1960 changed the political agenda and focused on economic nationalism instead of promoting further strengthening of military power in Japan. The famous philosopher and pundit Tsurumi Shunsuke (1991: 15) analyzed this change of semantics very convincingly:

> The time of Kishi Nobusuke, who was member of cabinet during the war, ended tarnished by the huge demonstrations of protest in the anpō-crisis. Ikeda Hayato, who appeared instead on the stage as prime minister, utilized a vocabulary and rule of grammatical transformation which deviated from classical nationalist theories. He held speeches which focused on explanations of economic growth. "Economic growth," "gross national product" and "standard of living" became important words of the political vocabulary.

The Tokyo Olympics were the ideal event to overcome the anpō crisis and perform national unity. The anpō crisis also demonstrated the potential of unrest as a threat to a mega-event. Though the immediate societal frictions were patched, criticism lingered on. Student organizations in particular kept protesting against the government throughout the 1960s and were willing to risk forceful clashes (Takagi, 1985).

Defining safe Olympics

A major political crisis with protest and clashes between police and demonstrators had shaken Japan in 1959–1960. Nevertheless, various opinion polls taken before and during the Olympics suggest that security was a minor concern not only for the media but also for the citizens. State television Nippon Hōsō Kyōkai published detailed results of these polls as a book in 1967. The polls were partly conducted by the state television and partly by state institutions. A review of the questions asked in the polls shows that very few actually address hōan, anzen and antei, which suggests that, at least for those who designed the polls, security was not a topic of concern.

A set of questions regarding the upcoming Games, which were included in a poll taken in April 1964 by the Prime Ministers Agency, provide some insight into the issue of security in relation to the Games. The poll participants were asked whether they thought that the Games would be a success.

Notably, only a minority of 22.8% in Japan overall and 14.8% of Tokyoites had any doubts about this.[10] Asked to rank likely problems, most saw general infrastructural deficiencies of Tokyo as a possible obstacle. Interestingly, 32% were concerned about misconduct of young people.[11] Unfortunately, the category "misconduct of young people" was not specified precisely. I suggest, that it probably refers to students and their organizations who had played a very active role in the anpō demonstrations and continued to raise their voice. Of the poll participants, 12% saw minor incidents of violence as a threat, another category of problems which was not scrutinized closely in the poll.[12] The poll did not even bother to ask about other topics, which are today related to security, such as assassinations or other high-risk scenarios. The state television also took many polls itself.[13] Yet, this television station did not see it important to ask any questions related to security.

Judging from social unrest and various incidents in the decade when the Tokyo Olympics took place, one might be tempted to ask why the public and the participants did not see this issue as a higher priority. In this one opportunity where the polls offered to reflect on this topic, both the polls and the participants seem to have ignored questions of hōan, antei and anzen.

This public sentiment on matters of hōan, anzen and antei before the Games was also reflected in the activity of the institutions of public order. The final report of the Organizing Committee contains a chapter entitled "Security and Traffic Control," which is only about seven pages long.[14] It consists nearly entirely of details about which measures were taken by the police to cope with traffic and crowds watching events both in and outside stadiums. Other sections deal with "Traffic Control Around the Games Sites,"[15] "Police and Traffic Control on the Days of Opening and Closing Ceremonies at the National Stadium"[16] and "Police and Traffic Control on Road."[17] Only a few sentences in the whole chapter do not deal directly with traffic. The section "Guard and Traffic Control Around the Olympic Village" explains the number of police staff employed in guarding the village and the case numbers of lost-and-found items in addition to the traffic situation.[18] Because the report stated that traffic "was one of the most important and difficult problems at the time of the Games,"[19] this is no surprise.

When Tokyo won the bidding race in 1959 against competitors like Detroit, one of the major concerns of city officials, national politicians, members of the Organizing Committee and pundits was indeed Tokyo's traffic system. After being the target of heavy air raids during World War II, the city had been hastily rebuilt. It lacked major routes for diverting traffic around the center. Additionally, cars became popular in the 1960s due to rising living standards, so metropolitan infrastructure had to be modernized.[20] One of the major achievements for the Games was a new system of inner-city highways. These highways were built in the early 1960s in preparation for the Olympics and financed by the metropolitan government as well as by the state. Staging of the Olympics accelerated these infrastructural ameliorations, which had been deemed necessary anyway (Igarashi, 2000; Tagsold, 2002). Yet traffic caused major headaches for the metropolitan police of Tokyo in charge of security and traffic control. In order to avoid traffic congestions around the Olympic venues, two routes with limited rights to drivers were set up around the Meiji Olympic Park and National Stadium. Cars were not allowed to park inside this area, and routes were limited to one-way traffic. Restrictions were lifted again after the Games.

Similarly police concluded that spectators had to be controlled in order to channel the participants smoothly in and out the stadium. Especially during the closing of the Opening Ceremony, when 75,000 people would leave the stadium at the same time, the police had to consider measures to divert the participants. They took a light approach: "These measures included the brass band music at the National Stadium and the display of fireworks outside the National Stadium to divert the attention of sections of the crowds. These performances proved quite effective in preventing confusion, in that a large number of people both inside and outside the Stadium paused for a short while to enjoy the performances."[21] Beyond traffic control and some sentences on guarding the Olympic Village and managing crowds during the Opening Ceremony, the report does not touch on other matters.

The infrastructural ameliorations for the roads not only were a step to a better flow of traffic to and from the venues and thereby better to safety standards; they also helped to convey the image of Tokyo as a modern city to the world. Another measure by the city also aimed at a safer and cleaner image, but this measure was not mentioned in the official reports and went mostly unnoticed by the public. The homeless and the beggars were removed from the inner city.[22] They were either simply driven away or were allotted to council housing for homeless far from the center of the city (Seidensticker, 1990: 235; Sakurai, 1993: 32).

Not only did official sources touch security only in passing, but the media before, during and after the Olympics were not concerned with hōan, anzen or antei either. As early as the start of the Tokyo campaign in 1959, only traffic problems got major attention. Shortly after winning the bid race, newspapers asked critically whether the city would be able to resolve pending problems such as traffic or accommodation for foreigners.[23] But even during the anpō crisis in late 1959 and 1960, questions about the Olympics and security were not on the agenda of the media.

Avoiding the carnivalesque

For the most part, the Organizing Committee of the 1964 Games did not see any threat to hōan, anzen and antei. However, there was a general under-standing that the behavior of the Japanese could easily lead to problematic situations in terms of hōan. The organizers of the Games were concerned that Japanese carnivalesque behavior would tarnish the image of the people and the country internationally. In other words, there were doubts that the right version of Japanese culture – at least in the eyes of Japanese officials – would prevail. This fear had been strongly articulated by political leaders before the 1940 Olympic Games, which had to be canceled shortly before their start due to Japan's role as an aggressor in Asia (Hashimoto, 1994; Collins, 2007). In preparation for these Games, the right attitude of the Japanese had been widely discussed in the late 1930s. Nagai Matsusa, member of the Organizing Committee wrote in 1938:

> there is a strong tendency among normal citizens to exaggerate the matsuri [festival]. But on the occasion [of the upcoming Olympics] one has to be mindful of the real standing of Japan and one has to adapt the real spirit of sportive competition. It will not be tolerated that someone slips into a mood of degeneration!...We have to welcome the foreign guest with firm pride and beautiful noble-mindedness.[24]

Since the goal of the ruling ultra-nationalist elite was to present Japan as a civilized and, at the same time, superior country, forms of acceptable behavior for the duration of the Games were narrowly defined. *Bushidō*, the way of the samurai, amongst many others, was invoked constantly by Nagai as the right attitude. The ideas of "firm pride" as well as "beautiful noble-mindedness" refer directly to the concept of bushidō as the Japanese form of chivalry. As Stephen Vlastos (1998) has shown, bushidō is much more a construct of the late 19th and early 20th centuries than a traditional virtue widespread in Japan. The emblematic book for this process of construction is surely Nitobe Inazō's (1900) *Bushidō: The Soul of Japan.*[25] Bushidō served the political leaders as legitimation in imperialist expansion but also as a tool against the commoners. In the words of Nagai: "The base of the honorable bushidō is the willingness of Japanese to sacrifice themselves for the *tennô* [emperor]."[26] Folk style of living was countered by an austere vision of Japaneseness. A symbol for "degeneration" – as Nagai called it – of folk was the *matsuri*.

Matsuri are traditional festivities most often conducted by a local shrine or temple. Markets and carnivalesque festivities are typical, and processions through the quarters of the organizing shrine or temple take place. Often young men carry a deity on their shoulders through the narrow streets. The deity's wooden housing is heavy, and up to 30 or 40 young men are needed to carry it. These processions serve to condemn behavior deemed hurtful to the community. Families that have posed problems for others find their houses utterly destroyed during matsuri when the young men push the deity into it (Schnell, 1995). It is hard to make out the culprits under these circumstances so there is no way to sue for compensation. During matsuri, alcohol flows freely, and there is "collective excitement, spontaneity and confusion," as Elizabeth Moriarty (1972: 93) has pointed out.

The fear of the Olympics turning into a matsuri was not as strong in 1964, but nevertheless it did prevail. In one of the debates of the Olympic Preparational Committee of the government in 1962, one member of the House of Councilors put it very similar to Nagai two-and-a-half decades earlier: "I think that concerning the staging of Olympics, that they are originally a pure sports festivity. I think, it is very important to underline this nationally and internationally. In my opinion we cannot allow for a 'matsuri-sawagi.'"[27] *Matsuri-sawagi* is a pejorative term for passion shown during matsuri, "sawagi" meaning uproar or disturbance. Quite similarly on May 26, 1964, the *Asahi Shimbun*, Japan's leading liberal newspaper titled an article, "Don't rampage like in a Matsuri!" The Metropolitan Educational Board of Tokyo had admonished schools to avoid everything recalling a matsuri outbreak and take an orderly and humble approach to the Games. Similar warnings about the possibility of the Games turning into an unruly matsuri were voiced by the economic newspaper *Nikkei Shimbun* more than once (Tagsold, 2002).

An educational campaign was created to make sure that citizens would behave accordingly. In 1964 the Organizing Committee formed a Citizens Movement for Olympic Education with branches in each prefecture.[28] This movement, defying its name, was rather bureaucratic. It was mostly the prefectural governors who were installed as head of their prefecture's branch, showing its importance. The movement disseminated informational brochures to the Japanese in which the citizens were informed about the proper conduct. One of the central brochures started out with a number of points. The first was: "Let us improve our self-image as Japanese, stressing pride to be Japanese."[29] Two decades after the end of World War II, strengthening patriotism was one of the main goals for the government. The second point asked for a general understanding of foreign countries and their customs. The next point outlined concrete steps for the Olympics: "Let us internalize the right attitude and situation to approach foreigners: (a) Attitude and situation of approaching foreigners; (b) etiquette against foreigners."[30] The presence of foreigners in this way was used to regulate citizens' conduct.

In the end, the Organizing Committee was not successful in fully suppressing matsuri-sawagi. The Olympic Flame Relay caused joyful mass gatherings in the province even though the educational movement had been set up to avoid this. For many Japanese, the relay was even more important than the Games themselves (Fujitake, 1967). Many had no chance to see the Games live except for the torch passing through their village or town. Tickets were sparse, and most could not afford a trip to the capital anyway. After the torch arrived on Japanese soil, it was divided into four flames. These were being carried through the country on four different routes, so all 47 prefectures were able to greet the flame. Cities on the route, and especially prefectural capitals that hosted the flame for a night, were heavily crowded when the Olympic torch came into town.

"Everywhere sawagi [disturbance]," reported *Asahi Shimbun* on September 18, 1964, detailing incidences in Miyagi prefecture as well as in Sapporo, the very north of Japan. The article enumerated "problems of the Olympic torch relay" and held that "the degree of confusion was too high and many places fell into utter chaos." In Miyagi more than ten people were injured, while in Sapporo a phone booth was heavily damaged. Even though *Asahi* reported these disturbances, the articles rather stressed the great joy and enthusiasm of people everywhere.

The prefectural police were not often able to control the crowds. For example, the small capital Tsu of Mie prefecture saw about 50,000 spectators turning up when the torch arrived. The city itself at this time had roughly 150,000 inhabitants. The Olympic torch was escorted by one of the four patrol cars the prefectural police owned. When I interviewed the driver of the day in 1998 – later head of the prefectural police of Mie – he remembered that streets were heavily overcrowded in all parts of the prefecture:

> In Seki [a small town near the prefectural capital Tsu] already many lined the streets, but in Ishinden [a suburb of Tsu] it was incredible. The street over there is pretty smallish, isn't it? Even today a patrol-car barely passes through. With people lining the street you have to be very careful. It cost us some nerves to pass through without hitting anyone.

Beyond some police bicycles and the one patrol car, prefectural police were only able to secure the relay with a few dozen policemen facing tens of thousands of spectators (Tagsold, 2002).

An American photographer who followed the flame on its route was quoted by *Asahi Shimbun* with a highly interesting observation in the context of securing the Games: "I took photos in Hokkaidō and Kyūshū. The atmosphere was incredible everywhere. In America the police would have coerced the crowed using weapons."[31] The Japanese police did not use such methods and did not interfere with the celebratory crowd.

The Organization Committee and the metropolitan police were proven right about fearing outbreaks of what they deemed to be unruly behavior in matsuri style. However, the pedagogical approach coupled with clever inventions during the Games – such as the brass band music diverting crowds after leaving the stadium mentioned earlier – did help to avoid such problems during the Games. The regional outbursts of joy surrounding the passing of the Olympic torch through the country were the only major examples of what the organizers would consider trouble with hōan.

Bringing the Self-Defense Forces into the Games

To the international spectators, the presence of the Japanese defense forces at the Games was probably the most obvious sign of security efforts. The role of the Self-Defense Forces (SDF) was particularly visible to the outside world during the Opening Ceremony. The defense forces administered most of the symbolic tasks such as bringing the Olympic flag into the stadium and hoisting it.[32] The Self-Defense Forces were installed in 1954, due largely to the fact that the United States pushed Japan to set up its own army. This push on Japan to create an army led to a problematic situation.

Japan, in its postwar constitution, had abdicated all rights to wage war and even to maintain an army of its own. This was stated in the famous Article 9 of the new constitution, which had been passed in 1947. The constitution was based on a draft of the American General Headquarters in charge of affairs until Japan regained sovereignty in 1952 (Inoue, 1991). Because the imperial army of prewar times had been the backbone of ultra-nationalist rule, it is quite understandable that in the late 1940s the American General Headquarters did not want the Japanese to reinstall their army. Therefore Article 9 also was part of the package the American General Headquarters handed over to Japanese legislation. However, as Cold War conflicts deepened in Asia, the United States decided that Japan should have an army of its own. Ruling conservatives in Japan willingly consented. They had harbored a strong wish to again set up an army for themselves. Article 9 was never revised. To cover this breach of the constitution, at least semantically, the new army was named Self-Defense Forces.[33]

Because Article 9 had gained broad backing in Japan in the postwar period, the defense forces were highly unpopular. Petitions signed by millions of citizens were handed to the government to no avail. Citizens also objected to the cost of maintaining an army. The defense forces were termed "tax thieves" regularly (Morris, 1960: 250). Even the Imperial Household tried to maintain a distance from the defense forces in order to avoid raising prewar memories when the Japanese emperor was commander of his imperial army. The first modern constitution of Japan from 1889 stated this in Article 11. After the Japanese defeat, the imperial supreme command was seen as one of the reasons for militarization of the society in the prewar era. Preserving the new peaceful image of the *tennō* and cutting the connection to the discredited army was much more important than lending symbolic legitimacy to the new Self-Defense Forces. The Imperial Household Agency, which was in charge of controlling the emperor's public appearances, refused any symbolical concession linking the emperor and the defense forces (Yamauchi, 1976). The 1964 Olympics were therefore an excellent chance for the conservatives and the defense forces themselves to alter their image. Or as the final report of the Agency for Self-Defense put it: "The SDF's cooperation [during the games] did result in deepened trust and understanding for the SDF by Japanese citizens."[34]

More than 7500 soldiers from the Self-Defense Forces participated in the organization of the Games – a number that had been unseen until then. The total number of people involved in organizing the Games was about

60,000. The defense forces sent more than 10% of these people,[35] justifying their presence by drawing on the historical example of the 1936 Games in Berlin:

> Through the thorough cooperation of the army, the unprecedented smooth execution of the Berlin games was possible. Especially the opening ceremony was staged uninterrupted due to the efficient military control. The spectators in and outside the stadium were deeply impressed. There have been critical voices on the ban of Jews or the political and tactical use of the games. But it cannot be denied that because of the cooperation of the army the games got a success.[36]

Clearly the official interpretation of the Self-Defense Forces here was that the role of the military could be exempted from criticizing the Games. In the Self-Defense Forces' reading, the critique was directed toward political problems and inherent racism and did not concern the role of military in 1936. Such high esteem of the Berlin Olympics was widely shared among the International Olympic Committee circles in the 1960s. Indeed, as Schiller and Young (2010) have been able to prove, the perceived success of the Berlin Games also deeply influenced the awarding of the 1972 Games to Munich.

The identification with the German Wehrmacht is telling. While the defense forces saw their role as maintaining quiet and orderly Games, their involvement in the Opening Ceremony was highly representational. The military used the peaceful image of the Olympics to shape its own image. Only two minutes after thousands of doves of peace had been released into the sky, the jet-fighter planes appeared to paint the Olympic rings. As the spectators were still looking upward, the jet fighters flew over the last doves dispersing to paint the rings. The classical symbols of peace served to prepare the sky for the new symbol of peace. This was not the only symbolic coup for the Self-Defense Forces. The two weeks of the Olympics and the Closing Ceremony also helped to raise the esteem of the defense forces so that even the famous left-wing novelist and later Nobel laureate Ōe Kenzaburō praised their efforts.[37]

Though the symbolic side was likely paramount for the involvement of the defense forces, the army was clearly also important for hōan, anzen and antei. The latter's role, however, was not emphasized. The official report of the Self-Defense Forces treats the latter role in a marginal subchapter discussing administrative management toward the end of the report.[38] This included traffic management, patrolling, guidance of spectators and tourists, bodyguard work, and finally analysis of crimes (broadly defined in the sources) in close cooperation with the police. Of these, traffic received the most attention in the report – a total of about three pages – while other tasks were briefly listed without any specific detail.

The Olympic Village was certainly intensely patrolled. The Self-Defense Forces and the police shared the work in this area. Again, traffic to and from the village was the main focus and nearly 200 soldiers were allotted to this task. In addition, guards from a private security company were employed in the village, something quite novel in Japan. Nihon keibi hoshō had been founded only two years earlier and was the first security company in Japan.[39] Its involvement in the Games helped to advertise its services nationwide (Haraguchi, 2010).[40] However, its overall role in the security of the Games was rather minor. Along with patrolling and offering guidance, gatekeeping was the task for the soldiers.

Other examples of control, which are today considered a "security matter" during the Olympics, also included seemingly minor tasks like controlling the guns of the shooting competitions.[41] The possession of firearms was and still is illegal in Japan. This of course greatly eases the task of protecting mega-events for official organizers since the number of illegal firearms is indeed very low in the country. Defense forces also actively cooperated in other sports such as horse riding and sailing competitions, in which its expertise outdid that of other state institutions.

For the defense forces, the Olympic Games were a huge success. Issues of security and surveillance technologies and procedure, other than regular crowd control, only played minor roles. It was the symbolic tasks that helped to alter the image of the army in spite of its problematic constitutional context. It may have been more important for the military to not be very visible and avoid the use of force even when intervention may have appeared necessary. In fact, this image of the Self-Defense Forces was also prevalent in the other Olympics staged in Japan. As Kiyoshi Abe discusses in Chapter 5 of this book, by the time of the Sapporo Games in 1972, perceptions of threats to security have changed, yet the role of the military remained largely symbolic. While it was broadcast widely during the Sapporo Games that numerous young soldiers in uniforms were clearing the ski run from heavy snowfall, their role in maintaining order during the Games was largely played down.

Concluding remarks

For the Tokyo Olympics in 1964, the peculiar features of what would today be referred to as "Olympic security" relate to their specific historical context. The Games were historically embedded between two major national crises, which could have created anxieties about security of the Games. However, in the decades after World War II, the Olympics were seen as a strictly nonpolitical event by the International Olympic Committee and Japanese citizens alike (Tagsold, 2009). For these reasons, as far as the Japanese were concerned in the early 1960s, the Games were not to be mixed with political protest against the security treaties with the United States. In the eyes of organizers as well as the public, therefore, political terrorism was considered a highly unlikely threat.

Within this context and reflecting the political agenda of staging the Games, the metropolitan police and the Self-Defense Forces shared the burden of ensuring that the Games took place without disruption. The emphasis on presenting Japan as a modern, civilized and peaceful country had important implications. The educational programs instructing the Japanese citizens to engage in "proper conduct" (or sportsmanship), competition, pride, and noble-mindedness, shifted the emphasis from an indigenous matsuri-style joyful carnival toward a bureaucratically organized and controlled state ritual. This ritual was, however, void of direct military and police intervention even when the public did erupt into an unruly, spontaneous joy, as was the case during the Olympic Flame Relay. After all, despite drawing on the organizational success of the 1936 Berlin Games as the justification for the involvement of the military in the staging of the Olympics, the 1964 Tokyo Games were not to be a show of military strength. Rather, this was an opportunity for Japan to revive nationalism, shed the shadows of the not too distant past, find a new place for its military, prove its ability to stage well-organized Games in an atmosphere of economic progress, and push aside elements of tradition to embrace the notion of order of Western modernity.

Notes

I would like to thank an anonymous reviewer for comments. All translations are my own.

1. *New York Times*, "Japanese Throwing Off Cloak of Isolation: Hirohito, Now 63, Reviews Parade at Start of Games," October 11, 1964.
2. Until 1971 the yen's exchange rate was fixed: ¥360 equaled US$1. The sum named in the article therefore roughly translates into US$270 million – a quite exorbitant sum in the mid-1960s taking the gist of the discussion in *Asahi Shimbun*.
3. Leading national newspapers such as the *Asahi Shimbun* or the *Yomiuri Shimbun* did not publish many articles on this topic. I reviewed nearly all *Asahi Shimbun* articles on the 1964 Olympics between the time of the bid for the Games in 1957 through the 1964 Games. Hōan and antei were not discussed more than a dozen times in this time span.
4. As a foreign loanword, security is written in Katakana syllabary, not in Kanji (adopted Chinese characters): セキユリテイ.
5. A simple search on Google demonstrates that sekyuriti within the context of the Olympics has mostly replaced hōan. The combination of the Olympics (*orinpikku*) and sekyuriti yields five times more hits than the Olympics and hōan (roughly 1.2 million vs. 246,000, respectively).
6. *Yomiuri Shimbun*, another leading national newspaper, has been using the word "sekyuriti" since 1947. The word appears only five times up to 1970 but starts to be used regularly from the mid-1980s and on.
7. *Nihonkoku to amerika gashhū koku to no aida no anzen hoshō jōyaku.*

8. Japanese names in this article follow the Japanese convention to have the family name (Kishi) before the given name (Nobusuke).
9. *Nippon-koku to Amerika-gasshūkoku to no Aida no Sōgo Kyōryoku oyobi Anzen Hoshō Jōyaku.*
10. Nippon Hōsō Kyōkai [NHK], Tōykō orinpikku, 261.
11. Ibid., 259.
12. Ibid., 259.
13. Ibid.
14. Organizing Committee for the Games of the XVIII Olympiad. 1964. The Games of the XVIII Olympiad Tokyo 1964: The Official Report of the Organizing Committee. vol. 2, Tōkyō, 461–468.
15. Ibid., 461.
16. Ibid., 462.
17. Ibid., 465.
18. Ibid., 466.
19. Ibid., 461.
20. According to the Japanese Statistics Bureau, the number of vehicles in Japan doubled between 1960 and 1964. Car ownership normalized in this decade. See http://www.stat.go.jp/english/data/nenkan/1431-12.htm (last access October 25, 2009). Japan followed the example of Western nations that had already motorized.
21. See Organizing Committee for the Games of the XVIII. Olympiad, The Games, 464.
22. In preparation of the Tōkyō Olympics 1940, the city council had also decided to remove unwanted groups from the inner city. Tōkyō's Koreans were targeted for removal to hastily built shabby housing on a former garbage pit to exclude them from the center (Chan-jung, 1997: 57f). These houses were among the few structures finished before the Games were canceled.
23. See, for example, "The Olympics are coming but…Part 2: More than 100,000,000,000 Yen? Early Fears of Bribery," *Asahi Shimbun*, May 29, 1959.
24. Nagai, Matsusa (1938) *Orinpikku seishin* [*The Olympic Spirit*]. Tōkyō: Dai jūnikai orinpikku Tōkyō taikai soshiki iinkai, 23f.
25. Nitobe wrote the book in English for an international readership. In his very first sentence of the book, he made clear that for him, bushidō was a very current guideline for the Japanese: "Chivalry is a flower no less indigenous to the soil of Japan than its emblem, the cherry-blossom; nor is it a dried-up specimen of an antique virtue preserved in the herbarium of our history." (Nitobe, 1900: 1)
26. Nagai, *Orinpikku seishin*, 24.
27. See online parliamentary records: http://kokkai.ndl.go.jp/cgi-bin/KENSAKU/swk_dispdoc.cgi?SESSION=27023&SAVED_RID=2&PAGE=0&POS=0&TOTAL=0&SRV_ID=3&DOC_ID=25&DPAGE=1&DTOTAL=9&DPOS=7&SORT_DIR=1&SORT_TYPE=0&MODE=1&DMY=29980
28. Monbushō (ed.) (1965) *Orinpikku Tōkyō taikai to seifu kikan no kyōryoku* [*The Tōkyō Olympics and the Cooperation of govermental institutions*], Tōkyō, 198–202.
29. Ibid., 197.
30. Ibid., 197.
31. See "Taishū ga momiau" ["The crowd bounced each other"], *Asahi Shimbun*, September 9, 1964.
32. The final report remarks that eight members of the Japanese Maritime Self-Defense Force brought the flag into the stadium and hoisted it. See Organizing Committee for the Games of the XVIII. Olympiad, The Games, 231.

33. Since the conservative Liberal Democratic Party's rule was uninterrupted for more than four decades, opposition coming mainly from the left was not able to effectively intervene. Communists and socialists did stress that Self-Defense Forces were unconstitutional but did not succeed in enforcing Article 9. The majority of LDP held that setting up national self-defense was no breach of Article 9.
34. Bōeichō [Department for Self-Defense] (1965) Dai-18-kai orinpikku Tōkyō taikai: Un'ei kyōroku no kiroku [The 18th Olympic Games of Tōkyō: Report of the Administrative Cooperation], Tōkyō, preface.
35. Akiyama, Josui (1965) *Tōkyō orinpikku no uchi to soto: Hōdō shitsuchō no mita butai ura* [*Inside and outside the Tōkyō Olympics: The Backside of the Stage as Seen by the Head of Media Relations*], Tōkyō: Bēsuboru magajin sha, 169.
36. Bōeichō, Tōkyō orinpikku, preface.
37. ōe, Kenzaburō (1964) "73,000-jin no 'kodomo jikan' [The childhood of 73,000 people]." In *Tōkyō orinpikku: Bungakusha no mita seiki no saiten* [*The Tōkyō Olympics: The Festival of the Century as Literates Saw It*], ed. by Shōichi Noma, 36–43. Tōkyō: Kōdansha, 42.
38. Bōeichō, Tōkyō orinpikku, 156–158.
39. The company's name translates to Japanese Guarding and Security. Today it is called Secom and has become the largest security company in Japan. It has also expanded to other Asian countries.
40. Ishii, Ryōichi (2009) "Ajia no minna san, 'sekomu shitemas?': Tetteishita jizen-shugi de gurōbaru hatten" ["You in Asia: 'Do you know Secom?': Global development through consequent self-financing']. *Nikkei bijinesu*, http://business.nikkeibp.co.jp/article/pba/20090106/181958/?P=2&rt=nocnt (last accessed March 30, 2012).
41. Bōeichō, Tōkyō orinpikku, 82–91.

4
Repression of Protest and the Image of Progress (Mexico City 1968)

Kevin B. Witherspoon

In 1963, the International Olympic Committee awarded the 1968 Summer Olympic Games to Mexico City based largely on the perception that Mexico – unique among Latin American nations – was a peaceful land led by a stable government. This image of Mexico had been decades in the making and incorporated a blend of celebrating Mexico's rich history and indigenous culture along with its growing promise as a modern, urban, cosmopolitan nation. Marketing these ideas began in the late 19th century, when a group of elite Mexican leaders and experts, described by historian Mauricio Tenorio-Trillo as the "wizards of progress," began portraying such an image through displays at the world's fairs (Tenorio-Trillo, 1996: 18–19). As historian Eric Zolov has explained, these developments continued in the tourism advertising campaigns of the 1960s, exemplified by the slogan, "So foreign...yet so near" (Zolov, 2001: 248).

Despite the government's successful marketing campaign, this image of Mexico as a peaceful and contented land concealed the reality of a nation whose citizenry was tightly controlled and repressed by its government. As historian Tanalis Padilla and others have argued, Mexico was quiet not so much because its populace was content, but rather because it was too terrified to protest publicly (Padilla, 2008). As this chapter will demonstrate, it was internal disruption, far more than any external threat, which consumed the attention of Mexican officials. Thus, preserving its peaceful image while hosting a massive global event, became a vexing problem for Mexican Olympic organizers. Successfully hosting such an event would signal Mexico's entry into the ranks of the world's most modern and developed nations. With that in mind, Mexico marketed its Olympics as a festival of peace, and symbols such as the dove and the peace sign were ubiquitous in Mexico as the Games approached. The slogan *"Todo es posible en la paz"* ("All is possible in peace") was featured prominently on billboards throughout Mexico City.[1]

On the other hand, in order to ensure that this image of a "harmonizing" nation was maintained, Mexican officials had to be prepared to suppress any threats to that image (Zolov, 2004: 163). While there was virtually no reference to what is today often referred to as "Olympic security" in publications released by the Mexican Olympic Committee, behind the scenes officials were gravely concerned that the carefully constructed image of Mexico would be challenged through disruption. If the Olympics were interrupted or disturbed, then the image of a peaceful Mexico would be tarnished, perhaps even shattered. As such, Mexico maintained an extensive network of repressive institutions, from local police, to a large standing army, to secret police and special forces, including a unit whose sole responsibility was enforcing peace at the Olympics, known as the Olympia Battalion.

To outsiders, for whom Mexico was a misunderstood and mysterious nation, Mexico seemed to be a simple, rustic land, whose people lived contented country lives. The urban centers like Mexico City were depicted as modern, bustling places. Construction was ubiquitous – during the 1950s, the government sponsored innumerable projects to improve roads, the water system, and the university. The United States Department of State commentary preferred to accentuate these positives, while playing down the troubles of the lower classes. Memoranda within the Department praised the high growth rates of the Mexican gross national product. Its economy was "growing rapidly," with the future showing nothing but "sustained economic growth." Most important for United States business interests, this growth meant "favorable prospects for U.S. traders to build on the billion-dollar market which Mexico has become for them and for U.S. interests to make further productive investment [there]."[2] Experts in the State Department deemed Mexico to be "in the vanguard of progressive Latin American nations."[3]

Mexico had successfully polished its image enough to impress the international community, despite its combustible internal problems. So, to casual commentators representing foreign magazines such as *Sports Illustrated* and *Time* magazine, Mexico would have to struggle with environmental issues such as the altitude and smog, with cultural concerns like the mythical mañana attitude – that is to say, the laziness – of its people, and with urban problems like traffic and overcrowding; however, issues associated with security were rarely mentioned in such magazines in the years leading up to the Olympics.

But Mexican government officials and Olympic organizers understood the profound dangers lurking beneath the veneer of calm. Such officials recognized that, despite the image promulgated internationally, the Mexican populace simmered with discontent, and threatened to boil over by the summer of 1968. That year, of course, was one of the most tumultuous years in modern history, with violent protest movements springing up all over the world. As student protests gripped many nations, most notably the United States and France, Mexican students soon caught the fever. One participant in the event, and later chronicler of it, Paco Ignacio Taibo II recalled that Mexican students heard and read about the "May events in France...the Prague Spring, the student mobilization in Brazil, the occupation of Columbia University in New York, and the Cordoba Uprising in Argentina," and that they, too, became influenced by this "international contagion" (Taibo II, 2004: 29). In July, a simple street fight between rival student factions sparked a protest movement that swelled to frightening proportions as the summer wore on. As cartoon images distorting symbols such as the Olympic rings or athletic competitions became common currency for the students, Mexican leadership could not ignore the possibility that the students might attempt to disrupt and ruin the Games. It was this internal threat of student dissention that was the primary security concern for Mexican Olympic organizers.

The Olympia Battalion

The connection between security and athletics is symbolized by the central figure in the preliminary stages of Mexico's application to host the Games, General José de Jesús Clark Flores, whose life had been dedicated to two passions: the military and sport. Not only was he the highest-ranking military official in Mexico, he could claim legitimate title as the highest-ranking sporting official as well. Skilled in fencing and basketball, Clark presided over the Mexican Basketball Association and the Mexican Sports Confederation, and had been on the organizing committees of both the 1954 Central American and Caribbean Games and the 1955 Pan American Games. Elected Vice-President of the International Olympic Committee in 1966, Clark had reached the highest post ever achieved by a representative from a Latin American country. It was General Clark who chaired an Executive Commission that supervised the completion of various tests and reports and also outlined preliminary plans regarding security. Clark envisioned a special force charged with maintaining order during the Games, a vision that would be realized in the Olympia Battalion. The Battalion was a special force of 300 men, "made up of soldiers and young officers, members of the Federal District Police Force, the Federal Judicial Police, the Federal Security Agency, and the Federal Treasury Agency" (Poniatowska, 1993: 259). They were identified by their signature white gloves and white helmets. Their primary role in the months prior to the Olympics seemed to be to stand in formation at various locations among the Olympic venues and put a nice, clean face on the issue of security. The often-photographed Olympia Battalion became part of the symbolic imagery surrounding the event, their pristine white gloves and helmets complementing the ubiquitous white dove and other symbols of peace.

As the student movement escalated that summer, the issue took on a heightened state of urgency, and the images grew more ugly. Increasingly, the Olympia Battalion took to wearing plain clothes and could be recognized only by their white gloves. In addition, Mexican President Gustavo Díaz Ordaz charged the Mexico City police and members of the regular Mexican army with keeping order as well, meaning that as many as 10,000 heavily armed soldiers were ready for action at a moment's notice. In short, the full might of the Mexican military was responsible for ensuring the security of the Games. This made for a dramatic contradiction between the message organizers had hoped to send through the Olympics – a message of peace, cooperation, and harmony – and the reality of a heavily surveilled, even militarized, Games. Foreign observers who once made little mention of the issue of security now made it a prominent theme in their writing about the Olympics, and photographs of the Olympic venues often featured members of the regular military, machine guns in hand. As *Sports Illustrated* aptly predicted, "When the big show moves into the stadium on Opening Day, there will be almost as large a crowd of soldiers outside the place – guarding it."[4]

Mexico's efforts to prevent the disruption of the Games were made in secret. The massive four-volume report published by the Mexican Olympic Committee after the Olympics concluded, which spent dozens of pages describing the various services and programs offered by the Mexicans, makes no mention of the issue of security or the military presence so evident during the Games. It described in detail arrangements regarding air and ground transportation, the *edecanes* – Olympic "hostesses" whose outfits resembled those of airline stewardesses – the post office, tickets, lodging and hotels, the Olympic Villages, and other services, but never mentioned security or extensive surveillance put in place. However, pictures in the volume could not hide what the committee was unwilling to discuss. Several photographs show members of the Olympia Battalion wearing telltale white helmets standing watch near some of the Olympic venues.[5]

A history of unrest

Early planners of the Olympics could not have envisioned the explosion in protest activity during the summer of 1968. Years of pent-up frustration at many elements of the Mexican government were unleashed in a summer of massive popular protests. The Mexican student movement had its origins in a series of other protest movements in previous decades, all of which had been summarily crushed by the Mexican government, but each one had added to the crescendo of popular unrest. These episodes demonstrate that the public image of Mexico as a peaceful, contented nation obscured the reality of deep dissatisfaction within the population and of a government all too ready to wield force to maintain order.

The Mexican government, even as it had achieved the economic boom known as the "Mexican miracle" in the 1940s and 1950s, and even as it was lauded by the rest of the globe for its political stability, had always had its detractors. Various strikes and protest movements over the years had inspired specific mechanisms within the government for handling such problems, and by the time the students began their protest in 1968, the government was well practiced in dealing with troublemakers. With rare exception, violence was not the modus operandi of the Mexican government; it preferred to extinguish opposition in quieter and more devious ways. Leaders of groups that started to speak too loudly were usually co-opted into the government and thus silenced. "Often such groups found their voices squelched by a publicity infrastructure that was entirely controlled by the government – paper and ink for printing pamphlets or newspapers, space on billboards, air-time on radio or television, and virtually any other means of reaching a wide audience were either owned by the government, or sympathetic to it" (Witherspoon, 2008: 106). Other methods employed by the government included propaganda campaigns, launched in those same government-owned newspapers or over the radio. The president and his aides, too, thwarted opposition groups by either ignoring them or refusing to meet with their representatives publicly. Finally, and only if all of the above mechanisms had failed to quiet the protest, the government might resort to force. Swiftly and completely, the most vocal dissenters were made to disappear. Only rarely had this happened in the revolutionary era, so rarely that the incidents barely dented the Mexican reputation for stability.

These methods for controlling protest had been tested several times prior to 1968, and always things had ended badly for the protestors. In 1940, troops fired upon labor leaders who sought improved working conditions, leaving 11 people dead. The worst massacre prior to 1968 came in 1952, when the army attacked a group protesting the policies of President Ruíz Cortines, killing over 200 people. A general strike in 1958–1959, involving telephone workers, electricians, teachers, railroad workers and others, suffered repeated attacks at the hands of Mexican police and army forces. Historian Elaine Carey, describing the strike, writes that at one time or another "*granaderos* harassed and beat many teachers... police brutally dispersed the marchers," and that railroad "leaders were arrested and imprisoned" (Carey, 2005: 23–26). In the years prior to the Olympics, such forces were also deployed throughout the country in an attempt to dismantle any potentially disruptive groups, carrying out a "secret war" in the countryside and an aggressive campaign to suppress the Communist Party in Mexico (Padilla, 2008: 1–25). The members of the Communist Party were especially targeted for their perceived revolutionary goals and had been subjected to violent attacks and arrest many times during the 1950s and 1960s. Carey, utilizing interviews and other original documents, builds a compelling case that many of the students involved in the 1968 protests were influenced by their parents, who had experienced violent government reprisals in the 1950s and 1960s. One such student explained, "Before 1968, the authoritarian state had brutally beaten workers, also *campesinos*, and it had destroyed leftist opposition parties. It was in this vacuum, that students injected their demands, aspirations, and desires that were not exclusively of student interest, but also of interest to *campesinos*, workers, intellectuals, political parties, etc." (Carey, 2005: 29). Thus, by the time of the Olympics, both the ideology and framework of protest – and the government mechanisms of repression and response – had been formulated over decades of previous experience.

The student movement

It was into this atmosphere that the students launched their movement in 1968. The protests began in late July, when students from several schools marched through the streets in celebration of the 15th anniversary of Fidel Castro's revolution in Cuba. A chance encounter between student groups led to fisticuffs in the street. The *granaderos*, Mexico's feared riot police, dispersed the students, swinging their clubs and injuring many demonstrators. They pursued both groups back to their schools, where they continued to attack both students and teachers. In extending their brutality onto the school campuses, the granaderos breached the barrier of university autonomy that was a tradition in Mexico. As reporter John Spitzer put it, "The students and the teachers were outraged," along with their parents, university officials, and other sympathizers.[6] In the charged atmosphere of 1968, Mexican students now caught what Taibo II calls the "virus," and the student movement was born (Taibo II, 2004: 29). The movement escalated rapidly, and on July 26, a massive student march was again met with violence. Granaderos and the city police assaulted the students with clubs and bayonets, injuring many and killing four.

As tensions mounted on both sides, Mexican President Gustavo Díaz Ordaz chose to escalate the cycle of repression, leading to more student protest, and the pattern continued throughout the summer. On July 26, government officials created a "Strategy Committee" headed by Secretary of the Interior Luis Echeverría, who played the central role in directing government response to the students.[7] Overall, this early strategy allowed the movement to carry on its activities largely unchecked, while planting subversives within the movement to weaken it from within and at the same time hoping that student enthusiasm for the movement would wane. They purchased full-page advertisements criticizing the student movement and attempted to alienate the students from the rest of the population by leveling accusations of communist agitation. The police arrested many student leaders, several of them foreigners older than typical students, for contributing to rumors of communist involvement.

Such government efforts were counterbalanced by student publicity campaigns, as growing armies of students distributed flyers, conversed with people on the street, and emblazoned buses and walls with their slogans and demands, including one of many new slogans: "*NO QUEREMOS OLIMPIADOS*" ("We don't want the Olympics").[8] By August, several marches were estimated to include more than 100,000 participants. The protests became more vocal and their calls for change more radical, including not only more personal and vicious insults of the president himself, but also more direct jabs against the idea of hosting the Olympics. By late August, the movement was becoming truly disruptive, including several instances in which students attacked and damaged government buildings or facilities, and marches clogged the streets and exacerbated already difficult traffic conditions. On August 29, American official Thomas Hughes noted, "President Díaz Ordaz has had enough of student demonstrations and insults and has decided to use force to put down future disorders." He continued, "Tanks and armored vehicles have been employed to rout student groups and keep them dispersed in the narrow streets feeding into the main square in Mexico City."[9] The size, disruptive nature, and increasingly revolutionary tone of the protests contributed to Díaz Ordaz's belief that the students posed a genuine threat to the Olympics, and that the violent repression of the students was necessary. In his annual presidential address on September 1, Díaz Ordaz warned the students against further action and reminded them that the full might of the army stood ready should the activism continue. In addition, he reminded the nation that "The army intervenes to safeguard order and not to oppress the people."[10] According to historian Dolores Trevizo, while the rank-and-file student protestors were moderate in their demands, a small group of radical students contributed to the revolutionary tone of the movement, sparking Díaz Ordaz's response (Trevizo, 2006: 197–229). To American diplomats stationed in Mexico, conflict seemed inevitable. Unbeknownst to the students, Díaz Ordaz was making preparations for such a conflict, requesting and receiving radios, riot gear, and heavy weapons from the United States State Department, whose interest in the growing clamor was hardly casual.

Conditions worsened until a pivotal moment on September 18, when Díaz Ordaz authorized military force to occupy Autonomous National University of Mexico, where protesting students had taken up their headquarters, and where they used campus grounds to plan their next protests and organize the brigades for their daily marches. Equally important, the university campus was "the location of a number of important Olympic installations," which the Mexican government could not allow to be threatened.[11] It was later reported that the attack was a preemptive strike to thwart a student march on the Olympic Village. In describing the attack, an American official explained that "The action seemed to be of a preventative nature with the Government of Mexico hoping to gain control of the situation before the Olympics."[12] Autonomous National University of Mexico would be restored to its normal operation procedures, explained Minister of the Interior Echeverría, but probably not until after the Olympics were completed.

Further complicating Mexico's handling of maintaining order was the role of the United States government, and specifically its Central Intelligence

Agency. Cold War tensions contributed to their concern, as early reports seemed to indicate that the student movement of Castro-friendly Mexico had been infiltrated by communist radicals. For years, the United States State Department had kept tabs on communism in Mexico and was leery of the Left gaining influence. As the student movement grew, the State Department documents reflected growing concern that communists controlled the movement, fears exacerbated by Mexican authorities blaming the protests on foreign agitators. These worries over losing Mexico to the communists inspired the United States government to support Díaz Ordaz even as he encouraged the repression, and ultimately destruction, of the student movement. Central Intelligence Agency operatives and others in the United States government eventually decided that the communist threat had been exaggerated and discussed the Mexican handling of the student uprising with a critical eye. The Central Intelligence Agency's Agent Philip Agee, stationed in Mexico for months prior to the Olympics, writes derisively of Luis Echeverría in his famous memoir, *Inside the Company*. "Echeverria is responsible... for re-establishing order but so far has only made matters worse... claiming that five 'riot coaches' from France, and other communist agitators had plotted the insurrection from outside the country. No one believes such trash which makes the government look ridiculous and makes compromise more difficult" (Agee, 1975: 553). On August 28, another diplomat assessed Díaz Ordaz's methods by writing that "The evidence thus far is that Díaz Ordaz has not distinguished himself in handling the student crisis. He apparently has: (1) under-estimated the depth of student hostility toward the Government of Mexico; (2) overestimated the role played by alleged 'Communist' agitators; and (3) failed to follow up on possible opportunities to settle the problem."[13] Agee wrote in late September that one of his colleagues came away from a meeting with Díaz Ordaz with the impression that "the President [was] confused and disoriented, without a plan or decision on what to do next" (Agee, 1975: 556).

The Tlatelolco massacre

With the opening ceremonies of the Olympics only ten days away (October 12, 1968), the conflict between the students and government forces reached its tragic conclusion. On the afternoon of October 2, about 10,000 people gathered at the Plaza of Three Cultures in Tlatelolco Square in Mexico City. The assemblage was entirely peaceful and included many children and parents of the students. Local police and the military hovered at the fringes of the crowd, but the students had grown accustomed to their presence after months of similar protests. The hum of helicopters, too, seemed little cause for concern.

Suddenly, at about 6:20 p.m., two helicopters swooped low over the square. A few moments later, thousands of army troops, who had quietly observed the protest for most of the afternoon, moved to seal off all exits from the square. Members of the Olympia Battalion opened fire on the crowd from a number of balconies and rooftops that lined the square. Elena Poniatowska's gripping account of that night, translated as *Massacre in Mexico*, recounts the evening's events from numerous perspectives. Poniatowska cites Mexican newspapers that described an awesome array of firepower directed against the students: "all sorts of armaments, including heavy-caliber machine guns mounted on twenty jeeps or more... some three hundred tanks, assault troops, jeeps and troop transports... surrounded the entire area" (Poniatowska, 1993: 205).

The crowd was helpless. The unarmed students formed a panicked human wave, rushing from one end of the square to the other, seeking desperately for some escape. As one witness explained, "The troops didn't even use tear gas to disperse the crowd. The soldiers just fired into the people."[14] The killing continued for over an hour, subsided for a few minutes, and then resumed. For two hours, the firing was nearly constant, and stray shots were heard into the night. Students fled into the apartments that ringed the square, huddling on floors with strangers who took them in. Soldiers and tanks saturated these buildings with bullets and grenades, blowing out windows and wounding many people inside. The troops then stormed the apartments, arresting not only anyone who looked like a student, but many of those who had tried to help them. Those arrested were sent through a gauntlet of soldiers and police, beaten and groped as they were pushed toward the trucks awaiting them.

One worker, not connected to the students but arrested anyway, explained, "a panel truck full of *granaderos* drove up, and the soldiers formed two lines and made us go down the middle, with each of them hitting us with their rifle butts as we went past them" (Poniatowska, 1993: 132). By the time the slaughter had ended, somewhere between 300–500 people had been killed. Several thousand student leaders were taken into custody. Many were tortured by methods that included beatings, electric shocks, mental torture, food deprivation, and simulated castration. One victim, Luis Tomás Cervantes Cabeza de Vaca, after describing in great detail the tortures enacted upon him, summarized: "More tortures, then, more blows, more electric shocks" (ibid., 107). It would be years before most of the students could consider public protest again, and many were too emotionally scarred to participate in any protests after that night.

The students and the Olympics

The day after the massacre, the United States ambassador to Mexico wrote that "there [did] not seem to be any connection between [the] shootings and [the] Olympics."[15] In fact, the evidence suggests that the student movement grew increasingly linked to the upcoming Olympics as the summer wore on, and thus suppression of the students was perceived by Olympic organizers as fundamental to preserving security at the Olympics. From the government's perspective, eliminating the "student problem" was tantamount to preserving Olympic peace.

Connections between the student movement and the Olympics are many. Most important, the timing of the Olympics, "the Olympic deadline" as one United States government document described it, required that the crisis be resolved quickly.[16] Students and government officials interpreted this deadline differently. Leaders of the student movement declared that "time was on their side because the Mexican government had to show [the] International Olympic Committee ... that political stability could be maintained" leading up to the Olympics.[17] At least one American official agreed, noting that, "With the Olympics only two months away, the students are in a much stronger position than usual."[18] For Mexican government officials, and Díaz Ordaz in particular, the approaching Olympics meant fewer options for quieting the students. As American intelligence official Thomas Hughes wrote on August 6, "As the date of the Olympics approaches, the administration of President Díaz Ordaz will step up its efforts to head-off student demonstrations and the security forces will grow increasingly sensitive to any indication of trouble." He continued, "The security forces will remain alert and ready to react at the first sign of trouble."[19] By September, members of the United States State Department wondered if the window of opportunity for a peaceful settlement had passed. The student movement had gained so much momentum that violence and repression seemed the only possible solution. As a State Department memo dated September 26 explained, "All indications are that the Government of Mexico is completely determined to restore order by any means."[20] Díaz Ordaz himself said plainly, "We are not going to let the student protest interfere with the Olympics."[21] Indeed, with only a few weeks to the opening ceremonies, and with international media already arriving, Díaz Ordaz had run out of time. As one American diplomat put it, the "significance of [the] Olympic deadline should not be underestimated. [The] government obviously felt that concessions under pressure would only strengthen [the] hand of radicals and encourage terrorist elements who might jeopardize [the] Olympics." Swift and violent force was the only way to subdue the students before they could threaten the Olympics.[22]

Student rhetoric and other symbols are the second connection between the two movements. From the beginning, students vowed not to disturb the Olympic Games. They recognized that the Olympics were hugely important in building Mexican pride and nationalism, and that the vast majority of Mexicans supported the undertaking. To attack them directly would be self-defeating. Still, the Olympics exemplified much that was wrong with Mexico, and the students increasingly drew connections between their own grievances and this ultimate symbol of Mexican extravagance and waste.

While the government spent millions of dollars in construction, beautification programs, training, and organizing for the Games, the masses remained mired in poverty. One student summarized their views:

> We weren't against the Olympics as a sports event, but we were against what the Games represented economically. We're a very poor country, and the Olympics meant an irreparable drain on Mexico's economic resources... [the president] made this commitment simply to make a big splash, to enhance our country's outward image, which had nothing at all to do with the country's real situation. (Poniatowska, 1993: 310)

By the end of July, the first slogans and banners decrying the Olympics had appeared. On one sign, the Olympic rings were replaced with five smoking bombs. Another read, "Mexico: Gold Medal for Repression." The popular Olympic jingle "1968: Year of the Olympics," was replaced with "1968: Year of the Repression" (Ali and Watkins, 1998: 166). By the end of August, the crowds of protesters waved countless signs against the Games. At a march on August 27, nearly half a million people joined the students in chanting, "We don't want the Olympics, we want revolution."[23] Similar slogans were spray-painted on buses and buildings, often directly on top of the Olympic logo or Mexico's logo for the Games, which read "Mexico '68."

The third link between the two was the security force that helped put down the rebellion. Witnesses at the Tlatelolco massacre recall seeing white-gloved soldiers interspersed in the crowd, some in civilian clothes (while still wearing the telltale white gloves). One United States State Department report explained that the "Students did not start [the] violence at Tlatelolco, but rather [a] well-armed group identifying [them]selves by gloved left hand[s] started firing and provided pretext for army firing."[24] Testimony at later hearings indicates that a total of some 65 soldiers from the battalion had been sent to the square and played a key role in blocking the panicked students as they tried to flee. They also stormed the apartment buildings surrounding the square, as witnesses recall hearing soldiers calling to one another, "Olympia Battalion! Olympia Battalion!" and such things as "Don't shoot! They're wearing white gloves!" (Poniatowska, 1993: 218, 221). Surely the Mexican military could have squashed the student movement without the participation of these 65 soldiers, but their presence was a telling reminder that the protection of the Olympics was at stake.

A fourth connection between the two was heightened media attention. Just as there was a buildup of surveillance and order maintenance forces for the Olympics, there was dramatically increased media in the country. With only a few weeks before the opening ceremonies, the number of reporters and film crews in Mexico City was growing by the day. Those reporters who did arrive received specific instructions from the Mexican government regarding their coverage of the student movement. Jack Zanger, a writer for the *New York Times*, resigned from the press corps in protest over being censored. "We should have known what was coming at the first meeting," said Zanger, "when an official told us: 'There are no riots. If anyone asks you about riots, say it's not your department.'"[25] Many papers, including the *New York Times*, carried daily updates of both the Olympics and the student movement. Many such reports were critical of Díaz Ordaz's handling of the students and wondered what protests they had planned for the Olympics. Such speculation grew louder as more and more crews arrived. If the student movement was to be put down, it needed to happen before the full media crush that was to arrive in the following days.

Finally, the widely held perception that the student movement aimed to damage the Olympics created a connection between the two. The international media began linking the two movements very early, and as the Games drew nearer, scarcely an article could be written that did not speculate whether the protests would threaten the Olympics. An article running in the September 2 issue of *Newsweek* quoted one student as saying, "The committee is considering different projects to use the Olympics to embarrass the Mexican Government. Violence is definitely being considered – but right now it would be a last resort."[26] A government propaganda campaign contributed to this misconception. A headline in one government-run paper on the morning after the massacre read, "The Objective: Preventing the Nineteenth Olympic Games from Being Held" (Poniatowska, 1993: 201). These campaigns were largely effective, as most international readers or visitors to the country believed that the students were trying to disrupt the Games. One French tourist commented, "The students' acts of bravado and the turmoil they were causing were threatening to ruin the Olympic Games" (ibid., 307). Another said, "What happened was that students wanted to steal the spotlight from the Olympics" (ibid.). At its height, such concern over the safety of the Olympics led to discussion of postponing the Games until the student movement was silenced, a rumor that the International Olympic Committee was quick to dispel.

Coupled with such beliefs were legitimate concerns about the safety of visiting athletes and tourists. The United States State Department grew more alarmed in the weeks prior to the massacre, and remained so in its aftermath. It issued bulletins speculating that there might be more trouble during the Games, and certainly that there would be a heightened presence of the surveillance apparatus and order maintenance forces. Indeed, on the day of the opening ceremonies, the front page of the *New York Times* ran a large picture of the Olympic Stadium, ringed with hundreds of riot police. But the movement had been crushed, its leaders either dead or jailed, and the Games went on undisturbed. As one historian wrote, "by mid-week of the final week before the Opening there was much more threat of turmoil than actual turmoil. Mexico City was outwardly peaceful and serene" (Kiernan and Daley, 1969: 420–421).

The student movement, hindsight shows us, had been silenced, its leaders incarcerated and its rank-and-file demoralized. Díaz Ordaz and his officers, though, still wondered whether there might be some backlash during the Games. In secret, students continued to discuss the movement, even visiting their jailed comrades. During the Olympics, an ad appeared in the newspaper *El Dia* signed by 59 jailed students, blaming "the 'Olimpia Batallion' made up of army and police for firing without discretion at innocent people in Tlatelolco."[27] The students also claimed to have been beaten and tortured, and that many of the jailed had never participated in the protest movement. Letters such as this indicated that the students still showed the will to resist, and thus the government had to respect the possibility of further action. In addition, pockets of student resistance carried on in rural areas and might have somehow revived the urban movement. Just in case, the Mexican government arranged for troops to be ever-present, so that athletes approaching the stadium might have understandably thought they had walked into a war zone. One journalist described Tlatelolco days after the massacre, as the Olympics was about to open, writing, "while children played on swings and slides, the area resembled an armed camp with hundreds of soldiers, armored cars, trucks and jeeps surrounding it."[28] Another wrote, "Outside the stadium troops and tanks were poised beyond the view of television cameras" (Gutmann, 2002: 65). An Olympics that was supposed to symbolize peace, prosperity and good will instead opened in an atmosphere of fear, tension and distrust.

After the massacre: the Olympic Games

While the student massacre was the most indelible incident related to security around the 1968 Olympics, it was not the only one. We must recall that these Olympics were contested in the midst of the Cold War, and several competitions featuring combatants from opposite sides of the Iron Curtain raised concern within the Mexican Organizing Committee that violence might erupt. As one example, on the opening day of the competition, the Soviet Union faced Czechoslovakia in a women's volleyball match. Only a few weeks before, the Soviet army had rolled into Czechoslovakia, conquering its peaceful neighbor after only minimal resistance.[29] The match drew thousands of enthusiastic fans, even more excited by the political overtones surrounding it. One American player speculated on the potential for violence, "If the Czechs have any class, there is going to be some blood tonight."[30] Under heightened surveillance, the match carried on without incident. The Czechs played better than expected, winning a set from the Soviets for the first time in six years, but in the end the Soviets won convincingly.

There were other, lesser tensions during the Olympics as well. Students in several rural states stopped classes in support of those killed or arrested in the massacre. Those in Tijuana organized several marches, including one of nearly 1000 people on the eve of the Olympics, and they reiterated the demands of the original student movement. Students in Chihuahua, too, continued to protest, engaging in several marches between the massacre at Tlatelolco and the beginning of the Games. Their protests centered on the disappearance of a student reporter named Sergio Sáenz, who had gone to Mexico City to cover the student movement and had not been seen since the massacre. The unrest in Chihuahua grew so intense that the students were eventually sent on an "Olympic holiday" to prevent further problems during the Games, which successfully quieted the protests. As one American official stationed there wrote, "Chihuahua City is now tranquil as her students cluster about the nearest television set to cheer on the Mexican Olympic athletes."[31]

Such continued activity was not unnoticed by the United States government, which worried whether these limited incidents might explode under the spotlight of the Olympics. One internal memo expressed such concerns: "The continuing violence raises two concerns for the U.S.: (1) the safety of U.S. athletes and visitors to the Games and (2) U.S. participation in scientific and cultural activities associated with the Olympics."[32] Even minor developments, rumors and speculation heightened the concern. The State Department took note of a leaflet, issued by a radical wing of the student movement a week before the opening ceremonies, which read "It will be necessary to mount a major military operation against the government during inaugural ceremonies of Olympic Games."[33] Given such activity, the United States ambassador to Mexico speculated that "The Olympic Games will be held, although marred by sporadic violence. Students are not likely to attract significant support from other important sectors and will not threaten the stability of the Government in the short run."[34]

The State Department needn't have worried much about the prospect of student unrest. Not only were the students in Mexico City terrified into submission, but also the Mexican police and other operatives were constantly on the lookout for any troublemakers and kept the United States government abreast of any developments. Rumors of possible sabotage of Olympic facilities, or even kidnapping of athletes, proved unfounded. The event was not without incident, though. A State Department memo cited one incident that threatened the peaceful atmosphere, in which a student named Ramón Hernández Vallejo was hired by a group of Cubans to kill an American athlete. Hernández had second thoughts and failed to carry out the attack, and was then himself attacked by a group of Cubans and nearly killed. In another incident, a student attempted to incinerate an Olympic bus, but all athletes and passengers escaped without harm. In yet another, "A Mexican spectator shot himself at the start of a cycling team trial...in protest of the Mexican government's treatment of students" (Chester, 1971: 164). These incidents notwithstanding, aside from a few small student gatherings, all of which were understandably peaceful and relatively quiet, there were no serious protests during the Games. The city was consumed in the Olympic spirit, and those students who were not incarcerated either joined in the celebration of the Games or kept quiet, not wanting to revive the ire of the government.

While the Games themselves were conducted peacefully, the Mexican people never forgot the horrors of October 2, 1968. Mexico's inability to maintain peace during the Olympic year had done irreparable harm to its international image and symbolized a profound loss of innocence for the Olympic Movement. As demonstrated by Jørn Hansen in Chapter 6 of this book, organizers of the 1972 Munich Olympics sought to distance themselves from both the memory of the "Nazi Olympics" of 1936 and the heavily militarized Olympics in Mexico City. It was, in part, the recollection of ever-present soldiers and police forces in Mexico City that encouraged organizers of the Munich Games to pursue a more open, peaceful atmosphere. That atmosphere was, of course, tragically and irrevocably crushed by the terrorist action of the Palestinian Black September Organization and the murder of 11 Israeli athletes. Never again would Olympic planners attempt to shroud the issue of security. Thus, Mexico City takes its place on the continuum defining the evolution of the Olympics from a genuinely peaceful international sporting event to one requiring ever more stringent security measures imaginable.

Notes

I thank an anonymous reviewer for valuable comments.

1. *Mexico '68*, vol. 4 (Mexican Olympic Committee, 1969): 738–739.
2. Department of State Airgram, From Amembassy MEXICO to Department of State, Feb. 24, 1967, *National Archives and Records Administration (NARA)* RG 59, Box 642, folder E 2–2 Mex 1/1/67.
3. United States State Department Research Memorandum, June 12, 1968, *NARA* RG 59, Box 643, folder E 12 Mex 1/1/67.
4. Bob Ottum, "Grim Countdown to the Games," *Sports Illustrated* (October 14, 1968): 43.
5. *Mexico '68*, vol. 3, 165–201.
6. John Spitzer and Harvey Cohen, "In Mexico, '68," *Ramparts Magazine* 7:6 (October 26, 1968): 39.
7. Intelligence Note, "Mexican Student Riots Highly Embarrassing But Not a Threat to Stability," Aug. 6, 1968, *NARA* RG 59, Box 2343, Pol 238.
8. Henry Giniger, "50,000 Mexico City Students March in New Protest Against Police and Army," *New York Times* (Aug. 2, 1968): 11.
9. United States Dept of State Intelligence Note, from Thomas L. Hughes to the Secretary, Aug. 29, 1968, *NARA*, RG 59, Box 2343, folder 23–28 Mex 1/1/68, POL 23 Mex to POL-MEX-US.
10. State Department Telegram from Amembassy Mexico to SecState, Sept. 1, 1968, *NARA*, RG 59, Box 2341, POL 15–1 Mex 1/1/68.

11. State Department Telegram, Sept. 19, 1968, *NARA*, RG 59, Box 2340, folder POL 13–2 Mex 9/1/68.
12. State Department Airgram, "Review of Mexico City Disturbances," Oct. 20, 1968, *NARA*, RG 59, Box 2340, folder POL 13–2 Mex 9/1/68.
13. Dept. of State Memorandum, from Covey T. Oliver to Acting Secretary, Aug. 28, 1968, *NARA*, RG 59, Box 2343, folder 23–28 Mex 1/1/68, POL 23 Mex to POL-MEX-US.
14. "On Olympic Eve – Biggest Flare-Up Yet," *U.S. News & World Report* (Oct. 14, 1968): 10.
15. Dept. of State Telegram, from Amembassy Mexico to Sec State, Oct. 3, 1968, *NARA*, RG 59, Box 2340, folder POL 13.2 Mex 9/1/68.
16. Dept. of State Memorandum, from Covey T. Oliver to the Secretary, Sept. 26, 1968, *NARA*, RG59, Box 2343, folder 23–28 Mex 1/1/68, POL 23 Mex to POL-MEX-US.
17. Central Intelligence Agency, secret intelligence summary, "Mexican Government Stalls Student Movement," Sept. 6, 1968, National Security Archive, "The Tlatelolco Massacre," document 66, http://www.gwu.edu/~nsarchiv/NSAEBB/NSAEBB99/#usdocs
18. United States Dept. of State Airgram, Aug. 9, 1968, *NARA*, Box 2337, folder POL 2 Mex 7/1/68.
19. United States Dept. of State Intelligence Note, from Thomas L. Hughes to the Secretary, Aug. 6, 1968, *NARA*, RG 59, Box 2343, folder 23–28 Mex 1/1/68, POL 23 Mex to POL-MEX-US: 1, 4.
20. Dept. of State Memorandum, from Covey T. Oliver to the Secretary, Sept. 26, 1968, *NARA*, RG59, Box 2343, folder 23–28 Mex 1/1/68, POL 23 Mex to POL-MEX-US.
21. Goodsell, "Why Students Rioted," 33; United States Dept. of State Telegram, Oct. 5, 1968, *NARA*, Box 2340, folder POL 13.2 Mex 9/1/68.
22. United States Dept. of State Intelligence Notes, from Thomas L. Hughes to the Secretary, and Aug. 6 and 16, 1968, *NARA*, RG 59, Box 2343, folder 23–28 Mex 1/1/68, POL 23 Mex to POL-MEX-US.
23. Henry Giniger, "Mexico Keeps Up Calm Exterior," *New York Times* (Aug. 15, 1968): 11.
24. Dept. of State Telegram, from Amembassy Mexico to SecState, Oct. 6, 1968, *NARA*, RG 59, Box 2343, folder 23–28 Mex 1/1/68, POL 23 Mex to POL-MEX-US.
25. "Spell of the Olympics," *Newsweek*, Oct. 21, 1968, 65.
26. "Plot to Kill the Olympics," *Newsweek*, Sept. 2, 1968, 59.
27. The ad appeared in the Oct. 17 *El Dia*, cited in Dept. of State Telegram, Oct. 17, 1968, *NARA*, RG 59, Box 2340, folder POL 13.2 Mex 9/1/68.
28. Henry Giniger, "Mexican Student Protest Appears to be Crushed," *New York Times* (Oct. 5, 1968): 14.
29. Thomas J. Hamilton, "14 Athletes Set to Leave Today," *New York Times* (Sept. 15, 1968): V, 9.
30. Robert Lipsyte, "Return from Olympus," *New York Times* (Oct. 26, 1968): 45.
31. Dept. of State Airgram, from Amconsul Chihuahua to Amembassy Mexico City, Oct. 18, 1968, *NARA*, RG 59, Box 2340, folder POL 13.2 Mex 9/1/68.
32. Dept. of State Memorandum, Oct. 3, 1968, *NARA*, RG 59, Box 2340, folder POL 13.2 Mex 9/1/68.
33. Dept. of State Telegram, from Amembassy Mexico to SecState, Oct. 6, 1968, *NARA*, RG59, Box 2343, folder 23–28 Mex 1/1/68, POL 23 Mex to POL-MEX-US.
34. Dept. of State Memorandum, from Covey T. Oliver to the Secretary, Sept. 20, 1968, *NARA*, RG 59, Box 2343, folder 23–28 Mex 1/1/68, POL 23 Mex to POL-MEX-US.

5
Fear of Radical Movements and Policing the Enemy Within (Sapporo 1972)

Kiyoshi Abe

Before considering the organization of the 1972 Winter Olympic Games in Sapporo, it is important to understand linguistic and semantic differences between safety and security. As briefly discussed by Christian Tagsold in Chapter 3 on the 1964 Winter Tokyo Games, in Japanese, "safety" and "security" are generally translated as *anzen* (安全). When a more subjective, perceptional, and emotional dimension of these terms is considered, the word *anshin* (安心) is preferred. The word *chian* (治安) has been used in discussing concerns of public safety and national security, while *chian-jousei* (security situation) or *chian-iji* (maintaining security) are often used in official discourses like police reports on tasks concerning "law and order." Actually, chian may imply both public safety and national security, depending on the contexts in which it is used. In recent mass media discourse on criminal activities, we find sensational reporting on police concerns for *chian-akka* (治安悪化), which means corruption of public safety. This has become a way of legitimizing introduction of tight surveillance policy. In these cases, threat to the public safety is regarded as "crime as violation of law." In a mundane way of talking about how to realize order in society in response to real or imagined threats, it is often said that we have to ascertain security, or *sekyuritii*, as the word has been incorporated into Japanese. In recent sociopolitical context of Japan where the threat of crime is somehow exaggerated, the terms chian or sekyuritii could be understood as the counterpart of "public safety" in English.

On the other hand, the word chian-jousei is often used in describing the sociopolitical conditions concerning national security. In periods of political instability in Japan, one of which was the era of rising student movements in the 1960s and 1970s, the crisis of security (*chian-jousei-no-akka*) became a deep concern for political leaders as well as the public. In those cases, threat to the public is regarded as "crime as disturbance of society." In formal discourse, such as reports published by governmental ministries, it is emphasized that maintaining security through policing and surveillance is one of the most urgent and indispensable tasks for the government. In those cases, the term chian could be equated with "national security" in English.

126

This analytical clarification of the complicated connotation of chian in the historical-political contexts of postwar Japan is important if we want to understand how the task of public safety and national security was considered, estimated, and carried out during the hosting of the Sapporo Olympic Games in 1972. Below, I analyze how the Sapporo Organizing Committee and the police concerned about chian at the time, estimated threats and carried out policing. Through this discussion, I would like to shed light on the sociopolitical significance of guarding the Emperor at such public occasions. Given the constitutional status of the Emperor in postwar Japan as "the symbol of the state and the unity of the people," guaranteeing safety of the Emperor is an indispensable means of ascertaining the security and well-being of the nation.

Sociopolitical significance of the Sapporo Olympic Games in 1972

As Christian Tagsold points out in Chapter 3, the Tokyo Olympics functioned as an international opportunity through which Japan could gain confidence, self-pride and satisfaction in entering into a postwar relationship with other countries. By the time of the Sapporo Games in 1972, Japan had completed its ambitious ten-year economic growth plan, which aimed to double the income of its citizens within ten years, beginning in 1960. While the sociopolitical objective of the Tokyo Olympics related to Japan's recovery from the war and its postwar ambition to enter the international community, the Sapporo Olympics was expected to be an opportunity by which Japan could show the world its economic and technological development as well as the peaceful and wealthy nation that it had become.

The prospect of hosting the 1972 Sapporo Olympics was a happy one but worrisome for those who had responsibility for planning and managing the Games. The reason for this outlook is that the political situation in Japanese society in the late 1960s and early 1970s was unstable owing to the rise of a radical student movement that exerted political power and influence over the public. These developments were readily reported by the mass media in the United States. Under the heading "Police Rout Radicals at Japanese University," for example, the *Los Angeles Times* reported the clash between students and the police at Hokkaido University in which 30 policemen and 15 students were injured, and other such clashes in Sapporo as well as Tokyo University, and alluded to the fact that Sapporo was to host the coming Winter Olympics.[1] Faced with political instability and tensions threatening to undermine the image Japanese society was seeking to project to the world, the government and the police treated the student movement as a potential risk that could have threatened the security of the Sapporo Olympic Games. This response was also reported by the United States media, emphasizing that "up to 4000 police [would] be mobilized every day during the next month's Winter Olympic Games in Sapporo in case of trouble from right and left wing extremists."[2]

From "student movement" to "radical sects"

As Oguma (2009) shows, the student movement began with protests against poor research and learning conditions and the rise of tuition fees caused by popularization of higher education. Later, the movement became more politicized, questioning the legitimacy of the postwar regime as well as the growing United States military bases in Japan. As the student movement became more radical and violent in the late 1960s and early 1970s, public perception of the political demonstrations and actions organized by active student groups grew more negative and unsympathetic. While at the beginning the general public was sympathetic toward students drawing attention to the problem of mass education at universities, public opinion turned against the movement by the early 1970s as some of the students became excessively violent, attacking police stations and banks, hijacking an airplane, and murdering members of other political groups.[3] Under these conditions, it became very difficult for members of radical leftist student organizations to gain public support for their political appeals. As confrontations between the student groups and the police escalated, there emerged a sort of sociopolitical discrepancy between the student movement and the general public, in which groups considered "radical" were isolated from the majority of students and from the larger population.

However, these shifts in public perception of the student movement did not occur as a result of political consequences alone. What had a profound effect on public perception was the categorization of the student movement as radical. As much research on the media's representation of these political events has clarified, the process of categorization depicted through media reports and coverage has ideological effects on an audience's perception and recognition of those matters (Hall et al., 1978). This categorization was constructed by the police bureau in its documentations of crime. In 1960, the Japanese Ministry of Justice began to publish the so-called *White Paper on Crime*.[4] As is easily imagined, the *White Paper* aimed at including all sorts of crimes that were perceived to exist in Japanese society at that time. In the *White Paper on Crime*, the category of "collective crime committed by students" first appeared in 1969.[5] Given that the late 1960s was the time of the rising of student movement throughout the industrialized Western societies, the *White Paper* used the category of "collective crime committed by students" in describing the changing political situation concerning the student movement in Japan. This category refers to the incidents caused by student political groups and the related criminal activities.

The extension of the Security Treaty with the United States, which allowed the presence and action of the United States military on Japanese territory,

was a major issue. While the majority of the public was against the extension of the Treaty, it was left-wing student groups who were one of the most
vocal and active elements engaging in political struggles with the government. Conflict over the construction of Narita Airport, the newly planned
international airport near Tokyo, became one of the most symbolic incidents of the violent confrontation between students and the government.
The government decided to build an airport in the Narita area and articulated its basic plan in the 1960s. When many landowners refused to sell
their property for this purpose the project came under intensive criticism.
As the Japanese government stubbornly continued to advance its original
plan, it caused serious political tensions between the state administrations
and members of the student movement who supported the landowners and
peasants who refused financial offers made by the government. As the political negotiations began to seem impossible and as the political confrontation became more harsh and violent, the Japanese government feared the
destructive potential of the rising radical student movement.

Considering the sociopolitical situation surrounding the student movement in the early 1970s, the term "collective crime committed by students"
used in the *White Paper* can be regarded as a category implicating the danger
of the "enemy within" at that time. The growing fears about radicalization of
the student political demonstrations and actions could easily cause the actual
student movement to be identified with the image of the "enemy within."

We see that in 1971, the category that referred to crimes related to the
student movement was slightly changed. The *White Paper on Crime* published
the same year uses the term "collective violent crime committed by students."[6]
"Violent" was newly added to the former category of "collective crime." The
new category probably reflected the deepening fear and anxiety, shared by
political leaders and the public alike, about the radical student movement.
Here we can perceive the rising trend of criminalizing the student movement through categorization accomplished by official documents.

In 1974, another category appeared in relation to the student movement:
"radical sects of political extremism."[7] The very negative, violent and anti-
social image of "radical sects" to which the student movement was now
attached resulted in ruthless criminalization of the student movement and
isolation of students from the larger public.[8] It is important to understand
that it was not the content of student protests, but rather the images of
"radical sects" constructed through the media's sensationalistic representations and through the official categorization of "radical sects of political
extremism" that pervaded the majority of the population from the 1970s
onwards. This category has persisted to the present day. It calls forth the
typical image of a "public enemy" that threatens the peaceful way of life of
ordinary people through its violent actions and demonstrations. While the
term "political extremism" implies the dangers of terrorism and guerrilla in
general, one of the characteristics of the category of "radical sects" as used in

the *White Paper on Crime* is that it mainly focuses on left-wing radical movements of students, not right-wing ones. With the rise of radical religious
groups in the 1990s, such as Aum Shinrikyo whose members committed the
sarin gas attack at the Tokyo Metropolitan Subway station in 1995, killing 13
and injuring some 6000 people, the category "radical sects" came to imply
extremist movements in general.

Symbolic meaning of guarding the Japanese Emperor

As a result of the official categorization of left-wing social movements as
"radical sects," public perception of the political activities of student groups
became very negative and unsympathetic. One of the reasons for this categorization, which had connotations of a typical public enemy, was the movement's questioning of the legitimacy of the postwar system of the Japanese
Emperor. In contrast to the prewar Emperor system, which functioned as
the fundamental normative ground of the Japanese Imperial regime, the
constitutional position of the postwar Emperor is that of the symbol of the
Japanese nation. Article 1 of the Constitution of Japan describes the position of the Emperor as follows: "The Emperor shall be the symbol of the
State and the unity of the people, deriving his position from the will of
the people with whom resides sovereign power." However, as critics of the
Japanese postwar Emperor system pointed out, there existed not only the
discontinuity but also the continuity between the pre- and postwar regimes
with respect to the legitimacy of the Japanese Emperor system (Gluck and
Graubard, 1992; Miyoshi and Harootunian, 1993; Morris-Suzuki, 1984). In
other words, while the militant regime of prewar Japan was abolished under
the occupation policy led by the United States, the status of Emperor that had
been the center of Japanese people's loyalty and spirituality during wartime
has not changed. Therefore, even in the period of postwar democracy in
Japan, the legitimacy of the Japanese Emperor has been a sanctuary that has
been immune from critical discussions among the public and the discourse
of mass media. Therefore, questioning the political status and legitimacy of
the Japanese Emperor system has been socioculturally prohibited among
the public imagery in Japanese society.

The left-wing movement of radical students tried to challenge that taboo
through political demonstrations and direct action against the Emperor
system. While the majority of the population supported the symbolic system
of the Japanese Emperor in the postwar period, the conservative political
leaders of the Liberal Democratic Party seem to have been concerned with
the threat caused by political protests of students against the Japanese
Emperor. Since the legitimacy of postwar Japanese society relied heavily
on the symbolic system of the Emperor (Dower, 1999), those who clung to
the postwar political regime had to forbid any critique of the constitutional
status of the Emperor. For those who hold political power in postwar Japan,

the sociopolitical significance and legitimacy of the political system based on the Emperor must be taken for granted. It should not be regarded as a political issue that is up for discussion.

Considering the political indispensability and significance of the Emperor system in Japanese society, it is conceivable why the "security tasks"[9] for postwar Japanese society have been closely related to the need to protect the members of the Imperial Family. In the context of postwar Japanese society, granting the legitimacy of the Emperor and guaranteeing the safety of the Imperial Family has been one of the most important sociopolitical objectives for political leaders to accomplish. The reason why is that the security tasks, it is presumed, could be realized, as long as those safety tasks concerning the Emperor system are perfectly met. In this sense, the safety of the Emperor at public occasions is not just a matter of protecting the "individual" body of the Emperor, but also of ascertaining the "collective" polity of the nation as a whole, which is symbolically embodied by the public presence of the Emperor. Therefore, the Japanese establishment has regarded protest movements against the Emperor as the most dangerous and harmful political activities in that they threaten the legitimacy and security of Japanese society.

The symbolic status and position of the Emperor in postwar Japan seems to have influenced how and to what purpose measures of public safety are taken in preparation for events such as the Olympics. It is common that members of the Imperial Family in Japan participate in public ceremonial events of sport and culture held by the Japanese government and administration. The National Festival of Sports is a typical event in which the Emperor or the Crown Prince appears before the public at the Opening Ceremony. Utilizing such public occasions, the symbolic system of the Japanese Emperor has tried to perform and ascertain its sociocultural legitimacy through ritualized ceremonies. For those ceremonies to be completed successfully, it is vital that potential risks that question or threaten the legitimacy of the Emperor are completely eliminated from entire events and festivals. In the context of protecting public functions while welcoming a member of the Imperial Family, the objective of the task of protection essentially means protecting members of the Imperial Family so that neither obstructions nor violations undertaken by those who oppose the Emperor system can occur. Only one month before the beginning of the Sapporo Olympics, an 18-year-old boy with a firecracker tried to tackle Crown Princess Michiko when the Princess visited the National Festival of Sports at Nikko on January 6, 1972.[10] This incident made the police even wearier about the safety of the Imperial Family during public events.

Then, as today, when potential threats to the Emperor system can be foreseen in advance of public events, the police show no hesitation in engaging in tighter policing and surveillance practices even when these may cause a serious intervention in civil liberties and human rights. These activities are usually accepted and permitted without harsh criticism or dissent from the public. During public events, particularly if they are attended by members of the Imperial Family, measures are easily introduced and quickly practiced without reasonable and democratic discussion. Indeed, by law, the Imperial Guard Headquarters, a part of the National Police Agency, has the right and responsibility to guarantee the safety and comfort of the Imperial Family. For those involved in such a task, protecting the Emperor from risk and maintaining Japan's symbolic system can be equated with national security. The close relationship between the safety of the Emperor and the safety of the public at large is unquestionably presupposed. Therefore, just as the legitimacy of the Emperor system should not be questioned in Japan's postwar political regime, the indispensable task of insuring public safety through harsh policing practices of potential disruptions that could violate the legitimacy of the Emperor system is taken for granted in the case of culturally and symbolically important public events.

Reading the documentary report of policing activities at the Sapporo Winter Olympics

During the time of the Sapporo Games, the police were expected to guarantee peace and order. Unlike the Tokyo Games where, as discussed by Christian Tagsold in Chapter 3, Japan's Self-Defense Forces took the main responsibility for providing order, during the Sapporo Games, the Self-Defense Forces were mainly responsible for constructing the course for sky competitions and supporting transportation and telecommunications. The police took the main responsibility for providing order, which was regarded as nothing less than national security. "Considering the recent condition of public security threatened by the illegal, excessive cases committed by radical violent groups," the police report stated, "the police prepared for the Sapporo Olympic Games by establishing the policy of 'plan of defending security at the Games' in December 1971."[11] As Tagsold points out, during the Tokyo Olympics the issue of security – *hôan* (保安), *anzen* (安全) and *antei* (安定) – was not seriously considered. In contrast, the task of ensuring security – *chian* (治安) – was the primary goal for police during the Sapporo Olympic Games.[12]

Looking back at the result of their activities at the Games, the head of Hokkaido Prefecture Police proudly estimated their success this way:

> At the time of hosting the Sapporo Olympic Games, the situation of security was very severe as there happened several threatening incidents like the intruding into the Palace of Japanese Imperial Family and bombing struggles by radical violent groups in the latter half of 1971. It should be acknowledged that under such hard conditions the police perfectly completed the jobs of guarding VIPs, ascertaining the safety of audience, managing traffic, preventing and detecting the criminal cases through its systematic activities.[13]

In this section, I will focus on an official report on police activities concerning the Sapporo Olympics. In 1973, the police of Hokkaido prefecture, where the city of Sapporo is located, published a document titled "Documentary report of the activities of police at Winter Olympics at Sapporo 1972."[14] Its contents and coverage are very wide ranging. We can learn a lot about how and through which processes and procedures the security tasks at the Sapporo Olympic Games were perceived, prepared and carried out by the police and about its collaboration with other institutions such as the Japanese military. Through reading the official document of police activities, we can shed new light on policing strategies at the Sapporo Olympics.

Policy of "inspection and research"

According to the documentary report, Hokkaido Prefecture Police took on "the policy of inspection and research" of previous cases in which the police completed the task of ascertaining safety during large-scale public events.[15] This policy included sending their staff to learn about security tasks at huge public events like the Olympics from other places to best articulate the planning of guarding the Olympics in Sapporo. In January 1968, two members of staff were sent to Grenoble while two went to Tokyo for six months. The Hokkaido Prefecture Police sent other officials to the Tokyo Metropolitan Police as well as to the Osaka Prefecture Police where they were to learn from the experience of the Japan World Exposition in 1970.

However, it seems that Hokkaido Prefecture Police did not think it indispensable to send their staff to Mexico City, where the 1968 Olympics were held. Considering that, as analyzed by Kevin Witherspoon in Chapter 4 of this book, the standoff between the Mexican government and the student movement at the time of the Games led to a massacre, it is somehow strange that the documentary report made no mention about the case in Mexico City. Even though both Mexican and Japanese authorities had a similar task with respect to how to control the protest movements by students, the documentary report fails to include any dialog between the two countries regarding this matter.

Estimation of threat

According to the description of the expected threat concerning the Olympic Games in the documentary report, it is apparent that the Sapporo Organizing Committee and Hokkaido Prefecture Police were deeply concerned with the relatively unstable political situation surrounding the Games.[16] Their estimation of potential threats included the following:

1. Judging from conditions of security in both Japan and abroad, the cases concerning the ultra-leftwing violent group were expected to become more serious. In fact, there were instances of abuse and harassment against members of the Imperial Family and other VIP. On the other

hand, it seemed that the rightwing group that worried about the movement of the leftwing groups showed more aggressive attitude towards
them. As a result, the situation was assessed to be very crucial.
2. The social movement was expected to raise issues such as transferring
of the Self-Defense Forces to Okinawa and opposition against the rise of
tuition fees. Because these movements were regarded as stimulating the
student movement at universities, it was expected that there would be
gathering and demonstration around Sapporo city area.
3. Given that member of North Korea, South Korea, and the Republic of
China were expected to participate in the Games and a group of observers
from the People's Republic of China was to come to Hokkaido, there were
concerns that it could lead to conflict among political groups in Japan
which supported each nation. It was also expected that there may be
attempts to flee.[17]

Reflecting the sociopolitical tensions between the political establishment
and the counter-social movements embodied mainly by vocal students, the
basic tone of the police documentary report was alarming. As is easily imagined considering the political landscape in late 1960s and early 1970s, the
most dangerous group that might violate and destroy the Olympic Games
was assessed to be radical left-wing groups like the Japanese Red Army. We
can find in the documentary report several mentions of incidents and criminal cases that were committed by those left-wing groups. For example, with
respect to guarding the Imperial Family, the documentary report mentions
the following:

Judging from the threatening movements of radical sect groups against
the Imperial Family and the conditions of European nations to which
Emperor and Empress had visited before the Games, it is expected that
through fundamentally assessing the traditional way of guarding of the
Imperial Family the practice at the Sapporo Olympic Games should be
the guard that is enacted through ascertaining security in advance.[18]

Through noting the past criminal cases, the documentary report legitimizes
the tightening of policing in preparation for security tasks at the Sapporo
Games. The documentary report summarized the lessons the police had
gained from activities at the Sapporo Games in this way:

The general conditions of security with regard to the Games were in an
uproar as the cases like using explosives and threat of bombing committed
by violent ultra-leftwing groups had occurred. In spite of that, Hokkaido
Prefecture Police declared its policy to firmly face against those cases in
briefing to the media. Through tight investigation of criminal cases and
thorough search and inspection of potential risks, the police succeeded

in preventing the groups from acting out. Thanks to the support from the riot police at the Tohoku jurisdiction, Hokkaido Prefecture Police could perfectly prevent any criminal cases from happening through practicing intensive and active policing and making the attitude of the police absolutely sure.[19]

Interestingly enough, as we see in the estimation of threats quoted above, while the danger of the radical right-wing movement is also alluded to in the documentary report, this movement was regarded as only a "reaction" against the political demonstrations and actions of the left-wing groups. It appears that it was assumed that how and to what extent the right-wing movement might be harmful depended heavily on the conditions created by "the ultra-left-wing violent group."[20] According to the presupposition written in the documentary report, the more vocal and visible the left-wing political demonstrations, the more probable and violent the potential of right-wing reaction against them. In other words, for the police's goal of assuring public safety, the threat of left-wing groups was primary and that of their right-wing counterparts was secondary. The reasons have to do with the question of loyalty. Since the right-wing groups are very loyal to the Emperor they cannot be a threat to the symbolic Emperor system in postwar Japan even though their activities are actually very harmful to the public.

While the radical left was regarded as the "enemy within," some foreigners coming to Japan to visit Sapporo were considered to be a potential "enemy outside" who might commit crimes like illegal trading.

As many foreigners come to Hokkaido, there will be crimes that relate to those people from abroad. Owing to those criminal cases, the international status of the Japanese government might be threatened. Therefore, it is vital that those cases should be treated cautiously and properly.[21]

Pre-investigation and pre-inspection during preparations for the Games

Based on the recognition that threats aimed at the Olympic Games that would be caused by an enemy within would be serious and harmful, the police initiated the policy of investigating potential dangers in advance. The year before the Sapporo Games in 1972, the police regularly undertook systematic and total investigations of targeted people and areas considered potentially risky. In terms of civil liberties, those policing policies were violations of human rights. However, it seems that the police's tough and intolerant treatment of potential suspects was smoothly legitimized because the anticipated security dangers at the time of the Olympic Games were so threatening that extraordinary measures were considered indispensable by the police for properly preparing for security in advance.

In the pre-investigations, the targeted criminal acts and areas by the police were pickpocketing, drug dealing and illegal business in the red light districts. The Japanese Mafia (*bourykudan*) was also a focus of these pre-investigations. For example, according to the documentary report, in October 1971 the police performed special undercover investigations of pickpockets throughout Hokkaido prefecture, and recognized the names of 154 usual pickpocket suspects. From October 1, 1971, to January 25, 1972, police carried out and found 110 cases of pickpocketing, arresting 15 people. Beginning in September 1971, the police initiated large-scale investigations of the red light districts in Hokkaido prefecture three times. The results included 783 cases of illegal business, 58 cases of illegal prostitution and 24 cases of public indecency.[22]

Certainly, the police could show the public that they were doing their job of policing questionable people and areas well. However, the threats that were eliminated through the investigations were not extraordinary at all. While the risk of having pickpockets in public spaces might represent a danger for ordinary people, it is not certain whether eliminating those relatively minor risks might actually contribute to achieving the safe and peaceful Olympic Games, which, according to the documentary report, were considered to be severely threatened. Here we can see some sort of discrepancy between the expected threats described in the report, which sound very damaging for public safety, and the actual practice of the police in coping with those risks.

Surveillance and policing during the Games

Just as they did in preparing for the Sapporo Games, the police maintained tight and systematic policing during the Olympic Games period. As a result, they detected several crimes and arrested some of the criminals during this time. The documentary report tells us "thirty-five Olympic-related cases occurred." But, it also says "twenty-one of them were the stealing of Olympic flags." With respect to policing red light areas, the documentary states that "during the period of the Games, thirty shops (and forty-eight people) were arrested for illegal business," and "ten cases of prostitution were detected." While the police had been concerned about the illegal trading of tickets for the Games, in the end, "there was no illegal trading of entrance tickets for Games."[23]

Other criminal cases mentioned in the documentary report were: two cases of individuals drawing graffiti on a building related to the Games, and a blackmail incident at Sapporo whereupon the police were notified of bombs being placed in the car of the Crown Prince and Princess. With respect to the student movement, the documentary mentions "the student strike and boycotting at Hokkaido University and other universities took place. The number of people who were involved in gathering, demonstrating and spreading pamphlets at twelve points all over Hokkaido was 665."[24] Also, the report states "at thirty-three places in Hokkaido, the number of right-wing group members who collectively paraded and spread pamphlets at busy streets was 2,885."[25]

In contrast to the expected threats to Olympic Games safety, the actual resulting dangers were not so serious insofar as we can judge from carefully reading through the documentary report by the police. Though some crimes took place, most of them did not hurt the Games at all. According to the report analysis of the sociopolitical situation surrounding the Games, the low crime that occurred during the Sapporo Games was just a successful consequence of the long-lasting tough policing undertaken in preparing for them.

> It seems that the radical, violent left-wing groups, which were regarded as the most serious threat to the Games abandoned their policy of protesting against the Olympic at Sapporo. The reason for this decision is that they seemed to realize that direct demonstrations and actions were difficult to carry out, owing to the rise of a welcoming atmosphere toward the Sapporo Games among the public at large, and to the tight and tough policy of the police. As a result of these circumstances, no serious incidents were carried out by those groups that were said to be threatening to the Olympic Games at Sapporo. Reflecting the relative calmness of the vocal left movements, it seems that the radical right-wing groups, which were planning to demonstrate themselves against their leftist counterparts, changed their original plan as well. As a result, events in general with respect to the antagonistic political groups proceeded peacefully.[26]

The documentary report proudly declares that the abovementioned fact that no serious incidents took place is nothing but the consequence of the safety policy that the police had advanced. It further points out three main reasons that contributed to the successful results:

1. The police's tough policy on illegal activities was publicized through media reports and news coverage, and it effectively functioned as a mechanism for preventing potential crimes.
2. The prevention of potential dangers caused by radical left-wing groups was effective as a result of tough pre-investigations of areas near the Olympic Stadium and of the Emperor's parade route, the pre-inspection of the activities of suspected criminals, and the tracing of past incidents of bombing by left-wing groups.
3. Thanks to their cooperation with the riot police at Touhoku jurisdiction, the police at Hokkaido jurisdiction had enough resources so that they could establish a tighter and seamless defense system for policing.[27]

In terms of a literal reading of the documentary report, the results of the strict policy of surveillance and the policing of potential risks related to the Olympics seem to have been very successful and satisfactory for both the police and the general public. However, utilizing a sort of hindsight, we might have some questions and suspicions with respect to the effectiveness of this policing. Certainly, the police self-legitimately declared the effectiveness of its tough policy for assuring safety of the Games. Those policies were regarded as indispensable in response to anticipated threats that might have come from the left-wing radical movement. Upon reading the entire documentary report, we cannot get rid of the suspicious feeling that the estimation and expectation of potential risks might have been excessive. In comparison with the degree of threats that actually happened, it seems that the police might have overestimated the risk that the left-wing group might represent. It was true that the leftist radical groups were harsh and often violent at that time. Therefore, the anxiety and concern that the police had with respect to the activities of those political organizations are fairly reasonable and understandable. However, it also seems that the police might have utilized the Olympic Games as an opportunity to further its own objective of legitimizing its policing activities both in scale and scope. The targets of the investigation and detection in advance preparations for the Olympic Games do not seem to be particularly relevant for establishing the safety of the Games as a whole. However, for the police, it must have been quite significant to tighten and strengthen their everyday practices in coping with potential crimes like pickpocketing or illegal business activities conducted in the red light districts.

Guarding of the Emperor

The Emperor and Empress, the Crown Prince and Princess, and other members of the Imperial Family, a total of 13, came to see the Sapporo Olympic Games. In preparing for their arrival at Sapporo, the police seem to have employed a special policy for guarding and keeping the Emperor and other members of the Imperial Family safe. Interestingly enough, the term used in reference to the activities of guarding the Emperor is different from the term used in protecting other VIPs like the heads of other countries. The word for the former is *keiei* (警衛), and the word for the latter is *keigo* (警護). While keigo is a word with an ordinary meaning, keiei is a special term mainly used in the police bureau. This distinction between the two technical terms, depending on the individuals being guarded, suggests to us that protecting the Emperor has a special significance for the police in insuring security. The total number of police staff who engaged in keiei during the period of the Games was 19,679.[28]

The threat of the radical left-wing student movement, which apparently was expected to protest against the legitimacy of the Emperor system, was estimated by the police to be quite serious and potentially dangerous. The Emperor and Empress as well as the Crown Prince and Princess were scheduled to attend the Sapporo Games. Considering these sociopolitical conditions in which the police had to provide safety, it is understandable why they were so eager to advance the policy of policing and the surveillance of potential risks that might threaten the safety of the Emperor and the legitimacy of the Emperor system. As no serious incidents happened with respect to the safety of the Emperor and other members of the Imperial Family, the police's documentary report could include the details of its activities concerning keiei and proudly declare its success. Reading through the report, we can recognize how and to what extent the protection of the Emperor's safety is paramount in order for the police to realize public safety.

Presence of the Self-Defense Forces

In the same documentary report, we can also find references to the role of Japan's Self-Defense Force. As the report reveals, the military afforded police accommodations for their staff who worked during the Olympic Games. In addition, the military also completed a variety of jobs and tasks related to preparations for the Games, as was also the case with the 1964 Tokyo Games.[29] Considering its controversial political status related to Article 9 of the Japanese Constitution, which calls for the abolishment of the military forces, the indispensable role and presence of the military at the Olympic Games, also pointed out in the document, should not be understood only as an efficient part of the staging of the Games. Under the condition of heavy snow during the Winter Games, a large number of people were needed to set up competition courses. The United States media approvingly reported that "the Japanese are ready to roll out a vast array of equipment and an army of 3,500 men to stage a snow-removal operation such as few if any places have ever seen."[30] Therefore, cooperation with and mobilization of the military was indispensable in completing the Sapporo Games. However, the presence of the military in the Olympics should also be recognized as a matter of political and symbolic legitimacy of the Self-Defense Forces. Just as was the case with the 1964 Tokyo Olympic Games discussed by Tagsold in Chapter 3, the Sapporo Games were also an opportunity for the military to demonstrate its peaceful presence and its significant role to the Japanese people.

The indispensable role of the military was readily acknowledged in the official documents of the Sapporo Olympics.[31] In the section titled "Support," the formal document published by the Sapporo Organizing Committee expresses appreciation to the organizations that supported the realization of the Games. Noteworthy is the order of the acknowledgment: the Self-Defense Forces first, next the police bureau, and lastly, the fire departments.[32] While the police organization seems to have carried enormous tasks of policing criminals, controlling protest movements and regulating the traffic in Sapporo City at the time of the Games, the first appreciation is given to the activities enacted by the military, whose main contributions were building the ski courses and supporting transportation and communications. One of the reasons for this emphasis may be that for the military, collaboration with other public organizations such as the Sapporo Organizing Committee was very important in legitimizing its political status, which has been questioned and criticized ever since the Self-Defense Forces were established in 1954. As we learn from the Tokyo Games discussed by Tagsold in Chapter 3, the military's commitment to the Games prompted the public to support the military despite its controversial status. Criticisms against the military, however, did not subside. A terrible air accident on July 30, 1971, between an F86 jet fighter and an All Nippon Airways Boeing 727 that killed 162 people[33] added to that sentiment. The acknowledgments in the official report issued by the Sapporo Organizing Committee can, therefore, be understood as an attempt to promote a positive image of the military.[34]

The military's contribution at the Sapporo Games can be said to be "peaceful" in nature. Based on the official report by the Sapporo Organizing Committee and the police's documentary report of the Sapporo Games, neither standard military activities nor forceful surveillance were undertaken by the Self-Defense Forces. Its main role in the Olympics was largely pragmatic and symbolic. As we will see in the succeeding chapters, however, the work of the police and the military contrasts sharply with the role these institutions are expected to perform in securing the later Olympic Games under the political condition of rising threats of terrorism.

Concluding remarks

Surveillance and policing in relation to the Sapporo Olympics reflect the specific sociopolitical contexts of the Japanese society at the beginning of 1970s. As threats to the Emperor system due to the radical student protest movements became worrisome, it is quite understandable that the police would enact such policies and such activities would be supported by public anxiety. Utilizing hindsight by which we can understand the history of policing and surveillance in the Japanese society after the 1970s (Abe, 2004), however, we can state that the excessive estimation and expectations of the potential risk had great significance for the legitimization of police activities in the years to come. Even if foreseen threats at public events do not occur, the police are not blamed for the misconception of potential risks. On the contrary, the police are able to self-legitimately declare the success and effectiveness of a preventive surveillance policy by showing that nothing serious and harmful happened during the events.

This is a typical logic that enables the introduction and legitimization of increasing surveillance procedures and technologies. We have seen this sort of reasoning functioning quite smoothly in periods of sociopolitical crisis. For example, the Aum Shinrikyo panic in 1995, the aftermath of the events of 9/11, and the fear of hooligans attending the 2002 Korea/Japan World Cup Soccer event, were used as opportunities to install closed-circuit television cameras in public places and face recognition systems at airports with public support and without due discussion (Abe, 2004; Lyon, 2003; Murakami Wood, and Abe, 2011). In retrospect, with regard to surveillance and public fear in Japan after the 1970s, it can be said that the overestimation of the police of potential threats in hosting the Sapporo Olympic Games had established the practical template for the government and the police on how to enhance surveillance without public debate or dissent. The excessive and imaginative estimation of threats contributed to legitimizing the increased surveillance in Japanese society thereafter. Indeed, such a way of introducing and legitimizing the need for tighter policing has become a cliché in implementing surveillance measures in Japan. In this sense, the practice at the Sapporo Olympic Games can be seen as an "innovation" in that it succeeded in legitimizing tighter policing policy that mainly focused on pre-investigation of potential risks, utilized and supported by the seemingly excessive fear for the "enemy within."

While it is the demonized image of a visible, concrete, and dangerous "enemy within" that is mobilized to implement more control through surveillance, the main reasons for such policies are often much more mundane. It is simply that they are willing to accept larger budgets and to legitimize everyday activities for their own organizational reasons and interests. As a result, surveillance of ordinary people and society at large proceeds smoothly without rational public discussion about whether or not such policies are really needed in order to ascertain public safety.

Here we can depict the sociopolitical uniqueness concerning the relationship between surveillance and security in Japan. As scholars have pointed out, public safety and national security have very different historical origins and very different sets of institutions responsible for each one, respectively (Zedner, 2009). This is based on the modern concept of sovereignty and state, which presupposes the distinction between "interior" and "exterior" of the entity of nation-sate (Lipschutz, 1995). Security scholars have also pointed out that in recent decades we are increasingly seeing attempts to conflate national security concerns with issues not directly related to state sovereignty, such as public safety (Wæver, 1995). The case of the 1972 Sapporo Olympic Games as analyzed in this chapter may be an early example of this trend. The presence and safety of the Emperor at public occasions like the ceremony at the Olympic Games is politically and symbolically significant in securing Japan as a united nation-state. Considering this, it is fairly understandable why the main activity of the police – "security task" (*chian-iji*) – was to perfectly guard the Emperor. Through the policing practice leading up to and during the Sapporo Winter Olympics, ascertaining public safety as well as national security of Japan was the primary goal.

As this chapter clarified through analyzing the documentary report by the police, given the deep concern of the police for the safety of the Japanese Emperor and other members of the Japanese Imperial Family during the Sapporo Games, the security tasks related to prominent people coming from other countries, relatively speaking, did not seem to be considered serious.[35] Judging from the documentary report, the guarding practice of keigo was regarded as not so crucial as that of keiei, the main purpose of which was safeguarding the Emperor. In that sense, the basic policy of ascertaining safety at the Sapporo Olympics was surely domestic-oriented in that the targets of policing and the object of protection were mainly "within" the nation. Though the threats coming from abroad were recognized in relation to the potential crimes committed by foreigners, the main focus of policing and surveillance was on domestic matters. In the case of Japan in 1972, guarding the Emperor at public events symbolically ascertains the security of the state and the nation as a unity. Yet, as analyzed by Jørn Hansen in the following chapter, it is a threat that comes not from within but from outside of the host nation that was tragically realized at the Munich Olympic Summer Games, just seven months after the Sapporo Olympics.

Notes

1. "Police Rout Radicals at Japanese University." *Los Angeles Times,* November 9, 1969. See also "Japanese Police Rout Students from University," *Hartford Courant,* November 9, 1969.
2. "Police at Olympics." *Washington Post,* January 22, 1972.
3. *The White Paper on Crime,* 1972, 81–82.
4. *Hanzai Hakusho (The White Paper on Crime)* [1969–1974], Research and Training Institute, Ministry of Justice, Japan.
5. *The White Paper on Crimes,* 1969, 121–134.
6. *The White Paper on Crimes,* 1971, 85–88.
7. *The White Paper on Crimes,* 1974, 91–96.
8. *The White Paper on Crime* in 1974 uses the terms guerrilla (*gerira*), inner-group violence (*uchi-geba*), and terrorism (*tero-koui*) to depict the recent conditions of student movements citing several incidents, such as "the first Haneda case," "University of Tokyo case," "Day of Okinawa case," "International Anti-War Day case," "Prevention of Prime Minister's visiting to US case," etc. (pp. 91–96).
9. In Japanese: *chian iji* (治安維持)
10. *Asahi Shimbun,* 動機きかれても答えず美智子妃事件の少年 (Not answering the motive when asked: A boy committed an attacking incident for Crown Princess Michiko) January 7, 1972.
11. Hokkaido Prefecture Police, 1973, "Sapporo orinpiccu toukitaikai no keisatsukat-sudou kiroku" (札幌オリンピック冬季大会の警察活動記録/Documentary report of the activities of police at Winter Olympics at Sapporo 1972)30.
12. Ibid., Preface.
13. Ibid., Preface.
14. This report covers the activities of police in preparing for hosting Winter Olympics at Sapporo 1972 in details with a lot of photos and charts.
15. Hokkaido Prefecture Police, 1973, 15.
16. Ibid., 42.
17. Ibid., 42.
18. Ibid., 32.
19. Ibid., 89.

20. In Japanese: kyokusa bouryoku shuudan（極左暴力集団）
21. Hokkaido Prefecture Police, 1973, 40. 多数の外国人が来道するので、外国人に関する犯罪などの多発が予想され、特に、外国人が関係する犯罪については、その処理いかんによって国際問題にまで発展するおそれもあったため、円滑な処理が必要とされた。
22. Ibid., 40–41.
23. Ibid., 74–75.
24. Ibid., 76.
25. Ibid., 76.
26. Ibid., 77. 最も警戒を要する極左暴力集団は、市民の間にオリンピック歓迎ムードが盛り上がり、かつ厳重な警戒態勢の中での反対運動は困難であるとの判断から、大会に対する直接的な行動計画を変更放棄したため、大会行事および警衛、警護に直接関連する事案の発生はなかった。一方、右翼関係勢力も左翼の動きが平穏であったことらから、当初計画を変更するなど全般的に問題なく終始した。
27. Ibid., 77. 1. 道警察が、不法行為に対しては、き然たる態度で臨む方針をマスコミなどを通じて広報したことから、これが抑圧力として効果的に作用したこと。2. 会場周辺および行幸啓路線周辺における徹底した事前検索、ぐ犯者の行動確認、爆弾事件等既発事件の追跡捜査によって、過激派のしゅん動抑制対策奏功したこと。3. 東北管区機動隊の応援により、警備体制に余裕を得て、重要な警備対象に対して適切な警備措置を講ずるなど、間げきのない警戒を実施したこと。
28. Ibid., 58.
29. The Organizing Committee for the XIth Olympic Winter Games, Sapporo 1972, 1973, 400–404.
30. *Christian Science Monitor*, "Sapporo a lavish spectacle," February 3, 1972.
31. The City Office of Sapporo, 1972, "Dai jyuittsukai orinpiccu toukitaikai Sapporo-shi houkokushyo"（第11回オリンピック冬季大会札幌市報告書）[The city of Sapporo's official report on the XIth Olympic Winter Games Sapporo 1972], 202–204; Organizing Committee for the XIth Olympic Winter Games, Sapporo 1972, 1973, Official Report, 400–404.
32. The Organizing Committee for the XIth Olympic Winter Games, Sapporo 1972, 1973, Official Report, 400–404.
33. *Chicago Tribune*, Japanese Pilot Faces Arrest in Worst Air Crash; 162 Dead, July 31, 1971.
34. The Organizing Committee for the XIth Olympic Winter Games, Sapporo 1972, 1973, Official Report, 400–404.
35. Ibid., 140–145.

6
"The Most Beautiful Olympic Games That Were Ever Destroyed" (Munich 1972)

Jørn Hansen

The overriding purpose for the organizers of the 1972 Summer Munich Olympic Games was to demonstrate to the world that the post–World War II Federal Republic of Germany (from now on, West Germany) had become a modern democratic and open society. There were two key persons in this process: Willi Daume, the head of West German sport and President of the Munich Organizing Committee, and Hans-Jochen Vogel, the mayor of Munich and Vice-President of the Munich Organizing Committee. Daume and Vogel, together with others on the Committee, wanted to erase the negative memories of Hitler's 1936 Olympic Games in Berlin. As has been shown in the research literature, however, this purpose was not supported by all Germans (see Schiller and Young, 2010; Pfeiffer, 2001; Dwertmann and Pfeiffer, 2001). Especially the other Germany, the German Democratic Republic (from now on, East Germany) was eager to suppress the initiative that the Olympics should be given to Munich.[1]

After World War II, the Allied powers that defeated Nazi Germany divided Germany West of the Oder-Neisse Line into four occupation zones. The American, British and French zones formed the so-called West zone and the Soviet occupational zone the so-called East zone. The same partition was made in Berlin even though it belonged to the East zone geographically. In 1949, the West zone became the Federal Republic of Germany or West Germany, and the East zone became the German Democratic Republic or East Germany. In West Germany the capital became Bonn, and in East Germany the capital became Berlin – in fact, East Berlin was identical to the Soviet occupational zone in Berlin (Hobsbawm, 1994).

East Germany formed part of the Soviet, or Eastern, Bloc in terms of both power politics and ideologically, while West Germany joined the ideology of the West, which meant subscribing to its principles of market economics and democratic politics. This meant that the two countries came to address Nazi atrocities in two very different ways. The leaders of East Germany could relatively easily distance themselves from Nazism because communists had always been among the most virulent opponents of Nazism and, as is well known, communists all over Europe were persecuted by the Nazis. This meant that in the self-perception of its political leaders, East Germany could in no way be held responsible for the crimes of Nazism. As they saw it, this was far from being the case with their neighbor, West Germany. According to the official East German ideology, West Germany was burdened with the crimes of Nazism not the least because its acceptance into the world of Western imperialism meant that there were elements of continuity with regards to Nazi Germany.[2] We will see what significance this had in East Germany's criticism of the decision to allow the Olympic Games to be held in Munich.

West Germany's position in relation to the issues sketched here was more difficult. Nazism presented a problem for West Germany from the very start. Officially the political leaders of West Germany wanted to work together with the allies from the West to create an open democratic society that would be in direct contrast to Nazi Germany. On the other hand, in order to get the new social order to function as smoothly and as soon as possible, it was necessary to carry out a relatively rapid denazification of a fair number of people who would take up central positions in the establishment of Western Germany. Any real public confrontation with what had actually been widespread popular support for Nazism would, therefore, have to wait. Indeed, public protest only began to make itself felt at the end of the 1960s.[3] This awareness of the popular support for Nazism and the denazification of a number of political figures made West Germany particularly vulnerable to judgments of both the East and the West.

The International Olympic Committee and the German problem

In 1951, the International Olympic Committee was confronting a problem with two German Olympic national committees, one for West Germany and one for East Germany, both of which were seeking to be adopted into the Olympic Family. The application from West Germany was approved, while at the time, the International Olympic Committee had no intention of going along with the application from East Germany. To solve the problem, the Committee proposed to create a joint committee that would underwrite a joint German Olympic team. The hope was that this decision would not get in the way of a different issue, which was an important focus of attention during these years, namely the integration of the Soviet Union into the International Olympic Committee (Dwertmann and Pfeiffer, 2001; Hansen, 2004: 73). The Soviet Union had realized that the Olympic Games were an important arena for the international contest between the two ideological systems of the postwar era. For this reason they were keen to relinquish the self-imposed isolation of the interwar years. The International Olympic Committee for its part wanted them on board.

The Committee asked its West German member, Karl Ritter von Halt, to open negotiations with East Germany about the creation of a joint German Olympic team for the Games in 1952. This initiative was met with opposition from both East and West Germany. As a result, it was only West German athletes who took part at the 1952 Games in Helsinki. From 1954 onward, however, prior to the Games in Melbourne in 1956, a series of crucial changes in the German question took place. It had become clear that East Germany could not permanently be kept out of the International Olympic Committee and the Olympic Games. Ritter Von Halt, however, managed to persuade his friend and Committee President Avery Brundage that what was expected to be a full recognition of the East German National Olympic Committee at the International Olympic Committee meeting in Paris in 1955 would only be provisional. It was only after German Chancellor Konrad Adenauer visited Moscow in 1955, which was the result of diplomatic relations having been established between the Soviet Union and West Germany, that further progress was able to be made in earnest. This resulted in an agreement to create a joint team, which came into being before the Games in Melbourne. The selection of athletes was made according to the rules of West Germany, and the national anthem would be the hymn from Beethoven's 9th Symphony. That same year, at Karl Ritter von Halt's instigation, Willi Daume was chosen as a member of the International Olympic Committee. Daume was a member of the Nazi Party from 1937 to 1945. In 1950, he became the president for the West German Sports Federation. In this capacity, beginning in the early 1960s, Daume began to work with West Germany's National Olympic Committee to bring the Olympic Games to Munich (Dwertmann and Pfeiffer, 2001: 74, 101).

The provisional approval of the East German National Olympic Committee lasted until the International Olympic Committee's 63rd congress in Madrid in 1965, when the International Olympic Committee accepted East Germany as a full-fledged member. This recognition was in line with the world order prevailing at the time. After the Cuban Missile Crisis in 1962, it became obvious that the Eastern and Western Blocs did not want any direct confrontation. Instead the peaceful competition in the field of sport took over. In the shadow of the building of the Berlin Wall in 1961, however, the decision in Madrid ended up creating major problems in West Germany.

One consequence of the recognition of the East German National Olympic Committee was that at the 1968 Olympic Games in Mexico City and in Grenoble, the two Germanys were allowed to compete as independent nations, though with the proviso that they should enter jointly in the opening procession and share a national anthem. On the other hand, the International Olympic Committee decided during the Games in Mexico that at the next Olympics in Munich in 1972, East Germany would, for the first time, march into the stadium as an independent nation using its own national anthem (Pfeiffer, 2001). In doing so, the East German athletes would compete for the first time as a completely independent nation at the Olympic Games in the "homeland of the class enemy" – that is, in the "wrong" Germany. All of this had transpired after Munich and the West German National Olympic Committee sent in their application to host the Games in 1972. It should also be noted, however, that the authorities in East Germany made it clear all along that they would do everything in their power to prevent the International Olympic Committee from accepting the application (Pfeiffer, 2001: 95; Hartmann, 1998:72).

The application to host the Games and the ensuing debate in the East and the West

At the end of October 1965, Munich's mayor, the Social Democrat Hans-Jochen Vogel, undertook the initiative to support the application to host the Games. Throughout December, he took the initiative to the parliament and the West German National Olympic Committee. On December 30, 1965, the International Olympic Committee received the official application from Munich alongside applications from Detroit, Montreal and Madrid. In the application from Munich, Willi Daume stressed that the Games should first and foremost be a sporting festival *"ohne Gigantismus,"* a reference to the Nazi monumental staging of the Games in Berlin in 1936. In contrast to Berlin in 1936, Munich proposed to avoid gigantic, colossal undertakings of any kind, and to stage, instead, the Olympic Games with "a human face" in a city where Pierre de Coubertin's idea of uniting art and sport had every chance of being realized. To underline the significance of the Games as a festival of joy, the German chancellor at the time, Ludwig Erhard, emphasizes this position with the following words: "We must not constantly be looking at the negative side of things" (Hartmann, 1998: 72).[4]

At the time Munich applied with the International Olympic Committee to host the Games, East Germany was not yet a member of the Committee and therefore could not take action against the application. Instead, the case was taken up by its neighbor, former Czechoslovakia. Referring to the Berlin Games in 1936, for example, the Czechoslovakian press maintained that "history does not speak in favor of Munich's candidacy" (Pfeiffer, 2001: 96). In addition, Czechoslovakian Committee member Frantisek Kroutil emphasized that Munich was the city with *Feldherrnhalle*, the "Commander Hall" and "near Dachau" (Hartmann, 1998: 72). It was a clear reference to Munich's relation to the Nazi past. Hans-Jochen Vogel responded that these concerns were justified and understandable. Referring to an amicable dialog he had had with the mayor of Prague, Vogel assured Kroutil that the desire of Munich was to promote peace and friendship. Vogel also assured that, should the International Olympic Committee so decide, Munich as the host of the Games would accept East German athletes competing under their own flag and banner (Hartman, 1998: 72–73; Pfeifer, 2001: 96–97).

This agitation on the part of Czechoslovakia actually had no decisive significance for the decision as to where the Games should be hosted. In April 1966, a majority of the International Olympic Committee was in favor of giving the Games to Munich, and, as the monthly *Der Spiegel* reported, the international press promoted the idea that sport and the Olympics could be used to rehabilitate Germany. West Germany also saw the Games as a chance to demonstrate that its population wished to promote peace and democracy, an agenda that was entirely in line with the official position of the Organizing Committee.[5]

The actual process of organizing and staging the event, however, proved to be not as simple because, even though East German criticism did not prevent Munich from being awarded the hosting of the Games, it did manage to raise the most delicate issue for West Germany and Munich. *Der Spiegel*, for example, warned readers of the danger of the festival of reconciliation in Munich going haywire. It wrote that a backlash would ensue if people witnessed that Germany, "a country which had started a war and which had undergone a defeat it had brought upon itself," was "using a new-found national pride to allow German blame for the past to burn up in the Olympic flame under the rings in Munich."[6] And in the same article one could read that even though "Munich was an important center for European culture; Munich was also the city where Dachau is lying just outside the town's gate."[7] In other words, a successful hosting of the Games was going to be a difficult balancing act.

West German leaders and the Organizing Committee in Munich were perfectly well aware of this. Were they to forget, they would be reminded by criticism from East Germany. As quoted in Pfeiffer (2001: 97–99), a series of articles in East Germany's official newspaper, *Neues Deutschland*, under the headline "Don't two times 36 make 72?" stirred up the view that West Germany's policies had their roots in fascism, imperialism and militarism. Other deadlines talked of "the Nazis getting their way ... the Olympic peace is in danger ... In Munich revanchism is out of control ... Munich as the city of revanchism and revisionism ... the home of the smear campaign of Radio Liberty and Free Europe" (Pfeiffer, 2001: 97–98). This agitation gradually died out after 1970 when West German Chancellor Willy Brandt introduced a policy of reconciliation with East Germany and the rest of the Eastern Bloc countries. Nevertheless, the East German criticism of "the abuse of the Games in Munich for imperialistic and revanchist goals"[8] and West Germany's fear of the ghosts of the past had taken on crucial significance for the staging of the 1972 Games in Munich, including their thinking about security and policies implemented to this end. According to the official report, "the Games of the XXth Olympics were to be animated, informal, and peaceful." Accordingly, "the concept of security had to be adapted to this context."[9]

In what follows, I first look more closely at the framework for the staging of the Munich Games, particularly the Olympic Stadium, and then analyze the security measures that were – or were not – put in place.

Munich: an airier stadium and a freer Opening Ceremony

The Olympiastadion (Olympic Stadium) for the Berlin Games was a gigantic, imposing, neoclassical structure with plenty of space for various activities, including the so-called Maifeld. This was an area for display and practice that lay between the Marathon Gate of the stadium and the Glockenturm, a bell tower with a huge cast iron bell with the insignia *"Ich rufe die Jugend der Welt,"* calling the youth of the world to Berlin. The foundation of the bell tower was the great Langemarckhalle, a series of large halls that made the connection between the Olympic Stadium and the Nazi death cult (Kluge, 1999: 76–78, 104–105).[10]

The 1936 Berlin was the capital of Hitler's Third Reich. The 1972 Berlin was an occupied city, divided by the Wall and lacking prospects for the future. Munich, in contrast, had by 1972 developed into a modern cosmopolitan city with a rich and lively cultural life that boasted 23 museums, four large orchestras, 17 theaters, and a tradition of both local and international art. In the eyes of the Organizing Committee, this was an excellent platform from which to stage the Olympic Park as an easygoing, transparent and open area that would present a stark contrast to the militaristic and nationalistic Games of the past.

The Olympic Park was to be situated in the northern part of the city in a neglected area that had long been lying fallow and waiting to be developed. The area was originally completely flat, but with the aid of heavy machinery it was transformed into an undulating landscape with a lake created by damming the water from a canal that ran through Munich to Nürnberg. The park was equipped with training areas for the athletes, swimming pools, theaters, a number of restaurants, the press center, Olympic Village, and the Olympic Stadium with seating for 80,000 spectators. By this means a sports and leisure landscape was established that was richly diverse and in complete contrast to Berlin's monumental sporting architecture (Gold and Gold, 2007: 34–36).[11]

The jewel in the crown of the Olympic Park was the airy and elegant stadium (see Figure 6.1) with its spectacular roof construction that in the form of a giant tent extended over the stadium and was mirrored in similar roof constructions over a number of the other sports arenas. The Opening Ceremony itself was designed to underline the easygoing nature of the staging of the Games. At the entry procession, fragments of well-known

Figure 6.1 Openness, simplicity, and comprehensibility: the 1972 Munich Olympic Park (Official Report Munich 1972)

music from each of the participating nations replaced the military music played during the Berlin Games (Hansen, 2009: 137).

With a total of 7121 contestants, 6065 men and 1058 women from 121 nations, the Games in Munich broke all previous records for the Olympics. One significant cause of this was to be found in the dissolution of the colonial dominance of the West, which resulted in a large number of new independent nations. This development presented a challenge to the Western thinking that hitherto had marked the Olympic Games. This found expression in a number of the new African states exploiting the International Olympic Committee and the Olympics to make an issue of the racial discrimination prevailing in South Africa and Rhodesia, pointing out that whites and blacks did not have equal opportunities for competing in the Games. The African countries demanded, therefore, that South Africa and Rhodesia be excluded from participating in the Olympics – an action in which they were supported from the outset by the Soviet Union and other Eastern Bloc nations (Mandell, 1991: 100–101; Pfeifer, 1987).

Initially, both Avery Brundage and the West German National Committee had supported South African participation in the Games in Mexico in 1968, but once it became clear to the West German delegation that this might cost Munich the Games in 1972, West Germany chose not to be at loggerheads with the Third World, and Avery Brundage suffered one of his few defeats. South Africa became the first country to be explicitly excluded from the International Olympic Committee and thereby excluded from taking part in the Olympic Games.

Immediately prior to the Games in Munich it looked as if the awkward customer at the Munich Olympics would be Rhodesia. In 1965 southern Rhodesia had broken away from English sovereignty, and under the purely white supremacy rule of Ian Smith, it had turned itself into an independent African state under the name of Rhodesia. At the 1968 Games in Mexico, the United Nations' sanctions had made it easy for the Organizing Committee to exclude Rhodesia. It was more of a problem in Munich, where Rhodesia had declared that it would take part under the English flag, whereby they fulfilled in principle the International Olympic Committee's rule regarding racial discrimination. If it had been implemented successfully, this strategy would have led to a large-scale boycott of the Games in Munich by the independent African nations. A boycott was avoided because the West German Organizing Committee was able to point to an error in the use of incorrect passports at the Rhodesian team's entry into West Germany and used this as a basis for refusing the team's permission to compete (Hansen, 2004: 100–101).

Once both the South African and the Rhodesian problems were solved, the Games looked as though they would pass off easily and painlessly, following the wishes of Organizing Committee President Willi Daume. As is well known, things turned out quite differently. As I demonstrate below, to the Regulation Service (*Der Ordnungsdienst*),[12] which prepared a strategy for Identification and Control (*Ausweisswesen und Kontrolldienst*),[13] it seemed paramount that West Germany of 1972 be placed in stark contrast to Germany of 1936.

Sicherheit und Ordnung[14] *in the Olympic Park and the Olympic Village*

On April 1, 1970, the Organizing Committee made an agreement with the president of the Munich police force, Manfred Schreiber, that he would be their special commissioner for security, or *Ordnungsbeauftragte*,[15] the authority responsible for law and order and principal adviser in these matters (Schiller and Young, 2010: 148). According to the Olympic Report, under the heading "The Given Facts," the basis of the agreement was "the basic conception of these Games, which was intended to project the image of the Federal Republic of Germany in a joyous, relaxed atmosphere in a conscious contrast to the image of Germany in 1936."[16] An image of a man

Figure 6.2   Spectators: the 1972 Munich Olympics (Official Report Munich 1972)

who climbed up a tree (Figure 6.2 above) in order to better see what was taking place on the stage was published in the official report. The image speaks perhaps most powerfully to the perception of what constituted an acceptable distance between the public and the event.

Indeed, by the end of 1969, Vogel and Schreiber were of the opinion that there were two potential threats that would demand engagement of the *Ordnungsdienst*: one were the militant, anarchist activists attracted by the extraordinary publicity of the Olympics and the other were countries, such as East Germany, seeking to prove their national superiority outside the sporting arena (Schiller and Young, 2010: 149).

In conjunction with the preparation of security measures, the Organizing Committee gathered information about what had been done previously in other places at similar large-scale sporting events.[17] This involved obtaining information from the 1960 Olympics in Rome, 1964 in Tokyo, and 1968 in Mexico City. There were, however, a whole range of experiences that would be difficult to transfer to Munich in 1972. For example, about 90,000 police officers were involved in Tokyo, but this would have been unthinkable in 1972 Munich and would have run counter to the image of the Games.[18] In addition, to the Olympics, Schreiber also investigated security measures adopted in conjunction with the Asian Games in Bangkok in 1970, a large-scale sporting event in Moscow in 1971, and sports Games in a number of large cities in South America.[19]

Security procedures were also assessed by the security authorized from the Bavarian government in relation to the 1972 Winter Olympics in Sapporo as well as at the major spectator catastrophe at the Glasgow football stadium in 1971.[20] Following the Olympics Report we are lead to conclude that while the idea was to have open and democratic Games without any military flavor, the most elementary security measures were most certainly not omitted. As I point out next, in one particular area they even introduced a special regulation.

This special regulation was related to right to demonstrate. In order to avoid demonstrations prior to and during the Olympic Games, West Germany's Ministry for Internal Affairs approved a law on May 31, 1972, the official purpose of which was to ensure Olympic Peace.[21] In reality, this entailed a ban on demonstrations and on marches inside the Olympic Park. Neither the regulation itself nor the Olympic Report give any direct reference that this ban may have been put in place to prevent a repeat of the violent demonstrations that had preceded the 1968 Games in Mexico, as discussed by Kevin Witherspoon in Chapter 4 of this book. The official report states only that: "The Olympic Committee had to take into account demonstrations and their potentially negative accompanying effects on the Olympic sports sites, on living quarters and the organizers' area."[22] We can reasonably assume, however, that these decisions were related to the events in Mexico and the radical left-wing groups in West Germany. This meant that, from July 25 on, the Bavarian government interdicted demonstrations in the following areas. First was "the Olympia Park with the Olympic Village, the media city and the Olympic mountain. This was the center of the Olympic events." Second was "the centrally situated trade exhibition south of the Theresien meadow where many sports competitions took place." The third area where demonstrations were prohibited was "the area for the marathon, the 20 km and 50 km walking distance and for the torch relay and the welcome ceremony at the Königsplatz."[23] The law apparently worked, for there was only one occasion during the Games, on September 3, where there was a threat of a minor demonstration, and even this soon fizzled out.[24]

The design of the Olympic Village and the security precautions judged necessary when so many people were to assemble in one place also had to be in accordance with the general concept of the Olympic Games in Munich. This was clear from the security considerations discussed by the Organizing Committee. The considerations of the official report on security in the Olympic Village in Munich are reflected in the following:

> The design and the security ("Die Gestaltung und die Sicherheit") of the Olympic Village as well as the approach to these aspects were fitted to the overall conception chosen for the Olympic Games. Everything was avoided which would allow the Olympic Village to resemble an armed fortress. Thus its outer barrier was a two-meter high wire netting fence without barbed wire. The ten outer gates and the twelve inner gates were manned by guards. Of these, the main gates 6 and 7 (south and north gates on Lerchenauer Strasse) as well as the gates 28a and 30a were always open. The remaining gates were closed between midnight and 6 am.[25]

The village itself consisted of three separate sections: one for male athletes, one for female athletes, and a semi-public zone. Access to the village was only permitted for people in possession of a pass issued jointly by the Organizing Committee and the International Olympic Committee. According to the report, the following types of groups had permanent access:

The athletes and their coaches;
The administration personnel;
The service personnel (including stewards and drivers supplied by the army);
The operators and staff of the amusement center and the shopping precinct as well as their delivery personnel; and
The Regulation Service (*Der Ordnungsdienst*) and post office employees.

Passes without an attached photograph were valid only with a photo ID.[26]

Der Ordnungsdienst was responsible for maintaining both law and order in the entire geographical area of the Olympic Games. The service had no police jurisdiction and staffs were armed only at night. In the Olympic Village, they were responsible for controlling pedestrian as well as motor traffic entryways, patrolling the areas, preventing disruption of order, and preliminary action involving punishable offenses. Regular police stationed in the Olympic Village was responsible for further action in such cases. Security personnel worked in shifts of about 60 people per shift, among which five women were responsible for surveillance of the quarters for female athletes. If needed, reinforcement was available from the general services.[27]

Protecting the Israeli athletes

At 4:30 on the morning of September 5, 1972, in the throes of the Olympic Games in Munich, eight members of the Palestinian Black September Organization broke into the Israeli team's quarters in the Olympic Village. Dressed in training gear, with their sports bags full of powerful firearms, they had no difficulty in gaining access. Two Israelis got away, two were shot, and nine were taken hostage. The presence of the world's media ensured the best possible direct news exposure and communicated Black September's demand to exchange the hostages for 200 prisoners in Israel and an airplane to an Arab country. International Olympic Committee President Avery Brundage had no choice but to temporarily suspend the Olympics.

The Palestinian commandos negotiated with West German authorities and the plan was that the Palestinians would make their getaway to Egypt. With the nine hostages as human shields, the Palestinians were transported to the airport, where two helicopters awaited them – and a group of German marksmen. Israeli Prime Minister Golda Meir refused to negotiate with the hostage-takers: not one prisoner would be freed. Egypt would not accept the Palestinians. West German Chancellor Willy Brandt was left with no options, and in this checkmate situation the German marksmen went into action. Unfortunately, everything that could go wrong did go wrong. During the exchange of fire, the nine Israeli hostages were killed. Five Palestinians and a German policeman also lost their lives, while three of the Palestinians were captured.

Perhaps most significantly for the future of the Games, the entire drama, moment to moment, was televised live by a German television station, which meant that millions around the world were watching. Since the 1960 Games in Rome, the Olympics have been a media event. With 4250 journalists covering the Olympics in Munich – among them 1200 radio and television journalists – the whole world could follow the drama in Munich (Schiller and Young, 2010: 52). The International Olympic Committee, the city of Munich, and the world were in a state of shock (Hansen, 2004: 100–103; Mandell, 1991: 127).

The action of Black September in Munich was a decisive moment in the history of the Olympic Games, for even though political events had cast a shadow over the Games on a number of occasions, the sporting events themselves had always carried on uninterrupted once the Games were under way. Munich was different. For the first time in the history of the Olympics, a direct action meant that course of the competitions had to be temporarily halted, breaking with the ritual pattern of the way the Games were to unfold. Brundage, however, decided to lead the Olympic Games forward when he made his famous speech at the Memorial Ceremony at the Munich Olympic Stadium in front of 80,000 mourning spectators and countless TV viewers:

> We mourn our Israeli friends... Sadly, in this imperfect world, the greater and the more important the Olympic Games become, the more they are open to commercial, political and now criminal pressure... I am sure that the public will agree that we cannot allow a handful of terrorists to destroy this nucleus of international cooperation and goodwill we have in the Olympic Movement. The Games must go on and we must continue our efforts to keep them clean, pure and honest and try to extend the sportsmanship of the athletic field into other areas. (Quoted in Guttmann, 1984: 254)

The Games were resumed, but the events in Munich were a watershed in the history of the Olympic Games. At all subsequent Games, the greatest attention was to be paid to the security of the athletes and other participants of the event.

As I have demonstrated above, a number of security measures were put in place, for which, no doubt, the Organizing Committee, working together with the Munich police chief, must have felt to be sufficient to guarantee law and order during the Games. However, in addition to this the organizers were perfectly aware that the tense situation in the Middle East made it necessary to take special steps to ensure the safety of athletes from Israel.

Prior to the Games the various authorities in West Germany had, in fact, also received a number of reports predicting politically motivated actions and unrest during the Games. In an interview in *Der Spiegel* after the Games, Manfred Schreiber equated the amount of credible information received with a capacity of five laundry baskets. He also mentioned eight bomb threats before the opening of the Olympic Stadium.[28] According to the official report, all such reports were investigated, but none of them contained any concrete clues either about time and place or the actual targets of such action.[29] As regards the attack from Black September on September 5, no concrete warning was received either by West German authorities or by the Organizing Committee.[30]

In his book *One Day in September* (2000 and 2006 with a new Epilogue), Simon Reeve makes a number of statements: that "German security officials were warned of a possible terrorist attack at the Olympics"; that "A German psychologist told the Munich police that there was a danger of a terrorist assault on the Israelis"; and that "the Interpol issued an alert just weeks before the Games that Arab terrorists appeared to be grouping in Europe for a possible 'spectacular' attack." Reeve also states that "On August 21, 1972 the German secret police sent a letter to the Munich police warning of Palestinian plans to do 'something' at Munich" (2006: 228). These statements are based on a conversation with Ankie Spitzer, widow of Israeli fencing coach Andre Spitzer, in which the widow claims to have gained access to 3808 files of information from an archive in Munich, alleg-edly closed until 1992.[31] Ankie Spitzer's story may well be credible, yet it is important to emphasize that with the knowledge we have today it would be extremely difficult to judge the specificity of these warnings.

Reeve also states that the Israeli officials "had told the Germans they would prefer to be billeted at the top of one of the taller accommodations buildings" and that "military security specialists had flown to Germany to suggest ways of protecting the team. At the insistence of the Germans, all security protection was left to the host country."[32] Reeve, unfortunately, cites no sources for these claims.[33] The official report, however, contradicts these claims. According to the report, several months before the Games, representatives of the police department had held a number of meetings with agents from the Israeli embassy and the Israeli team about security measures for the Games. On August 9, police authorities in Munich informed the Israeli security agent about the security measures that were in place for the Israeli guests of honor and for Israeli athletes in the Olympic Village. Those taking part in the meeting agreed that there was no specific reason for concern about the security of the Israelis and no sense of dissatisfaction on the part of the Israeli security authorities.[34]

Meetings were held again on August 24 and 25 between the police in Munich and the delegates from the Israeli team, again discussing security for guests from Israel. At neither of these two meetings was there any sugges-tion of suspicion about an imminent attack, be it on the Israeli athletes, Israeli equipment, or other individuals from Israel.[35] We are thus led to conclude that the Palestinian attack on September 5 must have come as a surprise to German security authorities in Munich as much as Israeli secu-rity forces.

The outcome: "the most beautiful Olympic Games that were ever destroyed"[36]

With the beautiful design of their stadium and the lack of pomposity of their Opening Ceremony, the Games in Munich were to present West Germany to the world-at-large as a new democratic and open country, and no measure was spared to avoid shadows of the past spoiling the Games. It was, there-fore, all the more tragic that terror should strike Israelis on German territory. West Germany had made huge efforts to atone for Nazi atrocities toward the Jews, and Israel and West Germany had been reconciled. Terrorism, however, destroyed any joy that might have been generated in this process. Hans Klein of the Organizing Committee expressed it as follows: "We are not only some of the most sensitive people on earth but ... also some of the most easily wounded ... It seems now that there is no wounded we could still suffer where we have not yet been hit."[37]

Purely symbolically, the catastrophe in Munich was also given a sporting expression. During Hitler's Games in Berlin in 1936 the large clutch of medals reaped by African American Jesse Owens was bound to create problems for Nazi ideology about the Germanic Superman. In this context Hitler and the rest had to put a brave face on it when they saw Owens being feted on the victory podium. In Munich the most prolific medalist was the devout American Jew Mark Spitz, who, despite winning seven gold medals, chose to return to the United States earlier than planned after the September 5 tragedy. For him there was nothing to celebrate. And that was equally true for the German organizers.

After the Olympics, in a column called "Terror und kein Ende" ("Terror without an end"), the founder and editor of *Der Spiegel*, Rudolf Augstein, wondered why the people from Israel and Germany who were responsible for the protection of the Israeli team had acted so deficiently. Were the Olympics not the best public platform for the Arabic underground army?[38] There is no simple answer to the questions raised by Augstein. Terror has been a well-known word in history since the French Revolution and the so-called Reign of Terror and had also played a role in the anti-colonial movements in, for example, Algeria during the 1950s. But in 1972 Europe, terror had just started to be a serious problem. West Germany did have to deal with radical left-wing terror from the Baader-Meinhof Group, but the Olympics in Munich were the first time that a global event of this kind was disrupted by an international terror organization. No one in the Organizing Committee could have foreseen the massacre in Munich. More importantly, at the time, the organizers of the Olympics were not expected to envision all the possible scenarios of how the Olympics could conceivably be disrupted. Instead, their attention was focused on a different issue: the balance between open and free Olympics and the security arrangements.

Postlude

In the interview in *Der Spiegel* mentioned earlier, Manfred Schreiber, the person responsible for order and security, discussed with the journalist whether the policemen in the airport were sufficiently skilled in shooting. Following Schreiber, some of them were; however, Schreiber was of the opinion that trained riflemen belonged to the army, not the police. It also became clear during the interview that, at the time, West Germany had no special antiterror corps. Schreiber said, "a specific group which would act only against terror did not exist in Germany."[39] One will never know what a special antiterror corps could have done at the airport, but the lesson from Munich 1972 was that such a corps should be established in West Germany. This was realized on September 26, 1972, when an antiterror group under the name Grenzschutzgruppe 9 (GSG 9) was established. Later the name of the group changed to Grenzschutzgruppe 9 der Bundespolizei. One of the group's most successful actions was the rescue mission of the hostage in a German airplane in Mogadishu 1977.[40]

In turn, Munich also seems to have been a watershed for the Palestine Liberation Organization. As one of the planners of the terrorist action, Mohammed Oudeh, previously known by the name of Abu Daoud, stated in 2006: "Before Munich, we were simply terrorists. After Munich, at least people started asking: 'Who are these terrorists? What do they want?' Before Munich nobody had the slightest idea about Palestine" (cited in Toohey and Veal, 2007: 108).

No less, the events in Munich left a permanent legacy within the International Olympic Committee and in relation to the organization of the future Olympic Games. As Bruce Kidd demonstrates in the next chapter, four years later, at the opening of the 1976 Olympic Games in Montreal, nothing was left undone as regards the security arrangements. All personnel were protected, locked away behind a security fence, and required to repeatedly present proof of their identity. The days of open and unfettered Games were over.

The 1972 Munich Olympics was a global event, broadcast live to millions of people around the world. The exposure was used to draw attention to political causes, this time on a massive scale and with far-reaching consequences. With television cameras transmitting to audiences worldwide the drama surrounding the hijacking from minute-to-minute, attention was diverted away from the Games, leaving behind a negative legacy for the city of Munich as much as for Germany. As the following chapters demonstrate, ever since, the host city and country, as much as the International Olympic Committee, have been doing everything in their power to make sure that global attention is – and remains – focused only on the Games and the carefully constructed self-image the host country wants to present to the world.

Notes

I thank an anonymous reviewer for valuable comments.

1. At the time, there were two German nations: the Federal Republic of Germany or FRG (*Bundesrepublic Deutschland* or BRD) and the German Democratic Republic or GDR (*Deutsche Democratische Republic*, or DDR).
2. It should be emphasized that I am referring here to East German self-perception rather than historical facts.

3. This was also one of the common explanations in understanding the radicalism of the youth rebellion of West Germany, in that it was also a revolt against their parents' generation's suppression of the truth.

4. See also Die Spiele. Der offizielle Bericht, herausgegeben vom Organisationskomitee für die Spiele der XX Olympiade München 1972 (The Games. The Official Report of the Organizing Committee for the Games of the XXth Olympiad Munich 1972), vol. 2, 5.

5. Die Spiele, vol. 1, 23.

6. *Der Spiegel*, 19/1966, 33.

7. Ibid.

8. Ibid., 99.

9. CHeiter, ungezwungen und friedlich sollten die Spielen der XX Olympiade verlaufen. ... Auch die Sicherheitskonzeption hatte sich ihr anzupassen." Die Spiele, vol. 1, p. 32.

10. Also instructive is the exhibition of the German Museum of History in Langemarckhalle, which opened in conjunction with the renovation of the Olympic Stadium for the 2006 World Championship in football.

11. See also Die Spiele, vol. 2, 31–36.

12. Die Spiele, vol. 1, Der Ordnungsdienst, 340.

13. Ibid., Die Organisation, 316.

14. Ibid., 340. The headline to this section of the Report reads: "Problem der Sicherheit und Ordnung im Kompetenzbereich der OK." OK stands for Olympischer Komitee (Olympics Committee). The 1991 edition of the *Collins German–English/English–German Dictionary* translates *Sicherheit und Ordnung* as "law and order." The connotation of this expression to national security arrangements seems to be a later development.

15. Die Spiele, vol. 1, 340. Schreiber was responsible for "Beratung des Vorstandes des Generalsekretärs und des ständigen stellvertretenden Generalsekretärs in allen Sicherheitsfragen und Ordnungsproblemen."

16. Ibid., 340. "die Grundkonzeption dieser Spiele, die in heiterer, gelöster Atmosphäre das Bild der Bundespepublik in bewusstem Kontrast zum Deutschlandbild des Jahres 1936 zeigen sollten."

17. Ibid., 340. "Das OK baute bei seinen Entscheidungen und Massnahmen in Sicherheitsfragen auf den Erfahrungen ähnlicher Grossveranstaltungen auf."

18. Ibid. "Die tatsächlichen und rechtlichen Verhältnisse wären nicht vergleichbar. So setze das japanische OK während der Olympischen Spiele in Tokoy ca. 90.000 Polizeibeamte ein."

19. Ibid., 340. "Der Ordnungsbeauftragte informierte sich ... – über Erfahrungen sowjetischer Sicherheitsbehörden bei sportlicher Großveranstaltungen im Juli 1971 in Moskau. – über Sicherheitsprobleme in Grossstadien und Terroranschläge auf eine Reise nach Rio de Janeiro, São Paulo, Buenos Aires und Lima in November 1971."

20. Ibid. "über den Besuch der Olympischen Winterspiele in Sapporo im Februar 1972 durch den Sicherheitsbeauftragten der Bayerischen Stattsregierung. – über die Katastrophe im Fussbalsstadion von Glasgow im Januar 1971."

21. Ibid., 341. The regulation was called "Gesetz zum Schutz des Olympischen Friedens vom 31. Mai 1972."

22. Ibid., 341.

23. Ibid., 341. 1. "Den Olympiapark mit Olympischem Dorf, Pressestadt und Olympiaberg: Er war das Zentrum des olympischen Geschehens." 2. "Das zentral

gelegene Messegelände südlich der Theresienwiese. Viele Sportwettkämpfe fanden dort statt." 3. "Die Streckenbereich für den Marathonlauf, das 20-km- und 50-km-Gehen und den Fackellauf einschliesslich der Empfangszeremonie auf dem Königsplatz."

24. Ibid., 341. "Es sei festgestellt, dass es nur eine einzige Demonstration in Olympiapark am 3. September 1972 gab, die von der Polizei rasch zerstreut wurde bezw. sich von selbst wieder auflöste."
25. Ibid., 138.
26. Ibid.
27. Ibid., 138.
28. *Der Spiegel*, 38/1972, 34.
29. Die Spiele, vol. 1, 32.
30. Ibid., 32 and 340.
31. Ibid., 226.
32. Ibid., 228.
33. Ibid., 227.
34. Ibid., 32. The report states that "Die Gesprächspartner waren sich einig, dass keine konkreten Hinweise auf Störungen oder Attentatsabsichten gegenüber israelischen Sportlern oder Besuchern vorlagen."
35. Ibid., 32.
36. From a Munich daily, cited here from Mandell, 1991, op. cit. 178.
37. Ibid., 178–179.
38. *Der Spiegel*, 38/1972, 20. "Ich verstehe nicht, wieso die Israeli und die gastgebenden Deutschen für die Mannschaft Israels einen so unzulänglichen Schutz durchexerziert haben. ... Gab es eine bessere geeignete Plattform für die arabischen Untergrundkämpfer als die Olympischen Spiele?"
39. Ibid., 34. "Eine spezifische Gruppe die nur gegen Terroristen eingesetzt wird, gibt es in ganz Deutschland nicht."
40. *Der Spiegel*, 44/1977.

7

"The Army's Presence Will Be Obvious" (Montreal 1976)

Bruce Kidd

There was nothing discrete about the surveillance organizers undertook at the 1976 Winter Olympic Games. In the largest Canadian military operation since World War II, 8940 Canadian soldiers guarded the Olympic venues, hotels and transportation hubs in Montreal and the satellite cities of Bromont (equestrian), Kingston (yachting) and Toronto (soccer preliminaries). They worked in close coordination and communication with 1376 officers of the Royal Canadian Mounted Police, 1140 from the Quebec Police Force, 533 from the Ontario Provincial Police, 1606 from the Montreal Police Department, 424 from four other municipal police services, and 2910 private security guards. Most of these officers were heavily armed, equipped with the most technologically advanced communication devices and in full uniform. In airports and the various border crossings, customs and immigration officers were on alert, empowered by temporary legislation that gave them the authority to turn anyone without an Olympic identity card or a Canadian passport away at will. Visitors from Middle East countries entering from the United States were required to have special visas. Along extended stretches of the unguarded Canada-United States border, electronic sensors were installed and air, ground and waterway patrols were initiated in the period leading up to and during the Games.

The International Olympic Committee headquarters, in the Queen Elizabeth Hotel in downtown Montreal, was turned into a fortress, surrounded by soldiers, with credential checkers and metal detectors at every entrance, security personnel in every room, and International Olympic Committee President Killanin was given an around-the-clock bodyguard. The Olympic Village in east Montreal was protected by a ten-foot barbed wire fence and patrolled by soldiers with automatic weapons, hovering helicopters, and dogs trained to detect bombs, while sharpshooters were posted on the terraces. Inside the village, teams were housed according to a security calculation, with the Israelis lodged in separate quarters with extra protection. Hidden cameras and listening devices were placed throughout the village and monitored around-the-clock. Every athlete, coach, official, journalist or dignitary

Figure 7.1 Be discreet by Aislin, 1976

who entered the village (or any other special area) had to present approved photo accreditation, printed on specially prepared paper to thwart forgeries, walk through a metal detector and submit all bags and other belongings to search. Even the prime minister of Canada was required to undergo accreditation.[1] Soldiers also guarded the buses athletes and dignitaries took to training and competition sites. Bus routes were changed on a daily basis and teams were mixed up so that no individual team would be targeted.[2] While some security personnel were told to "be discreet," it was an impossible task, as the Aislin cartoon shows above (Figure 7.1).

These measures were not just for show. Those who found themselves in the wrong place were roughed up and arrested. A German journalist who had unwittingly entered a restricted area for photographers was "removed violently," arrested and deprived of his accreditation. In another formal complaint to the International Olympic Committee Executive Board, a German photographer who "had taken up position in the swimming hall in an unoccupied seat, was without any warning brutally beaten by eight policemen, clapped into handcuffs, and taken temporarily into custody."[3]

An American fan who tried to join Bruce Jenner's victory lap was also arrested (Ludwig, 1976: 62). Prior to the Games, the Montreal police apprehended political activists, gays and lesbians and advised them to "get out of town."[4]

The strategy behind such a "conspicuous, uniformed" display of force was to safeguard the conditions for successful Olympic Games by "showing that the police are present." According to official statements before and after the Games, the idea was to

> have the Olympic Games take place in a joyous atmosphere of peace and tranquility ... (through) prevention, reaching people and groups suspected of being likely to cause trouble and dissuading or diverting them from committing criminal or illegal acts. ... It was agreed that the best way to deter suspected trouble-makers was not to adopt a plan of operation which would interfere with civil rights, but one that would leave no doubt in their minds they were under continual close surveillance.[5]

The 1976 strategy thus anticipated the distinction that underlies this book between the idea, perception, and vision of a "safe" social reality from the technology and procedures of "surveillance" that enabled the idea and vision to be achieved. In the organizers' minds, the latter was necessary for the former, so much so that in their documents and reports, they conflated these two concepts into the single term, "security."

To what extent were the organizers required to justify the "continual close surveillance" put in place for Montreal? How did implementation affect the Olympic spirit and the conduct of the Games? What was the legacy for the Olympic Movement and Canada? These are the questions I will address in this chapter. Worrall reports heavy-handed surveillance already at the 1976 Olympic Winter Games in Innsbruck.

> The usual security fences were constantly patrolled by visibly-armed police, often accompanied by menacing guard dogs. Motor vehicles entering the Village, even when bearing proper accreditation stickers, were thoroughly examined. This was the first time I had seen mirrors used to check underneath the vehicles for any hidden bombs or other devices. All accreditation badges and personal belongings were also examined and checked before you could enter the Village.... Although not as obvious, security was also provided for the IOC members and other Olympic Family people living outside the Village. (Worrall, 2000: 145)

I will argue that along with the equally heavy-handed surveillance of the Innsbruck Games five months previously, Montreal legitimized a much greater investment in surveillance at the Olympic Games. While the Games in Montreal were exuberantly joyous and intercultural, as much as any Games since World War II, the "security" arrangements confined the festival to certain areas of the city. The result was rewarding Games for those who were there but marginalization and exclusion for those who contested the Games and its leadership. I will also argue that the Montreal strategy was as much a response to domestic political issues – especially labor strife, political opposition, and the gay rights movement – as the threat of a repeat of the Munich tragedy. Like many other aspects of the Montreal legacy, the impact of the security arrangements was therefore multifaceted: while they upped the ante for Olympic surveillance and strengthened the expertise of the security state, they also contributed, even if unintentionally, to its increased public scrutiny and new human rights protections for gays and lesbians.

My perspective is that of a critical insider. I have been involved in the Olympic Movement all my life, as an athlete, coach, artist, educator and member of the National Olympic Committee. In 1976, I was coauthor of *The Athletes' Show*, a play about Canadian athletes in the Olympic sports that was performed by Theatre Passe Muraille in the Olympic Village; the coordinator of the Artists-Athletes Olympic poster project; and I covered the Games as a journalist. I had two official accreditations and a parking space in the village. The army changed its patrols outside our theatre tent, and I had to navigate the various checkpoints every day. Doug Booth (2004: 22) has called me a "partisan eye-witness." I remember those Games fondly but full of contradiction, and I have watched those contradictions unfold ever since (Kidd, 2004).

The plan

Montreal promised "modest Games" that would create an exemplary experience for the athletes "by giving a distinctly human dimension to this great festival *where the amateur spirit counters that of materialism.*"[6] "Security" was to be at a minimum; in fact, the original design for the Olympic Village suggested that it would be fenceless.[7] But all that changed with the invasion of the Olympic Village in Munich in 1972 by eight Palestinian Black September Organization terrorists and their seizure of 11 Israeli athletes – with the murder of two, and the eventual deaths of the remaining nine Israeli hostages, five of the eight terrorists, and one policeman in a shootout at the Munich airport. The three-person team of Canadian military and police officers responsible for planning security for Montreal were in Munich at the time of the massacre. They also visited sporting events held in Mexico, Tehran and Innsbruck. They concluded from these experiences that the relatively relaxed security of Munich had given the terrorists opportunity. According to a subsequent presentation by Quebec Justice Minister Jérôme Choquette to the Quebec legislature, Munich officials had kept security hidden because of an "anti-military and anti-police psychosis stemming from the Nazi experience.... But they later regretted it. That move probably opened the door, at least the psychological door to the terrorists who committed the well-known raid." The Montreal planners also concluded that relying solely upon the various police forces in the jurisdictions that would host the Games would be inadequate, and Canadian Armed Forces participation would be essential. They recommended that "as far as the physical presence of security forces is concerned, a conspicuous, uniformed presence was the best means of prevention." While they cautioned that the "security measures must be shrouded in the greatest secrecy to be effective," they recommended that "the whole world had to be advised through the media that security measures were properly planned and well in hand." Doing his part, Choquette told the Quebec legislature 14 months before the Games that "the army's presence will be obvious, there'll be soldiers or policemen present in many places."[8]

Previous Canadian joint efforts involving different police forces and the army, such as the emergency surveillance deployed during the 1970 October Crisis when the Front de Libération de Québec kidnapped a British consul and a Quebec cabinet minister, had almost foundered on poor coordination, so the planners made an integrated command the priority. Early in 1973, the federal government and the Organizing Committee jointly established the Chief Committee on Public Safety for the Olympic Games. It was chaired by an assistant director of the Montreal police, with membership from the various police departments and the Canadian Armed Forces, plus 13 broadly representative subcommittees, including one for public relations. This was the working organization. The Chief Committee reported to an advisory committee of police department directors (the Security Forces' Directors' Committee) and a decision-making committee (the Superior Committee on Olympic Security) of senior representatives of the federal, Quebec, Ontario and Montreal governments and the Organizing Committee. The Chief Committee not only achieved coordinated planning but also gave priority to the development of specialized weapons units, such as the Tactical and Reserve Units created by the Ontario Provincial Policy, and training. The lead time it enjoyed enabled it to stage several simulation exercises in the spring of 1976 with a focus on intergovernment and interagency partnership on the ground. The result was "hitherto unforeseen areas of communication and cooperation between policy and military personnel," in the words of the Official Report.[9]

To anticipate, investigate and prevent a threat from outside Canada's borders, in 1973 the Royal Canadian Mounted Police Security Service established a special group known as the International Terrorist Guerrilla Section. The Section strengthened communication with foreign intelligence services and closely monitored the activities of foreign embassies and Canadian groups who were thought to be subversive, increasing electronic and physical surveillance, mail openings, the infiltration of meetings and the recruitment of "informants." These relations were formalized in 1974 when Canada signed the United National Convention on the Prevention and Punishment of Crimes against Internationally Protected Persons, including Diplomatic Agents. [10] To strengthen border security, in 1976 the federal government passed the Temporary Immigration Security Act to give Minister of Manpower and Immigration Robert Andras the power to deport

> any person who is not a Canadian citizen and not lawfully admitted to Canada for permanent residence and who, in his opinion, is likely to engage in acts of violence that would or might endanger the lives or safety of persons in Canada or in other violent criminal activity if admitted to Canada or permitted to remain there.[11]

The Act removed the right to an appeal hearing – with the right to hear and challenge the evidence used against one – to anyone about to be deported. The government kept it in effect until the end of 1976, in part to have it for the first United Nations Habitat conference that was held in Vancouver later that year, and in part to see whether it should be enacted permanently. According to Minister Andras, "in the case of suspected terrorists...it is often impossible to meet such evidentiary requirements since the information available to me and my department is obtained from sensitive or protected sources which, frankly, cannot be revealed at an inquiry hearing." Andras said that the legislation was intended to block "dangerous aliens," who might target the Games, the Canadian government and/or representatives of other governments or countries attending the Games. [12] With these preparations, the budget grew apace. While a mere $500,000 was identified for security in 1973, the ultimate cost was estimated to be $100 million, with many additional expenditures assumed by the contributing agencies.[13] The Organizing Committee and the Canadian government jealously guarded their responsibilities for security. Reports in the International Organizing Committee Executive Board Minutes are terse, with President Killanin repeatedly "pointing out that security is the responsibility of the Canadian Government."[14]

The justification for intensified surveillance

Were these measures warranted by the circumstances? Were the organizers ever pressed to justify them? The attack on the Israeli athletes in Munich had been condemned around the world, even in the Arab/Muslim world, providing some hope that it would not be repeated. In fact, former Canadian diplomat Eric Morse, who was responsible for sport in the Department of External Affairs at the time, has suggested that the attack on "an event that was and still is a 'sacred ceremony' not only for the West but for almost everyone else on Earth" led to an unofficial "Olympic truce," a "silent consensus" that the Olympic Games and other major sports events would not be attacked. According to Morse, this tacit understanding prefigured the official Olympic Truce established by the International Organizing Committee and United Nations during the 1990s. The "silent consensus" lasted for 37 years, until the assault on the Sri Lankan cricket team in Lahore in 2009.[15] Morse's observations come in hindsight. In the buildup to Montreal, there could be no such confidence. In the early 1970s, the use of terrorism to bring about political change and even to bring down the entire system of democratic government was on the rise. In Ireland and Britain, the Provisional Irish Republican Army assassinated politicians and bombed, shot and maimed soldiers and civilians in an effort to win Irish unification. In Spain, radical Basque nationalists (the Euzkadi Ta Askatasuna) did much the same in the interests of Basque independence. In Germany, the Red Army Faction led by Andreas Baader and Ulrike Meinhof, bombed military installations, assassinated soldiers, police, and corporate executives, robbed banks, and kidnapped politicians in an effort to completely dismantle the federal government. According to Tony Judt (2005), similar groups operated in Italy (Red Brigades), the United States (Weather Underground), Japan (Japanese Red Army), and South America (Tupamaros).[16] The Red Army Faction had been trained by Palestinian guerrillas and had provided local assistance to the Black September group in their assault on the Israeli athletes in Munich. Would it, or one of the other groups like it, decide to make another attack in Montreal? There were certainly newspaper reports of potential international threats to Canada and the Games, although the government was quick to dismiss them.[17] There were at least two staff members of foreign embassies, including the Soviet Olympic attaché, who were expelled for what the government considered improper activities in the buildup to the Games.[18] The international situation remained uncertain, especially after the 1973 Yom Kippur War in which Israel retained the territory it had won six years previously against a coalition of Arab armies led by Egypt and Syria. The Yom Kippur War precipitated the Arab oil embargo, more than doubling the cost of oil in Western countries.

The situation in Montreal was almost as volatile. During the 1960s, Quebec society was transformed by a broad state-led secularization and modernization often referred to as the "Quiet Revolution." Seeking to be *maître chez nous*, French-speaking Quebeckers, who comprised 80% of the provincial population, aggressively challenged the Anglo-Canadian elite's economic and cultural hegemony, particularly the expectation that everyone speak English in the workplace and commerce. Though united in the desire for language rights and cultural recognition, French-Canadians were divided about the best strategy to realize their interests. Quebec nationalists sought French unilingualism and even greater powers for the provincial legislature – their *assembleé nationale* in Quebec City. Some even called for complete

Quebec independence. Fiercely opposing separatism were federalists like Pierre Trudeau, who became Canada's prime minister in 1968. Trudeau sought to advance francophones' interests through a greater presence in the federal government; he championed a bilingual pan-Canadianism. There were many gradations of these positions across the political spectrum. Many, like Montreal's astute and charismatic Mayor Jean Drapeau, the driving force behind the 1976 Olympic Games, incessantly lobbied both levels of governments and tailored his appeals accordingly. A federalist, Drapeau sought to celebrate *la survivance*, the will of French Canada to survive two centuries of English-Canadian attempts at assimilation, with the Games. The largest and most visible English-Canadian presence was in Montreal, where Anglophones made up just 16% of the population (French-speakers comprised 64%; those from other backgrounds, 20%), but dominated business and cultural life, including sport. Prior to the 1976 Olympic Games, French-speaking Quebeckers made up less than 2% of Canadian Olympic and other representative teams, although they comprised almost a quarter of the Canadian population. They were even less represented in positions of leadership (Boileau, Landry, and Trempe, 1976). Montreal was the site of the fiercest debates about the national question, the most boisterous demonstrations for and against language laws, and a small but growing number of bombing attacks against federal institutions and English-Canadian corporations by self-styled Quebec revolutionaries.

In October 1970, the Front de Libération de Québec kidnapped the British consul and murdered the Quebec labor minister. There were concerns that outside interests, especially the Palestinian Liberation Organization, Algeria and France were involved. Fearing "a state of apprehended insurrection," Drapeau and Quebec Premier Robert Bourassa persuaded Trudeau to invoke the War Measures Act and mobilize the army to protect public buildings and politicians. Therefore, 10,000 soldiers drawn from units from across Canada were deployed. Although the nature and extent of operations remain classified, the army raided the Front de Libération de Québec training camp and "on at least five and possibly eight occasions, security forces prevented le Front de Libération de Québec cells from conducting violent acts."[19] Police were given arbitrary powers, and in Montreal they arrested and detained without bail 497 persons, many of whom were Drapeau's political opponents. All but 62 of them were later released without charges. It was the only time in Canadian history that the War Measures Act was used to deal with a domestic crisis.

The military intervention was welcomed by the overwhelming majority in both French- and English-speaking Canada. In fact, polls suggest it was one of the most popular government actions in Canadian history (Bothwell et al., 1981). Yet it did little to dampen the flames of Quebec nationalism and militant activism. On the contrary, support for the separatist movement and the Parti Quebecois continued to grow and organized labor increasingly took to the streets in strikes and mobilizations. In 1971, a five-month lockout of typesetters at Montreal newspaper *La Presse*, with strong nationalist overtones, pushed the three provincial trade union centrals – the Confederation of National Trade Unions, the Quebec Federation of Labor, and the Quebec Teachers' Corporation – to join together in what became known as the Common Front. In part, they wanted to bring their members the new benefits that the Quiet Revolution had brought the middle class. They also sought to protect them from the economic downturn of the early 1970s, especially the spiral of high inflation and low growth ("stagflation") that pushed governments into ever greater debt, with serious long-term consequences for public spending. In 1972, the Common Front led a prov-ince-wide general strike that brought government and business activities to a halt. Radio stations were seized, factories were occupied, and entire towns were brought under workers' control. The strike was only ended by provincial legislation. When the Quebec government then jailed the three leaders of the Common Front, the walkouts resumed spontaneously. It was only when the three leaders were released from jail that workers return to work (Drache, 1972).[20]

Under these circumstances, the Olympic organizers were never really called upon to justify the plan for increased surveillance – the need to avoid a repeat of Munich and the Front de Libération de Québec kidnappings were taken for granted by insiders and outsiders alike. As one opposition spokes-person said in the House of Commons, "all agreed that every precaution must be taken and no effort spared to prevent an incident such as that which occurred at the 1972 Olympics in Munich."[21] I had spoken out against the invocation of the War Measures Act and was a vocal critic of many aspects of the Olympic preparations, but in reviewing what I wrote in those years and the (primarily English-language) clipping files I kept, I am struck by how little opposition was expressed to the idea of increased surveillance. In part, the details were never announced in advance. In part, there were many other Games-related issues to discuss – the tremendous delays in construc-tion, the frequent reports of corruption, the environmental and poverty protests, the escalating expenses. To be sure, concern was expressed about the potential for abuses – one opposition member of Parliament even asked the Solicitor General "to see that his security people do not trespass on the rights of decent Canadians because they happen to be related to people from the Arab world."[22] But in the wake of Munich and similar acts of terrorism around the world, there was a widespread consensus that effective protec-tion for athletes, dignitaries and visitors was in order. The only outright opposition came from the militant left.[23]

The international and Canadian crises strongly influenced the prepa-rations for Olympic surveillance. It was during the War Measures Act, for example, that the various forces realized the necessity of careful planning and an integrated, coordinated command.[24] The spirit of the Common Front inflamed labor relations for years to come and enormously complicated the construction of the Olympic facilities. In 1975, for example, a province-wide strike by construction workers stopped all work on Olympic facilities, with labor leader Louis Laberge suggesting that the Games could be postponed to 1977, causing enormous panic among Olympic authorities.[25] According to the terms of reference of the Chief Committee on Public Safety for the Olympic Games, the protection of construction sites was one of its responsibilities.[26]

The "cleanup" in Montreal

In his response to the 1975 construction strike, Quebec Premier Bourassa said that the preservation of the social order was more important than any single event, even the Olympic Games.[27] In fact, throughout the 1970s, this spirit led many governments in Canada to step up their regulation of political activity and their police surveillance of individuals and groups they feared or opposed; and in some cases, police forces did it for them without authorization.[28] In Montreal, the Drapeau-led city council and the municipal police used every opportunity to stifle debate and protest. In 1967, the city had passed a by-law requiring anyone who wished to parade or demonstrate to obtain a police permit. When the courts declared the by-law ultra vires, Drapeau refused to repeal it. Then in 1971, in the midst of the lockout at *La Presse*, the city banned pickets and protests within 50 blocks of the plant. When 15,000 supporters of the lockout workers showed up in solidarity, the police charged and clubbed everyone they could catch. One woman died in the fighting and more than 100 were injured. Nor did Drapeau allow any public consultation on the plans for the Games and their implications for the city. The details were simply announced. When an environmental group, Espaces Verts – supported by the city's director of planning, the Quebec minister of the environment, and a petition with 22,000 signatures – objected to the plan to build the Olympic Village on a public park, the mayor forced through the decision and publicly humiliated those who opposed him (auf der Maur, 1976: 28, 69–75; McKenna and Purcell, 1980).

Other groups that were targeted were gays and lesbians, social activists, and critical artists. While Montreal had a discreet gay quarter from at least the 1920s, the quiet toleration that the police had long extended began to break down in the early 1970s when gays became more politically active through groups, such as the Front de libération des homosexuels, and conservative groups called for moral cleansing. In 1975 and the early months of 1976, gay and lesbian bars, bathhouses and washrooms in Montreal (and one in Ottawa) were repeatedly raided, in some cases with police wielding axes and machine guns. Although homosexuality had been legalized by Prime Minister Trudeau in 1969, patrons were photographed, charged as "found ins" under the "bawdy house" and "acts of indecency" provisions of the Criminal Code, and their names were reported to the media; as further intimidation, membership lists were seized. For a short period in May–June 1976, all of the gay bathhouses in Montreal were closed. The Royal Canadian Mounted Police began to collect information about gay activist groups across Canada (Kinsman and Gentile, 2010: 310–317). Simultaneously, as political friends told me at the time, police visited activists at their places of work and homes, and they were told to "get out of town." Most took the advice and made other plans for the summer. The "cleanup" even extended to the official Arts and Culture Program. Four days before the opening ceremonies, shortly after midnight, work crews dismantled and destroyed Corridart, a 20-installation outdoor art and photographic exhibit along nine kilometers of a major thoroughfare (and the marathon route) that was mildly critical of the city's wholesale demolition of single-family housing, including a number of grand 19th-century mansions, to clear the way for high-rise apartments and commercial offices. According to the city, Corridart was "a dangerous demonstration which threatened public safety" (Jule, 1997: 179–180; van Toorn, 2008: 22–23). The destruction of the exhibit underscored the mayor's dictatorial style and his antagonism to conservationists, environmentalists, antipoverty activists, and advocates of alternative public investments.

A joyous Olympic Games

There were no terrorist attacks and very few "problem areas," as the Official Report for the Games referred to them, in Montreal. Three "breaches of security" were reported – a Canadian athlete smuggled a friend into the Olympic Village, a journalist succeeded in meeting the Queen, and a spectator jumped over the barrier, all of which may well have been minimized or even dismissed at other Games. No doubt there were others: a streaker evaded security to join the dancers during the Closing Ceremony. Although 700 scalpers were apprehended, arrests as a whole dropped by 20% during the period of the Games. Nevertheless, a number of Olympic participants were troubled by the heavy-handed display. Monique Berlioux, the International Olympic Committee's senior staff person at the time, complained that "the traditional spirit of gaiety had been muted by thousands of armed soldiers, plus extraordinary security precautions at the Olympic Committee's headquarters in the Queen Elizabeth Hotel" (Lukas, 1980: 225). Lord Killanin (1983: 127) "agreed with much of what she said (but) her timing was inappropriate." The American 800-meter runner Mark Enyeart complained to *Track and Field News*: "I got tired of being hassled about wearing my ID on the outside of my shirt and being checked every five steps to see if I was really who it said. I doubt that the security could have protected themselves, much less us."[29]

Many others, including this writer, experienced the 1976 Olympic Games in Montreal as remarkably festive and intercultural, much as the organizers had hoped. While the Olympic Village, the transportation corridors, and competition sites were closely and visibly guarded, the open plazas of the vast Olympic Park – the location for 12 sports plus the opening and closing ceremonies – were sites of extraordinary interchange among participants and spectators from all countries and cultures. According to anthropologist John MacAloon (1989: 6–23):

> There were streams of fans, domestic and foreign, bartering for tickets, killing time between events inside one of the venues around them, lingering after a sports event had concluded. They paused seriatim to focus around performers of many types – musicians, dancers, jugglers, clowns, religious proselytizers, political leafletters, soapbox orators, pin traders, commercial vendors authorized and outlaw, uniformed COJO workers taking a break from their routines of ushering and ticket-taking, the occasional media unit (usually uncredentialled), and athletes saun-tering on their way to and from the Village or practice fields. Exchange is the idiom of festival. Exchanged above all in this daily free-form performance were looks and conversation. Paradoxically, although nothing was planned and one never knew what or whom one might see, it was here that one could count on a central part of the Olympic experience.

Once an athlete, coach or official left the village or the protected area of a venue s/he was free to mingle, and many did. In addition, the Métro and the many entertainment quarters in the city were alive with the same spirit, and here, security was participatory. In one of my favorite memories, one early morning on St. Catherine's Street I encountered a wildly celebra-tory German Oom-pah band, followed by a snake line of revelers, that was being led by a young police officer into a police station, apparently to arrest them for making too much noise. The sergeant on desk simply told him to forget it, and the entire line marched into the station and out again. By the second week, as the accompanying drawing illustrates, many of the security personnel were able to breath a little easier.

MacAloon (1989) has attributed Montreal's spirit to the city's French and Catholic character, its rich festival tradition, and the genius of Olympic Park, including "a sufficiency of eating and drinking establishments all clustered around a central plaza (that) ensured a continuous flow of crowds." It was enabled by fine weather, faultless organization, courteous

Figure 7.2 Bored security by Aislin, 1976 (reprinted with permission of Terry Mosher)

and enthusiastic volunteers, and superb performances. After the delays, scandals, and departures – 24 African, Asian, and Caribbean teams withdrew from the Games to protest the International Olympic Committee's seeming indifference to the New Zealand rugby tour of apartheid South Africa – as illustrated above in Figure 7.2, the Games went off without a hitch. By the closing ceremonies, as another one of Aislin's famous cartoons illustrates (Figure 7.3), the security even became a source of humor.

Figure 7.3 Podium security by Aislin, 1976

The legacy

The 1976 Olympic Games in Montreal were watershed Games. Although it was not appreciated at the time, the Organizing Committee developed many new sources of revenue, including much more ambitious sponsorship agreements; the Games actually generated a surplus on operations, convincing the International Olympic Committee to separate the capital budget from the official accounts for future Games, and placing the responsibility for facilities and infrastructure much more squarely on the hosting authorities. The Games demonstrated the wisdom of the new eligibility rules – and the new events for women; they showcased the dazzling new generation of female stars that the advocacy of second-wave feminism enabled. Thanks to an advance in pharmaceutical analysis in 1974 – the methodology to test for anabolic steroids – the 1976 Games also constituted an intensification of the other form of surveillance now commonplace in modern sports: biomedical testing for banned substances. There were 2001 tests in the new International Olympic Committee–accredited lab in Montreal, 269 in swimming, 257 in athletics. As a result, eight athletes were disqualified from the Games, including three medalists.[30]

The African boycott and the refusal to require the National Olympic Committee from the Republic of China (Taiwan) to compete as Taiwan, rather than the Republic of China, which in turn led to the Republic of China's boycott of the Games, caused much bitterness within the International Olympic Committee and many Western governments. These events, however, ultimately turned the International Olympic Committee toward full support of the African-led campaign against apartheid sport and the admission of the People's Republic of China (China). Both policies significantly enhanced the Games' legitimacy within the Two-Thirds World.[31] The politics of Montreal mentored a new generation of leadership as well. Juan Antonio Samaranch had a firsthand vantage point on the complexities of hosting and international sport in the years leading up to the Games as a member of the International Olympic Committee Executive Board, while Richard Pound (see Chapter 2 of this book) cut his teeth as a rising leader of the Canadian Olympic Association. Pound became the Canadian Olympic Association's president in 1977 and an International Olympic Committee member in 1978.

The physical and electronic surveillance put in place for the 1976 Olympic Games in Montreal (and the Olympic Winter Games in Innsbruck previously that year) changed international sport forever. As Jim Worrall, the Canadian member of the International Olympic Committee Executive Board at the time, observes in his memoirs, "the security measures (are) commonplace to the IOC now, but a big change back then" (Worrall, 2000: 154). While soldiers were present at earlier Olympic Games – I distinctly remember the Japanese forces policing the Closing Ceremony at the 1964 Games, as discussed by Christian Tagsold in Chapter 3 of this book – lest athletes conduct a spontaneous celebration the way we had at the British Empire and Commonwealth Games in Perth two years earlier, they had never been so numerous or so visible. Innsbruck and Montreal initiated the use of acoustic, closed circuit television and other means of electronic surveillance; the securing of transportation hubs and athletes' and dignitaries' travel between sites; the enhancement of accreditation requirements, including the accreditation of site workers; and the establishment of integrated command and communication structures. Future Olympic hosts would continue to perfect these measures (Fussey, 2011: 96–97). But while insiders like Worrall (2000: 154) reported that they "never felt so safe," the surveillance had the effect of legitimizing, without full public debate, a radical new level of social monitoring, while strengthening the hands of those who, like mayor Drapeau, sought to take advantage of potential threats to silence critics and harm those they disapproved. It is telling that even some of the police establishment worried that their new powers, and the tremendous funds required, were too much to justify. In its final report on Olympic activities, the Ontario Provincial Police concluded, "the extent and cost of security operations for the Olympic Games bring into doubt whether or not there will be Games in the future."[32]

But in the aftermath of the Games, as details about the abuses committed by police forces emerged, and people had further opportunity to reflect upon the arbitrary powers obtained for surveillance, discussion of the Olympic experience contributed to several efforts to strengthen civil rights. In parliament, the opposition parties returned to their concerns about the arbitrary, subjective power given immigration officers to turn away visitors without review or appeal, expressed during the debates on the Temporary Immigration Security Act. Despite the government's original intention to abolish the right to appeal deportation permanently, when a new Immigration Act was introduced later in 1976, the opposition parties prevailed and that right was restored. In 1977, in response to allegations that the Royal Canadian Mounted

Police had frequently broken the law in its surveillance of political and social activists, the federal government was forced to appoint a royal commission to investigate. The Inquiry into Certain Activities of the Royal Canadian Mounted Police (known as the McDonald Commission after the chair, David McDonald) did in fact find that the police had acted illegally on numerous occasions, especially in its surveillance and interference with political activists, including one case relating to the 1976 Olympic Games. The commission recommended that police be held accountable for strict compliance with the law and that the Royal Canadian Mounted Police be stripped of the responsibility for security. The government quickly acted upon these recommendations, and a new civilian security agency, the Canadian Security Intelligence Service, was established in 1984.

Perhaps the most encouraging example of successful pushback against the arbitrary and discriminatory aspects of Olympic surveillance came from organized gays and lesbians. In response to the various raids in 1975 and early 1976, the communities formed a Gay Coalition against Repression, bringing together Francophone and Anglophone gays and lesbians, with links to the left and feminist movements. On June 1976, more than 300 gays, lesbians and supporters marched through the streets of Montreal chanting "Down with police repression." The immediate effect was to end the closure of gay bars and bathhouses, and build a movement that would stand up against future raids. It also led to the formation of the L'association pour les droits de gai(e)s du Québec (the Association for the Rights of Gays and Lesbians in Quebec), which successfully lobbied for the inclusion of protection for sexual orientation in the provincial Charter of Rights and Liberties (Kinsman and Gentile, 2010: 313). The courage of Montreal gays and lesbians in 1976 has long been remembered within the Canadian Olympic community, inspiring the fight against homophobia in sport while reminding bid committees that Games surveillance must be consistent with civil and human rights. In one heartwarming outcome of these struggles, at the 2010 Olympic and Paralympic Winter Games, Pride Houses were established in Vancouver and Whistler – the first in Olympic history – to provide a welcoming space for lesbian, gay, bisexual, trans-identified/two-spirited sportspersons, communities and their allies; a place to celebrate diversity and accomplishments of these athletes, and a rallying point and resource for the ongoing struggle against homophobia and other abuses of human rights.[33]

Notes

I am extremely grateful for the research assistance and advice of Martha McIntosh and Melanie Belore and the helpful comments of Vida Bajc.

1. Olympic Games Organizing Committee, "Accreditation", The Official Report of the XXIst Olympiad Montreal 1976 (Montreal: OCOG, 1976), 532–541.

2. These details are drawn from OCOG, "Security", The Official Report, 556–571; Martha McIntosh, "Security Measures at the Summer Olympics," unpublished paper, School of Physical and Health Education, University of Toronto, 1986; and International Olympic Committee, Minutes of the 78th Session, Montreal, October 4–6, 1975, 23.

3. For the first episode, see Willi Daume's complaint, IOC, EB Minutes (July 24, 1976): 50–52. Canadian IOC member James Worrall's (2000: 154) response was that the Germans were in the wrong and the "police had naturally met force with force." For the second incident, see letter from Erich Baumann, president of the AIPS Special Commission of Sports Photographers, to IOC President Killanin, August 31, 1976, Annex 11, Minutes of the IOC Executive Board, Barcelona, October 13–17, 1976.

4. Personal communications, summer of 1976. None of the activists I worked with in the years prior to the Games stayed in Montreal during the Games; they all feared that they would be arrested.

5. OCOG, "Security," 556–558; and Dennis Trudeau, "Army to be out in force for Games," *Montreal Gazette*, May 23, 1975.

6. City of Montreal, *Jeux Olympiques Olympic Games 1976* (Bid Book), 1969, 43. Italics in original.

7. Neil Amdur, "Growth of politics in future games seen," *New York Times*, September 7, 1972.

8. Trudeau, "Army to be out in force for Games"; and OCOG, "Security," 556.

9. OCOG, "The 1976 Summer Olympics Public Safety Objectives and Terms of Reference Project 063", February 6, 1975; OCOG, "Security"; Sean Maloney, "Homeland Defence," DLSC Research Note 01/02, Directorate Land Strategic Concepts, Department of National Defence, January 2001, Kingston Ontario, 28–34. See also King, 1997: 60.

10. Canada, *Royal Commission of Inquiry into Certain Activities of the RCMP* (MacDonald Commission), vol. 1, 1981, 67; and vol. 3, 1981, 329–330.

11. Canada, "Bill C-85," House of Commons Bills, 30th Parliament, 1974–1976.

12. Canada, House of Commons Debates, 1st Session, 30th Parliament, Vol. XIII, February 26, 1976, 11282.

13. Glen Clark, "Olympic security: a $100 million task," *New York Times Magazine*, June 6, 1976, 72.

14. IOC Executive Board Minutes, Montreal, July 1976, 33.

15. Eric Morse, "Sport's truce with terror is over," *Globe and Mail*, March 9, 2009; and personal communication, July 27, 2011.

16. These groups are all cited in the *Inquiry into Certain Activities of the RCMP* as concerns of the RCMP Security Service, vol. 1, 268.

17. For example, see the exchange between Gerard Laprise and Solicitor General Warren Allmand in the House of Commons on May 18, 1976, *House of Commons Debates*, 13613–13614.

18. For the Soviet attaché, see Doug Gilbert, "'Miffed by spying reports, Gresko vows he'll return'", *Montreal Gazette*, June 14, 1975; for the other, see MacDonald Commission, vol. 3, p. 330.

19. Maloney, "'Homeland Defence'", pp. 31–31.

20. Gruneau and Neubauer (forthcoming) argue that the breakdown of the post–WWII Keynesian compromise, the Arab oil embargo and the resulting "'stagflation'" contributed significantly to Montreal's financial problems.

21. Jake Epp, *House of Commons Debates*, February 26, 1976, 11282–11283. Epp was a Conservative. The New Democratic Party's Andrew Brewin said exactly the same, 11283.
22. The request was made by Heath Macquarrie, *House of Commons Debates*, November 6, 1975, 8940–8942.
23. For example, "Against Capital's Games," *The Old Mole*, July 1976, 5.
24. Maloney, "Homeland Defence," 30–31.
25. In the end, the workers agreed to return to the Olympic sites, but not without a flurry of political activity on both sides of the Atlantic. See IOC Executive Board Minutes, Rome and Lausanne, May 14–16, 19, and 23, 1975. See also Killanin (1983) and Worrall (2000: 140–142).
26. OCOG, "The 1976 Summer Olympics Public Safety Objectives and Terms of Reference," 3.
27. Dennis Trudeau and Dave Thomas, "Bourassa would sacrifice Games," *Montreal Gazette*, May 14, 1975.
28. Royal Commission of Inquiry into Certain Activities of the RCMP, throughout.
29. "Olympic Team Poll," *Track and Field News*, March 1977, 41.
30. OCOG, The Official Report, 455.
31. Following Esteva and Prakesh (1998), I use the terms "Two-Thirds World" and "One-Third World" to represent the social majorities and minorities, while attempting to remove geographical and ideological binaries in such terms as Global North/Global South.
32. Ontario Provincial Police, *Olympic Security 1976* (Toronto: OPP, 1977), 32.
33. Jennifer Birch Jones, *Pride House Legacy Report.* Vancouver: Pride House Steering Committee, November 2010.

8
"To Guarantee Security and Protect Social Order" (Moscow 1980)

Carol Marmor-Drews

According to the Soviet Deputy Minister of Interior Affairs B.T. Shumilin at a meeting in December 1979, the Soviet leadership saw the 1980 Summer Olympic Games in Moscow as not only a unique opportunity but also a huge responsibility: "For the first time in the history of the Olympic Movement, the Games are taking place in a socialist country, a country which advocates the strengthening of security of nations, facilitates a wide international cooperation, and is unshakable...in its implementation of Leninist world politics of peace."[1] During the Cold War, international sport was one of the areas where the East and the West would seek to demonstrate to each other the superiority of their respective political systems. Interestingly, however, Robert Edelman (2006) notes that, during the pre-Olympic period, the theme of the Cold War was largely absent from the Soviet discourses. The Olympics were already popular in the Soviet Union by 1952, following the first successes of the Soviet athletes in Helsinki. To the Soviet sport leaders at the time, the Olympics would be an opportunity to leave the international isolation of the Stalinist period behind and present to the world the new Soviet leadership as peaceful and progressive (Prozumenshchikov, 2004: 191).

The Soviet Union saw the awarding of the Olympics to Moscow as an acknowledgment of its peaceful foreign policy. This long-awaited international approval made it possible for the Union of Soviet Socialist Republics to present itself to the world as a nation of venerable culture and heritage and a comfortable standard of living (Edelman, 2006: 150). The XXII Olympiad would present Moscow as an exemplary capital city [2] with modern facilities and a superb infrastructure,[3] "the culture and professionalism of the Soviet Police, the successes of our government in providing reliable legal security,"[4] as well as "the Soviet way of life, our socialist democracy, political and ideological unity of the Soviet society, our discipline, the high moral nature of the Soviet people, our hospitality, internationalism, and friendliness."[5]

Underlying this eagerness on the part of the Soviet leadership to present to the world an image of its own making was an astute awareness that the live televising of the Games to an unprecedented number of viewers at home as well as worldwide would put the Olympic hosts under intense international scrutiny:

> All of us must keep in mind that during the Olympic Games the work of the police and the Ministry of the Interior Affairs will be closely watched – not only domestically but by people from almost every country in the world. Through the help of television this will be an audience of two billion people. Any mishaps and any mistakes, including in the handling of security and social order, will be witnessed by the entire world.[6]

The organizers were well aware that to be able to show that the Soviet Union was, at the same time, a nation with its own distinctive political culture and national heritage yet also a modern state much like those in the West, it was necessary to demonstrate that the Soviet Union was capable of organizing the Games according to Western expectations and following Western standards.[7] Managing the projected unprecedented influx of visitors was a challenge.[8] The Soviet Union at the time was a relatively closed society, more accustomed to hosting small, controlled delegations than to accommodating many large tourist groups simultaneously (Parks, 2009: 274–275). The visitors coming to enjoy the Olympics would demand accommodations with amenities they expected and commodities from their home environments they took for granted. Parks (2009: 279) reports, for instance, that in 1975, Moscow only had 42,000 beds available for international and domestic tourists. To put this in perspective, some 150,000 foreign and 100,000 domestic tourists were originally expected to attend the Games.[9] Western consumer goods, from Pepsi-Cola to Camel cigarettes, were put on the shelves to help create aesthetics of "normality" in the Western sense.

At the meeting in Vienna in 1974, the International Olympic Committee insisted that those who attended the Moscow Olympics be able to move freely within as well as between the host cities (Parks, 2009: 257). For a country with a particular residential policy and a limited contact between locals and foreigners, both discussed in more detail below, this represented another kind of challenge. The Games were organized in five cities, located in four different republics: Moscow and Leningrad in Russia, Kiev in Ukraine, Minsk in Belorussia, and Tallinn in Estonia. The air distance between Leningrad (today St. Petersburg) to the north and Kiev to the south is about 740 miles or 1200 kilometers, while Moscow to the East and Minsk to the West are about 430 miles (700 km) apart. The decision about this geographical layout of the venues may have reflected the effort to demonstrate diversity of the multinational state and equality and unity among the Soviet Socialist Republics, considered to be "the brotherly family of the Soviet peoples."[10] All five cities were open to international and domestic tourism. Most of the competitions took place in Moscow, a city of over eight million people. The Olympic Sailing Regatta was organized in Tallinn, a city of 450,000 people, and the preliminary matches of the Olympic football tournament took place in Leningrad with over four million, Kiev with over two million, and Minsk with 1,309,000 inhabitants (Stuart, 1984: 28). The Olympic Flame had to pass 1500 miles (2300 km) from the Moldavian Republic across Ukraine to Moscow. Comparing these numbers and distances with those of the previous Games discussed in this book, the 1980 Moscow Olympics were a formidable undertaking.

Given this ambition to have an exemplary Olympics, the organizers were very sensitive to Western perceptions of their efforts. The highly respected German magazine, *Der Spiegel*, in its June 1979 issue criticized the preparation process for the Games – which were scheduled to take place in July 1980, 13 months later – stating that the Soviets had still not managed to build the needed facilities, particularly the hotels and the catering establishment.[11] Such negative commentaries by Western media were considered alarming and a potential threat to security of the Games.[12] By July 1979, the Committee for State Security (also known as the KGB) became concerned that Western media outlets may actually have been giving their journalists instructions to focus their reporting on "the shortcomings in the Soviet economy, trade, service, and preparations for the Olympics."[13] Such reactions to perceptions of the West seem to be consistent with the early 1960s policy that saw the fight against Western actions aimed at weakening the influence of the Soviet ideology as a priority (Hilger, 2009: 105). Indeed, as I demonstrate below, correspondence between the Committee for State Security and the Central Committee of the Communist Party of the Soviet Union suggests that perceptions of threats to security of the Moscow Olympics were based on the Cold War confrontation between communist and capitalist values.

The two main bodies responsible for facilitating the movement of people and ensuring security of the Games were the Ministry of Interior Affairs and the Committee for State Security.[14] In both institutions, new departments were set up specifically for the organization of the Olympics. The Olympic department was founded within the Ministry of Interior Affairs in 1975 to manage the organizational aspects of the Games while another department was established within the Committee for State Security in 1977 with the purpose to "enforce field security operational measures to prevent clandestine activities by hostile elements during the preparations for and the course of the summer Olympics in Moscow."[15] Its tasks included the investigation of sabotage activities abroad and identification of links between these actions abroad and the opponents at home.[16] The Deputy Minister of Interior Affairs oversaw the entire preparation process,[17] and representatives from the Ministry of Interior Affairs and the Committee of State Security were involved in the process right from the start.

In this chapter, I reconstruct how the Ministry of Interior Affairs and the Committee for State Security understood threats to security and how they prepared for the Olympic Games. Focusing on cultural aspects that influenced their thinking about security, I demonstrate that the Soviet concept of *bezopasnost*, translated in today's language as "security," played a crucial role. To understand this framework of the Soviet conceptions of security, I examine surveillance practices, which emerged during the Stalinist and post-Stalinist years but were still in place during the time of the Olympics; namely, *propiska* (the registration system in urban centers), *profilaktika* (preventive measures to minimize social causes of crime),[18] *ochistka* (policies dealing with anti-social behavior), and *druzhina* (civil police). I suggest that these surveillance procedures, which were practiced intensively during the preparation for the Olympics, coupled with conceptions of *bezopasnost*, reflect not only Soviet cultural understandings of security but also ways in which the organizers and the security apparatus strove to meet the expectations of the West.

Accessibility of sources has been cited as the reason why scholars have paid little attention to the Moscow Olympics, and particularly to the specific institutions responsible for the organization and the security of the Games. In the Russian Federation, while the archives are to be opened after 30 years, there is a provision that allows for many documents to remain closed (see Knight, 1990). The correspondence about the Olympics between the Committee for State Security and the Central Committee of the Communist Party between 1978 and 1980 can be found on the website *The Soviet Archives*,[19] established in 1999. Documents presented in this archive were discovered and copied by a known Soviet dissident and later made available online.[20] The same records can also be found in the Fund 89 of the Russian Archive for Contemporary History. This archive also includes records of correspondence between the Committee for Physical Culture and Sport and the Central Committee of the Communist Party (Funds 4 and 5). I also make use of materials I have collected in the archives in Tallinn and Moscow, particularly files from the Estonian State Archive, including those of the City Government of Interior Affairs in Tallinn and the Ministry of Interior Affairs of the Estonian Soviet Republic where some preparations for the 1980 Olympics were conducted (Fund ERAF-17SM). These documents pertain to planning the Olympic Sailing Regatta and communication with the Ministry of Interior Affairs of the Soviet Union in Moscow. Another important source is the internal schooling materials of the Soviet Ministry of Interior Affairs for the Olympic security preparation in December 1979.[21]

Perceptions of threats to security

When the Soviet functionaries talked about security, they did not mean the everyday safety of its citizens, but rather their integration into the orders of the society and the state (Gestwa, 2011: 454). The Soviet society was in a process of perpetual transition, moving from socialism toward communism.

To reach this utopia, the population needed to overcome elements left over from the former capitalist order, such as religion, petit bourgeois mentality, and the prejudices of the former aristocratic value system.[22] The envisioned society of *developed socialism* was characterized by different values, specifically the spirit of collectivism, internationalism, and high social and moral ideals. According to Field (2007), the value of morality seems to have acquired a special status in the post-Stalinist years. As quoted in Anweiler (1976: 248), this understanding of morality is reflected in the 1971 speech by General Secretary Leonid Brezhnev: "The new face of the Soviet Man, his communist morality and his worldview will be shaped in a constant, uncompromising battle against the survivals of the past. There can be no victory of the communist morality without a decisive battle against its opposites, namely greed, corruption, idleness, slander, betrayal, drunkenness, and other similar behavior." This code of morality and behavior was supposed to govern all aspects of private life. It required political loyalty, hard work, collectivism, and proper behavior in everyday life. Convincing the Soviet people to act according to these ethical standards would ideally produce loyal, enthusiastic citizens, who would work voluntarily to fulfill these goals (Field, 2007: 12–13). At the same time, it was assumed that this morality would also prevent people from drifting into criminality.

The spheres of uncertainty in the Olympic project were identified according to the bureaucratic terminus "to guarantee security and protect social order."[23] The paradigm was a general expression in the language of the Soviet state institutions, describing measures against domestic and foreign enemies. The aim was to communicate that the Soviet Union should be aware of the dangers at home, such as crime and non-conformist ideas, and also be careful of non-domestic threats like international terrorism and ideological interference from abroad. Domestically, the goal was "to protect the social order" as envisioned through the moral code. Externally, the goal was "to guarantee security," which meant the integrity of this envisioned state. The entire territory of the Olympic cities was treated as one big security problem. In the case of the Moscow Olympics we do not find a discourse of separation. The geographical areas where the Olympics took place were not articulated as different from the rest of the city, separated through concrete blocks, walls, fences, checkpoints, and other tightly controlled barriers as observed by Bajc (2007b, 2011b) in her analysis of public events today. Rather, the Soviet security officers treated the entire metropolitan area as one single zone in which security was to be ensured.

Zero tolerance for crime

In order to purify a large geographical area from all possible internal and external threats, as a precondition, the Soviet authorities started to reduce the criminality. Crime was considered one of the relics of capitalism, and it was assumed that crime would disappear once its social causes were eliminated (see Kaiser, 1969: 1118). The state's understanding of morality helped to determine which behavior would be considered undesirable. According to the Soviet Criminal Law in 1975, persons refusing to work were "punished by deprivation of freedom for a term of one or two years or by corrective labor for the same term" (Feldbrugge et al., 1985: 555). These parameters defined the way the security apparatus decided who should be included or excluded from the Olympic festivities. Knight (1990: 325–332) tells us that the notion of *bezopasnost* included a fight against treason, espionage, terrorism, sabotage, and subversive acts as well as anti-Soviet agitation and propaganda. The Soviet security apparatus intended to counteract all these activities in the run-up to the Olympic Games. There is evidence that, for the duration of the Games, the Soviet security apparatus tried to eliminate crime completely.[24] The Soviet security establishments were obliged to battle all crime. Extremely low crime rates would have served as an exemplary self-presentation of the Soviet society to the world and would also function as evidence that public space had been purified of "undesirable behavior." Shelley (1984: 118) suggests that the Soviet police often left crimes unrecorded to exaggerate its success in controlling crime and solving criminal cases.

Increased efforts at crime prevention in all Olympic cities were supposed to ensure that there would be no unwanted incidents during the Games. Yet, the officials noticed that crime was increasing in the Olympic cities.[25] In Minsk and Tallinn, there was more crime committed by underage persons and the number of armed robberies and purposeful murders grew as well. As more tourists came into the country, incidents involving foreigners were also growing. In 1978, three Swedish tourists were killed and two citizens of the German Democratic Republic were violated in Moscow.[26] The authorities grew increasingly alarmed at a possibility that it might be problematic to guarantee security of foreign individuals and their property, not only in the Olympic cities but also in all regions of the country. In response, the security apparatus had to take more serious steps to improve its ability to prevent further crimes because "in some cities the implementation of measures... for the prevention of recidivist crime was still not adequate."[27] Self-evidently, the organizers could not allow similar incidents during the Olympic Games because "despite the fact that the overall crime was actually insignificant," any crime whatsoever committed during the Olympics would nevertheless cause "irreparable damage to the prestige of our country and to the honor and dignity of the Soviet citizens."[28] The Olympic cities were given the task to "strengthen social order, legislation, crime prevention, and crime investigation" through cooperation between multiple organizations, including "the Central Committee, the government, the Ministry of Interior Affairs, as well as the local party and civic organizations which have proven and continue to prove to be a big help for the Olympic cities, by providing them with assets such as the workforce, technology, and transport."[29]

Suspects of crime included particularly persons who were not officially inhabitants of the Olympic cities. The Soviet system controlled internal migration, particularly immigration to major urban centers, by implementing residential policies that required *propiska* (registration) at one's place of residence. Individuals who were born in a city, married a resident of the city, or were offered employment that included a residence permit were issued a document that established them as legal residents of a city.[30] As Shelley (1984: 114) reports, the majority of crimes had been committed by nonresidents, and so the image of newcomers, mostly rural immigrants without *propiska*, as potential criminals was widespread in the large urban centers. Therefore, the authorities concentrated their attention on this group: "Under the current circumstances, measures aimed at preventing and solving crimes committed by citizens from parts of the Soviet Union [other than the Olympic cities] and by persons without permanent residence and employment [in these cities] will be an important means of strengthening social order."[31] For these purposes, the Ministry of Interior Affairs developed a system to collect information about persons who did not possess a residency permit for Olympic cities: "Arrangements should be made for the exchange of information about persons intending to be in Moscow during the Games with the goal of violating the law. The measures for *ochistka* of the city from vagabonds and from arriving criminals should be pursued much more actively."[32]

The authorities reasoned that the inhabitants of a city were interested in its well-being and, therefore, would not take part in criminal activities. In contrast, *inogorodnie* (nonresidents) were thought to be more likely to commit crime because three out of four people persecuted for crimes were nonresidents.[33] The authorities found it particularly troubling that the number of crimes committed by nonresidents in Moscow was growing. For this reason, for the duration of the Olympic Games, the authorities put in place a policy of separation through which contact between individuals who could potentially commit crime and international visitors would be minimized.[34] Hilger (2009: 79–80) suggests that the policy of *profilaktika*, that is, of removing such individuals from the cities, had been in use as an alternative to arrest since the Stalin era. This policy was also meant to have a preventive and educational impact on those individuals who tended to drift into criminality.[35] Future crimes were to be prevented by prophylactic conversations and informal punishments to change the worldview of the citizens.

In the run-up to the Games, the Ministry of Interior Affairs organized a series of operations called *Profilaktika-80* to "discover and arrest vagabonds and persons without confirmed employment."[36] In the Estonian Republic, for example, there were three "specific prophylactic operations for the identification of…anti-social elements" in the period from June 24, 1980 to July 15, 1980. During each operation approximately 2500–3000 persons took part in raids, undertaken in apartments, cellars, buses, cars, bars, restaurants, and shops.[37] In most cases, the civilians underwent a thorough search. While the policemen were looking for 53 people who had previously committed a crime, they arrested altogether 2016 people for various reasons.[38] The surveillance mechanisms were meant to have a disciplinary effect with a positive impact on crime rates. On August 1, 1980, the police chief in Tallinn reported that the number of crimes, including juvenile delinquency, was reduced. At the same time, the rate of disclosure of crimes by residents was also reported to be improving.[39]

As told by the famous dissident Andrei Sakharov (1991: 603), by the beginning of 1980, the security apparatus received the authority to arrest dissidents, including members of Helsinki Watch groups in Moscow and in Ukraine, Christian activists, and Crimean Tatar leaders. In March 1980, the *New York Times* reported that Sakharov called for a withdrawal of the Soviet troops from Afghanistan,[40] and on the International Olympic Committee to "refuse to hold the Games in a country which is waging a war." Sakharov argued that the Olympics had a peace-supporting mission, which was itself based on an old Greek tradition to stop wars during the Games. For these reasons, preparations and staging of the Olympic Games was not the time when such activities could be tolerated. Dobrynin (2011: 513) explains that the authorities decided "Sakharov and his wife had turned into a constant focus of anti-Soviet campaigning abroad and therefore had to be deprived of all access to foreigners through the exile to a place closed to foreign reporters."

Fear of non-domestic terrorism

The Cold War United States were intensely unhappy about the fact that the Olympic Games were awarded to the Union of Soviet Socialist Republics. By 1978, a boycott campaign began to gain traction. When it became known that the Soviet authorities wanted to exclude from the Olympic Games representatives from "Radio Free Europe" and "Radio Liberty," both set up by the Americans in Munich to spread pro-American and anti-Soviet propaganda, American politicians publicly called for a boycott of the Games (Mertin, 2009:103). Knecht (1980) reports that a number of influential international figures denounced human rights violations in the Soviet Union, and in August 1978, the Australian parliament debated whether Australian athletes should abstain from the Olympic Games if the human rights situation in the Soviet Union did not improved. As widely discussed and pointedly analyzed by Sarantakes (2011), this boycott campaign had far-reaching political implications and eventually also succeeded in weakening the international participation in the Moscow Olympics.

For the purposes of my argument here, it is important to consider how this Western campaign against the Moscow Olympics was understood by Soviet authorities as an attempt to discredit the Games: "Recently there

Figure 8.1   "Podnozhka" ("Stumble") by Andrei Krylov, published in *Krokodil*, No. 6, 1980

Note: *Krokodil* was a satirical magazine, which has been in circulation in the Soviet Union since 1922. All materials published in the issues that were printed during the time of the Soviet Union are in public domain and are not registered with the international copyright.

have been attempts to defame the entire work for the preparation of the Games, including expressions of skepticism about readiness of Olympic facilities...and fulfillment of international demands."[41] The cartoon featured on the front page of *Krokodil* (see Figure 8.1) suggests that the Soviet people may have thought of the boycott as a campaign by some anonymous administration of the United States to create obstacles for their own athletes to participate at these Olympics. The Soviet authorities, however, saw these campaigns as threats: "An active role in this campaign is played by diverse anti-Soviet organizations abroad."[42] The Committee for State Security was working to discover these opponents. In June 1978, a number of such groups were identified, among them the Committee for the Return of Crimean Tatars to Their Homeland. This group was planning to exclude its athletes from the national teams in protest against the mass deportation of the Crimean Tatars to Central Asia in 1944. The group planned to use the global publicity during the Games by appearing at the Opening Ceremony with a number of posters communicating messages in support of the Crimean Tatars.[43] The Soviet authorities monitored a number of other groups that protested the Games, including the Estonian National Council, Jewish organizations in the United States, Israel and West Berlin, the Latvian National Fund, Estonian emigrants, and the Baptist organization known as The Crusade at the Universities for Jesus Christ.[44]

In 1979, the security apparatus noted that the tactics of the groups attempting to sabotage the Olympic Games had changed: "While in 1977 and in the first half of 1978 their activities were characterized by appeals to boycott the Moscow Olympics," the security apparatus now believed that they put their main emphasis "on the idea of using the 1980 Olympic Games to conduct on the Soviet territory acts of terrorism, sabotage, and other subversive actions of an extremist character."[45] The security apparatus suspected that the nationalist movements abroad were collaborating with intelligence services in a number of capitalist countries with the intention of being included in a number of national delegations and tourist groups traveling to the Soviet Union before and during the Olympics: "Foreign agents and their associates within the ranks of the Soviet citizens were given the task to study the social and political situation in the country and create conditions that would provoke social disturbance." This would include acts by nationalist and religious organizations, trying to import massive amounts of materials with the purpose of "inundating Moscow, Kiev, and the Baltics" with anti-Soviet literature during the Olympic Games.[46] The security apparatus also suspected that terrorists were trained in the capitalist countries, including the Federal Republic of Germany, with the purpose of being sent as tourists to Moscow.[47]

In its calculations, the Committee for State Security did not exclude a possible cooperation between the secret services of Western countries and the Soviet dissidents. They reasoned that in order to discredit the Moscow Games, the "enemy's intelligence services and foreign anti-Soviet centers" would attempt to use "various kinds of insinuations about the violation of human rights in the Soviet Union."[48] In some cases, the security apparatus "exposed provocations on the part of the foreign agents who were able to persuade the anti-state elements inside the country to make slanderous public statements that inflame the anti-Soviet hysteria in the West."[49] To date, no archival material is available to either confirm or deny the suspicions by the Soviet authorities that international groups were indeed planning to commit terrorist acts during the Games with the help of groups inside the Soviet Union. Emotions were tense on both sides of the ideological divide, the Cold War hysteria influenced Soviet as well as Western security calculations, both intending to embody the Olympic Flame of liberty.

The Committee for State Security considered all actions of dissent, from negative news coverage to terrorist activities, as a possible danger to security. In doing so, the security apparatus interpreted apparently harmless activities as an appeal for terrorism in Moscow. The novel *The Jericho Commandment* by James Patterson, published in 1979, for example, was understood as a possible instruction for hostage-taking of athletes because the plot of Patterson's book takes place during the Moscow Olympics.[50] The authorities were very concerned about the book, which was published in Great Britain in mass circulation because it described "in detail...how to disrupt Moscow's electric, water, and communications systems, and how to commit acts of hooliganism and set things on fire during the Olympics."[51] None of these fears came to pass. A security operative in Moscow remembered that only one man from a Middle Eastern country was identified as a terrorist and promptly arrested.[52] The Soviet authorities were clearly concentrating on the Cold War, while internal terrorist threats received less attention.

This is interesting because terrorism in the Soviet Union was discussed seriously in the 1960s and 1970s.[53] In 1969, a lieutenant in the Soviet army tried to assassinate Leonid Brezhnev by opening fire as the government entourage was on its way to an official ceremony in honor of cosmonauts after their successful space flights "Soiuz-4" and "Soiuz-5." Though Brezhnev was not hurt, the assassin killed the driver and wounded two cosmonauts (Zubok, 2009: 297). Eight years later, in 1977, bombings of the metro in Moscow claimed seven lives and 37 people were injured. While three members of an Armenian nationalist organization were executed for the act, the political causes of the bombing remain unexplained to date (Kunze, 2008: 172–173). Following these events, the seventh department against terror and diversion was established within the Committee for State Security (Hilger, 2009: 63) and in 1974, we also see the establishment of a special forces unit named "Alpha." While, to date, researchers have not yet discussed possible connections between the founding of Alpha and the events during the 1972 Munich Games, I suggest that establishment of Alpha may have been an answer to the failed German response. In 1977, Alpha included 52 soldiers; in 1979, 100, and in May 1980, its staff again doubled to 200.[54]

Despite this background, terrorism was nevertheless considered to be a foreign problem: "As we prepare for the XXII Olympiad, we have to consider the international situation and the certain increase of terrorism in Western countries."[55] As also noted by Bruce Kidd on the 1976 Montreal Games in Chapter 7 of this book, the 1970s were marked by intensive terrorist activity. The same document emphasizes that "In Europe's capitalist countries alone, more than 100 terrorist organizations are currently operating, which have thousands of members in their ranks. In most cases, these are well hidden organizations, equipped with the most advanced weapons and explosives." The Soviet security apparatus had intelligence that "according to testimonies given by security services of the Western countries, those terrorist organizations have not only false bank accounts with tens of millions of dollars, West German marks, and French francs, but also laboratories for production of explosive substances and falsified travel documents."[56] Given the availability of such resources, the document notes, more than "500 cases of airplane hijackings by criminals have been registered" in the West in recent years. The possibility of terrorism inside the Soviet Union, however, was excluded because "our country lacks the social conditions that favor the development of terrorist and other extreme organizations or groups."[57]

Indeed, the security apparatus was focused on persons assumed to be active in international terrorist organizations and strategies of preventing such persons from entering the Soviet Union. The Chairman of the Committee for State Security wrote to the Central Committee of the Communist Party of the Soviet Union in May 1980 about the "main measures for guaranteeing security during the period of the preparation and hosting the Olympics." The measures were the following:

> The main attention is focused on counteracting the extremist tendencies of the opponents. Specifically for this purpose, a catalog with the data on 3000 known members of international terrorist organizations was compiled and sent to all relevant security units, border control posts, and security units of the countries in the socialist alliance with the goal to prevent entry of these persons into our country.[58]

This information was used not only during passport checks at the entry into the Soviet Union but also at the entry into other countries of the socialist alliance.

Additionally, the security apparatus identified another 6000 people it considered able to enter the Soviet Union with the purpose of executing "hostile activities" during the Games: "The entry to the Soviet Union is closed to 6000 foreigners that represent danger from the standpoint of possible conduct of hostile activities during the Olympics. The work of identifying foreigners of this category with the purpose to bar them entry into the Soviet Union continues." The control procedures on the border were immensely important because they were put in place to block the import of illegal weapons, bombs, and anti-Soviet and other political material.[59] The apparatus was working diligently and with full speed: "In the Consular

Department of the Ministry of Foreign Affairs, a temporary provision was put in place to guarantee an investigation of persons applying to enter the Soviet Union using the most recent intelligence – as recent as two months – acquired by the Committee for State Security."[60] From June 20 up to August 5, 1980, the Soviet customs control processed 2 million civilians crossing the Soviet border. The customs found 53 firearms, 8900 cartridges, 1000 "cold weapons," 1050 grams of narcotics, and an "enormous number" – 37,500 – of examples of "ideologically dangerous materials."[61] The operation named "Krepost-79" suggests that authorities were also looking for weapons inside the Soviet Union. In the Estonian Republic, for example, the Soviet police found altogether 173 weapons.[62] In this way, any external or internal possibilities to conduct an act of terrorism were to be eliminated.

Creating "normality" in Moscow

Creating "normality" in Moscow for the duration of the Olympics gave rise to many humorous descriptions. Tamara Eidelman (2010: 19) gives us the following sense of Muscovites' first impression of the Olympics: "The streets of Moscow became oddly empty and store shelves were suddenly filled with items such as Pepsi-Cola, which they started to produce at a factory in Novorossiysk in honor of the Olympics." [63] The spectators who attended the Games were supposedly visiting Moscow but found themselves surrounded, instead, with Western consumer goods.[64] For many Muscovites, the sudden Western flavor of the city left a confusing impression: "The visitors were welcomed to the Games by Mishka, the smiling little bear who was the symbol of the Moscow Olympics, and the Metro stations were suddenly announced in English, all the while the police and the secret service continued to control the streets"[65] – as if, as the sentiment implies, no police is visible and no secret service present in the subways in the West. Such changes in the cityscape, coupled with the presence of policemen and the blue-shirted security apparatus operatives, made up the mix of many Olympic experiences.

Muscovites were poking fun of other measures, too. While the 1980 Olympics were promoted as a festival of the people and the youth, it became clear that neither the youth nor the rest of the population would be allowed to take part in the celebrations for reasons of security. More than a year before the Olympics began, the decision was made to put in place a short-term prohibition of entry to the capital for those "not involved in participating or servicing" the Olympic Games. From June 15, 1980 to August 15, 1980, all seminars and conferences in the capital were canceled and all tourist excursions to Moscow rescheduled. The Ministry of Interior Affairs was made responsible for closing entry to the capital by rail and designing new ways to move around the city. Inside Moscow, the Ministry of Civilian Aviation and the Ministry of Railways worked out measures to cancel all city transit, including airports and train stations.[66] In this way, the Soviet capital was effectively declared a closed city for Soviet inhabitants, where not even a train could stop. In addition, Muscovites and their municipal neighbors were encouraged to leave the scene of the Olympics and go to the country-side to "build lots, play sports, attend pioneer camps, or go to other vacation places for the summer."[67] To minimize unplanned contacts with foreign visitors, schools were obliged to change the dates for entrance examinations. University students and secondary school pupils not volunteering in the Olympic Games were sent off on internships, to do agricultural work, work on a building lot somewhere outside the city, or attend sportive or pioneer camps.[68] Promoted as a festival of youth, the Olympic Games seem to have been accessible to adults with conformist behavior and communist youth, both active as service personnel on the Olympic venues. People poked fun at the measures, saying that the security apparatus was afraid of an uncontrollable influx of masses into the city – not to participate in the Olympics but to buy all the newly available Western products.[69]

During the Games, cooperation of all security organizations was required. In Moscow, 30% of the city's *militsiia* (police force), 8525 people in total, were ordered to be on patrol.[70] Security was ensured by 4100 people in the Olympic Village, while 4409 people worked in the Moscow region, in airports, and on the railways. In the Luzhniki sports complex, where more than 140,000 spectators were expected, over 6808 people were positioned to maintain order. The 22 remaining Olympic objects were guarded by 21,758 people. In the nine hotels where accredited tourists were staying, 6813 people were on duty. In the other 120 public places, 3482 operatives maintained social order. A total of 12,000–15,000 officers were active during the Games: 7800 of them were working in plain clothes and 10,000 in uniform. They followed sports competitions from the Olympic venues and looked with binoculars for suspicious activities. Just how many of these operatives patrolling the Games were actually from the Committee for State Security is still unknown except that they were wearing plain clothes as well as official uniforms.[71]

Another organization that contributed in this effort to achieve order and security was *druzhina*, a kind of civil police, in use since 1959. The *druzhin-niki* were supposed to fulfill a practical function in the realm of "individu-al-prophylactic work." They were to look for marginalized individuals like prostitutes and drunkards and get them off the streets. From June 15 to August 15, 1980, the number of *druzhinniki* in Moscow was to increase to 30,000 people.[72] These people were released from their employment in order to work as civil police in the city, and this form of participation was fostered by the state. The involvement of the public in administrative tasks was seen as a way to bring state and people closer together and was mentioned in the Constitution of 1977 as one of the elements of socialist democracy. It was consistent with the political philosophy that the state would eventually wither away and in its place the Soviet people would participate in the affairs of the state and society (Makepeace, 1980: 271). From the perspective of the citizens, service in the *druzhina* was often used to get a paid day off from work and stroll around the neighborhood. Nevertheless, the requested cooperation of *druzhinniki* and *militsiia* shows that the mobilization had to be taken seriously. In this way, the Soviet security apparatus exerted control over those adults who remained in Moscow in the summer of 1980 and also over the *inogorodnie*.[73]

A chronicler described, with a good measure of sarcasm, the changes experienced in the Olympic Moscow. New facilities were built "with a speed that could be listed in the Guinness book of records." The city was fully decorated by its inhabitants in less than a week. When the inhabitants of "the city of high culture" of ballet, opera, theater, symphony, and art museums were called to clean up the "Olympic railway" in June 1980, the city demonstrated "its own theatre of war activities" as a "battle of great local significance." The Olympic Games, the chronicler wrote, turned the monumental city of Moscow into a Potemkin village of elaborate structures and colorful façades that reflected the bright side of communism. During the two Olympic weeks, Moscow was turned into a city of an exemplary social order where the streets were absolutely clean and the public transport more punctual than ever.[74]

Conclusion

Successful enforcement of security during the 1980 Moscow Olympics was a matter of honor where it was important to show the values of the Soviet society and to convince the guests that the Soviet Union was a state like any other in the West. This notion of "normality" meant that the Soviet Union was capable of professionalism and impeccable organization according to Western standards. This idea of "the state like any other" also had to deliver to Western expectations of "spontaneity" and "free movement." This approach, however, created tension in the Soviet understanding of *bezopasnost*. In order to create the appearance of "normality," the Olympic guests were allowed to move freely in Moscow and in the other participating Olympic cities. At the same time, there had to be an oversight over the large number of tourists because Western influence deemed unfriendly to the Soviet value system could potentially be dangerous for the society and jeopardize its project of transitioning into socialism and then communism. To play it safe, with the exception of those who were directly involved in the staging of the Olympics, the urbanites were sent out of the city while non-Muscovite Soviet inhabitants found themselves unable to come in.

The Soviet moral code also influenced the way the Committee for State Security defined threats. Terrorism was taken as something very specific to the Western political system, which supported criminals with weapons and bank accounts in Central Europe. In contrast, it was assumed that the Soviet society lacked the social conditions under which terrorist organizations could develop. The Western protest campaign and criticism were considered anti-Soviet activities that could potentially turn into terrorist acts, prompting the security apparatus to react decisively. In fact, I suggest that the political boycott by the West and the extensive media coverage of Western protest campaigns had the effect of often being misinterpreted; at times leading the security apparatus to fall back into Stalinist patterns of thought and action.

In the run-up to the Olympics, the apparatus drew on already existing practices. The Olympic preparation was connected with long-established discourses on criminality and the stereotypical other. So, too, the use of *profilaktika* or *druzhinniki* was no invention of the organizers of the Olympic Games. Rather, the security apparatus simply relied on practices already rehearsed for decades during the Soviet festivals and other public celebrations. In response to the imposed requirement by the International Olympic Committee that all the venues be open for free movement, the Soviet organizers had to broaden the radius of the surveillance mechanisms. To this end, and contrary to the way Bajc (2007b, 2011b) has observed security and surveillance practices in public events today, the security apparatus did not spatially differentiate between "the uncertain and insecure everyday life" and the "security zone" specifically set up for the event. Rather, the security apparatus treated the entire metropolitan areas where the Olympics took place as one unified security problem. The criminality discourse and the ambition to eliminate crime completely for the duration of the Olympic Games helped to this end.

As the security apparatus was mobilized by the fear of the unknown and the never before experienced, its response to a massive influx of foreign people, foreign ideologies, and possibly foreign terrorists brought contradictions to the fore. On the one hand, extreme surveillance mechanisms were expanded to the whole urban areas, while on the other hand, public spaces of interaction were broadened to guarantee free and spontaneous movement. This paradox brought about two corresponding contradictory developments: a paranoid fallback into the Stalinist patterns of thought and, at the same time, an opening of the capital of the Soviet Union, the Soviet people, and the Soviet way of life to global audiences. In the end, the Soviet security apparatus overcame this dilemma by using Stalinist practices to deliver to Western requirements and expectations.

Notes

I would like to thank, Martin Aust, Vida Bajc, Alexei Yurchak, Volker Zimmermann, and the two anonymous reviewers for invaluable comments on earlier versions of this chapter. I am very grateful to Ivo Mijnssen for editing various drafts of this chapter.

I would also especially express my appreciation to the Olympic Studies Center at the International Olympic Committee headquarters in Lausanne, which provided me with a Postgraduate Research Grant to work in the International Olympic Committee archives. All mistakes in this chapter are my own.

1. "Osoboe vnimanie etikh Igr sostoit v tom, chto oni v pervye za vsju istoriju olimpijskogo dvizhenija sostojatsja v sotsialisticheskoi strane – v strane, kotoraja neuklonno ja posledovatel`no provodit leninskuju politiku mira, vystupaet na ukreplenie bezopasnosti narodov i shirokoe mezhdunarodnoe sotrudnichestvo." Министерство внутренних дел СССР: Материалы всесоюзного совещания-семинара руководящих работников органов внутренних дел, July 4–7, 1979, Moscow, in: ERAF, f. 17SM, op. 4, d. 892, l. 206.
2. Minutes of the First Meeting of the Organizing Committee for the 1980 Olympic Games, March 7, 1975, in: GARF f. 9610, op. 1, d. 3, l. 21.
3. Report of the Meeting of the Organizing Committee for the 1980 Olympic Games, "Olimpiada-80," under the direction of I. T. Novikov, January 4, 1976, in: GARF, f. 9610, op. 1, d. 33, l. 6.
4. "Zdes´ my imeem vozmozhnost´ i dolzhny dostoino prodemonstrirovat´ pered vsem narodom uspekhi nashego gosudarstva I obespechenii nadezhnogo pravoporjadka, prodemonstrirovat´ vysokii professionalizm i kul´turu sovetskoi militsii." Министерство внутренних дел СССР: Материалы всесоюзного совещания-семинара, l. 242.
5. Постановление Секретариата ЦК Коммунистической Партии Советского Союза, August 12, 1980, Об итогах Игр XXII Олимпиады 1980 года, *Soviet Archives*, http://psi.ece.jhu.edu/~kaplan/IRUSS/BUK/GBARC/pdfs/olympiada/ct223e80.pdf (accessed June 9, 2012), ll. 1–2.
6. "Nado vsem pomnit´, chto v dni Olimpiady rabota organov vnutrennikh del I militsii budet na vidu ne tolko moskvichei, zhitelei strany, no i inostrantsev pochti iz vsekh stran mira, a posredstvom televidenija – u auditorii v 2 mlrd. chelovek. Ibo esli budut dopuschcheny nedostatki ili oshchibki, v tom chisle po sluzhbe okhrany obshchestvennogo porjadka, o nikh nemedlenno budet znat´ ves´ mir." Министерство внутренних дел СССР, Материалы всесоюзного совещания-семинара, l. 237.
7. Постановление Секретариата ЦК КПСС о создании пресс-центра для советских и иностранных журналистов, August 26, 1980, in: RGANI, f. 4, op. 24, d. 1368, l. 58.
8. As discussed below, the boycott campaign, declared by United States President Jimmy Carter on January 20, 1980, reduced the number of expected tourists drastically. In May 1980, a total of 130,000 tourists were expected to visit the Soviet Union: 60,000 of them in Moscow, 1100 in Tallinn, 10,500 in Leningrad, 5500 in Kiev, and 3000 in Minsk. A. Shibal', B. Patuhov, S. Nikitin to the Central Committee of CPSU, May 20, 1980, in: RGANI, f. 5, op. 77, d. 133, l. 55.
9. Yu. Andropov, V. Makeev, I. Novikov, N. Shchelokov: О введении временных ограничении на вьезд в г. Москву в период Олимпиады и направлении граждан г. Москву и Московской области в строительные отряды спортивные, пионерские лагеря и другие места отдыха летом 1980 года, July 24, 1979, in: RGANI, f. 89, op. 31, d. 9, l. 2.
10. Справка о ходе выполнения постановлений ЦК КПСС от 2 и 20 февраля 1975 года: О подготовке к XXII летним Олимпийским Играм 1980 года в Москве, in: ERAF, f. 1, op. 302, d. 245, l. 1.
11. Bis drei Uhr morgens, in: *Der Spiegel*, June 4, 1979, 175–176.

12. Выписка из протокола No 186 заседания Политбюро ЦК КПСС от 29 февраля 1980 года: О мероприятиях в поддержку Олимпиады-80, July 5, 1980, *Soviet Archives*, http://psi.ece.jhu.edu/~kaplan/IRUSS/BUK/GBARC/pdfs/olympiada/pb186–80.pdf (accessed September 16, 2012), l. 1.
13. Yu. Andropov to KGB USSR, О враждебной деятельности противника в связи с Олимпиадой, November 30, 1979, *Soviet Archives*, http://psi.ece.jhu.edu/~kaplan/IRUSS/BUK/GBARC/pdfs/olympiada/kgb79–2.pdf (accessed April 16, 2012), ll. 1–2.
14. Record of Meeting of the Orgcom Presidium, May 4, 1975, in: GARF f. 9610, op. 1, d. 5, l. 28.
15. Sever, Aleksandr (2008) *Istorija KGB*, Moscow: Algoritm, 299. (In Russian: Север, Александр. 2008. История КГБ, Москва: Алгоритм.)
16. Smykalin, Aleksandr (2011) "Ideologicheskii kontrol' i Pjatoe upravlenie KGB SSSR v 1968–1989 gg," *Voprosy istorii*, 8: 30–40.
17. Record of Meeting of the Orgcom Presidium, May 4, 1975.
18. Токарев, А. Ф.: *Профилактика правонарушений*, in: Некрасов, Владимир (Сост.) 2002: МВД России. Энциклопедия, Москва: Обьединенная редакция МВД России, Омма-пресс, 442.
19. Olimpiada-80, Collected documents of Vladimir Bukovskii, *Soviet Archives*, http://psi.ece.jhu.edu/~kaplan/IRUSS/BUK/GBARC/pdfs/olympiada/olym-rus.html (accessed October 16, 2011).
20. Julia Zaks, Leonid Chernikhov: *Soviet Archives*. "Introduction to Web-Master," *Soviet Archives*, http://psi.ece.jhu.edu/~kaplan/IRUSS/BUK/GBARC/intro.html (accessed Ocober 16, 2011).
21. Министерство внутренних дел СССР, Материалы всесоюзного совещания-семинара.
22. Tadevosjan, Eduard (1979) *Obshchestvennye otnoshenija v razvitom sotsialis-ticheskom obschchestve*, Moskva: AN SSSR INION, MID SSSR, 41–42.
23. Even the institutional body was named according to the term "to guarantee security and protect the social order": Комитет по безопасности и общественному порядку. GARF, f. 9610, op. 1, d. 5, l. 28.
24. Министерство внутренних дел СССР: Материалы всесоюзного совещания-семинара.
25. Ibid.
26. Ibid., l. 219.
27. "V otdel'nyh gorodakh eshche ne dostignuto kachestvennoe vypolnenie mero-prijatii programmy sovershenstvovanija dejatel'nosti po preduprezhndeniju retsidivoi prestupnosti." Ibid., l. 211.
28. "V obshchem kolichestve prestuplenii neznachitelen, oni nanosjat nepopravimoi uron pristizhu nashei strany, chesti i dostoinstvu sovetskikh grazhdan." Ibid., l. 219.
29. "Takim obrazom, v olimpiiskikh gorodakh predstoit provesti v szhatye sroki ogromnyi ob'em raboty po ukrepleniju pravoporjadka, zakonnosti, preduprezh-deniju i raskrytiju prestuplenii. No vozmozhnosti dlja reshenija takoi zadachi est'- tem bolee, chto ZK KPSS, Pravitel'stvo, MVD SSSR, mestnye partiinye i sovetskie organy okazali i okazyvajut organam vnutrennyh del olimpiiskikh gorodov bol'shuju pomoshch, v tom chisle shtatami, tehnikoi, transportom." Министерство внутренних дел СССР: Материалы всесоюзного совещания-семинара, l. 212.
30. Tsalik, Stanislav (2012) *Kiev. Konspekt 70-h. Rasskazy o povsednevnoi zhizni goroda i gorozhan*, Kiev: Varto, 37–53.

198   *Carol Marmor-Drews*

31. "V nastojashchikh uslovijakh bol´shoe znachenie dlja ukreplenija pravoporjadka v olimpiiskikh gorodakh imejut meroprijatija po svoevremennomu preduprezh-ndeniju i raskrytiju prestuplenii, sovershaemykh grazhdanami, prozhivajush-chimi v drugikh gorodakh i oblastjakh Sojuza SSR, i litsami bez opredelennogo mesta zhitel´stva i zanjatii." Министерство внутренных дел СССР, Материалы всесоюзного совещания-семинара, l. 212.
32. "Nalazhen obmen informatsii o litsakh, namerevajushchikhsja pribyt´ v g. Moskvu i olimpijskie goroda s tsel´ju sovershenija pravonarushenii. Bolee aktivno provodjatsja meroprijatija po profilakticheskoi ochistke goroda ot brodjag, pres-tupnikov-gastrolerov." Ibid.
33. Ibid., l. 213.
34. Об основных мерах по обеспечению безопасности в период подготовки и проведения игр XXII Олимпиады 1980 года, May 12, 1980, *Soviet Archives*, http://psi.ece.jhu.edu/~kaplan/IRUSS/BUK/GBARC/pdfs/olympiada/kgb80–1.pdf (accessed July 10, 2012), ll. 2–3.
35. Mitrokhin, Vasilii (2002) *KGB Lexicon: The Soviet Intelligence Officer's Handbook*. London: Cass, 329ff.
36. О мероприятиях МВД Эстонской ССР по обеспечению безопасности и общестиенного порядка в период подготовки и проведения Игр XXII Олимпиады, August 1, 1980, in: ERAF-17SM-4–902, l. 49.
37. О мероприятиях МВД Эстонской ССР по обеспечению безопасности, l. 49–50.
38. Ibid.
39. Ibid., l. 48.
40. "Sakharov proposes Soviet withdrawal," *New York Times*, March 1, 1980.
41. Yu. Andropov to KGB USSR, О враждебной деятельности противника в связи с Олимпиадой, July 30, 1979, l.1.
42. Yu. Andropov to KGB USSR, О враждебной деятельности противника в свяи с Олимпиадой-80, April 25, 1979, *Soviet Archives*, http://psi.ece.jhu.edu/~kaplan/IRUSS/BUK/GBARC/pdfs/olympiada/kgb79–3.pdf (accessed July 10, 2012), l. 1.
43. Ibid., l. 2.
44. Yu. Andropov to KGB USSR, О враждебной деятельности противника, July 30, 1979, ll. 2–3.
45. "Esli v 1977 godu i pervoi polovine 1978 goda naibolee harakternymi dlja ego dejalten´nosti javljalis´prizyvy boikotirovat moskovskuju Olimpiadu, to v poslednee vremja na pervyi plan vydvigaetsja ideja ispolzovat Olimpiiskie igry 1980 goda dlja osushchestvlenija na territorii SSSR terroristicheskikh, diversion-nykh i inykh aktsii ekstremistskoho kharaktera." Yu. Andropov to KGB USSR, О враждебной деятельности противника, April 25, 1979, ll. 1–2.
46. "Pered emissarami i svjazannymi s nimi vrazhdebnymi elementami iz chisla sovetskikh grazhdan protivnik stavit zadachu po izucheniju obstanovki i sozdaniju uslovii dlja provedenija provokatsionnykh aktsii." Yu. Andropov to KGB USSR, О враждебной деятельности противника, April 25, 1979, l. 2.
47. Yu. Andropov to KGB USSR, О замыслах западных спецслужб и зарубежных антисоветских организаций в связи с Олимпиадой-80, June 16, 1978, *Soviet Archives*, http://psi.ece.jhu.edu/~kaplan/IRUSS/BUK/GBARC/pdfs/olympiada/kgb78–1.pdf (accessed June 11, 2012), l. 3.
48. Ibid., ll. 2–3.
49. Ibid., ll. 3–4.
50. Yu. Andropov to KGB USSR, О враждебной деятельности противника, July 30, 1979, l. 2.

51. "V Anglii, naprimer, massovym tirazhom izdana kniga, v kotoroi podrobno izlagajutsja rekomendatsii po narusheniju v Moskve sistem elektro-vodosnabzhenija, svjazi, soversheniju huliganskih deistvii, podzhogov i t.d. v period Igr XXII Olimpiady." Министерство внутренных дел СССР, Материалы всесоюзного совещания-семинара, l. 209.

52. Alidin, Viktor (2001) *Gosudarstvennaja bezopasnost` i vremja*, Moscow: Izo-grafus, 293.

53. Sever, Aleksandr (2008) *Spetsnaz KGB. Grif sekretnosti snjat!* Moscow: Jauza, Eksmo, 630–634.

54. Sever, *Spetsnaz KGB*, 637.

55. "Gotovjas' k provedeniju Igr XXII Olimpiady, my dolzhny uchityvat' mezhdunarodnuju obstanovku I osobenno rost terrorizma v stranakhZapada." Министерство внутренных дел СССР, Материалы всесоюзного совещания-семинара, l. 225.

56. Po svidetel'stvu spetsial'nyh sluzhb zapadnyh gosudarstv terroristicheskie organizatsii v bankakh na podstavnykh lits imejut ves'ma krupnye summy deneg, ischisljajushchiesja desjatkami millionov dollarov zapadnogermanskikh marok ili frankov, imejut laboratorii po izgotovleniju vzryvchatki i poddel'nykh dokumentov." Министерство внутренных дел СССР, Материалы всесоюзного совещания-семинара, l. 225.

57. Ibid., l. 226.

58. "Osnovnoe vnimanie udeleno protivodeistviju ekstremistskim ustremlenijam protivnika. Dlja etogo, v chastnosti, podgotovlen al'bom s ustanovychnymi dannymi na 3 tysjachi izvestnykh uchastnikov mezhdunarodnykh terroristicheskikh organizatsii, kotoryi napravlen vsem zainteresovannym organam KGB, na kontrol'no- propusknye punkty v`ezda inostrantsev v SSSR, a takzhe organam bezopasnosti stran sotsialisticheskogo sodruzhestva s tselju predotvrashchenija v`ezda etikh lits v nashu stranu." Об основных мерах по обеспечению безопазности в период подготовки и проведения игр XXII Олимпиады 1980 года, May 12, 1980, l. 2.

59. Ibid., l. 3.

60. "Zakryt v`ezd v Sovetskii Sojuz 6 tysjacham inostrantsev, predstavljajushchim opasnost´ s tochki zrenija vozmozhnogo osushchestvlenija vrazhdebnykh aktsii vo vremja Olimpiady. Rabota po vyjavleniju inostrantsev ukazannoi kategorii i zakrytiju im v`ezda v SSSR prodolzhaetsja. Po linii Konsul'skogo upravlenija MID SSSR vveden vremennyi porjadok vydachi viz, kotoryi garantiruet proverku lits, zhelajushchikh v`ekhat v SSSR, po operativnym uchetam KGB za dva mesjatsja do v`ezda." Ibid., l. 2.

61. M. R. Kuz'min to Central Committee of the Communist Party, August 12, 1980: Информация Министерства Внешней Торговли СССР в ЦК КПСС о результатах работы таможенных учреждений СССР во время проведения Олимпийских игр в Москве, in: RGANI f. 5, op. 77, d. 133, ll. 178–179, cited in: Konova, Tat'jana and Prozhumenshchikov, Mikhail (Eds) 2011. *Pjat´ kolets pod kremlevskimi zvezdami. Dokumentalnaja hronika Olimpiady-80 v Moskve*, Moskva: MFD, 787–788.

62. A. M. Martin to I. E. Lozhkin, February 4, 1980: Докладная записка о проделанной в 1979 году работе по подготовке к обеспечению охраны общественного порядка и безопасности на Играх Олимпиады, in: ERAF f. 17SM, op. 4, d. 892, l. 92.

63. "XXII Summer Olympic Games. July 19–August 3, 1980," Tamara Eidelman, *Russian Life*, July/August, 2010, 19–21.

64. Olümpiaregatt tõi Tallinna Aseri töölised, Vigri ja Fanta, in *Eesti Päevaleht*, August 16, 2008.
65. "XXII Summer Olympic Games. July 19–August 3, 1980," Tamara Eidelman, *Russian Life*, July/August, 2010, 19–21.
66. N. Shchelokov, V. Cherbikov to the Central Committee of the Communist Party, May 20, 1980: О мероприятиях МВД СССР и КГБ СССР по обеспечению безопасности и охраны общественного порядка в период проведения XXII Олимпийских Игр в г. Москве и об использовании в етих целях сотрудников территориальных органов, учебных заведений и войск МВД СССР, in: RGANI, f. 89, op. 25, d. 60, l. 3.
67. Yu. Andropov, V. Makejev, I. Novikov, N. Shelokov, July 24, 1979: О введении временных ограничении, l. 4.
68. Ibid., ll. 3–4.
69. Tallinna olümpiaregatt ja unised nõukogude mesilased, in: *Õhtuleht*, July 24, 2010.
70. Ibid., l. 4.
71. Ibid., l. 7.
72. Министерствовнутреннныхдел СССР, Материалывсесоюзногосовещания-семинара, l. 217.
73. Ibid.
74. Titarenko, Vitalii (1998) *Proshchai Vysotskii: Dokumental'naja khronika pohoron.* Tambov: Izd-votamb. Gostipografii Prolet. Svetoch.

9
Cross-National Intelligence Cooperation and Centralized Security Control System (Seoul 1988)

Gwang Ok and Kyoung Ho Park

The 24th Seoul Summer Olympic Games were a significant mega-event for both South Korea and the international sporting community. South Korea was able to showcase its economic progress following the devastation left by the civil war and, through this event, enter the world of the developed countries. Modern sport, introduced to Korea about a hundred years ago, was now transformed successfully into a global phenomenon through the Olympics (Ok, 2008). The choice of Seoul as the host city, however, highlighted the conflict on the Korean Peninsula, including protests by North Korea to the International Olympic Committee, the fatal bombing of high-ranking South Korean officials in Myanmar in 1983, and the bombing of South Korean Air Flight 858 on route to Seoul in 1987. In this context, the Seoul Organizing Committee for the Olympic Games, a number of international intelligence agencies, and the security and surveillance agencies in South Korea collaborated closely to establish a nationwide security and surveillance system. The Seoul Organizing Committee commissioned two South Korean private computer and software-related companies, Sangyong Computer and Hangooksoft, to develop what they named Seoul Olympic Management System. This system built on measures implemented during the domestically hosted international events such as the 1986 Asian Games, as well as on the experiences of other cities that hosted the Games. An integral war room was set up during the Games to jointly resolve matters related to performance and safety.[1] Various agencies conducted coordinated operations and rounds of comprehensive rehearsals at each venue to strengthen measures against North Korea and international terrorist organizations and to practice dedicated personal security for participants (Kim, 2004).

The Korean Peninsula divided

It may be useful to briefly sketch out the events that lead to the division of Korea in 1948 to give a sense of the Cold War sentiment in which the

Seoul Olympics were conceived and carried out. After the Japanese colonialism ended, following the fatal American bomb attack on Hiroshima and Nagasaki in 1945, the declaration of Korea's independence was overshadowed by a civil war in which the former Union of Soviet Socialist Republics supported the North and the United States supported the South. The war was preceded by failed negotiations between the two superpowers under the auspices of the United Nations. This resulted in the declaration of the Republic of Korea (from here on South Korea) in August 1948 with the capitol in Seoul and the Democratic People's Republic of Korea (from here on North Korea) in September 1948 with the capitol in Pyeongyang [often known as Pyongyang]. The three-year civil war, 1950–1953, left behind huge destruction with a million homeless, and hundreds of thousands of killed, wounded, and missing, and a demilitarized zone at the 38th parallel, which separated the communist Korea to the North from a pro-Western Korea to the South.

The idea to host the Olympics in Seoul was conceived under a military government. The military rule began with the May 1961 coup d'état lead by Major General Park Chung-Hee. Under the military dictatorship, democratic principles in politics and social life deteriorated, and the political right became more extreme in its relationship with North Korea. The intensification of the political confrontation with North Korea served as a momentum to solidify the nationalistic ideology in South Korea and sport was used politically as a means to do it. The process for hosting the Seoul Olympics can be understood in this context. Park Chung-Hee and Park Jong-Kyu, the two key players in the politics of hosting the Seoul Olympics were both nationalists from the military. Park Jong-Kyu, who had been the central force of the May 1961 coup d'état became afterward the main figure of the Yushin regime, serving as the Chief Officer of the Presidential Security of the Park Chung-Hee regime. Park Jong-Kyu, the man with enough boldness and drive to be called "Pistol Park," later resigned from the position in connection to the 1974 murder of Yuk Young-Soo, President Park's wife (Kim, 2000: 49–50).

Soon after, President Park, who was the leading power for the competition to host the Olympics, was assassinated by one of his close staff. At the time it seemed that the movement to host the Games was losing momentum. However, the movement resumed under the control of Chun Doo-Hwan, who took over the regime through another coup d'état in December 1979. This time, the push to host the Olympics was facing a strong public opposition. There was such a sharp division of opinions between those who approved and others who disapproved of the competition to host the Games that a delegation was formed only three weeks before the 1981 International Olympic Committee Session where the host city was selected.[2] In light of this situation, President Chun Doo-Hwan, who was the core of the political regime, simply declared that because it was not in his power to alter the decision of the former president without any specific reason, South Korea would be obliged to host the Games and claimed that the government should carry forward this historical project rather than being overwhelmed by a sense of defeat.[3]

It has been argued that this action reflected the intention of the military government to justify a number of agendas, particularly its brutal suppression of the so-called Gwangju Democratization Movement, the coup d'état through which it won the power, and the push for ideological superiority in relation to North Korea. While there was a public discussion about the decision to compete for hosting the Games, the military regime of the time was able to push through the decision to go to Baden-Baden and bid to host the Games. It was the military regime that deteriorated the South Korean democracy that was able to exert power, which made "the miracle of Baden-Baden" possible. The public opposition to hosting the Games during the bidding process was organized around two concerns. The first concern was related to the burden of the costs of hosting the Olympics and the distrust of the military regime by the public (Kim, 2000). The winning of the bid and the government's determination to support the event did little to dissuade the public. The second concern had to do with the relationship with North Korea and the insistence that North Korea cohost the Olympics. This initiative was supported by the popular uprising against the military dictatorship in 1980, called the Gwangju Democratization Movement. The slogan of the demonstrations read "Desperately Oppose to Hosting the Ruinous Olympic Games."[4] There was another wave of demonstrations against South Korea's push to exclusively host the Olympics in 1988, which included students of Seoul National University and Korea University, as well as citizens who demanded the liberation of the imprisoned president of the National Association of College Students for Democracy, and threatened to interrupt the events of the Olympics.[5] Despite these protests, as the day of the Opening Ceremony was approaching, South Koreans agreed that it was important to have successful Games, which ultimately led to the successful hosting of the event.[6]

Not surprisingly, North Korea did everything in its power to oppose the Games. The pressures felt by North Korea are best described by a statement of its President Kim Il-sung, who stated, "The Olympic matter is not just a sporting problem but a political one" (Kim, 1987: 52). Seoul's hosting of the Olympics was indeed a serious political problem for North Korea because it would legitimize in the eyes of the international world the division between the North and the South and enhance the status of South Korea and its economic development in relation to the North.

Pyongyang initially proposed that the Games be shared by both countries in the following way: the name of the Olympic Games would be either the Joseon Olympic Games or the Pyongyang-Seoul Olympic Games, the 23 sports Games would be halved in order to be held in either of the two nations, revenues from fees for broadcasting rights would be halved between the two nations, the Seoul Organizing Committee would be jointly formed, and the opening and closing ceremonies would be held separately in Pyongyang and Seoul. However, the International Olympic Committee turned down this proposal by arguing that it was against Article 4 of the Olympic Charter, which states that the honor of hosting the Olympic Games is granted to only one city, and the selection of the host city is an exclusive right of the International Olympic Committee.[7]

After these negotiations failed, North Korea intensified its activities to sabotage preparations for the Seoul Games. While bidding activities were being carried out in Baden-Baden in 1981, the Bid Committee was under alert after receiving information that a great number of North Korean Taekwondo masters were gathering in Baden-Baden with the purpose of disturbing the bidding activities (Lee, 1989). North Korea also lobbied International Olympic Committee members from other countries to retract the decision by arguing that Seoul was at risk of war (Kim, 2000), that South Korea won the bid by manipulating the result of voting using bribery at the Session, that the people of South Korea opposed the hosting of the Games, and that Seoul was an insecure city both politically and socially. These arguments were in line with the initiative to let Greece be the permanent host of the Games, which was on the rise among International Olympic Committee members at the time because of the loss of the Olympic spirit due to the boycott of the Moscow Games by Western countries and subsequently of the Los Angeles Olympics by communist countries.[8] North Korea also emphasized that South Korea would use the Games to finalize the division of the peninsula. They argued that if the Games were held in Seoul, it would be a disgrace for the Olympic history as well as the Olympic Movement. This promoted antigovernment and anti–United States sentiment in the South (Senn, 1999: 220–221).

North Korea also conducted numerous activities in order to disturb the Olympics, including assassination attempts at the President of South Korea. This resulted in one of the most serious tragedies in modern history of South Korea where 17 high-ranking government officials were killed in Rangoon, Myanmar (formerly Burma) in 1983 while they were paying homage to Aung San Mausoleum. The bomb was aimed at killing President Chun Doo-Hwan, who was fortunately 1.5 km away from the place of the bombing. Right after the incident, President Chun canceled his schedule and returned home to dispatch a fact-finding team while calling an emergency cabinet meeting to counter another North Korean provocation. He also instructed the army to prepare for emergencies related to a worsening relationship with

North Korea. As a result of investigations conducted by the governments in Myanmar and South Korea, two people were arrested who turned out to be North Korean spies. It was found a year later that the bombing incident was committed by North Korea with the goal of causing political and social confusion in South Korea by killing its president. If successful, this may have hindered the 1986 Asian Games and the 1988 Olympic Games (Ok and Ha, 2011).

After the Rangoon bombing, North Korea suggested forming a unified Olympic team for the 1984 Los Angeles Olympic Games. South Korea accepted the suggestion, but these negotiations also failed when North Korea refused to cooperate with the investigation into the Rangoon bombing. This led the North Korean Olympic Committee to request from the International Olympic Committee chairman to change the site of the Olympic Games. Citing the Olympic Charter specifying that if the site of the Olympic Games is at war, it can be canceled, North Korea requested cancelation of the Seoul Olympic Games. This was rejected with the Lausanne Resolution adopted by the 89th International Olympic Committee Special Plenary Session held in 1984.[9] In November 1987, ten months before the Games, South Korean Air Flight 858 exploded, killing the crew and 115 passengers who were mostly overseas workers.[10]

As the news of the Flight 858 bombing was officially unveiled, the United States government immediately invoked various sanctions against North Korea, defining it as a terror-sponsoring nation, and the Japanese government prohibited North Korean government officials from entering Japan. On February 10, 1988, the United Nations Security Council called an emergency meeting where representatives from various countries denounced North Korea for terrorist acts, and the incident seriously hurt North Korean diplomatic capacity on the global stage.

The Seoul Olympic Games were held amid ceaseless concerns about the imbalance of the inter-Korean relationship and terrorist threats by North Korea, which was technically still at war with South Korea. As the 22nd Moscow Olympic Games and the 23rd Los Angeles Olympic Games were reduced to the "half" Olympic Games in the wake of accelerated disputes between the Soviet Union, which invaded Afghanistan, and the United States, which invaded Vietnam, conflicts between the East and the West escalated. Amid this international turmoil, South Korea, under the military dictatorship since the Park administration, went through serious discords with North Korea. The tragic terrorist activities and threats need to be understood against this backdrop. Despite these tumultuous events, the Seoul Olympic Games, held from September 17 through October 2, 1988, were the largest-ever global sports event in which a total of 160 countries participated including the Soviet Union and China (Pound, 1994).

The surveillance system

The Security Control Center

To make thorough security checks and surveillance procedures possible, the government of South Korea established a Security Control Center in March 1987. The center was based on a plan to lay the foundation for a peaceful sports festival by ensuring absolute security while endeavoring to elevate national status and make a leap forward to join the ranks of advanced countries. The Security Control Center, which consisted of 170 government officials from 13 ministries, established measures for 20 sectors including immigration control and anti-terrorism activities. It also organized 16 task force teams to guard influential figures, protect sports stadia, and secure Athletes Village. South Korean government requested that the Security Control Center make the tasks a top priority.

The government also drew up basic plans to block terrorist attempts by North Korea and international terrorist organizations, provide dedicated security and protection to key figures and participants in the Olympic Games, prevent pro-communist activities, and take measures to counter crimes against foreigners. Toward this end, the government focused on securing an appropriate level of police force, a balanced budget, and high-tech equipment. A total of roughly 48,000 police, accounting for 40% of the entire police force, were mobilized and placed to guard sports facilities. In order to safely and effectively support reporters' air coverage, aircraft operation was controlled and coordinated. A day-to-day council for daily safety activities was formed for this purpose, which had joint participation by the International Olympic Committee and its South Korean counterpart (Kim, 2004).

The Safety Measures Committee

The Security Control Center for the Seoul Olympic Games was operated by the Safety Measures Committee with the Safety Coordination and Control Headquarters as its subsidiary organization. Under the umbrella of this committee and its headquarters there were 16 authorized bodies and 264 sub-organizations known as site safety headquarters. The center's purpose was multiple: to preempt maneuvers to obstruct the Games; to ensure safety of stadia and special venues while maintaining free atmosphere for the Games; to provide a safe and comfortable environment to participants; to establish the public peace and order for the Games; and to construct preparedness against contingencies for fast response. Its major tasks included obtaining and administering personnel for entrance and exit management and materials for safety, ensuring safety of facilities, and investigating identity of persons associated with the Games.[11]

Laws to protect peace of the Olympic Games

Another notable characteristic of security management of the Seoul Olympic Games was the enactment of a set of laws aimed to "maintain peace of the

Olympic Games."[12] As South Korean intelligence organizations continued to discover attempts by North Korea to disrupt the Olympic Games, the Security Control Center invited the head of the Munich Police Agency who took charge of security management during the Munich Olympic Games to visit Seoul. Emphasizing the importance of providing maximized security based on minimized inconvenience, the chief of the Munich Police introduced an example of enactment of a special law during the Munich Olympic Games. Learning from this example, the Korean government pushed for the enactment of a special law on the Seoul Olympic Games and promulgated it on August 5, 1988, one month before the Games began.

A legislative bill to keep peace during the Olympic Games was unanimously passed by the ruling and opposition parties on July 22, 1988, after revising it so that punishment of those who violated the provision banning assembly and demonstration was governed by the law on assembly and demonstration. On the morning of July 23, however, the process met with difficulty due to the opposition parties' objection. The four ruling and opposition parties immediately met. Secretary-level talks and the Legislation-Judiciary

Table 9.1 Laws to protect peace of the Olympic Games

Article 1 (Purpose) It aims to contribute to making the Olympic Games a success by prohibiting rallies and demonstrations that might hurt the peace of the 24th Olympic Games held in Seoul.

Article 2 (Designation of Olympic Peace Zone)

  (1) Mayor of Seoul City or Mayors and Governors of Olympic Cities ("Mayors and Governors" hereinafter) shall be allowed to designate Olympic Peace Zone ("Peace Zone" hereinafter) in order to maintain peace for the Olympic Games.

  (2) The Peace Zone above shall include Olympic Games facilities, accommodations facilities for participating athletes, officers and tourists, related roads and sites and surrounding areas.

  (3) The peace zone shall be designated for a certain period of time before and after the Olympic Games.

Article 3 (Notification on Peace Zone and etc.) If Mayor of Seoul City and Mayors and Governors want to designate Peace Zone, they shall notify the period and pertinent areas to the general public.

Article 4 (Compliance with Peace Zone)

  (1) Everyone shall make effort to keep the peace of the Olympic Games in the Peace Zone and not engage in rallies or demonstrations that might hurt the peace of the Olympic Games.

  (2) Despite Law on Assembly and Demonstration, all assemblies and demonstrations shall be prohibited in the Peace Zone except for assemblies that pertain to Article 9 of Law on Assembly and Demonstration.

Additional Rules <No. 4014, August 5, 1988>

  (1) (Effective Date) It shall take effect from the date of promulgation.

  (2) (Effective Period) It shall take effect until October 31, 1988.

Legal Information by Ministry of Government Legislation.

Committee's executive committee meeting were held to completely delete provisions on penalties, and a legislation having a declaratory meaning was agreed on. Still, without such provisions on penalties, violators were subject to punishment pursuant to the law on assembly and demonstration.[13]

From the 475 districts in Seoul, all but 37 were designated by the Law for Peace during the Olympic Games as "peace districts," meaning peace zones for the Olympic Games (See Table 9.1). The law was effective only until the end of October 1988. All assemblies and demonstrations were banned within the peace districts and it was prescribed that efforts be made to keep peace in the districts.[14] The law aimed to designate Olympic Games facilities, accommodations facilities for participating athletes, officers and tourists, related roads and sites, and surrounding areas as the Olympic Peace Zone and prohibit assemblies and demonstrations within that zone. As per Article 9, there was an exception for assemblies related to academic activities, arts, sports, religion, ceremony, social gathering, entertainment, four ceremonial occasions, and national festivals. The exceptional cases specified in Article 9 also pertain to a formal objection in the wake of notification of prohibition of assemblies and demonstrations, so it is taken as meaning fundamental prohibition.

These laws were meant to prevent activities by groups that opposed the military regime of Chun Doo-Hwan and his push for the Seoul Olympics as well as anti-regime demonstrations by pro-North Korean students in South Korea. At the time when huge efforts were made abroad to induce the Olympic Games, the Gwangju Demonstration Movement in 1980 and various rallies and demonstrations were held at home to protest against the administration, which took over the power through a military coup. These demonstrations continued until right before the Olympic Games.[15] In this regard, as far as Chun's government was concerned, the enactment of the special laws to maintain the peace for the Seoul Olympic Games is taken as meaning that not only terrorism from outside but also various opposition forces inside posed a serious threat to the Olympic Games.

International security cooperation and intelligence sharing

Since the 1972 Munich Olympics, significance of safety management for the Games has increased, and in most Games thereafter we see the host country collaborating with other states. In the case of the 1984 Los Angeles Games, we learn from the United States Federal Bureau of Investigation's website that the Los Angeles Police Commissioners Board maintained a collaborative relation with the Bureau, France's Services des Voyages Officials, and Israel's Mossad. For these Games, the Bureau specially created an elite unit called Hostage Rescue Team and also formed the Computer Analysis and Response Team. The Hostage Rescue Team was trained to prepare for possible crimes and acts of terror while the Computer Analysis and Response Team was set up to retrieve any evidences or possibilities of such activity from computers.

The Computer Analysis and Response Team eventually expanded as a full program in 1991.[16]

Given that the Seoul Games were held in a divided country in an acute conflict situation, there was more intense cooperation between the host country and its political allies. In particular, there was close collaboration with the United States and Japan. This included sharing all kinds of anti-terrorism information, specifically identity information about some 6000 international terror suspects and 600 terrorist organizations.[17] Through close cooperation, intelligence organizations of these countries exchanged with each other various kinds of information on terrorist attempts against the Seoul Olympics.

Undersecretary of the United States State Department expressed his concern about possible North Korean terrorist attempts against the Seoul Games in a forum held in Washington in May 1988. Since the bombing of South Korean Air Flight 858, there were ongoing discussions related to the safety of the Seoul Olympics with the United States, then South Korea's closest ally, which presented measures such as dispatching more of its naval forces and strengthening military collaboration. In fact, the Washington forum was a part of a series of security meetings between the two countries following the bombing. There was a lot of other support as well, including countless discussions in meetings by related parties as well as the visit of United States Deputy Secretary of State Edward Joseph Derwinski to South Korea right before the Games.[18]

According to one of these intelligence agencies, Red Army Faction in Japan was plotting to destroy Olympic facilities in Seoul, abduct influential South Korean figures and International Olympic Committee officers, occupy South Korean embassies and legations abroad and foreign embassies in South Korea, and rise in arms. In response, the Metropolitan Police Department in Japan arrested the No. 2 man in the Japanese Red Army Faction in November 1987. The analyzes of secret codes on his note concluded that they plotted to assassinate South Korean government officials including President Chun Doo-Hwan. In addition, a person associated with the Red Army Faction who participated in the Yodo incident in 1980 before defecting to North Korea was arrested in Japan in 1985. Members of the Red Army Faction who remained in North Korea declared through the media that they would not sit idle with the arrest, and there were signs that those ordered by North Korea were planning to conduct terrorist acts against the Seoul Olympics.[19] In addition, when the Ministry of Foreign Affairs in Japan provided intelligence that one of the people involved in the Yodo incident staying in North Korea was frequently contacting members of the Red Army Faction in a third country in April 1988, the South Korean government issued a high alert.

Amid terrorist threats at home and abroad, the South Korean government established a network with intelligence agencies in the United States, Japan,

West Germany, the United Kingdom, France, and Israel for the purpose of securing the Seoul Olympics. In particular, since the Rangoon bombing, the South Korean government had established a proactive cooperative system with intelligence agencies in the United States and Japan by disclosing the entire intelligence on North Korea. At that time, these states spared no effort to support South Korea by transferring as many as 140 cases of intelligence on international terrorists, falsified passports, and asylum attempts.[20]

The Red Net

As concerns on air security had been heightened since the South Korean Air Flight 858 bombing, the South Korean government needed to strengthen related surveillance. Regarding this, the United States suggested installation and operation of the Red Net to identify counterfeited or falsified passports to the Ministry of Justice of South Korea and at the Gimpo International Airport. The two countries exchanged data on counterfeit or falsified passports. The Red Net refers to a computer network that identifies forged or altered passports. This system strengthened computer programs used for immigration checks, utilizing close collaboration with domestic intelligence agencies and the International Criminal Police Organization (INTERPOL) in order to identify people of concern based on information like terrorists' photos and profiles. The Red Net system was proposed by the United States. INTERPOL provided the data on international crime while the South Korea Ministry of Justice carried out its operation.[21]

The United States Federal Bureau of Investigation and Central Intelligence Agency as well as the Japanese Cabinet Intelligence and Information Office provided information on international terrorists and Yakuza in Japan to South Korean security control computer terminals to help prevent unwanted individuals from entering the country. The terrorism-related computer network detected 30 suspects including 20 international terrorist suspects from seven countries and 13 counterfeited or falsified passport owners from seven countries in the immigration process from January 1988 to the time of the Closing Ceremony. In the process, personal information on 16,000 participants in the Olympic Games, including detected international terrorist suspects, was transferred to the Ministry of Justice of South Korea and the Federal Bureau of Investigation for identification, and those suspected of being involved in terrorist acts were monitored while staying in South Korea.[22]

Bomb detection training

The Federal Bureau of Investigation and the Central Intelligence Agency provided information on how to detect explosives and crack down on terrorist acts at least ten times. At the same time, it conducted anti-terrorism training for security of the Games. South Korea began to develop interest in international terrorism in 1981, and the interest was further enhanced around the

Asian Games. South Korea's antiterrorist tactics, therefore, lagged behind in experience. In this regard, joint training with the Delta Force, one of the United States Special Operation Forces, which had taken part in various antiterrorist campaigns in the Middle East since its inauguration in 1977, played an important role in transferring know-how in anti-terrorism activities.[23] In the meantime, the South Korean military strengthened combined forces between the United States and South Korea in an effort to counter North Korean provocations during the period of the Olympic Games, and officials with the United States State Department visited South Korea twice to promise an enhanced cooperative system between the two countries. Specialized agencies like the Federal Bureau of Investigation Bomb Data Center provided training on how to detect explosives and train explosives-detecting dogs, and the Central Intelligence Agency offered anti-terrorism know-how such as data on analysis of terrorist incidents and how to direct the quelling of terrorist incidents. The Seoul Organizing Committee invited the Central Intelligence Agency's expert instructors to educate agents selected from the National Safety Planning Agency, the Ministry of Internal Affairs, and the Ministry of Defense about guarding and anti-sniping in 1987 and identifying forged passports, performing foreign surveillance, maintaining airport safety, researching the mentality of hostage-takers, and negotiating with them in 1988.[24]

By the time the 1988 Olympic Games were about to begin, a total of 42 anti-terrorism agents had visited South Korea in order to provide 13 rounds of anti-terrorism education.[25] Regarding the October 1987 anti-terrorism joint training with members of Delta Force, Min Byeong-don, then special operations force commander and former principal of South Korea Military Academy, attested that: "In the indoor anti-terrorism training hall for special operations force, our members performed live-fire exercises facing each other. The members of the Delta Force who visited South Korea in order to perform military exercises with its 707th Special Mission Unit members witnessed them and could not close their open mouths."[26]

Deployment of the military forces

The United States Navy deployed core military power in the Far East including Midway Aircraft Carrier Battle Group and Enterprise Aircraft Carrier Battle Group to areas surrounding the Korean Peninsula, and the United States Air Forces stationed in South Korea enhanced their around-the-clock air patrol duty. The South Korean military also maintained high alert termed Jindo Dog 1.[27] "Jindo Dog" refers to the South Korean Army's defense readiness conditions against North Korea's potential local provocation such as infiltration of armed guerrilla agents. It was divided into Jindo Dog 1, 2, and 3. Its alert system begins with Jindo Dog 3. This is elevated to Jindo Dog 2 when conditions like infiltration of armed guerrilla agents occur. When more severe conditions happen, the level goes up to Jindo Dog 1. Jindo Dog

1 is the highest level of alert ordered in case an enemy certainly infiltrated the nation. At this level, the ground for a charge against the communist regime is unquestionable and valid and all operation forces such as the army, police, and reserve force are immediately dispatched to designated locations to get ready for battle in accordance with a given command.

Training of volunteers

Despite the fact that the Seoul Olympic Games were held amid tight security, International Olympic Committee Chairman Juan Antonio Samaranch thought the Games to be a successful and peaceful sports festival: "This atmosphere not only helped the world peace," he announced, "but also provided valuable aid for the sporting world through the Olympic Movement."[28] One of the reasons why the Games were seen as successful was attributed to the smooth security management throughout the entire process. This included coming up with a thorough security and surveillance system for the participants and for South Koreans. This system enabled the government to select and post sufficient human resources in advance to protect key figures and major facilities, making it possible to produce the biggest security effect with the smallest number of personnel. The military and the police provided support in the background and pretrained civilian volunteers responded to participants in the foreground. According to the operation of the police force as described in *A Detailed Security Plan for the Seoul Olympic Games*,[29] human resources were designated and trained in advance to guard major facilities and important figures. This also included occasions where large numbers of people were needed to fill up the space such as the Opening Ceremony, the Closing Ceremony, the marathon, and street festivals. The volunteers who were mobilized during the Games numbered 27,221 – 12,746 men and 14,475 women. The total included students (15,513), workers (3929), housewives (1300), businesspeople (767), and others.

Volunteers received four stages of training. The first stage was from October 1987 through March 1988. The volunteers received a basic course related to the Olympic Games and 86 safety measure outlines. This training included phases of international terrorism, North Korea's provocative maneuvers, site entrance and exit management, and measures against contingencies. During the second stage, from March 1988 through April 1988, volunteers were trained in support for safety and entrance and exit management, volunteering work, identity investigation-related work, materials and equipment demonstration, and firefighting. The third stage took place between April 1988 and May 1988. This stage involved entrance and exit demonstration training, and magnetic-strip-reader operation demonstration training. A temporary pass operation demonstration training was performed for site adaptation. The fourth stage, between May 1988 and August 1988, was used to identify deficiencies from four rounds of rehearsals and how to correct them. During this time, they also established interoperation and collaboration systems with relevant organizations and other fields.[30]

Members of South Korean National Police Veterans Association with vast amounts of experience in pertinent areas as well as members of the Photo Artist Society of South Korea also played a proactive role in minimizing the exposure of the police. Volunteers from Gyeongwuhoe, which was comprised of former police officers, played their role on the frontline on behalf of the police force by controlling those who entered and left the Olympic Village. Meanwhile, volunteers from the Photo Artist Society of South Korea were committed to detecting explosives that may have been disguised as cameras based on their camera knowledge. Safety management for the Seoul Olympic Games was performed by deploying volunteers on the frontline with the army and police on the back line, to prepare for contingencies. The police force was committed to facilities requiring guarding and safety only at a minimum level and mostly volunteers served Olympic families on the frontline and the army was on standby.[31]

Rehearsing the three-step security check

During the Seoul Olympics, the police force was positioned based on three zones according to the tickets' variation. This was to enable the police to protect large areas designated for the Games by creating a three-zone security check system. The police force's three zones refer to dividing participant entrances into three zones of checkpoints. In each zone, the police force scanned the Olympic Identity and Accreditation Card first, followed by a body search and luggage check with X-ray, and then a final check of the Olympic Identity and Accreditation Card more closely for possible falsification. In other words, accessible zones were restricted according to levels of access cards,[32] and even with an access card; the owner of the Card could gain access to core zones only through these three checkpoint steps. It should

Figure 9.1 Ticket for the 1988 Seoul Olympic Opening Ceremony

be noted that Cards were issued to certain persons to allow them to enter specially designated zones, while an event entrance ticket allowed a spectator into a specific arena for a particular event. Figure 9.1 shows an example of the entrance ticket for the Opening Ceremony. The ticket confines the spectator to a specific area within a given arena.

The goal of this plan was to protect key figures, participants, visitors, and facilities. It was performed through rounds of rehearsals such as the 87 Hodori Rehearsal.[33] The rehearsal was carried out during general rehearsal, which was a rehearsal of the whole Olympic program; during the tactic rehearsal, which was rehearsal for a command post exercise specific to security; and during partial rehearsal. The Hodori Rehearsal was carried out between August 26 and October 15, 1987, and included four major rehearsals: partial preparation; overall realistic rehearsal, which included the Olympic Flame Relay; International Olympic Committee General Meeting, other international meetings, cultural activities, youth camp, athletic teams and special guests; 25 event operations, and the opening and closing ceremonies; and athletic operation of the Paralympic Games and their overall rehearsal. In particular, under close collaboration with the government's safety agencies, civilian volunteers were drawn and trained and safety liaison officers were deployed at major locations in order to resolve participant safety matters during the Games.

Computerized accreditation system

The three-step security check was supported by the Seoul Olympic Management System, an electronic system developed in 1984 by Sangyong Computer, one of the two private South Korean companies mentioned early on in this chapter. The system was put in place to manage over 4.6 million tickets sold for 2093 different kinds of events as well as to register members of the International Olympic Committee and the national sports federations, human resources related to the Games, athletes, press, and special guests. The task included classification of the admission tickets. The Seoul Olympic Management System issued identity cards to athletes from 161 countries, executives, and all other personnel who gained access to facilities for the opening and closing ceremonies, and controlled their entrances and exits. Furthermore, this system supported personnel management, registration management, admission tickets, the Olympic Village, and protocol management. This system certainly contributed to the security of the Olympics.

There were, in fact, three other electronic systems to support the Olympics. Games Information On-line Network System dealt with the information about the Games. Wide Information Network System serviced electronic postings. Seoul Olympic Support System supported transportation, accommodation, supplies, and practice gymnasiums. Table 9.2 shows electronic data processing and usages of the Seoul Olympic Management System.[34]

Table 9.2 Data processing and usage of the Seoul Olympic management system

	Human Resource	Tickets	Registration	Athletes' Village	Press Village	VIP	Total
Usages	704,282	5,125,219	133,129	195,251	75,583	44,622	6,278,086
Rates	11.2%	81.6%	2.2%	3.1%	1.2%	0.7%	100%

Source: Seoul Olympic Organizing Committee, Official Report for the 24th Seoul Olympic Games: supplement – formation of the Games' condition, September 1989, p. 107.

South Korea at the time had a lot of loopholes in anti-terrorism response tactics but was able to establish more a modern and systematic surveillance system with support from other states. Certain national or international events might promote the development of a national security system as well as private policing. While, as Lee (2004) suggests, the Seoul Olympic Games may have been one of the factors that stimulated the development of private security businesses, South Korean economic growth might also have contributed to demands for the expansion of security and surveillance technologies at both national and private levels.

Conclusion

The willingness of France, Israel, Japan, the United Kingdom, the United States, and West Germany to share their surveillance and security expertize with South Korea during the 1988 Seoul Olympics stems from ideological conflicts of the Cold War. After the Japanese colonial rule was over, following the nuclear bombing of Hiroshima and Nagasaki, the Korean Peninsula became a victim to power struggle between the United States and the Soviet Union, resulting in a division of a people against its will. As conflicts between the capitalist camp and the communist camp accelerated, the area became the symbol of ideological conflicts. While the Olympic Flame of the Seoul Olympic Games was successfully lit and the Games were able to take place without disruption, the event left another tragic memory about the Korean Peninsula divided. Rather than an international sport festival, the Games took on the character of a battlefield without guns. Unlike concerns about terrorism surrounding the earlier Games, terrorist acts aimed at the Seoul Games were related to ideological conflicts between the two Cold War superpowers that made the Korean Peninsula their strategic geopolitical playground. In making sure that the Seoul Olympics would go on uninterrupted, the so-called friendly countries spared no efforts to prevent terrorist attacks, the South Korean government enacted special laws, civilian volunteers and supporters played an important role to ensure security, and ordinary citizens made all the efforts to make the sports festival a success supported by a smooth security management. Following the example of the

Munich Games in 1972 discussed by Jørn Hansen in Chapter 6 of this book, temporary special laws were also put in place for the Seoul Olympics. These laws, in turn, were used as a blueprint for the Beijing Olympics in 2008, discussed in Chapter 15. The Games Information On-line Network System and the Wide Information Network System also proved to be highly effective, and the organizers of the 1992 Barcelona Games, discussed by Stephen Essex in the next chapter, showed interest in installing those systems for their Olympics.

Notes

We thank Vida Bajc and an anonymous reviewer for valuable comments.

1. Seoul Olympic Organizing Committee, *Seoul Olympic Anjeon Gwangri Gyeolgwa Bogo* (Report of the result of safety management for the Seoul Olympic Games), 1988.
2. Seoul Olympic Organizing Committee, Official Report for the 24th Seoul Olympic Games: supplement – formation of the Games' condition, September 19, 1988.
3. National Archives of Korea, December 13, 2010.
4. *Kyunghyang Shinmun*, "Hwayeombyeong, Cheoyrutan...Olympic Bulan" ("Firebombs and Tear Gas...the Uncertain Olympic Games"), June 15, 1988.
5. *DongA Ilbo*, "Ilbu Daehaksaeng Olympic Banghae Uihyeop Simindeul Yongnap Mothal Il Jajae Chokgu" ("Citizens Urging Students to Refrain from Unacceptable Threat to Interrupt the Olympic Games"), September 29, 1988.
6. *DongA Ilbo*, "Olympic Seonggongbaraneun Shiminjeongshin..shiwi, Nongseong Keugaejuleo" ("Demonstrations and Protests Have Been Reduced by the Spirit of Citizenship Aspiring to Success in Hosting the Olympic Games"), September 12, 1988.
7. *DongA Ilbo*, "88 Gongdong gaecheo Jujanggwa Hyeonshil Sai" ("Disparity between the insistence on joint hosting of the 88 Olympic Games and reality"), June 8, 1988.
8. *Monthly Chosun*, "HanKuk hyeondaesa eui gyeoljeongjeok sungandeul" ("The Tragic Moments in the Modern Korean History"), October 2003.
9. Ibid.
10. "Suspect in Korean Crash Recovers from Poisoning," *New York Times*, December 6, 1987.
11. Seoul Olympic Organizing Committee, *Seoul Olympic Anjeon Gwangri Gyeolgwa Bogo* (Report of the result of safety management for the Seoul Olympic Games), 1988.
12. The law was named *Olympic Pyeonghwareul Jikigi Wihan Beoprul* (Laws to Protect Peace of the Olympic Games).
13. *DongA Ilbo*, July 23, 1988.
14. *DongA Ilbo*, August 15, 1988.
15. Gwang Ok, *Sport Loving Nation: Cultural Legacy of the '88 Seoul Olympics*, presented at the Beijing Forum, November 8, 2008.
16. Federal Bureau of Investigation, "A Brief History of the FBI," History, retrieved from www.fbi.gov, on August 4, 2011.
17. *Maeil Business Newspaper*, May 4, 1988.

18. Ibid.
19. *Monthly Chosun*, "HanKuk hyeondaesa eui gyeoljeongjeok sungandeul" ("The Tragic Moments in the Modern Korean History"), October 2003.
20. Ibid.
21. *DongA Ilbo*, "Jangwe Junbi Isang Eupna(4) Hwakin ddo Hwakin…Terrobangji Geomijul Gyeongbi" ("Repetitively check whether there is no problem with out-of-stadium preparation(4)…anti-terrorism cobweb guard"), June 27, 1988.
22. *Monthly Chosun*, "HanKuk hyeondaesa eui gyeoljeongjeok sungandeul" ("The Tragic Moments in the Modern Korean History"), October 2003.
23. "Delta Force," retrieved from Encyclopedia.com on August 11, 2011.
24. *Monthly Chosun*, "HanKuk hyeondaesa eui gyeoljeongjeok sungandeul" ("The Tragic Moments in the Modern Korean History"), October 2003.
25. Ibid.
26. Ibid.
27. Ibid.
28. See Juan Antonio Samaranch, President of the International Olympic Committee (1980–2001), Opening Address at WACSO (The World Academic Conference of the Seoul Olympiad '88), August 21, 1988.
29. *Seoul Olympic Daehoe Saebuanjeon Gaehoik*, 1987.
30. Seoul Olympic Organizing Committee, Official Report for the 24th Seoul Olympic Games: supplement – formation of the Games' condition, September 19, 1988.
31. Ibid.
32. The access cards were verified whether the holders were ordinary spectators (ticket holders) or special participants (AD cardholders) such as the International Olympic Committee members, VIPs, athletes, and press.
33. Hodori was the Seoul Olympic official mascot that was shown after national contest in 1983.
34. Seoul Olympic Organizing Committee, Official Report for the 24th Seoul Olympic Games: supplement – formation of the Games' condition, September 1989, 104–107.

10
Platform for Local Political Expression and Resolution (Barcelona 1992)

Stephen Essex

The 1992 Barcelona Summer Olympics are remembered as a model of urban regeneration, especially in terms of their ability to change the spatial structure and image of the city (Garcia-Ramon and Albet, 2000; Marshall, 1996, 2000, 2004; Monclús, 2003). These outcomes were partly facilitated by the safe and secure staging of the event, which, while not considered to be "high risk" by the organizers, did present some potential challenges. At the global level, there was some thinking about possible reprisal attacks on competing nations in the Olympics for their involvement in the Gulf War (1990–1991) (Coaffee and Johnston, 2007: 146). Domestically, there was some concern that the Olympics might be used as a platform for publicity by those seeking greater political autonomy from the centralist state based in Madrid. Notably, there had been long-standing tensions in the Basque Country, Catalonia and Galicia, where a strong sense of social and cultural identity had underpinned demands for greater political and economic independence (Conversi, 1997). The location of the Games in Barcelona, the most populous and powerful city within these potentially divergent autonomous regions, obviously had particular reso-nance. By analyzing the spatial organization of the four main Olympic venues across the city, the coordination between the multi-sectoral agencies involved in surveillance and their strategies to counter any potential threat of disrup-tion, the argument taken in this chapter suggests that, in terms of security, the success of the event had more to do with political debate and the recognition that any disruption would be counterproductive to the respective causes. The principal threats to the tranquillity of the Games stemmed more from political and regional tensions within Spain than from externally generated instability. However, in terms of security, the success of the event was partly determined by the recognition by potential dissidents that disruption to such a globally high-profile event would be counterproductive to their causes.

Barcelona as the host city

The background to staging the Olympic Games in Barcelona provides an important context within which to understand perceptions of security and implementation of surveillance technologies and practices in the local and global circumstances. Barcelona, with a population of about three million, has been the economic and cultural capital of Catalonia for many centuries. During the 20th century, the city had experienced urban and industrial decline from both changes in the global economy and General Franco's centralized dictatorship after the Spanish Civil War (1936–1939). Franco's regime, based in Madrid, stifled the local government's ability to respond to the changing economic trends and acted to repress any expression of regional identity and culture. However, the death of Franco in 1975 unleashed forces for immense change that had built up by that time, including the establishment of more local powers and considerable autonomy for the regions of Spain. In Barcelona, these changes led to the establishment of a relatively powerful new city government and an autonomous government for Catalonia, together with the reassertion of Catalan identity and culture and a desire to position the city as a modern, post industrial and prosperous city of world standing to attract international investment (Marshall, 1996; Monclús, 2007).

Over the decades following Franco's death, Barcelona had modernized its port and manufacturing sectors to advance its status as an economic powerhouse and transformed its older industrial urban districts into the dynamic post industrial capital of culture that it is today. The staging of the Olympic Games in 1992 was a catalyst for much of the physical transformation, although the redevelopment was part of a longer-term strategy. The General Metropolitan Plan of 1976 set out a 50-year strategy to guide the spatial adjustments necessary to modernize and sustain the port and logistics-based activities, to revitalize the waterfront and public spaces, to restore polluted and derelict industrial sites, to invest in road systems and new layouts, and to emphasize architectural design (Monclús, 2007: 222–223).

Barcelona has a proud history of using mega-events to drive forward its urban development, which has included World Expos in 1888 and 1929 and, more recently, the Forum 2004 (a cultural exposition) in 2004 (Monclús, 2007). At the time that the Games were awarded to Barcelona in 1986, International Olympic Committee President Juan Antonio Samaranch, who had been a Catalan Francoist, seemed to have been aware of the potential of the event for "fast-tracking" the development process in his home city (Hargreaves and Ferrando, 1997: 82; Hargreaves, 2000: 139). Hargreaves and Ferrando (1997: 86) record, for example, that when the Mayor of Barcelona, Narcís Serra, told Samaranch of the city's desire to stage the Olympics, Samaranch is said to have replied, "I accept your challenge."[1]

Security was one of the initial concerns. When the *New York Times* reported about 1987 bombings by Terra Lliure – which means "free land" – a Catalan separatist organization, and Euzkadi Ta Askatasuna, the Basque separatist group, it also noted that "Maragall, the Mayor [of Barcelona], said that security was of prime concern to the city's Olympic organizers." The success of this strategy in creating a new urban identity for Barcelona, and indeed for the Spanish state, therefore, seems to have depended, at least in part, upon the Olympics being perceived as well organized and, above all, a safe and secure event.[2]

The award of the Olympic Games to Barcelona represented an opportunity for both the Castilian state and Catalonia to promote their respective political causes. The Spanish state wished to use the Olympics as a means of marking the end of the Franco regime[3] and to celebrate the emergence of a new, fully modernized, politically mature and unified democratic state to the rest of the world (Hargreaves and Ferrando, 1997: 67). 1992 was a critical year for the country as a whole as it attempted to stage not only the Olympics in Barcelona but the World Expo in Seville and the cultural capital of Europe in Madrid, in what became known as the "Spanish Project" and the "Year of Spain." The benefits of staging these three international events were perceived by the Spanish government as fostering pan-Spanish cooperation and better regional working relationships, as well as serving as an equalizing force throughout Spain's disparate regions and attracting inward investment.[4] 1992 was also perceived by some as Spain's final exam for membership of the club of First World, rich, democratic and organized countries (Pi-Sunyer, 1995: 37). Although Spain had joined the European Community in 1986, the year of 1992 marked the creation of the Single European Market, involving the removal of economic barriers to form a "free market" in the European Community (Wise and Gibb, 1993). Spain was positioning itself at the forefront of this emerging new Europe. The perception and anticipation of the potential of the Olympics for improving the international image of Spain and encouraging inward investment is nicely captured in the words of the President of the Spanish Olympic Committee and first Vice-President of the Organizing Committee of the 1992 Barcelona Olympic Games (COOB, 1992), Carlos Ferrer Salat:

> It's important and fundamental that the opening and closing ceremonies of the Games help to modernise the image that foreigners have of Spain, because currently we continue to be bullfighters and flamenco dancers. If we are able to do this, this will be the best benefit possible and compensation for the effort it takes to organise the Games.[5]

In contrast, public opinion in Catalonia wished to utilize the Olympics as an expression of their already existing economic wealth, aspirations for urban regeneration, and the distinctive character and culture of their region. Their goal, too, was very different; namely, to further the political cause of autonomy and greater independence. The *New York Times* wrote, for example, that "Catalonia, the prosperous autonomous region that has Barcelona as its capital, never misses a chance to promote its name and its nationalism – and what better chance than the Olympics?" In that same report, Catalan President Jordi Pujol was quoted as saying, "Strictly speaking, these are Barcelona's games... But spiritually, yes, and politically and sentimentally too, these are also very much Catalonia's games."[6] Recognition by the International Olympic Committee was seen as a powerful symbol of legitimacy for the aspiration of nationhood within Catalonia (Pi-Sunyer, 1995: 37). On the eve of the Olympics, the Generalitat (regional government) took a two-page advertisement, at a cost of about $5.6 million, in several European and American newspapers to promote awareness about the status of Catalonia as a "country" within Spain. Page one of the advertisement showed the location of Barcelona on a blank map of Europe asking the question "What country do you situate this city in?" The second page gave the answer "Catalunya, of course. This is where Barcelona is, in Catalunya, a country in Spain with its own culture language and identity."[7]

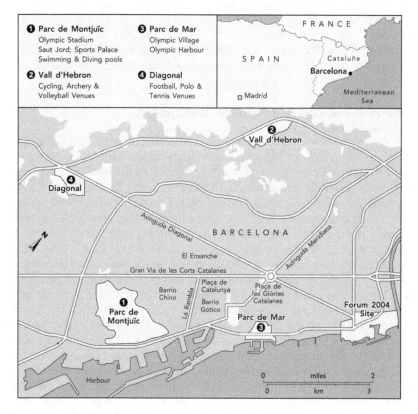

Figure 10.1 The location of the main venues used in the 1992 Barcelona Olympic Games

Source: Adapted from Essex and Chalkley (1998: 198).

In addition, there were political groups in other regions in Spain, such as the Basque Country and Galicia, which could have used the Olympics as a platform to promote their claim for greater independence but not in the same way. While Catalonia recognized that it had the opportunity for entirely legitimate promotion of identity, Euzkadi Ta Askatasuna had few options other than the threat of disruptive action. The movement from the Basque Country – Euzkadi Ta Askatasuna – was more extreme and had a record of terrorist acts within Spain (Hooper, 2006). Euzkadi Ta Askatasuna was established in 1959 as a cultural movement to protect the distinctiveness of the region, but by 1963, it had become more militant and had adopted revolutionary armed struggle and violence as a means of achieving its objectives (Conversi, 1997: 96). Euzkadi Ta Askatasuna's campaign involved assassinations of police, the military, politicians, businessmen, journalists and academics, as well as occasional bombings in the seaside tourist resorts visited by international visitors. Such actions claimed the lives of over 800 people by 2009. The staging of the Olympics on Spanish soil presented Euzkadi Ta Askatasuna with a potential target and platform to promote its cause to a global audience (Hargreaves and Ferrando, 1997: 68), although it might also have been conscious that such actions might prove counterproductive in terms of negative public opinion.

Geography of Olympic facilities in Barcelona

The geography of the sporting facilities and other infrastructure utilized for the Olympic Games of 1992 presented a fundamental challenge for the security of the event (see Figure 10.1). The sporting facilities were provided at four main locations across the city. The main venue for the Olympics was the Montjuïc area, which is a piece of higher ground southwest of the city center used as a defensive location and fortification throughout history. This location contained the redeveloped main stadium, originally built for the International Exposition in 1929, together with the Sant Jordi Sports Palace and the swimming and diving pools. The area had become a well-established park in the city and presented numerous access routes into and across the site. The second main venue for the Olympic events was the Vall d'Hebron area, which was a large, isolated and unstructured neighborhood in the west of the city. This site provided the venues for cycling, archery and volleyball.

The Olympic Village was developed on a 130 ha/1.3 km² site previously occupied by declining industries on the coast northeast of the city center (at Parc de Mar). Extensive redevelopment took place in this location involving the transfer of the rail route inland, the building of a coastal ring road, the removal of old industries, the construction of the Olympic Village and a new marina (Olympic Harbour). Parc de Mar was constructed as a continuation of the Eixample district and opened up 5.2 km of coastline previously blocked by railway lines (Essex and Chalkley, 1998; Chalkley and Essex, 1999). The fourth Olympic site, on the Diagonal, hosted the football, polo and tennis. A ring road linked the Olympic venues together, along with new traffic interchanges and a computerized traffic management system (Hargreaves, 2000: 155).

Organization of surveillance to deliver a secure event

Security considerations had been a central part of the bid process and evaluation by the International Olympic Committee. The Olympics had been awarded to Barcelona on October 17, 1986, and by June 1987, a Higher Commission for Olympic Security had been set up in the city to plan and implement the surveillance procedures and technologies needed to deliver a safe and secure event. A Technical Security Cabinet, involving representatives from the Organizing Committee and the Higher Commission for Olympic Security, was formed in 1988 to analyze lessons from previous Olympic Games, including observation of the Calgary and Seoul Games, and to propose a model for the Barcelona event. According to the Olympic Organizing Committee report, "the Olympic security operation began in stages and in 1989 the surveillance and counter-surveillance services at the Olympic building sites and information gathering tasks, among others, were already underway."[8] With 39,462 accredited members of the "Olympic Family" (including athletes, officials, media, VIPs and guests of sponsors) and nearly 500,000 spectators, together with the eyes of the world on Barcelona (estimated to be 2.3 billion for the Opening Ceremony),[9] the preparations to deliver security required just as much time and planning as the infrastructural developments.

The proposed model to deliver security was an integrated system of public and private plans and resources under the command of the Higher Commission for Olympic Security. Collaboration involved a huge range of surveillance operatives (see Table 10.1). The Olympic Security Master Plan[10] was organized around three types of operational projects: (1) functions (e.g., public safety, road safety); (2) specifics (e.g., information security, explosive deactivation, VIP protection); and (3) activities (e.g., sports competition, accommodation, telecommunications, logistics).[11] A total of 17 broad security operations were identified, within which there were 86 specific projects covering a broad range of measures to protect aspects as diverse as public safety, ticketing, telecommunications, transport and Olympic sponsorship and image rights (see Table 10.2). This structure evolved during the preparations for the Games. The mayor of Barcelona was reported saying,

> We have met with teams from America's State Department and National Security Council: we're in touch with private security firms; we talked to security people from Los Angeles, and the IOC is advising us.... We're getting a lot of advice. The IOC told us we had too many agencies, 70, involved in security. We've cut that down and named a single person to be in charge of security planning.

Each specific project was assigned to an organization with a director and its own Olympic Security Office to supervise, coordinate, monitor, control and manage the risk to security.[12] All projects were ready by June 1990.[13]

During the Games, the so-called standard operations plans noted above were translated into "territorial operations plans," involving a highly coordinated task force approach. Three territorial units were established with command centers (CEMAN) and coordination centers (CECOR): Level 1 (base level), where surveillance operations were carried out by the operatives at each sports venue or center; Level 2 (area level), which brought all level 1 operations into a territorial area; and Level 3 (command level) comprising the centralized Olympic Security Center for the whole city (Centro de Seguridad Olímpica) (see Figure 10.2). This hierarchical structure ensured that the lines of communication were centralized to allow operations to be properly coordinated. Centro de Seguridad Olímpica was itself linked to a Crisis Center in Madrid should circumstances require. Such arrangements

Table 10.1   Security forces deployed during the 1992 Barcelona Olympic Games

Security force	Responsibility	Personnel deployed
National Police	80% of Olympic facilities (venues, training sites, Olympic Village and official hotels) and most of the functional plans	15,500
Guardia Civil	Airports, Port of Barcelona, four venues, essential public services (water, fuel, electricity, telecommunications, transportation)	5,000
Mossos d'Esquadra (Catalan police)	Two competition venues, crime prevention activities (e.g., ticket touting and commercial crime)	385
Barcelona City Police	Traffic and street public safety; dealing with victims of crime	2,890
Local Police Forces	Within municipal territories	1,700
Army	Supported Guardia Civil to protect essential services and human resources for COOB, 1992	3,000
Air Force	Protection of air space	250
Navy	Territorial waters and water competition areas	Undisclosed
Total		28,725

Source: United States Senate Committee on Commerce, Science and Transportation; Barcelona Olympic Organizing Committee.[14]

Table 10.2 Olympic Security projects at the 1992 Barcelona Olympic Games

Program	Project	Responsible agency
Intelligence and special services	Interior and exterior staff, accreditations and ticket control	Department of State Security
	Special operations	National Police
	Explosives detection and deactivation	Guardia Civil
Internal Security 1: COOB, 1992 company security	COOB, 1992 company security, staff control, logistics	COOB, 1992
Internal Security 2: accident and intrusion	Physical security of Olympic facilities and surroundings	COOB, 1992
Internal Security 3: access control	Accreditations, tickets and access	COOB, 1992
Transport Security	Official transport security	National Police
	Mobility and road security	Barcelona City Council, local police forces, Generalitat of Catalonia
Accommodation Security	Accommodation and Olympic Village security	National Police
Competitions, Events and Ceremonies Security	Security for Olympic torch, ceremonies, competition and training, congress, cultural event and Paralympics	National Police
VIP and Special Risk Delegation Security	VIP security and special risk delegation security	National Police
Olympic Support Services Security	Olympic support services security, doping control security, security air cover	National Police
	Information security	Ministry of Transport and Communications
	Arrival and departure management and security	Guardia Civil
Public Safety	Crime prevention, judicial police, public order, commercial crime	National Police
	Dealing with victims of crime	City Councils

Continued

Table 10.2 Continued

Program	Project	Responsible agency
Public Services Security	Essential public services security, transport and communications security and frontier security	Guardia Civil
	Administration and control of territorial waters and air space affected by the Games	Ministry of Defense
Emergencies	Internal security and emergencies at Olympic sites and power	Fire Extinction and Rescue Services and Generalitat of Catalonia
	Internal security and emergencies: water supply and flood	Junta d'Aigües
	Internal security and emergencies: telecommunications	Department of Telecommunications
	Internal security and emergencies: land passenger transport of dangerous materials	Dirección General de Transporte
	Internal security and emergencies: air transport	National airports
	Internal security and emergencies: sea transport	Dirección General de la Marina Mercante
	Internal security and emergencies: chemicals	Gerencia de Protección Civil
	Thermal inversion emergency	Barcelona City Council
Planning	Olympic Security Plan, monitoring basic infrastructures, tests	Higher Commission for Olympic Security
Administration	Agreements, economics, logistics, office, legal, administration	Higher Commission for Olympic Security
Human Resources	Human resources management, staff selection, training, food and accommodation, transport, medical and health, social and labor relations	Higher Commission for Olympic Security
Telecommunications and Computers	Telecommunications networks and equipment	Higher Commission for Olympic Security
	Computer networks and equipment	Department of State Security
Relations with the Community	Image and relations with media	Higher Commission for Olympic Security

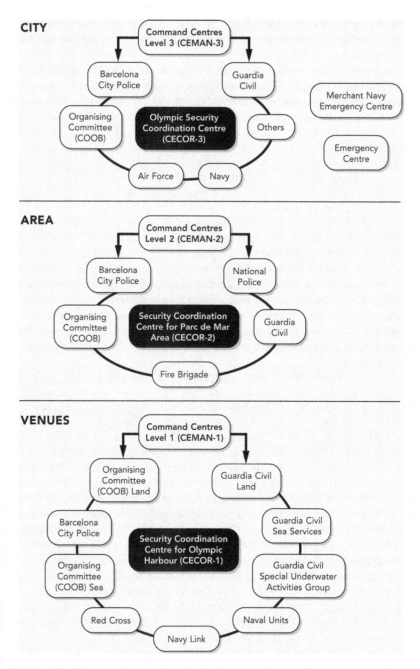

Figure 10.2 The organizational framework of security forces at the Barcelona Olympic Harbour

Source: Barcelona Olympic Organizing Committee (1992: 307).

contributed to the creation of multi-scalar partnerships in Spain and to assist in reducing potential tensions and suspicions through collaboration and consensus.

The surveillance technologies and practices for the Olympic Games involved the "Olympic Adaptation Project." Hargreaves (2000: 133) notes that most measures were implemented discreetly and were not overbearing. However, at some strategic locations, these practices and technologies were obviously conspicuous (Coaffee and Johnston, 2007: 147). According to the Organizing Committee's report to the International Olympic Committee, "security considerations made it advisable to seal off the whole of the Olympic Village with a double line of steel fencing, and to place very strict access controls at the entrances to the residential area and the international zone." This zone included "each of the various sports facilities in the Parc de Mar Area" which also "constituted a sealed area." In addition, "the mouth of the Olympic Harbour and the beaches of the Olympic Village were protected by underwater fencing as well as by coastal patrols." So, too, "the Parc de Mar Village was a sealed area," adding to the list of strict access controls imposed at entrances to residential areas and the international zones.[15] About 28,725 police and armed forces personnel were deployed during the Olympics, together with an additional 8624 volunteers and 145 contracted staff, who were hired by the Organizing Committee to deal with its internal company security and security at Olympic facilities during the Games period.[16]

These arrangements proved successful to the organizers and the local and international audiences in that there was no serious incident. Barcelona Director of Security Santiago de Sicart has subsequently acted as a security adviser for the International Olympic Committee Coordination Commissions for the Summer and Winter Olympic Games of 2000, 2002, 2004 and 2006, demonstrating that the development of intellectual capital can become highly marketable in terms of transnational knowledge transfer for future events. The influence of these "security experts" has therefore been long-standing, although their identity has not always been known. As the International Olympic Committee acknowledged in one of its reports, it was the "Director of Security at the Games of the XXV Olympiad in Barcelona in 1992 and [the] security expert on the 2000, 2002, 2004 and 2006 IOC Coordination Committees" who contributed research reports to the Security Working Group evaluating the bids for the 2010 Winter Olympics.[17] Their names were made public by the *New York Times* during the time of the Salt Lake City Games: "the security chiefs from the 1992 Barcelona Olympics and the 2000 Sydney Games, Santiago de Sicard [sic] and Peter Ryan, were acting as advisers for Salt Lake and for future Games."[18]

According to Coaffee and Johnston (2007: 146), a total of $66.2 million was spent to ensure security for the Barcelona Olympics, or about $7,072 per athlete. Interestingly, this figure is considerably less than the Games

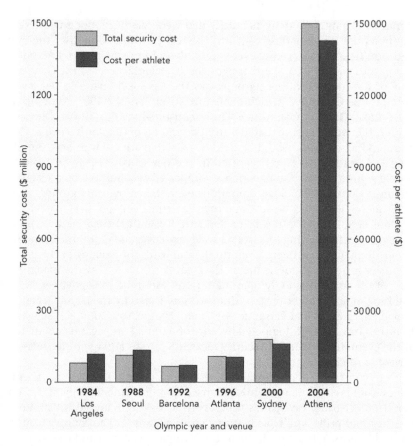

Figure 10.3 Security costs of the Summer Olympic Games, 1984–2004

immediately before or after the Barcelona Olympics (see Figure 10.3). The reason may be that key personnel were drawn from the Spanish military and police forces rather than private security companies. It also reflects perceptions and estimates of threats from domestic or international terrorism by the organizers of the Games.

Perceptions and estimates of risks to security

There was recognition that the use of the Barcelona Olympics as a platform for publicity by regional groups seeking greater political autonomy from the state, especially in Catalonia itself and the Basque Country, had the potential, however small, to be a destabilizing force for the event (Hargreaves, 2000: 165), although these tensions were largely played out in symbolic terms. The "physical" dangers anticipated were relatively modest, whereas the potential for embarrassment was the real concern. Soon after the city had won the bid to stage the event, a number of pressure groups and political parties based in Catalonia sought the "Catalanization" of the Games.[19] One of the most prominent groups was the Associació per a la Delegació Olimpica de Catalunya, which demanded, from January 1987, recognition of a Catalan Olympic Committee. The establishment of the Catalan Olympic Committee would ensure that identifying symbols of Catalonia, such as flag and national anthem, would be used if a Catalan athlete won an Olympic medal. According to a poll reported in the newspaper *El País* on January 5, 1990, 86% of the Catalan public supported recognition of a Catalan Olympic Committee.[20] Such aspirations were shared by other groups, such as Esquerra Republicana de Catalunya (a republican political party), La Crida a la Solidaritat (Appeal for Solidarity), a militant *independista* pressure group campaigning for Catalan independence, and Omnium Cultural/ Acció Olímpica, an influential cultural group with the backing of the party in power in regional government (Hargreaves, 2000: 62). At the inauguration of the refurbished Olympic stadium on Montjuïc in September 1989, the King of Spain and the Spanish team were jeered by the largely Catalan crowd (Hargreaves and Ferrando, 1997: 68). Hargreaves (2000: 65) suggests that the crowd were ill-tempered because of national propaganda circulated at the event, heavy-handed security measures, bad weather and the delayed arrival of the King.

It was concluded that a repeat of such actions during the Olympics themselves would represent a potential source of political embarrassment, which could reflect badly on Spain's progress in achieving national integration, identity, and pride, and have negative ramifications for the country's international status. The act positioned the Olympic organizers and the Spanish government in front of a dilemma. On the one hand, they saw a need to give surveillance measures utmost priority to ensure that the Olympics in Barcelona were a successful and trouble-free event. On the other hand, allowing the regional groups to have some voice would permit the Spanish government to display its democratic credentials. After 40 years of dictatorship, the state would not wish to continue to appear as a police state by suppressing and/or overriding such claims. Similarly, the regional groups were aware of the potential for alienating any support for their cause through unreasonable demands and/or unpopular acts. Neither the state nor public opinion in Catalonia had any interest in using violence as a means to achieve its goal. Consequently, there was a lot of good will and diplomacy at work, which reduced the actual risk of disruption.

The political process helped to manage the public debate over the extent of state and regional symbolism to be used in the Barcelona Games and ultimately to ensure that an appropriate compromise was reached between excessive Castalianization and excessive Catalanization. The Organizing

Committee of the Games comprised Barcelona City Council, the Catalan regional government (Generalitat), the Spanish government and the Spanish Olympic Committee, reflecting the multi-scalar collaboration required in the organization of international events. Barcelona City Council played the key role in the preparations and was run by the Catalan Socialist Party led by Pasqual Maragall (as Mayor). The Catalan Socialist Party is affiliated with the Spanish Socialist Workers Party, which formed the Spanish national government in Madrid at the time. Former Mayor of Barcelona Narcís Serra, who had instigated the Olympic bid and appointed Maragall, had become a key figure in Spanish national politics as Deputy Prime Minister and Minister of Defense (Hargreaves and Ferrando, 1997: 67).[21] Maragall's task was to stage a sufficiently Catalan event without unduly distressing opinion in Madrid (Pi-Sunyer, 1995: 43), although his overriding objective was the urban regeneration of the city. In contrast, the Generalitat was run by Convergencia i Unío, a Catalan nationalist coalition, led by Jordi Pujol, a center-right pragmatic nationalist, who was more strident in promoting regional interests with less deference to Madrid (Pi-Sunyer, 1995: 43).[22] His public statements often expressed strong pro-Catalan views, while others were couched in more conciliatory terms.[23] Therefore, the potential political tensions were not simply between the Spanish government and the regional government but also, to some extent, between the interests of the regional government and the city government. The views of politicians from the city and region were constantly in the forefront of mass media coverage, while contributions from Madrid were sidelined. Politicians in central government avoided any public engagement in the symbolism debate and were non-confrontational.[24]

Nevertheless, the "Catalanization" of the Olympic Games began to gain a higher profile in the pre-Olympics period. In April 1992, Esquerra Republicana organized a three kilometer banner around the Olympic Stadium promoting their cause. It gained publicity by being the largest banner in the world for the *Guinness Book of World Records*. A cardboard effigy of the Barcelona Olympic mascot, Cobi, was burned. Supporters of Catalanist movement La Crida distributed materials including stickers, posters, clothing and a leaflet explaining the case for the "Catalanization" of the Games.[25]

On May 7, 1992, at a press conference hosted by the Catalan Olympic Committee, the local political groups (La Crida, Esquerra Republicana and Omnium Cultural/Acció Olímpica) announced five minimums for the Catalan presence that would be acceptable during the Games.

- Catalan athletes must march separately under the Catalan flag.
- The Catalan hymn must be used with other national anthems.
- Catalan athletes who win medals must be able to choose between the Catalan and Spanish anthems at awards ceremonies.

- The participating countries must march according to the alphabetical order of the Catalan language.
- The International Olympic Committee must publicly state that there is no legal reason that the Catalan Olympic Committee cannot be recognized.[26]

The groups stated that if these minimums were not met, then there would be community demonstrations in the lead-up to the Opening Ceremony of the Olympic Games in Barcelona. A pact (Paz Olímpica) between the Mayor of Barcelona and the President of the Generalitat, less than two months before the Opening Ceremony, attempted to pacify the Catalan cause. The main concessions and agreements were:

- The credit for a successful Games would be shared by all participants.
- The Games should be carried out peacefully in order to enhance the prestige of both Barcelona and Catalonia.
- The symbols of Catalonia would be showcased at the Games.
- The Spanish, Catalan and Barcelona flags would have equal status during the Opening Ceremony, and the King of Spain would enter the stadium to the Spanish national anthem and the Catalan "Els Segadors" hymn. Catalan would be an official language.
- Residents of Catalonia were encouraged to show their support for the Olympics by hanging banners of all types outside their homes.[27]

These concessions were accepted by the Esquerra Republicana political party as they sensed that public opinion had become tired of the ongoing debate. As reported in *La Vanguardia*[28] newspaper on June 10, 1992, the party's president announced a "cease-fire" over the symbolic content of Olympic ceremonies and that public pressure had stopped Spanish centralists from hijacking the Games.[29] La Crida and the Catalan Olympic Committee were less content with the pact, especially regarding the use of the *senyera* flag during the awards ceremonies for Catalan athletes.[30] However, public reaction against these continued demands of the Catalan groups, as reflected in newspaper editorials and letters to editors, began regarding them as unreasonable and disloyal.[31]

The threat of disruption continued in the immediate buildup to the Opening Ceremony on July 25, 1992 (Hargreaves, 2000: 65). The 5570 km Olympic Flame Relay through all 17 autonomous regions of Spain in June 1992 was disrupted by demonstrations, flags and slogans. At various points along the Olympic Flame Relay through Catalonia to Barcelona, the flame was surrounded by demonstrators with Catalan flags chanting slogans.[32] Security remained low profile and discreet to avoid inflaming the situation and perhaps as a deliberate attempt by the authorities to show that democratic rights in the "new" Spain were no longer restrained. It was at one such demonstration, in the coastal town of Empúries on June 13, 1992, that press coverage, particularly in *La Vanguardia*, and public opinion began to turn against such protests. The display of the "Freedom for Catalonia" flag[33] during a saxophone solo of "El Cant dels Ocells," itself a symbol of the region, was portrayed as a shameful and inane act in newspaper coverage. The incident was not shown in the television coverage of the event.[34] It soon became clear through editorials and letters to editors, that the public was growing increasingly intolerant of any further disruption that might threaten the success of the event, and the public wanted the Games to be allowed to "play out" peacefully (Hargreaves and Ferrando, 1997: 84).

In March, shortly before the Games, a dozen Euzkadi Ta Askatasuna members were arrested because the authorities reasoned that such an arrest would diffuse the threat of attacks during the Games. As the *New York Times* reported, "The arrest last month of ... the leader of the Basque Homeland and Liberty organization, known by its Spanish initials, ETA, and 11 of his associates heartened authorities that ETA might be diffused enough to pose a lesser threat to the Olympics, which begin July 25."[35] This act seems to have earned broad public support and a wave of positive feedback for the central government.[36] Nevertheless, according to Toohey (2008: 435), Euzkadi Ta Askatasuna did bomb electricity pylons to disrupt electricity supplies during the Opening Ceremony.

Outside of the regional political disputes, Grupo de Resistencia Antifascista Primo October ("Grapo"), a Marxist group, which inflicted attacks in various parts of Spain between 1975 and 2000, exploded bombs on a gas pipeline about 30 miles outside Barcelona during the Games. The incident was reported in the United Kingdom media:

> Juan Antonio Samaranch, the president of the IOC, denied that yesterday's bomb attack on a pipeline 30 miles outside Barcelona at Vilafranca, said to be the work of the extreme left-wing group, *Grupo de Resistencia Antifascista Primo October*, posed any threat to the Games, which were taking place under tight security. "I don't think you can say that it is a threat because the incident took place nowhere near an Olympic site," he said. Police dismissed any possibility that the explosion was the work of either Basque or Catalan separatists.[37]

The United States media also makes reference to the potential threat from Grapo:

> But one security expert in the region said the resurgence of a left-wing guerrilla group known as Grapo [Grupo de Resistencia Antifascista Primo October] also bears watching, particularly by United States interests. Grupo de Resistencia Antifascista Primo October was actively involved in the campaign several years ago to close two United States military bases

in Spain, in Torrejon and Zaragoza. The Air Force finally left Torrejon two weeks ago, and the remaining American ground crews at Zaragoza will be gone by the Olympics. "Grapo was very active a couple of years ago," said the expert, who spoke on condition of anonymity. "Most of the leaders ended up in jail, and six months ago, I wouldn't have thought they posed much of a problem. But then they were involved in a couple of low-grade bombings, and their leader escaped from jail last week. So I don't know what they're capable of."[38]

According to Cottrell (2003: 311), both incidents caused inconvenience but did not gain global media attention and did not disrupt the event.[39]

During the Games, important gestures to Catalonia were made: most notably, the King declared the Games open in Catalan. Even the Spanish flag, which is perceived as a symbol of past oppression in Catalonia, appeared more frequently in the stadium and on the streets (Hargreaves and Ferrando, 1997: 73–74). Some Catalan groups continued to use the Games to publicize their cause by claiming that the surveillance procedures threatened freedom of expression and civil liberties. La Crida described the deployment of the surveillance and security operatives as an occupation of Catalan territory (Hargreaves, 2000: 80). Over 30 people were arrested for being members or supporters of Terra Lliure (Hargreaves and Ferrando, 1997: 74), which had been established as a Catalan attempt to emulate Euzkadi Ta Askatasuna (Tremlett, 2006: 332). The group, in turn, understood these arrests as evidence of ongoing state oppression and intimidation (Hargreaves, 2000: 84). Disruption of the Olympic Games was nevertheless minimal, yet surveillance procedures during the Games appeared for the most part discreet and not overbearing. Police and paramilitary drafted in from other parts of Spain were issued with guidelines on how to treat Catalans and their culture with respect. Plain clothes police were disguised as volunteers and what was deemed "dangerous propaganda material" was confiscated (Hargreaves, 2000: 132). It may well be a testament to the measures used at the event that, in a survey of 800 Catalan residents undertaken for *La Vanguardia* following the Games, the achievement of a secure event was regarded as the most successful aspect of the Barcelona Olympics by the majority of the city's population (Hargreaves and Ferrando, 1997: 75–76; Hargreaves, 2000: 133).

Conclusion

The organizers of the Barcelona Olympics saw domestic political groups interested in furthering their cause of regional autonomy and independence as a potential threat to security of the event, rather than any disruption from external sources. Despite the extensive surveillance measures, which have become a model for subsequent Olympic Games, much of the "threat" was dissipated through dialog, compromise, some arrests, and careful public relations and media management, together with common sense rather than confrontation or aggression. In this respect, the organizers had shown to the world that Spain was no longer ruled by a fascist regime but was an open and democratic state. The Games played a big role in bringing maturity and pragmatism to relations between Spain, Catalonia and Barcelona and hence reduced overall political tensions. The benefits of the Olympic Games for both the greater Spanish nation-state and the regions were ultimately recognized by most interest groups and led to a struggle largely fought out in symbolic terms. The Olympic Games were allowed to be staged without being affected by terrorist acts (Hargreaves, 2000: 161). Some argue that, as a result, the Barcelona Olympics acted to advance the cause of Catalan nationalism for a greater degree of autonomy within the existing democratic constitution (Hargreaves, 2000: 165). Others regard the Barcelona Olympics as a missed opportunity to strengthen the region's political identity (Pi-Sunyer, 1995: 50). The International Olympic Committee, for example, refused to recognize the Catalan Olympic Committee some months after the Games in Barcelona on the grounds that Catalonia was not a state. Despite the potential threats, the Olympics were safe and secure, which ultimately enabled Barcelona to establish itself as a cultural capital of Europe and a truly global city, helped the country to consolidate its rapid socioeconomic maturity, and brought greater mutual acceptance to late-20th-century Spain.

Notes

The author wishes to thank Clive Charlton, Geoff Wilson and an anonymous reviewer for their valuable comments on an earlier draft of this paper. Thanks also to Brian Rogers, Tim Absalom and Jamie Quinn for the cartography in the School of Geography, Earth and Environmental Sciences, Plymouth University.

1. Quoted from *La Vanguardia*, June 14, 1992.
2. "Barcelona Plans a Lasting Olympics," P. Delany, *New York Times*, October 21, 1987.
3. "Olympic Games as Showcase" [online article], S. A. Harris (1992) Centre d'Estudis Olimpics UAB, Barcelona, 5. http://olympicstudies.uab.es/pdf/wp013_eng.pdf
4. Ibid., 8. The government also undertook international publicity, involving a nine-part series of advertisement supplements in *Time* magazine (November 1988–January 1992). The nine supplements covered various topics: "Goodbye Mañana, Hello Tomorrow," "Renewing Spanish Industry," "Fashionable Spain," "An Olympic Champion," "Telecommunications and High Tech," "A Thriving Cultural Paradise," "Spain Spearheads Europe," "Spanish Banks Go Global," and "1992 – The Year of Spain" (cited in "Olympic Games as Showcase," p. 12). The final supplement noted: "The end of 1992 marks Spain's full-fledged membership in the European Community and its integral role in Europe's emerging single market. These events together have created a six-year economic surge in which Spain has had the fastest growth rate in Europe. Not only did the government embark on a massive public-spending campaign to prepare for 1992 and

upgrade an outmoded infrastructure, but foreign companies flocked to Spain to take advantage of the thriving domestic economy" (cited in "Olympic Games as Showcase," p. 9).

5. *ABC Catalunya* newspaper, July 25, 1990, cited in "Olympic Games as Showcase," 11.
6. "Catalonia is pressing ahead as Olympic 'Country'," A. Riding, *New York Times*, July 18, 1992.
7. Cited in "Olympic Games as Showcase," 23.
8. Barcelona Olympic Organizing Committee (1992) Official Report of the Games of the XXV Olympiad, vol. 3, COOB 1992, Barcelona, 310.
9. *Economy of the 1992 Barcelona Olympic Games* (1993), F. Brunet. Documents of the Museum, IOC, Lausanne, 33 and 36.
10. Plan Director de Seguridad Olimpica.
11. COOB, 1992, 305.
12. "Barcelona Plans a Lasting Olympics," P. Delany, *New York Times*, October 21, 1987.
13. COOB, 1992, 305; United States Senate Committee on Commerce, Science and Transportation (2004) *Lessons Learned from Security at Past Olympic Games: Testimony of Mr. David Maples,* May 4, 2004. The Information Warfare Site: http://www.iwar.org.uk/homesec/resources/olympic-security/maples.htm
14. United States Senate Committee on Commerce, Science and Transportation (2004) *Lessons Learned from Security at Past Olympic Games: Testimony of Mr. David Maples,* May 4, 2004. The Information Warfare Site: http://www.iwar.org.uk/homesec/resources/olympic-security/maples.htm; COOB 1992, Barcelona Olympic Organizing Committee, Official Report of the Games of the XXV Olympiad, Barcelona, vol. 3, 310–312.
15. COOB, 1992, 253–254.
16. COOB, 1992, 315.
17. *Candidature Acceptance Procedure: XXI Olympic Winter Games in 2010,* IOC, Lausanne, 2002, 6.
18. "Olympics: Salt Lake Olympics to review security," by Anon, *New York Times*, September 13, 2001.
19. "Olympic Games as Showcase," 19.
20. Ibid., 19.
21. Ibid., 13.
22. Ibid., 10.
23. Ibid., 24.
24. Ibid., 11.
25. Ibid., 21.
26. Ibid., 21.
27. Ibid., 27.
28. *La Vanguardia* is a relatively conservative newspaper based in Barcelona, but written in Spanish.
29. "Olympic Games as Showcase," 27.
30. *El País,* June 19, 1992, cited in "Olympic Games as Showcase," 28.
31. "Olympic Games as Showcase," 28.
32. Ibid., 21.
33. The fact that the "Freedom for Catalunya" flag was written in English to have maximum international impact in the media was regarded by some Catalans as counter to their cause; "Olympic Games as Showcase," 28.
34. Ibid., 18.

35. "Spain's Objective: Peaceful Games," M. Janofsky, *New York Times*, April 16, 1992.
36. "Olympic Games as Showcase," 12.
37. "Barcelona 1992: Security threat played down," M. Rowbottom, *The Independent*, July 25, 1992.
38. "Spain's Objective: Peaceful Games."
39. Cottrell, R.C. (2003) The Legacy of Munich 1972: Terrorism, Security and the Olympic Games, in de Moragas, M., Kennett, C. and Puig, N. (Eds.) *The Legacy of the Olympic Games 1984–2000*, Documents of the Museum, International Olympic Committee, Lausanne, pp.309–313. See Fussey and Coaffee (2012).

11
Rupturing Performer-Spectator Interaction

Ingrid Rudie

Audience-spectator-performer interactions are central to public events because they are meant to encourage interpersonal relations and collective sentiments in public spaces. This is particularly the case with the Olympics because their original purpose was to bring together performers and spectators from different parts of the globe. When surveillance procedures dominate the organization of the event, these interactions take on interesting forms. I became aware of these restricted relations while studying the Lillehammer Games of 1994 as part of a team of anthropologists. I shall draw attention to these interactions through methodology by trying to show how the organizational design of the Olympics as a global event and the strategies of surveillance put in place to ensure its success set specific conditions for fieldwork and hence affect the research process. More specifically, I shall discuss how these conditions shape the questions that we are able to pose and the kind of data we are able to collect. When I studied the Winter Olympics in 1994 as member of a research team, I did not see surveillance as a research topic in its own right. I just found myself subject to the rules and regulations that surrounded the arrangement.

My approach will, therefore, to a large extent, be an exercise in self-reflection and hindsight using my field notes,[1] newspaper reporting, the official report from the 17th Winter Olympics, and the research works published by members of the team in which I took part. Our team's research is necessarily a reflection of a series of methodological solutions and theoretical and perspectival choices we made in relation to specific conditions "in the field." I demonstrate how, in the study of public events, these conditions affect the core activity of anthropological fieldwork, namely, observation. Our team experienced a particularly frequent oscillation between what I call a *spectator mode* and a *participant mode* (see also MacAloon, 1999; Archetti, 1999). This oscillation seems to be related to the organizational and technological aspects of the event, namely that the Games seem to be unavoidably designed to enhance a festive experience under more or less strict limitations imposed by surveillance procedures.

I shall now take the reader through the following steps: After a brief introduction to the Lillehammer Winter Olympics, I discuss the challenges to fieldwork during the two peak phases in which all team members took part in situ: the Olympic Flame Relay and the two weeks of competition at Lillehammer. These two phases must be described as "fieldwork on the move" – in constant movement between a series of particular events – sportive, festive, and more purely ritual. My most in-depth discussion will deal with my own sub-project, the athlete as a key symbol, which was designed as a study of public discourse and public imagery surrounding the athletes, including their publicly visible role management. In this context, I discuss regulation of mobility, inaccessibility of athletes, and the ubiquitous nature of media communication. I was pulled into a position in which I participated as a spectator and, at the same time, as a researcher while the persons on whom my research interest was focused – the athletes – became untouchable ritual objects. I conclude by reflecting on the fate of the "anthropological ambition" to study global events in the modern world where local and global experiences blend inextricably.

Lillehammer was awarded the 1994 Winter Games by a narrow victory at the ballot in Seoul in 1988. This victory started a new phase in the planning, strategizing, and debating already under way for some years. Hosting the Games was a national and a regional project. Lillehammer is centrally placed in Eastern Norway between the mouth of a valley, Gudbrandsdalen, and the low-lying districts around Norway's largest lake, Mjøsa. This region was lagging somewhat behind the more densely populated area around Oslo on a number of economic parameters, and both political authorities and the business community in the region hoped that the Games would boost development. Preparations for the Games soon became fueled by an official rhetoric about national challenge, local progress, cooperation, and creativity. Although public opinion differed about the coming Olympic event, with some seeing the Games as a blessing and others as a burden, the undertaking gained momentum as a quest for local and national excellence and resources were poured into infrastructure and Olympic venues.

To understand efforts to ensure success of the Games of which surveillance was an important element, it is necessary to consider the rhetoric and symbolism of the political process before the event. At the state and municipal levels, a pro-Games majority of both socialist and conservative convictions engaged in rhetoric about the giant common undertaking for which it was important to create a favorable public attitude in order to ensure success and smooth running of the Olympics. The Prime Minister at the time is still quoted for saying that "it is typical for Norwegians to do a good job." Public appeals were made to revitalize the spirit of *dugnad* – a time-honored tradition of communal effort. *Dugnad* is a Norwegian word for communal or neighborhood undertakings, a kind of collective practice which we find in most societies. In Norway the concept has been brought into modern times as an honorary metaphor for cooperative spirit. The dugnad metaphor could be seen as a means to win public confidence and an encouragement to inhabitants of the district to contribute actively by presenting local culture at its best, by showing a helpful and welcoming attitude to visitors, and by putting up with cumbersome traffic regulations.

The Games were not a matter free of controversies. Many opponents considered them a waste of taxpayers' money and came up with examples of other, more "worthy" needs that should have been given priority. Many leftist politicians and intellectuals saw the Olympics as a spearhead of market-driven megalomania. There were also more deeply value-laden tensions between alleged Norwegian egalitarian ideals and the more outright elitist orientation of international Olympism. Shortly before the opening of the Games, tensions escalated into a serious conflict when a newspaper revealed that the Norwegian public was generally critical of the leadership of the International Olympic Committee. In addition, cross-country skier Vegard Ulvang had publicly criticized the Committee's lack of democracy and also dropped an unfortunate reference to Committee President Samaranch's former affiliation with Franco's regime. The conflict became so serious that members of the Committee threatened to leave, and the Lillehammer Olympic Committee leadership, aided by the Prime Minister, had to use high-level diplomacy to solve the crisis (Klausen, 1999b: 42–43).

The political part of ensuring the success of the Games was, therefore, concerned with disputes on values, major decision-making, high-level strategizing, and allocation of resources. The practical part, in turn, dealt with *quality assurance,* which was defined as "all of the systematic procedures and measures which prevent errors from occurring and ensure adequate quality."[2] Thus, quality assurance included a host of organizational, engineering, constructive, logistic and artistic efforts, all of which have elements of surveillance in them. The planning explored in the most minute detail all possible weather conditions, camera angles under conditions of sunlight (or the lack of it) on specific dates in February, designs for sluicing a multiplied population between venues and through the tiny streets of a small town, to mention but a few. To enforce quality assurance, the Lillehammer Olympic Committee built a complex organizational apparatus in the broadest possible sense, including the department responsible for events support, which dealt with accreditation, ticketing, computer services, health services, accommodation, security, telecommunication, and transportation. Two security-related principles were laid down early in the planning process.[3] First, security measures should not cast a shadow on festivities; surveillance technologies and procedures must be sufficient, but should not detract from the positive atmosphere. Second, the Lillehammer Olympic Committee cooperated with the police to scan their records for information on all candidates for accreditation. The police, together with the young conscripts to the military were responsible for traffic regulation and patrol. The most potent tool for surveillance lay in the computer and telecommunication functions, as about 60% of the security budget was spent on technological equipment. This included surveillance equipment as well as television and radio systems serving the public and the media personnel.[4]

While these surveillance tools and security measures were fully integrated in the planning process, fear of serious political upheaval or terrorist attacks on the general public or the athletes was not a major topic in public discourse and did not take front stage in the Lillehammer Olympic Committee's self-presentation. This may have been the case because the goal that security measures should have a low-key appearance in order not to spoil the festive mood was made very explicit. In addition, the low rate of public violence in Norway is related to relatively little fear of violence on the part of the Norwegian public. To give an example, police forces are normally not armed, and it takes an extremely dangerous situation and a formal procedure for the police to carry weapons. These dynamics came to the stark attention of the Norwegian as well as international public in July 2011, when the country was shaken by an unbelievable terror attack. The perpetrator first detonated a bomb causing vast damage to the government quarters in Oslo, then swiftly made his way to an island some 40 kilometers outside of the city where the Labor Party's youth organization had gathered for their annual summer camp. There he shot dead 69 youths, and severely injured many more. In the aftermath of the tragedy, as critical questions have been posed about the adequacy of police resources and surveillance practices in its wake, the public discourse nevertheless seems to be dominated by a strong commitment to regain confidence and avoid an escalation of fearful thinking.

The biggest challenge to the Lillehammer Olympic Committee as well as the inhabitants in the district likely was traffic control. The small town of Lillehammer was the hub of the Games, but a number of important competitions in alpine skiing and long-distance as well as figure skating were to take place in four neighboring townships, venues situated at distances from 13 to 60 kilometers outside of the center of Lillehammer. One major threat, severely affecting thousands of inhabitants in the district, was a possible breakdown of transportation and the decision to ban private cars in Lillehammer and around the Olympic venues for the duration of the Games. Work commuters from the rural municipalities that neighbored the city had to rely on bus services while spectators and Games employees used special shuttle buses to transport them to the venues.

The establishment of an Olympic space

Vida Bajc (2007b, 2011a, b) invented the concept *security meta-ritual* to analyze the process designed to create an undisturbed space for other rituals going on under its canopy. Building on Bajc's analysis, I shall add an exploration of the idea of *ritualization* in order to facilitate a processual approach to the complex event of the Olympics, and to be able to stress the interconnectedness between a public ritual and its sub-rituals and other social actions, including surveillance. Here I follow Catherine Bell, who suggests the term *ritualization*

> to draw attention to the way in which certain social actions strategically distinguish themselves in relation to other social actions. (In a preliminary sense) ritualization is a way of acting that is designed and orchestrated to distinguish and privilege what is being done in comparison to other, usually more quotidian activities. (Bell, 1992: 74)

While Bell makes clear that the concept of ritualization has been used by a number of scholars before her (ibid.: 88ff), she stresses that her own effort will be "to focus more clearly on (1) how ritualization as practice distinguishes itself from other practices and (2) what it accomplishes in doing so"(ibid.: 89).

The transformation of a whole landscape to which I will turn in a moment can aptly be seen as a security meta-ritual, in Bajc's sense. By applying the notion of ritualization, it also becomes possible to stress the temporary nature and even different degrees of "ritual-ness." It also becomes easier to switch between different aspects of the Olympic event, from the landscape to the particular persons in focus, such as the athletes, and the event itself. In this sense, ritualization helps us to switch between *performance* and *ritual* at the venues as well as other public gatherings. The observational modes of the public and of the fieldworkers as members of the public seem to be related in subtle ways to ritualization and deritualization, and more widely, to the way in which these processes are embedded in the organizational and technological devices of the surveillance apparatus. The strategies of the security meta-ritual, particularly as they are implemented through the communication technology, may not only protect the rituals under its canopy, they may also reinforce them.

For the two weeks of the Games, Lillehammer and its neighboring townships were transformed into a new and temporary spatiotemporal zone. We experienced it as an Olympic Space, which was superimposed on, and partially annulled or glossed over the existing local differences and borders. Following Bajc (2011b), this space had elements of a "sterile zone of safety," although, in tune with the Lillehammer Olympic Committee's idea of quality assurance, surveillance took on a low-key appearance in most public places. This means, among other things, that there was free pedestrian movement in the downtown area of Lillehammer and between the venues. Checkpoints were placed at the entrance to venues and living quarters for the athletes and the international VIP guests such as the Committee representatives. Road travelers following the highway E6 for the 100 kilometers from the southernmost to the northernmost venue are still today reminded of the 1994 Olympic Space. Every time they cross the boundary to a township that hosted competitions in 1994, they meet a road sign with the five rings, reading "OL1994."

Within this space the landscape was physically and administratively transformed. Some of these transformations are permanent, such as buildings, arenas, and some infrastructural improvements that were needed anyway and were speeded up for the sake of the coming Olympics. Other transformations were temporary, such as traffic regulations, tents, kiosks, grandstands, and stages. There were no specific measures taken to distinguish between residents and guests in public places. Pedestrians thronged the small streets within Lillehammer and were sluiced in unaccustomed tracks to the venues at the outskirts of the town. With the ban on private cars and a calculatedly parsimonious use of collective transport, it was a "natural" expectation that as many inhabitants and visitors as possible would walk to the nearest venues. Walking trails to the venues were strewn with sand to prevent slipping, and marked with temporary road signs. The walks were quite long, and the experience was bodily and material in nature – "good," for some, but very "arduous" for others. A peculiar bodily feel also emerged in the throng of the streets downtown. In a nearly untranslatable pun, the main shopping street, normally a pedestrian street, was renamed by the locals from "Walk Street" (*gågata*) to "Standstill Street" (*stågata*). Not all the changes in the Olympic Space were related directly to surveillance; some were examples of local creativity in the joint effort of *dugnad*. One such example of local initiative left a lasting mark in a forested hillside opposite the Hafjell alpine venue: The pine and fir wood was cut down in the shape of a huge representation of the "Torch Man," one of a series of logos created for the Lillehammer Games. This clearing has later been maintained at intervals so that it still appears white in winter and with a lighter shade of green from grass and deciduous shrub vegetation in summer.

All along, everyone was reminded that the transformation of the landscape and the unusual patterns of movement were necessary for the good of a common cause. This is consistent with Bajc's (2011b: 61–62) argument that security meta-ritual requires cooperation; that public approval of the surveillance procedures is required if such a ritual is to succeed, and that the cooperative spirit is shown in a willingness to accept a degree of discomfort. Regardless of the fact that many remained critical of the Olympics in 1994, this common cause was, to varying degrees, internalized as a "local duty" and linked to the feeling of being chosen for the world's biggest sportive happening. Perhaps we could say that the security meta-ritual in the strict sense of a strong apparatus of surveillance and quality assurance not only created a canopy for other ritual to go on undisturbed but also it entered into an alliance with a rhetoric of cooperation that transposed experience and brought it under some collective spell. It is a case of ritualization of a

Ingrid Rudie

landscape, in which the cooperativeness that Bajc draws attention to, and the internalization and feeling of chosenness, seemed to be established as a temporary state of mind in the Olympic Space.

Research on the Olympics

A great deal of research on the Olympics was planned and carried through in the 1990s. Most of this dealt with economic and demographic consequences of the Games. The anthropological project in which I took part was of a different kind. The project was called "The 1994 Olympics and Culture" and was broadly designed to attempt to study the process of planning and carrying through of the Games. This project was initiated and led by Arne Martin Klausen at the University of Oslo. It was obvious from the outset that a team would be necessary in order to cover the various aspects of preparations and the peak events, all of which would have to take place within a strictly delimited time period.

Klausen approached four researchers from the anthropology department in Oslo, and one from the Regional College at Lillehammer, with an offer to take part in a team. Apart from our common commitment to anthropology, we were interested in different aspects of the Games. Each team member had his or her own sub-project dealing with different organizational or symbolic aspects of the Olympics. Klausen took the responsibility to arrange ad hoc seminars for the group, spent ample time at Lillehammer throughout the planning period, and stayed in touch with the Lillehammer Olympic Committee to be continually updated. We divided our research interests to focus on the development of the design program, the planning of opening and closing ceremonies, and the "tug-of-war" about the Norwegian and the Greek flames; the rituals of modernity and the lasting transformation brought about by the construction of a new alpine course; the international media coverage of the Games; the public discourses on athletes; and the cultural shows and theatrical performances before and during the Games. I should mention that two members of our team were immigrants to Norway while two of us were born and bred in the Lillehammer district. These backgrounds may have added specific angles to the way the four of us perceived the events going on at Lillehammer. Also, two worked full time on the project, while the rest of us devoted as much time as we could in addition to our regular departmental duties. All team members engaged in intensive fieldwork during the two peak phases, when we followed the Olympic Flame Relay from November 1993 until February 1994 and throughout the two weeks of the Games at Lillehammer. The project resulted in a number of publications that appeared during the planning period and after the Games were over, a full reference of which is beyond the scope of this book.

Klausen's leadership was flexible; each team member was free to follow his or her particular interest and theoretical preferences as long as these were compatible with the overarching intentions in the project. We had some perspectival orientations in common, such as an interest in the effects of globalization and in points of articulation between the "traditional" and the "modern." Importantly, we also discussed ideas about the Olympics as a ritual of modernity in relation to the theoretical debates on *drama, performance* and *spectacle* (MacAloon, 1984a, 1989; Handelman, 1990; Hughes-Freeland, 1998; Hughes-Freeland and Crain, 1998).

Challenges to fieldwork

The complex design and long duration of our project necessitated a number of different strategies in order for us to be able to produce data. During the years of planning, we had an ongoing consultation with the press and the mass media. We conducted intermittent ethnographic observations of the practical preparations in Lillehammer and the neighboring townships, as well as more or less formal interviews booked as needs arose. It is noteworthy that our experiences of working as a team were positive throughout the years of planning as well as during the write-up period. We hit a productive balance between the common goals of our research group and our specific individual research interests, which was made easier by the fact that we all knew each other beforehand, with five of us working in the same department at the University of Oslo. John MacAloon (1999), who visited us during the planning period and also wrote a chapter for the book in which our sub-projects were published (see Klausen, 1999), emphasizes the importance of our shared background and contrasts this to his own attempt at building a team to study the 1984 Los Angeles Games. That teamwork resulted in good individual contributions but did not yield to team-related publications. MacAloon (1999) also draws attention to other circumstances that might have enhanced the success of our teamwork, particularly a close rapport between the academics and the government officials in Norway and the never to be underestimated smaller size of the Winter Olympics in comparison to the Summer Games.

Our multifaceted field approaches reflect, first, our limited access to the people and the events we studied, and second, the need to be constantly on the move spatially as well as temporally. Temporally, we tried to hang on to a series of parallel events that had a specific beginning and a specific end. The awareness that there would be no coming back for more data when the Games were over was haunting. Spatially, we faced a need for a multi-sited approach in order to study "social phenomena that cannot be accounted for by focusing on a single site" (Falzon, 2009: 1, quoting Marcus, 1995). A specific and extreme form of multi-sited approach is what I prefer to call "fieldwork on the move," or as Clifford (1992) put it, "fieldwork as travel practice." The fieldworker is continually moving between events of focal interest that may be widely dispersed yet linked together within one common thematic, organizational, or symbolic scheme. This became the routine nature of our fieldwork during the two peak phases: the Olympic Flame Relay and the two weeks of the Games at Lillehammer.

The problem of getting access to the persons in focus, a challenge in all fieldwork, becomes exacerbated in the case of the study of an event such as the Olympics. The accreditation system puts people in categories with precisely defined access rights. Members of our team were accredited as *observers*, a small yet quite mixed category that included organizers of other large events and those interested in specific aspects of the Lillehammer Olympics. Our *observer* status was specified according to arenas and zones. My identification card was valid for the freestyle, cross-country, figure skating and alpine arenas – disciplines that would allow me to focus on gender issues. At these venues I had access to the zones of administration and organization and the zones for the press without press rights. In addition, we needed regular admission tickets for events at which we had accreditation as well as for any other events that we might want to watch. All these tickets had to be booked in advance. This meant that we had to plan our specific fields of observation and our movements well in advance so that not much was left to the spontaneity of regular fieldwork. We also had accreditation to the public area in the Olympic Village, but not to its residential quarters. In my one visit to the Olympic Village, I found myself in a reception room where it was possible to study posters and leaflets. There was no one present, apart from a young priest, who was there as a Lillehammer Olympic Committee employee. While I was having a relaxed conversation with him, I received an issue of the New Testament, a slim paperback designed for the Games with the snowflakes and Northern Lights logo on the cover. The priest was updated on all the competitions, but no athlete was in sight.

The athletes whom I wanted to study were protected in their living quarters to be admired only at a distance as they gave their performances and appeared at the ceremonies of victory. It was already in the early stages of my preparations for the fieldwork that it dawned on me that to get data, I would need to rely heavily on a spectator mode of observation as well as on textual material drawn from the media coverage. The focus of my research design was therefore on public discourses – a practicable solution, indeed the only solution that seemed possible. Our movements were predestined, and the routes of movement were pretty well laid down in advance through the careful logistics of the Olympic Flame Relay and the quality assurance of the Olympic event itself. Particularly in the latter, we were up against a number of barriers built to prevent transgression between the inside and the outside of the zones. Strong limits to accessibility breed fear of transgression, which is one among several emotive elements in ritual and *ritualization* in the broadest possible sense of the term. The ritualization of the athletes is part of the overarching security meta-ritual, perhaps we could say that the security meta-ritual not only protects and shapes the rituals going on under its canopy (Bajc, 2007b, 2011a, b) but also can directly add specific emotive qualities to the public experience of them.

Fieldwork on the move

Instead of following everyday routines as anthropologists are used to doing in a more conventional fieldwork, ours was a fieldwork that was constantly driven by major events and major decisions. There was nothing "ordinary" about it. Instead of being stuck with a relatively approachable group of informants close at hand, we were constantly on the move, caught between focal events and their different sets of performers as "quasi-informants." These were performers at various cultural shows and commentators at the venues who were extremely skilled in the "art" of informing and inspiring the audience. Our fieldwork on the move peaked in two different experiences: the Olympic Flame Relay covering two months ahead of the Games and the 16 days of Games at Lillehammer. We took turns to follow the Olympic Flame Relay and, in this way, were able to cover most of the route. Because this was a single process without complementary events, it was possible to follow it closely and near completely. We visited scores of townships and community centers along the coastline and across inland districts, finally ending up in the inner part of Eastern Norway, the heartland of the Games. Our fieldwork on the Olympic Flame Relay was published with all six team members as a "collective of authors" (Klausen et al., 1995).

Our stay at Lillehammer placed us in situations that required moving fast between venues, some of which were situated in neighboring townships at distances from 13 to nearly 60 kilometers away from the city. In between the major events, we were just members of the crowd that filled the streets of Lillehammer. At the venues we were part of an audience with the same kind of tickets as the ordinary onlookers. The only privilege that separated us from the rest of the audience was our strictly defined accreditation, valid for some but not all venues. Within Lillehammer we walked considerable distances every day between our rented flat in the town center, venues at the outskirts of the town, and other points of research interest. To attend events at venues outside Lillehammer we needed to use charter buses and adhere to their schedule.

Between these two intensive phases of fieldwork on the move there had to be differences in data collection because they involved different varieties of participation and observation and because there was a difference in the way fieldwork had to be organized in order to obtain data. The Olympic Flame Relay was characterized by strict logistics with the surveillance of events more relaxed and low-key. In contrast, surveillance peaked during the Games around the focal events at the sports arenas, but movement on foot was free in most of the downtown area.

Traversing Norway with the torch

The torch was lit in Morgedal in late November 1993, a place considered to be the "cradle of skiing" in Norway. For more than two months, up to the opening of the Games, this flame was carried around Norway to finally end at Lillehammer, where it was replaced by the flame brought from Greece. The Lillehammer Olympic Committee had engaged the national postal service to organize a convoy and take care of the transportation. Our team obtained permission to follow the convoy, and we did so individually, taking turns to cover shorter or longer stretches. For most of the time, we were passengers on the bus that carried local volunteers to run legs with the torch. We were actually able to hold the torch and take part in the small talk on the bus. We spent the nights in prebooked hotels and stopped in rapid succession at festive arrangements along the route. These bus rides and hotel stays brought us the closest to participant observation. Our objects of study on the bus were drivers and representatives of the local population who were on the bus to take turns carrying the torch certain distances. When we took part at festive performances along the route, our approach became highly interpretative as we studied their themes focused on nature, occupational structure, mythical and literary figures, important historical events, sports heroes native to the place, and other cultural elements of these locations. Some of us came close to places that we knew particularly well from having lived there, in which case our understanding broadened because we had an incorporated experience that made us sensitive to subtler markers.

All through the Olympic Flame Relay we were observers either in a participant or a spectator mode. This was a very intensive fieldwork because we had no private quarters to which we could withdraw before the end of the day. In our participant phases we were sometimes not able to, or chose not to, take notes, but rather relied on our memory. During the spectator phases, we made extensive use of cameras as well as pocket-size tape recorders. Into my recorder went both the public utterances and my reflections on what I saw and heard. To sum up so far, the following of the Olympic Flame Relay was an extreme case of multi-sited approach to data collection with very fast movement and versatile fieldwork techniques. The bulk of our data consisted of photographs and sound recordings from festive arrangements, as well as comments from local newspapers when these could be obtained. It was a tour at which logistics became more important than surveillance in the sense of separation of the inside from the outside. The "inside" was, strictly speaking, the moving convoy with the flame, carriers, fieldworker guests, drivers, and technical personnel. The majority of places that we visited were small towns and rural community centers where security and surveillance did not present a major problem. A few loosely erected provisional fences and sufficient loudspeaker capacity for outdoor arrangements would usually do the job.

In the middle of the Olympic space

During the Games our positioning as fieldworkers was changed. The insider membership we had in the convoy that offered us an opportunity for participant observation was lost. Our *observer* accreditation to the Games offered only limited access, which was not sufficient to make up for the loss. In my own sub-project, the spectator mode became by far the dominant mode, as we went along with the crowds, watching sportive and other performances, exhibitions and public behavior. By implication, we were spectators and so a part of the public. Our overreaching experience was being part of a multifaceted crowd. While some in our research group were particularly aware of the spatial transformations of the Games from having lived in the city as fieldworkers, we were mostly spectators who were only slightly more reflective than the average onlooker.

From this point on I will carefully distinguish between speaking for myself and speaking for the group. As a group, we kept in touch nearly every day. Four of us shared the same flat and met at least twice every day, at breakfast before we went out to disappear in some crowd and late in the evening when we shared experiences and discussed whatever Olympics coverage the television offered. Speaking for myself, I shall quote a passage that went into my fieldnotes a few days after the opening of the Games:

> I have landed in this exotic culture, and am trying to grasp a bit of it. What strikes me first is the seething crowd in the downtown streets. At intervals during the day, part of the crowd organises itself and heads for the arenas. There, the athletes show their skills within strictly defined procedures. During the competitions as well as the ceremonies of victory, public and performers are rigorously separated. The athletes are also extremely protected in their living quarters. The audience is like a huge, live organism. The speaker intensifies this feature by eliciting cheering and the wave.

This brief passage foreshadows a great deal of the observations that went into my fieldnotes. My field recordings followed the same techniques that I had used during the Olympic Flame Relay. I recorded events on soundtracks, adding my own comments and explanations to what came through the loudspeaker, and I wrote notes on the computer, a diary that was quite selective as it highlighted some experiences and ignored others. Watching sports competitions, we become participants and observers in complex ways. As observers we can keep a disinterested distance or take the role of supporter, cheer or keep quiet, feel joy or despair at the victories or losses of our favorite competitors. The victories of our local favorites can boost up our national or local self-images. Competitions which take place in a tightly limited space such as an ice rink or a ski jump can be experienced in total without much technical aid. Others, like alpine and cross-country skiing, are widely dispersed in a landscape so that it is impossible for one spectator to have a full view without technical aid. For our research team, the cross-country competitions offered a peak into a technically aided spectatorship. The athletes were partly followed by moving cameras, partly shot by stationary cameras strategically placed along the track, so that they could always be followed on a giant video screen at the main arena at the same time as the commentators kept the public informed about the development of the competition along the track. The commentator also took responsibility for activating the spectators by frequent elicitation of cheers or "the wave." This phenomenon needs a brief explanation. "The wave" was initiated at one of the first broadcast arrangements during the Olympic Flame Relay, as a recipe for good spectatorship. One person starts it by raising a hand at one end of a crowd of spectators. The neighbor follows, and so on, so that a wave of raised hands moves through the crowd from one end to the other. The cross-country stadium could take 31,000 spectators and was filled close to capacity at the most popular competitions.

The spectator area was subdivided into numbered zones. Since my accreditation gave me the right to stay close to the rostrum and the press zone, I was a somewhat privileged spectator. While I had the choice to enter the administrative and the press zones, nevertheless I opted for staying with the crowd of spectators and immersing myself into a spectator role. This choice certainly had to do with my timidity, but it also reflected my sense that the dynamics between the speaker and the crowd were the most interesting part of the event. The design of the event had made an impact on my focus. Both cheering and the wave were instantly thrown back on the screen and through the loudspeakers, so that, at least as far as sound was concerned, it was impossible to distinguish between live voices on the ground and voices coming through the loudspeakers. This is an instance of observation in which the participant and spectator modes are mixed, or rather, an instance of oscillation between the two modes. Focused on the competition, the public as a spectator watches a meticulously directed performance, which includes the athlete on whom their attention is focused, the commentators who act as dramatic directors, and the video screen that ensures a near-complete overview of how the competition develops.

As participants in spectatorship, we experience our bodily and mental presence through the throng of the crowd, the possible discomfort of weather conditions, the suspense of the tight competition, and our communication with other bystanders. The more devoted spectators are also active in cheering the athletes along and in breaking out in joy or disappointment over results. If the outbreaks are not sufficiently enthusiastic, the "director-commentator" exhorts the audience to give a louder cheer, or the wave. Then the experience is transposed from partly distant spectatorship to emotive involvement as the audience is suddenly included in the scheme of a more total performance, learning to be a better audience and led to participate directly in a ritual of spectatorship. Just as there is an oscillation between participant and spectator modes of observation, there is an oscillation between ritual and performative accents on the whole event. At the time of fieldwork, I was intrigued by the use of information technology and its effects on the social dynamics at the arenas. While, at the time, I did not see surveillance as a topic of research in its own right, I can now add that the clever use of technology at the arenas, which molds the experience of the audience along with their behavior, is perhaps also one aspect of surveillance of the crowd. Further, the same technology can be used to transmit all kinds of information, including possible threats to security. All these aspects were built into the Lillehammer Olympic Committee's overarching ambition of quality assurance.

With an analytic focus on person and gender

"The sports champion as a key symbol" was the title I chose for my own sub-project. I concentrated on sports champions not because I was particularly interested in competitive sport as such. Rather, I was interested in competitive sport as a cultural phenomenon, its power of fascinating and creating enthusiasm, and the way in which champions become models for personhood and objects of identification. As such, champions "belong" to the public and can aptly be used to enhance the pride of a community, a district, or a nation. If *person* is in focus, *gender* follows by necessity. There are two reasons why gender is an important issue in the study of sport: for one, sport is highly gender segregated, and second, women have, for a century, fought for the right to participate in, and not only watch, sports competitions. A discourse on gender politics in sport formed one important backdrop for my approach to the 1994 Olympics, at the same time as I raised the question whether the contrast between gender segregation in sports competitions and the general gender equalization in modern society at large might lead to a kind of double bind between essentialist and constructivist conceptions of gender. I analyzed three different disciplines: cross-country skiing, downhill skiing, and figure skating – disciplines that carry distinctly different symbolic loads and have different histories as regards women's placement in them (Rudie, 1999).

My focus was on the athletes, and yet I did not have access to them as a researcher would in normal fieldwork circumstances. To study the athletes in a traditional anthropological sense, I would have had to have access to their own self-understanding through repeated close-up conversations and preferably also informal interaction with them in different settings. This would have been a standard participant observation approach to their daily life. I have a strong interest in an understanding of the person as a "node" in cultural processes, and I understand the importance of *embodiment* and *experience* (Csordas, 1994). So, what could have been more rewarding than studying athletes as cultural products and cultural heroes? Before the start of the Games I did manage to arrange several interviews with former champions, particularly women cross-country skiers who had ended their sports careers and were leading more "normal" lives. One of them had actually fought at the forefront for the acceptance of cross-country skiing as a women's discipline. These former champions were ready to reflect and to discuss with me the costs and rewards of elite sport and to answer my questions about how early-life experiences had molded their ambitions. I was also present at an occasion at which aged heroes, former male skating champions, were looking back on their formative experiences and sporting careers with a kind of reflective distance. This was as close as I came to the experience and self-identification of elite athletes.

Privileged interviewers in the heat of competitions were commentators at the venue, reporters, and television journalists at the evening shows. The interview at the venue immediately following the competition catches an athlete still somewhat out of breath. The standard approach here is congratulations and a question about the *feelings* of victory. The medalists are then briefly hailed in a flower ceremony, before they are sluiced back to their living quarters. They reappear at the Olympic Medal Ceremony in late afternoon and finally in a television show in the evening. In this tightly structured interview schedule, no room is left for researchers and their academic interests.

Ritualization and deritualization

This sequence, starting with the competition, then through the flower ceremony and the Olympic Medal Ceremony to the evening television show, can be described in terms of ritualization and deritualization. The competition is an event in which the performance and person of the athlete are ritualized through a set of classical markers. It is highly formalized and follows a strict pattern in which certain rules for the purity of the competition are sacred. The person in focus, the athlete, becomes a ritual object, set apart and inaccessible to the common public, only to be hailed at a certain distance. There is an unbreakable barrier between the inner sphere of the arena and the outer sphere of the spectators. The commentator, relying on a more anonymous technical staff, takes the responsibility for a clever staging of the performance through which he or she has the power of turning the public into ritual cooperators. The "ritual-ness" takes several fleeting shapes, and the experience of the public oscillates between distant spectatorship and devoted participation. The flower ceremony and the Olympic Medal Ceremony are simpler incidences of rituals in which the "truth" of the day's efforts are celebrated and made known to everyone present. In the Olympic Medal Ceremony the truth is sealed with flags and national anthems, a ritual high point that is prone to bring out the tears of those whose anthem is played. The ritualization of the athlete is part of the surveillance strategies guiding the Games; it is directly derived from *the security meta-ritual,* to follow Bajc's phrasing. The dynamic just described is also an example of how the security meta-ritual not only protects the public event from disturbances but also is an example of how a skilled commentator can "educate" an audience to become better spectators by making them participate in a ritual of spectatorship. The ritualization attains a point at which it seems to "afford a fit among the main spheres of experience – body, community, and cosmos" (Bell, 1992: 109; also Rudie, 1998).

The evening television shows stand in contrast to the formalized sequence described. These shows are studied informally, and so deritualization takes over. The atmosphere is relaxed, the champions have changed into ordinary clothes, and the interviewers encourage them to speak about themselves as complete persons, to reveal part of their "non-sportive" self. The television interviewer poses questions akin to the kinds I would have asked had I had access to the athletes. Relative to me as the researcher, television journalists were the privileged interviewers. The questions they posed, however, were only partly relevant for my purposes because they had a different focus. Still, these interviews may allow us to reflect on ways in which this deritualization represents a well-known feature of the television medium; namely, its power to create a kind of surrogate familiarity by tempting people to make their personal life publicly visible. In this respect, these shows had some direct bearing on my project in which public discourse was an important element in that they could be seen as possibly adding to, confirming, or modifying the myths about the most famous athletes that appeared on the screen. The deritualization in the television presentation did not turn the athletes into close-up informants, because it did not give an in-depth access to their existential experience. It did, however, give a glimpse of their self-identifications as Italian, Russian, Norwegian, or as the case might be. Above all, the process contributed to the public discourse in which they were already placed. In that case, it also contributed to a store of myths already present in the public mind. Some myths might be modified, others strengthened. It may have also enriched the force of the athletes as role models. In other words, the athletes' presence in ritualized and deritualized situations lent itself to textualization and symbol analysis – one important but not exhaustive intake to the understanding of championship as cultural process.

Concluding remarks

How do we collect data on perceptions of what constitutes security and threats to security, and what kind of surveillance practices and procedures are put in place to ensure such security in a global event? At the outset of this book, I flagged the ambition of approaching these questions in a reflexive methodological perspective by suggesting that surveillance in public events creates specific conditions for the researchers' access and freedom of movement and then asking what impact this may have on the quality of our data. Thinking about surveillance as a topic in its own right was indeed a new challenge for me, so I had to tease it out from my memories, my remaining fieldnotes, official reports and media coverage, and the already published works from our project "The 1994 Olympics and Culture." The high points of our team fieldwork I discussed were concerned with the fullest cases of this *public event*. I have zoomed in on my own sub-project because it is the one that I can describe with some degree of authority.

Among the part-projects, mine may also be the one in which the conflict between ingrained ethnographic fieldwork ideals and what the research field actually offered was most intensely felt. These fieldsites demanded mobility, entailed a great deal of observation in a spectator mode, were characterized by a high degree of ritualization, and were phases in which surveillance was put to its final test. The fieldwork conditions and the impact they made on the character and quality of the data are twofold; some I could foresee, and others emerged more unexpectedly from the specific experience of fieldwork on the move in a transformed landscape. The foreseen conditions were those we understand to be a part of the modern society. Because small local communities never contain the full life of our informants, multi-sited approaches will always be necessary to a certain extent, and we cannot do without taking in information from literature, press and the mass media. I had already taken these conditions into consideration and planned my part-project in such a way that public discourse and the publicly visible role management of the persons in focus would be important parts of my data. The unforeseen conditions were those that arose more specifically from the organizational strategies behind the big public event, from the ambition of *quality assurance* with its built-in surveillance.

These conditions were partly a source of frustration and partly opened a new path to unexpected insights. It was tiring to always have to follow a tight logistic schedule, so different from my previous fieldworks, which had always given much leeway for improvisation. The strict limits between the inside and the outside gave rise to a constant feeling of never coming to the *core* of events (however fictitious the idea that there is a *core* might be). But unexpected insights also emerged from the experiences of being in a ritual-ized landscape and of being a part of a focused crowd. This culminated in interpersonal interaction at the venues and the dynamics between athletes, commentators and the audience where all those involved switched between different kinds of presence. The athletes went from performers and competi-tors to ritual objects, the commentator from informative speaker to ritual and performative manager, the audience from interested spectators to active ritual participants. Above, I referred to "the wave" as a mode of cheering that had been instituted at a broadcast gathering during the Olympic Flame Relay. It was cleverly used at the venues, it was integral to the ambition of *quality assurance*, and it was a means of educating a public by teaching it to become better spectators. These experiences at the venues fascinated me so much that they became important ingredients of my field material and gave rise to dominant analytical points in my publications. Working on this book has alerted me to the importance of studying the many aspects of public interactions that surround a big public event: the elicitation of cooperativeness with the security meta-ritual (Bajc, 2011b: 61–62); the elicitation and "teaching" of good spectatorship at specific gatherings; and the broader experience of being an audience to mass media and a spectator at focused events simultaneously. The methodological lesson that seems most important to me was the experience of oscillation between participant and spectator modes of observation. The organizational strategies behind the Games frequently forced the researcher into a spectator mode, a situation that could next be turned into participant observation of spectatorship. In this way, we may be able to take back the classical fieldwork strategies in a historical time and in particular situations where spectatorship dominates public life.

Notes

I wish to thank an anonymous reviewer for comments.

1. My field notes have not resisted time as well as I would wish, because they were mostly written on floppy disks that could only partially be converted to a more recent computer system. What has been rescued is still able to support my memory.
2. The Official Report of the XVII Olympic Winter Olympics, vol. 1.
3. The Official Report from the XVII Olympic Winter Games, vol. 3.
4. Ibid.

12
National Special Security Event (Salt Lake City 2002)

Sean P. Varano, George W. Burruss and Scott H. Decker

The 2002 Salt Lake City Winter Olympic Games began in February, just five months after the events of September 11, 2001.[1] This tragedy, combined with the memory of the Centennial Olympic Park bombing during the 1996 Atlanta Summer Games created a sense among some that such global public events bring unnecessary risks. In fact, a group of security experts convened by the Jane's Information Group in the days after the attacks debated about the relative merits of moving forward with the Olympics considering the uncertain future public safety landscape. Some wondered if this event might "divert security resources from airports and other public facilities where critics say security is inadequate and underfunded."[2] The decision to move forward with the Games sent a clear message to the public that the spirit of the Olympics would not be deterred. In the months leading up to the Games, there was a sense of foreboding and anticipation of an extended period of uncertainty, fear, and economic instability. For many in the United States, the pending Olympics represented both an opportunity and a threat, a time for healing but also a time of anxiety. As Bellavita (2007: 1) observed, "The Games became a symbol of national resolve in the face of barbarism." These sentiments underscored the importance of the symbol of the Olympic Games, something that prompted the host organization to spend more and more money, increasingly involving the federal government and its security institutions.

Funding the Games

The mounting financial costs[3] and a major bribery scandal that hit the local Salt Lake City press in November 1998 nearly derailed the Games before they even began. Local news, for example, ran stories about the daughter of a deceased International Olympic Committee member who was attending American University in Washington, DC, on a scholarship paid for by the Salt Lake Organizing Committee. The following investigation revealed a sophisticated bribery scheme that had existed for some time whereby "brokers" and other dealmakers would "deliver" IOC member votes for money, trips, and other benefits. The news heavily tarnished the image of the Salt Lake Organizing Committee and their capacity to generate the necessary political will and financial support to pull off the Games, and several key sponsors put their substantial donations on hold to see how the scandal was addressed (see Mallon, 2000). This placed additional financial strain on the already tenuous budget process. Some linked the scandal to the resistance of some influential United States politicians to providing federal aid to support this private enterprise.[4]

It was not just the corruption scandal that cast shadows over the Games but also the mounting financial costs. The Salt Lake City Games, said to be the "most expensive Winter Games ever" by December 2001, were estimated to cost more than \$2 billion, or just over \$790,000 per athlete.[5] These estimates put the Games at \$1.8 billion *more* than the original \$200 million estimate. The increased costs were a result of both actual cost increases and the implications of reduced private investments in the aftermath of the bribery scandal. Concerns were further complicated by uncertainties about what portion of the public obligations would be absorbed by local, state, or federal governmental authorities, respectively. From the early planning days, attempts to push costs onto the government, particularly the federal government, ignited opposition. The United States is a government founded on the principle of limited federal government, and the authority of the federal government to involve itself in events like the Olympics is questionable. The United States Constitution, for example, limits federal power to those explicitly authorized by the Constitution. Through provisions established by the Tenth Amendment, any such powers not explicitly afforded to the federal government are therefore reserved for states. The amendment specifically reads: "Each state retains its sovereignty, freedom, and independence, and every power, jurisdiction, and right, which is not by this Confederation expressly delegated to the United States, in Congress assembled."[6]

This system of federalism has important implications for the organization of the law enforcement and public safety apparatus in the United States (Provine et al., 2012). In contrast to other Western countries, the United States has no national police force. Policing is instead a function of government that is relegated to states. Each state authorizes its own state, county, and local units of government to enforce laws on its behalf. This can create a variety of responses that can overlap and are sometimes also contradictory (Junger-Tas and Decker, 2006). National law enforcement agencies such as the Federal Bureau of Investigation, Drug Enforcement Administration, and the Immigration and Customs Enforcement are agencies of limited jurisdiction. Their authority is restricted to particular areas of crime they are legislatively and/or administratively mandated to "police" (Decker et al., 2009). In the case of a "typical" crime such as homicide or some other form of assaultive behavior, federal law enforcement agencies have no legal authority to directly intervene in an investigation. The absence of a national police force was not a historical oversight but instead a deliberate attempt to minimize the involvement of the federal government in local affairs for fear that such a force could function as a de facto standing army. In the United States, then, law enforcement is primarily a function of state and local units of government.

The constitutional restrictions of the role of the federal government in what is otherwise the responsibility of each state provide a critical backdrop to the history of the Olympic Games in the United States. Plainly put, the federal government has no inherent authority to get directly involved in supporting the Olympic Games. As the United States Government Accountability Office noted in its report to Congress, "In the United States, unlike in other countries, the host city, not the federal government, is generally responsible for hosting the Olympic Games."[7] Absent clear legal authority to fund or otherwise directly support private sporting events, several politically powerful United States senators aggressively pushed for limited federal involvement during the early planning stages of the Salt Lake City Games. In a speech on the Senate floor in October 1999, one of the most outspoken senators and critic of the increased federal commitment to the Salt Lake City Games was quoted as stating, "I do not know if we will ever stop this practice of earmarking and pork barreling,[8] but I will never stop resisting it."[9]

The federal commitment, by April 2000, was estimated to be $254 million for projects directly related to planning and staging the Games themselves, with another estimated $1 billion in larger infrastructure projects including $645 million for highway construction.[10] Funding by the federal government for large highway construction projects is not inherently controversial in the United States, and the federal government, through its Department of Transportation, maintains responsibility for building and maintaining the interstate highway system. These and other costs provided a target for crusaders who argued these costs should be assumed by the Salt Lake Organizing Committee and the International Olympic Committee. Arguing that promoters of the Olympics were using security concerns as a way of gaining unwarranted financial support from the federal government, one United States senator argued, "I believe it was Mark Twain [who] said, patriotism is the last refuge of a scoundrel; security is the last refuge of the scoundrels [who] are running these Games and ripping off the American taxpayer."[11] As costs continued to rise exponentially along with the federal government's financial interests, the backlash and mounting political resistance to the governmental movement into funding the 2002 Games continued to mount. These debates underscore the tension between the public role of security and the private nature of financing the Games. While public safety is the general responsibility of law enforcement, particularly local and state law enforcement, taxpayers generally only underwrite these costs for events that are directly sponsored by municipalities. Private entities like businesses, sports venues, and private universities historically absorb public safety costs associated with hosting events as part of normal operating costs.

The legislative authority for the federal government to assume this level of investment in what are essentially locally sponsored and privately owned events remained uncertain through much of 2000 and even into 2001. Although there was a history of using federal resources to support prior Olympic Games and similar sporting events (Decker et al., 2005), the approach can be best characterized as a patchwork of funding through temporary legislative provisions. The request for clarification on this very authority by the United States Senate's Judiciary Committee resulted in congressional testimony that generated the United States Government Accountability Office 2000 report. The request itself provides evidence that many of the most experienced federal legislators were unclear on the role of the federal government in the Olympics.

Domestic bombing attacks and their impact on the Olympic experience

The expansion of governmental involvement in such sporting events can be traced, in part, to a series of domestic attacks that occurred in the United States in the years leading up to the 2002 Winter Games. Although interests of the United States had been vulnerable to terrorist attacks for much of modern history, prior to the 1990s, fears were largely directed at external threats to targets within the territory of the United States. Much of the sense of isolation and protection people in the United States felt began to crack with the bombings at the World Trade Center in February 1993 and in downtown Oklahoma City in April 1995. These events changed the emotional landscape for many, and for the first time in generations, many Americans felt vulnerable to large-scale domestic attacks. Several national polls confirmed that people across the United States were becoming increasingly concerned about politically motivated domestic attacks.[12] State and federal legislators began to respond to this new threat by providing increased levels of resources toward thwarting future attacks.

In citing these events as justification for the increased military presence in the 1996 Atlanta Games, one United States senator remarked that "[the bombings at the World Trade Center and Oklahoma City] demonstrate that we are not [as] impervious to terrorist threats as we once thought, either from abroad or from here at home."[13] Experts, including the Chief of the Federal Bureau of Investigation Counter-terrorism Section, offered testimony about the dangers, and witnesses noted that the these tragedies in the United States, as well as others experienced internationally, were still "fresh in [the] minds" of most Americans.[14] Others emphasized that "recent atrocities in this nation, such as the heinous bombing in Oklahoma City and the World Trade

Center, have sent a sobering message that terrorism has come to America."[15] There is little doubt these domestic bombings were used to generate support for a variety of political agendas in the years that followed.

The planning for the 1996 Summer Games in Atlanta had a tremendous impact on the 2002 Winter Games. The congressional testimony discussed above, for example, was offered in anticipation of the 1996 Summer Games in Atlanta and demands by some segments of the security apparatus that the business-as-usual approach to public safety around global sporting events was no longer sufficient. In the days and months leading up to the start of the 1996 Games, there were growing demands for a greater presence of the federal law enforcement and the military to help secure the areas in and around the Olympic venues. While the involvement of the federal government in securing multinational domestic athletic games was not new, the $609 million of federal money for the 1996 Olympics in Atlanta was far and above the $75 million spent on the 1984 Summer Games in Los Angeles.[16] United States federal authorities, including the military, were to have a "massive presence on the ground" that would involve "tens of thousands of eyes and ears watching for even the slightest abnormalities."[17]

The scope of the federal investment in the 1996 Games was unprecedented. The estimated amount of support for safety and security strategies alone was $96 million, up from $68 million in security spending for the 1984 Los Angeles Games. Thus, increased governmental commitment to providing financial support for otherwise private industry interests was evident. This slow movement by the federal government into providing more and more security was much bigger than just financial. It is, however, better understood as a slow, deliberate shift that included a wide array of law enforcement and military assets that are traditionally prohibited for use for domestic security events. The 1996 Summer Games were heralded as the "largest peacetime security operation" in American history.[18] During his congressional testimony, one senior senator arrogantly warned those considering attacks, "we are ready...so don't even think of coming to Atlanta."[19] The unthinkable, however, did happen during the 1996 Summer Games when a bomb exploded on July 27, killing two and injuring 111 bystanders. The bombing demonstrated the fragile nature of public safety at large public gatherings with multiple avenues of access, and with thousands of onlookers and participants (Decker et al., 2005, 2008). The Atlanta bombing reinforced the reality that public safety was an incredibly difficult thing to guarantee even after unprecedented infusion of resources.

Expansion of the federal involvement: the creation of the National Special Security Event

The Atlanta bombing helped create another momentum: the passage of a series of executive orders. The Presidential Decision Directive 62 became public law in 2000 and set a legal path for changes in how public safety is coordinated for large-scale events deemed to be of national significance. Presidential Decision Directives (PDDs) are executive orders issued by the President of the United States that are not subject to legislative review or rejection.[20] Presidential Decision Directive 62 is a classified document and not subject to public review, and the only information available is from executive summaries. In addition, President Clinton at the time also issued Executive Order 13010: Critical Infrastructure Protection, which established a national interest in protecting key private and public infrastructure projects deemed to be at risk for attack. Like Presidential Decision Directive 62, this was an executive order not subject to legislative review. Executive Order 13010 read, in part, that identified governmental entities were instructed to "consult with ... elements of the public and private sectors."[21] Executive Order 13010 also provided that identified agencies were to "determine what legal and policy issues were raised by efforts to protect critical infrastructures and assess how these should be addressed."[22] In a letter to President Clinton arguing for greater investments by the federal government in protecting important private assets, the chairman of a congressional oversight committee argued that "Because the infrastructures are mainly privately owned and operated, we concluded that ... [protecting these assets] ... is a shared responsibility of the public and private sectors."[23] The report later recognized that privately owned infrastructures "make it possible for us to enjoy our inalienable rights and take advantage of the freedoms from on which our nation was founded."[24] This justification expanded the scope of governmental interest to any private interest that is judged to facilitate the enjoyment of "inalienable rights" by the public. While Executive Order 13010 provided the political cover for expanding the reach of the federal government, none of these executive orders identify the constitutional authority or a deep substantive rationale to do so.

Federal involvement was also expanded by passage of Public Law 104–201,[25] which permitted the use of the military for domestic security. "[T]he Secretary of Defense may authorize the commander of a military installation ... to provide assistance for ... the Olympics, and any other civilian sporting event in support of essential security and safety."[26] The legislation never defined the concept of "essential security and safety," therefore leaving the decisions about the applicability of the law to the Secretary of Defense and unspecified civilian authorities. Presidential Decision Directive 62 and Public Law 104–201 provided a baseline of authority for federal involvement and for the expanded use of the military, but the exact responsibilities of individual agencies and sources of funding remained uncertain. Prior to these, authorizations were funded on a case-by-case basis in response to specific legislative requests, but not part of a more comprehensive legislative framework that actively encouraged such investments. In short, prior to

PDD 62 and Public Law 104–201 these decisions are best understood as the outcomes of political negotiations that lacked clear legislative authority.

Presidential Decision Directive 62 (PDD-62) was significant in that it made explicit the role of the federal government in the Olympics and other large-scale global events with the creation of a special classification of events collectively referred to as a *National Special Security Event*.[27] This designation was implemented in direct response to growing concerns of domestic terrorism, particularly in the aftermath of the 1996 Centennial Olympic Park bombing. The designation, National Specific Security Event, for the 2002 Winter Games was due to the perceived security failures in the 1996 Summer Games.[28] According to a Congressional Service report, a National Special Security Event is any occasion deemed by the President of the United States or the Secretary of Homeland Security as an increased terrorist or criminal threat.[29] PDD-62 is general in terms of its classification of events as qualifying for such designation, indicating "some" of the events that might qualify for special designation include "Presidential nominating conventions, Presidential Inaugurations, Presidential Summits, State of the Union addresses and Olympic games."[30] In 2000, Congress also passed the Presidential Threat Protection Act, which further authorized the United States Secret Service to participate "in the planning, coordination, and implementation of security operations at special events of national significance, as determined by the President."[31] According to the United States Secret Service, several factors can suggest an elevated risk of terrorist attack, including the size of the gathering, presence of dignitaries, or the symbolic nature of the event.[32] The same source specifies that, often, a state's governor requests a National Special Security Event designation when a major national or international event is planned, and these requests are reviewed for approval by the National Special Security Events Working Group.

In his 2007 statement to a United States House of Representatives Subcommittee, the Assistant Director for the Office of Protective Operations, which oversees the National Special Security Event program, noted that the role of the United States Secret Service in protecting security plans for major events represented a "natural evolution" in their mission. He noted that "[t]he Secret Service has a long history and expertise at planning and implementing security at major events" and it has a strong reputation for "communicating and coordinating with our local, state and federal law enforcement partners in those jurisdictions where the major events take place."[33] The use of the term "evolution" is noteworthy as it reflects the image of governmental movement into areas outside original missions that was influenced heavily by 15 years' worth of domestic terrorist attacks and demands for more coordinated approaches to security.

Presidential Decision Directive 62, Executive Order 13010, Public Law 104–201, and ultimately the National Special Security Event designation taken together represent much of the framework for federal and military involvement in the Olympic Games in the United States. This piecemeal approach lacked a cogent, formal approach that went through the more typical legislative processes. The lack of clarity on this authority resulted in a request by the United States Senate to the Government Accountability Office to enumerate the authority of the federal government to provide financial and programmatic support. The request itself was prima facie evidence that there were serious internal debates among many segments of the United States Senate about the legal authority for using military and non-military federal assets to secure a private sporting event. In the end, however, the report was clear that "[n]o government-wide law or policy exists that defines the federal government's overall role in funding and supporting the Olympic Games when hosted in the United States."[34] The report, taken as a whole, seems to imply that the cumulative legislation action up until that point created a piecemeal approach that allowed certain actions in certain circumstances but in no way created affirmative obligations and/or mandatory statutory obligations. In the end, more than $300 million was spent on securing the 2002 Winter Games, more than 90% of which was funded directly and indirectly by the federal government (Decker et al., 2005: 69). But regardless of the exact sources of the original and expanded federal authority, the passage of the National Special Security Event designation was crucial in that it codified the role of the United States Secret Service in providing vast levels of support for large-scale public events.

The United States Secret Service as the lead agency

As the lead agency in security matters, the United States Secret Service is to implement its security plan in coordination with local, state, and federal agencies.[35] Table 12.1 provides a summary of all designated National Special Security Events from 1998 through 2008. The support includes planning, training, and employing security technology, such as accreditation[36].

Like all operations with this enhanced security designation, the 2002 Olympics had the United States Secret Service functioning as the lead federal agency responsible for coordination of federal public safety and security assets. Moreover, the Secret Service provided guidance and input for the development of operational security plans to local and state police officials. The purpose was not to replace local law enforcement experts, "but rather to augment them when a crisis exceed their capabilities,"[37] as a senior senator from Utah argued in a 2001 hearing before the Senate Judiciary Committee. According to Decker et al. (2005), the designation assured considerable funding for security from the federal government and guaranteed that state and local law enforcement would give up command responsibilities during the Games.

At its most basic level, the security apparatus for the 2002 Salt Lake City Winter Games was coordinated under the umbrella of the Utah Public Safety

Table 12.1 National Specific Security Events designations, 1998–2008

	Event	Location	Year	Type of event
1	World Energy Council Meeting	Houston, TX	1998	International
2	NATO 50th Anniversary Celebration	Washington, DC	1999	International
3	World Trade Organization Meeting	Seattle, WA	1999	International
4	State of the Union Address	Washington, DC	2000	Presidential
5	International Monetary Fund Meeting	Washington, DC	2000	International
6	International Naval Review (OpSail)	New York, NY	2000	International
7	Republican National Convention	Philadelphia, PA	2000	Political
8	Democratic National Convention	Los Angeles, CA	2000	Political
9	Presidential Inauguration	Washington, DC	2001	Presidential
10	United Nations General Assembly 56	New York, NY	2001	International
11	State of the Union Address	Washington, DC	2002	Presidential
12	Super Bowl XXXVI	New Orleans, LA	2002	Sporting
13	Winter Olympic Games	Salt Lake City, UT	2002	Sporting
14	State of the Union Address	Washington, DC	2004	Presidential
15	President Reagan State Funeral	Washington, DC	2004	Presidential
16	Sea Island G8 Summit	Sea Island, GA	2004	International
17	Democratic National Convention	Boston, MA	2004	Political
18	Republican National Convention	New York, NY	2004	Political
19	Presidential Inauguration	Washington, DC	2005	Presidential
20	State of the Union Address	Washington, DC	2005	Presidential
21	State of the Union Address	Washington, DC	2006	Presidential
22	President Ford State Funeral	Washington, DC	2007	Presidential
23	State of the Union Address	Washington, DC	2007	Presidential
24	State of the Union Address	Washington, DC	2008	Presidential
25	Democratic National Convention	Denver, CO	2008	Political
26	Republican National Convention	St. Paul, MN	2008	Political
27	G-20 Economic Summit	Washington, DC	2008	International

Source: United States Secret Service (2011b).

Command. This group was created by State of Utah statute in an effort to coordinate the entire security operation. The group included members of local, state, federal agencies, and the private sector.[38] The Utah Public Safety Command model was effective in that it statutorily created not only a mechanism for coordinating security but also codified the appropriate partners at the table and loosely defined their roles. Beyond creating the framework for relationships across levels of government, this group was interdisciplinary and included representatives from law enforcement, fire, emergency medical services, emergency management, public works, and the National Guard. Thus, it created an expanded definition of "public safety" that moved far beyond the concept of physical security alone (Decker et al., 2005).[39] The Secret Service, a key member of the Utah Public Safety Command was responsible for coordinating the federal effort and now the primary agency responsible for public safety.

Although Presidential Decision Directive 62 created the mechanism for federal engagement and identified the United States Secret Service as the lead agency responsible for coordinating public safety, its effectiveness in doing so was unclear during the early stages of planning. The 2002 Winter Games were the first real "test" of the impact of this directive. The impact of this approach, particularly one that spans levels of government and is interdisciplinary, was all but uncertain. The law enforcement community is generally not well coordinated. In a profession where "jurisdiction" (both physical and substantive areas of responsibility) is a defining dimension of work dynamics, local, state, and federal agencies generally work independent of each other. The expanded involvement of the military, which represented over 32% of all public safety personnel, resulted in the single largest federal law enforcement presence ever deployed in the United States (Decker et al., 2005). These relationships can often be most graciously characterized as "loosely coupled" – fragmented at best (Hagan, Hewitt, and Alwin, 1979) and antagonistic at worse. Jurisdictional disputes, lack of cooperation, and outright hostility are not altogether uncommon. Thus, the true impact of PDD 62 remained uncertain at the outset.

The involvement of the United States military

The designation National Special Security Event, together with previous federal statutes identified above, also provided for extensive involvement from the United States military. This is something frowned upon in the United States. In addition to the federal law enforcement presence, the United States military added 3500 personnel,[40] which was the largest single allocation of security workforce from one branch among the various contributing organizations – military, local police, state law enforcement, federal law enforcement, law-enforcement volunteers, and fire and emergency management services personnel. This indicates that the military, which is traditionally kept separate from civilian law enforcement operations, had a much larger role in security at the Olympics than would have typically occurred. The military was primarily responsible for "aviation communications, explosive ordinance disposal, physical security, and temporary facilities...that are essential to security and public safety of the Winter Olympics"[41] perimeter security, which was critical both symbolically and in an instrumental sense to the safety of the Salt Lake City Olympics.

In the United States, the use of military forces, particularly the United States Army or Navy, in domestic law enforcement is historically prohibited. Title 18, United States Code section 1385, commonly referred to as the Posse Comitatus Act, prohibits the use of these assets in general law enforcement roles. The law reads, in part, "Whoever, except in cases and under circumstances expressly authorized by the Constitution or Act of Congress, willfully uses any part of the Army or Navy...to execute the law...shall be fined...or imprisoned." The Posse Comitatus Act applies most explicitly to the Army and Air Force.[42] The purpose of the law is to send a clear message that in the United States, policing is a non-military responsibility. Moreover, absent exigent circumstances, the military is an outwardly facing function of government that has no domestic public safety and/or national security role. There are two primary functional impacts of the Posse Comitatus Act on public safety, particularly as it relates to the Olympic Games. Notwithstanding exceptional events such as large riots and/or natural disasters, the law restricts the use of military for domestic policing functions. When the military does operate domestically, its role is often a supporting role whereby it provides access to equipment and other military assets generally inaccessible to civilian authorities. It should be noted that military assets are traditionally mobilized domestically in response to actual or impending public safety crises and historically are not mobilized to function in a prevention role.

Although the Posse Comitatus Act created a legal framework that limits the role of the military domestically, there had been a steady expansion of the use of the military in domestic public safety for large-scale public events. As documented previously, the 1996 Games were pivotal in that the threat of terrorist attacks was used to justify pushing the boundaries of law and tradition. "Terrorism," one United States senator argued during congressional testimony, required that the federal government provide the "equipment, expertise, technology, intelligence, communication, resources, and manpower required for a massive counterterrorism operation."[43] Similar references were made to "terroristic threats" throughout all testimony referenced during the 1996 hearing before the Senate Judiciary Committee. References to threats of terrorism, however real, arguably functioned to quell dissent. In the end, the 1996 Atlanta Games included the single largest "deployed" military presence in the United States at that time in history. The threat of terrorism was driving the political discourse at the time and functioned as the justification behind an expanded military involvement. As one United States senator argued in a 1996 U.S. Senate hearing specifically about the role of the military in the Atlanta Games, "It is my idea that the threat of terrorist activity, regardless of the venue chosen by the perpetrator, is of fundamental concern to our national security interests."[44]

While the attacks leading up to the 1996 Games provided much of the political justification for the expansion of military involvement, how the military would be involved continued to be controversial in the United States Senate. There was a perception among some that the new threat was little more than a political power grab that resulted in access to federally funded and trained personnel to perform benign tasks that civilians should otherwise assume. Stated plainly, some believed military personnel were little more than cheap labor that would be exploited in the name of national security. One United States senator strongly opposed the expansion of federal funding for the 1996 and 2002 Olympic Games, warning that military personnel would be underutilized and have very little public safety value. He pointed out the dubious nature of the military presence and its limited capacity to create a real sense of public safety because it had no arrest power: "This means that the 13,000 military personnel who will be on the ground ... have no authority to arrest or even detain individuals who engage in criminal activities."[45] As an example, the same senator questioned the value of having uniformed military personnel driving buses to and from Olympic venues.

The issue of military personnel driving buses became a significant issue of debate in the 1996 Senate Judiciary Committee meeting between two politically powerful senators. One senator who strongly opposed the expanded use of the military in the Olympics argued that not only did it demean highly trained military personnel by using them as "chauffeurs" for international athletes but it actually decreased their personnel safety since they would replace better-trained bus drivers. The senator from Utah, however, argued that there would be a net increase in security because military personnel are "armed and ... watching over the people in the bus." The senator opposed to the use of the military instead insisted that "The military is certainly not trained to provide that kind of security. That is not in their training." He further argued that if that type of protective service was really the motivation, then the Secret Service were a more viable option as that falls in their area of expertise: "[I]f we are going to have to give them additional training [to] provide the kind of protection the Secret Service does, then let's get the Secret Service or [Federal Bureau of Investigation] driving those buses." The Utah senator responded with a sense of blind faith that military personnel would be used in an effective way to enhance security: "Well, I have been led to believe they are trained for it and they can be trained for it and they can do a good job and that is one of the ways they protect these athletes and others."[46] This impassioned debate continued through much of the planning stages for the 2002 Salt Lake City Games.

The 9/11 Commission Report

The tragedy of 9/11 represented a moment in history where governmental bureaucracies were explicitly implicated by being blamed that they failed to anticipate the event. The vast array of intelligence and public safety communities were blamed for not "connecting the dots"[47] in ways that understood the connections between disparate pieces of intelligence suggesting that such an attack was both plausible and indeed operational.

In the weeks and months that followed, intelligence and law enforcement agencies received scathing criticism for not using more "imagination" in their assessments of threats and for not effectively moving beyond Cold War notions of the conventional enemies and modalities of attacks. For example, although intelligence available at the time suggested that some international terrorist organizations were planning to crash planes filled with explosives into Central Intelligence Agency headquarters, "little thought had been devoted to the danger of suicide pilots" among the likely scenarios actively considered among highly ranked intelligence experts.[48] "Imagination," they noted, "is not a gift usually associated with bureaucracies."[49] *The 9/11 Commission Report* also noted that although the Central Intelligence Agency was once "central to our national intelligence capabilities,"[50] their role was diminished following the end of the Cold War. Intelligence operations were largely shared among three large bureaucracies located within the Department of Defense and, in fact, were not centralized and adequately coordinated. No single agency, for example, had the authority to establish national intelligence priorities or to prioritize resource allocation. One of the most pressing observations was that the intelligence capacities were far too divided among too many agencies. This created intelligence silos that served the need of "home agencies" and not "joint missions."[51]

The *9/11 Commission Report* was critical of nearly all aspects of governmental preparation as it related to the possibility of terrorists attacks. In addition to being criticized for a lack of "imagination," the intelligence and public safety communities were also criticized for not establishing early warning signs for growing terrorist plots, for a lack of coordination and communication within and between bureaucratic agencies, and for sacrificing public safety due to jurisdictional disputes about which agency owned the authority and/or responsibility for particular security concerns.

A Utah Public Safety Command official at the time noted that in the aftermath of the attacks, public safety took on an entirely different meaning: "The public safety community began to consider what the new terrorism threat meant for Olympic security operations, with the *national government leading most of those discussions* [Emphasis added]" (Bellavita, 2007: 1). This new threat redefined questions of jurisdiction, the role of the federal government, and questions about the use of the military. "Olympic security was *now too important to remain exclusively under local control* [Emphasis added].

A variety of federal agencies wanted to make sure there were no flaws in it" (Bellavita, 2007: 1). As a direct response to increased threats, United States congressional members provided millions more in federal funding for security.[52] The Bush Administration made it clear to the American people and the world that security was a top concern as the 2002 Winter Games approached: "We will show the world we can safeguard the Olympic ideal without sacrificing our American ideas – openness, mobility, diversity, and economic opportunity."[53]

From a political level, the effects of 9/11 were felt almost immediately. For example, the President of the United States submitted an emergency appropriations request on October 17, 2001, that outlined $1.1 billion in additional spending for the Department of Justice "responsibilities arising from the September 11th terrorist attacks."[54] According to one public safety expert closely involved in planning, "it was very easy to get money and people – two resources hard to obtain before the attacks" (cited in Bellavita, 2007: 1). Political opposition to federal spending for the Olympics was also largely decimated in the aftermath of 9/11. One of the staunchest critics of increased federal spending in the United States Senate, for example, dropped all public criticisms and instead was purported to "support... 100 percent" additional money for public safety.[55] The public safety and political stakes were high, and no politician wanted to be on the wrong side of this issue.

Amending the Posse Comitatus Act

The shift in political will in the aftermath of 9/11 was notable not only in terms of funding but also in terms of support for the expanded role of military assets related to the Salt Lake City Games. The emergency spending bill submitted by the President of the United States put into place new rules for the use of military assets related to the 2002 Games that bypassed conventional civilian oversight processes. The request, for example, "would temporarily waive the requirement to obtain Attorney General certification" that the support in question was "necessary to meet essential security and safety needs" for the 2002 Winter Games.[56] This level of civilian oversight, particularly by the Attorney General of the United States, who functions as the chief law enforcement officer in the nation, is noteworthy. Finally, the President's emergency funding plan also expanded the scope of military involvement in the Salt Lake City Games. Whereas previous provisions allowed for federal reimbursement of pay for "members of the reserve components serving in an active duty status," the new rules would "temporarily"[57] permit reimbursement for "a member of the Army National Guard or Air National Guard while performing State of"[58] the Posse Comitatus Act. The justification for this "temporary waiver" or how such a waiver is reconciled with the Posse Comitatus Act was never offered in the funding request.

Concerns about the apparent conflict between the expanding role of the military and the potential for legal problems associated with the Posse Comitatus Act were evident and ultimately had to be addressed legislatively. A new code was passed, stating that while the basic principles of the 1878 act remained intact, "[T]he *Posse Comitatus Act* is *not a complete barrier* [Emphasis added] to the use of the Armed Forces for a range of domestic purposes, including *law enforcement functions* [Emphasis added]." Such use was justified "when the use of the Armed Forces is authorized by Act of Congress or the President determines that... [its use]... is required to fulfill the President's obligations... to respond in a time of war... or serious emergency."[59] Although this code was written after the completion of the 2002 Winter Games, it reflects the prevailing conceptual shift about the use of the military in the weeks that followed 9/11. The exact source of this more relaxed interpretation is unclear but was likely influenced by both the evolving legislation discussed above and the impacts of 9/11. As the 2002 Games approached, the commitment and central command authority of the federal government were clear.

Conclusion

The National Special Security Event designation was critical in the movement of the federal government, and the Secret Service more specifically, into the forefront of public safety for large-scale events such as the Olympics. Its establishment through an executive order rather than a legislative process moved the question of the involvement of federal law enforcement or the military in the Olympics and related events out of the shadows of backroom legislative bargaining and instead formalized the process of seeking authorization and funding. For the United States, these developments represent important substantive shifts in federal authority that need to be further studied. Although the National Special Security Event designation has been so consequential in creating the legal framework for the expansion of the United States federal government, including the Department of Defense, in what are otherwise private events such as large-scale sporting events, much of this has been accomplished under the veil of secrecy. In fact, until March of 2014, PDD-62 was deemed a "classified" document that was not available for public review. The authors of this chapter went through a three-year process to have this document declassified through formal channels with the William J. Clinton Presidential Library. While the initial request for declassification was denied without justification, a subsequent appeal of that decision to the Interagency Security Classification Appeals Panel resulted in a public release of a redacted version of the document, after more than three years.

A review of PDD-62 revealed what can best be classified as a tremendous expansion of the authority of the United States federal government, through the mechanism of the National Special Security Event classification, in otherwise private events. A more substantive review of this document reveals a legal framework that is both enabling and, by all accounts, open-ended. By enabling, we mean to suggest there are essentially no limits to the type of events and/or venues that could be classified as of "national significance" and therefore likely targets of "unconventional attacks."[60] Importantly, the regulation merely lists *examples* of events that might be classified as falling under this special designation, but ultimately gives discretion to the Counterterrorism Security Group to make recommendations to the "Attorney General and Secretary of the Treasury of events when it believes they should [be] designated [as] a 'National Special Security Event.'"[61] By open-ended, we mean there are no limits, financial or otherwise, placed on the involvement of the federal government in such events. It reads, in part, "I have decided that for such National Special Security Events, the full protective and consequence management capabilities of the Federal Government shall be available as necessary ...."[62]

The public safety apparatus that supported the Salt Lake City Olympics had been going through a steady shift away from local, privately funded events and toward increased involvement of the federal government. The difficulties of executing the agreements that led to security arrangements at the Salt Lake Olympics are mirrored by the Greek experience during the Athens Olympics discussed in the next chapter. A full and complete documentation of the shift in the United States seems nearly impossible because it is buried deep in congressional testimonies, executive-level orders, administrative regulations, and legislative action – many of which are not easily made available to the public. Be they publicly legislated or executively ordered, such policies stand in strong opposition to centrality of "local government" in the United States and a long-held resistance against the use of the military for domestic policing programs.

Notes

This research was supported in part from Roger Williams University's Foundation to Promote Scholarship and Teaching. We thank an anonymous reviewer for valuable comments.

1. Salt Lake City competed with Quebec City, Canada, Sion, Switzerland, and Östersund, Sweden. On June 16, 1995, the IOC awarded the Games to Salt Lake City. Just two months earlier, on April 19, 1995, a bomb explosion in the Alfred P. Murrah Federal Building in Oklahoma City, OK, killed 168 people and devastated the downtown area.
2. "Security at Games stiffens won't let fear stop Olympics," M. O'Keefe, *NY Daily News*, September 26, 2001, 95.
3. All funding references are in constant 1996 dollar terms.
4. "Games have been golden for Utah; GAO [the U.S. Government Accountability Office] says state will get $1.4B in federal money for projects related to 2002 Olympics," L. Fantin, *Salt Lake City Tribune*, December 22, 1999.

5. "Completely united: Heightened security to cost $40 million more," *CNN Sports Illustrated*. October 4, 2001. Retrieved from http://sportsillustrated.cnn.com/olympics/2002/news/2001/10/03/security_request_ap/

6. The Constitution of the United States, Amendment 10.

7. *Olympic Games: federal government provides significant funding and support* (No. GAO/GGD-00-183). Washington, DC: U.S. Government Accountability Office, 2000, 5.

8. In the lexicon of American politics, "pork barrel" projects are those funded merely for political gain. Such language resonates with the American public in important ways as it represents political corruption.

9. "In Olympics success, Romney found new edge," K. Johnson, *New York Times*, September 19, 2007. Retrieved from http://www.nytimes.com/2007/09/19/us/politics/19romney.html?_r=2&pagewanted=all

10. GAO, 2000, 82.

11. Senate Judiciary Committee (1996) The Olympics and the threat of terrorism. Committee on the Judiciary (2nd ed.), Washington, DC: U.S. Government Printing Office, 2.

12. In one national poll, by late 1995, half of American citizens predicted an additional attack was "very likely" while the other half predicted "somewhat likely." See Polling Report (2011), retrieved from http://www.pollingreport.com/terror9.htm

13. Senate Judiciary Committee, 1996, 3.

14. Ibid., 13.

15. Ibid., 1.

16. GAO, 2000, 5.

17. Senate Judiciary Committee, 1996, 3.

18. "Bomb at the Olympics: the stakes; pipe bomb in a park trumps Games' advanced security," J. Kifner. *New York Times*, 1996, A1. Retrieved from http://www.nytimes.com/1996/07/28/us/bomb-olympics-stakes-pipe-bomb-park-trumps-games-advanced-security.html

19. Ibid.

20. Relyea, H. C. (2008) *Presidential Directives: Background and Overview*, Washington, DC: Congressional Research Service.

21. The President (1996) Executive Order 13010: Critical Infrastructure Protection, Washington, DC: Federal Register, 37 and 348.

22. Ibid.

23. President's Commission on Critical Infrastructure Protection (1997) *Critical Foundations: Protecting America's Infrastructures*, Washington, DC: The White House, p. i.

24. Ibid., 3.

25. 10 U.S.C. 2554, 1996. United States Congress (2001) Tilte. In & Committee on Appropriations. Washington: U.S. Government Printing Office.

26. Ibid., 2496.

27. All references to PDD 62 are taken from a variety of primary (declassified but redacted copy of PDD-62) and secondary sources, in particular congressional summaries completed by S. Reese in 2008 and 2009 and the 2000 GAO report to the Senate Committee on Commerce, Science and Transportation. S. Reese. *National Special Security Events*. Washington, DC: Congressional Research Services, 2008, 2009. For 2000 GAO report, see Note 5.

28. John Buntin, Kennedy School of Government case study, Parts A–C: "Security Preparations for the 1996 Centennial Olympic Games (Part A)," Case No. C16–00–1582.0.
29. Reese, *National Special Security Events*, 2008, 2009.
30. PDD-62, 10.
31. Public Law 106–544 sec. 3.
32. T. J. Koerner (2007) Full statement of Timothy J. Koerner, Assistant Director, Office of Protective Operations, United States Secret Service. U.S. House of Representatives Subcommittee on Intelligence, information sharing and terrorism risk assessment. Aurora, Colorado.
33. Ibid., 2.
34. GAO, 2000, 8.
35. United States Secret Service (2011a) *National Special Security Events*. Retrieved November 3, 2011. Retrieved from: http://www.gpo.gov/fdsys/pkg/FR-2011–11–03/pdf/FR-2011–11–03.pdf
36. Ibid.
37. Senate Judiciary Committee (2001) *The 2002 Winter Olympics in Salt Lake City, Utah: Cooperation between federal, state, local and private agencies to address public safety concerns*. Salt Lake City, 2.
38. Senate Judiciary Committee, 2001. See also Oquirrh Institute (2003) *The 2002 Olympic Winter Games Security Lessons Applied to Homeland Security*. Salt Lake City: Oquirrh Institute.
39. See also Oquirrh Institute, 2003.
40. Oquirrh Institute, 2002.
41. Senate Judiciary Committee, 2001, 16.
42. Although the law does not explicitly include the Navy and Marines Corps, both organizations function as if it is applicable.
43. Senate Judiciary Committee, 1996, 3.
44. Ibid., 1.
45. Ibid., 6.
46. Ibid., 8.
47. Ibid., 408.
48. Ibid., 336.
49. Ibid., 344.
50. Ibid., 409.
51. Ibid., 408.
52. "Winter Olympics: Rings of steel to surround Games in response to terrorist attacks," T. Knight, *Telegraph*, December 17, 2001. Retrieved from http://www.telegraph.co.uk/sport/othersports/olympics/3018942/Winter-Olympics-Rings-of-steel-to-surround-Games-in-response-to-terrorist-attacks.html
53. The White House (2002) *Preparing for the World: Homeland Security and Winter Olympics*, Washington, DC.
54. United States Congress, 2001, 5.
55. *CNN Sports Illustrated*, 2001.
56. United States Congress, 2001, 15.
57. The Emergency Supplemental Appropriations request sent by the President of the United States to Congress on October 17, 2001 (United States Congress, 2001) used the term "temporarily" many times but never clearly defines a time range.

58. Ibid., 15.
59. Title 6, United States Code, section 466 titled "Sense of Congress reaffirming the continued importance and applicability of the Posse Comitatus Act," November 25, 2002.
60. PDD-62, 10.
61. Ibid.
62. Ibid.

13
Asymmetric Power Relations (Athens 2004)

Anastassia Tsoukala

> We were facing the dilemma: either you buy the security system or we boycott the Games.[1]

This above statement was made in 2010 by the Minister of Defense before the Greek Parliament's investigation committee in the lead-up to the 2004 Athens Olympics. The committee was investigating the security scandals involving Siemens and the security system called Command, Control, Communications, Computers and Information (C4I).[2] In some respects, it could perfectly sum up asymmetric power relations between Greece, the host country of the first post-9/11 Summer Olympics, and what could be qualified as a United States–led hegemonic group[3] of Western countries (Australia, United Kingdom, France, Germany, Israel, and Spain) that sought and eventually managed to shape the Greek Olympic security dispositif. To highlight what lies beneath this rather unusual official confirmation of fierce left and radical left denunciation of the "Olympic fiesta that endorses collaboration between domestic bosses and multinational firms, foreign political command centers and security agencies,"[4] one has to go back in time. Unraveling the way 21st-century concerns over security threats mingle with protection of economic, political and geopolitical interests in the Athens Olympics' context cannot be achieved unless this web of interactions is seen inter alia in light of the evolution both of security policies and international relations in the postwar era.

As discussed in other chapters in this book, security became a key issue for the Olympics, following the Games in Munich in 1972 and Atlanta in 1996. The overall reassessment of the planning regarding security, however, only took place after the events of 9/11 in the United States. As I explicate below, what started as an essentially quantitative upgrading of security policies in the 2002 Salt Lake City Olympics led to deep qualitative shifts in the Athens Olympics through the setting up of a vast international security network and the introduction of high-tech surveillance technologies. At first glance, the very existence of such a security dispositif was highly predictable to the extent that it fully complied with the henceforth predominant international collaboration pattern in counter-terrorism.[5] The ensuing security measures, ranging from surveillance mechanisms and intelligence-led policing to military involvement, and their conceptual background – that is, preemptive risk assessments – might also be seen as expectable. Securing the Olympics could not be dissociated from the broader security context in postmodern risk societies that was precisely focused on technology-based proactive risk management strategies (Bajc, 2007b, 2011a; Boyle and Haggerty, 2009; Klauser, 2009; Giulianotti and Klauser, 2010; Tsoukala, 2010; Fussey et al., 2011). From this standpoint, the main novelties of this extensive security dispositif would only be related to its unprecedented (for Olympic standards) extent and formality. Notwithstanding the appropriateness of such an approach, summing up the 2004 Olympics security policy as the outcome of the implementation into the sports field of otherwise prevailing security concerns, strategies and practices, to highlight increasing securitization of sport mega-events, is somewhat misleading. It downgrades the interplay between the security field and the political and economic ones. In assuming, on the contrary, that security management in the context of the Games cannot be divorced from politics and economics, this chapter aims at highlighting how the setting up of relevant security measures by a minor player in the international political and economic arena also has to be understood in terms of hegemonic versus subordinate state relations.

The impact of asymmetric power relations on the shaping of 2004 Olympic security dispositif has been at the heart of the Siemens / Command, Control, Communications, Computers and Information security system scandal. Yet, as of the time of writing, Siemens-related trials are pending, and the veracity of both the hearings of witnesses and many different statements made by Greek officials deemed to be involved in the scandal is so questionable that I cannot ground analysis on these sources. Moreover, I believe that the severity of punishment to be brought upon those who are found guilty for corruption-related crimes undermines the already doubtful objectivity of potential interviewees. Given these constraints, I will address the security issue at the Games through thematic content analysis of all relevant articles published from January 1, 2001, to August 12, 2004, by two American and two French upmarket daily newspapers. The former (*The New York Times* and *The Washington Post*) are chosen because they covered extensively the issue in a country that played a leading role in shaping the Olympic security dispositif; the latter (*Libération* and *Le Figaro*) are chosen because they are nationally distributed and are thought to be representative of the ruling parties[6] of a country that, along with the United States of America, has been involved both in the Olympic Security Advisory Group and the run for the Olympic security bid.

This comparative analysis is further likely to uncover state power relations at work. This is so for a number of reasons. Both countries share the same definition of the threat posed by religious fundamentalists after 9/11 (Tsoukala, 2009b). Both countries are also high-ranking at the international scene, but only the United States seeks to play a worldwide hegemonic role. The United States and French Olympic security-related economic interests diverged from March 2003 on, when the United States–led Science Applications International Corporation[7] Consortium (seven from the United States, three Greek, four other European, and two Israeli firms) won the Olympic bid at the expense of the American/French-led Thales France and Raytheon System consortium (two American, four Greek, and four other European firms). As a member of the European Union, France has divergent political interests from the United States. Also, Greek-American relations have been marked by tensions throughout the postwar period, but no such tensions are to be found in Greek-French relations. My analysis of this media coverage below shows that the United States took a hegemonic position toward Greece while France did not exhibit the same attitude. To shed light on why this was the case and also why the Greek authorities did not stand their ground under pressure, I first discuss the influence of security-related political and economic interests on these dynamics. This preceding discussion rests upon secondary sources and 11 interviews I conducted with Greek senior security officers during the lead-up to the Olympics.

While in line with the argument that security-related political discourses are embedded into the application and institutionalization of technologies of government, as part of a broader process of securitization (Wæver, 1995; Buzan et al., 1998) the present analysis differs from prior discursive approaches to security. I do not address the way security discourses interact with security policies within an (inter)national territory. What I seek to grasp instead is a deterritorialized threat assessment with forceful indirect effects in space and time. Regarding the hegemonic discourses in particular, I have argued elsewhere (Tsoukala, 2006: 44) that the United States media discourses on security issues at the 2004 Olympics, widely broadcast in Greece, targeted first and foremost the Greek public. For this reason, theses media discourses can be seen as part of a broader strategy to determine all major parameters of the Olympic security dispositif following the threat perception in the United States and the interests of their security-related firms. These discourses were not meant to persuade a given public on the necessity to adopt a given policy, but rather to inform, from a hegemonic position, on the direction of decisions to be taken by Greek officials. This hegemony has been bluntly confirmed by the Greek Minister of Public Order who, on his way to the United States, said, "We are invited by a superpower that plays a hegemonic role all over the world. Of course we have to go to the U.S.A. for the Olympic security issues, where did you expect us to go, to Tanzania?"[8]

And the winner is...

In the euphoria which followed the International Olympic Committee announcement in 1997 that Athens was chosen as the host city for the 2004 Olympics, Greek national pride was mingling with ambitious dreams of a rise in power in regional political and economic fields. Successful hosting of the Games was expected to turn Greece into a security know-how exporting country in both Southeastern Europe and cities hosting future Olympic Games (Floridis, 2004). From a different standpoint, successful management of security-related issues was meant to be met with an array of both avowable and non-openly admitted challenges. Protection of the people participating and attending the Games was going along with the safe staging of a sport mega-event that was believed to be highly vulnerable not only because of the so-called threat of global terrorism but also because the 2004 Athens Games were the first in the new Europe with abolished internal border controls within the Schengen area.[9] Coping successfully with these challenges was, however, continuously linked with pressure by the ruling parties to allay international and especially United States criticism on lax tackling of domestic urban guerrillas. This criticism was based on the argument that no single member of the two major post-dictatorial armed groups, Revolutionary Organization 17 November and Revolutionary People's Struggle, was ever arrested.

Islamist threat

In fact, the United States' distrust of the Greek handling of domestic political violence was embedded in a much broader and multifaceted international skepticism about Greece's capacity to cope with security issues at the Olympics. Doubts were fueled by the country's geographical position and geological specificities. As post-9/11 security threats became increasingly connected with Islamist armed groups, geographical proximity both to Middle East and Balkan countries was seen as likely to cause serious security problems. Potential attackers were deemed to easily reach Athens not only because they would not have to expose themselves to long and risky travels but also because the existence of countless points of entry into the country, at any island of the archipelago, made efficient border controls practically impossible. These concerns were shared by most Western governments.[10] Authorities of the United States, however, were linking this issue to the bilateral negotiations about adding Greece to the United States Visa Waiver Program and the plan for central control over passport issuance in order to minimize forgery.[11]

At first glance, these worries seem well grounded. Yet, a more detailed look into these issues suggests something different. The rock-solid cordial relations between Greece and the entire Arabic world in the postwar period are well known (Arvanitopoulos and Koppa, 2005). Also, there were consistent reports from all major Western intelligence services that radical Islamist groups were not a threat to security of the 2004 Athens Games.[12] Safety of the Games had even been implicitly guaranteed by Yasser Arafat, who, in announcing unilateral cease-fire on the part of Palestinians during the Olympics, had called for a global respect of the Games so that they might play out peacefully.[13] In an equally implicit way, Colonel Muammar el-Qaddafi pledged to keep the Games safe by asking Libyans living in Greece not to engage in any acts of violence during the Olympics.[14]

Greek urban guerrilla

Fear of being the target of Islamist-originating attacks was coupled with concerns raised by the activity of Greek urban struggle groups. As the latter had frequently targeted United States officials and interests, they were more worrisome to American rather than French authorities. Greek armed groups were thought to be all the more dangerous as they were allegedly backed by Greek officials. Widely broadcast American official denunciations of collusion between high-ranking Socialist officials and armed groups that had marked out Greek-American relations throughout the post-dictatorial era, once again, were influencing the bilateral political agenda. In 2000, for example, American Foreign Policy Council Senior Associate Wayne Merry implied that 17 November was connected with Greek high-ranking officials, among them Foreign Minister Papandreou.[15] Similarly, former United States Central Intelligence Agency Director James Woolsey stated that Greece had not been doing enough to capture the group's members (ibid.). According to Fakitsas (2003), a 2000 report issued by a United States Congressional Commission designated Greece as "not cooperating fully" in counterterrorism. Even after the dismantlement of 17 November in 2002, following close collaboration between police and intelligence agencies in Greece and the United Kingdom (Fakitsas, 2003; Floros and Newsome, 2008), a 2004 report for the Congress shows that the State Department kept the organization on its annual list of foreign terrorist organizations, insisting that "additional members of the group are at large, and investigations are continuing."[16]

This report also mentions that the insistence by the United States on a "terrorist threat" at the Games was also related to the activity of numerous minor anarchist groups thought to be apt to target, alone or in collaboration with domestic or foreign anti-globalization groups, the United States and other Western interests.[17] Arguably then, it is this context of distrust and discontent that lies beneath the wiretapping scandal that unraveled after the Athens Games whereby Greek officials were convinced that United States intelligence agencies were involved in wiretapping more than a hundred high-ranking Greek officials, including the prime minister, before and during the Olympics (Samatas, 2007, 2011). At the time of this writing, there is new evidence that strongly suggests the involvement of the United States Embassy in Athens, and Athens' prosecutor filed an action for "a major case of attempted espionage."[18]

International relations

In addition to the increased sense of vulnerability of Western countries after 9/11, particular United States security-related claims have to be understood in light of the traditionally strong anti-American feelings in Greece as well as evolving European Union and United States relations. In terms of American-Greek relations, in the more recent phases of what Greeks perceive as the long-standing United States "meddling" in Greek internal affairs, resentment is fueled by their support of the 1967–1974 military junta[19]; their alleged involvement in the 1974 Cyprus invasion by Turkey[20]; and their support of Turkey with regard to the contentious issue of delimitation of the Aegean Sea and the Cyprus question.

At the scale of the European Union, political restructuring of former Eastern European countries and the correlated emergence of the European Union as a potentially powerful actor on the international political scene, and on global trade and finance, have reshaped both the scope and the objectives of United States regional politics. For what matters here, more often than not promotion and legitimization of United States policies in Europe have rested upon management of security-related issues. In the former Eastern European countries, the expanding strategies of influence by the United States seem primarily to be related to security. This is shown by the establishment of the International Law Enforcement Academy in Budapest in 1995[21] or the launching of the Southeast European Cooperative Initiative in 1996, inspired by the United States (Papanicolaou, 2011: 116f). Concerning relations between the European Union and the United States, management of security concerns usually rests upon consensus, as was the case with the extraordinary rendition practices (Satterthwaite, 2006; Geyer, 2007). Otherwise, it is the pro–United States outcome of contentious bilateral negotiations, as is shown by the controversial 2004 and 2007 Passenger Name Record Data Transfer agreements, where the European Commission had to take into consideration inter alia that "a failure to transfer the data [to the United States] would lead to sanctions in the United States which might extend to heavy fines and ultimately to a loss of landing rights."[22]

The security market

As in the aforementioned example of economics-backed security-related politics between the European Union and the United States, economic factors may also play a key role in shaping politics to the extent that the latter have to take into account the security market that is embedded in the global security industrial complex (Molnar and Snider, 2011). In this respect, setting up the Olympic security dispositif offers a broad field of action to firms supplying security equipment, technology and know-how. When the city hosting the Games is in a country endowed with powerful security industry it ensures the Games may become an essentially domestic affair. This was not, however, the case with the Athens Olympics. Foreign security-supplying firms that were attracted by the highest security budget ever adopted in an Olympic context were practically free from Greek pressure since there was no significant competition from Greek security firms.

Economic interests at stake were all the more important as security infrastructure prior to the Games was limited. Besides, the winner of the Olympic security bid could plausibly hope to have more chances to win future bids in Greece and in other Olympic Games host cities. Concerning promotion of American economic interests in particular, it has to be bore in mind that Greece could hardly oppose a policy driven by a country that, from another point of view, was its largest foreign investor.[23]

In 2003, following serious delays due to hard negotiations conducted between the Greek government and the Science Applications International Corporation and Thales France and Raytheon System consortiums,[24] the $255 million Olympic security bid was won by the former. As it was established after the end of the Games, this victory was in many respects ill-grounded, thereby leading to a series of trials. Firstly, the C4I security system was subcontracted to German Siemens, which was promoted through bribes. Secondly, what was meant to be the most extensive security shield in Olympic history was of such a technical complexity, and was delivered so late, that it failed to work during the Games. As Samatas demonstrates (2007, 2011), conventional security systems and methods were in fact sufficient to guarantee disturbance-free Games. Yet, this was not discussed during the Games and was not reported by the United States. This lack of awareness is clearly shown by an article published in September 2004 in *Washington Technology*: "The 2004 Summer Olympic Games in Athens went off without a hitch... IT infrastructure was laid out... the advanced systems deployed for the Olympics will serve Greece for years to come."[25] In fact, since the Command, Control, Communications, Computers and Information system was also to be used after the Games for counter-terrorism purposes, it was agreed that it would be fully installed in October 2005 (Samatas, 2007). In May 2010, after numerous rounds of heated negotiations, the Greek government refused to sign final acceptance of the Command, Control, Communications, Computers and Information security system and submitted a complaint against the Science Applications International Corporation for failing to install on time the security system and to train Greek personnel to work with it.[26]

Of course, the Greek officials could not have possibly imagined that their preparations for the Games would ever lead to such an outcome. According to my interview with a senior Greek Army officer in July 2003, security concerns were taken very seriously. The cost of $1.5 billion was almost five times higher than the expense for the 2000 Sydney Games. As Boyle (2011) notes, security strategies implied signing 38 security agreements with 23 countries and accepting close collaboration with the seven-nation[27] Olympic Security Advisory Group, which was involved in decision-making and was providing intelligence services and training to Greek civil and military security personnel in counter-terrorism units. Taking security seriously also involved receiving security advice from other governments, notably

Russia.[28] Following the 2004 Madrid bombings, this also included asking for assistance from the North Atlantic Treaty Organization in requesting air and sea patrols, and protection against nuclear, chemical or biological attacks.[29] Olympic security rested upon the unprecedented deployment of 70,000 security personnel and, for the first time since the military dictatorship, also a deployment of around 10,000 soldiers. A no-fly zone was imposed around Olympic venues and other sites. Civil and military security personnel, who were expected to guarantee 24-hour police surveillance, as well as 24-hour aerial and open-sea surveillance, were relying in turn on technological surveillance provided by submarine control systems and seabed detectors, a blimp mounted with ultra-sensitive sensors and ultra-high-resolution cameras, radiation detection devices along Greece's borders, and around 1200 supersensitive cameras installed in stadiums and other venues (Tsoukala, 2006: 45).

Whose security?

In what was seen as a major national challenge, security came to be solely identified in law enforcement terms, both in the public debate and the security field, thereby neutralizing any counter definitions likely to draw attention to legal, human, or ecological security-related issues. Efforts to guarantee secure hosting of the Games were certainly met with disapproval by certain political circles and parts of civil society, but critical voices were rapidly dismissed because they remained marginal. Fierce criticism stemming from the Communist Party, the Coalition of the Left, Movements and Ecology, and numerous anarchist and far-left milieus against the strengthening of security and surveillance devices, and exploitation of workforce employed in the construction of Olympic venues, thus found no significant echo in Greek society or ruling parties. With the exception of left-wing newspapers, mainstream media remained silent on the unsafe working conditions on Olympic venue construction sites that caused at least 13 deaths and hundreds of injuries among Greek and migrant workers.[30] Exclusion of members of trade unions from the Athens Organizing Committee only provoked isolated reactions among left-wing deputies.[31] Denunciations that, in evacuating student residences so that housing could be used to host journalists during the Games, foreign students had to sign a document stating they would lose their rights to return to the residences if they participated in anti-Olympic protests[32] did not raise particular concerns. Ecological objections that the construction of a rowing center would destroy the Schinias wetland[33] occupied a marginal place in the public debate. As similarly noted by Vanolo in his contribution on the Turin Olympics in Chapter 14 of this book, there was no noteworthy reaction to protests stemming from the United Nations Committee on Economic, Social and Cultural Rights with regard to the "extrajudicial demolition of dwellings and forced evictions of Roma from their settlements by municipal authorities, often under the pretext of construction projects for the 2004 Olympic Games, and frequently without payment of adequate compensation or provision of alternative housing."[34] Interestingly, the only objections that were taken seriously were those of Greek and foreign archaeologists about the construction of a canoe/kayak slalom center at an area adjacent to Marathon Battlefield. In implicitly admitting primacy of (inter) national cultural heritage over the Games, the Greek Minister of Culture announced that the venue would be transferred "to respect the overall landscape, because of its proximity to Marathon."[35]

Security in the press

Greeks "have been asked to pay the sum of our fears" stated the *Washington Post* one day before the opening of the Games,[36] thus admitting the outstanding importance of the United States' influence on shaping security policies for the Games. This apparently sincere confession is, however, misleading. As I explain below, this grounding of the excessive security-related claims by the United States on emotional factors silences the role played by an array of other, wholly rational factors not only in managing security in general but, especially, in inflating the security budget. Moreover, in transforming fear into the sole explanatory factor of pressure on the part of the United States, it somehow makes this pressure excusable. Fear may be criticized for producing undesirable effects, but to the extent that it is grounded on genuine facts, its very existence is morally acceptable. Attributing American pressure to fear justifies the whole United States policy as it obfuscates the morally questionable promotion of their political and economic interests. Yet, since fear was presented as the ground of its security-related pressure and since fear was being fueled by rise in religious extremism after 9/11, analyzing the way security policies and threats have been framed in the American and French press should allow us to see what part of relevant claims may be attributed to fear and what part arguably reflects political and economic interests at stake.

In quantitative terms, attention drawn by the United States to security issues at the Games is revealed by the volume of relevant articles. The security subject is addressed in 114 American articles[37] and 38 French articles.[38] In both cases, however, and rather unsurprisingly, coverage of the security issue grows as the Games get closer: 75.4% of American articles and 81.5% of French articles were written in 2004. Thematic content analysis uncovered two main themes: the security policy assessment and the threat assessment. Due to practical reasons, presentation of each theme will rely on a selection of quotations that are believed to be representative of its whole coverage.

The security policy assessment

In both the United States and France, newspapers often describe security measures in detail and insist heavily on the close cooperation established between Greece and the Olympic Security Advisory Group. This supportive approach is further reinforced by frequent release of reassuring statements made by high-ranking Greek officials, who affirm that "everything is under control"[39] or that "we have done everything humanly possible [to secure the Games]."[40]

Reassuring statements could not, however, conceal rising unease due to wide-scale delays. Athens succeeded in completing construction of all venues on time, but by late March 2004, for example, some Olympic projects were still behind schedule. In France, these delays were seen as worrisome because they might jeopardize the quality of the Games if they prevented the public from having access to all sport venues. Being thus limited in the sports field, delays were mentioned in 10.5% of the articles but were usually commented through the reassuring voice of the International Olympic Committee president. On one occasion, the president commented playfully that ensuring security of the Games is "like syrtaki: it starts very slowly, it accelerates all the time, and by the end you can't follow the pace."[41]

In the United States articles, by contrast, delays were a source of concern because they were seen as likely to endanger security. Newspapers mention a number of issues. They report that delays disturbed installation of the security devices: "contractors cannot install surveillance cameras without walls on which to affix them."[42] The American newspaper articles also suggest that delays prevented familiarization with the security apparatus: "police officers cannot familiarize themselves with all the nooks and crannies where terrorists might lurk while the venues are still construction sites."[43] We also read that delays reduced the "time to fully test systems to detect or respond to an attack."[44] Yet, while delays were extensively covered in 5.9% of the articles, the fact that Science Applications International Corporation was unable to deliver the whole security system on time, and that even the deliverable parts of it would be delivered so late that there would not be enough time for its surveillance systems to be completely checked; and references to fully trained Greek personnel were hardly mentioned at all – only in 2.5% of the articles.

In the American press, unease was further reinforced by extensive criticism of Greek officials and law enforcers (15.3% of the articles). Totally absent in France, unfavorable representation of Greek government and security agencies in the United States press features, in 66.6% of the cases, in articles published in 2002 and 2003, the rest being essentially published in 2004. Criticism concerned both international and homegrown security threats. In the former case, reporting of problems related to disorganized police forces and lax maritime patrols[45] was combined with remarks that Greek security agencies could not deal with the mass casualties that a chemical or biological attack could cause, in spite of considerable progress being made.[46] As suggested above, similar Olympic-linked comments should also be seen in light of the extent of American-Greek tension over Greek counter-terrorism policies. Quite unsurprisingly then, concerns over the Greek government's ability or even willingness to counter political violence were expressed well before 9/11. In July 2001, it was reported that the Greek government had been criticized by the United States State Department for not doing enough to prepare for potential attacks at the Games.[47] After 9/11, such criticisms rise in number and become unambiguous. In April 2004, for example, according to a 2000 report from the United States State Department, Greece was shown to be "one of the weakest links in Europe's efforts against terrorism,"[48] and a congressionally mandated commission on global terrorism in 2000 had considered that "there may have been affinities between the radical leftist terrorists and the political elite that emerged after the military junta."[49]

Civil rights and liberties

Installation of about 1200 closed-circuit television cameras in Athens stirred vivid civil society protests because only 293 of them were authorized to function, on an exceptional basis, from July 1 to October 4, 2004. This illegal and uncontrolled surveillance became a key political issue in Greece and eventually led Amnesty International to ask the Greek government to protect civil rights and liberties by limiting the scope and duration of this measure to the strict Olympic context, and by specifying the length of time these data would be preserved and who would have access to them.[50] Despite its importance, jeopardizing civil rights and liberties was only mentioned in 3.4% of the American articles. Being framed in implicitly depreciating terms, in general, the small amount of coverage included statements such as "the surveillance video has provoked howls of protest from privacy watchdogs, who consider it too intrusive."[51]

When compared to media coverage of the same issue in France, we see again contrasting differences. In the French press, the issue was extensively covered in 5.2% of the articles. More importantly, it was not framed in pejorative terms. So, for example, the French media reported that hostility to closed-circuit television cameras was broadly grounded in the Greek society and also widely shared by mayors of certain districts in Athens, human rights nongovernmental organizations, and leftist groups. Furthermore, the French coverage explained to readers that fear of political regression to authoritarianism was at the heart of the 2004 Greek legislative election campaign, stating that human rights defenders believed "strengthening of [Olympic] security measures will endanger civil rights and liberties [on a permanent basis]."[52]

The threat assessment

Introduction of extensive and extraordinary security measures in what were the first Summer Olympics after 9/11, could be seen as highly predictable and reasonable if we think of them as seeking to counter key security threats posed on the Games by radical Islamist groups. On closer inspection, however, this assumption is problematic. In 9.4% of the American articles, it was reported that neither American nor European or Greek intelligence services had ever received information that Al Qaeda or other radical Islamist groups were planning an attack at the Games. Discrepancy between threat assessment and security measures is not uncommon to organizers of mega-events (Bajc, 2007a, b, 2011a, b). Yet, far from regularly informing public opinion on the low probability of an attack, these reassuring threat assessments were being published between June and August 2004, when setting up of the security dispositif was practically over. On this point, there is no significant difference between American and French press since, in the latter's case, too fear-appeasing threat assessments appeared from April 2004 on and were being published in a very small part (5.6%) of the articles. French journalists diverged from their American counterparts only once, two days before the opening of the Games, when they reported that Greece had never had to face any serious Islamist threat and, on the contrary, due to its long-standing cordial relations with the Arabic world, it had frequently been denounced for allegedly hosting training camps for Palestinian and Kurdish extremists.[53]

Differences in American and French threat assessments become momentous when it comes to defining the core elements of the threat. As will be shown below, in most cases core elements are only featuring in the American press. For example, 12.8% of the articles in the United States put forward the potentially limitless nature of the risk. There was a general assumption in the United States media that "no one entity...can ultimately guarantee protecting the Olympics from terrorism"[54] because, ever since 1972, "there is always something to fear before every Olympic Games,"[55] and threats originating from radical Islamists could never be fully contained due to the natural unpredictability of human behavior. For example, Interpol's secretary-general stated, "in today's world, prudence requires us to recognize that terrorists could attack at any point in time and any place in time."[56] The media reports further strengthened the ensuing risks by both human and technological limits of the security apparatus itself. A United States officer overseeing North Atlantic Treaty Organization's preparation to help guard the Games affirmed that "the absence of such threat indicators is no cause for complacency...there could be something deeply buried that we just haven't seen or anticipated."[57] Other voices reminded readers that "security fences and maritime patrols are not always successful"[58] or "the reality is that computers still can't analyse faces well enough."[59]

The absence of similar arguments from French public discourse that, in other contexts, had unambiguously put forward the limitless nature of radical Islamist threat (Tsoukala, 2009b) suggests that United States discourses did not only reflect broadly shared perceptions of security threats among Western politicians and security officials but also sought to legitimize debatable Olympic security dispositif. In weakening the effect of reassuring threat assessments, it was therefore possible for the *New York Times* to conclude, one month before the opening of the Games, that "while no intelligence agency has picked up any specific threat by Al Qaeda or any other group, no one will deny that Athens is a tempting target."[60]

In the American press, potentially limitless risk was further linked to a broader insecurity context that was going well beyond the Olympics. Athens was seen as a tempting target because, according to the United States Department of Homeland Security Secretary, it ranked high on a list of possible targets among high-profile public events likely to influence the outcome of the United States presidential election in November 2004.[61] Athens was also believed to be a prime target because, in the words of the chairman of the United States House Permanent Select Committee on Intelligence, it might simply be the next choice in a probably never-ending series of attacks on United States and Western interests, ranging from New York and Bali to Madrid and Istanbul, since "Athens is at a crossroads to a part of the world where a lot of terrorists come from."[62]

Security concerns related to Greek geographical position and geological specificities are put forward both in the American and French press, in quite similar quantitative terms (9.4% and 7.8%, respectively). From this standpoint, vulnerability stemmed from close proximity to Balkan and Middle East countries and, above all, from these "hundreds of kilometres of coastline [that] offer countless points of entry to commandos."[63] In the United States, porosity of Greek borders was further linked to alleged rise in security deficit due to abolition of internal border controls within the Schengen area. The (then) new legal rule that "visitors arriving in Greece from fellow European Union nations are not subject to immigration checks," stressed the fact that "there are lots of Islamic radicals living in Europe with French and British and other passports, and they'll be able to travel to Greece without having their documents checked."[64]

In the United States, security concerns related to Islamist extremism were further fueled by the worrisome image of Greece as a country that "has long had a reputation as a heaven for terrorists, according to numerous intelligence officials."[65] Despite the fact that experts believed "the biggest security threat to the Olympics comes from international terror organizations and not homegrown militants,"[66] 23% of the American articles focused on Greek armed groups. This issue is totally absent from the French press. Undoubtedly, the significant place held by homegrown-threat-related arguments is to be attributed to wide-scale Greek anti-American feelings and the ensuing long-standing targeting of American officials and interests by Greek urban struggle groups. Contrary then to domestic Muslim threat that was briefly mentioned under the form of sleeper cells in only 2.5% of the articles, the 17 November case was covered in 44.4% of the articles, with the rest of the articles covering low-level bomb attacks that were carried out in May 2004.

Both of the United States dailies insisted heavily on the 27-year impunity of 17 November that had led to many explanations spanning "from pernicious corruption to profound incompetence [of Greek authorities]."[67] As noted above, the commonly shared belief that "Greece turned a blind eye to terrorism on its soil"[68] was not changed after dismantlement of 17 November. Far from considering that Greece could henceforth efficiently control domestic political extremism, both of the United States newspapers regularly released statements from American and foreign officials and experts that the group still had members at large, thereby calling into question the trustworthiness of Greek officials. A former Federal Bureau of Investigation special agent who had been involved in the investigation on 17 November was "still view[ing] it as a threat"[69]; former head of Mossad believed "one cannot rule out the possibility that somewhere there are still operatives of this organization thinking, plotting and planning to make havoc of an event like the Games"[70]; and United Kingdom security agents were reported to have "refused to cooperate closely with Greece in providing security for the Olympics because of fears that Greece would compromise sources and methods of gathering information."[71]

Threats allegedly posed on the Games by homegrown extremists were further strengthened due to vivid activity of the Greek anarchist movement. But, as it was highly unlikely that anarchists would be able to get through the Olympic security dispositif, anarchist threat could not be presented as serious enough to cause concern unless it was amplified. The blasting of three low-level bombs near a police station in May 2004 was mentioned then in 66.6% of the American articles referring to Greek security threats, and it was compared with the bloody attacks carried out in Madrid or Riyadh, though no one was injured in Athens.[72] Amplification of anarchist threat was also obtained through displacement of its effect from a probably minor, if any, physical danger to a vaguely defined emotional menace. It was thus stated that "the biggest concern remains that some Greek anarchist group will set off a small explosive device in a public area removed from the Olympics, and cause a panic that could affect the Games."[73]

Devious ground of security threats in press coverage from the United States becomes clearer when relevant articles in the their press are compared to French ones. In 10.5% of the French coverage, Islamist extremism was thought to be threatening, but presentation of the threat remained brief, while the issue of sleeping cells was never addressed. Concerning homegrown extremism, there was no allusion to members of 17 November being at large; the collusion thesis was mentioned in 5.2% of all articles but only to report Americans' distrustful attitude toward Greek authorities. Anarchist groups and the May bombing were more broadly covered (15.7% of all articles) but were not seen as serious enough to cause concern. In the aftermath of the bombing, reassurance of public opinion was obtained by excluding comments of security officials and inviting instead the president of the coordination committee of the International Olympic Committee, who stated that the attack "could occur anywhere" and, consequently, did not affect "IOC's security assessment of the Games."[74]

Strong divergences are also observed when comparing American and French press coverage of a major potential consequence of fear-producing threat assessment: boycotting the Games. In France, there was never question of French athletes being hesitant about their participation at the Games. The issue was raised in 7.8% of the articles but only with regard to American and Australian threats of boycotting the Games. On the contrary, both of the American dailies covered extensively, in 7.7% of all articles, athletes' worries about security. In 88.8% of the cases, these articles were published between April and May 2004, and did not suggest a (practically impossible to justify) institutional boycott. Pressure was exerted indirectly, by broadcasting a probable individual withdrawal of some athletes. Venus Williams, for example, was quoted as saying, "My security and my safety and my life are a bit more important than tennis. And so if it became a real concern to where I personally wouldn't feel comfortable, then I wouldn't go to Athens."[75] Similarly, it was reported that even though "no [National Basketball Association] players have cited security concerns as a reason to stay home, global instability could affect their decisions."[76] Another example stated that "the [Australian] organization was not considering withdrawing the team, but individual athletes were free to pull out."[77]

Security in context

To grasp what lies beneath these frequently diverging press representations, one has to take into account the aforementioned web of overlapping and mutually interacting (inter)national political and economic interests at stake. Drawing a clear dividing line between genuine fear and artificially amplified fear, between prevailing ideological patterns and manipulation, and between security as a goal to be achieved and security as a means to promote economic interests, is not an easy task and, in any case, can never claim utter precision. Insights provided by comparative analysis have then to be confirmed and even expanded by taking into consideration the way evolving political and economic fields may be reflected in the timing of publishing of a given set of Olympic security-related arguments.

Politics by the European Union

Time of publishing, thus, plays a key informational role first of all with regard to the way perception of security threats per se impacts on the setting up of the Olympic security dispositif. After 9/11, most Western governments share American dominant perception of radical Islamist threat as potentially limitless and unpredictable (Rasmussen, 2002; Tsoukala, 2008). It may be assumed then that security and threat assessments in the Olympic context are greatly influenced by this perception, thereby leading to a potentially limitless introduction of security measures. However pertinent, this linear explanation reaches its own limits when one considers that both French and United States government and security officials share the same perception of security threats but are unequally involved in Olympic security matters. To the extent that threat assessment has also taken into account Greek anti-American feelings and Greek armed groups targeting United States interests, diverging involvement in the shaping of the Olympic security dispositif may be attributed to national specificities. But to the extent that threat assessment has further relied on the geographical position of Greece and porosity of its borders, time of publishing of most relevant articles suggests that, far from being closely associated to the Olympics, this part of threat assessment addresses European Union and United States tension on, and European worries over, the efficiency of European Union migration controls. In fact, 70% of the United States' geography-related arguments and 66.6% of the same arguments from French press articles are advanced between April and July 2004, right before and after the European Union enlargement that has fueled deep concerns on both sides of the Atlantic about the efficiency of European Union border controls. It is telling that in France, where such worries are rejected by left-wing parties, geography-related arguments are only put forward by the Conservative *Figaro*. Even in this case, however, these arguments are limited to Greek geological specificities and, contrary to American press coverage of the issue, do not entail direct questioning of efficient border controls within the Schengen area.

Economic interests

Regarding security policy assessment, contextualization of criticism of Greek officials and security agents clearly suggests that representation of the issue has been influenced by several factors that are not related to securing the Olympics. Not only are these criticisms being expressed by American journalists but also 66.6% of them are being published in 2002, during the initial hard negotiations for the Olympic security bid, and in 2003, while the winner of the Olympic bid was seeking and eventually managed to convince Greek officials to increase the initial security budget.[78] The idea that these criticisms should be seen as part of a media-orchestrated strategy to promote Science Applications International Corporation's interests is corroborated if one considers deafening silence on the part of the United States about the Olympic bid-related economic interests at stake. This silence acquires its full meaning when discreet handling of these issues is left alone by the French side in March 2003, when it is clear that the Olympic security contract would be won by Science Applications International Corporation. French journalists admit then that American-French rivalry over the Olympic security bid led to such a fierce lobbying that finalization of the Greek government's decision was seriously delayed.[79] The issue is raised again in 2004 to denounce at length the United States' commercial practices that "under-evaluated the cost [of the security system] because the United States government wanted at all costs to be involved in the security of the Games and kick the French out of the market."[80]

While American pressure on Athens was commented on in 15.7% of all French articles, the interplay between security claims and promotion of economic interests was only denounced from July 2004 onward. Criticisms of the Olympic security dispositif from the United States were then met with irony and qualified as "paradoxical" since they were being put forward by those precisely who, by definition, should remain discreet about it as they were heavily involved in setting it up.[81] On the eve of the opening of the Games, the French media designated Greece as the "field of securitarian Games," and reported that the Greeks had been so disgusted by [security] claims coming from the United States, United Kingdom and Australia, along with threats about boycotting the Games, that "authorities have had no other choice but to…opt for the inflationist solution."[82]

Greek sovereignty

Arguably, protection of American economic interests went together with promotion of the United States' political-based security claims. Once taken into account, time of publishing of most articles referring to athletes' concerns over security suggests that press coverage of the issue was correlated to the contentious question of foreign agents carrying weapons in Greece. This claim of security agents from the United States, Israel, United Kingdom and other countries was frontally opposing Greek national sovereignty since Greek law prohibits foreign personnel from carrying weapons within the country. Hence, Greek authorities sought by all means to resist as foreign pressure intensified in the last months before the opening of the Games.[83] Being unwilling to admit compromise on such a sensitive issue that was believed to stir up anti-American feelings, besides, the Greek government firmly denied the broadcast news from the United States that "under intense pressure from the United States, Greece will allow 400 American Special Forces soldiers to be present at the Olympic Games next month under NATO auspices and will also permit American, Israeli and probably British security officers to carry weapons."[84]

In the course of heated negotiations that preceded this alleged arrangement, security claim-makers were, however, supported by frequently broadcast threats of boycotting the Games. Of course, some of the American articles on athletes' hesitations to attend the Games for security reasons were published following the May 2004 bombing. Consequently, they could plausibly be seen as natural fearful reaction of ordinary people. Yet, massive publishing of boycott-related articles in April and May 2004, along with the length of the May articles, totally disproportionate to the threat of bombs, suggests that press coverage of the issue was in fact a hardly veiled pressure to reach the abovementioned objective. This correlation is indirectly corroborated by the United States' silence on two Molotov cocktails hurled, on July 21, 2004, at the Greek Ministry of Culture in charge of Games organization.[85] By then, relevant negotiations were over. Arguably then, there was no more reason for minor attacks to be amplified and fuel insecurity. This hypothesis seems even more plausible when American press coverage of the issue is compared to French coverage. In France the armed escort issue was never raised in direct terms. Security of French athletes, delegates and officials was addressed in 21% of the articles, but the question of non-Greek security agents carrying guns in Greece was only mentioned in relation to the United States' relevant pressure. In any case, whenever journalists were referring to this issue they were stressing its impact on Greek national sovereignty, displaying relevant Greek law, and explaining why Greek government could not accept this measure. Lastly, they remained silent on the alleged final arrangement.

The day after

Comparative analysis of French and American press discourse on Athens Olympics security uncovers that the latter has been part of a broader United States strategy to impose its own vision of security over the host country's vision. Comparative analysis further reveals that the United States involvement in shaping the Olympic security dispositif went well beyond its initial ideological ground to promote its economic and political interests that, more often than not, were irrelevant to the Games. In this tangled web of United States–vested interests, the subordinate position of Greece toward the United States made possible, for the first time in the history of the Games, the unhindered establishment of a circular process of mutually reinforcing risk-based perceptions, counter-risk technologies and procedures, and market-oriented strategies.

Yet, as I have argued elsewhere (Tsoukala, 2006: 52), implementation of such a security planning would not have been possible if it had not met with the interests of other Western security agencies. As a lead security officer has stated with regard to the Olympic preparation in Sydney, "the intelligence community is really rediscovering itself in terms of international cooperation."[86] Notwithstanding, then, a United States–dominant position, security governance at the Athens Games is also to be seen as part of an ongoing reshaping of the security field at the international level with sport mega-events serving as laboratories for testing new security systems and multinational security collaborations (Bajc, 2007b, 2011a; Boyle and Haggerty, 2009; Tsoukala, 2009a).

From this standpoint, given Greece's inferior position in these power struggles, it was highly predictable that Greek officials could not resist multifold pressure being put on them. Yet, it should be kept in mind that, in doing so, they expected to achieve certain benefits such as turning Greece into a security know-how exporting country and consolidating the international image of Greece in a perspective of encouraging foreign capital investment, as well as making Athens a key tourist destination. Promotion of tourism was greatly inspired by the Barcelona Olympics; if Greece could improve its international image by showcasing its managerial capacities at successfully hosting a sport mega-event, and allaying security concerns and international criticism on its lax problem-solving ability regarding domestic political violence, then foreign investment would likely increase. Needless to point out, the global economic crisis of 2008 – and, above all, the current Greek financial crisis – seriously undermined any chance of achieving the aforementioned economic objectives. Greece did manage, however, to become a security exporting country. As preparation for the Beijing Games gathered pace, Athens signed a memorandum of cooperation on security issues, Greek security experts were invited to consult with Beijing, and Chinese security agents were sent to Greece for additional training (Yu et al., 2009) in much the same way as described in other chapters in this book.

Poor post-Olympic Greek performance in (inter)national political and economic fields, however, goes together with a successful achievement in the domestic security field that, regretfully, has been made at the expense of domestic civil rights and liberties. While most Olympic venues were eventually abandoned after the end of the Games,[87] the use of around 1200 Olympic closed-circuit television cameras rapidly became a highly controversial issue. Criticism about surveillance in the public space escalated immediately after the end of the Games. In August and September 2004, protesters became aware of the fact that Olympic cameras were monitoring them despite the Greek Data Protection Authority's banning. Government officials denied political monitoring,[88] but they announced that the cameras would continue functioning to monitor road traffic. In November 2004, police obtained a six-month authorization for 208 cameras. In May 2005, police demands for authorization to extend the use of closed-circuit television cameras for security and counterterrorist purposes was rejected. From then on, police engaged in a judicial fight (Samatas, 2008) that in November 2008 led to the resignation of the Greek Data Protection Authority president and all members. In 2009, Law 3783, in a highly controversial section regarding its conformity to the Greek Constitution and European Human Rights law (Katrougalos, 2010; Mitrou, 2010), excluded from Greek Data Protection Authority's control gathering and preservation of data provided by the cameras. In April 2010, under its new composition, Greek Data Protection Authority authorized permanent installation of closed-circuit television cameras and accepted extension of their use to protect national security and public safety, control serious offenses, and monitor road traffic.[89] It seems then that, with regards to the security facet of the Olympics in Athens, the sole Olympic legacy of what would be recalled as a fine case of asymmetric power relations has been a permanent introduction of extensive surveillance devices and the ensuing contraction of civil rights and liberties.

Notes

I thank an anonymous reviewer for valuable comments.

1. "Mas ethesan dilima: systima asfaleias i boycottage ton Agonon," *Eleftherotypia*, May 3, 2010.
2. There is evidence that from 1998 to 2006 high-ranking members of both Socialist and Conservative Parties, and numerous public officials, received bribes from Siemens regarding the purchase of the Command, Control, Communications, Computers and Intelligence system (C4I) and other security equipment.
3. Though the United States is seen as a hegemonic power in international relations, in the Gramscian sense of the term (Cox, 1993), hegemony is understood as dominance of one country (or group of countries) over others.
4. Anarchist/Anti-authoritarian Assembly (2004) *Let the Games die in their birth-land* (in Greek).
5. See European Union Network of Independent Experts in Fundamental Rights (2003) *Balance of Freedom versus Security in the Response of the European Union and Its Member States to the Terrorist Threat*.
6. *Libération* is a left-wing newspaper; *Le Figaro* is a conservative one.
7. This major provider of security systems for the U.S. Army installed the security system for the 2002 Salt Lake City Olympics.
8. "Floridis-Nasiakos kai EYP spevdoun stis IPA," *Eleftherotypia*, January 13, 2004.
9. "Schengen area" refers to the territories of 26 European countries that have implemented the Schengen Agreement. The area operates like a single state without internal border controls.
10. Interview with senior police officer (2003).
11. Migdalovitz, C. (2004) *Threat of Terrorism and Security at the Olympics* (Greece: CRS Report for Congress), 4. Retrieved from http://hsdl.hsdl.org
12. Ibid., 3.
13. In 2005 U.S. Embassy Athens noted, "Greece has longstanding ties to the Palestinian cause and Arafat personally" (leaked diplomatic wire 05Athens2529); "Asfaleis agones vlepoun oi Palestinioi," *Forthnet*, June 28, 2004.
14. "Stepped-up police activity irks an Arab area in Greece," *New York Times*, July 26, 2004.
15. Greek Counter-Terrorism. Have the lessons been learned?" by Tally Kritzman. International Institute for Counter-Terrorism. August 8, 2000 Retrieved from http://212.150.54.123/articles/articledet.cfm
16. Migdalovitz, op. cit., 2. In addition, in 2005, the U.S. Embassy Athens related that "some 17N members remain at large; others have never been identified" (leaked diplomatic wire 05Athens2529).
17. Migdalovitz, op. cit., 3.
18. "Martyria-fotia anoigei pali ton fakelo ipoklopes," *To Vima*, August 31, 2011.
19. "Clinton concedes regret for U.S. support of Greek junta," *Topeka Capital-Journal*, November 21, 1999.

20. "U.S. involvement in 1974 Cyprus invasion questioned," *CNSNews*, July 7, 2008.
21. The International Law Enforcement Academy aims at providing assistance to the police services of former communist countries to reduce international crime, combat terrorism, and share in knowledge and training "in the interests of the United States and the international law enforcement community." Retrieved from http://www.ilea.hu/en
22. House of Lords (2007) The EU/U.S. Passenger Name Record (PNR) Agreement, 14 Retrieved from http://www.publications.parliament.uk
23. http://www.state.gov
24. "SAIC completes security talks with 15 months to go," *Athens News*, May 2, 2003.
25. http://washingtontechnology.com/articles/2004/09/14/after-olympics-contractors-leave-behind-it-legacy.aspx
26. "Meriki katagelia tis simvasis gia to sistima C4I," *Kathimerini*, May 26, 2010.
27. United States, Australia, United Kingdom, France, Germany, Israel, and Spain.
28. Migdalovitz, op. cit., 6.
29. "NATO's First Operations," 6. Retrieved from www.aco.nato.int
30. "Paraplevres apoleies stin Athina 2004," *Eleftherotypia*, May 2, 2004.
31. "Apokleismo 17 sundikaliston apo tis olympiakes diapistefseis," *Skai*, July 28, 2004.
32. Anarchist initiative against the Olympics...*And the winner is...Athens*, 2003 (in Greek). Retrieved from http://athens.indymedia.org/front.php3?lang=el&article_id=18483
33. www.asda.gr/elxoroi
34. United Nations (2004) Committee on Economic, Social and Cultural Rights: E/C.12/1/Add. 97.
35. "Marathon and the Olympic Rowing Venue," *Archaeology*, March 19, 2002.
36. "We've prepared the Games our own way," *Washington Post*, August 12, 2004.
37. *New York Times*, 49; *Washington Post*, 65.
38. *Libération*, 12; *Le Figaro*, 26.
39. "Le chantier grec s'éternise," *Figaro*, March 19, 2003.
40. "Delays in Athens raise concern on Olympic security readiness," *New York Times*, July 3, 2004.
41. *Figaro*, March 19, 2003.
42. "Uneasy Greeks focus on Olympic safety," *New York Times*, April 7, 2004.
43. *New York Times*, April 7, 2004.
44. *New York Times*, July 3, 2004.
45. "For Athens Olympics, a security gap: tests show porous defences," *Washington Post*, September 27, 2003; "Greek, U.S. officials talk security," *Washington Post*, January 16, 2004.
46. "Report cites bioterror concerns," *Washington Post*, October 29, 2003.
47. "Olympics: More to it than Games," *New York Times*, July 20, 2001.
48. *New York Times*, April 7, 2004.
49. "Arrests destroy noble image of guerrilla group in Greece," *New York Times*, July 23, 2002.
50. "I Diethnis Amnistia zita egiuseis gia ta dikaiomata mas," *Eleftherotypia*, May 12, 2004.
51. "High-tech security's Olympic moment," *Washington Post*, August 12, 2004.
52. "Face à la menace terroriste, les Grecs ont fait de la sécurité leur priorité," *Figaro*, February 19, 2004.
53. "Athènes: la sécurité à tout prix," *Figaro*, August 10, 2004.
54. "The hurdles before the Games," *New York Times*, July 18, 2004.

55. "Olympic doomsayers as cyclical as cicadas," *New York Times*, May 22, 2004.
56. "Interpol detects no specific threats against Games," *Washington Post*, June 30, 2004.
57. "NATO guardian at Games sees no specific threat," *Washington Post*, August 1, 2004.
58. *Washington Post*, September 27, 2003.
59. *Washington Post*, August 12, 2004.
60. "Providing security, with the help of some friends," *New York Times*, July 18, 2004.
61. "USOC asks athletes for top behavior," *Washington Post*, April 21, 2004.
62. "New fears about Olympics," *Washington Post*, May 6, 2004.
63. "Les jeux en joue," *Libération*, April 19, 2004.
64. "Greek domestic security an issue before Olympics," *Washington Post*, May 14, 2004.
65. *Washington Post*, September 27, 2003.
66. "Experts say Greek verdicts don't dispel Olympic threat," *New York Times*, December 10, 2003.
67. "Greece to begin trial involving long-elusive terror group," *New York Times*, March 3, 2003.
68. "Athens Olympic work makes chaos the norm," *New York Times*, September 22, 2002.
69. *Washington Post*, September 27, 2003.
70. *New York Times*, December 10, 2003.
71. "Euro worried," *Washington Post*, March 21, 2004.
72. *Washington Post*, May 6, 2004.
73. "Pressured by U.S., Greece will allow troops at Olympics," *New York Times*, July 21, 2004.
74. "Un groupe terroriste revendique l'attentat d'Athènes," *Figaro*, May 13, 2004.
75. "Security to be boosted for U.S. athletes," *Washington Post*, April 1, 2004.
76. "Security at Summer Games in Athens is topic A, B and C for U.S. Basketball," *New York Times*, April 29, 2004.
77. "Bomb blasts in Athens cause unease," *Washington Post*, May 6, 2004.
78. In September 2003, after many rounds of heated negotiations, Science Applications International Corporation warned Greece that it would not install the Olympic security system unless it could add to it €50 million in new elements (Tsoukala, 2006: 52).
79. "Athènes dans le marathon des chantiers olympiques," *Figaro*, March 3, 2003.
80. "Athènes 2004: bilan encourageant pour les entreprises françaises," *Figaro*, August 10, 2004.
81. "La Grèce refuse la présence de gardes armés étrangers," *Figaro*, July 22, 2004.
82. "La Grèce, terrain de jeux sécuritaires," *Libération*, August 9, 2004.
83. Interview with senior police officer (2004).
84. *New York Times*, July 21, 2004.
85. "La Grèce accepte des hommes armés aux JO," *Courrier international*, July 21, 2004.
86. "Greece playing it safe with Olympics," *Washington Post*, January 4, 2003.
87. "After the party: what happens when the Olympics leave town," *Independent*, August 19, 2008.
88. "Systimata ilektronikon chafiedon," *Rizospastis*, August 8, 2004.
89. "Prasino fos gia kameres alla me elegkho," *Eleftherotypia*, April 14, 2010.

14
Spatialities of Control (Turin 2006)
Alberto Vanolo

Turin, a city in northwestern Italy with a population of about 900,000 and a metropolitan area of about 1.5 million was the host of the 2006 Winter Olympics. As the capital of the Piedmont region of 4.3 million inhabitants, Turin is the fourth-largest Italian city. Thanks to the headquarters of automobile manufacturer Fiat, the city was recognized as the Italian capital of automobile production, and as such, Turin has often been compared to Detroit (see Vanolo, 2008, 2015). As in many other cities dominated by one corporation, the general crisis of the Fordist-style factory manufacturing, beginning in the late 1970s, has been dramatic, thus laying the foundation for a debate on the economic future of the city. Following a devastating automobile crisis in 1996, the metropolitan administration launched an initiative to support the city's economic diversification and a change in its industrial image.

The Torino Organizing Committee of the XXth Olympic Winter Games was officially created the same year Turin won the bid in Seoul; that is, 1999. Agenzia Torino 2006 and other organizations were later added to the complex governance mechanism that constituted the management of the Games. There was substantial political and popular support for this new policy, which aimed to change Turin from an industrial city to an economically diversified international city. The successful bid for the Games needs to be understood in this context. This attitude was well expressed by the mayor:

> As the biggest sporting event, the Games constitute an opportunity for urban regeneration, visibility, and international positioning. Already started and well on the way, the Olympics are an attempt to build new Turin which will connect its economic tradition with renewal of its infrastructure and cultural and tourist attractions.[1]

The Olympic Games provided an opportunity to show the world Turin's "new" urban profile. In this sense, in the eyes of politicians and urban promoters, it was imperative to avoid any kind of problems, including threats to security, in order to sustain a narrative of urban success, perfection, and impeccable organization. This narrative was broadcast on television screens all over the world. As a person responsible for the police forces explained:

> The attention of the whole world was not only on Turin and other municipalities involved in the Games but also on the presence of grassroots movements opposing the Games. This situation imposed on us adoption of a security system encompassing the venues as well as the urban and provincial spaces where the Games took place. This security system ensured a planned execution of the Games and safety for everyone who participated, be it directly or indirectly. The relevance of the XXth Winter Olympic Games and IXth Winter Paralympic Games is such that, to guarantee the international image of Italy, the Games must proceed within a framework of maximum security.[2]

In popular and political discourses, the Olympics have, for the most part, been celebrated as a great success for the city, particularly in terms of its international promotion. Yet, the Games represented a major challenge for the redevelopment of both the physical layout of the metropolitan area as much as the Olympic valleys. The Olympic "theater" was much wider than the city boundaries and included seven municipalities in the mountain valleys of the Province of Torino. This Olympic geography also included five logistic warehouses, two parking structures, media villages, and an anti-doping laboratory.

As is well known, the Winter Olympic Games are significantly smaller than the Summer Olympic Games. As we can see in Table 14.1, Torino hosted 2633 athletes and 84 medal events. This pales in comparison to the previous host city, Athens, where 10,600 athletes competed in 301 medal events during the 2004 Summer Games. Nevertheless, Turin's 900,000 inhabitants were swamped by the 1.1 million tourists who visited the city to attend the Games from February 10 to February 26, 2006. The shortage of hotel rooms was such that city officials asked the residents to help accommodate this huge influx of tourists by renting their homes or rooms to visitors.

Below I analyze the complex governance and management system designed to coordinate between the Organizing Committee and the surveillance and security forces. I focus on how technologies were implemented through the organization of space, describe surveillance practices, and discuss the experiences and perceptions of surveillance by the people involved in the Games. For this analysis, I consulted a number of different documents: Olympic management documents, the Olympic bid, the Host City Contract, the final report on the Games, debriefing materials, documents from the Italian police forces, strategic planning documents from security and safety managers, media reports, and secondary data. Between June and September

Table 14.1 Torino 2006: some figures

The event
15 winter sport disciplines, 84 medal events, 1,026 medals awarded
2,700 paid staff and 18,000 trained volunteers
2,633 athletes, 2,704 officials and companions, 80 National Olympic Committees
688 journalists from printed press, 6,720 radio and television journalists
7 villages dedicated to the media in the metropolitan area
345,000 meals served to staff and volunteers

The spectators
About 900,000 tickets sold (out of 1,128,000 available tickets)
     59% of the purchased tickets were for urban sporting events, 36% for
         mountain events, 5% for ceremonies
     172,000 tickets (19%) sold to corporate partners
     70% of sales to the general public were to persons from Italy, followed by
         Switzerland (6%), Germany (6%), France (6%), Norway (3%), US (3%)
About 1.1 million tourists in 2006

The material structures
5,100 computers
90,000 accreditation badges
8,000 square meters of PVC applied to the outside of the buildings with Games
     logos

The safety system
1,740 Torino Organizing Committee personnel (paid and volunteer) with tasks
     connected to safety and surveillance
202 X-ray machines
463 metal detectors
922 hand-wands (hand-held metal detectors)

Source: All data from Torino 2006, *Final Report* (official concluding report developed for the International Organizing Committee).

2009, I also conducted formal interviews and informal conversations with various people who were involved in the Games.

Defining threats to security

Prevention of threats to security entails what Michel Foucault referred to as biopolitical practices. Such practices control actions of individuals – for example, denying them access to specific places and in this way, limiting their mobility in space. The definition of what is allowed and what is not allowed, that is, the boundary between "reasonable" and "excessive" control over the practices of the local population and the actors in the Olympic event is a delicate issue that is often politically and socially contested.

    The question of detection and classification of potential threats to security became an interesting issue. An initial list of potential perils was compiled by a technical team led by the Torino Organizing Committee safety manager and presented in a preliminary strategic plan elaborated by the Torino Organizing Committee in 2002.[3] Threats compiled in this list were divided into two general categories. The first category included risks connected to traffic conditions, bad weather, fires, floods, and other environmental disasters; accidental and malicious technological risks; and risks connected to image of the national prestige and the Olympic Family. The second category of risks was referred to as "severe risks" and included terrorism in the form of violent demonstrations and public protests, disorders by non-global movements, and organized crime. The Minister of the Interior responsible for security matters was quoted as saying that "security planning for the Olympics means continuously updating elements connected to scenario dynamics," implying that the list had to be considered as merely indicative rather than complete.[4] Indeed, there was a striking difference between the abovementioned list of "severe risks," which was published in a confidential document meant to be used only internally, and all successive Torino Organizing Committee documents, which were made public. In fact, this list of security threats disappeared from the later documents all together, creating a possibility – at least publically if not internally – for more amicable attitudes toward demonstrations and social movements. An official responsible for the police forces later explained to me that "respect of constitutional freedoms and respect for the right of those intending to manifest and express their ideas in a peaceful way had to be guaranteed" but did not comment about the disappearance of the initial list of security threats.[5]

The local imaginary of fear was articulated in mass media coverage and in planning documents in the form of two "severe risks." At the forefront of terrorist fears was Islamic fundamentalism. Examples of this "threat" were newspaper articles titled "Torinistan and the Olympic truce" or "Assault risk for Olympics and elections," which warned the public that "among recurrent menaces of Islamic-inspired attacks, attempts to revise a new armed party alarmed no global itches... but this is not a reason to be joyful."[6] As also expressed by the Minister of the Interior, "because of their worldwide echo, the Turin Olympics run the risk of raising a great interest in the eyes of Al Qaeda's strategists."[7]

Equally threatening to security of the Olympics was a long-lasting conflict surrounding a high-speed railway project in Val di Susa, a valley northwest of Turin, which was a part of the Olympic landscape. The local population and environmentalist organizations, only partially interested in sports events, were fiercely opposed to the railway project. Their activism was seen as a threat and was represented by the mass media as responsible for terrorist attacks. Apprehension concerning these activists grew even stronger after protesters succeeded in altering the path of the Olympic torch, prompting the local media to turn against them with titles such as

"The torch surrenders to anti-[rail]."[8] As an official connected to the police explained in an interview,

> The national political situation, the international scenario, the situation emerging in Val di Susa as a consequence of the [high-speed railway] works required, at least for the duration of the Olympic and Paralympic Games, the planning of a system which would guarantee order and public security, it required setting up a complex system of vigilance over potential targets in Turin and the province.[9]

Some protest movements denounced severe repression by the police during that period and the impossibility of practicing what Lefebvre (1968) calls people's "right to the city." Part of it was related to the evacuation of squatter houses in the city center shortly before the Games. One of these squatter houses had been occupied since 1986 and was evacuated in July 2005. Today, the building houses a travel office for students.[10] By September, only four months before the Games, two other squatter houses were evacuated. The official reasons behind these evacuations were not connected directly to the Games but to some violent incidents that occurred during a protest a few months earlier. The timing of these evacuations, however, raised suspicions, and the independent media firmly denounced what it called a repressive policy aimed at "hindering" dissident voices.

This is a particularly sensitive topic, because of the risk that security measures could be used in order to limit the possibility of public participation. The major local protest movements, named *Nolimpiadi*,[11] denounced, particularly through the Internet and unofficial posters, a number of issues fully in line with the police framing presented above; for example, the lobbying the urban elite in order to manage the Games, environmental damage, waste of money, and corruption. In particular, in 2003, the movement asked, without success, for a public referendum in order to decide whether to host the event.

A public protest against companies providing surveillance technology, particularly companies that also provided technologies for warfare in Iraq, took place as well. Technologies involved in the organization of the event were often provided by northern Italian enterprises (as Elsag Datamat) and implemented by Italian experts. In some cases, this has led to criticism from social movements that opposed the Games. For example, police forces acquired new radios, called Tetra (terrestrial trunked radio), produced by Italian firm Selex Communications. According to the protest movements, the purchase was just a business transaction in order to enrich Selex Communications.[12] According to other voices[13], acquiring the new radio system has provided and has left in the province a valuable technological heritage for local police forces. In other cases, technologies came from outside Italy, like metal detectors provided by the American company Garrett, a well-known provider of Olympic security technologies.[14]

Internet threats

A threat not explicitly mentioned in the official documents, but discussed in popular news,[15] referred to hackers and Internet attacks. The topic has been often associated with ideas of "antagonism." According to a newspaper article:

> The antagonist area is also under the control of police, not just for potential clamorous acts, but because of informatics attacks. Last Friday, in fact, a so-called "netstrike" against both the official website of the Games and the Coke website has been organized.[16]

It is curious, for example, to note the use of the expression *cybersquatting* with reference to the registration of commercial Web domains with names similar to those of official organizations (in this case, www.torino2006.it), a phenomenon that was effectively faced by the Italian police before the Games. Put differently, Internet security has been imbued with a sort of spatial imaginary, with websites represented as spaces that may be "occupied," "attacked," and "squatted," and therefore are to be "defended" and "protected."

Public-private security partnership

The Host City Contract between Turin and the International Olympic Committee was quite explicit with reference to security, giving full responsibility to host countries:

> Responsibility for all aspects of security is a matter to be dealt with by the appropriate authorities of the Host Country. The City, the National Olympic Committee [i.e., CONI] and the Organizing Committee for the Games [i.e., Torino Organizing Committee] undertake that all appropriate and necessary security measures shall be taken accordingly.[17]

In the Italian case, by law, the national government is formally responsible for security. In the case of the Torino Winter Games, without denying in any way the full responsibility of the government, the public sector (the police service, but also military forces, fire brigades, medical services, etc.) cooperated with the private sector, represented by the Torino Organizing Committee. Specifically, the Organizing Committee was assigned coordination tasks, particularly with reference to the management of what is referred to as "passive" security functions in the Olympic venues such as choices and locations of technologies and practices for security, from fences to ticket control. In the official documents, the distinction between "passive" and "active" security is only implicit and nowhere defined. By reading the documents, however, it becomes apparent that "passive" security functions refer to technologies, including identification cards, keys, locks, fences, lights, and alarms. As I discuss below, Torino Organizing Committee staff were also involved in scrutinizing identification cards.[18]

According to Italian laws (n. 121/81), the Ministero degli Interni (Ministry of the Interior), responsible for security, specifically through the National Council for Security, assigned the planning and management of security issues for the Olympics to the Prefect (the representative of the Italian government in the province) of Torino. In order to develop security coordination functions, the Organizing Committee organized a taskforce named Torino Organizing Committee Games Security with the aim of planning and organizing surveillance for people (e.g., with metal detectors), vehicles (in specific Vehicle Screening Areas), goods (by a Vendor Certification Program) and venues (by cameras, patrolling and other technologies). In July 2003, a Memorandum of Understanding was signed by the Prefect and Torino Organizing Committee, further clarifying the functions assigned to the Torino Organizing Committee.

The strategic planning of security, coordinated by the Prefect of Torino, started about five years before the event, leading to the publication of a guideline document[19] at the end of 2004, which indicated specific goals to be reached, in terms of security. The operative planning, coordinated by the Questura di Torino (Turin's provincial police office), was intended as the way to reach those goals. The 2005 planning document established two more institutional bodies: one technical taskforce, including Questore, various representatives of police forces, firemen, majors, health sector and other stakeholders; and one operations center, a command and control center for all police forces.[20]

The activities carried on by the police were managed by a central body, Centro di Coordinamento,[21] and by a series of units in the various Olympic venues. Among the various functions of the central body were the coordination of external security forces in case of major accidents and military forces in cases of terrorism, the circulation of information between the various police and military forces, and the coordination with security activities of local municipalities – particularly Protezione Civile, a voluntary service for supporting eventual emergencies. The use of police forces, by the end of the Games, constituted about 9279 personnel, with about 170 police officers from small municipalities in the province and 316 military personnel with specific surveillance tasks.

Regarding the Games Security function of the Torino Organizing Committee, a complex governance system was implemented during the planning period before the event. The highest level was the head of Games Security, whose duty was to organize the Torino Organizing Committee planning functions, supported by an impressive number of specific managers, including the various Venue Security Managers; the Security Integration Manager, with coordination functions; the Workforce Manager, responsible for workers, with the help of a Volunteers Manager and a paid Staff Manager; a Transport & Logistics Manager, regarding security in transports; a Law Enforcement Liaison Manager, for cooperation with the police; Security Technology Systems Management, for security instruments and technologies; and a Sponsor and National Olympic Committee Manager, to oversee enterprises and external national Olympic committees. Inside every Olympic venue, apart from the Venue Security Manager, there were a number of other managers; for example, several Deputy Venue Security Managers for various support activities, and a Control Room Supervisor and Sectoral Commanders, responsible for security systems, security volunteers with patrolling and authorization-check functions, and private security guards.

During the Games, the Torino Organizing Committee Games Security function included a staff of 204 employees, 202 temporary external contractors, and 1536 volunteers. For the coordination of problems that could not be solved in specific venues or management areas, the Torino Organizing Committee created the Main Operations Center, a unit internal to the Organizing Committee, whose function was to guarantee information flows during the Olympic Games to all interested organizations (e.g., providing event timetables to police forces) and to manage possible critical events. Each of the potential problems emerging during the Games had to be reported to the Main Operations Center, which classified according to severity (low, medium, high, crisis) and management scale for resolution (venue or central level, favoring when possible the lower level). A specific plan, named the Incident and Crisis Management Plan, was ready to be implemented in case of severe crisis. The physical collocation of the Main Operations Center was coterminous to the central body for the management of police forces (the abovementioned Centro di Coordinamento), favoring dialog between the two bodies (see Figure 14.1).

The whole security system was developed on the basis of the experience of previous Olympic Games. In the framework of the process of knowledge transfer promoted by the International Olympic Committee, the manager for security of the Torino Organizing Committee visited and discussed the topic with managers of other Olympic cities. From my conversations with a Torino Organizing Committee safety manager,[22] it became clear that the Barcelona Olympics – and the work of their main manager, Santiago de Sicart – was considered a sort of "best practice" in the field. As reported in the newspapers after the Games, the head of Games Security of the Torino Organizing Committee declared that the experience of Torino could now also be considered a successful example.[23] According to my interview, this process of knowledge transfer from the Torino experience to the next Games started with a debriefing in Vancouver in 2006, where the purpose of the

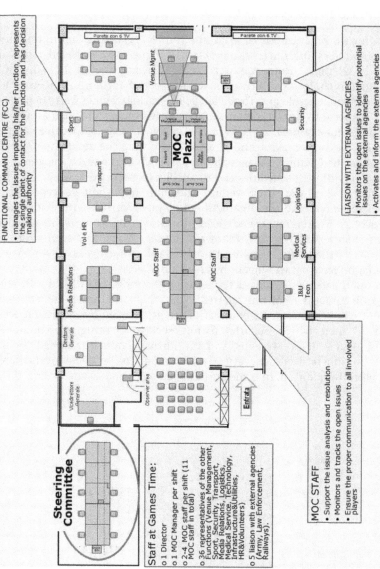

FUNCTIONAL COMMAND CENTRE (FCC)
- manages the issues impacting his/her Function, represents the single point of contact for the Function and has decision making authority

LIAISON WITH EXTERNAL AGENCIES
- Monitors the open issues to identify potential issues on the external agencies
- Activates and inform the external agencies

MOC STAFF
- Support the issue analysis and resolution
- Monitors and tracks the open issues
- Ensure the proper communication to all involved players

Staff at Games Time:
- o 1 Director
- o 1 MOC Manager per shift
- o 2-4 MOC staff per shift (11 MOC staff in total)
- o 36 representatives of the other Functions (Venue Management, Sport, Security, Transport, Media Relations, Logistics, Medical Service, Technology, Infrastructure&Utilities, HR&Volunteers)
- o 5 liaison with external agencies (Army, Law Enforcement, Railways).

Figure 14.1 Main Operations Center: physical layout

Source: File #31, "Analysis of command, control and communication operations," in *The Torino 2006 Olympic Experience: The Official Debriefing & Final Analysis of the XX Olympic Winter Games*, Torino 2006 dvd.

meeting was to disseminate the Italian experience by presentations, discussions, and diffusion of materials.

Technologies and spaces of security

Regarding the organization of space, the Torino Organizing Committee and the police forces introduced various classifications. On a wide geographical scale, the Olympic theater was organized in three areas with three distinct personnel in charge of security: the urban space of Torino; Val di Susa and Pragelato; and Pinerolo and Torre Pellice. The various venues were then classified further into three categories. Competitive venues included all tracks and courts: for example, ski runs or hockey fields. Non-competitive venues included the medal plaza and the media village. The residential venue referred to the Olympic Villages and hotels. Each of the three categories of venues had different schedules and timetables for security.

At the level of the single venues, the most important conceptualization of space refers to the organizing of a system of concentric rings (see Figure 14.2). Each venue was divided into three rings: the *soft ring* at the outer edge, the *hard ring* further toward the center, and the *security ring* in the heart of the venue. Looking through various documents, I found no explanation for what was meant by "hard ring."

Most of the venues are characterized by just two rings: hard and soft. The hard ring contains what was referred to as "vital structures." The concept was not clearly defined. Its boundaries are delimitated by security fences about 2.7 meters high, security patrols, security lighting, closed-circuit television surveillance systems, and anti-intrusion systems. Closed-circuit television cameras were set every 60 meters along the perimeter of the hard ring, with the addition, in some areas, of "dome" cameras characterized by

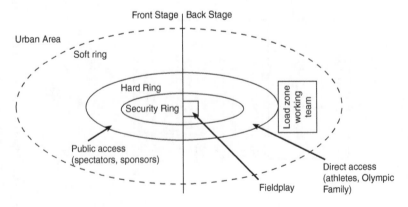

Figure 14.2 Security rings

high resolution (about 100 meters in range). All the cameras were linked to a closed-circuit television monitor room inside the venue and supervised by Organizing Committee staff 24 hours a day.

In each of the three Olympic Villages, a third ring named security ring was planned inside the hard ring, and isolated by a 2.7-meter high fence: all persons entering this ring were fully inspected. I have not had the possibility to clearly define which physical structures were located inside and outside the ring, because the venue manager I interviewed had doubtful memories about that,[24] and no specific mention of it can be found in planning documents. We may probably assume that the security ring hosted the rooms of the athletes.

Outside the hard ring, a soft ring includes "load" and "drop off" zones for passengers accessing the venue, parking for the vehicles with specific passes issued by the Torino Organizing Committee, and check-in for spectators. I discuss the check-in process in more detail below. The intensity of these controls depended on the nature of the venue. Competitive venues, such as the medal plaza and the Olympic stadium for the occasion of the opening ceremony had temporary security controls. The Olympic Villages and media villages had permanent security controls.

Both the hard and the soft rings are each divided into the "front stage" space, or "front," and the "back stage" space, or the "back of the house." Access to the back of the house was granted only to workers. This included the Olympic Family, the athletes, the media, and the Torino Organizing Committee team.

The soft ring does not have physical boundaries but is encircled by a wider area where the planned activities include:

- wide-area controls along the perimeter of urban or mountain centers,
- random controls over suspicious vehicles or persons,
- notification of activities of groups of demonstrators wishing to get closer to the venues or important places in order to start demonstrations,
- immediate verification of alarms or signals of suspicious activity, if necessary, by asking the help of police dogs or explosive experts, and
- sensitizing personnel about the need to signal to the operations center every anomaly or ambiguous situation that may cause troubles to the Games.

The management of these security spaces implied a large set of technologies and practices. Concerning physical enclosures, for example, different types of fences were utilized according to the material layout of spaces: strong metallic fences where possible, lighter plastic fences in areas with trees and rocks, and cement-based fences near highways. Another example was video surveillance, implemented with 700 cameras, 100 km of optical cables, and many hours of staff training.

As mentioned, it is also possible to refer to the defense of the virtual Internet space, since experts prevented an undefined number of intrusion attempts by hackers. It is interesting to consider from a technical point of view that the most sensitive information was located in a separate intranet called Info2006, which was not accessible from the standard, global, Internet, reproducing the spatial imaginary of the rigid separation between the hard and the soft ring.[25]

Control of behavior and movement of spectators

Control over the body, the behavior, and the movement of spectators – what Michel Foucault famously referred to as biopolitics – was implemented in different ways. As emphasized in various documents, including the webpage of the Ministry of the Interior, the presence of the police had to be noninvasive and as invisible as possible, guaranteeing an enjoyable experience for the public.

> An organization of security adequate to possible menaces has been implemented. Overall, the "Olympic Spirit" has prevailed, and the visibility of the police force has been kept as low as possible, always maintaining a high and vigilant level of surveillance.[26]

Controls over the spectators started with the sale of the entry tickets for sporting competitions. The sale started in November 2004. Tickets were available through a website, a call center with a toll-free phone number, branches of a local bank, and a number of other authorized vendors. Events such as the medals ceremonies were not available for purchase to the general public. These tickets were distributed by the Torino Organizing Committee free of charge only to specific guests and some locals. On the front of each ticket there was information in English and Italian about the venue for which the ticket was issued, the gate through which the visitor must enter with his or her specific ticket, the seating zone within which the spectator must be positioned, the seat number to which that ticket holder is assigned, the time of the event, the price, and an anti-duplication hologram (see Table 14.1). Visitors had to abide by terms and conditions specified on the back of each ticket, which were also published on the Internet and in the spectator guide that I discuss below. When seeking access to an event using such a ticket, the visitor waives a number of rights, particularly the right to disseminate for public or commercial use photos taken by the visitor at the event, the right not to be filmed or photographed by the organizers during the event, and eventually even the right to access to the venue if the spectator opposes specific rules of the venues.

Together with the ticket, the viewer receives the official spectator guide,[27] a 176-page document describing rules, suggestions, and information.

Concerning the rules, it was strictly forbidden for the spectator to carry objects deemed by the organizers as dangerous, including beverage glasses, drugs, weapons, lighters, and even coins. In addition, other objects were restricted, such as large objects, cameras, smelly or noisy objects, food, and anything showing a logo or a commercial, political, or religious message. Once admitted, the spectator was not allowed to leave the premises. If the spectator left the premises, he or she would not be allowed to return to that same venue. The spectator guide also included "suggestions" about appropriate behavior such as not using a private car to arrive at the event venue and general information about the city and various events.

The limitation of the "commercial" messages is an interesting point. As it is well known, sponsors pay for the exclusive exploitation of the marketing of the Games. For this reason, a specific part of the security activity was carried out by a team called Brand Protection Unit, which sought out and eliminated the display of any non-sponsor logo – so-called ambush marketing. In order to carry out this function, for example, adhesive tape was used to hide non-sponsor logos, even in the case of instrumentation used for the Games (e.g., brand of the personal computer monitors), and commercial activities of restaurants and bars could be fined for showing Olympic logos and brands. In the case of spectators and the working team, for example, they were not allowed access to the front rows of venues if found wearing a T-shirt with an obvious logo, and adhesive tape was used also in this case – even on some athletes.[28]

Control of spectators' bodies was extended by banning the consumption of any food or drink not sold by venue sponsors inside, apart from non-commercial water. As affirmed by an International Organization Committee spokeswoman, "the IOC works hard to protect the investment of our partners. Without their contribution the Olympic Games couldn't happen the way they do."[29]

The most evident moment of control refers to the checking and limiting of access to specific places, and particularly to the hard ring. The control procedures for admission to the venues were quite similar to those of an airport. First, an Organizing Committee employee called a "pacer" organized the queue, gave instructions (recounting, for example, objects not allowed within the venue), and checked tickets. Then police officials checked spectators with a metal detector. In cases where metal was detected, the spectator would be told to empty his/her pockets into a specific box and move through the portal again. A second check was then conducted by hand-wand detectors. Often the hand-wand detector was the only method employed for checks in such cases as for the disabled and/or spectators attending in wheelchairs. At the same time, an X-ray machine would screen specatators' bags. The procedure for checking bags was referred to as "mag and bag." Objects eventually found to be prohibited had to be disposed of in a specific box. Finally, a Torino Organizing Committee employee stamped the ticket and indicated to the spectator where to go in order to enjoy the event.

Surveillance of staff and special guests through the accreditation system

Security measures were organized for the various workers connected to the event, such as deliveries staff, athletes, journalists, Torino Organizing Committee members, cleaners, etc. The management of their bodies happened through a complex accreditation system, always associated with the exhibition of a proper identity card. I wish to draw attention to the fact that the accreditation system is so powerful as to represent a space of "exception to the norm" with reference to standard European immigration policies. Members of the International Organization Committee, national federations, national Olympic committees, and specific journalists and sponsors had access to a special Olympic card that, together with a passport, allowed them to enter Italy independently from a visa.[30] Members of the Olympic staff received just one card, independent of the number of tasks they may have been associated with. The cards were inspected visually.

The accreditation system was managed by the Torino Organizing Committee, and about 90,000 badges were produced.[31] The system was organized in four steps: registration of potential accredited persons, confirmation, checking (either by workers of the Ministero degli Interni or by police) and, finally, printing and delivery of the badges. All the accreditation requests come from organizations involved with the Games, and not from single persons. The printing and delivery of the badges happened as late as possible, in order to avoid risk of forgery. Even police forces had their accreditation badges.

Inside every venue, six different areas were accessible to people with different types of accreditation cards. For example, a specific access applied just to journalists, another one for television camera operators, and another one for athletes. Moreover, in particularly sensitive areas, such as the playing field or the anti-doping center, access was further restricted, allowing just those with specific additional passes. In case of loss of the pass, this was to be immediately communicated to the Organizing Committee accreditation center, and badges could be withdrawn in case of violation of the norms. It was obligatory to keep the badge visible at all times when on duty.

A Torino Organizing Committee environmental manager described the inspection in the following way:

> Every morning I was submitted to *mag and bag*, independently of the fact that, after months of work, I knew the policeman at the entrance very well, and of my accreditation badge. It was a control similar to that in airports.[32]

Finally, specific security measures were implemented for the movement of guest stars, like celebrities or athletes receiving awards in the medal plaza. Technical details defined the distribution of police forces, vehicular movements, and the organization of radio contacts. In specific situations, snipers were located in unseen places. The management of celebrities is a complex task, partly because of the overlapping of functions between local police and foreign bodyguards and security teams.

In the case of athletes, the management of bodies was strictly connected to a complex system of transports and movements referred to in the documents as "bubble to bubble," which included bus movements and security escorts to and from villages and competition venues (including airspace surveillance) and using specific supervised drop-off/load-in zones. From the arrival at the airport, and specifically from a guarded area, buses departed every 20 minutes for one of the three Olympic Villages (in total, nine buses every hour), escorted by police officers. The movements between the villages and the venues took place along predefined routes and inside checked buses. This system allowed the athletes to move from a "secured" place (one "bubble") to another one without having contact with the "external" world, thus making it unnecessary to check the athletes on arrival at a venue. Of course, the athletes were free to exit from the village and then come back (where they would once again be checked by security agents at the entrance), but it was quite unusual for them to do so. In the case of ceremonies (like medals awards), specific escort services were organized and provided by police from the Olympic Village to the medal plaza and back. Three central cars were arranged to transport the three athletes winning gold, silver and bronze medals, respectively. It is worth noting that this is just one of the many configurations of the escort services, with variations, for example, according to the presence or absence of the anti-doping service.

A similar system was implemented for vehicles, which were considered potentially even more risky than people, because of the many possibilities to hide forbidden objects. Every vehicle attempting to access the hard ring had to display a particular pass (VAPP) on the windshield. In specific "vehicle screening areas" located close to the hard ring, vehicles were checked by the police with hand-wands and physical inspections. In case of goods deliveries, a system of "keys," including reviewing the delivery schedule, the certification of inspection, and the seals of the delivered boxes, was put in place.[33] Moreover, in the soft ring, the access to vehicles was limited to specific categories, such as residents' cars. In order to access the soft ring by car, residents had to display a different specific pass showing the car's registration plate and the soft ring code.

Finally, it has to be mentioned that, throughout the city, Olympic Lanes, marked by yellow stripes and Olympic symbols, were established by the mayor of the city in order to allow the effective movement of police forces, ambulances and other assistance vehicles, and Olympic athletes.

Life inside the Olympic Village

Inside residential zones in the Olympic Villages, further controls occurred in the security ring and adjacent streets. For example, the village in Torino was the largest at more than 100,000 square meters of space, hosting about 2600 people, mostly athletes and journalists. Life in the villages was basically separate from the rest of the urban space, with specific events and amenities (like disco parties), which were communicated to the athletes through newsletters and contributed to creating a sense of community (e.g., birthday celebrations). A shopping center and a relaxation area were provided inside the village, as were interfaith prayer sessions, Broadway shows, and all sorts of live concerts, special parties, and videogames for the duration of the Games. This kind of internal organization of village life makes the metaphor of the "bubble" used by the Organizing Committee even more pertinent. Its environmental manager puts it this way: "there was everything inside the village, the barbers, the flower shop, the mini-market...it was a sort of *Love Boat.*"[34] He was referring to the famous television series from the 1980s, where all the stories and relationships took place on a cruise ship. This analogy fully grasps the idea of an ideal small world, where everything is provided in order to avert the need to interact with the outside world.

As a form of surveillance over athletes, attention must be paid to drug tests as well. According to the guidelines of the World Anti-Doping Agency and the International Organization Committee, controls aim at detecting the use, or potential use, of illicit substances, so as to deter the refusal or faking of biological inspections. Anti-doping analyzes have been considered part of the medical services. Every competitive venue and every Olympic Village included a doping control station, where biological samples were collected every day from a random sample of athletes. After the daily casual selection of athletes' names to be checked, volunteers of the Olympic team, called "escorts," had to quickly reach the athletes and alert them to be at the doping control station within an hour. Escorts were supposed to follow the athletes during the next hour, in order to avoid actions that could potentially falsify the anti-doping analysis. Once at the doping control station, biological samples from the athletes were collected and stored in specific bags. Then, an official from the doping control station carried the samples to the central anti-doping lab, where doctors qualified by the Italian Federation for Medical Sport performed the analysis. In case of the detection of drugs, it was the president of the medical commission's job to inform the International Organization Committee executive committee.

How participants evaluated surveillance

As mentioned above, the head of Games Security of the Torino Organizing Committee considered the Torino experience a successful best practice, and many local politicians celebrated the good performance of the Games. For example, the Minister of the Interior, who was responsible for security, in a public conference immediately after the Games, stated, "The wide and sophisticated security system for the Olympic Games has worked perfectly."[35] As he proudly reported on the Ministry of Interior website, it even impressed the former New York Mayor Rudolph Giuliani, who saw the Torino performance as "A perfect example of what to do in the presence of terrorist menaces."[36]

When it comes to measures taken to ensure security, it is difficult to evaluate the perception of the public. A relevant survey was carried out during the events by Lisa Delphi Neirotti.[37] It refers to questionnaires submitted to three samples of spectators, in the pre-Games period, with questions referring to expectations, motivations and services during the Games; issues on the nature of services received; and impact/overall satisfaction post-Games. The questionnaire also asked the spectators to express how they felt about security and the surveillance system to which they were exposed during the Games. The results show that a large majority of the people (62.7%) described the measures as appropriate. The word evokes ideas of meaningful, reasonable and effective surveillance. The remaining 37.3% of the respondents in the Torino case were divided between those who perceived the surveillance system as too lenient and others who perceived it as too intrusive. A comparison with the Athens Olympics is interesting. As Tsukala analyzes in the previous chapter, two years earlier, the Athens Games were conspicuously saturated with surveillance technologies and procedures, and yet over 73% of the respondents agreed that these measures were appropriate.

This general survey confirms the interviews I conducted for the purposes of this chapter. Of the 20 people interviewed, most described the surveillance practices without any particular emphasis. That is, during our conversations, these respondents had no particular memories and no vivid emotions about surveillance practices and technologies used during the Games. I asked the respondents, "Do you think it was appropriate, lenient or intrusive?" Of the 20 interviewees, 17 reported surveillance as "useful," "appropriate" and "not particularly invasive." Only 3 people found it excessive. These three people were relatively young spectators, one female and two males between 25 and 35 years of age. All three felt that surveillance was "annoying" and "too rigid" because it prevented them from moving around inside the venues. A young female spectator related the following:

> I was going to see half pipe: I had a place in full tribune, but I wanted to move to the pipe border in order to see the evolution more closely, but there was no way to convince the loyal and dreadfully elderly volunteers.[38]

"Half pipe" is a snowboard competition, and by "full tribune" she meant that she had bought a quite expensive ticket in a privileged part of the spectator area. Her reference to the too-rigid elderly volunteers refers to the fact that, not infrequently, Torino Organizing Committee volunteers in mountain areas were elderly, retired persons who were well trained to perform this task. Here we see that practices of control over space hampered the spectators from moving outside the sector assigned with their ticket. My respondents noticed that these spaces were vacant, in that nobody was sitting on those chairs, so in their mind, these seats were "free," "available" and actually "more enjoyable" because they provided an even better visual angle to the competition. At the same time, in their perception, moving to those chairs would in no way compromise security or the general management of the event. A male spectator related that "It was excessive to block the access to Bardonecchia to every nonresident: in order to get to the venue I had to make an impressively long walk."[39] Put differently, he considered the practice of limiting vehicle circulation annoying and excessive, probably because he perceived no particular perils or threats to security. The evaluation of the effectiveness of security is more complicated in the case of working staff, due to the lack of data sources. According to a Torino Organizing Committee manager, "It always seemed to me an accurate service; I don't know if it was excessive, but I think it was inspired by a prevention approach."[40]

Journalists and sponsors had something different to say. In a file from the Vancouver debriefing after Torino 2006, for example, it is reported that in the main press center it was "relaxed," with "effective security; enough mag/bag machines to avoid delays."[41] Another file describes media security as "redundant," affirming that "the venue became a police station rather than a media center: the constant issue was too many police officers in the venue without proper roles and often without accreditation."[42] Most criticisms come from the sponsors, such as Omega, Samsung, Atos Origin, and Visa: they saw surveillance as something "to be improved" due to difficulties of access to the venues, inconsistent behavior of security representatives and, according to Atos Origin, not enough secure access to the Torino Organizing Committee headquarters.[43]

A different and interesting technical debate following the Games took place during the Vancouver debriefing of 2006, when Cesare Vaciago, Chief Executive Officer of the Torino Games, affirmed that the use of the mag and bag system was "a waste of money," basically because it required too much personnel, and it could not stop nonmetallic weapons.[44] This position has been strongly criticized by many experts, while others sympathized, affirming that such technologies just gave a "security feeling" and no real control over risks, and that the Olympic committees are lobbied by the producers of such technologies (ibid.).

Concluding remarks

The case of Torino confirms that the management of security involves highly spatialized practices: as described in the chapter, the organization of surveillance involved massive classifications of spaces and flows. Security rings, fences, and rules for the movement of spectators, athletes, workers, cars, and goods are all examples of dispositives for controlling the space and the movement of people within the space of the Games. Because of the relatively small dimension of Torino and its neighboring territories, the Games had a massive impact over space in both physical and discursive ways, being intended as an opportunity for the promotion of alternative development paths and for showing the world a renewed image of culture and hospitality. The public enthusiasm concerning the Games, with an impressive participation of volunteers (about 18,000) has to be framed in this general imaginary and confirms the nature of the event as a "recruitment agency" providing, for the local society of Torino, a strong *communitas* experience (MacAloon, 1984b; see also Vanolo, 2015). This probably contributed to a relaxed attitude toward surveillance practices: voices opposing the Games had a limited role (Dansero et al., 2012), and no particular resistance to the Games and to the practices of body and space control spread during the event. This frames the Torino experience in quite a different way with respect to Beijing 2008, which will be examined in the next chapter.

Notes

I wish to thank an anonymous reviewer for comments.

1. "I Giochi, grandissimo appuntamento sportivo, per una città costituiscono anche l'occasione di rigenerazione urbana, visibilità, riposizionamento: sono il tentativo, ormai avviato e consolidato, di realizzare una nuova Torino, che affianca alla propria vocazione economica originaria il rinnovamento delle infrastrutture e dell'offerta culturale e turistica"; as written by the mayor himself (Chiamparino, 2006, p. 15); my translation.
2. "L'attenzione del mondo intero sulla città di Torino e sugli altri Comuni interessati ai Giochi, nonché la presenza di movimenti contrari allo svolgimento degli stessi, hanno imposto l'esigenza di predisporre ed attuare, sia all'interno dei siti, sia nei contesti cittadini e provinciali in cui essi insistono, un sistema di sicurezza volto a garantire, oltre che il regolare svolgimento dei Giochi Olimpici, l'incolumità di quanti, in maniera diretta o indiretta, sono chiamati a parteciparvi. La rilevanza dei XX Giochi Olimpici Invernali e dei IX Giochi Paralimpici Invernali impone che gli stessi si svolgano in una cornice di massima sicurezza, anche per tutelare l'immagine internazionale dell'Italia" (interview with an official of Questura di Torino).
3. Torino Organizing Committee, *Security Preliminary Strategic Plan*, Doc. PSP/1–31/01/2002. Natural risks are not considered in this paper, but see Giordano (2005).
4. http://www.interno.it/olimpiadi/pages/sicurezza_giochi_olimpici/ruolo_mi/ruolo_mi.html (consulted September 2009), my translation.
5. "Il rispetto delle libertà costituzionali di coloro che intendono manifestare ed esprimere le proprie idee in maniera pacifica deve essere garantito" (interview with Functionary of Questura di Torino).

316   *Alberto Vanolo*

6. "Torinistan e la tregua olimpica," *Il Foglio*, February 14, 2006, 3; "Rischio atten-
   tati per olimpiadi ed elezioni," *Il Giornale*, February 18, 2006, 11. The sentence
   quoted in text is extracted from the latter; the full original Italian sentence is
   "Fra ricorrenti minacce d'ispirazione islamica, tentative di rielaborazioni di un
   nuovo partito armato, preoccupanti pruriti no global e sbandate politicizzate
   negli stadi, non c'è da stare poi così allegri."
7. In December 2005; quoted in M. V. Rizzo (2006), "Il sistema di sicurezza delle
   olimpiadi di Torino 2006," *Obiettivo sicurezza*, 1: 22–24; see also S. Ghieth (2005),
   "Italy May Suffer Attack Before Olympics, Elections, Pisanu Says," *Bloomberg
   News*, retrieved from http://www.bloomberg.com
8. See, for example, "La fiaccola si arrende ai No Tav," *La Stampa*, February 6, 2006,
   pp. 1, 6–7.
9. "La situazione politica internazionale, lo scenario internazionale, la situazione
   venutasi a creare in Val di Susa a causa dei lavori per la realizzazione della TAV
   richiedono, in occasione dei Giochi Olimpici e Paralimpici, la predisposizione di
   un dispositivo a tutela dell'ordine e della sicurezza pubblica che prevede anche
   un complesso sistema di vigilanze agli obiettivi sensibili presenti in Torino e
   Provincia" (interview with an official of Questura di Torino, my translation).
10. Information from independent media: http://www.glomeda.org/documenti.
    php?id=428;   http://www.informa-azione.info/chiamparino_impera_sullo_
    sgombero_del_nuovo_fenix
11. www.nolimpiadi.8m.com
12. www.nolimpiadi.8m.com/militarizzati.html
13. Personal conversation with Torino Organizing Committee Safety Manager,
    July 20, 2009. For a (basically) positive account, see also "Tutta colpa del soft-
    ware Tetra. Ha reso inutili i vecchi scanner," *La Repubblica*, August 27, 2009;
    see also http://www.protezionecivilecomuneroma.it/sito/upload/documents/
    torino.pdf
14. As denounced on the website, http://nolimpiadi.8m.com/sponsor.html (consulted
    September 2009).
15. "Torino 2006, sventato un attacco informatico," *Il Messaggero*, February 14,
    2006, 9; "Olimpiadi, scacco alla sicurezza," http://www.01net.it/01NET/
    HP/0,1254,0_ART_67692,00.html (accessed July 2009).
16. "Sotto controllo degli investigatori c'è anche l'area antagonista, non solo per
    possibili gesti clamorosi ma anche per attacchi di pirateria informatica. Proprio
    venerdì scorso, infatti, era previsto il cosiddetto 'netstrike' contro il sito ufficiale
    dei giochi e quello della Coca Cola," in "Hacker sui cinque cerchi," *Il Sole 24 ore*,
    February 14, 2006, 11.
17. Host City Contract, 1999, subpara. 20.
18. Torino Organizing Committee, *Security preliminary strategic plan*, Doc.
    PSP/1–31/01/2002.
19. *Direttiva per l'organizzazione dei servizi d'ordine e sicurezza pubblica*.
20. *Tavolo tecnico* and *centrale operativa*, in Italian.
21. *Centro di Coordinamento della sicurezza e di gestione delle emergenze olimpiche*; the
    units in the Olympic venues were called *Sale Comando di Sito Olimpico*.
22. Interview, Torino Organizing Committee manager, Torino, July 20, 2009, my
    translation.
23. Francesco Norante (2006) "Il ruolo della security nelle manifestazioni sportive
    a carattere mondiale," *Essecome*, 4: 30–38, http://www.securindex.com/articoli/
    essecome/e4_06Norante_p30–38.pdf (consulted September 2009).

24. Interview with Torino Organizing Committee environmental manager, Torino, September 25, 2009.
25. "Torino 2006, sventato un attacco informatico," *Il Messaggero*, February 14, 2006, 9; "Hacker sui cinque cerchi," *Il Sole 24 ore*, February 14, 2006, 11; "Olimpiadi, scacco alla sicurezza," http://www.01net.it/01NET/HP/0,1254,0_ART_67692,00.html (accessed July 2009).
26. "E' stata pertanto resa attiva un'organizzazione dei dispositivi di sicurezza adeguati con le possibili minacce. Su tutto è prevalso 'lo spirito olimpico,' ed è stato perciò limitato al massimo l'impiego visibile delle Forze di Polizia pur mantenendo sempre alto e vigile il livello di sicurezza"; http://www.interno.it/olimpiadi/pages/sicurezza_giochi_olimpici/ruolo_mi/ruolo_mi.html (consulted September 2009), my translation.
27. Available in both Italian and English, on http://www.torino2006.it/ENG/OlympicGames/vieni_a_torino2006/guide.html (consulted September 2009).
28. Interview with spectator, Torino, July 12, 2009; interview with Torino Organizing Committee environmental manager, Torino, September 25, 2009, my translations.
29. "Excuse me, but your label is showing," www.msnbc.msn.com/id/11414718 (accessed July 2009).
30. European Union Regulation n. 2046/205.
31. Torino 2006, Final Report (official concluding report developed for International Organization Committee).
32. "Ogni mattina ero sottoposto al mag and bag, a prescindere dal fatto che, dopo mesi di lavoro, il poliziotto e io ci conoscevamo benissimo, e dal mio badge di accredito. Era un controllo simili a quelli degli aeroporti" (interview with Torino Organizing Committee environmental manager, Torino, September 25, 2009, my translation).
33. For a full description, see G. Pisapia (2006) "Security and logistics in a major sport event: the vendor certification program (VCP) of the XX Winter Olympic Games" and G. Pisapia (2006) "The security system of the XX Winter Olympic Games," both available at www.itsitme.it (consulted October 2009).
34. "C'era tutto nel villaggio: il barbiere, il negozio di fiori, il mini-market...era una specie di Love Boat" (interview with Torino Organizing Committee environmental manager, Torino, September 25, 2009, my translation).
35. "L'ampio e sofisticato sistema della sicurezza messo in campo per le olimpiadi di Torino ha funzionato alla perfezione," *Viminale*, February 27, 2006; http://www.interno.it/olimpiadi/pages/news/Conf_stampa_viminale.html (consulted September 2009), my translation.
36. "Esempio perfetto di quello che bisogna fare in presenza di minacce terroristiche"; http://www.interno.it/olimpiadi/pages/news/giuliani.html (consulted September 2009), my translation.
37. A short presentation of the results is available as: File #72, "Spectator and General Public Experience," in *The Torino 2006 Olympic Experience: The Official Debriefing & Final Analysis of the XX Olympic Winter Games*, Torino 2006 dvd. A deeper survey on the data and analysis has been kindly furnished by the author. However, no specific data concerning the statistical size of the sample were presented.
38. "Ero andata a vedere l'half pipe: sebbene avessi il posto in piena tribuna, volevo spostarmi a bordo del pipe per vedere più da vicino le evoluzioni ma non c'è stato verso di convincere i ligi e temibili anziani volontari" (interview with spectator, July 14, 2009, my translation).

39. "Era assurdo bloccare l'accesso a Bardonecchia ai soli residenti; per accedere alla struttura della gara c'era da fare un giro impressionante" (interview with spectator, July 14, 2009, my translation).

40. "Mi è sempre sembrato un servizio accurato; non so dire se fosse eccessivo, ma immagino fosse ispirato a un principio di prevenzione" (interview with Torino Organizing Committee environmental manager, Torino, September 25, 2009, my translation).

41. File #42, "Torino 2006 Olympic Experience. Part 3, Olympic Stakeholder Experience," in *The Torino 2006 Olympic Experience: The Official Debriefing & Final Analysis of the XX Olympic Winter Games*, Torino 2006 dvd.

42. File #79 in *The Torino 2006 Olympic Experience: The Official Debriefing & Final Analysis of the XX Olympic Winter Games*, Torino 2006 dvd; see also, "A Few Words about Security at the Olympics," http://olympics.about.com/b/a/000024.htm.

43. Respectively, Files #62, #64, #68, #69, in *The Torino 2006 Olympic Experience: The Official Debriefing & Final Analysis of the XX Olympic Winter Games*, Torino 2006 dvd.

44. A full description of the debate is available on *The Torino 2006 Olympic Experience: The Official Debriefing & Final Analysis of the XX Olympic Winter Games*, Torino 2006 dvd; see also "Just how much security do those X-ray machines provide? Not much"; http://communities.canada.com (access July 2009).

15
People's Olympics? (Beijing 2008)

Gladys Pak Lei Chong, Jeroen de Kloet and Guohua Zeng

A safe and secure Olympics represents a successful Beijing Olympic Games, it is a very important symbol to showcase our national image.

Xi Jinping, vice president of the People's Republic of China and Liu Qi, president of the Beijing Organizing Committee for the Olympic Games[1]

The kind of security one does not see is the best form of security.

Wang Shilin, host of *Focus Today* of Channel 4 of China Central Television[2]

One world, one dream

Granted, the question mark was not included in this main slogan of the 2008 Beijing Olympics. The Beijing Olympics generated heated debates worldwide on China's authoritarian governance, environmental pollution, human rights situation, alleged indulgence of humanitarian disaster in Darfur in southern Sudan, and its policies toward Tibet. Indeed, many observers believed that not all people shared the same dream. The charge of China's indulgence of humanitarian disaster in Darfur made Steven Spielberg withdraw in January 2008 from his cooperation with Zhang Yimou to design the spectacle of the Opening Ceremony – a step that did not cause much debate within China itself. The months preceding the Olympics were thus ridden with events unplanned by the authorities, events that disrupted the intended promotion of the Olympics.

The Beijing Olympics were promoted as a "Green Olympics," a "High-Tech Olympics" and a "People's Olympics."[3] According to the website of the Beijing Organizing Committee of the Olympic Games, a "Green Olympics" emphasized the use of environmentally friendly technologies and measures to design and construct Olympic facilities and the promotion of environmental awareness to the general public; a "High-Tech Olympics" stressed the importance of scientific innovativeness and high-tech achievements in the

Games and also their popular use in daily life; a "People's Olympics" aimed to showcase Chinese culture, its historical and cultural heritage and the population's positive support of the Games, as well as to promote cultural exchanges and "harmonious development between mankind and nature."[4] The official manual for Olympic volunteers states that "The Beijing Olympic Games will fully express the common aspiration of the Chinese people to jointly seek peace, development and common progress together with the peoples of the world, and it will highlight the fact that the 1.3 billion Chinese people of 56 ethnic groups, along with 50 million overseas Chinese, are all most enthusiastic participants in the Beijing Olympic Games."[5] It follows up by listing eight high-quality features: "high-level sporting venues, facilities and competition organizations; high-level opening ceremonies and cultural events; high-level media services and favorable press commentary; high-level security work; high-level volunteers and services; high-level transportation and logistics; high-level urban civility and friendliness; high-level performances by Chinese athletes."[6] Security was highlighted as an important feature here.

This theme of security rapidly gained importance in popular discourse as well as in government circles – the two domains are closely intertwined – in relation to the uprising in Tibet and global protests surrounding the Olympic Flame Relay. Protests in London, Paris, Tokyo, and Seoul interrupted the Olympic Flame Relay; in San Francisco, the protest forced the Olympic Flame Relay to change the route. These protests made headlines all around the world. They caused counter-protests within China because many Chinese interpreted these protests as yet another case of China bashing from the West (see de Kloet and Liu, 2008: online). Both events inspired the International Olympic Committee and the authorities – it remains difficult to disentangle both actors in the organization process surrounding the Olympic Games – to emphasize that this would also be a "safe and secure Olympics."[7] The words suggest a sense of predictability, plain and foreseeable like everyday life, and stability, with no disruption of everyday life.

This theme was mediated to the public through numerous television items, poster materials, and brochures, and was translated into policy by changing visa regulations and creating ample security measures throughout the city of Beijing. For example, posters about security issues appeared on bulletins of every community in Beijing. Security advertisements were repeatedly broadcast on television and on mobile TV in taxis, buses and the metro. Banners were placed in neighborhoods asking residents to pay special attention to safety and security issues. For example, a banner we came across said "Deal with hidden risks, prevent accidents – secure a safe Olympics, build a harmonious Chaoyang [the most populated district in Beijing]."

In some residential areas, posters gave citizens detailed instructions with as many as 20 guidelines. These guidelines instructed property owners to have a valid permit to lease out their properties; hoteliers to follow all safety regulations and keep closed-circuit television footage for a required period of time; hoteliers to also inform the police right away if they see suspicious behaviors or objects; foreigners or visitors to Beijing to register at local police stations within 24 hours after arrival in China. The regulations came with cartoon figures that connoted cuteness and cheerfulness. This is a general trend in the 2008 Beijing promotion materials, inspired by the hugely popular aesthetics of Japan's cute culture; police figures have big eyes and cute faces, thus softening and popularizing the message it promotes.

Our analysis mainly draws on eight months of fieldwork in Beijing between November 2007 and November 2008. Although our research purpose was not solely related to security, this issue had spontaneously become an integral part of fieldwork because it turned out to be one of the core issues of the Beijing Olympics. During the fieldwork, we observed how security measures were integrated into the event, and we also experienced how security was integrated and entangled with everyday life. In addition, we participated in several Olympic-related cultural and sporting events, and gained participant experience of surveillance for Olympic events and venues. We interviewed officials of the Beijing Organizing Committee, volunteers, journalists, and other participants and local people. We also collected mass mediated materials. After the fieldwork, we continued to follow the Olympic-related media reports in which security issues were a crucial part. In our analysis, we include both ethnographic data and media reports and representations. The latter includes TV recordings recorded during our fieldwork, an Olympic documentary called *Dream Weaver*, and Internet news.

In this chapter we analyze the ideas and notions of security and surveillance practices and procedures as employed by the state and the Beijing Organizing Committee and scrutinize their impact upon everyday life in Beijing. We aim to pay particular attention to the specific local translations of security measures – not to claim that globalization always implies localization, but more as to show how the global discourse of security is inherently flexible and malleable, so that it can be translated toward different cultural contexts and circumstances. To structure our analysis, we take our inspiration from the security lecture series of Foucault. In these lectures, Foucault distinguishes four features of the apparatus of security: the spatial arrangements, the treatment of the uncertain, normalization of security, and the idea of a population (Foucault, 2007 [1978]: 11). In our view, the fourth feature runs as a thread throughout the previous three features. We will show how in spatial arrangements, the treatment of the uncertain, and processes of normalization, the Chinese state constantly involves the cooperation of the population. This massive mobilization of the citizenry constitutes, in our view, the most salient and culturally specific characteristic of the Beijing Olympics. We hence do not discuss this as a separate theme. Instead, we add a fourth dimension: the role of media and technology as a tool to address and discipline the citizenry. We will show in our analysis how these four aspects of securitization unfold in a Chinese context.

Spatial arrangements

Whereas Foucault engages with town and city planning to show how security relates to space, one can also do so on the level of Olympic venues and spaces. According to Foucault, "the specific space of security refers then to a series of possible events; it refers to the temporal and the uncertain, which have to be inserted within a given space" (2007 [1978]: 20). This is not so much to fix locations and establish limits as it is to "making possible, guaranteeing, and ensuring circulations: the circulation of people, merchandise, and air, etcetera" (ibid.: 29). The Olympic Green, located in the north of Beijing, is one space in which security measures help establish a "correct" flow of people and things. The best way to get to that space is by metro. That line, the "Olympic line," was only open to those people who had a valid ticket. Physical boundaries – in the form of security checkpoints – were established to scrutinize the welcome "insiders" from a mass of unknown crowds.

Who could pass through these checkpoints was determined by a set of rules, rules that were established in accordance with the Beijing Organizing Committee, the Chinese officials, and the International Organizing Committee. As Roberto Vanolo also observes discussing the Turin Olympics in the previous chapter, the boundaries of what is and what is not permissible in controlling the local population is a highly sensitive and contested issue. The physicality of the checkpoints – just like roadblocks – subjected individuals to a disciplinarity that required them to queue up patiently and follow the requirements of the organizers and have their bodies and belongings checked by machines and strangers. The architectural design of these checkpoints – holiday-like, white party tents (Figure 15.1) – disguised these stringent and highly discriminatory security acts, giving individuals the illusion that they were queuing up for something exciting and fun instead of threats and dangers associated with security discourses.

But security measures were still very much in place in this cheerful environment. First of all, potential spectators needed to follow the rules and regulations set by the organizers (i.e., the conditions of entry) and the instructions given by the staff. That also meant that they needed to go through a security check. Second, they needed to show that they possessed valid tickets. Third, there was a list of prohibited items that they were not allowed to bring: alcoholic beverages; musical instruments, bulky items, flagpoles or flags of non-Olympic participating countries; unauthorized professional video equipment; sharp objects or any items that could cause injury; any fire-starting devices; animals (except guide dogs); any vehicles or transportation devices (except wheelchairs and strollers); unauthorized

Figure 15.1 Security checkpoints before entering the Olympic lines

sound-amplifying equipment; and weapons that are controlled under Chinese laws. Fourth, people were not allowed to dress inappropriately. An example of such inappropriate dress was the demonstrators in the equestrian events who were dressed in orange, with T-shirts showing support for the pro-Free Tibet movement, and also carried a Tibetan flag. They were deterred from entering the venues. Although the list of prohibited items did not mention it, spectators were also not allowed to bring in any food or drinks that were not sold by event sponsors. In this case, the whole surveillance practices resonated with what Vanolo discusses in the previous chapter in the case of the Turin Olympics.

The Olympic Green is located at the north end of the central axis of Beijing, which runs from the south (the Temple of Heaven), through the center (Tiananmen Square and the Forbidden City) to the Olympic Park. This location – heavily promoted and made clearly visible on maps – grants the space with an aura of historicity and establishes a clear link with the political center. It grants the space an aura of Chinese-ness. Yet, simultaneously and paradoxically, the Olympic Green is a placeless place, a cosmopolitan zone that almost feels surreal. There are no cars, it is a clean and green space, full of joyful people, children who play in fountains, and where many different nationalities walk peacefully – indeed, it is a space that above all produces a sense of security for all the visitors on site, including the Chinese public. Here, the visitors could rest assured that they would have a good time enjoying the Games, just like a holiday. The rather invisible security measures inside the Olympic Green reminded us of the saying by China Central Television host Wang Shilin with which we opened this chapter: "the kind of security one does not see is the best form of security."[8]

Security measures were anything from absent inside the Olympic venues. The Beijing Organizing Committee and the state even managed to persuade the International Organizing Committee to allow an army of 100 fully armed soldiers to lurk in a huge basement under an artificial lake in the center of the Olympic Green. The captain of a team of Chinese People's Armed Police Force, Zhao Yongjun said,

> Our team, at that time [before and during the Olympics] were mysterious and secretive, we were equipped with 4 types of weapons, 136 guns, 95 assault rifles, 88 sniper rifles, 92 handguns, we also had light machine guns. ... As for the IOC, [I] must say we got a special permission from them, we were in the core of the Olympic area, 10 meters under the lake, we stationed there before and during the Olympics.[9]

It is unknown whether the Chinese People's Armed Police Force really got permission from the International Organizing Committee. Suffice it to say, surveillance technologies and operatives were rendered not too visible, as that would take away the cheerful spirit of the Olympics, but visible enough to let the spectators know that they were being taken care of, or being watched. These dialectics of visibility and invisibility of surveillance help discipline individuals. According to our interviews with Olympic Games volunteers, various forms of security personnel were present inside the Olympic venues – some more visible than others. In the words of one volunteer:

> There were two kinds of security personnel. According to my observation, [the training] did not say how many kinds [of security personnel], one of them was the usual policemen, [they] didn't wear their usual uniforms in Bird's Nest, the other one was the P[eople's] L[iberation] A[rmy] ... if you pay attention, every section would have a few of these guys, the policemen would wear white shirts, the PLA would wear blue shirts with white caps, we could find some of them standing next to us during our service.[10]

In an interview, a high-ranking official in the Organizing Committee's security department admitted to us that some seats were not sold to the public as they were reserved for security reasons. Although he refused to reveal the number of such seats, he did say that this was a procedure in compliance with the International Organizing Committee requirements.

Since mid-May, very strict regulations were in place to control the movement of specific goods or materials. On July 1, when trying to transport the newly invented "ancient instrument" *Fou*, the drums used in the first minutes of the Opening Ceremony, into the Bird's Nest, the manufacturer encountered great problems: the truck was pulled over by the police a number of times, though finally the manufacturer managed to fulfill his duty.[11] During the Games, the surveillance became even more rigorous. For example, the lunchboxes for the volunteers in the Olympic venues had to go through eight steps of control when being moved from the collective kitchen to the Olympic venues. These boxes were prepared by cooks, in bioscientist-like uniforms, who had to pass through body temperature inspectors and fingerprint identifiers before entering the kitchen.[12]

Being located on such a historical and political axis, yet stripped of all political connotations, the Olympic Green represents a milieu that establishes a relationship between the government and the Olympics. It is a space outside the nation-state yet intimately linked to it; it transports the citizen toward a zone of perceived safety that seems to justify all security measures taken by the nation-state. It is a ritual space, as Bajc writes in the context of the transformation of Washington for the 2005 presidential inauguration, it "makes public the efforts of the modern state to provide personal, communal, and state security under conditions of uncertainty. These efforts are based on surveillance practices whose goal is to provide security on the basis of prospects for maximum control over all mobility" (2007b: 1649). Those who cannot afford, or cannot manage to obtain, a ticket[13] are not allowed to enter the Olympic Green. To create a clean and tidy city, nearly all migrant workers – those who constructed the venues – were forced to leave the city, as all construction work was halted and they lacked the proper papers or resources to stay in the city.[14] Similar measures were also applied to the city of Beijing as a ritual space of Olympic city. Small businesses (mainly run by the migrant population), such as low-end restaurants, snack carts and fruit trolleys, and small barbershops, were also closed down for the duration of the Olympics.[15] From late July to the end of August, though there was no publicized policy in this regard, those persons (especially people from remote areas) who had no tickets for the Games would very likely encounter problems buying train tickets to Beijing. These exclusionary measures were far larger in the scale than those reported by Vanolo in the case the 2006 Turin Olympics or reported by Kennelly in the case of the 2010 Vancouver Games.

The control over space also became clear to us when the Olympic Flame arrived in Beijing on August 6, 2008. Being the symbolic center of the nation, the flame would of course start its journey at Tiananmen Square, where we had been waiting since five in the morning. We were slowly but steadily being pushed away and replaced by various forms of "security guards" (in different uniforms with badges saying "security") and groups of official supporters; these were people from work units that were mobilized by the authorities to cheer for the flame. The first line thus consisted of "security guards," marked by their recognizable set of outfits. On the second line we could find the recruited supporters, again visually marked by their clothes, as they would all wear similar T-shirts (sponsored by corporations), and only behind them the regular visitors were allowed to watch. The Olympic Flame Relay was to be a ritual, celebrating this grand achievement of China. China wanted to show to the world how much the Chinese embraced and supported the Games. It was a counter-message to the global contestations and boycott of China as the host of the Games. As such, the authorities needed the public to appear and perform their support. Yet, the public also posed unpredictable threats and potential chaos, so they were therefore also guarded and monitored – first by the official security guards, and then by the recruited supporters who were hired particularly to cheer for the torch (Li, 2011).

The Chinese visitors around us complained. "Are we second-class citizens?" one sneered toward the police, as they were forced to move away from the Olympic activity so that those who were officially recruited and trained by the authorities could move into that space. The spatial arrangements are thus closely connected to managing the circulation of people and rendering the "right" people most visible, while pushing others toward more invisible zones.

These dialectics of visibility and invisibility are what characterizes the spatial control. It has to be visible, so that people will be aware that they are being watched; at the same time, it has to be invisible, so that it will not disturb the cheerful image the authorities wish to convey locally and globally. When the implied hierarchy is rendered so visible, for example, during the Olympic Flame Relay in Beijing, moments of resistance arise as people start to complain. A young female explained to us how disappointed she was when she tried to attend the passing of the torch in her own neighborhood of Tongzhou, located at the far east end of Beijing:

> Finally, we reached the point. Unfortunately, we couldn't see anything because there were four lines of people building up a "wall" to separate people. For this point to the canal, it was still quite far away. The four of us were stuck at there. For me, it was very disappointing. You can see two lines of people with their red shirt, and the other two lines with their uniforms. ... The government has been broadcasting for such a long time about the Olympics and the excitement, and also, we all know how much we have spent on the Games, and in those advertisements, they say, welcome... but when we are ready to join it, we just couldn't. Also, the way they do it was like we were enemies. There were hundreds of them blocking our way. They even said that it was all for our safety.

Her remarks point at how the arrangements of space, driven by the security apparatus, block citizens from actively participating in the celebrations. These are moments the state does not succeed in producing a sterile and sanitized zone like the Olympic Green; on the contrary, these are moments that citizens start to question the Olympic project, and with it, the intentions and goodwill of the nation-state. When the Beijing Olympics excluded people, even if it is said for the purpose of security, the people still felt betrayed and discriminated. This resonates with a general mistrust in the authorities, in particular the disjuncture between what is promoted (a People's Olympics) and what is enacted (but only for some people...). One more related element here is that the security issue, which resonates with the globalized narrative of the "war on terror," is relatively "new" in China. People do not easily accept the security-related logic and are reluctant to take relevant measurements. Finally, the young female's skeptical attitude toward the government is an attitude that one very often encounters in everyday life in China, as well as on the Internet. More often than not, it is the political system discussed in cynical terms, full of parody. The full-fledged support for the Olympic Games on the part of the citizenry – "full-fledged" as only very few voices of opposition have been heard[16] – does not equal wholehearted support for authorities that rule the country, which explains why the latter were so keen in involving the people.

Apart from these specific spatial arrangements around the Olympic sites and events, the safety of the city of Beijing was propagated as a source of security concern. Various measures were being put in place around the city, and throughout the city, some of these measures resembled security measures taken in wartime. An indicative example is the setup of three defense lines with a few hundred checkpoints around and in the city of Beijing. The first defense line was to inspect any incoming flows of people and objects to Beijing. Checkpoints were set up at highways leading to the city and at the national airports. The second defense line was set up nearby the six counties around the city of Beijing. The third defense line was placed around the main roads of the eight urban districts in Beijing. Besides the three defense lines, checkpoints were set up on all the roads connecting to Beijing in order to keep danger and uncertainty away from the city. Furthermore, in cities throughout the country, especially big cities and cities in "sensitive" areas such as Xinjiang and Tibet, security was reinforced to create a "peaceful and harmonious" atmosphere for the Games. In other words, the "security lines," to some extent, expanded to the whole country. The Beijing municipal government had issued clear instructions to all drivers.

> All vehicles that are going to the city of Beijing should be well-prepared in accordance with regulations issued by the local municipality for the Olympics; when checked by the local police officers, drivers should stop the engines and let the officers perform security check; when being questioned, drivers should provide their driving licenses and car permit, open the trunk and assist the officers to perform the security check; passengers are required to show their personal identification documents and

their household registration documents, allow and assist the officers to check their personal belongings; all the checkpoints to enter Beijing are equipped with water and medicine for emergency situations, if needed, the police officers will provide help and assistance.[17]

The defense lines paralleled the security checkpoints being placed around the Olympic sites; they were being put in place to intercept, identify and control the incoming flows of people and objects. To command control over accessibility and mobility of the people exemplifies "the state's push for flexibility to act on the future, its ability to deal with ambiguity and scale, and its power to identify and remove outsiders from everyone else" (Bajc, 2007a: 1584).

Throughout the Olympics, the population was actively recruited to act "voluntarily" as security guards. News reports in the period leading up to the Games would often present high-ranking officials such as Zhou Yongkang (member of the Politburo Standing Committee) visiting local neighborhoods in the city to encourage residents' active participation in ensuring a safe and secure Olympics.[18] These officials would shake hands with the neighborhood security volunteers, a gesture of approval and a sign of encouragement to the population. Because of the need to include the mass in its security force, the number of volunteers for the Beijing Olympics had expanded enormously from 70,000 for the Olympic Games and 30,000 for the Paralympics (De Kloet et al., 2008: 15) to almost 2 million volunteers in total when the Games ended. Volunteers came from all walks of life, ranging from retired citizens, unemployed citizens, waiters and waitresses in neighborhood restaurants, and street cleaners in neighborhoods (Figure 15.2), to the young and handsome university students serving in the Olympic venues.

The authority had classified and categorized the population (i.e., potential volunteers) into different types of volunteers according to a set of recruitment criteria, training practices and responsibilities. There were six categories of volunteers: (1) Pre-Games Olympics volunteers, (2) Games volunteers, (3) Paralympic Games volunteers, (4) Beijing Organizing Committee Pre-Games volunteers, (5) city volunteers, and (6) society volunteers.[19] Hierarchy and prestige were tactically placed in such ways that volunteers would know their roles and responsibilities (see Chong, 2011). According to Chong (2011), Games volunteers, followed by Paralympic Games volunteers, were the most prestigious; of relevance, recruitment criteria were most demanding on these categories. Once selected, these volunteers would be assigned to the most important Olympic venues. City volunteers and society volunteers were not as prestigious as the aforementioned, but they constituted the majority of the volunteer population. During the Olympics, one could easily spot society volunteers (a.k.a. the capital city's security volunteers), who were responsible for the safety of neighborhoods through patrol and observation. These volunteers were given a list of phone numbers, and

Figure 15.2   Street sweepers/cleaners also took up the security task, as shown by the red armbands

in case of emergency or security violation, they were told to contact authorities immediately. The volunteers serving at the prime Olympic sites would receive security-related training. These volunteers, working in the forefront of the Games, were expected to take up an active and responsive role in securing a safe Olympics. During a rehearsal related to the potential threat of demonstrations, politician Wang Anshun said,

> I think it's better to let the volunteers deal with them [protesters] first, persuade them to leave, and warn them, if they don't listen, then we need to mobilize the police to implement some measures and solutions.[20]

The everydayness and normality of volunteers is preferred above the uniform-wearing policemen, most likely as they will seem less threatening, less clear representatives of the state, and hence better capable to ask protesters to leave. This shows how volunteers were actively involved in the security practices, which also involves a spatial regulation and specific distribution of the population as well as of the volunteers themselves.

The treatment of the uncertain

Concerns about security make it legitimate for a government to take all possible precautionary measures in order to minimize possible threats and damages. But what are these threats? On national television, a security expert explained that they covered a broad spectrum of unpredictable events, which included: (1) natural disasters, (2) any kind of contagious diseases, (3) criminal activities, (4) demonstrations, and (5) international conflicts. On *Road to Beijing*,[21] an entire episode was devoted to the discussion of "unexpected events and how to deal with these events." The program discussed at great length all possible risks that might happen during the Olympics. These threats unfolded in the order of significance: (1) terrorist attacks, (2) demonstrations, (3) unfavorable weather, (4) logistic issues, (5) technical failure, (6) problems that might be caused by beverage and food, (7) medical care, and (8) problems related to accommodations. In other media sources, mentally unstable people were also included as potential threats to the Games.[22] The expert assured the audience that it would be impossible to avoid all unforeseeable events. In an effort to take sensible precautionary measures, the authorities had chosen to focus on risks that might be caused by mankind.[23]

In the lead-up to the Games, we witnessed shifts in the discourse of risks and uncertainties revolving around the notion of "Safe Olympics." During our first fieldwork in 2007, risks – in the form of unexpected events – pertaining to the notion of "Safe Olympics" were mainly about reminding the public of domestic and everyday hazards such as fire hazards. For example, a banner displayed inside Yonghegong subway station reads "Everyone be vigilant of fire safety, together we build a safe Olympics." It also dealt with maintaining law and order; for example, a subway poster reads "Wait behind the lines, getting on and getting off the train in order, order brings safety." Small tombstone-like signage reading "Ping'an Aoyun" would often be found next to the elevators inside apartment buildings or outside the buildings (Figure 15.3).

The Tibet protests in March and the events surrounding the Olympic Flame Relay had led to a shift of discourse that demanded more stringent security measures. As early as March, there had been reports of attempts of terrorist attacks targeting the Beijing Olympics: on March 7, 2008, two Uyghurs tried to hijack an airplane to crash the Olympic venues, but they failed.[24] By July, there were frequent reports about explosions and alleged terrorist attacks nationwide: two explosions happened in Kunming, a big city in southwestern China, with the East Turkestan Islamic Movement claimed responsibility for both.[25] These events both intensified and legitimized the discourse of threats and security that emerged alongside the hitherto dominant "proud and joyous" narratives of the Olympics.

As explained earlier, this discourse of threats borrows its power from the global discourse on the "war on terror." For example, *Handbook of Olympic Security*, a television program launched by Channel 7 of China Central Television on July 26 and August 2, 2008, reviews the development of security issues after the Munich Olympics, and especially after the 9/11 attacks, emphasizing the increasing importance of security issues

Figure 15.3 "Avoid fire hazards; we make a safe Olympics"

in the Olympic Games and thus justifying the high-profile security measures in Beijing. "From the recent Olympics, including both the Summer Olympics in Sydney and Athens and the Winter Olympics in the Salt Lake City, employing technology to ensure a safe and peaceful Olympics has been a global trend."[26] Such an antiterrorist system is basically focused on a possible event, "an event that could take place, and which one tries to prevent before it becomes reality" (Foucault, 2007 [1978]: 33). As the Games drew closer, in the months before the Opening Ceremony, the discourse of potential terrorist attacks grew stronger. One of the tactics of making this "war on terror" more imminent was to identify and categorize these potential troublemakers. Listed according to the level of threats these groups posed, they were the East Turkestan terrorists,[27] Tibetan separatists,[28] practitioners/followers of the Falungong cult,[29] international terrorists who attempt to seize the Olympic spectacle to make a statement (e.g., Islamic fundamentalists), overseas civic groups (potential demonstrators), and – a deliberately vague category that holds the power to include potentially everybody that voices critique – discontented citizens.[30] After the Tibet uprisings in March and the global contestations during the Olympic Flame Relay, the training for volunteers included a special focus on security, and some groups had special training in relation to terrorist attacks inside the Olympic venues.[31]

In this discourse of terrorism, in particular the Uyghurs, identified as participants of global terrorist group East Turkestan Islamic Movement,[32] featured prominently, as their Islamic beliefs tied in most neatly with the war on terror discourse. A bomb attack by Uyghur "terrorists" in the week preceding the Opening Ceremony thus helped the authorities in "proving" that the risks were real and the corresponding security measures thus were necessary. Risks are infinitely reproducible (Beck, 1994: 9); they can easily glide from Tibet activists in London to Uyghur activists in West China to migrant workers' protests in the capital city. In Beck's view, risks are produced by an excessive demand for control, resulting in "the realm of the uncertain" (ibid.: 10) According to Beck, this, in turn, leads to a self-critical society. "Within the horizon of the opposition between old routine and new awareness of consequences and dangers," writes Beck, "society becomes self-critical" (1999: 81). This causality, however, does not apply to China because its space for public critique is very confined. Instead, what we observe here is how the global discourse on terror was adopted in a local context by assigning "Chinese features": threats posed by separatists, religious cults, demonstrators, and discontented individuals.

Foreigners were also perceived as a potential threat. After all, it was foreigners who snatched the Olympic flame away. They, thus, needed to be under constant surveillance of the local police, just as their travel opportunities needed to be contained by imposing stricter visa regulations. All visitors (outsiders), including Chinese citizens of non-Beijing household registration (*hukou*), were required to report to the local police within 24 hours and 72 hours, respectively, of their arrival. Posters about this regulation were placed in all neighborhoods. While we stayed in the city, the police would indeed check if we had registered ourselves properly. Acquaintances who did not register were required to leave the country.

Since these outsiders might not follow the required procedure, it was therefore the responsibility of the local communities and authorities to pay vigilant attention to the arrivals of any strangers and report any suspicious activity to the police. Notices and posters were found in all local communities and all residential areas. Volunteers who are assigned to patrol local communities and streets are specifically trained in this regard. As one volunteer explained to us:

> During the (training) meeting, we were told to pay special attention to those who wore Tibetan or Xijiang ethnic clothes, who spoke in north-western dialects, spoke with Xinjiang accent and Tibet accent, who had big bags or odd-shaped baggage, and anyone who looked suspicious. We were also told to pay attention to foreigners, especially those who had a banner, poster or something alike. If we found anything suspicious, we were asked to clarify to them, with the premise of being aware of our own safety and being friendly and polite to them ... But if we had truly found anything, we wouldn't have to talk to them – in such a case we were asked to report it immediately.[33]

Her explanation echoes the priorities of the listed threats mentioned above, and a practice of demarcating the non-locals from the locals. Non-locals, especially members of ethnic groups from Western China, were related to potential threats. The solution was to mobilize the mass, supplemented by the police, to maximally reduce the uncertainties (which will be discussed in detail later). It was precisely the endless and seemingly imminent potential and unknown threats that required the public to stay alert at all times – something emphasized repeatedly in the media. By elaborating extensively on possible threats, the state actually managed to induce a mixture of crisis and being in control, with the latter performed through repeated images of tests and rehearsals. This helped to justify the state's role as the omnipresent protector of its citizenry.

Security and normalization

In the wake of the events in March, surveillance and security practices entered everyday life in Beijing. As the Games approached, banners and posters promoting the concept of "Safe Olympics" seemed not tangible enough. In order to induce a more tangible security act, luggage X-ray control, which is similar to those used at airport checkpoints, appeared at all subway stations a month before the Games, and formal security checks were put into practice on July 29, 2008. It is important to note that after the Olympics, these machines stayed in place.[34] The attention paid to the monitors and flow of people by security guards was often so insufficient, in our eyes, that it would not be too difficult to circumvent the security system.

In all subway stations, there would be a sign reading "Security Check" in both Chinese and English, with a big arrow pointing in the direction of that checkpoint. During the Olympics, a subway officer would be standing right next to the sign. Unlike the more stringent security check at the important sites (like the Olympics), these subway checkpoints did not seem to function as an interception point and they appeared to be rather loose: no special personnel were assigned to guide the flow of people to form a queue or to maintain order, and no personnel were holding metal detectors or hand-wand detectors to check passengers or their baggage. Although a police officer would be standing next to the X-ray machine, they hardly inter-vened. Based on our multiple observations, the personnel did not seem to understand why it was important to x-ray passengers' personal belongings; what one could observe was a performativity of security – it was a public display of the state watching over its citizenry.

In its justifications, a discursive link is created between security and a happy, cheerful life. For example, Beijing Organizing Committee Security Director Liu Shaowu claims in a brochure explaining the security measures that

> We have worked closely with the law enforcement departments of the Chinese Government to build a safe and secure environment for the Games. All participants will be able to enjoy the games to the utmost. ... We are sure that we can avoid any potential security threat to the Games.*

First, the direct link between security and enjoyment is relevant, as it points at how policies are legitimized by claims related to a happy and enjoyable life. Second, the claim that total security is guaranteed is a performative statement in which the ruling authorities claim absolute control, even over what is in the end uncontrollable. It is a performance of an omnipotent nation-state that guards over its citizenry like a mother over her child: "within China and the larger Chinese communities globally, the party-state always assumes the role of a patriarchal figure in a big Chinese family, as prescribed in Confucian and Mencian theories" (Chong 2011: 44).

Surveillance practices not only interrupted "ordinary" everyday lives, they were also costly practices. The state guided the population to believe that the governing body was a capable government in control of unexpected events. International practices on security issues (e.g., the security measures employed in the Athens Olympics) were invoked to convince the popula-tion that security measures were not only normal practices but also abso-lutely necessary during the time of the Games. Ample references would be made to the International Organizing Committee's concern about security, so much so that a quote by its president, Jacques Rogge, was translated into Chinese: "Olympic security is more important than the competitions."[35] At other occasions, senior government officials such as Colonel Tian Yixiang (military minister of the Beijing Olympic Security Coordination Group) repeatedly emphasized that "all host countries of the previous Games placed strong emphasis on security issues," and the modern Olympics were such an international spectacle that troublemakers would seize the Games to reach their goals.[36] This may not happen, as China had promised to host great Olympics that met all international requirements and standards. Wu Jingguo, a member of the Organizing Committee's coordination team, said on national television:[37]

> In terms of preparation and safety, Beijing is full of confidence, also IOC trusts us in this regard, because Mainland China will not let any unexpected event take place during the Games. In this regard, China does more than is required by the IOC, the IOC is therefore very satisfied with our promise and measures.

A safe Olympics was presented as part of this national promise to the international community. Moreover, to validate and normalize for the citizenry the involvement of the People's Liberation Army and their military facilities – such as two missiles close to the Bird's Nest – in the supposedly "politics-free" Olympics, ancient Olympic history and recent Olympic experiences were invoked.[38]

Besides, previous security problems related to the Games were often highlighted to emphasize the importance of having a good security master plan. The narrative often started with the 1972 Munich Olympics, in which members of Black September killed 11 members of the Israeli team. Images of the event – masked terrorists, ambulances, injured policemen, and how German law enforcement failed to rescue the hostages – were used repeatedly to remind viewers of the atrocity terrorists could commit, on the one hand; and on the other hand, the failure of Germany's security measures during the Games. The underlying message is related to China's fear of being shamed globally, the fear of losing face. "How the Beijing Games were received by the world and its citizens was read as the fate of the country. If the Games were not approved or praised by the world, then it meant that China lost 'face' – a shameful thing – signifying failure, something the Chinese state had worked hard to avoid. The Games needed to be impeccable" (Chong, 2011: 35). Incidents of other Games were also presented as examples of unpredictable events and cases of security failure.[39] For instance, the bomb explosion in Centennial Olympic Park during the 1996 Atlanta Olympics and the pushing out of the marathon trail of a Brazilian marathon athlete by a stranger in Athens 2004. Previous failures were presented as a form of mis-governance: a failure in managing the uncertain and the unexpected. In recalling these Olympic histories and linking these to the importance of not losing face, it helped to justify the necessity and the importance of securitization.

Mobilization of the media

The earlier mentioned case of the Olympic Flame Relay is indicative of the role the media played. For example, the images of Tibet protestors snatching the torch away from the Chinese female Paralympic fencer in a wheelchair, Jin Jing, caused a strong nationalistic response in China. The Olympic Flame Relay as well as the protests it evoked was, above all, a media spectacle, with authorities and protesters doing their utmost best to make global headlines. Angry calls appeared on the Internet to resist and boycott French goods and the French supermarket Carrefour, following allegations that Carrefour is aligned to the Tibetan movement, which resulted in group protests against Carrefour branches in Kunming, Hefei, Changhai, Wuhan, Qingdao and other big cities across China (see de Kloet and Liu, 2008).

In particular, the media are used to presenting an image that the governing body is in control of the public's safety and to inducing a sense of fear and crisis to the public that helps to legitimatize its security measures. In many Olympic security television programs, images about anti-terrorism rehearsals often borrowed their aesthetic style from Hollywood action films: the heroes were the People's Liberation Army, masculine men in tight uniforms, with bulletproof jackets, fully equipped with advanced weapons. Their actions were swift and well trained, and they all acted as a unit to protect the innocent and harmless ordinary people. The villains, on the other hand, were the terrorists: people wearing masks, denoting a sense of secrecy and threats. These spectacular images, resonating with *Mission Impossible* aesthetics, would often be accompanied by interviews with soldiers, who would talk in great detail about their daily training:

> We had trained for a long time, till every procedure became part of our habits, our goal was to be able to act swiftly in unexpected circumstances without wasting time to think about how to react. Every step in our training has its procedure and requirement, if you don't follow the procedure, you may lose seconds, which may cost your life, then you were doomed.[40]

Their professionalism is further underlined by their serious and formal presentation. Yet, they were also humanized by showing their weaker moments when they expressed how tired and bored they felt after long and demanding training sessions. A member of a Special Weapons and Tactics Team said: "We had been training so much that we were a bit fed up with it."[41] *Dream Weaver* is the official documentary film about the Beijing Olympic Games. It documents how the Chinese people prepared for the Beijing Olympics since China got its bid in July 2001. The documentary shows how hard the Special Weapons and Tactics Team trained, sometimes failing to do the required movements; and like other ordinary men, also showing fear. One of the team members, afraid of heights, hesitated and wanted to backtrack to safe ground. Here one could see his weakness – fear – something generally not shown about the Special Weapons and Tactics Team. In a reflection session after the training, the team leader asked him what he was afraid of. The team member said, "I stood there I felt very dizzy, my legs were shaking, my hands and my feet were like frozen."[42] Through invoking such stories, the documentary personalizes and humanizes the security efforts of the state, a move that helps to legitimize these efforts. After all, if the Special Weapons and Tactics Team are able to express but also overcome their fears, the task they face must be a truly important one.

Media were also mobilized to explain the important role technology plays in optimizing security. High-tech equipment for the Games was publically paraded. Images of weapons like helicopters, missiles, explosives-detecting dogs, and the like were shown on various programs on China Central Television.[43] When reporting about the security procedure for the transportation of food to the venues, the media highlighted the advance technology used in the process, such as the tracking system that could estimate delivery time, route, and arrival time.[44] Also mentioned above, the army officer not only gave a detailed description about what kinds of weapons they had, but also the technology used to make sure their stay in the underground would be safe. Reports also showed that the Chinese authorities had deployed ten "secret weapons" for the security of the Olympics: bomb-detecting and -detonating robots, closed-circuit television cameras, portable X-ray inspection system, infrared video detectors, explosives-detecting dogs, protective gear for dealing with explosive materials, powerful crossbows, police helicopters, surface to air missiles, and hazardous liquids detectors.[45]

Whenever security issues were mentioned in the media, technology would have its place in the discussion – in particular, digital and advanced communication technologies. High-tech police equipment used for anti-terrorism and centralized security systems connecting all the Olympic venues provided further proof of the government's technological sophistication. The media also constantly enumerated the technological innovations of the Beijing Olympics: a satellite was sent into space to orbit and broadcast the Games all over the world, which was a first for modern Olympic history; chip-inserted tickets of the Games claimed to contain the holder's personal information[46]; the self-innovated Nuclear Quadruple Resonance Explosive Detection System solved the world-class technological difficulties on explosive objects detection; and so forth.[47] In the media, these technological innovations were specifically presented as achievements of the "High-Tech Olympics."

Detailed reports about security rehearsals and high-tech security equipment were meant to be broadcast to the population to underline how well prepared and organized the governing body had been, and therefore how well uncertainties invoked in the risk discourse were governed.[48] As Bajc writes, "mass media provide a crucial link through which the general public is made aware of, and informed about, different practices of surveillance in service of securitization...the mass media are a venue through which state agencies seek public legitimacy for their surveillance" (Bajc, 2007a: 1585). It was partly through the media that the governing body sought its justification and legitimacy in implementing various security measures and presented itself as being capable and in control of unexpected events.

Conclusion: power to the people?

Through the production of allegedly safe spaces related to controlling the circulation of people and things, through normalizing security practices and referring to a wide range of threats and uncertainties, using new technologies and employing the media to interpellate the citizenry, and by actively engaging all citizens in the production of a safe Olympics, the intense securitization of Olympic China was part and parcel of the tactics of governmentality of the Chinese authorities. These tactics allowed "the continual definition of what should or what should not fall within the state's domain, what is public and what private, what is and is not within the state's competence" (Foucault, 1991: 109). The four elements identified in this chapter – space, risk, normality, and media and technology – mutually reinforce and constitute each other.

What connects them, and what we consider the most characteristic element of the securitization of the Beijing Olympics, is the massive involvement of the citizenry. Beijing Organizing Committee President Lui Qi said "a safe and secure Olympics is like 'a people's war,' it needs the general population's support."[49] Official promotion encouraged the public's active participation in the Games from the time China won the Olympic bid on July 13, 2001. In particular, following the events on March 7, 2008, this participation was discursively linked to the issue of security. For example in the slogan, "A safe and secure Olympics is extremely important, the safety of Olympics is everyone's responsibility," the population was explicitly made part of the security apparatus. In the period around the Games, one could easily spot banners and posters addressing citizens directly, such as "Your attention, my participation, our safe Olympics." The authorities, aware that they could not keep an eye on everybody, needed to include the population – its citizens – to be part of its surveillance team.

The emphasis on the population's support was linked to the larger discourse of China's century-old Olympic dream. Three factors make this such a powerful discourse: first, its connection to the discourse of humiliation; second, its connection to the assumed power of the people in the foundation and consolidation of the People's Republic of China; and, third, its connection to Confucianism.

Hosting the Olympics was an important symbolic marker indicating China's ascendency to the league of global power and, as Chong writes, "a crucial moment to cleanse the long-held discourse of national humiliation" (2011: 35). The discourse of humiliation recounts "how at the hands of foreign invaders and corrupt Chinese regimes, sovereignty was lost, territory dismembered, and the Chinese people thus humiliated. The Opium War, whereby the British Navy pried open the Chinese empire to Western capitalism in 1840, is usually seen as the beginning of the century of national humiliation, and the communist revolution in 1949 as the end" (Callahan, 2006: 180). The discourse of humiliation helped to successfully mobilize the population to embrace every bit of the Games so as to demonstrate to the world China could host an impeccable Games (Chong, 2008, 2011; de Kloet et al., 2011). It can be read as the ultimate public ritual through which China overcame the burden of the humiliation it experienced in the past.

The "mass route,"[50] which means to mobilize, organize and rely on the masses to achieve the Communist Party's goals, is regarded as the determinant factor of the Party's success in the revolution and socialist construction. Today, it is also broadly used in China by the government to solicit support and legitimacy for its policies, political campaigns and mega-events like the Beijing Olympic Games (see Perry, 2007). The legitimacy of the state is rooted in the "government's capacity to sustain stability and social order" (Shue, 2004: 41). For this, it needs to actively engage its citizenry, especially at moments like the Beijing Olympics.

The involvement of the people cannot only be traced back to China's recent communist history. Nor can it be reduced to the discourse of national humiliation. Rather, we also need to consider the teachings of Confucianism. According to Confucianism, the leaders of the state are always evaluated by the people; the active involvement of the citizens is therefore translated into a sign of good governance. The state, according to Confucian values, is to bring order and peace to the world and its leaders, and, as Daniel Bell writes, it "should be morally upright" (2008: 10). It should not disrupt the population's everyday lives. Contrary to what people commonly believe, the Chinese government does not simply impose policies on its people; rather, it deploys strategies and tactics that guide the population to its desired ends (Chong, 2011).

The Games offered China an opportunity to showcase a positive face of China so as to gain international recognition and reputation. Viewed in this light, China had tried its very best to avoid any depreciation of face. In our interviews and chats with various volunteers, many of them did express a sense of crisis and anxiety, and sometimes hostility, that the unknown "others" – often foreigners – would pose threats to the Games and therefore jeopardize China's Games. As such, they all shared the imminent responsibilities to protect the nation from the unexpected and potential threats. Meanwhile, during and after the Games, also many other cities in China mobilized huge amounts of volunteers and adopted more stringent security measures to secure local safety in the name of a safe Olympics. The governing body had not only succeeded in mobilizing a broad spectrum of the population in its security force but also subjected them to behave and act according to its will. As Bajc writes (2007a: 1577), "biopolitics is fully successful when subjects come to govern themselves according to state specification." In a similar vein, Callahan (2006: 181) argues that "'security' is not about defending us so much as telling us who we must be." Questions regarding the human, material, environmental, social, political and financial costs involved in the intensification of security and surveillance are pushed backstage; what counts is the front-stage performance of a safe and happy nation, ready for the 21st century, with a supportive and cheerful citizenry. But our example in this chapter of the discontented citizens during the Olympic Flame Relay in Beijing hints at the flipside of this narrative of surveillance and control. As Vivienne Shue writes, "in any system of domination's own logic of legitimation we should be able to find encoded the basic grammar for protest, the 'raw material' that is available to be used most powerfully in opposition to that system" (2004: 34). Nevertheless, during the Olympic year of 2008, the authorities managed to sustain and legitimate its dominant position, in the midst of a whirlwind of protests, natural disasters and scandals. It did so partly through the increased securitization of society in which the citizenry was actively involved. The skillful adaptation and appropriation of the discourse of security attests to the continued power of the state in China, and helps to obscure the possible "raw materials of protest," thus keeping possibilities of fundamental social and political change out of reach.

Notes

*Safe Olympics [Ping'an Aoyun平安奥运]. By Beijing Chaoyang District Office.[北京市朝阳区人民政府].
All images by Gladys Pak Lei Chong. We wish to thank an anonymous reviewer for helpful comments.

1. http://cn.reuters.com/article/wtNews/idCNChina-1634920080709 (accessed on August 13, 2010) and http://www.chinanews.com.cn/olympic/news/2008/-02/1300374.shtml (accessed on August 13, 2010). Xi Jinping, the Vice President of People's Republic of China (PRC) and member of the standing committee of the Politburo of Chinese Communist Party. The Beijing Organizing Committee of the Olympic Games was set up on December 13, 2001, as an organization responsible for the Beijing Olympics. Liu Qi, originally the mayor of Beijing, was then appointed as the president of the Beijing Organizing Committee of the Olympic Games. This quote was an official statement informing the public the significance of a safe and secure Olympics to China.
2. Channel 4 of China Central Television (CCTV 4), July 16, 2008, *Focus Today: Security in Beijing* (Hosted by Wang Shilin) (中央电视台4台，2008年7月16日，"今日

关注: 奥运安保[王世林主持].") *Focus Today* is a daily news program that discusses domestic and international current affairs, broadcast on CCTV4 (the Chinese International Channel) at 9:30 p.m. It always invites various government officials and experts to participate and share their views with the public.

3. In Chinese, these slogans are "Green Olympics" (绿色奥运), "High Tech Olympics" (科技奥运) and "People's Olympics" (人文奥运).

4. http://en.beijing2008.cn/bocog/concepts/index.shtml (accessed on June 13, 2011).

5. "Chapter 3: The Beijing Olympic Games and the Olympic Volunteering" http://en.beijing2008.cn/upload/readerupdate/3.pdf (accessed on September 3, 2008) 79–80.

6. Ibid., 80.

7. 平安奥运, the character 平 means peaceful, equal and quiet; the character 安 means safe, stable and calm. Collectively they refer to "safe and secure Olympics" or "peaceful and safe Olympics."

8. Channel 4, July 16, 2008, *Focus Today: Security in Beijing.*

9. Channel 5 of China Central Television, "Army in the Underground Square," Episode 5 (Section 2), *Olympic Archive.* (中央电视台五台, "屯兵地下广场", 《奥运档案》第五集[下]), http://space.tv.cctv.com/video/VIDE1231492965703355 (accessed June 14, 2010).

10. The National Sports Stadium of China is also called Bird's Nest for its nest-like shape.

11. Channel 5 of China Central Television, "The Song of Fou," Episode 1 of *Aoyun Dang'an,* (中央电视台五台, "缶之歌", 《奥运档案》第一集), http://sports.cctv.com/special/fouzhige/01/index.shtml (accessed April 6, 2011).

12. Channel 5 of China Central Television, "The Story of Lunchbox," Section 4 of Episode 6, *Aoyun Dang'an* (中央电视台五台, "盒饭的经历", 《奥运档案》第六集第四部分), http://sports.cctv.com/20090112/110355.shtml (accessed April 6, 2011).

13. The cheap tickets were sold for approximately US$5 but were very hard to obtain; on the black market, ticket prices were often much higher.

14. See, for example, http://www.reuters.com/article/2008/07/21/us-olympics-migrants-idUSSP26521520080721

15. These exclusionary measures were not specifically created for the Beijing Olympics. During every March, when the National People's Congress and National Committee of the Chinese People's Political Consultative Conference are open, similar measures are also put into practice. Part of its purpose is to present the city in neatness and to minimize the uncertainties that may be brought by the migrant population. However, during the Olympics, Beijing conducted the exclusion in an ever-larger scale.

16. According to the International Organizing Committee evaluation report, 96% of the Beijing population supported China hosting the Olympics (p. 60), Report of the International Organizing Committee Evaluation Commission for the Games of the XXIX Olympiad in 2008. International Olympic Committee Evaluation Commission, see: http://www.olympic.org/Documents/Reports/EN/en_report_299.pdf (accessed August 15, 2010).

17. "Important notes for security check" by the municipality of the city of Beijing http://ggaq.beijing.cn/aqzxsm/n214071618_1.shtml (accessed August 15, 2010).

18. Channel 4, July 16, 2008, *Focus Today: Security in Beijing.*

19. *Volunteer Manual,* 127.

20. Channel 4, July 16, 2008, *Focus Today: Security in Beijing.*

21. A program providing information related to the Beijing Olympics, broadcast from June till October 2008 on Channel 5 of China Central Television.

22. In an Olympic security-related episode shown on CCTV 5 法国黑豹在北京 (about French security forces coming to train the Beijing security force) in summer 2008. For more information, see http://bugu.cntv.cn/sports/talk/tiyurenjian/classpage/video/20100330/100867.shtml and http://sports.cctv.com/20090112/110142.shtml (accessed on July 30, 2010).

23. Channel 4, July 16, 2008, *Focus Today: Security in Beijing.*

24. http://news.163.com/10/0212/09/5VAHK1BT0001124J.html (accessed May 7, 2011).

25. East Turkistan Islamic Movement (东突厥斯坦伊斯兰运动/东突厥斯坦伊斯兰党). In August, several attacks happened in Xijiang, the Autonomy Area of Uyghurs in Northwestern China. One of these attacks claimed the lives of 16 soldiers http://www.caijing.com.cn/2008-08-05/110002722.html (accessed August 11, 2009).

26. CCTV 7, July 26 and August 2, 2008, *Handbook of Olympic Security*, http://v.youku.com/v_show/id_XMzY3NTQ3MjQ=.html, http://v.youku.com/v_show/id_XMzc1Nzk4MTY=.html (accessed May 10, 2011).

27. In Chinese it is called "东突恐怖势力," which is often related to Xinjiang independence organizations.

28. In Chinese it is called "藏独势力," referring to organizations and individuals who strive for Tibetan political independence.

29. In Chinese it is called "法轮功组织," a religious movement, which has been prohibited in China since 1999.

30. *International Herald Leader*, June 29, 2008, "Main Threats of Beijing Olympics from East Turkestan Terrorist and Tibetan separatists" (国际先驱导报, 2008年6月29日, "北京奥运主要威胁来自东突藏独 美FBI助阵反恐"), http://mil.news.sina.com.cn/p/2008-07-04/0944508715.html (accessed April 6, 2011).

31. As explained to us during the interviews with volunteers.

32. 东突厥斯坦伊斯兰运动/东突厥斯坦伊斯兰党.

33. From an interview with Ms. Liu, a governmental employee in her 50s, who patrolled on the streets from late June to August 25, 2008.

34. Whereas surveillance increased, media censorship was reduced during the Olympics, presenting an open society to the outside world. Soon after the Olympics, it became impossible to access Facebook, Twitter or YouTube.

35. The original interview could be found on http://www.neurope.eu/articles/What-I-really-want-is-good-Games-for-the-athletes/89034.php (accessed August 25, 2010). Here, Rogge said, "Security is a number one priority" in English, but the Chinese media translated it into "Olympic security is more important than the competitions." This was repeatedly mentioned in the Chinese media; see, for example, http://news.xinhuanet.com/mrdx/2008-07/20/content_8587550.htm (accessed August 25, 2010) and Channel 4, July 16, 2008, *Focus Today: Security in Beijing.*

36. http://gb.chinareviewnews.com/doc/1006/4/0/5/100640553.html?coluid=7&kindid=0&docid=100640553&mdate=0509140806 (accessed August 25, 2011).

37. CCTV 5, June 23, 2008, *Road to Beijing: Emergency Measure, Security and Safety for BOG* (Hosted by Sha Tong, 沙桐) (中央五台, 2008年7月23日, "北京之路: 突发与应对(沙桐主持)").

38. http://big5.china.com.cn/military/txt/2008-07/09/content_15976539.htm (accessed August 15, 2010).

39. CCTV 5, July 23, 2008, *Road to Beijing*; see also Channel 7, July 26 and August 2, 2008, *Handbook of Olympic Security*.

40. CCTV 11, August 27, 2008, *Law Online: "Security of BOG: The Olympic Defenders"* (中央电视台11台，2008年8月27日，"法制在线：奥运保卫者").

41. Ibid.

42. *Dream Weaver* (2007), directed by Gu Yun; and also in CCTV 11, July 21, 2008, *One on One: Interview with Gu Yun: Security Military of BOG* (中央电视台11台，2008年7月21日，"面对面：顾筠：七年奥运梦：北京奥运的安保部队").

43. For example, Channel 4, July 16, 2008, *Focus Today*; CCTV 5, July 23, 2008, *Road to Beijing*.

44. Channel 5 of China Central Television, "The Story of Lunchbox," Section 4 of Episode 6, *Aoyun Dang'an*.

45. http://military.cnnb.com.cn/system/2008/07/23/005692086.shtml (accessed August 15, 2010); http://mil.news.sina.com.cn/p/2008-07-23/0857512778.html (accessed August 15, 2010); http://bbs.voc.com.cn/topic-1576891-1-1.html (accessed August 15, 2010).

46. It is unclear to what extent this was the case; the tickets we bought for various events were not personalized or linked to our names.

47. See CCTV 7, July 26 and August 2, 2008, *Handbook of Olympic Security*; http://www.space.cetin.net.cn/index.asp?modelname=new_space%2Fnews_nr&FractionNo=&titleno=XWEN0000&recno=50402 (accessed May 10, 2011).

48. They were shown frequently; see, for example, in *Dream Weaver, Focus Today, Road to Beijing*, etc.

49. http://www.chinanews.com.cn/olympic/news/2008/07-02/1300374.shtml (accessed August 13, 2010); similar saying was mentioned by Zhou Yongkang, http://news.xinhuanet.com/legal/2008-08/05/content_8959976.htm (accessed August 13, 2010).

50. In Chinese, the mass route is known as 群众路线.

16
Promoting "Civility," Excluding the Poor (Vancouver 2010)

Jacqueline Kennelly

The 2010 Vancouver Winter Olympics ushered in "the most complex domestic [surveillance] operation ever undertaken in Canada."[1] Preparations began at least four years prior to ensure the smooth interinstitutional collaboration between the Royal Canadian Mounted Police (Canada's federal policing arm), municipal police forces, the Canadian Armed Forces, and private security firms, which together became the Vancouver 2010 Integrated Security Unit. These "official" aspects of surveillance for the Vancouver Games were supplemented by legislative changes, the implementation of new bylaws, and city "guidelines" for residents of Vancouver. This chapter traces these initiatives, as represented within media reports, legislature records, and official documentation, and asks: for *whom* are these practices intended? Through a qualitative research project designed to investigate the experiences of homeless and street-involved youth in the year prior to and during the Vancouver Winter Olympics, the chapter attempts to illuminate the effects of such surveillance regimes on the most marginalized members of host cities. In doing so, I wish to highlight larger issues pertaining to the neoliberalization of city spaces, intensified under the auspices of Olympic preparations, and the implications these have for marginalized residents' citizenship rights within urban spaces.

The qualitative data from which this chapter is derived was collected as part of an ongoing comparative study documenting the experiences of homeless, street-involved, or marginally housed youth before, during, and after the Olympic Games in Vancouver (2010) and London (2012). Specifically, data for this chapter was collected the year before the Vancouver 2010 Games (February to April 2009) and during the Games themselves (February 2010). Interviews, focus groups, and an arts-based project were conducted with a total of 33 youth in the first fieldwork period; interviews and focus groups were conducted with 27 youth in the second fieldwork period. Participants ranged in age from 15 to 24; the groups were highly diverse in both ethnicity and gender, including a fairly even mix of male and female, as well as some transgendered, participants. There was also a disproportionately high number of Aboriginal participants, reflective of the specific histories of colonialism and subsequent impoverishment experienced by Aboriginal youth and children in Canada (Downe, 2006).

The chapter proceeds as follows: I begin with a discussion of the surveillance preparations put in place for the Vancouver Olympics, tracing the semantics and logistics of Canada's largest peacetime surveillance operation. I use the experiences of the youth participants with whom I worked to critically assess the effects of these surveillance practices on the city's most marginalized populations. Looking not only at surveillance during the Games, this first part of the chapter also examines the effects of pre-Olympic policing practices, and their meanings for young homeless people. Next, the chapter turns to what I call the "soft" aspects of surveillance – that is, the educational and regulatory efforts made to ensure that the entire city population is "on-side" and "on-message" with the Olympic promotional apparatus (as opposed to the more overt, or "hard," forms of surveillance that take the form of policing and security checks, for example). I conclude with some reflections on the implications of both "hard" and "soft" surveillance practices associated with mega-events such as the Olympic Games for marginalized young peoples' sense of inclusion, safety, and belonging within Olympic host cities.

Justifying security measures: terrorists, activists, and those who protect the sponsors

Critical theorists of contemporary security culture note that much of the rhetoric on which enhanced surveillance is justified promulgates *risk* as the central category of concern, where surveillance practices are directed at "the pre-emption of the catastrophic event" (Dean, 2010; see also Bajc, 2007a). As noted by Bajc (2007b: 1653), "Surveillance has become the primary means through which states control uncertainty, act on perceived threats, and facilitate the resulting change within their borders." It is within this context that states justify huge and ascending expenditures for Games-related surveillance. In the case of the Vancouver Games, an initial security budget of $175 million ballooned to roughly $850 million by the time the Games were held.[2] Such amplifications of costs were explicitly justified in terms that referenced the yet unknown but always potential existence of threat:

> The RCMP-led Vancouver 2010 Integrated Security Unit acknowledged it can't protect the Games for the $175 million it has been given. ... Into this mix add a host of world events – the rapid rise of militant extremism, Millenium Bomber Ahmed Ressam, the Sept. 11 attacks, the wars in Iraq and Afghanistan, and the four London bombings – which has the impact of driving up threat levels.[3]

While potential terrorist acts were most frequently cited as the rationale for enhanced security, concerns about "protest groups" were also noted; for instance, in 2008 the *Vancouver Sun* reported that police planners for the Winter Games were seeking permission to ignore public requests for information under the federal Access to Information Act because "such information can be put to nefarious counter-intelligence use by terrorist or protest groups compromising the security of the 2010 Games."[4]

Not included in Olympic security spending estimates are the costs of refocused policing practices in marginalized neighborhoods deemed to be a danger to the "quality of life" in Vancouver. For example, the 2009 business plan of the Vancouver Police Department included an explicit focus on the Downtown Eastside, a low-income neighborhood that has often been the target of policing efforts, and a locale that is characterized by city elites as a blight on the reputation of Vancouver as a tourist destination and global city.[5] The plan included additional numbers of police patrolling the neighborhood, more street spot checks (whereby a person can be stopped and asked for identification or other questions), and more by-law violation tickets issued.[6] The plan suggested that "with more officers being dedicated to the area, and more of their shift spent enforcing the law on the street, the disorder and offending associated with this area will decrease, increasing the quality of life and safety for all residents and visitors in the area."[7]

While the chimera of safety makes for persuasive public rhetoric, an important question to be asked is, *which residents'* quality of life is being enhanced through these practices? When asked in a focus group how homeless youth – most of whom had recently lived in the Downtown Eastside and still spent time there[8] – felt about seeing more police on the street, the group was unanimous about feeling less safe, rather than more. As one participant remarked in an interview, "The police are the ones I don't feel safe about." When I asked why, he replied that the police are "the ones who can hurt you. Other people aren't going to hurt me because I don't have anything on them. They don't have anything on me. They've seen me walking around since I was a kid. I know some pretty crazy dudes. And they would actually protect me, right? But the cops you can never trust."

Such remarks are unsurprising, given the degree to which homeless people in general, and street youth in particular, are subject to criminalization and negative interactions with police (Mitchell and Heynen, 2009; Mayers, 2001). They also signal the long-standing issues of entrenched impoverishment within Canada, and in the Eastside of Vancouver in particular, issues which have worsened over the past several decades and taken on a distinctively youthful character in the process. Vancouver's Downtown Eastside has been reported to be the "poorest postal code in Canada,"[9] where average incomes are substantially lower than in the rest of the city, an illegal drug trade and street prostitution are highly visible, and the HIV infection rate is as high as that of the poorest countries in Africa. Vancouver also carries the dubious distinction of belonging to the province with the highest degree of child and youth poverty in Canada.[10] Vancouver's Eastside, which consists of both the Downtown Eastside and residential neighborhoods such as Grandview-Woodland and Strathcona, has historically seen the highest concentration of child and youth poverty in the city.[11] Although the Vancouver Olympic events were largely situated outside of this impoverished neighborhood, the "Olympic lane," which was a designated street lane reserved for Olympic traffic, ran right through the main thoroughfare of the Downtown Eastside (along Hastings Street). The Athletes Village was walking distance from the neighborhood, and the Olympic media center was mere blocks away.

The shifting priorities of policing in pre-Olympic Vancouver were felt by the youth most strongly in the year before and the month immediately preceding the Games; in both 2009 and 2010, youth reported being more frequently harassed for offenses that were previously disregarded, such as jaywalking, littering, and possession of drugs. In each of the instances, the youth remarked upon both the increasing pressures they were experiencing from the police and the degree to which it seemed disproportionate to the actual offense. Their overall impression was of being specifically harassed, particularly in the period leading up to the Games; the youth believed this to be an effort to "clean the streets" in preparation for the arrival of the "rich people" they associated with the Olympic Games. For example, in 2009, Alison reported that "they're arresting you more for possession. They didn't care for possession before. They'd just smash your pipe. And try to intimidate you. But that [was] it." In the same year, Artemis reported that:

> Cops are ticketing people for like jaywalking, ridiculous reasons. They're searching, like, they aren't supposed to just stop somebody on the street and search them or whatever and they're doing that. And actually one officer told me his boss demanded that he hand out tickets, and he wouldn't have given me a ticket otherwise but he's going to lose his job. So I didn't ask him if that had anything to do with the 2010 [Olympics], but that could be it very well.

Similar comments were made during a focus group discussion in 2009, where one participant reported that "people are getting arrested left, right, and center." In 2010, Justine remarked that the arrival of the Olympics in her city had been heralded by "more laws." "If you throw a [cigarette] butt on the ground they'll stop you and charge you for that. [For] littering." When I asked her to elaborate on this experience, she reported, "[The police] let us go but they said to throw the butt in the garbage can or in an ashtray outside. I'm like, there's tons of butts on the ground." She explained that this experience happened about a month before the Games began.

The accounts above clearly demonstrate that the business plan of the Vancouver Police Department was being rolled out in the period before the Games, and homeless and street-involved youth were feeling its effects. Indeed, they often experienced such policing as differentially applied, and they felt themselves to be the unfair targets of these increased interventions. Justine believed that she was singled out by the police, who used the excuse of enforcing an obscure littering law; as she noted, "there's tons of butts on the ground." Likewise, Artemis suspected that his increased encounters with police were spurred on by Olympic-related incentives.

By contrast, while low-income and homeless youth felt themselves to be the target of increased policing, corporate sponsors of the Olympics were hiring private security firms in order to enhance their own sense of safety.[12] Such security took the form of bodyguards hired to protect key employees, and in one case the securing of an entire hotel "on behalf of a major communications firm that's a major partner for the Olympics."[13] Such increased security is justified on the basis of the sheer size of the Olympics, whereby "companies realize the police will have difficulties dealing with day-to-day security issues, and are taking it on themselves to ensure security for their own key staff and events."[14] Not coincidentally, those who are able to afford such extra protection also happen to be wealthy outsiders to the city in question; their presence is simultaneously used as justification for the increased policing imposed on low-income neighborhoods. This raises again the question of *for whom* the streets are being made safe: for local residents and the most marginalized members of the city's population? Or for corporate sponsors of the Games, temporary visitors who will be spending tourist dollars, and global media conveying images of Vancouver around the world?

Of relevance to such a question is to consider the experiences of the youth *during* the Games. While many reported intensified police interactions in the year before and particularly the month immediately preceding the opening ceremonies, the youth were mostly unanimous in feeling that their interactions with police dropped substantially while the Games were happening. As mentioned above, policing and security for the 2010 Olympics was governed by Vancouver's Mounted Police–led Integrated Security Unit. The goal of this body was to have police "on every corner" during the Games themselves[15]; this was achieved through the secondment of approximately 6000 additional police officers from 119 agencies across Canada, approximately 5000 Canadian Armed Forces troops, and approximately 4800 private security guards (not including the private security that was already on hand through individual businesses and property owners).[16] This was in addition to the 1327 Vancouver Police Department officers available as of January 2010,[17] a number that had grown from 1124 in 2004.[18]

Given the swell of security officials within the city, it is somewhat remarkable that the youth reported a drop in police interactions: surely the behavior of the youth did not change so much during the Games that *less* police intervention was warranted? And surely the presence of approximately *fifteen times* the normal number of security personnel would imply that *more* rather than less interactions would be likely? That this did not manifest suggests that the surveillance apparatus constructed around the Vancouver 2010 Games was concerned not only with surveillance practices but also with projecting the appearance of the city as liberal, tolerant, and welcoming. Given the intense focus on Vancouver by global media during the Games, any incident that might suggest that the police were engaging in targeted enforcement that infringed on the human rights or civil liberties of marginalized peoples within the city would not have enhanced the image that Vancouver elites were hoping to convey. The Canadian Armed Forces were particularly sensitive to this dynamic; reflecting back on the Vancouver Games, Rear-Admiral Tyrone Pile notes that "with all the effort put into preparing, just as much effort was taken to maintain a low profile throughout the Olympics."[19] This was achieved by "using an array of surveillance technologies, including closed-circuit cameras, electronic sensors, and unmanned vehicles flying high over the Olympic venues in Vancouver and Whistler."[20]

Such sensitivity to appearances by the Vancouver Integrated Security Unit meant that homeless and street-involved youth experienced a welcome reprieve from constant police interactions during the Games themselves. For instance, Sandy conveyed being harassed by police, with escalating degrees of violence, in the weeks and months leading up to the Games, particularly when she and her friends were sitting on the steps of the Vancouver Art Gallery. Significantly, the art gallery is located adjacent to Robson Square, the center of Olympic celebrations within Vancouver. However, once the Games began, she reported that being moved on by the police "doesn't usually happen anymore, with that big TV screen there [near the steps of the Vancouver Art Gallery]." When I asked why she replied: "Because the TV screen's there. ... It's a big fucking TV screen, have you seen it? ... Because now we're not loitering." She laughed. "Now we're not loitering *because* we're watching TV. Isn't that awesome?"

Captured in this vignette is the malleable nature of so-called criminal behavior; what had been intensely surveilled and punished in the weeks preceding the Games had now become banal or innocent in light of the media spectacle of the Olympic Games ("now we're not loitering *because* we're watching TV"; see also Kennelly and Watt, 2011). Thus the "hard" aspects of Olympic surveillance did not produce monolithically negative interactions for homeless youth with police; in this case, it had a mitigating effect and permitted youth, temporarily, greater mobility and freedom from surveillance than they typically experience within Vancouver. Such freedom is certainly short-lived, and not predictable; nor does it outweigh the intensification of surveillance experienced by the youth in the year preceding the Games.

Self-regulation in the global Olympic city: civility, censorship, and city marketing

The official implementation of security protocols, through the establishment of the Integrated Security Unit and the 2009 business plan of the Vancouver Police Department, form one arm of pre-Olympic and Olympic surveillance practices. The picture would not be complete, however, if we did not also consider the "soft" forms of Olympic surveillance, particularly relevant in liberal democratic states where populations are encouraged to be self-regulating through both the threat of legal consequences and non-coercive means such as education and media (Rose, 1999; Brown, 2005). In the case of the Vancouver Olympics, these took the form of bylaws, legislation, and informal practices and protocols designed to ensure that the members of a host city comply with the efforts to "secure" a city in preparation for the Olympics; affective language such as "civility," "pride," and "patriotism" are often bandied about in support of this goal. Several elements are disguised by these practices and their attendant language; one such is the disproportionate burden laid on marginalized members of a city's population. Another is the degree to which these practices are designed not to ensure the safety of a population within the host city but to prop up the business interests of the corporate sponsors to the Olympics. This section of the chapter examines some instances of these practices and the effects they had on the youth with whom I spoke.

Just before the Olympics arrived, the City of Vancouver released a Vancouver Olympic protocol guide, directed at 600 City of Vancouver employees. The protocol includes such detailed instructions as ensuring that one's socks match one's pants, the proper manner in which to shake hands, and the degree of openness with which to smile:

> A smile denotes warmth, openness and friendliness. Smile "gently" and with sincerity. Be careful not to overdo it. False smiles can look artificial, and never-ending smiles may invite suspicion. A frown or a furrowed brow suggests anger or worry, even if your words are positive.[21]

The protocol guidelines make it clear that the task of City of Vancouver employees during the Olympics is not only to perform their jobs but also to stay "on message" with city marketing strategies, ensuring through their own good behavior that the city is represented in the best possible light. The City of Vancouver also spent $25,000 on a supplement entitled *Host City 101* for the *Vancouver Sun*, one of the major daily newspapers in the city. In it, city residents were given a top ten list for how to be a good host, "including offering directions, telling people where to get visitor information, or directing them to police or hospitals. Beyond all that it urges people to 'share your love of the city' and 'enjoy yourself.'"[22] Mayor Gregor

Robertson writes in the supplement: "With the world's spotlight shining on Vancouver for the 2010 Winter Games, we have an unprecedented opportunity to boost our local economy and showcase our city to the world."[23]

How do such initiatives fit into an investigation of Olympic-related security? One way to understand their relationship is by turning to the concept of "city marketing." E.J. McCann (2009: 119) notes that city marketing schemes generally promote "the city as welcoming and safe, vibrant and fun, tolerant and accepting of social and cultural difference, environmentally friendly, culturally rich, business friendly, and as strategically and conveniently located." In order to enhance such an image, McCann suggests that cities will often engage the following tactics:

> [T]he provision of packages of business incentives, the (re)building, policing, and cleaning of the urban built environment to keep its appearance in line with the city's marketing image, and continual efforts to maintain coherence in the city's marketing message by keeping disparate interest groups either "on message" or out of the spotlight. (McCann, 2009: 119)

When the logic of city marketing is at the fore, the stage is set for not only the publication of somewhat comical protocols and top ten lists but also strategies of city cleansing that rely on policing and security to ensure that a city "looks its best" when the Olympics come to town. As noted by Christian Tagsold in Chapter 3 on Tokyo in this book, city cleansing strategies were used for just this purpose in Tokyo in 1964. In the case of Vancouver, these strategies could not be explicit, as part of the image of a tolerant, liberal, Western democratic city is that it does *not* engage in such practices. In other words, it was in Vancouver's marketing interests to appear safe yet simultaneously *not* appear like a repressive police state that might deter tourism or investment. This is in contrast with the practices of Moscow in 1980, as documented by Carol Marmor-Drews in Chapter 8 of this book, which focused quite openly on cleaning the streets of the homeless and drug users as part of their preparations for the Games.

The balance between appearing safe yet also ensuring that a city "looks its best" seemed to be struck in Vancouver by ensuring that police interventions happened gradually, incrementally shifting the sites of visible poverty into less prominent areas of the city. For instance, the year before the Games many of the youth remarked on the disappearance of activity from a community park in the middle of the Downtown Eastside, locally referred to as "Pigeon Park." During a focus group, Alison pointed out that "the people that are getting arrested are the people that are really out in the open, like Pigeon Park and stuff. Like, every night I go home [after] work. And when I go by...the cop is always sitting by Pigeon Park now." When asked what had happened to the people in Pigeon Park, another woman replied, "They're in the alleys." This was confirmed by another, who said, "Yeah. They're in the alleys. Now the cops don't go down the alleys anymore. Like even I still walk around there. When I first came here [Pigeon] park was crammed with people fighting, doing whatever. Now you're lucky to see more than one person sitting there for more than five minutes."

Youth also reported various individual experiences with the police pressuring them to move out of highly visible downtown neighborhoods, both the year before the Games began and during the weeks immediately preceding the opening ceremonies. One young man reported, "I've been told [by the police] to get off Granville Street for the whole night just because I was alone and had a suitcase." When asked when that had happened and whether the police had given a reason, he replied: "Just before the Olympics" and that he thought it was "because I was homeless."

One manner in which such pressure was applied to homeless youth was via a project introduced in 2006 by former City of Vancouver Mayor Sam Sullivan. In his Project Civil City initiative, he was explicit about its goal being to ensure that the city was ready for the arrival of the Olympics in 2010.[24] Part of the Project Civil City initiative was the Downtown Ambassadors program; unlike other ambassador programs in major Canadian cities, this one made use of trained security guards to patrol city streets and ensure that the codes of "civility" implied by the title of "Civil City" were respected (Sleiman and Lippert, 2010). Run by Genesis Security and the Downtown Vancouver Business Improvement Association, Ambassadors are "trained to provide hospitality assistance and crime prevention services" with a focus on what they term "quality of life" issues "such as panhandling, litter, theft, illegal vending, and graffiti."[25] The youth I spoke to in 2009 had many negative reports of interactions with the Ambassadors. Marianne, a young Aboriginal woman, described the following encounter:

> I remember when [the Ambassadors] first came out I was pregnant and I was sitting down on Granville Street. Like, I wasn't panhandling. I wasn't asking people for money and they were like, you need to move. And I was like, what?...I'm eight-and-a-half months pregnant. They're like, we don't care. It's not our job, we're trying to make our city look more nice. You know? They told me, it doesn't help to have homeless people kicking around on the streets....You're making our city look bad. Don't you know? We have the Olympics coming.

Marianne was not alone in experiencing the Downtown Ambassadors as extremely problematic. In 2009, Pivot Legal Society and the Vancouver Area Network of Drug Users launched a complaint against the Ambassadors, which was heard by the British Columbia Human Rights Tribunal.[26] Pivot and the Network alleged that the group "discriminates against the homeless and drug users in the city," stating that they "'act very much like homeless police' because they tell people who sit, sleep or panhandle on sidewalks to move along, and that they are not welcome."[27] Although the suit was dismissed in 2012, Tribunal Member Tonie Beharrell made the following important caveat:

> My finding that the complainants have not established a connection between the adverse treatment alleged and a prohibited ground of discrimination should not be taken as a finding that I accept the DVBIA's assertion in this regard. In particular, I note that the evidence...raises the potential that the Ambassadors were not acting solely on the basis of illegal behaviour, but were also targeting certain types of individuals. I also note that the removal of individuals...is, intuitively, much more likely to occur with respect to individuals who are or appear to be members of the Class than with other members of the public.[28]

As noted above, the Downtown Ambassadors program was begun in order to prepare the city for the arrival of the Olympics, through recourse to the euphemistic language of "civility." In doing so, the program succeeded in making the lives of marginalized people within the city significantly more difficult. We must question here what concept of "civility" is being promoted through the "Project Civil City" initiative, and who are perceived as "uncivil" under this definition.

New legislation was not required to affect the results described above; nonetheless, new legislation was introduced at the provincial level that gave the police even more powers to move homeless people off the streets. Officially titled the Assistance to Shelter Act, activists dubbed it the "Olympic Kidnapping Law," in light of the authorization it granted to police to forcibly move a person from the street to a shelter. Ostensibly limited by police assessment as to whether the person in question is considered to be "at risk" due to inclement weather, the British Columbia Civil Liberties Association decried the law, stating that "This bill would have police arrest citizens who are not guilty of any crime, and detain them without any charge, simply because they are homeless."[29] Likewise, the City of Vancouver introduced an "Olympic By-law Package" in July 2009 that the Civil Liberties Association successfully challenged on the basis of its infringement on free speech and Canada's constitutional guarantees. The bylaws were designed to protect the interests of the Olympics' corporate sponsors by ensuring that small businesses did not make use of copyrighted terms such as "Olympics," "Winter," "Gold" and other Olympic-related terminology without paying for the rights. If violated, the bylaws carried a maximum fine of $10,000 a day and a jail term of six months. Critics were concerned about the chilling effect that these bylaws could have on anti-Olympic protesters; as noted by Robert Holmes, president of the Civil Liberties Association at the time, "Telling people who exercise free speech that local authorities may barge in, rip down signs inside your property, fine you or throw you in jail will under-score the growing impression that our governments care more about their own camera appearances at Olympic events than about people's rights."[30] While the City of Vancouver eventually changed their bylaws "'to make sure it's crystal clear that' constitutional rights 'can't be abused,'" according to Mayor Gregor Robertson, the modified bylaws remained in place for the duration of the Games in order to protect corporate interests.[31]

Despite the victory of the Civil Liberties Association in softening the language of the bylaws, they were still used in one significant case to justify the removal of an anti-Olympic mural located in the Downtown Eastside. The graffiti by-law required "occupants as well as owners to remove graffiti from private property, thus providing for more timely removal of graffiti from buildings that are not owner occupied, and improving the look of the city leading up to the Games."[32] This by-law was proposed to become a permanent change, remaining in place after the Olympics were gone. At the implementation stage, the City of Vancouver made it clear that "public art" was to be exempted from its sign by-law provisions; nonetheless, a mural depicting the Olympic rings as four sad faces and one smiley face was ordered removed from the outside wall of a Downtown Eastside gallery. The City claimed that its removal was ordered on the basis of its new graffiti by-law, rather than the sign by-law, which required owners and occupants to remove graffiti from their habitation in preparation for the Games.[33] The gallery curator felt that the removal was ordered due to the context of the work, noting, "over the years she has hung about 30 murals there, and has never had any trouble."[34] The City denied that the mural was removed due to content, stating that a city inspector described the work as "black graffiti tags on wood paneling covering a window."[35] Whether the City ordered the mural removed on the grounds of content or through their perception that it was undesirable graffiti, the introduction of the Olympic By-law Package had the effect of censoring the artistic expression of at least one Vancouver artist. Taken in combination with other Olympic-related legislation and by-laws, this example adds to a broader picture of a city's population being required to shape their behavior in alignment with the demands of the Olympic Games. The youth participants were quite clear about the reasons behind this intensified pressure, understanding the city's obligation to portray a particular image. As noted by Richard, "The Olympics mean you've got to fit a certain [image]. The city has to fit a certain look. Like a certain way." When asked to describe this look, he replied, "Well it's like clean and I've noticed that a lot of homeless people are getting locked up and put in jails because they're homeless and the city people don't want to address it. They'd rather just sweep it under the table." The youth also felt strongly that such practices were unfair, and resulted in their increased marginali-zation in order to make way for affluent outsiders. As noted by Jess:

Well I was on the street four months ago and all that I would hear people talk about is when the Olympics come here they're either going to find [temporary] housing for people or stick them in jail when they see them on the street because we don't want to look bad because we're getting the Olympics. So what? You're going to toss us out because some richie-rich people have the Olympics for a few days? That's bullshit. Right? They don't have any money to spend on low-income housing because they're spending all the money on the Olympics.

Such reflections raise the question posed earlier in the chapter: who benefits from Olympic security, and indeed from the hosting of the Games? Much is made within Olympic promotional materials of the so-called legacies of an Olympic Games for a host city, and it is on the basis of these legacies that bid committees convince local populations and governments to stand behind their bid. Yet increasingly empirical studies such as this one are documenting that the positive legacies of the Olympic Games are questionable at best, certainly appearing to create more difficulty than benefit for those who are already most marginalized within a host city.

Conclusions

This chapter has traced both the "hard" and "soft" aspects of surveillance in the name of security in Vancouver in the year preceding and during the 2010 Winter Games. It has done so in part by juxtaposing the "facts" of security spending, numbers of security personnel, and the introduction of new bylaws and legislation with the lived experiences of homeless and street-involved youth residing in Vancouver the year before and during the Olympic Games. Suggesting that a complete picture of Olympic security can only be obtained by considering both the official numbers *and* the regulatory practices imposed on a city as a result of hosting an Olympic Games, the chapter has attempted to illustrate the effects of such practices for a city's most marginalized members.

The experiences of the youth, as captured through qualitative methods, raise important questions about the priorities and focus of a city once it has secured the prize of hosting the ultimate in sporting mega-events, the Olympic Games. While bid committees make extravagant promises of social legacies, including expanded social housing, opportunities for young people, and a commitment to protect a city's low-income residents, the reality, after the Games are completed, is that the majority of these commitments remain unfulfilled.[36] What remains is a security legacy (Giulianotti and Klauser, 2010) as opposed to a social legacy and city marketing as opposed to enhanced citizen rights to their own city. In addition to the bylaws (some of which were permanent, such as the graffiti by-law) and the changes in legislation (such as the Assistance to Shelter Act), Vancouver continues to carry the security legacy of surveillance technology infrastructure that was put in place for the Games, including permanent wiring for Closed Circuit Television cameras and the construction of a new control room for their deployment.[37]

In light of such outcomes, it is important to return to the question with which this chapter opened: for whom are Olympic-related surveillance practices intended? Evidence documented here points clearly in one direction: surveillance is most decidedly *not* in place to benefit homeless and street-involved youth, nor, arguably, is it meant to assist in supporting the well-being of other marginalized people within a city. Rather, Olympic-related surveillance, at both the "hard" and "soft" levels, seems to be designed to protect the interests and bodies of Olympic corporate sponsors, affluent tourists, and the Vancouver business interests who benefit from city marketing practices. In light of this, it is imperative that we question the implications of hosting an Olympic Games for local democracy and the inclusion of the young and the poor.

Notes

The author would like to extend thanks to the many talented research assistants who worked on this project, including Ryan Boyd, Amelia Curran, Christopher Enman, and Meghan Johnston. Particular recognition is owed to Chris Enman, who spent countless hours gathering information used within this chapter, and to Amelia Curran, who did an expert job of collecting the relevant literature. Thank you also to the anonymous reviewer, who provided helpful feedback on an earlier version of the chapter. Finally, the author extends immense gratitude to the youth who participated in the research in Vancouver.

1. Blondin, Y. (2010) "Gold medal performance," *Air Force Crew Brief, 8*(2), 11. Accessed May 12, 2012, at http://www.rcaf-arc.forces.gc.ca/v2/cb-ca/nr-sp/index-eng.asp?id=10784#s4.
2. The Canadian Press (2010, December 21) "RCMP's drug probes hindered by Olympic security demands: WikiLeaks cable," *The Globe and Mail*. Retrieved May 20, 2012, from http://m.theglobeandmail.com/news/national/british-columbia/rcmps-drug-probes-hindered-by-olympic-security-demands-wikileaks-cable/article1846406/?service=mobile
3. Lee, J. and M. Cernetig (2007, August 5) "Security at Vancouver Olympics a complicated, costly problem," *Edmonton Journal*, A5.
4. Lee, J. (2008, November 10) "Games security eyed exemption to delay information requests," *Vancouver Sun*, A4.
5. Preston, G. (2006, August 18) "Beggars, drug dealers kill convention business," *Vancouver Sun*, A1.
6. Pablo, C. (2009, January 21) "Vancouver police plan Downtown Eastside crackdown ahead of Olympics," *Georgia Straight*. Retrieved May 4, 2012, from http://www.straight.com/print/197388.
7. Ibid.
8. The homeless shelter in which the interviews and focus groups were held was strategically located *away* from the Downtown Eastside, in part to move young people away from the difficulties associated with the neighborhood.

9. Downtown Eastside Community Monitoring Report (2000) *A Review of Demographic Data for Chinatown, the Downtown Eastside, Gastown, Strathcona, Victory Square*. Vancouver: Vancouver Municipal Working Paper Series.
10. First Call: BC Child and Youth Advocacy Coalition (2009) *BC Campaign 2000: 2009 Child Poverty Report Card*. Vancouver: First Call: BC Child and Youth Advocacy Coalition and Social Planning and Research Council of BC (SPARC BC).
11. Tupechka, T., Martin, K., and Douglas, M. (1997) *Our Own Backyard: Walking Tours of Grandview Woodland*. Vancouver: Our own backyard.
12. Lombardi, R. (2010) "Executive protection, Olympic style," *Canadian Security Magazine* Feb/Mar, 2010, 8.
13. Ibid.
14. Ibid.
15. *Times-Colonist* (2010, February 12) "Police to be 'on every corner,'" *Times-Colonist*, A9.
16. Lawson, D. (2011, February 16) Project management and the RCMP security mission for the Vancouver 2010 Olympic Games: safe and secure Games through Integrated Security model [PDF Presentation]. Retrieved May 20, 2012, from http://www.pmi.bc.ca/storage/presentations/CWCC%20PMI%20 Presentation%2016%20Feb%202011.pdf
17. Vancouver Police Department (n.d.) Vancouver Police Department: Organization. Retrieved May 20, 2012, from http://vancouver.ca/police/organization/index. html
18. Demers, S., Palmer, A., and Griffiths, C. (2007) *Vancouver Police Department Patrol Deployment Study*. City of Vancouver. Retrieved May 20, 2012, from http:// vancouver.ca/police/assets/pdf/studies/vpd-study-patrol-deployment.pdf
19. Pile, T. (2010) "The Canadian Forces: Supporting RCMP-led security for the 2010 Winter Games," *RCMP Gazette, 72*(2), 30–31.
20. Akin, D. (2008, May 21) "Military plans 'discreet' presence at 2010 Olympics," *Edmonton Journal*, A5.
21. Vallis, M. (2010, January 27) "Vancouver Olympics protocol guide gives workers advice on smiling and other tricky tasks" [Weblog comment]. Retrieved May 20, 2012, from http://pr1vacy.wordpress.com/category/vancouver-olympics-protocol-guide/
22. McNair, A. (2010, January 6) "Mind your P's and Q's during Olympics" [Weblog comment]. Retrieved May 20, 2012, from http://unambig.com/mind-your-ps-and-qs-during-olympics/
23. Slobogen, T. (2010, January 6) "Mind your manners during the 2010 Games: four page guide tells us how to welcome the world." *News 1130*. Retrieved May 20, 2012, from http://www.news1130.com/news/local/article/14274–mind-your-manners-during-the-2010-games. Interestingly, neither of these guides (in Notes 22 and 23) can now be accessed through the Web, though media accounts of their existence remain.
24. Project Civil City tackles crime, public disorder and social issues in Vancouver (2006, November 27). Retrieved May 20, 2012, from http://www.samsullivan. ca/2006/11/project-civil-city-tackles-cri
25. "Downtown Ambassador Program" (n.d.). Retrieved May 20, 2012, from http:// www.genesissecurity.com/content.php?section=23.
26. CBC News (2009, July 7) "Downtown Ambassadors to face B.C. Human Rights Tribunal," *CBC News*. Retrieved May 20, 2012, from http://www.cbc.ca/news/ canada/british-columbia/story/2009/07/07/bc-downtown-ambassadors-human-rights-tribunal-homeless.html

27. Canadian Press (2012, February 7). "Human rights case against Vancouver's Downtown Ambassadors dismissed," *CBC News*. Retrieved May 20, 2012, from http://www.cbc.ca/news/canada/british-columbia/story/2012/02/07/bc-vancouver-downtown-ambassadors.html

28. Bennett, D. (2012, February 7) "Tribunal member qualifies 'Downtown Ambassadors' decision" [Weblog comment]. Retrieved May 20, 2012, from http://www.pivotlegal.org/pivot-points/blog/tribunal-member-qualifies-downtown-ambassadors-decision

29. Paulsen, M. (2009, September 21) "BC Preparing New Law to Apprehend Homeless," *The Tyee*. Retrieved May 20, 2012, from http://thetyee.ca/News/2009/09/21/HomelessLaw/

30. CBC News (2009, October 11) "Anti-Olympic signs could mean jail: rights group," *CBC News*. Retrieved May 20, 2012, from http://www.cbc.ca/news/canada/british-columbia/story/2009/10/09/bc-anti-olympic-sign-law-bccla.html

31. Schneider, J. (2009, November 18) "Vancouver to change Olympic law that critics call 'Beijing 2.0,'" Retrieved May 20, 2012, from http://www.bloomberg.com/apps/news?pid=newsarchive&sid=a.9TPJ4DXPg4

32. City of Vancouver (2009, July 6) 2010 Winter Games by-law regarding the Vancouver 2010 Olympic and Paralympic Winter Games [Administrative report]. Retrieved May 20, 2012, from http://vancouver.ca/ctyclerk/cclerk/20090721/documents/a4.pdf

33. Lederman, M. (2009, December 11) "Vancouver orders removal of anti-Olympic mural," *Globe and Mail*, A4.

34. Ibid.

35. Ibid.

36. Impact on Communities Coalition (2009, April 19) 2010 Olympic oversight interim report card. Retrieved May 20, 2012, from http://iocc.ca/documents/2009-04-19_IOCC_2ndInterimReportCard.pdf.

37. Inwood, D. (2009, July 2) "Will surveillance cameras become an Olympic legacy?" *The Province*. Retrieved May 20, 2012, from http://vancouver.mediacoop.ca/olympics/will-surveillance-cameras-become-olympic-legacy/5833

17
Public-Private Global Security Assemblages (London 2012)

Joseph R. Bongiovi

On July 6, 2005, London was selected as the first host city to be awarded the Olympic Games for the third time, solidifying its prominent role in modern Olympic and international sporting history. Matthew Llewellyn (2011) offers a useful analysis of this history. Great Britain held local, national and empire Games as early as the 17th century and also contributed to the founding of the modern Olympics. In spite of early indifference on the part of the government as well as the public, the British Olympic Association was founded in 1905 which made Great Britain an important participant in the pivotal 1906 Intermediate Games in Athens. This helped London to be selected to replace Rome as the host city for the 1908 Games in which Great Britain accounted for more than one-third of the participating athletes and received the greatest number of medals. As discussed by Richard Pound in Chapter 2 of this book, the four decades between London's first and second hosting of the Olympics were marked by an ambiguous relationship between Great Britain and the Olympics, as the Games were canceled once during World War I and twice during the World War II. In 1948 London held the first Olympics in 12 years at the time when the city was still recovering from the devastation of the war, people lacked housing, and food was still rationed.

The 2012 Games were an opportunity to demonstrate how far London had progressed since the devastation and recovery from World War II. To press its case London selected two-time gold medal winner Sebastian Coe to lead the effort. Its ultimate selection was received with such enthusiasm that Royal Air Force fighter jets were sent flying over London, with each jet trailing red, white, and blue smoke. The United Kingdom celebrated the award as Prime Minister Tony Blair was hosting the Group of Eight summit in Scotland from July 6–8, 2005.[1]

This jubilation was shattered the next day by the news that a coordinated series of bombings, claimed by a self-described Al Qaeda affiliate, struck London commuters on three separate subway lines and a commuter bus during morning rush hour, killing 52 people and injuring hundreds. This was reminiscent of previous Irish Republican Army bombings in the United Kingdom and Al Qaeda attacks in other parts of Europe. Prime Minister Tony Blair left the Group of Eight summit to assure worried Londoners of his leadership while the International Olympic Committee issued statements of confidence in the selection of London for 2012. The police showed confidence: "We've seen all this before in a way... We've been fighting the [Irish Republican Army] for years in London. So bombs are nothing new. But the difference is that I.R.A. provided some warning for their attacks. It seems the hallmark of these attacks is we get no warning, whatsoever. It was a matter of when, not if." So, too, a spokeswoman for the International Olympic Committee emphasized that its President Jacques Rogge expressed "full confidence in London and a secure Games in seven years time." [2]

A tense environment following this event led to extraordinary measures, most notably representation from all branches of the military, civilian public security, and private security. While anti-aircraft missiles had been a part of the Olympics in Athens and Beijing,[3] for a time it seemed that the highly public display of these missiles would become the signature memory of the London Games. In the end, this was eclipsed by the failure of private security company Group 4 Securicor to meet its personnel quota and the highly successful last-minute effort on the part of the United Kingdom Armed Forces and police in closing that gap.

While surveillance practices and security concerns have always been a part of the Games, the preparation and reaction to perceived shortcomings led to new extreme. This was powerfully symbolically portrayed by Steve Nease in his "Slight Over reaction" cartoon (see Figure 17.1), showing an athlete approaching a pole vault only to find it covered in razor wire. The cartoon vividly captures the feel of the London Olympics, where at times it seemed that the Games were at the service of the imperatives of security, rather than the other way around!

Assessing potential threats to security

In light of these events, the London Organizing Committee for the Olympic Games commissioned Rand Europe, a subsidiary of Rand Corporation, originally founded by the United States Army Air Force as a research and development think tank,[4] to conduct a study and propose recommendations regarding threats to security of the Olympic Games. As advertised on its website, the mission of the corporation is to "help improve policy and decision-making through research and analysis" through its offices in many cities around the world, by offering "objective analysis" and "effective solutions" to policy makers worldwide.[5] As the website further informs, "Defense and Security Research" is one of the many topics in which the corporation offers its expertise.[6]

The corporation identified three primary risk categories: terrorism, targeted disruptions, and serious crime. We learn from the report, that in this analysis, the corporation used its own research model with the following analytical categories: "adversary hostile intent," "adversary operational capability," and "domestic/international influences on United Kingdom security." It is worth reflecting further on these categories because they helped inform preparation for the London Games. Each one of these three categories had three variables, leading to 27 "future security environments," from "legal, non-violent" threats to "terrorist mass violence," as well as the direction of the trend, from "some improvement" to "status quo" to "significant worsening." Each of the "future security environments" was positioned within a "three dimension range of possibilities, from most benign to most insecure," with the most likely and concerning deemed to be small-scale isolated incidents, considered to be the hardest to detect and prevent. Against these estimates, the study positioned what it referred to as "security capabilities" and assessed them against each of the 27 "future security environments."[7]

A detailed analysis of the content suggests that the ramifications of the report by the Rand Corporation for the planning of the 2012 London

Figure 17.1 Olympic security by Steve Nease, 2012

Games were profound. The report led the London Organizing Committee to believe that there was a need for a "highly flexible and infinitely scalable" approach. Given that in such a tense environment the political price for simply ignoring envisioned scenarios is too high to be considered – no matter how unlikely it may be – this meant that the organizers not only had to take each of these scenarios into account but they also had to plan for them. This would ultimately lead to an "all hands on deck" approach to securing the Games.[8] Simultaneously with all the policing agencies, the Games saw one of the largest engagements of private military and security companies, coupled with state military and security resources, ever used in concert for an event of this type. As early as 2007, *The Telegraph* made public a leaked Home Office report on preparations for securing the 2012 London Games, including plans for police package scans, increases and linking of closed-circuit television systems, and development and utilization of the DNA genetic databases. The newspaper informed the public about "a big leap in forensics, particularly with the 'volume of information now available on the national DNA database,' on which details of more than three million Britons are stored." It also informed that the police would make a greater use of "a technique known as 'familial DNA' where a suspect whose details are not on the database can be traced through a family member whose details are already recorded." The newspaper then quoted a memo stating that "Records could be trawled more routinely to identify familial connections to crime scenes, providing a starting point to investigations through a family member that is on the database to a suspect that is not."[9]

While surveillance techniques and technology helped to define security measures, the location of the Games also influenced planning and preparation. East London had been chosen as the location for the Olympic Park as a way to increase both development and security in a part of the city that had been seen as a site of danger and criminality (Fussey, 2011). In a series of journalistic analysis, *The Guardian* reported that while Olympic-related development was hoped to have a long-term pacifying effect, there was an immediate concern with the possibility of "native-born extremists" from the host boroughs. A restricted "counter-terrorism local profile" authored by the police and the Home Office reported "a high-level threat of [Al Qaeda]-inspired extremism from males aged between 20 and 38. The individuals of interest to the police are predominantly British-born second generation migrants from south-east Asia. There is also interest from a number of Middle Eastern political movements and [Al Qaeda]-affiliated groups from north Africa."[10]

A related threat seemed to have been the "lone wolf terrorist," either native born or foreign. *The Guardian* cited two examples: a female who purportedly radicalized herself using information from the Internet and listening to Al Qaeda sermons, ultimately stabbing a Labour Party Member of Parliament; and a male who apparently used information from the Internet to make a homemade nail bomb suicide vest, attempting to blow it up in a crowded restaurant. One unnamed security observer reported, "It is difficult to exaggerate the nervousness of the police and the security services over what is an unprecedented and enormous challenge ahead."[11]

In light of the report by the Rand Corporation, the nature of threats to security were considered ubiquitous so that virtually all types of potential threats were treated as equally probable and threatening, thereby exacerbating the level of technology and personnel assigned to the Games.[12] This threat perception was further exacerbated by the subsequent reports and analyzes noted above. As the assistant commissioner for counterterrorism of the London Metropolitan Police noted, "We have done some very detailed planning over the past few months on the counter-terrorism side... we have tried to learn from Olympic Games all around the world, and not just [the] Games, but other large-scale events, and from colleagues around the world. London is an attractive target in some respects... There is lot more work to do. I am not complacent."[13]

This led to the incorporation of the military, civilian public security, and private security – all in an effort to be able to meet the demands. While Group 4 Securicor was playing the lead role in the Olympic venue, other private security companies were filling gaps for government, corporate and individual needs more broadly. The British Security Industry Association coordinated the overall involvement of the private security industry. In an address at the International Fire and Security Conference, held in Birmingham, England, in May 2012, their Project Director laid out the association's understanding of challenges to security of the 2012 London Games.[14] He emphasized that this was the first Olympics to take place within a city limits. Previous Olympics had occurred in outlying areas, which were often separated into "Olympic Villages." Partly because the Olympics were being held in the city itself, security was considered to be particularly problematic. But other factors also contributed to the challenge. Two rivers, as well as a train line, ran next to the site. It was also in one of the most deprived areas of the city. The Project Director argued that the primary risk to the Olympics was expected to be the terrorism threat, although social unrest and crime were also concerns. After thousands took to the streets in London in protest over the killing of a black male by the police in August 2011, the city deployed an additional 10,000 police officers from around the country.[15] Security precautions were also built directly into the Olympic venue. An example of this is a police initiative named "Secured by Design," which promoted anti-crime solutions built directly into the Olympic Park using the so-called "holistic approach" to cover the environment, buildings, and provisions for physical security. Apparently, these preparations had lifted London 2012 to a higher standard, rendering the Olympic Park as both "world class" and "cutting edge."[16] As Coaffee (2011: 120) notes, this "holistic approach" was similar to previous attempts to "design out terrorism" through infrastructure innovation in the United Kingdom, namely during its conflicts with the Irish Republican Army.

On the eve of the Olympics, the General Director of the United Kingdom's Security Service (popularly known as MI5),[17] reiterated the most persistent threats to the Games, arguing that, while previous terrorist attacks in London had come from the Irish Republican factions, particularly in the 1990s, the bigger threat was from Al Qaeda and other anti-British "jihadists," namely those from Yemen and the Al Shabaab militia in Somalia, in the 2000s. He also expressed concerns regarding Iran under international sanctions and what he considered as Iran's allies, namely the Hezbollah. Potential cyber attacks from any source were apparently also an issue.[18] The scope of the challenge as outlined by the General Director not only echoed reports by the Rand Corporation and other public authorities, it also likely served to condition public receptivity to the cost and profile of security events. In addition, this public statement was a form of marketing on behalf of private security corporations. The message from the British Security Industry Association's representative was one part professional analysis, but another part very much a sales pitch.

The role of private security companies

As other contributors to this book demonstrate, particularly Tagsold in his Chapter 3 on Tokyo, Ok and Park in their Chapter 9 on Seoul, and Tsoukala in her Chapter 13 on Athens, the involvement of private security companies in the Olympic Games does not originate with the 2012 London Games. The report on the 2008 Beijing Games mentions various police forces and "guards from private security companies" as the primary security resources for their Olympics.[19] So, too, Contemporary Security Canada was formed for the 2010 Winter Olympics in Vancouver where a joint venture between the Contemporary Group (based in the United States), Canada's United Protection Security Group, and Canada's Aeroguard Security Limited received a $97 million contract from the Canadian government and provided 5000 private security guards for the event.[20] Most interestingly, we learn from the report of the evaluation of the finalists – London, Paris, Madrid and New York – for the 2012 Olympics that all discussed the inclusion of "private security" along with police and the military. Here, Moscow was singled out as an exception, the only city among the finalists that did not mention the availability of private security resources.[21] This is most likely a legacy of the Russian communist past and a subsequently underdeveloped private security sector.

The increasing presence of private military and security companies is not only an Olympics phenomenon. Private security has a long history in Europe, but the expansion of this industry has been particularly substantial over the past two decades. Today it accounts for thousands of companies, millions of workers and hundreds of billions of dollars in annual revenue, with operations on every continent and nearly all countries (Abrahamsen and Williams, 2009; McCoy, 2009). A recent French Parliament study estimated the total market for military and security services to be between $100 billion and $400 billion a year,[22] while another study suggested that the total market would be $2.7 trillion between 2010 and 2020,[23] up from $55.6 billion in 1990 (Mandel, 2002). Firms such as Canada's Garda World,[24] Spain's Prosegur,[25] Sweden's Securitas,[26] and United Kingdom-Danish Group 4 Securicor[27] each employ hundreds of thousands of workers, provide a broad range of services, operate globally and earn billions of U.S. dollars in revenues annually. Growth of this industry came as deregulation and (neo)liberal globalization provided a landscape receptive to its expansion (Kobrin, 1997; Tilly, 2001). These private companies have their own advocacy organizations, such as the British Security Industry Association mentioned above,[28] as well as their own International Code of Conduct.[29]

It appears that the United Kingdom has had a domestic private security industry since at least the 19th century. As we learn from the way these companies advertise their services on their websites, one early British private security company, Corps Security, was founded by returning war veterans in 1859.[30] In the period after World War II, the British established a global orientation for its security industry. Dunigan (2011) writes that a former British Special Air Service officer founded a number of early private military and security companies. Control Risks Group states that it was founded in 1975, which would make it a successful early firm that has today become one of the most important global companies in corporate security and risk management.[31] Another important pioneer seems to be Defense Services Limited, founded in 1981 and later merged with other firms to create the industry giant Aegis – today an important provider of security services in conflict zones.[32] This firm is led by retired a British Special Operations officer who previously founded Sandline International, another private military and security company. This particular corporate story is described by the officer in his own book (Spicer, 1999). It was estimated that by 1995 the United Kingdom–based private security firms were employing 162,000 people, compared to 142,000 public police.[33] A more recent estimate of the ratio of private to public security personnel was closer to three to one. [34]

As scholars have observed, these companies recruit heavily from former service members, police, and intelligence operatives (Singer, 2003; Carmola, 2010). A good example of this overlap and linkages between public and private organizations in the United Kingdom can be seen in a recent posting on the networking site, LinkedIn:

Looking at getting into the industry, please help!! Good evening everyone. I have recently left the Royal Air Force Regiment after a period of 6 and a half years, I am now hoping to start a new career within the surveillance industry. Having been involved with the planning and management of numerous covert and overt Observation Posts and Reconnaissance Patrols, both in the UK and on operational tours throughout the world, I felt it was natural for me to transfer my skills and experience into this sector. I have gained Level 4 BTEC qualifications in Covert Camera Construction and Concealment, Tactical Foot & Mobile Surveillance and also Tactical Surveillance Procedures, and aim to complete my Level 4 BTEC Professional Diploma in Tactical Covert Surveillance within the next 12 months. I have also gained a City and Guilds Level 3/4 PTLLS (Preparing to Teach in the Lifelong Learning Sector) qualification. Any help/advice/contacts/networks or even jobs that you could offer would be very much appreciated, as I understand that this can be a difficult in such a discreet industry. Many thanks, Ben. [35]

This entry provides but one very good example of the relationship between public military and civilian public security and surveillance agencies on the one hand, and the private sector security firms on the other. Public military and civilian security agencies provide training and expertise to individual people who enlist to serve in these institutions. These skills are then readily transferrable into the civilian sector, where they then provide capability to corporations, individuals, nongovernmental organizations, and sometimes even to the agencies by which they were previously employed. This both feeds and reinforces public and private security and surveillance links.

Group 4 Securicor and the United Kingdom

Although there are a large number of United Kingdom–based private military and security companies, many of which stand out as global leaders, by 2012, Group 4 Securicor (known universally as G4S) was the largest organization of its kind globally. The London Stock Exchange listed the firm as reporting $12.035 billion in revenue in 2011.[36] Its 657,000 employees in 125 countries[37] made it the third-largest commercial employer in the world after United States retail giant WalMart and Taiwanese electronics manufacturer Foxconn.[38]

According to its website, Group 4 Securicor was formed through mergers and acquisitions of some of the oldest and most prestigious private firms. Its origins are traced to the Denmark-based Falck, founded in 1906. Other predecessor companies mentioned are British Night Watch Services (later Securicor), founded in 1935; United States–based Wackenhut, founded in 1960; and Sweden-based Group 4, itself formed from predecessor companies in 1968. Each of these companies seem to have been busy acquiring and merging other companies across Europe and North America before merging together themselves. Group 4 and Falck merged in 2001 to become Group 4 Falck, which then acquired Wackenhut, the second-largest United States–based security firm, the following year. In 2003, Group 4 Falck and Securicor merged, becoming Group 4 Securicor, which became publicly listed in 2004 and has since acquired additional diverse global companies, including battlefield security provider Armor Group and humanitarian services specialist RONCO in 2008.[39] By 2011, the company continued to pursue other mergers and acquisitions in Brazil, China, India, and the United Kingdom, as well picking up the London 2012 security contract, worth $454.4 million.[40]

According to the news reports, the company is also noteworthy for the scope of its operations. Its Armor Group North America provided security for the United States Embassy in Afghanistan, in addition to numerous other diplomatic missions globally.[41] Its corrections division managed prisons and immigration detention centers in Australia, the United States, the United Kingdom and Israel.[42] In the United Kingdom alone it managed six prisons, an asylum center for detention seekers and security operations in hospitals.[43] It provided a variety of other services to governments and private firms. It guarded air and sea ports and specialized in energy and public and private utility guarding. It also focused on transport and tourism, including a number of United Kingdom airports, as well as financial and retail guarding.[44] More recently it ventured into anti-piracy operations.[45]

The scope of this operation made history in early 2012 when the company became the first private security firm to win a government contract to build and run a police station. The ten-year, $320 million deal included an optional five-year extension and put Group 4 Securicor in charge of running administration for the Lincolnshire Police Authority.[46] It also bid on $2.4 billion in contracts to run West Midlands and Surrey administrative, crime scene investigation and intelligence services.[47] This was only one of many United Kingdom public service contracts being tendered.[48] In fact, at least ten more police forces, including Cambridgeshire, Bedfordshire and Hertfordshire, announced privatization plans. Its government business grew from 15% of global revenues in 2006 to 27% in 2011, with 50% of its United Kingdom business being government services by 2012. In preparation for further police work, the corporation compiled a database of 17,000 former officer Policing Solutions.[49]

Even before proving its ability to successfully complete such work, the head of its United Kingdom branch outlined the company's plans for further business expansion.

> For most members of the public what they will see is the same or better policing and they really don't care who is running the fleet, the payroll or the firearms licensing – they don't really care...I have always found it somewhere between patronizing and insulting the notion that the public sector has an exclusive franchise on some ethos, spirit, morality – it is just nonsense. The thought that everyone in the private sector is primarily motivated for profit and that is why they come to work is just simply not accurate...we employ 675,000 people and they are primarily motivated pretty much the same as would motivate someone in the public sector.[50]

This statement reflects public statements made by other executives of such companies. Its claim is that private security and surveillance companies could provide the best of both worlds. These executives have always argued that private businesses were more efficient and effective than their corresponding public bureaucrats, providing flexibility, adaptability, and cost savings where needed. Now they were further arguing that these organizations were just as professional and committed to public service as their government counterparts. From their perspective, the profit motive would provide all of the advantages noted above, but none of the disadvantages of opportunism sometimes feared. The Olympics would be a test of whether that argument holds true in practice.

Planning for the Games: "bridging the gap" venture

Given the significant and growing role of private security in the United Kingdom, it is not entirely surprising that Group 4 Securicor was given responsibility for security at the Olympic Park in 2008.[51] As the media reported, in 2009, the British Security Industry Association, Skills for Security, Bucks New University, North Hertfordshire Further Education College, the Home Office, the Department of Business, Innovation and Skills, and the London Organizing Committee initiated a public-private joint venture. The venture was labeled "Bridging the Gap." Its goal was to increase the number of trained "recruits for the security and crowd management sectors." It was piloted with 14 "Further Education Colleges" before being expanded to 50 of these institutions, with the intent of training 12,000 students, including 9000 unemployed persons, in three years and "delivering" 6000 of them to support London 2012 with qualifications of supervisor and stewardship training. This was considered to be a "lasting legacy of the Games," increasing the pool of skilled security personnel, as well as providing work opportunities not previously available to these individuals. It was launched in November 2009 at Tower Hamlets Further Education College in East London. To this end, the Security Industry Association London 2012 Project Director stated the following:

> There has long been a need to encourage young adults to pursue a career in the security industry. Bridging The Gap will provide the security sector with a new supply chain of trained and qualified personnel direct from their local college. Coupled with this, a new stream of personnel will help meet the security challenge of London 2012, providing valuable support to the comprehensive security measures that will be in place.[52]

In late December 2010, the company was awarded a further contract to provide 2000 security staff for the Olympic venues and manage 8000 additional personnel made up of volunteers and other staff recruited from colleges of higher education. This contract commenced in March 2011. By

August 2011, in the wake of the street demonstrations in London mentioned above, conversations commenced regarding a substantial enhancement of resources for security. A United States Federal Bureau of Investigations and Central Intelligence Agency team assigned to monitor London 2012 security preparations warned of continued terrorist vulnerability, leading the Prime Minister of the United Kingdom to approve a five-fold increase in private, police and military personnel committed to the Games.[53] By December 2011, the total number of guards to be provided by Group 4 Securicor was increased to 10,400. In addition, the company was to take responsibility for managing the following additional guards: 735 existing Olympic Park guards; 3700 "Bridging the Gap" program graduates; 1000 William James guards in the Olympic Village; 5000 armed forces personnel; and 3000 London Organizing Committee "Games Makers," bringing the total number of security personnel under its management to 23,700.[54] At that time, the London 2012 security effort also included 12,500 London Metropolitan Police and 8500 services members in addition to those under direct company supervision.[55] By that point, the company's contract, originally worth $137.6 million, had grown to $454.4 million.[56]

Private opportunity, public show of force

By March 2012, the projected security costs had increased to over $1.6 billion, with venue-specific security alone more than doubling from an initial estimate.[57] Military service member commitment had grown to 13,500, or more than the number committed to the war in Afghanistan, as well as surface to air missiles, jet fighters, helicopters, and the Royal Navy.[58] The largest ship in the fleet, the 22,500 ton helicopter carrier Her Majesty's Ship Ocean was stationed in Greenwich. The 21,500 ton assault vessel Her Majesty's Ship Bulwark, the Royal Navy flagship, was moored in Weymouth to oversee the sailing events. Typhoon fighters, the most modern in the Royal Air Force, were assigned to the Royal Air Force Base Northolt and supplemented by helicopters operating from the Her Majesty's Ship Ocean, as well as surface to air missiles. While this arsenal was impressive, it was reported in the *New York Times* that "Organizers of the last two Summer Olympics, in Beijing and Athens, adopted similar air defense plans, deploying military aircraft and, as in London, batteries of ground-to-air missiles in a ring around the main Olympics sites. In London's case, that includes two missile detachments."[59]

In addition to the growing costs within the Olympic venues noted above, there was also a substantial increase to the original budgeted police expenses outside the Olympic venues.[60] This was related to the ambition that London 2012 be an opportunity to leave the installed surveillance infrastructure in place. There was an East London "Safer Neighborhoods" initiative, a DNA data collection initiative, another linking all closed-circuit televisions into a network of 500,000 cameras to be put at the disposal of the Metropolitan

Police, as well as a new command center built for the London Metropolitan Police.[61]

Expecting 25,000 athletes and 700,000 tourists, European Union passports were equipped with special chips that could be utilized in 11 airports in combination with special facial recognition software. Airspace within 30 miles of London was monitored by the Royal Air Force, and police and military paired up to detect chemical, biological, radiological, nuclear or explosive threats. This included Royal Air Force personnel in 14 observation posts equipped with thermal-imaging bomb detection equipment. Teams of military snipers patrolled the skies in helicopters while speedboats patrolled the Thames. An 11-mile 5000-volt fence, estimated to cost $150 million was installed around the Olympic Village and London's East End. The roughly 500,000 interconnected closed-circuit televisions photographed license plates on cars and cross-checked them automatically against any suspected criminal or terrorist activity. No outside food or water was allowed in the Olympic Park. Inside the park, roughly 2700 X-ray machines, metal detectors, vehicle scanners, and trace-explosive detectors provided additional surveillance.[62]

Group 4 Securicor was responsible for all activities within the Olympic venues, including training and assignment of all private and public security personnel.[63] In order to fill its positions, the company launched a massive recruiting effort. By April 2012, it had screened 50,000 applicants,[64] and by May, they had reviewed 100,000 applicants, with 67,000 interviewed and 21,000 selected to continue in the process. Hires were targeted for specific training. Newly hired security employees ranged in age from 18 to 65, with half being from the five host boroughs of the Olympics. Security roles for these new hires included searches, patrolling, X-ray, closed-circuit television and alarm monitoring, incidence response, asset protection, visitor assistance, and "command and control."[65]

The British Security Industry Association stated that the Olympics were an opportunity to showcase products and services.[66] One of the ways to promote the business was the International Fire and Security Conference mentioned above. It was the largest private security show of its kind with over 25,000 security professionals preregistered.[67] As we learn from the association's website, the Project Director for London 2012 was responsible for focusing on global events like the Olympics, seeking to portray the association's members as leading resources for private security services, and helping to broker opportunities for them.[68] The legacy hoped for by the Association was an increase in global market share for British firms. Its Project Director estimated that they had a 17% share of event security and they "only" had 5% of the global security market. A successful, private-led venture in London 2012, the Project Director argued, could give them a global marketing advantage.[69] This was further emphasized by the International Fire and Security event director for the 2012 conference who emphasized that this was the most crucial year for the industry in a decade. While the London Olympics and the Queen's Diamond Jubilee increased urgency, other major global events and scandals had already put a spotlight on the United Kingdom: data and privacy breaches in the news, the 2011 London demonstrations, and the threat of terror attacks.[70]

The Managing Director of Securitas in the United Kingdom and Ireland, who was also Chairman of the British Security Industry Association at the time, praised the Association's efforts in advocating for the industry in the United Kingdom and recognized the role of the Project Director for London 2012 in preparation for the Games. While noting that regulatory changes and austerity were proving opportunities for private companies, he emphasized the importance of getting London 2012 right:

> It's impossible to talk about forthcoming challenges without making mention of the London 2012 Olympic and Paralympic Games. While these events represent a significant long-term opportunity for our industry, they also bring with them a reputational challenge. Our industry is already firmly in the spotlight following the Diamond Jubilee celebrations which took place across the country – with a particular focus on London – earlier this month.
>
> As a precursor to the Olympics, the Diamond Jubilee was a very real test of our industry's capability, and one that received significant scrutiny by media and critics alike. In the months to come, the whole world's attention will be focused on Olympic security, and we must all work hard to ensure that the reputation of our industry is upheld while taking full advantage of the opportunities this brings to showcase our wide range of talent and innovation.[71]

The executive probably did not imagine how prescient those words would be. The Olympics would, in fact, be a monumental test of the ability of private security corporations to deliver on their commitments. Unfortunately for both security corporations and their public clients, the shortcomings of the prime contractor Group 4 Securicor would raise far more questions than would be addressed through their accomplishments.

Crisis as the Games begin

There are a number of arguments made in favor of private companies. One is that they offer flexible quantitative resources when there is a demand spike. London 2012 seems to be a clear example of a need for incremental resources. Another argument for private companies, made particularly by industry insiders, is that they bring a high degree of efficiency and effectiveness. This argument suggests that unlike their bloated and inflexible public counterparts, private companies are nimble and responsive, able to more quickly and effectively meet the changing needs. In response to this latter argument, organizational economists have a very different view. According to Williamson (1985, 1975) and Brauer and Van Tuyll (2008), services are best outsourced when the transaction in question is fairly routine and certain. When, however, the situation is unpredictable and uncertain, services are best delivered through internal hierarchies. The 2012 London Summer Olympics seem to be a clear example of the latter.

On the eve of the Olympics, after nearly $1.6 billion had been committed to securing them, and the hopes of the organizers had been placed in the efficiency and experience of private enterprise, the public was exposed to an unexpected surprise. The much-touted behemoth, Group 4 Securicor, announced that it could not fulfill its contractual commitment. In spite of weekly reviews involving its progress, the London Organizing Committee was informed "on the morning of July 11, 2012 that despite ongoing and recent assurances orally and in writing to the contrary, G4S would not be able to meet their labor pool target."[72] With Group 4 Securicor only having 4000 personnel ready, and another 9000 still in process, the Ministry of Defense agreed to step in with an additional 3500 service members.[73]

The failings were made especially egregious when compared to the London Organizing Committee's successful recruitment of 70,000 volunteer "Games Makers." The London Organizing Committee worked under the exact same time frame and environmental conditions and yet, unlike the corporation, it was able to recruit, train, uniform, and schedule all of these volunteers.[74] The London Organizing Committee Chairman recognized these volunteers in the Closing Ceremony, giving them more credit for the Olympics' success than any other group. As the International Olympic Committee President stated, "We will never forget the smiles, the kindness and the support of the wonderful volunteers, the much-needed heroes of these Games."[75]

Various factors were cited in the failings of Group 4 Securicor, including uncompetitive low wages, "totally chaotic" recruiting, and disorganized training.[76] In spite of this last-minute crisis, the additional military service members and subsequent recruitment and training of additional personnel closed the gap. The Olympics and the Paralympics were completed without a security incident. The company was nevertheless praised by the standing joint military commander for the Olympics who stated: "The day to day working with G4S has been exceptional and I would like to pay tribute to the G4S staff and volunteers. Working side by side I believe they are doing a very professional job providing Olympic security."[77] Regulatory compliance by private guards was found to be high by the Security Industry Authority, and crime was reduced during the Games.[78]

The security arrangements for London 2012, left many questions unanswered. Whereas private companies had expected to demonstrate their superiority over the public sector, it was the police and military that demonstrated their flexibility, reliability and efficiency. In its first-half report, the company acknowledged the shortcomings of its operations, was required to reimburse the government for police and military service member hourly costs, contributed $4 million to a service members relief fund, and took an $80 million charge against its first-half 2012 earnings for expenses and penalties incurred.[79] The parliamentary investigation into contract compliance continued through the end of September 2012. Needless to say, this was not what the government of the United Kingdom, the Security Industry Authority, or Group 4 Securicor had hoped for.

When the report was released, it not only identified the widely publicized shortcomings of the company's performance but juxtaposed it with the success of the public military and civilian security services, as well as the London Organizing Committee's own very successful recruitment and deployment of 70,000 "Games Maker" volunteers. The report recommended that the company, in addition to losses and payments already incurred, forfeit the $91.2 million management fee for the Olympics as a goodwill gesture to their biggest single global client, the United Kingdom taxpayer. The report also recommended a thorough review of all of the company's policies and procedures before renewing or adding any additional government business.[80] The corporation did not accept the management fee forfeiture but responded to the report by releasing its Chief Operating Officer and Chief Executive Officer for the United Kingdom and Africa, as well as its head of Global Events. The company also conducted its own internal review and submitted the corporation to organizational restructuring.[81]

London 2012 and the expansion of public-private and global-local security assemblages

Some scholars suggest that the increasing involvement of private military and security companies is a usurpation of what sociologist Max Weber famously characterized as the state's monopoly on the legitimate use of force (Avant, 2005; Mandel, 2002; Singer, 2003; Carmola, 2010). By analyzing shifting patterns in global governance, however, other scholars conclude that participation of private companies in this realm is actually complementary to public authority (Abrahamsen and Williams, 2007, 2009; Leander, 2005). The latter also argue that the state no longer acts alone or even necessarily with the greatest knowledge or authority and that these activities are no longer bounded by national borders. Rather, the emerging security networks are public-private and global-local, arising from a number of developments: first, the globalized demand for private security; second, processes that have allowed private firms to be accepted as legitimate authorities in the realm of security; and third, the resulting incorporation of these entities into hybrid networks.

The demand for private security can be observed in multiple realms. Multinational firms increasingly rely on private companies to protect property and activities wherever their production is located and their services

374 Joseph R. Bongiovi

offered (Avant, 2005). Individuals as well as the so-called gated communities hire private security companies rather than depend on local police (O'Reilly, 2011). States increasingly use these companies to support their military activities around the world (Singer, 2003), while nongovernmental organizations seek their support for international development operations (Joachim and Schneiker, 2012).

This involvement by the private security and military companies in various social and political spheres provides them with experience that, in turn, enhances their competence in the eyes of those who hire them. Through this legitimation as indispensable experts, they are able to enhance their own role in the shaping of the security agenda. By leveraging this experience and access, they are able to shape the perspective of key actors in terms of where priorities for security should lie, what the nature of threats to security may be, and how security should be achieved (Leander, 2005; Abrahamsen and Williams, 2007). This power to shape security discourse also provides them with structural power as these companies are able to position themselves into newly hybridized public-private and global-local security networks. Some have argued that these networks constitute a new form of governance in which nation-states neither fully cede their authority in the realm of security nor maintain their monopoly (Abrahamson and Williams, 2009).

The role of the Olympic Games and other such global events in legitimizing and accelerating this shift is being noted by industry advocates and opponents alike. Yet, it should be emphasized that, at least in the case of global events, the ultimate arbiter and backstop on the use of private corporations for security purposes is the state. As seen in the case of London 2012, the state is the only force as of yet capable of deploying warships, jet fighters, surface to air missiles, and thousands of trained and reliable personnel at the very last moment and under dynamic and ambiguous circumstances. However, states cannot replicate such experiences at the next Olympics as, next time around, these will be staged in a different country. For this reason, it is likely that, despite the fiasco of London 2012, interest in contracting global security firms for global events of this type may continue to grow. London 2012 is a case study of both the opportunity and shortcoming of this emerging hybridized form. Indeed, these companies were publicly recognized by the United Kingdom's military for their contribution in the London 2012 Olympics.

It will be interesting to see how this practice of combining private security corporations with state security agencies in the staging of the Olympics will continue to develop. Before the 2014 Sochi Winter Olympics, it was reported that the Russian Deputy Prime Minister was considering whether Russia should take a more active role in supporting such corporations, both domestically and internationally: "We are thinking about whether our money should go toward financing foreign private security [and] military companies, or whether we should consider the feasibility of such companies in Russia itself."[82] Nonetheless, the 2014 Sochi Olympics were guarded by the state institutions of the Russian Federation, including a large detachment of Cossack Militia.[83] It was not until after the Sochi Games that relevant legislation to potentially go in this direction was even introduced into the State Duma.[84] It appears that the only report of private security related to the 2014 Sochi Olympics was the engagement of the paramilitary evacuation company Global Rescue by the United States Ski and Snowboard Association, which accompanied the American team, as was also the case in the previous two winter Olympics.[85] We have yet to see how this march toward privatization of security in global sports events will play itself out in the future. It may be that the 2016 Rio de Janeiro Summer Olympics in Brazil will choose to follow the model of state-based security, which was so influentially demonstrated by the Russian Federation at the 2014 Sochi Olympics[86] as highly successful. In this case, we may see the emergence of different models, some based on Western privatization and outsourcing of security services, American style, and others continuing to follow the historic practice of state monopolies over the legitimate means of force.

Notes

I want to thank Vida Bajc, Charlie Kurzman, Arne Kalleberg, Shane Elliott, and an anonymous review for their input on various versions of this chapter.

1. "London wins right to 2012 Olympics," *New York Times,* July 6, 2005.
2. "After Coordinated Bombs, London Is Stunned, Bloodied and Stoic," Alan Cowell, *New York Times,* July 7, 2005; "With World Watching, London Looks to Shine," Christopher Clarey, *New York Times,* July 26, 2012.
3. "China tightens security, installs missiles near Olympics site," Stephen Wade, *Seattle Times,* June 25, 2008, and "Olympic threats fuel unease about security: China says heavy defense will secure Games, but clampdown is smothering," Associated Press, July 28, 2008.
4. Regarding this history, the company's website has a link to an essay by Virginia Campbell titled "How RAND Invented Postwar World: Satellites, Systems Analysis, Computing, the Internet – Almost all the Defining Features of the Information Age Were Shaped in Part at the RAND Corporation."
5. http://www.rand.org/about/glance.html
6. See the homepage for Rand Corporation: http://www.rand.org/randeurope/research/defence.html
7. The report is coauthored by 13 contributors. The website offers the following as the citation: Clutterbuck, Lindsay, Edward Nason, Lynne Saylor, Ruth Levitt, Lisa Klautzer, Michael Hallsworth, Lila Rabinovich, Samir Puri, Greg Hannah, Aruna Sivakumar, Flavia Tsang, Peter Burge and Cameron Munro. *Setting the Agenda for an Evidence-Based Olympics.* Santa Monica, CA: RAND Corporation, 2007. http://www.rand.org/pubs/technical_reports/TR516
8. "All hands on deck" is a naval term referring to a situation requiring that all available personnel put aside nonessential duties and participate in the fight, and it has entered into the common vocabulary in English-speaking countries when

referring to situations that are an existential threat and require the full effort and commitment of all involved.

9. "Ministers plan 'Big Brother' police powers," Patrick Hennessy and Ben Leapman, *The Telegraph*, February 4, 2007.
10. "London Olympics security report warns of extremist threat in host borough: high-level threat of al-Qaida-inspired extremism reported in Waltham Forest, home to part of the Olympic Park," Ryan Gallagher, *The Guardian (London)*, February 12, 2012.
11. "Unpredictable 'lone wolves' pose biggest Olympic security threat," Sanra Laville, *The Guardian (London)*, March 8, 2012.
12. *Setting the Agenda for an Evidence-Based Olympics*.
13. "Unpredictable 'lone wolves' pose biggest Olympic security threat."
14. Summary of the presentation by Peter Evans at the IFSEC 2012 Conference as reported on the Info4 Security website, http://www.ifsec.co.uk/Content/IFSEC-2012-Show-Highlights/25/
15. "Cameron Deploys 10,000 More Officers to Riots," John F. Burns, *New York Times*, August 9, 2011.
16. Summary of the presentation by Peter Evans at the IFSEC 2012 Conference.
17. See the homepage: https://www.mi5.gov.uk/home.html
18. "MI5 leader Jonathan Evans: 'The Olympics and emerging threats,'" Ashroff and Brian Simms, *Info4 Security*, June 26, 2012. http://www.info4security.com/story.asp?sectioncode=52&storycode=4129256
19. Security Industry Association (SIA) (2007) *China Security Market Report Special Supplement: Olympic Update*. Alexandria, VA: Security Industry Association; "China Finds American Allies for Security," Keith Bradsher, *New York Times*, December 28, 2007; Beijing Organizing Committee for the Games of the XXIX Olympiad (2007) Bid Documents and Analysis: Passion behind the Bid, Volume I of the Official Report of the Beijing 2008 Olympic Games, 150.
20. Contemporary Security Canada (www.contemporarysecurity.ca); "Defense Industry has its Sights on the Olympics: A look at some of the companies cashing in on 2010 security spending," Dawn Paley, *The Dominion*, February 20, 2010, http://www.dominionpaper.ca/articles/3189; Vancouver Organizing Committee for the 2010 Olympic and Paralympic Winter Games (VANOC) (2010) Vancouver 2010 Sustainability Report 2009–2010. Vancouver: VANOC.
21. International Olympic Committee Evaluation Commission (2005) Report of the International Olympic Committee Evaluation Commission for the Games of the XXX Olympiad in 2012. Lausanne, Switzerland: International Olympic Committee.
22. "Regulation, Expansion of French Private Security Firms Urged," Pierre Tran, *Defense News*, February 2, 2012.
23. "Olympics 2012 security: welcome to lockdown London," Stephen Graham, *The Guardian (London)*, March 12, 2012, http://www.guardian.co.uk/sport/2012/mar/12/london-olympics-security-lockdown-london?newsfeed=true
24. Garda World, http://www.garda-world.com/
25. Prosegur, http://www.prosegur.com/COM/
26. Securitas, http://www.securitas.com/en/
27. G4S, http://www.g4s.com/
28. British Security Industry Association (BSIA), http://www.bsia.co.uk/home
29. International Code of Conduct (ICoC), http://www.icoc-psp.org/
30. Corps Security, www.corpssecurity.co.uk

31. Control Risks Group, www.control-risks.com
32. Aegis, www.aegisworld.com
33. "Anti-Social Security," Julie Gallagher, *New Statesman & Society*, March 31, 1995.
34. *In Good Company: The Role of Business in Security Sector Reform* by Francesco Mancini, published by Demos in 2005. http://www.demos.co.uk/files/Goodcompanyweb.pdf
35. LinkedIn (2012) http://www.linkedin.com/groups/looking-getting-into-industry-please-2522879.S.112573383?view=&gid=2522879&type=member&item=112573383&trk=eml-anet_dig-b_nd-pst_ttle-cn
36. G4S "Investors News" http://www.g4s.com/en/Investors/News%20Events%20and%20Presentations/Announcements/2012/03/13/Preliminary%20Results%20for%202011/
37. G4S http://www.g4s.com/en/Who%20we%20are/Our%20Business/
38. "G4S faces down investors and protestors at annual meeting," Julia Kollewe, *The Guardian*, June 7, 2012, http://www.guardian.co.uk/business/2012/jun/07/g4s-faces-down-investors-protesters-annual-meeting/print
39. http://www.g4s.com/en/Who%20we%20are/History/
40. "G4S faces down investors and protestors at annual meeting" *The Guardian*, June 7, 2012.
41. "ArmorGroup Loses Kabul Embassy Contract," Daniel Schulman, *Mother Jones*, December 8, 2009 http://www.motherjones.com/mojo/2009/12/armorgroup-axed-kabul-embassy-contract
42. "Companies Use Immigration Crackdown to Turn a Profit," Nina Bernstein, *New York Times*, September 28, 2011 http://www.nytimes.com/2011/09/29/world/asia/getting-tough-on-immigrants-to-turn-a-profit.html?pagewanted=all and "G4S faces down investors and protestors at annual meeting."
43. "G4S faces down investors and protestors at annual meeting."
44. G4S http://www.g4s.com/en/What%20we%20do/
45. "G4S faces down investors and protestors at annual meeting."
46. "Private contractors to build and run police station," by Gill Plimmer and Helen Warrell, *Financial Times*, February 12, 2012.
47. "G4S UK boss expects bigger role for private security in policing," Rob Ratcliff, June 21, 2012, *Info4security* http://www.info4security.com/story.asp?sectioncode=9&storycode=4129239
48. "UK outsourcing drive gathers pace," Gill Plimmer, *Financial Times*, March 25, 2012.
49. "How G4S is 'securing your world': Budgetary pressure, political will and the lack of debate over public service privatization has seen G4S grow exponentially," Matthew Taylor, *The Guardian*, June 20, 2012 http://www.guardian.co.uk/uk/2012/jun/20/g4s-securing-your-world-policing
50. "G4S chief predicts mass police privatization: private companies will be running large parts of the police service within five years, according to security firm head," Matthew Taylor and Alan Travis, *The Guardian*, June 20, 2012 http://www.guardian.co.uk/uk/2012/jun/20/g4s-chief-mass-police-privatisation/print
51. "G4S chosen as official London 2012 Security Services Provider" http://www.london2012.com/news/articles/2011/3/g4s-chosen-as-official-london-2012-security-services-pro.html
52. "New security educational scheme to help plug gap for London 2012 launched," *Inside the Games*, November 9, 2009 http://www.insidethegames.biz/latest/7876 and IFSEC Show Highlights http://www.ifsec.co.uk/Content/IFSEC-2012-Show-Highlights/25/*info4security*

53. "Amid Reports of Ineptitude, Concerns Over Security at London Olympics," John F. Burns, *New York Times,* July 14, 2012, and "Britain Adjusts Security Plans in Tense Countdown to the Olympics," John F. Burns, *New York Times*, July 12, 2012.
54. Letter from Paul Deighton, Chief Executive of the London Organizing Committee of the Olympic Games and the Paralympic Games Ltd. to the Right Honorable Keith Vaz, Member of Parliament and Chairman of the Home Affairs Committee Office, House of Commons, dated July 16, 2012; "From cheers to jeers: chronology of the G4S cock-up," *4 News*, July 16, 2012 http://www.channel4.com/news/from-cheers-to-jeers-chronology-of-the-g4s-cock-up
55. "How G4S is 'securing your world': Budgetary pressure, political will and the lack of debate over public service privatization has seen G4S grow exponentially."
56. Ibid.
57. "Olympics 2012 security: welcome to lockdown London"; "Background: Faster, higher, longer: how bill for safe Olympics soared to more than 1Billion," Nick Hopkins and Owen Gibson, *The Guardian (London),* March 9, 2012.
58. "A New Amenity May Show Up on Some London Roofs for the Olympics: Missiles," Sarah Lyall, *New York Times*, May 12, 2012.
59. "An Olympics Vigil from 30,000 Feet," John F. Burns, *New York Times*, August 1, 2012.
60. "London Olympics security to be boosted by 13,500 troops: number greater than deployment in Afghanistan but defense secretary insists it will not affect operational capabilities," Owen Gibson, *The Guardian*, December 15, 2011 http://www.guardian.co.uk/sport/2011/dec/15/london-olympics-security-boosted-troops/print and "Snipers, jets and 13,500 troops on Olympics duty...4,000 more than Afghanistan," Ian Dury, *Mailonline*, December 15, 2011 http://www.dailymail.co.uk/news/article-2074669/London-2012-Olympics-MOD-drafts-13–500-military-troops-protect-The-Games.html
61. "CCTV Plan to Boost 2012 Security: Up to 500,000 CCTV cameras could be used as part of a highly sophisticated plan to police the 2012 Olympics," *British Broadcasting Corporation*, March 4, 2008, http://news.bbc.co.uk/2/hi/uk_news/england/london/7278365.stm and "Ministers Plan 'Big Brother' Police Powers."
62. "Security: A Locked-Down London," Andrew Rosenblum, *Fortune*, June 11, 2012.
63. "Olympics 2012 security: welcome to lockdown London"; "Greece is fastest-growing market for G4S" Gill Plimmer and Mark Wembridge, *Financial Times*, May 15, 2012; "Olympic security operation interactive map and graphic," Rob Radcliff, *info4security*, May 3, 2012 http://www.info4security.com/story.asp?sectioncode=9&storycode=4129001&c=1 and "Olympic military guards will not take orders from security staff," Peter Walker, *The Guardian (London)*, January 26, 2012.
64. "Background: Faster, higher, longer: how bill for safe Olympics soared to more than 1Billion."
65. G4S, http://www.g4s.uk.com/en-GB/London%202012/
66. Info4 Security, http://www.ifsec.co.uk/Content/IFSEC-2012-Show-Highlights/25/
67. International Fire and Security Conference (IFSEC), http://www.ifsec.co.uk/
68. In addition to the 2012 London Olympics, the conference also focused on the coincidental Queen's Diamond Jubilee and the Paralympic Games. While each of these is a separate event, the security industry referred to the Queen's Diamond Jubilee as a "dress rehearsal" for the Olympics and the Paralympic games. British

Security Industry Association (BSIA) (http://www.bsia.co.uk/); International Fire and Security Conference (IFSEC) (http://www.ifsec.co.uk/) and info4 Security (http://www.ifsec.co.uk/Content/IFSEC-2012-Show-Highlights/25/)

69. info4 Security http://www.ifsec.co.uk/Content/IFSEC-2012-Show-Highlights/25/
70. Ibid.
71. "BSIA Annual Luncheon 2012: Chairman's Address by Geoff Zeidler," Brian Sims *Info4 Security*, June 28, 2012 http://www.info4security.com/story.asp?sectioncod e=52&storycode=4129264&c=1
72. Letter from Paul Deighton, Chief Executive of the London Organizing Committee of the Olympic Games and the Paralympic Games Ltd.
73. "Amid Reports of Ineptitude, Concerns Over Security at the London Olympics."
74. House of Commons Home Affairs Committee, Olympics security: Seventh Report of Session 2012–2013, Vol. 1, September 21, 2012, 14.
75. "2012 Olympic Games: the real security legacy" *info4security*, Abbey Pekar, September 21, 2012.
76. "G4S Olympic security recruitment 'totally chaotic': Former police sergeant withdrew application to work at London 2012 due to concerns over employment process and pay," Nick Hopkins, *The Guardian*, July 12, 2012; "Olympic security chaos: depth of G4S security crisis revealed: recruits tell of chaos over schedules, uniforms and training while ex-police officers asked to help out," Robert Booth and Nick Hopkins, *The Guardian*, July 12, 2012.
77. "Olympics security chief highlights 'exceptional' work with G4S," Ron Alalouff, *Info4security*, August 13, 2012.
78. "Games time inspections yield high compliance for SIA," Brian Sims, *info4security*, August 28, 2012; "ACPO blog: an Olympian policing operation," Tim Holis, *info4security*, September 3, 2012; "Home Affairs Committee: evidence sessions on Olympics security and policing," Brian Sims, *info4security*, September 3, 2012.
79. G4S Half Yearly Results Announcement http://www.g4s.com/~/media/Files/ Investor%20Relations%20documents/2012%20interims%20announce- ment%20combined%20Final.ashx; Full Presentation Slides http://www.g4s. com/~/media/Files/Financial%20Presentations/G4S%202012%20HY%20 slides.ashx and Transcript http://www.g4s.com/~/media/Files/Investor%20 Relations%20documents/G4S%20Results%20Presentation%20-%20 28–08–12%20Transcript.ashx
80. House of Commons Home Affairs Committee, *Olympics security*.
81. "After London Olympics Debacle, Security Firm Shuffles Top Managers," Alan Cowell, *New York Times*, September 28, 2012; "Shake-up at G4S as two senior executives resign," Ron Alalouff, *info4security*, September 28, 2012.
82.. "Private Military Companies May Appear in Russia – Rogozin," *Sputnik International*. September 19, 2012.
83. Determined to Miss Nothing, Russia Trains All Eyes on Sochi: Intensive Security for the Winter Olympics," Steven Lee Myers, *The New York Times*, January 18, 2014.
84. Blackwater.ru: The Future of Russian Private Military Companies," Alexey Eremenko, *The Moscow Times*, November 12, 2014; "Private military compa- nies may be created in Russia – Izvestia daily: The companies' activity will be controlled by the Defense Ministry," *TASS*, July 7, 2014; "Russian lawmakers propose creating private military companies: Private military and security companies could specialize in providing military and security services to the state, individuals and legal entities on a contract basis," *TASS*, October 22, 2014;

"Russia's revised military doctrine lists foreign private military firms among threats: The previous version of the doctrine that was adopted in 2010 did not mention them in any way," *TASS*, December 26, 2014.

85. Olympic Fears Rattle Athletes and Families," Sarah Lyall, *The New York Times*, January 24, 2014; "Olympic Teams Prepare for Possible Security Crisis in Sochi," Yekaterina Kravtsova, *The Moscow Times*, January 23, 2014; and "Private Security Firms Tapped Ahead of Sochi as U.S, Prepares for the Worst," Jennifer Booton, *FOXBusiness*, January 15, 2014.

86. Brazil to share Russian Experience in Ensuring Olympic Security – Minister: Brazilian Minister of Defense Jaques Wagner said that Brazil will accept Moscow's proposal to share Russia's experience in ensuring security during major sports events," *Sputnik*, May 10, 2015.

18

Olympic Dilemmas: Surveillance, Security, Democracy

Vida Bajc

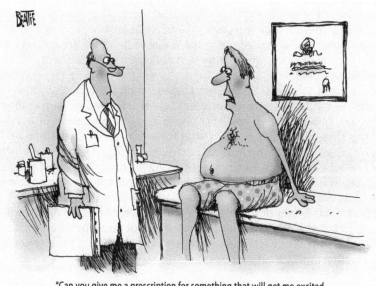

"Can you give me a prescription for something that will get me excited
about the Olympics?"

Figure 18.1   Olympics Ennui by Bruce Beattie

Attentive readers of this book might be in a similar state to that depicted in
Bruce Beattie's cartoon (Figure 18.1), intellectually confused, overwhelmed
by contradictions to the point of listlessness, and depressed by their own
indifference.

The billions of avid fans of Olympic competition and supporters of the
Olympic cause around the world appreciate the Olympics as the greatest
sports event in the world in which ideas of comradeship, inclusion, individual achievement, multiculturalism, respect of political differences, and

friendship through sports are promoted through fair competition. How could anyone with an appreciation of sportsmanship and internationalism not be excited about the Olympics?

And yet, this book suggests that the Olympic Games are also the world's most spectacular demonstration that surveillance and the surveillance–security nexus cover more than that invoked by the symbolism of the ubiquitous surveillance camera as Big Brother government and corporate snooping into people's private lives. To a bureaucratically organized Olympic assemblage surveillance is a supporting structure which sustains the working of the organization, supports its global expansion, enforces standards of purity in Olympic performance, and enables distinctions between athletes no longer perceptible to the human eye. When coupled with the imperative of security, surveillance becomes the means by which to encapsulate and encase the millions of people involved in Olympic activity to impose a secure social order for the duration of the Games. How could anyone who values diversity and inclusion be excited about the Games when they are a spectacular demonstration of the power to impose non-democratic social order on such a formidable scale?

Accustomed to demanding clear answers from experts and expecting immediate solutions from responsible authorities, Beattie's protagonist is sitting on a hospital bed, asking a physician for a miracle cure that can heal this Olympics Ennui, do away with these unbearable contradictions, so that he can experience the innocent excitement of the Olympics. Knowing how central competitive sports are in the life of many of his patients, the physician is not surprised to hear about this condition. Having a nuanced understanding of how surveillance works in modern democratic societies and how it has been put to use for the purposes of their security, however, the physician is well aware that such a magic potion cannot be concocted. Below I briefly outline the roots of these contradictions and suggest some possible directions for future research.

Enduring interest in the Olympic Games

While every Olympic Games can, and very often does become an occasion to express much public discontent about the event, the Olympics nevertheless continue to have ideological appeal and emotional resonance for immense numbers of people around the world. The enduring interest in the Games may be explained, at least in part, by the way the Olympics were designed. They are an example of modernity's invention of cultural and political projects of collective sentiment and bonding among huge numbers of otherwise unrelated individuals (Hobsbawm and Ranger, 1983; Roche, 2000). As Benedict Anderson (1983) well understood, such events espouse ideas that have been able to strengthen awareness of transnational connections and appeal to the sentiment of shared humanity. This invention of transnational collectivity also reflects the ethos of free market liberalism in which competition as means of cross-cultural interaction is revered as the noblest medium and the individual as supreme achiever is touted as the highest goal (Andrews and Silk, 2012; Zimbalist, 2015). This collective imagination and its neoliberal ethos are underwritten by media interests and corporate sponsorship through which the cult of celebrity and the culture of consumption have permeated the local lives of global audiences and shaped their national cultures (Andrews, 2003; Silk et al., 2005). Giulianotti and Brownell (2012: 200) point out that the Olympic Games today are a kind of transnationalism, which in one way or another engages some 70% of the world's population. Enthusiasm for the Olympics vary culturally and individually, from passion for competition, support for individual achievement, and fair play, to celebration of diversity, love of sports, excitement about internationalism, appeal to humanity, and more.

How intensive the ideological commitment and emotional attachment to the ideas the Games exemplify can be was well observed by journalist P.H. Mullen, who followed two male American swimmers through their preparations for competing at the 2000 Sydney Games, and is worth quoting here.[1] Mullen reminds us that for "every Olympics, legions of swimmers all over the world stop their lives to train for the opportunity to represent their country in the Olympiad." The International Olympic Committee well understands that this attraction to the Olympics is essential to the future of the Games. Most of these athletes, Mullen tells us, will remain anonymous: "Nearly all Olympic swimmers – and the tens of thousands who chased the Olympic dream but fell short – train more than a decade to live a moment like this." While their names may never be displayed on televisual screens, their efforts are, nevertheless, monumental: "Their arms have logged nearly enough miles to swim from Sydney's nearby harbor to Los Angeles – and back again." The physical struggle comes with personal sacrifice as these "athletes spend their whole lives backseating friends, social life, academics, and normal adolescence for the chance to chase this dream." Particularly for sports such as swimming, this is a lonely journey with little "team comraderies." Athletes "exist in an isolated, sensory-deprived world, where communications consist of barked commands, and external stimuli are limited to the rush of water in the ears and a fogged view of a pace clock." This isolation and seclusion carries all the way to the moment of the competition. The intimacy of an athlete's experience is exposed to "billions of television viewers [who] can see his ribcage rise and fall," while inside the arena thousands of surrounding spectators "are ready to scream themselves hoarse." And yet, Mullen writes, any sensation of collective sentiment an athlete could absorb is overwhelmed by "the singular, nonnegotiable passion to touch the wall first."

This immense passion to win is carefully and systematically nurtured by corporate interests, including the mass media, on which Olympic athletes increasingly depend for their success. A luge competitor at the 2006 Turin Games, for example, describes how she was "groomed from the tender age of 11," to spend her "childhood pursuing Olympic glory, which epitomizes the American dream of merit-based success." This "beautiful illusion," she writes, was an "experience she couldn't quite grasp as a child." It was "the creation of ingenious marketing mechanisms" which gave "meaning to the physical and emotional pain of [her] athletic struggle" and to "the fear that [she] would disappoint those [she] loved and those who had invested time and money in [her] athletic career." Her allegiance to her corporate sponsor was total and all encompassing. "All of my clothing was plastered with the [sponsor's] logo," she relates. She was "not allowed near any camera without giving a visual and verbal statement of thanks to [the sponsor] for making all of my dreams come true." This thanks giving, in turn, required grueling training of another kind. She was subjected to "intensive media training each year to reinforce this allegiance – to learn how to be a better spokes-person" for the sponsor. It also demanded a sacrifice of yet another nature where "during my Olympic year, I signed away my rights to use media time for just about anything other than gratitude to sponsors."[2]

This expectation that athletes are to completely devote themselves to their training and sponsors continues beyond their Olympic competition. As detailed in the case of the 1994 Lillehammer Games, even after the competition, athletes are made available only for a choreographed televised interview by selected journalists but are otherwise kept physically strictly separated from spectators and researchers alike. It appears that for some coaches and trainers, at least, competing at the Olympics means delivering their team on a private jet to the host city the day before the competitions, housing them separated from other athletes, and then whisking them away from the host city immediately after the Medals Ceremony. As described in the case of the 2006 Turin Games, athletes' living quarters are designed to encourage bonding and festivity and to cater to any taste and desire. These athletes, however, never once set foot into the Olympic Village and do not get to experience the Opening or the Closing Ceremonies because the absolute priority appears to be getting them back to their training facilities as soon as possible.[3]

This lonely journey towards wining is physically and emotionally taxing, but Mullen emphasizes that to sports enthusiasts "it is also noble... because one of the most important things to do in life is at least once [to] chase a dream with every ounce of power and conviction we can muster." This, Mullen suggests, may be the single most important appeal of the Olympic Games. "If you are a sports fan," Mullen tells the reader, "you believe that all sports build character and strengthen human will through tests, setbacks, and triumphs. You believe," he continues, "that all sports reinforce the notion that we improve ourselves through work and dedication." Therefore, he warns against the critics, "don't let anyone ever say sports don't matter. Sports matter more than almost anything else."

This strong sentiment and persuasion may be one of the reasons why athletes endure and their fans never tire of what Mullen calls "orderly sport...full of boundaries and enforced structure." It may help explain why athletes, their trainers, and their fans seem not to be encouraged to reflect on what it means that there is, in Mullen's words, "only one goal on everyone's mind: to move through the cool, blue water one-hundredth of a second faster than anyone else in the world." This ultimate, unshakable goal, to stand high in the center of the three-level podium, contributes little to interpersonal bonding and cross-cultural understanding. Instead, it encourages a continuous perfection of surveillance technologies and techniques to make minute distinctions between athletes possible, to allow for ceaseless random intrusions of purity tests, and to increase compliance to metal detectors and background checks. The glory of individual achievement and of chasing one's dreams with determination endures, first, within the strictures of bureaucratic regulations within each Olympic sport, is further subordinated to an international bureaucracy of the ultimate Olympic sports arbiter that is the International Olympic Committee, and is ultimately subjected to the parameters of the surveillance and security apparatus that ensures the safety of the Games. These dynamics point to the need for a more nuanced understanding of surveillance.

The naturalness of surveillance

Customarily, surveillance tends to be associated with an unnecessary intrusion of privacy on the part of the government and private enterprise. This aspect of surveillance has become symbolized through the rectangular prism-like closed circuit television camera mounted high on ceilings and street corners to peer at human activity below. This mystique about surveillance is compounded by the obscurity associated with the way surveillance apparatus works, the official secrecy through which the apparatus is legally protected from public scrutiny, as much as public expectations of getting things done. The International Olympic Committee, for example, has been adamant in its demand that surveillance procedures and technologies, from monitoring athletes for the use of unauthorized substances to scanning accreditation cards, be as inconspicuous as possible so as not to interfere with the festivity of the event. As suggested by its furious response to attempts by Julian Assange, Bradley Manning, James Risen, Edward Snowden, and others to bring surveillance to public attention, the surveillance apparatus itself seems to intensely dislike public discussion about the way it conducts its work. Rather than democratic participation and public input, the apparatus appears to value executive powers to make swift decisions that bypass public scrutiny and deliberation (see Sassen, 2008). No less important factors in this lack of understanding of how surveillance works is public expectation of efficiency and effectiveness. What we, as in situ spectators and media audiences scattered around the world, see are "results," that is, declarations and demonstrations that efficiency has been achieved, standards of performance upheld, and operational goals fulfilled. The actual workings of the surveillance apparatus that delivers and confirms these "results," however, are seldom explained to the public.

Such public discussion would help to uncover, in Harold Garfinkel's terms (1991), the common-sensical naturalness of surveillance in bureaucratically organized social orders and help to reveal why surveillance in the service of governance is so prevalent and so normalized that it is hardly noticed. It would facilitate an understanding of ways in which surveillance supports the functioning, management, planning, and governing of all bureaucratically organized institutions because the very existence of such institutions intimately depends on the ability to collect, analyze, and act on information about the lives of their members, customers, or clients. Such public discourse would also enlighten us about the fact that, while surveillance is central to bureaucratic organizations, the essence of this activity is, in principle, undemocratic and anti-social. It divides rather than unites, it imposes boundaries rather than encourages ties, it creates hierarchies rather than facilitates equalities, and subjects to authority rather than fosters deliberation. Why this is the case can be understood if we begin to grasp the fundamentals on which surveillance is based (Bajc, 2007a, 2010). Four elements which underlie the practice of surveillance are central in this regard: individuation, exclusionary classification, data analysis, and policy making.

Individuation assumes that every human being is identifiably unique (see Dumont, 1986). This enables collection and compilation of information about an individuals' behavior throughout their lifetime, from the moment when their birth certificate is issued and through to when their death is recorded. Individuation makes it possible to distinguish human beings from one another using different identifiers said to be unique to a particular human body, such as a bureaucratically assigned identity number, mug shot, fingerprint, retina scan, or DNA sequence. Based on such identifiers, information about each athlete's performance can be compiled throughout their career, and information about spectators', or volunteers behavior can be collected throughout their lifetime. So, too, it is on this basis that accreditation cards, as featured on the front cover of the book, can be granted to specific participants.

Exclusionary classification is a particular way of creating categories so as to enable the sorting out of compiled information into separate, non-overlapping categories (see Handelman, 2004, 1998). This information is organized through a particular way of seeing and understanding the world, which makes it possible to simplify the huge complexity of human behavior by classifying it into simplistic, mutually exclusive, clear-cut categories that can be easily invented according to the needs of those who sort out the information. To give but a few examples, the category "homegrown terrorist," became important at the London 2012 Games, the classification "foreign agent" was in use during the 1980 Moscow Games, while the category "radical sect" guided the workings of the apparatus at the 1972 Sapporo Games. While it is often pointed out that one person's terrorist is another's freedom fighter, exclusionary classification for the purposes of surveillance contains no such ambiguity. Rather, when information does not fit into any of existing categories, a new one is created. The ease with which exclusionary classification can be created makes it possible to efficiently handle huge amounts of information and helps to prevent those crises and confusions which could potentially result from information diversity and overload.

Individuation and exclusionary classification enable a separation of individuals from the information collected about them. It is not individuals as such that are object of surveillance but rather information about their behavior as it is recorded by surveillance technologies. Identity card swipes, credit card transactions, motion detector footage, communications interception recordings, records of athletes' performance in training and competitions codify information about how human beings behave. This takes away the burden of needing to engage with the persons directly or dealing with them face-to-face. This approach is based on the premise that human behavior can be treated as data, which can be analyzed for the purposes of social ordering. In this way, the apparatus works with the data and not the actual human beings to whom the information pertains. Through this process human beings become invisible, while the use of information about their behavior can acquire its own inertia and exert profound influences on their lives.

Classification-specific policy making pertains to the process of acting on the knowledge derived through data analysis. Classification and compilation of data are of no use unless policy specifications can be devised on how to act on this knowledge. This gives rise to rules, regulations, expert specializations, and a cadre of professionals who claim exclusive authoritative expertise on how to put such knowledge to use.

It is on this basis, as described in the case of the Montreal 1976 Games, that a photographer's behavior can be flagged as dangerous and thus the photographer promptly removed from an Olympic venue for changing his seat. This same logic makes it possible to pick out athletes as substance abusers and disqualify them from the Games.

Understood in this way, it becomes easy to see how, through the development of statistics and computational modeling, surveillance became a mode of governing for social institutions of all kinds as an efficient means for reducing the enormous diversity of human behavior into manageable activity (Desrosières, 1998; Foucault, 2008). Yet, left to its own terms, this skeleton of bureaucratic organization is void of ethics, anti-social, and undemocratic. Human and social qualities are not integral to the logic of surveillance. They need to be imposed on it from outside by the democratically enlightened citizenry and its ever vigilant civil society. It is for these reasons, as political philosopher Hanna Arendt (1951) and sociologist Zygmunt Bauman (1989) observed in the wake of the World War II, that modern nation-states are faced with an ongoing struggle between, on the one hand, authoritarian and totalitarian tendencies of its bureaucratic structures and, on the other hand, democratic values of human rights, privacy, equal participation, freedom of expression, collective deliberations, and collective decision-making on which modern social orders are based. These dynamics become strikingly visible when security is publicly acknowledged as the central collective priority.

Affinity of surveillance with security

The exclusionary, hierarchical, boundary-imposing, anti-social logic of surveillance pairs easily with security as value. Security is a particular kind of sentiment that is experienced as a feeling and felt as an emotion, and also has the capacity to become politically articulated as a specific agenda that takes on the character of ideology (Bajc, 2013). The logic of surveillance manifests itself in procedures, technologies, mathematical theorems, and computer modeling. This is a logic of practice in Bourdieu's (1990) sense. Security as value, in turn, comes to social life as a political persuasion of what constitutes acceptable order and safety, as espoused by the surveillance and security apparatus. This political persuasion is based on exclusionary premises so that it is able to unambiguously differentiate between safety and danger and clearly distinguish between what style of orderliness is acceptable and what type of chaos is deemed intolerable.

The case of the Olympic Games shows that, when coupled with security, the practice of surveillance, which is otherwise localized to specific institutions, is expanded to the domain of the systemic and to the level of the global, connecting practices of data accumulation and analysis between institutions worldwide. This surveillance–security nexus has a tendency to elevate the ideology of security to the top of collective priorities by overriding all other social values. Elsewhere I articulate this development which establishes a hierarchy rather than an equality by reducing the complexity of social life to simplified exclusionary categories, as security meta-framing (Bajc, 2011a). Security meta-framing is a logic of thought and practice which has the capacity to subordinate all social activity to its framing by establishing parameters and conditions of how collective public life is to be lived. These parameters are able to reduce the immense diversity of human life into categories of acceptable or not acceptable human behavior.

The exclusionary and hierarchical premise of security meta-framing can be understood in terms of Gregory Bateson's (2000 [1972]) theory of communication, where framing is an integral part of the process of how messages exchanged through interpersonal communication are to be understood and what kind of activity is to be related to that interpretation. I refer to one aspect of this communication process as meta-framing. The prefix "meta" signifies that, in this process, messages are communicated in such a way that they demand a hierarchical resolution, a zero-sum game affixed to dynamics which are in actuality very ambiguous and exceedingly complex. Meta-framing resonates with the Olympics as an event in which the complexity of what is understood as athletic performance by different cultures and huge cultural variations in the appreciation of athleticism are reduced to a competition which must generate winners and, by implication, losers. The supreme value of winning encourages standardization of sports and athleticism into categories which enable uniformly measurable outcomes (Chappelet and Kübler-Mabbott, 2008) and subordinates values of equal participation, comradeship, multiculturalism, and inclusion to these parameters. Olympic Medal Ceremonies, corporate sponsorship, mass media, and the ever more perfected performance surveillance technologies all serve this end.

In security meta-framing, "meta" signifies that there is a necessary hierarchy between distinct realities, organized according to exclusionary premises, where security stands for order, safety, progress, well-being, and achievement; while the alternative stands for disorder, destruction, fear, and potential violence. In this hierarchy of exclusionary thinking and action, security reduces the complexities of social life and the uncertainties these generate into mutually exclusive categories. The Olympic host is forced into a false dilemma, an erroneous choice between two mutually exclusive options. The first option is security, which can only be achieved through social order envisioned by the apparatus, in which privacy and democratic freedoms are necessarily compromised if surveillance is to be useful for security. The second option is the alternative in which chaos, disorder, destruction, and violence prevail because without effective surveillance stability is not possible and democracy cannot be practiced. The apparatus strives for the security meta-framing to be successful so that the public will easily choose security over the alternative. In the context of global planned events, such as the Olympics, security meta-ritual is one kind of social form that transpires through successful security meta-framing. Such social form generate, facilitate, and enable the emergence of a particular kind of social order. The specific goal of the security meta-ritual is to try to reduce dynamics and complexity with the hope of minimizing uncertainty in order to ensure that the performance of the Olympics will unfold as much as possible as a linear, predictable process. The kind of social order this generates is a sterile zone of safety, an enclosure with a controlled interior and an impermeable boundary that seals it off from its uncertain and dangerous surroundings.

Secure social order through surveillance–security nexus

A sterile zone of safety is an empirical manifestation of a particular vision of social ordering where uncertainty, indeterminacy, serendipity, and spontaneity in social interaction have been minimized for the sake of stability and predictability. This book outlines how this vision of society is made to happen by transforming the everyday social life of the Olympic host city into a secure kind of social order in which social life is lived under highly controlled conditions. This process follows the vision of the surveillance and security apparatus of what it means to live in a secure social and physical environment. In such social order, surveillance and security comprise a nexus in which surveillance technology, techniques, and operatives facilitate and manage social relations at a systemic level, while security dominates as a top collective priority. Conflicts are approached through the common interest in security in such a way that when tensions between different social and cultural groups arise, security is elevated to top priority over other collective values. In this process, the meaning of values central to democratic social relations such as privacy, human rights, equal participation, protection of minorities, freedom of speech, the right to public assembly, or collective political deliberation are adjusted in relation to the value of security and the specifications on the part of the apparatus for how this value is to be protected through surveillance.

Collective memories of violent disruptions to public social life are in many ways central to this process. Images and narratives of their destructive effects are broadcast live and in detail to the public locally and to media audiences around the world. Ceremonies and memorials at the site of destruction help ensure that these effects will continue to be commemorated and remembered. These collective memories of the past help encourage an expectation on the part of the public that such violent interruptions to collective life must be prevented. These public expectations are based on the assumption that the surveillance and security apparatus possesses the necessary expertise to preempt such activity in the future. The strategy on the part of the apparatus is to retrospectively reconstruct the process of the planning and execution of such interruptions using multiple surveillance sources and then treating this information as data to be analyzed for the purposes of envisioning how to prevent such interruptions from occurring at some future time. Conclusions from such analyses are accumulated as institutional knowledge on how to anticipate patterns of social life in the future. This knowledge of the past becomes central to how surveillance technologies and techniques are to be utilized to plan, manage, facilitate, and otherwise control social life in its becoming.

This approach to controlling the future through surveillance is systemic and it aspires to a global reach. Its systemic nature is evident through data sharing networks from the municipal to the state and beyond. Data collection is streamlined from local police, state intelligence agencies, the military, commercial, medical, educational, and religious establishments, and includes any other institution which generates surveillance data that can potentially be used for the purposes of securing the future. Its global reach is evident through the efforts to establish data sharing agreements with other such state-based systems around the world. The 1988 Seoul Games are an early example of such efforts. Institutions of order, otherwise subject to their own local rules and guidelines are reorganized hierarchically. In this effort, the principle of state sovereignty, as well as local and state legislation, may have to be adjusted to the needs of the security apparatus. The citizenry within this social order is also encouraged to contribute toward the common good of security. The public is expected to willingly offer to share private information for centralized data bases, subject themselves to surveillance of their communication and restrictions to their spatial mobility, follow instructions on how to behave in public spaces so as not to arouse suspicion, and help to accumulate information by actively reporting on the suspicious behavior of others.

The purified zone of safety is an exercise of a particular vision of social order in which democratic principles are adjusted to the needs of security. In this vision of sociality, public dissent is outlawed, perceptions of privacy are changed, and decisions about collective life are entrusted to a centralized authority. It is an opportunity for the military, secret services, police, private enterprise, volunteers, and event participants to practice how to work together under the umbrella of a centralized command and control authority. It is a laboratory for the surveillance and security apparatus to strengthen its network of experts and to test their power to impose on a sovereign government their latest surveillance technologies and techniques by testing how these work in real time. Security means that the social and physical environment of the Olympic city has been purified of individuals and groups who represent a threat to the security sanctioned social order and that the natural environment has been aesthetically purified into a surveillance-friendly landscape amenable to economic stimulus and appealing to potential foreign investment and tourism. The purified zone of safety is a demonstration of a commitment on the part of the citizenry, event performers, the state, and private enterprise that all available resources will be diverted to the value of the common goal of security even, as is frequently the case, when it leads to private and public debt. It is the evidence of capacity, power, and determination that a secure vision of social order can materialize with the cooperation of everyone involved.

It is worth recalling that this controlled transformation from everyday social life of the host city to sterile zone of safety is facilitated through a security meta-ritual. Importantly, as the name suggests, this social form resembles what scholars of culture and religion identify as ritual. Rituals are forms of collective activity found in every human society, throughout history. They are a medium through which social groups articulate collective sentiments and facilitate, shape, and control social change (Bell, 1997; Handelman, 1998). The secure social order that transpires through security meta-ritual espouses a particular nature of public social life, civic engagement, intellectual philosophy, structure or authority, and inter-personal interactions. It is based on excluding and boundary-making rather than including and facilitating social ties. It was invented by an apparatus of surveillance and security experts rather than an assembly of concerned citizens, community leaders, inspired intellectuals, or political philosophers. It transforms everyday life into a maximally controlled physical and social environment rather than embracing the complexities and ambiguities of collective social life. The apparatus insists that its vision of secure social order is the only acceptable version of sociality and vehemently resists public attempts to dissent. It has a strong preference for authoritarian decision-making and shows scant appreciation for privacy, spontaneous creativity, freedom of expression, and democratic participation. These characteristics suggest that sociality created through security meta-ritual is, in principle, not only anti-democratic but also anti-social.

This form of social organization has other notable characteristics. First, its nature is transitory. It is brought into existence for the duration of the Olympic Games with the specific purpose of protecting the event from unwanted disruption and is then disassembled. While the empirical manifestation of the sterile zone of safety is not lasting, its effects may continue to reverberate throughout the host country and beyond (Yu, Klauser, and Chan, 2009). Second, its nature has become global. We observe that it encapsulates planned events in cultures and societies worldwide, regardless of their political organization or the extent of their democratic culture. Third, its nature is flexible. The form can be adjusted to a wide range of global planned events, from state sponsored political events such as inaugurations and parades (Bajc, 2011b) to those with religious content (Bajc, 2007b), from sports events such as the Olympics or the World Cup to cultural events such as expos and carnivals. Fourth, it is also adaptable. It can mold itself to any physical environment, from rivers to mountains, from plains to forests and it can adjust itself to dense urban streets and high traffic avenues as much as sparsely populated remote areas. Lastly, the nature of this form is to continuously evolve. Each enactment is training in real time, an opportunity to put into practice new surveillance technologies, freshly trained operatives, and newly invented techniques. Each performance is a chance to adapt to new challenges in ever changing contexts.

Directions for future research

Given that the secure social order which transpires through security meta-ritual for the purposes of the Olympic Games is transitory in nature, how lasting are the effects of this transformation? When the curtain has dropped after the Closing Ceremony, the accreditation cardholders have left their assigned spaces, the huge white tents that housed the security checkpoints have been dismantled, the uniformed and undercover agents of order have returned to their regular assignments, the metal barriers and fences have been taken away, the military equipment has been removed, and the visitors at long last have had a chance to peek into the venues previously beyond reach – what is left behind from the just dismantled social and physical order in the sterile zone of safety?

These are questions that pertain to the effects of socialization on this particular vision of secure social order. Four come to mind. On the part of the participants, from spectators to athletes, how does this social ordering shape their individual experiences of the event? On the part of the agents of order – the police, firefighters, secret services, various military units, border patrol and others who were drawn from districts and offices from the host country and worldwide – as they return to their home offices, how will their experience in the Olympics shape the way things will be done in the home office? On the part of the political and business elites, who can now claim to have staged (perhaps yet another) successful Olympics, how will this experience of success shape their political culture? And on the part of the general public, which has just lived through weeks of intensive global attention and local excitement, what are the lasting effects in terms of their civic culture?

How surveillance procedures, whether in the service of governance or in the name of security, shape individual and collective experiences of the Olympics, and of global planned events more generally, remains an open research question, as yet largely unexplored. This is so not only in the case of the spectators and the general public but also the athletes, their trainers, their entourage, and other attendees. Strong ideological and emotional connections to such events may help explain, at least in part, how it is that despite been subjected to comprehensive and continuous surveillance it nevertheless becomes possible for many participants to burst into spontaneous expressions of collective excitement.[4] Detailed and nuanced ethnographic data help us understand possible cultural differences in the experience of collective sentiment as manifested during the Games in different host cities. The case of the Tokyo 1964 Games suggests that the Japanese government actively discouraged indigenous carnival-style festivity, while the streets of the 1976 Montreal Games did provide an environment for spontaneous public joy. In this light, the carnival culture in Rio de Janeiro, which is the host city for the 2016 Summer Games, is an important comparative case toward better understanding of cultural variations in individual and collective experiences of the Games.

The expectation is that state and state-empowered institutions of order will cooperate, not only domestically but also internationally, bringing together institutions with very different cultures of operation, technological levels of equipment, and sophistication in operational procedures. We gain some insight into what effects such encounters may have through the case of the 1988 Seoul Games. When the United States special operations force, Delta, arrived to train their South Korean counterparts in antiterrorism tactics through live exercises, their hosts were in such shock and awe that they forgot to close their mouths. This vivid description suggests that cooperation between agents of order likely has a strong impact on the host institution, not least in terms of how its leadership makes decisions about future training of its personnel. Such joint exercises, therefore, involve much more than training for a particular mission. They also tend to include contracts for purchasing equipment used in the exercises as well as training the weapons and equipment maintenance personnel, all of which, due to specificities of manufacturing and use, means a long-term commitment and dependency on the part of the host institution. Through this act of cooperation, the institution that is invited to train is also given an opportunity to mold the host institution according to its own template, which gives the invited institution additional advantages in terms of intelligence about activity and decision-making by the host institution. Lately it seems that such cooperation may also include highly paid public relations consultants who help shape the image of the newly trained host institution for its citizenry. In the effort to compete for attention on a global scale, cities may well have become laboratories for experimenting with how an opportunity to stage a global planned event, such as the Olympics, can be used as an occasion for such costly ventures to gain political approval.

Such demonstrations of enviable war and peacetime operations expertise may well serve not only as self-promotion for future potential contracts but also create a desire on the part of the aspiring elites in the host country, including police, military, and political officials, to be personally connected to such a global power. Instructive in this regard is an example of a politician explaining how the push to use all available resources for the 2004 Athens Olympics had prompted the organizers to turn to the United States for assistance. Utterly perplexed as to why anyone would find it unusual for Greece to turn to the United States for such advice, the official emphasized that, after all, he was invited on a visit to the country, which is the hegemonic global superpower, and then posed a disparaging rhetorical question: would he be expected to seek advice from a country like Tanzania instead? Such invitations tend to come with a carefully designed itinerary, which is structured in such a way as to imprint lasting desired impressions on the visitors. They may involve elaborate dinners with prominent political, military, business, and cultural elites, lavish socials in private homes and high-end entertainment venues, and visits to famous tourist attractions and state memorials, as well as gifts. Such visits support the accumulation of institutional knowledge. At the same time, they may also facilitate the creation, expansion, and strengthening of networks of surveillance and security experts and their supporting political elites.

Some possible ways in which the secure social order may shape the civic culture of the host country are suggested in the case of an official summary report on the effectiveness of policing of the 1972 Sapporo Games. The report asserts that the left-wing groups, which the organizers saw as potentially disruptive to the Games, gave up on public protest when they began to realize that public sentiment toward the Olympics had changed. The Japanese public had become welcoming and supportive of the Games as a direct result of sufficient resources made available to the police, specific surveillance strategies the police were allowed to use that would otherwise not be accepted by the public, and the extensive deliberately negative publicity in the news coverage of public protests by left-wing groups. This draws attention to the influence of the mass media on public sentiment. Which happening make front-page news and which are relegated to marginal columns toward the back of the newspaper, how long a story is run, what kind of mood the news conveys, and how the actors and their actions are reported and labeled, are all editorial decisions. This means that they are made by the newspaper's editorial team. It remains to be studied how people in the host country formulate their sentiments about the Olympics as they tune in to reporting by domestic and international mass media outlets and how these compete with messages communicated through the increasingly popular social media.

CODA

At this point, Beattie's unfortunate patient is burdened with more than the Olympics Ennui. He is now reflecting on how this version of social order compares to other kinds that transpire through meta-framing dynamics in other situations. Two come to mind, those pertaining to neoliberal economics and those related to modern warfare as exemplified through the, so-called, war on terror. The latter has been confronting the citizenry with a false choice between what are said to be two mutually exclusive versions of social order. One is based on the right to privacy, freedom of assembly, and individual legal rights. The other offers individual and communal safety and protection from social conflict through state surveillance and control. He has just been exposed to unbearable contradictions hiding behind the neoliberal meta-frame. The patient is contemplating how the citizenry is forced to face another false dilemma. The people are told that the emotional sentiment and ideological commitment to Western values, including solidarity, diversity, community, welfare, human rights, openness, and inclusion – are only possible under autocratic, hierarchical, anti-social, and anti-democratic neoliberal social order as envisioned by an apparatus made up of assorted state-empowered financial experts and elected political bureaucrats. The alternative is the illusion of democracy and sovereignty under conditions of bankruptcy, poverty, and violent outbursts of social conflict. In light of what exposure to the false dilemma of the neoliberal meta-frame has revealed so far, Beattie's patient may, at least for now, choose to relieve his physician of the pressure to help him resolve the contradictions of his Olympics Ennui and opt instead for a potion that will magically make these contradictions disappear.

Notes

1 All quotations are taken from P. H. Mullen's *Gold in the Water: The True Story of Ordinary Men and Their Extraordinary Dream of Olympic Glory*, published in 2001 in New York by Thomas Dunne Books, pages xi–xiv.
2 "Why the Olympics are a lot like 'The Hunger Games'" by Samantha Retrosi, *The Nation*, January 22, 2014.
3 Private communication regarding a team from the United States participating at the 2010 Vancouver Games.
4 Spontaneous collective joy and festivity, such as handholding, singing and dancing, have also been noted at other global planned events encompassed by the security meta-ritual, particularly pilgrims attending open-air mass officiated by the Pope on a visit to Jerusalem (Bajc, 2011b) and also visitors to the US presidential inauguration in Washington, DC. (Bajc, 2007).

Bibliography

Abe, Kiyoshi. 2004. Everyday Policing in Japan: Surveillance, Media, Government and Public Opinion. *International Sociology, 19*(2): 215–231.

Abrahams, Harold Maurice and David C. Young. 2013. "Olympic Games." In: *Encyclopædia Britannica. Encyclopædia Britannica Online*. Encyclopædia Britannica Inc.

Abrahamsen, Rita and Michael C. Williams. 2007. Securing the City: Private Security Companies and Non-State Authority in Global Governance. *International Relations, 21*: 237–253.

Abrahamsen, Rita and Michael C. Williams. 2009. Security Beyond the State: Global Security Assemblages in International Politics. *International Political Sociology, 3*: 1–17.

Agee, Philip. 1975. *Inside the Company: A C.I.A. Diary*. New York: Stonehill.

Ali, Tariq and Watkins, Susan. 1998. *1968: Marching in the Streets*. New York: The Free Press.

Anderson, Benedict. 1983. *Imagined Communities: Reflections on the Origin and Spread of Nationalism*. Revised Edition. London and New York: Verso.

Andrews, David L. and Michael L. Silk (Eds.). 2012. *Sport and Neoliberalism: Politics, Consumption, and Culture*. Philadelphia: Temple University Press.

Andrews, David L. 2003. Sport and the Transnationalizing Media Corporation. *Journal of Media Economics*, 16(4):235-251.

Anweiler, Oskar (Ed.). 1976. *Die sowjetische Bildungspolitik von 1958 bis 1973. Dokumente und Texte*, Berlin/Heidelberg: Quelle & Meier.

Archetti, Eduardo. 1999. "The Spectacle of Heroic Masculinity: Vegard Ulvang and Alberto Tomba in the Olympic Winter Games of Albertville." In: Arne Martin Klausen (Ed.) *Olympic Games as Performance and Public Event*. New York. Oxford. Berghahn Books, pp. 195–219.

Arendt, Hanna. 1951. *The origins of totalitarianism*. New York: Harcourt, Brace, Jovanovich.

Arvanitopoulos, Konstantinos and Koppa, Marilena (Eds). 2005. *Thirty Years of Greek Foreign Policy 1974–2004* (in Greek). Athens: Livanis.

Ashraf, Afzal. 2011. "Al Quaeda and the London Olympics." In: Anthony Richards, Pete Fussey and Andrew Silke (Eds) *Terrorism and the Olympics: Major Events Security and the Lessons for the Future*. New York: Routledge, pp. 32–48.

auf der Maur, Nick. 1976. *The Billion Dollar Game: Jean Drapeau and the 1976 Olympics*. Toronto: James Lorimer.

Avant, Deborah. 2005. *The Market for Force: Consequences of Privatizing Security*. New York: Cambridge University Press.

Avenell, Simon Andrew. 2010. *Making Japanese Citizens: Civil Society and the Mythology of the Shimin in Postwar Japan*. Berkeley: University of California Press.

Bacevich, Andrew J. (Ed). 2007. *The Long War: A New History of U.S. National Security Policy Since World War II*. New York: Columbia University Press.

Bajc, Vida. 2007a. "Introduction: Debating Surveillance in the Age of Security." In: Vida Bajc and John Torpey (Eds) Special issue "Watching out: Surveillance, Mobility, and Security." *American Behavioral Scientist, 50*(12): 1567–1591.

Bajc, Vida. 2007b. "Surveillance in Public Rituals: Security Meta-ritual and the 2005 U.S. Presidential Inauguration." Special issue "Watching out: Surveillance,

Mobility, and Security." Bajc and Torpey (Eds). *American Behavioral Scientist, 50*(12): 1648–1673.

Bajc, Vida. 2010. "On Surveillance as Solution to Security Issues." In: Graham Cassano and Richard Dello Buono (Eds) *Crisis, Politics, and Critical Sociology.* Leiden: Brill, pp. 183–196.

Bajc, Vida. 2011a. "Introduction. Security Meta Framing: A Cultural Logic of an Ordering Practice." In: Vida Bajc and Willem de Lint (Eds) *Security and Everyday Life.* NY, London: Routledge, pp. 1–28, 49–76.

Bajc, Vida. 2011b. "Collective Activity in Public Spaces: The Pope John Paul II in the Holy City." In: Bajc and de Lindt (Eds) *Security and Everyday Life.* New York: Routledge.

Bajc, Vida. 2012a. "Events, Global." In: Mark Juergensmeyer and Helmut Anheier (Eds) *Encyclopedia of Global Studies.* London: Sage.

Bajc, Vida. 2012b. Abductive Ethnography of Practice in Highly Uncertain Conditions. The *ANNALS of the American Academy of Political and Social Science, 642*(1): 72–85.

Bajc, Vida. 2013. Sociological Reflections on Security through Surveillance. *Sociological Forum, 28*(3): 280–293, 615–623.

Bajc, Vida. 2015. "The Future of Surveillance and Security in Global Events." In: Ian Yeoman et al. (Eds) *The Future of Events and Festivals.* London: Routledge, pp. 187–199.

Bakhtin, Mikhail M. 1968. *Rabelais and his world.* Cambridge, MA: M.I.T. Press.

Bale, John and Mette Krogh Christensen (Eds). 2004. *Post-Olympism: Questioning Sport in the Twenty First Century.* Oxford: Berg.

Bass, Amy. 2004. *Not the Triumph but the Struggle: The 1968 Olympics and the Making of the Black Athlete.* Minneapolis: University of Minnesota Press.

Bateson, Gregory. 1972. *Steps to an Ecology of Mind.* Novato: Chandler Publishing Company.

Bauman, Zygmunt. 1989. *Modernity and the Holocaust.* Ithaca, NY: Cornell University Press.

Bayly, Christopher. 1996. *Empire and Information: Intelligence Gathering and Social Communication in India, 1780–1870.* Cambridge: Cambridge University Press.

Beck, Ulrich. 1992. *Risk Society: Towards a New Modernity.* London: Sage.

Beck, Ulrich. 1994. "The Reinvention of Politics: Towards a Theory of Reflexive Modernization." In: Ulrich Beck, Anthony Giddens and Scott Lash (Eds) *Reflexive Modernization – Politics, Tradition and Aesthetics in the Modern Social Order.* Stanford: Stanford University Press, pp. 1–55.

Beck, Ulrich. 1999. *World Risk Society.* Cambridge: Polity.

Bell, Catherine. 1992: *Ritual Theory, Ritual Practice.* New York, Oxford: Oxford University Press.

Bell, Daniel A. 2008. *China's New Confucianism: Politics and Everyday life in a Changing Society.* New Jersey: Princeton University Press.

Bellavita, Christopher. 2007. Changing homeland security: A strategic logic of special event security. *Homeland Security Affairs, 3*(3): 1–23.

Benjamin, Walter. 1968. "The Work of Art in the Age of Mechanical Reproduction." In: *Illuminations: Essays and Reflections.* Hannah Arendt (Ed.) Trans. Harry Zohn. New York: Schocken Books.

Bennett, Colin and Kevin Haggerty (Eds). 2011. *Security Games: Surveillance and Control at Mega-Events.* London: Routledge.

Berkaak, Odd Are. 1999a. "A Place in the Sun: The Vernacular Landscape as Olympic Venue." In: Arne Martin Klausen (Ed.) *Olympic Games as Performance and Public Event.* NY, Oxford: Berghahn Books, pp. 137–172.

Berkaak, Odd Are. 1999b. "'In the Heart of the Volcano': The Olympic Games as Mega Drama." In: Arne Martin Klausen (Ed.) *Olympic Games as Performance and Public Event.* NY, Oxford: Berghahn Books, pp. 49–74.

Boileau, Roger, Fernand Landry, and Vincent Trempe. 1976. "Les Canadiens francais et le Grands Jeux Internationaux." In: Richard Gruneau and John Albinson (Eds) *Canadian Sport. Sociological Perspectives.* Don Mills: Addison Wesley, pp. 141–169.

Booth, Douglas. 2004. "Post-Olympism? Questioning Olympic Historiography." In: John Bale and Metta Krough Christensen (Eds) *Post-Olympism: Questioning Sport in the Twenty First Century.* Oxford: Berg, pp. 13–32.

Bothwell, Robert, Ian Drummond, and John English. 1981. *Canada Since 1945: Power, Politics and Provincialism.* Toronto: University of Toronto Press.

Bousfield, Dan and Jean Michel Montsion. 2012. Transforming an International Organization: Norm Confusion and the International Olympic Committee, *Sport in Society,* 15(6): 823–838.

Bowker, Geoffrey C. and Susan Leigh Star. 1999. *Sorting Things Out: Classification and Its Consequences.* Cambridge, MA: MIT Press.

Boyle, Philip. 2011. "Knowledge Networks: Mega-events and Security Expertise." In: Colin Bennett and Kevin Haggerty (Eds) *Security Games: Surveillance and Control at Mega-Events.* London: Routledge, pp. 169–184.

Boyle, Philip and Kevin Haggerty. 2009. Spectacular Security: Mega-Events and the Security Complex. *International Political Sociology,* 3(2): 257–274.

Boyle, Philip and Kevin Haggerty. 2012. Planning for the Worst: Risk, Uncertainty, and the Olympic Games. *The British Journal of Sociology,* 63(2): 241–259.

Brauer, Jurgen and Hubert Van Tuyll. 2008. *Castles, Battles & Bombs: How Economics Explains Military History.* Chicago: University of Chicago Press.

Brown, Wendy. 2005. *Edgework: Critical Essays on Knowledge and Politics.* Princeton and Oxford: Princeton University Press.

Brownell, Susan. 2008. *Beijing's Games: What the Olympics Mean to China.* Lanham, MD: Rowman & Littlefield.

Buzan, Berry, Ole Wæver and J. de Wilde (Eds) 1998. *Security: A New Framework for Analysis.* Boulder, CO: Lynne Rienner.

Callahan, William A. 2006. History, Identity, and Security: Producing and Consuming Nationalism in China. *Critical Asian Studies,* 38(2): 179–208.

Carey, Elaine. 2005. *Plaza of Sacrifices: Gender, Power, and Terror in 1968 Mexico.* Albuquerque: University of New Mexico.

Carmola, Cateri. 2010. *Private Security Contractors and New Wars: Risk, Law and Ethics.* New York: Routledge.

Chalkley, Brian and Stephen Essex. 1999. Urban Development through Hosting International Events: A History of the Olympic Games. *Planning Perspectives, 14:* 369–394.

Chan-jung, Kim. 1997. *Sainichi Korian hyakunenshi* [*100-Years History of the Korean Residents in Japan*]. Tôkyô: Sangokan.

Chappelet, Jean-Loup and Brenda Kübler-Mabbott. 2008. *The International Olympic Committee and the Olympic System: The Governance of World Sport.* Routledge.

Chatziefstathiou, Dikaia. 2011. Paradox and Contestations of Olympism in the History of the Modern Olympic Movement, *Sport in Society,* 14(3): 332–344.

Chester, David. 1971. *The Olympic Games Handbook.* New York: Charles Scribner's Sons.

Chiamparino, Sergio. 2006. "La città di Torino e i XX Giochi invernali." In Piervincenzio Bondonio, Egidio Dansero, and Alfredo Mela (Eds) *Olimpiadi, oltre il 2006,* Carocci, Roma. Chicago: The University of Chicago Press.

Chong, Gladys P.L. 2008. China op het Olympische erepodium. *Agora, 24*(2): 17–21.

Chong, Gladys P.L. 2011. Governing Citizens through Soft Power: Volunteers as the New Model Citizens. *China Information, 25*(1): 35–59.

Clifford, James. 1992. "Travelling Cultures." In: Laurence Grossberg, Cary Nelson, and Paula Treichler (Eds) *Cultural Studies.* New York: Routledge, pp. 96–112.

Coaffee, Jon. 2011. "Strategic Security Planning and the Resilient Design of Olympic Sites." In: Anthony Richards, Pete Fussey and Andrew Silke (Eds) *Terrorism and the Olympics: Major Event Security and Lessons for the Future.* New York: Routledge, pp. 118–131.

Coaffee, Jon and Lorraine Johnston. 2007. "Accommodating the Spectacle." In: John R. Gold and Margaret M. Gold (Eds) *Olympic Cities: City Agendas, Planning and the World's Games, 1896–2012.* London: Routledge, pp. 138–149.

Collins, Sandra. 2007. *The 1940 Tokyo Games: The Missing Olympics: Japan, the Asian Olympics and the Olympic Movement.* London: Routledge.

Comaroff, Jean and John Comaroff. 1992. *Ethnography and Historical Imagination.* Boulder, CO: Westview Press.

Connerton, Paul. 1989. *How Societies Remember.* Cambridge: Cambridge University Press.

Conversi, Daniele. 1997. *The Basques, the Catalans and Spain: Alternative Routes to Nationalist Mobilization.* London: Hurst and Company.

Cox, Robert W. 1993. "Gramsci, Hegemony and International Relations: An Essay in Method." In: Stephen Gill (Ed.) *Gramsci, Historical Materialism and International Relations.* Cambridge: Cambridge University Press, pp. 49–66.

Csordas, Thomas (Ed.). 1994. *Embodiment and Experience. The Existential Ground of Culture and Self.* Cambridge and New York: Cambridge University Press.

Dansero, Egidio, Barbara Del Corpo, Alfredo Mela, and Irene Ropolo. 2012. "Olympic Games, Conflicts and Social Movements: The Case of Torino 2006." In: Graeme Hayes and John Karamichas (Eds) *Olympic Games, Mega-Events and Civil Societies.* New York: Palgrave Macmillan, pp. 195–281.

Dayan, Daniel and Elihu Katz. 1992. *Media Events: The Live Broadcasting of History.* Cambridge, MA: Harvard University Press.

de Kloet, Jeroen and Wei Liu. 2008. "Flaming a Debate – On the Multiple Meanings of the Olympic torch Relay Spectacle." *Blind – Interdisciplinair Tijdschrift,* Issue 17.

de Kloet, Jeroen, Gladys Pak Lei Chong, and Wei Liu. 2008. The Beijing Olympics and the Art of Nation-State Maintenance. *Journal of Current Chinese Affairs, 37*(2): 6–37.

de Kloet, Jeroen, Gladys Pak Lei Chong, and Stefan Landsberger. 2011. "National Image Management at Home: Imagining the New Olympic Citizen." In: Jian Wang (Ed.) *Soft Power in China: Public Diplomacy through Communication.* Palgrave Macmillan.

de Moragas Spa, Miguel, Nancy Kay Rivenburgh and James F. Larson (Eds). 1995. *Television and the Olympics.* London: John Libbey.

Dean, Mitchell. 2010. Power at the Heart of the Present: Exception, Risk and Sovereignty. *European Journal of Cultural Studies, 13*(4): 459–475.

Decker, Scott H., Jack R. Greene, Vince Webb, Jeff Rojek, Jack McDevitt, Tim Bynum, et al. 2005. Safety and Security at Special Events: The Case of the Salt Lake City Olympic Games. *Security Journal, 18*(4): 65–74.

Decker, Scott H., Paul Lewis, Doris Provine, and Monica Varsanyi. 2009. "On the Frontier of Local Law Enforcement: Local Police and Federal Immigration Law." In: William F. McDonald (Ed.) *Immigration, Crime and Justice (Sociology of Crime, Law and Deviance, Volume 13).* Bingley, UK: Emerald Books, pp. 261–276.

Decker, Scott H., Sean P. Varano, and Jack R. Greene. 2008. Routine Crime in Exceptional Times: The Case of the Salt Lake Olympics. *Journal of Criminal Justice, 35*(1): 89–101.

Deleuze, Gilles. 1992. Postscript on the Societies of Control. *October, 59*: 3–7.

Despard, Erin. 2012. Cultivating Security: Plants in the Urban Landscape. *Space and Culture, 15*(2): 151–163.

Desrosières, Alain. 1998. *The Politics of Large Numbers: A History of Statistical Reasoning.* Cambridge, MA: Harvard University Press.

Dobrynin, Anatolii. 2011. *In Confidence: Moscow's Ambassador to Six Cold War Presidents.* Seattle: University of Washington Press.

Douglas, Mary. 1966. *Purity and Danger: An Analysis of the Concepts of Pollution and Taboo.* London: Routledge & Kegan Paul.

Dower, John W. 1999. *Embracing Defeat: Japan in the Wake of World War II.* New York: W.W. Norton.

Downe, Pamela J. 2006. "Aboriginal Girls in Canada: Living Histories of Dislocation, Exploitation and Strength." In: Yasmin Jiwani, Candis Steenbergen and Claudia Mitchell (Eds) *Girlhood: Redefining the Limits.* Montreal: Black Rose Books, pp. 1–14.

Drache, Daniel (Ed.). 1972. *Quebec—Only the Beginning: The Manifestoes of the Common Front.* Toronto: New Press.

Dunigan, Molly. 2011. *Victory for Hire: Private Security Companies' Impact on Military Effectiveness.* Palo Alto: Stanford University Press.

Dwertmann, Hubert and Lorenz Pfeiffer. 2001. "Zwischen Kontinuität, systematischem Neuaufbau und Transformation. Willi Daume – 'das neue' Gesicht im bundesrepubliknischen Sport." In: Michael Krüger (Hrsg.) *Transformationen des deutschen Sports seit 1939.* Czwalina Verlag Hamburg, pp. 135–152.

Edelman, Robert. 2006. "Moscow 1980: Stalinism or Good, Clear Fun?" In: Alan Tomlinson and Christopher Young (Eds) *National Identity and Global Sports Events: Culture, Politics, and Spectacle in the Olympics and the Football World Cup.* New York: SUNY Press, pp. 149–161.

Eidelman, Tamara. 2010. "XXII Summer Olympic Games. July 19–August 3, 1980. *Russian Life,* July/August: 19–21.

Essex, Stephen and Brian Chalkley. 1998. Olympic Games: Catalyst of Urban Change. *Leisure Studies, 17*(3): 187–206.

Esteva, Gustavo and Madhu Suri Prakesh. 1998. *Grassroots Post-modernism: Remaking the Soil of Cultures.* London: Zed Books.

Evens, T. M. S. and Don Handelman (Eds). 2006. *The Manchester School: Practice and Ethnographic Praxis in Anthropology.* New York and Oxford: Berghahn Books.

Fakitsas, Miltiadis. 2003. *The Rise and the Fall of Terrorist Organizations in Post-dictatorial Greece.* Master of Arts, Naval Postgraduate School, Monterey, USA.

Falzon, Mark-Anthony (Ed.). 2009. *Multi-sited Ethnography: Theory, Praxis and Locality in Contemporary Research.* Farnham: Ashgate.

Feldbrugge, Ferdinand J.M., Gerard Pieter van den Berg, and William B. Simons (Eds). 1985. *Encyclopedia of Soviet Law,* 2nd revised edition. Dordrecht: Nijhoff.

Field, Deborah. 2007. *Private Life and Communist Morality in Khrushchev's Russia.* New York: Lang.

Floridis, George. 2004. Security for the 2004 Athens Olympic Games. *Mediterranean Quarterly, 15*(2): 1–15.

Floros, Christos and Bruce Newsome. 2008. Building Counter-Terrorism Capacity Across Borders: Lessons from the Defeat of "Revolutionary Organization November 17th." *Journal of Security Sector Management, 6*(2).

Foucault, Michel. 1973. *The Order of Things: An Archeology of the Human Sciences*. New York: Vintage.

Foucault, Michel. 1991. "Governmentality." In: Graham Burchell, Colin Gordon, and Peter Miller (Eds) *The Foucault Effect: Studies in Governmentality*. Sydney: Harvester/Wheatsheaf, pp. 97–104.

Foucault, Michel. 1994 [1966]. *The Order of Things: An Archaeology of the Human Sciences*. New York: Vintage.

Foucault, Michel. 1995 [1977]. *Discipline and Punish: The Birth of the Prison*. New York: Vintage Books.

Foucault, Michel. 2004. *Naissance de la biopolitique: Cours au Collège de France (1978–1979)*. Paris: Seuil.

Foucault, Michel. 2007. *Security, Territory, Population: Lectures at the College de France 1977–1978*. New York: Palgrave Macmillan.

Foucault, Michel. 2008 [2004]. *The Birth of Biopolitics: Lectures at the Collège de France, 1978–1979*. G. Burchell (trans.). New York: Palgrave Macmillan.

Fujitake, Akira. 1967. "Tôkyô orinpikku: Sono 5-nenkan no ayumi [A road of five years]." In: NHK (Ed.) *Tôkyô orinpikku* [The Tôkyô Olympics]. Tôkyô: Nihon hôsô kyôkai hôsô yoron chôsajo, pp. 7–102.

Fussey, Pete. 2011. "Surveillance and the Olympic Spectacle." In: Anthony Richards, Pete Fussey and Andrew Silke (Eds) *Terrorism and the Olympics: Major event security and lessons for the future*. New York: Routledge, pp. 91–117.

Fussey, Pete and Jon Coaffee. 2012. Balancing Local and Global Security Leitmotifs: Counter-terrorism and the Spectacle of Sporting Mega-events. *International Review for the Sociology of Sport*, 47(3): 268–285.

Fussey, Pete, Jon Coaffee, Gary Armstrong, and Dick Hobbs. 2011. *Securing and Sustaining the 2012 Olympic City: Reconfiguring London for 2012 and Beyond*. Aldershot: Ashgate.

Garcia-Ramon, Maria-Dolors and Abel Albet. 2000. Commentary: Pre-Olympic and Post-Olympic Barcelona: A "Model" for Urban Regeneration Today? *Environment and Planning A*, 32(8): 1331–1334.

Garfinkel, Harold. 1991. *Studies in Ethnomethodology*. Wiley.

Gestwa, Klaus. 2011. "Sicherheit in der Sowjetunion 1988/89. Perestrojka als miss-glückter Tanz auf dem zivilisatorischem Vulkan." In: Matthias Stadelmann and Lilia Antipow (Eds) *Schlüsseljahre. Zentrale Konstellationen der mittel- und osteuropäischen Geschichte; Festschrift für Helmut Altrichter zum 65. Geburtstag*. Stuttgart: Steiner, pp. 449–469.

Geyer, Florian. 2007. "Fruit of the Poisonous Tree. Member States' Indirect Use of Extraordinary Rendition and the EU Counter-Terrorism Strategy." CEPS Working Document, no. 263.

Giordano, Roberto (Ed.). 2005. *La valutazione ambientale strategica dei XX Giochi olimpici invernali Torino 2006*. Edicom, Monfalcone.

Giulianotti, Richard and Francisco Klauser. 2010. Security Governance and Sport Mega-Events: Toward an Interdisciplinary Research Agenda. *Journal of Sport and Social Issues*, 34(1): 49–61.

Glaeser, Andreas. 2011. *Political Epistemics: The Secret Police, the Opposition, and the End of East German Socialism*. University of Chicago Press.

Gluck, Carol and Stephen Graubard (Eds). 1992. *Showa: The Japan of Hirohito*. New York: Norton.

Goffman, Erving. 1961. *Asylum: Essays on the Social Situation of Mental Patients and Other Inmates*. Anchor Books / Doubleday.

Gold, John R. and Margaret M. Gold. 2007. "Athens to Athens: The Summer Olympic, 1896–2004." In: John R. Gold and Margaret M. Gold (Eds) *Olympic Cities. City Agendas, Planning, and the World's Games, 1896–2012*. London: Routledge, pp. 34–36.

Graham, Stephen. 2011. *Cities Under Siege: The New Military Urbanism*. London: Verso.

Groussard, Serge. 1975. *The Blood of Israel. The Massacre of the Israeli Athletes at The Olympics 1972*. New York: William Morrow & Company.

Gruneau, Richard and Robert Neubauer. 2012. "A Gold Medal for the Market: The 1984 Los Angeles Olympics, the Reagan Era and the Politics of Neoliberalism." In: Helen Lenskyj and Stephen Wagg (Eds) *Handbook of Olympic Studies*. London: Palgrave Macmillan, pp. 134–162.

Gutmann, Matthew C. 2002. *The Romance of Democracy: Compliant Defiance in Contemporary Mexico*. Berkeley: University of California Press.

Guttmann, Allen. 1984. *The Games Must Go On. Avery Brundage and the Olympic movement*. Columbia University Press.

Guttmann, Allen. 2002. *The Olympics, a History of the Modern Games*. University of Illinois Press.

Haake, Steve. 2012. Material Advantage? *Physics World, 25*(7): 26–30.

Hacking, Ian. 1990. *The Taming of Chance*. Cambridge University Press.

Hagan, John, John D. Hewitt, and Duane F. Alwin. 1979. Ceremonial Justice: Crime and Punishment in a Loosely Coupled System. *Social Forces, 58*(2): 506–527.

Hain, Laura E. 1993. "Growth Versus Success: Japan's Economic Policy in Historical Perspective." In: Andrew Gordon (Ed.) *Postwar Japan as History*. Berkeley: University of California Press, pp. 99–122.

Hall, Stuart, Chas Critcher, Tony Jefferson, John N. Clarke, and Brian Roberts. 1978. *Policing the Crisis: Mugging, the State and Law and Order*. London: Macmillan.

Handelman, Don. 1998. *Models and Mirrors: Towards an Anthropology of Public Events* (2nd edition). New York: Berghahn.

Handelman, Don. 2004. *Nationalism and the Israeli State: Bureaucratic Logic in Public Events*. Oxford, UK: Berg.

Handelman, Don. 2007. "The Cartesian divide of the nation-state: emotion and bureaucratic logic." In: Helena Wulff (Ed.) *The Emotions: A Cultural Reader*. Berg Publishers, pp. 119–140.

Handelman, Don and Lea Shamgar-Handelman. n.d. *The Memorial Olympics of 1984: Israel and the Symbolism of Nationalism and Internationalism in Los Angeles*. Unpublished manuscript.

Hansen, Jørn. 2004. *Ringene samles – en fortælling om den olympiske bevægelse (The Gathering of the Rings – An Account of the Olympic Movement)*. Odense University Press.

Hansen, Jørn. 2009. "Mellem forførelse og overvågning – De Olympiske Lege i Berlin 1936, München 1972 og Beijing 2008." In: Ask Vest Christiansen (Ed.) *Kontrolsport. Big Brother blandt atleter og tilskuere*. Odense, Denmark: Syddansk Universitetsforlag.

Haraguchi, Kanemasa. 2010. "Succeeding by Destroying a Growth Model." In: Yôzô Hasegawa (Ed.) *Rediscovering Japanese Business Leadership: 15 Japanese Managers and the Companies They're Leading to New Growth*. Singapore: Wiley, pp. 1–16.

Hargreaves, John. 2000. *Freedom for Catalonia? Catalan Nationalism, Spanish Identity and the Barcelona Olympic Games*. Cambridge: Cambridge University Press.

Hargreaves, John and Manuel Garcia Ferrando. 1997. Public Opinion, National Integration and National Identity in Spain: The Case of the Barcelona Olympic Games. *Nations and Nationalism, 3*(1): 65–87.

Hartmann, Grit. 1998. *Goldkinder. Die DDR im Spiegel ihres Spitzensports.* Forum Verlag Leipzig.
Hashimoto, Kazuo. 1994. *Maboroshi No Tôkyô Orinpikku [The Olympics of Tôkyô that Stayed an Illusion].* Tôkyô: NHK books.
Hevia, James. 2012. *The Imperial Security State: British Colonial Knowledge and Empire-building in Asia.* Cambridge: Cambridge University Press.
Hilger, Andreas. 2009. "Sowjetunion (1945–1991)." In: Łukasz Kamiński, Krysztof Persak and Jens Gieseke (Eds) *Handbuch der kommunistischen Geheimdienste in Osteuropa 1944–1991.* Göttingen: Vandenhoeck & Ruprecht.
Hobsbawm, Eric. 1994. *Age of Extremes. The Short Twentieth Century.* Penguin.
Hobsbawm, Eric and Terence Ranger (Eds). 1983. *The Invention of Tradition.* Cambridge University Press.
Hooper, John. 2006. *The New Spaniards* (2nd Edition). London: Penguin.
Hoskin, Keith. 1996. "'The Awful Idea of Accountability': Inscribing People into the Measurement of Objects." In: Rolland Munro and Jan Mouritsen (Eds) *Accountability: Power, Ethos, and the Technologies of Managing.* London: International Thomson Business Press, pp. 265–282.
Hoskin, Keith W. and Richard H. Macve. 1995. "Accounting and the Examination: A Genealogy of Disciplinary Power." In: Barry Smart (Ed.) *Michel Foucault (2): Critical Assessments.* London: Routledge, pp. 99–138.
Hughes-Freeland, Felicia (Ed.). 1998. *Ritual, Performance, Media.* ASA Monograph 35. London and New York: Routledge.
Hughes-Freeland, Felicia and Mary M. Crain (Eds). 1998. *Recasting Ritual. Performance, Media, Identity.* London and New York: Routledge.
Hughes, Robert. 2001. *Barcelona.* London: The Harvill Press.
Igarashi, Yoshikuni. 2000. *Bodies of Memory: Narratives of War in Postwar Japanese Culture, 1945–1970.* Princeton, NJ: Princeton University Press.
Inoue, Kyôko. 1991. *MacArthur's Japanese Constitution: A Linguistic and Cultural Study of Its Making.* Chicago: University of Chicago Press.
Irokawa, Daikichi. 1990. Shôwashi [History of the Shôwa era]: Sesôhen [Volume Social Situation]. Tokyo: Shôgakukan.
Janowitz, Morris. 1960. *The Professional Soldier: A Social and Political Portrait.* New York: The Free Press.
Joachim, Jutta and Andrea Schneiker. 2012. New Humanitarians? Frame Apropriation through Private Military and Security Companies. *Millennium – Journal of International Studies* 40: 365–388.
Judt, Tony. 2005. *Postwar: A History of Europe since 1945.* New York: Penguin.
Jule, Walter (Ed.). 1997. *Sightlines: Printmaking and Image Culture.* Edmonton: University of Alberta Press.
Junger-Tas, Josine and Scott H. Decker. 2006. *International Handbook of Juvenile Justice.* New York: Springer.
Kaiser, Günter. 1969. "Kriminologie." In: C. D. Kernig (Ed.) *Sowjetsystem und demokratische Gesellschaft, Vol. 3: Ideologie bis Leistung,* Freiburg: Herder, p. 1118.
Katrougalos, George. 2010. "Security and Freedom: Surveillance of Public Space." (in Greek) In: Minas Samatas (Ed.) *Opseis tis neas parakolouthisis.* Athens: Vivliorama, pp. 159–178.
Katz, Charles M., Edward R. Maguire, and Dennis W. Roncek. 2002. The Creation of Specialized Police Gang Units: A Macro-Level Analysis of Contingency, Social Threat and Resource Dependency Explanations. *Policing: An International Journal of Police Strategies & Management,* 25(3): 472–506.

Kennelly, Jacqueline and Paul Watt. 2011. Sanitizing Public Space in Olympic Host Cities: The Spatial Experiences of Marginalized Youth in 2010 Vancouver and 2012 London. *Sociology*, *45*(5): 765–781.

Kidd, Bruce. 2004. "Montreal 1976." In: John Findling and Kimberly Pelle (Eds) *Encyclopedia of the Modern Olympic Movement.* Westport, CT: Praeger, pp. 191–198.

Kidd, Bruce. 2010. Human Rights and the Olympic Movement after Beijing. *Sport and Society*, *13*(5): 901–910.

Kiernan, John and Arthur Daley. 1969. *Story of the Olympic Games, 776 BC to 1968.* New York: J.B. Lippincott Co.

Killanin, Lord. 1983. *My Olympic Years.* London: Secker and Warburg.

Kim, Dal-sul. 1987. 88 SeoulOlympicgwa Nambukhangwangye (88 Seoul Olympics and Relationship between the South and the North Koreas), No. 189, North Korea, Seoul: Institute of North Korean Studies, pp. 48–55.

Kim, Je-hong. 2004. *Daegyumo Sportshaengsa eui gyeonghogyeongbie gwanghan yeon-gu (Study on the Protection and Security for the Mega Sports Events),* Unpublished Master Thesis. Seoul: Korea National Sports University.

Kim, Myeong-gon. 2000. *Terroyong pokbalmul geomcheuk eui hyoyuljeok chegye (A Study on the Effective Search System for the Terrorist's Explosives),* Unpublished MD Thesis. Seoul: Korea National Sports University.

Kim, Myeong-gon. 2006. *Sportsshiseol eui anjeonshiltae mit daeterrodaechaeke wanghan yeon-gu (A Study on Safety of Sports Facilities and Countermeasures against Terrorism),* Unpublished PhD Thesis. Seoul: Korea National Sports University.

King, Mike. 1997. Policing and Public Order Issues in Canada: Trends for Change. *Policing and Society*, *8*(1): 47–76.

Kinsman, Gary and Patrizia Gentile. 2010. *The Canadian War on Queers: National Security as Sexual Regulation.* Vancouver: UBC Press.

Klausen, Arne Martin. 1996. *Lillehammer-Ol og olympismen.* Oslo: Ad notam Gyldendal.

Klausen, Arne Martin. 1999a. "Introduction." In: Arne Martin. Klausen (Ed.) *Olympic Games as Performance and Public Event.* New York and Oxford: Berghahn Books, pp. 1–8.

Klausen, Arne Martin. 1999b. "Norwegian Culture and Olympism: Confrontation and Adaptations." In: Arne Martin Klausen (Ed.) *Olympic Games as Performance and Public Event.* New York and Oxford: Berghahn Books, pp. 27–48.

Klausen, Arne Martin (Ed.). 1999c. *Olympic Games as Performance and Public Event.* New York and Oxford: Berghahn Books.

Klausen, Arne Martin. 1999d. "The Torch Relay. Reinvention of Traditions and Conflict with the Greeks." In: Arne Martin Klausen (Ed.) *Olympic Games as Performance and Public Event.* New York. Oxford. Berghahn Books, pp. 75–96.

Klausen, Arne Martin, Odd Are Berkaak, Ellen K. Aslaksen, Ingrid Rudie, Roel Puijk, and Eduardo P. Archetti. 1995. *Fakkelstafetten – en olympisk ouverture.* Oslo: Ad Notam Gyldendal.

Klauser, Francisco. 2009. "Spatial Articulations of Surveillance at the FIFA World Cup 2006 in Germany." In: Katja Franko Aas, Helene Oppen Gundhus, and Heidi Mork Lomell (Eds) *Technologies of Insecurity.* London: Routledge, pp. 61–80.

Kluge, Volker. 1999. *Olympiastadion Berlin. Steine beginnen zu reden.* Parthas-Verlag.

Knecht, Willi. 1980. *Der Boykott. Moskaus mißbrauchte Olympiade,* Köln: Verlag Wissenschaft und Politik.

Knight, Amy. 1990. *The KGB. Police and Politics in the Soviet Union.* Boston: Unwin Hyman.

Knorr-Cetina, Karin. 2005. Complex Global Microstructures: The New Terrorist Societies. *Theory, Culture and Society*, *22*(5): 213–134.

Kobrin, Stephen J. 1997. "The Architecture of Globalization: State Sovereignty in a Networked Global Economy." In: Dunning (Ed.) *Governments, Globalization, and International Business.* Oxford: Oxford University Press, pp. 146–172.

Koss, Johan, Ann Peel, and Alexandra Orlando. 2011. "Athletes' rights and Olympic reform," *Sport in Society, 14*(3): 309–318.

Kunze, Thomas. 2008. *Russlands Unterwelten. Eine Zeitreise durch geheime Bunker und vergessene Tunnel.* Berlin: Links.

Leander, Anna. 2005. The Power to Construct International Security: On the Significance of Private Military Companies. *Millennium – Journal of International Studies, 33*: 803–826.

Lee, Dorothy. 1950. Codifications of Reality: Lineal and Nonlineal. *Journal of Psychosomatic Medicine, 12*: 89–97.

Lee, Bang-won. 1989. *Seoul Korea.* Seoul: Haengrim.

Lee, Chang Moo. 2004. Accounting for Rapid Growth of Private Policing in South Korea. *Journal of Criminal Justice, 32*(2): 113–122.

Lee, Dae-seong. 2008. *Terrobeomjoe eui donghyangbunseokgwa daeeungbangane daehan heonbeopjeok yeon-gu (A Constitutional Study on Trends Analysis and its Response of International Terrorism Occurred in South Korea).* Seoul: Korean Branch of International Association of Constitutional Law.

Lefebvre, Henri. 1968. *Le droit a la ville.* Anthropos, Paris.

Leonardsen, Dag. 2006. Crime in Japan: Paradise Lost? *Journal of Scandinavian Studies in Criminology and Crime Prevention, 7*: 185–219.

Levy, Daniel and Natan Sznaider. 2006. *The Holocaust and Memory in the Global Age.* Philadelphia, PA: Temple University Press. Translated from German by Assenka Oksiloff.

Li, Hongmei. 2011. The Gendered Performance at the Beijing Olympics: The Construction of the Olympic Misses and Cheerleaders. *Communication Theory, 21*(4): 368–391.

Lipschutz, Ronni (Ed). 1995. *On Security.* New York: Columbia University Press.

Llewellyn, Matthew P. 2011. Special Issue: Rule Britannia-Nationalism, Identity and the Modern Olympic Games. *The International Journal of the History of Sport, 28*(5).

Lucas, John. 1980. *The Modern Olympic Games.* Cranberry, PA: Barnes and Company.

Ludwig, Jack. 1976. *Five Ring Circus.* Toronto: Doubleday Canada.

Lyon, David. 2003. *Surveillance after September 11.* Cambridge: Polity Press.

MacAloon, John. 1981. *This Great Symbol: Pierre de Coubertin and the Origins of the Modern Olympic Games.* Chicago: University of Chicago Press.

MacAloon, John (Ed.). 1984a. *Rite, Drama, Festival, Spectacle: Rehearsals toward a Theory of Cultural Performance.* Philadelphia: Institute for the Study of Human Issues Press.

MacAloon, John. 1984b. "Olympic Games and the Theory of Spectacle in Modern Societies." In: John MacAloon (Ed.) *Rite, Drama, Festival, Spectacle: Rehearsals Toward a Theory of Cultural Performance.* Institute for the Study of Human Issues, Philadelphia, pp. 241–280.

MacAloon, John. 1989. "Festival, Ritual and Television." In: Roger Jackson and Tom McPhail (Eds) *The Olympic Movement and the Mass Media: Past, Present and Future Issues.* Calgary: Hurford, pp. 6–21.

MacAloon, John. J. 1990. Steroids and the State: Dubin, Melodrama and the Accomplishment of Innocence. *Public Culture, 2*(2): 41–64.

MacAloon, John. 1992. The Ethnographic Imperative in Comparative Olympic Research. *Sociology of Sport Journal, 9*(2): 104–130.

MacAloon, John. 1999. "Anthropology at the Olympic Games. An Overview." In: Arne Martin Klausen (Ed.) *Olympic Games as Performance and Public Event.* New York, Oxford. Berghahn Books, pp. 9–26.

MacAloon, John. J. 2006. "The Theory of Spectacle: Reviewing Olympic Ethnography." In: Alan Tomlinson and Christopher Young (Eds) *National Identity and Global Sports Events: Culture, Politics, and Spectacle in the Olympics and the Football World Cup.* State University of New York Press, pp. 15–39.

MacAloon, John. 2009. "Genre and Risk in Olympic Ceremonies." In: R.Schlesier and U. Zellmann (Ed.) *Ritual als provoziertes Risiko.* Berlin: Konigshausen and Neumann, pp. 31–52.

MacAloon, John J. 2012. Introduction: The Olympic Flame Relay. Local Knowledges of a Global Ritual Form. *Sport in Society, 15*(5): 575–594.

Makepeace, R. W. 1980. *Marxist Ideology and Soviet Criminal Law.* London: Croom Helm Ltd.

Mallon, Bill. 2000. The Olympic Bribery Scandal. *Journal of Olympic History, 8*(2), 11–27.

Mandel, Robert. 2002. *Armies without States: The Privatization of Security.* Boulder: Lynne Reinner.

Mandell, Richard D. 1991. *The Olympics of 1972. A Munich Diary.* University of North Carolina Press.

Marcus, George. 1995. Ethnography in/of the World System: The Emergence of Multi-Sited Ethnography. *Annual Review of Anthropology, 24*: 94–117.

Marshall, Tim. 1996. Barcelona: Fast Forward? City Entrepreneurialism in the 1980s and 1990s. *European Planning Studies, 4*(2): 147–165.

Marshall, Tim. 2000. Urban Planning and Governance: Is there a Barcelona model? *International Planning Studies, 5*(3): 299–319.

Marshall, Tim (Ed.). 2004. *Transforming Barcelona.* London: Routledge.

Martinkova, Irena. 2012. Pierre de Coubertin's Vision of the Role of Sport in Peaceful Internationalism. *Sport in Society, 15*(6): 788–797.

Mayers, Marjorie. 2001. *Street Kids and Streetscapes: Panhandling, Politics and Prophecies.* New York; Washington, DC: Peter Lang.

McCann, Eugene. 2009. "City marketing." In: Rob Kitchin and Nigel Thrift (Eds) *International Encyclopedia of Human Geography Vol. 2.* Oxford: Elsevier Ltd, pp. 119–124.

McCoy, Alfred. 2009. *Policing America's Empire: The United States, the Philippines, and the Rise of the Surveillance State.* Madison: University of Wisconsin Press.

McCoy, Katherine. 2009. Uncle Sam Wants Them. *Contexts, 8*(1): 14–19.

McKenna, Brian and Susan Purcell. 1980. *Drapeau.* Toronto: Clark Irwin.

McRoberts, Kenneth. 2001. *Catalonia: Nation Building Without a State.* Oxford: Oxford University Press.

Mertin, Evelyn. 2009. *Sowjetisch-deutsche Sportbeziehungen im "Kalten Krieg."* Sankt-Augustin: Academia Verlag.

Mitchell, Don and Nik Heynen. 2009. The Geography of Survival and the Right to the City: Speculations on Surveillance, legal Innovation, and the Criminalization of Intervention. *Urban Geography, 30*(6): 611–632.

Mitrou, Lilian. 2010. "Is there Privacy in Public Spaces?" (in Greek) In: Minas Samatas (Ed.) *Opseis tis neas parakolouthisis.* Athens: Vivliorama, pp. 179–210.

Miyoshi, Masao and H. D. Harootunian (Eds). 1993. *Japan in the World.* Durham, NC: Duke University Press.

Molnar, Adam and Lauren Snider. 2011. "Mega-events and Mega-profits: Unraveling the Vancouver 2010 Security-Development Nexus." In: Colin Bennett and Kevin

Haggerty (Eds) *Security Games: Surveillance and Control at Mega-Events*. London: Routledge, pp. 150–168.

Monclús, Francisco-Javier. 2003. The Barcelona Model: An Original Formula? From "Reconstruction" to Strategic Urban Projects, 1979–2004. *Planning Perspectives* (18): 399–421.

Monclús, Francisco-Javier. 2007. "Barcelona." In: John R. Gold and Margaret M. Gold (Eds) *Olympic Cities: City Agendas, Planning and the World's Games, 1896–2012*. London: Routledge, pp. 218–236.

Moriarty, Elizabeth. 1972. The Communitarian Aspect of Shinto Matsuri. *Asian Folklore Studies*, 31: 91–140.

Morris, Ivan I. 1960. *Nationalism and the Right Wing in Japan: A Study of Post-war Trends*. London: Oxford University Press.

Morris-Suzuki, Tessa. 1984. *Show: An Inside History of Hirohito's Japan*. London: Athlone.

Murakami Wood, David and Kiyoshi Abe. 2011. "The Spectacle of Fear: Anxious Events and Contradictions of Contemporary Japanese Govermentality." In: Colin Bennett and Kevin Haggerty (Eds) *Security Games: Surveillance and Control at Mega-Events*. London: Routledge, pp. 72–86.

Nakano, Osamu. 1997. Sengo no sesô o yomu [Reading Post-war Social Condition]. Tôkyô: Iwanami shoten. NHK. 1967. Tôkyô orinpikku [The Tôkyô Olympics]. Tôkyô: Nihon hôsô kyôkai hôsô yoron chôsajo.

Nederveen Pieterse, Jan. 2009 [2003]. "Three Paradigms." In: *Globalization and Culture: Global Mélange* (2nd ed.). Lanham, MD: Rowman & Littlefield.

Neiger, Motti, Oren Meyers and Eyal Zandberg. 2011. *On Media Memory: Collective Memory in a New Media Age*. Palgrave Macmillan.

Nitobe, Inazô. 1900. *Bushido: The Soul of Japan*. Philadelphia: Leeds & Biddle.

O'Reilly, Conner. 2011. "From Kidnapping to Contagious Diseases": Elite Rescue and the Strategic Expansion of the Transnational Security Consultancy Industry. *International Political Sociology*, 5: 178–197.

Oguma, E. 2009 [1968]. jou: wakamonotachi-no hanran to sono haikei, 1968 ge: hanran-no shyuuen.

Ok, Gwang. 2008. *Sport Loving Nation: Cultural Legacy of the '88 Seoul Olympics*, presented at the Beijing Forum, November 8.

Ok, Gwang and Nam-gil Ha. 2011. "Beyond all Barriers: the Significance of the '88 Seoul Olympics." In: William Kelly and Susan Brownell (Eds) *The Olympics in East Asia: Nationalism, Regionalism, and Globalism on the Center Stage of World Sports*, Yale CEAS Occasional Publications, Vol. 3. New Haven: Yale University Council on East Asian Studies, pp. 95–108.

Padilla, Tanalis. 2008. *Rural Resistance in the Land of Zapata: The Jaramillista Movement and the Myth of the Pax Priista, 1940–1962*. Durham, NC: Duke University Press.

Papanicolaou, Georgios. 2011. *Transnational Policing and Sex Trafficking in Southeast Europe*. Basingstoke: Palgrave Macmillan.

Parks, Jennifer. 2009. *Red Sport, Red Tape: The Olympic Games, the Soviet Sports Bureaucracy, and the Cold War, 1952–1980*. Unpublished Doctoral Dissertation. University of North Carolina, Chapel Hill.

Patterson, James. 1979. *The Jericho Commandment*. New York: Crown.

Perec, Georges. 1996. *W or The Memory of Childhood*. London: Harvill Press.

Perry, Elizabeth J. 2007. Studying Chinese Politics: Farewell to Revolution? *China Journal*, 57(Jan.): pp. 1–22.

Pfeiffer, Lorenz. 2001. "Die Olympische Sommerspiel '72 in München. Sportlicher Systemvergleich auf dem Boden des Klassenfeindes." In: Michael Krüger (Ed.)

Olympische Spiele. Bilanz und Perspektiven im 21. Jahrhundert. Lit Verlag Münster, pp. 90–110.

Pfeiffer, Rolf. 1987. *Sport und Politik. Die Boykottdiskussionen um die Olympischen Spiel von Mexico City 1968 bis Los Angeles 1984,* Verlag Peter Lang, Frankfurt am Main

Pi-Sunyer, Oriol. 1995. Under Four Flags: The Politics of National Identity in the Barcelona Olympics. *Political and Legal Anthropology Review, 18*(1): 35–56.

Poniatowska, Elena. 1993. *La Noche de Tlatelolco.* [*Massacre in Mexico.*] Helen R. Lane, Trans. Mexico: Biblioteca ERA.

Pound, Richard W. 1994. *Five Rings Over Korea, The Secret Negotiations Behind the 1988 Olympic Games in Seoul.* Boston: Little, Brown and Company.

Pound, Richard W. 2004. *Inside the Olympics, a Behind-the-Scenes Look at the Politics, the Scandals, and the Glory of the Games.* Toronto: John Wiley & Sons Canada Ltd.

Provine, Marie, Paul Lewis, Monica Varsanyi, and Scott H. Decker. 2012. A Multilayered Jurisdictional Patchwork: Immigration Federalism in the United States. *Law and Policy Quarterly, 34*(2): 138–158.

Prozumenshchikov, Mikhail. 2004. *Bol'shoi Sport i Bol'shaja Politika.* Moscow: Rosspen. (In Russian: Прозуменщиков, Михаил. 2004. Большой Спорт и Большая Политика, Москва: Росспэн.)

Puijk, Roel. 1999. "Producing Norwegian Culture for Domestic and Foreign Gazes: The Lillehammer Olympic Opening ceremony." In: Arne Martin Klausen (Ed.) *Olympic Games as Performance and Public Event.* New York, Oxford: Berghahn Books, pp. 97–136.

Pujadas, Xavier and Carles Santacana. 1992. The Popular Olympic Games, Barcelona, 1936: Olympians and Antifascists. *International Review for the Sociology of Sport, 27*(2): 139–149.

Rasmussen, Mikkel Vedbi. 2002. A Parallel Globalization of Terror: 9–11, Security and Globalization. *Cooperation and Conflict: Journal of the Nordic International Studies Association, 3*: 323–349.

Reeve, Simon. 2006. *One Day in September: The Full Story of the Munich Olympic massacre and the Israeli revenge operation "Wrath of God."* New York: Arcade Publishing, p. 228.

Richards, Anthony, Pete Fussey, and Andrew Silke (Eds). 2011. *Terrorism and the Olympics: Major Event Security and Lessons for the Future.* New York: Routledge.

Roche, Maurice. 2000. *Mega-events and Modernity: Olympics and Expos in the Growth of Global Culture.* London: Routledge.

Rose, Nikolas. 1999. *Powers of Freedom: Reframing Political Thought.* Cambridge: Cambridge University Press.

Rothschild, Emma. 1995. What is security? *Daedalus, 124*(3): 53–98.

Rowe, David. 2012. The Bid, the Lead-Up, the Event and the Legacy: Global Cultural Politics and Hosting the Olympics. *British Journal of Sociology, 63*(2): 285–305.

Rudie, Ingrid. 1998. "Making Persons in a Global Ritual? Embodied Experience and Free-Floating Symbols in Olympic Sport." In: Felicia Hughes-Freeland and Mary M. Crain (Eds) *Recasting Ritual. Performance, Media, Identity.* London and New York: Routledge, pp. 115–136.

Rudie, Ingrid. 1999. "Equality, Hierarchy and Pure Categories. Gender Images in Olympic Sport." In: Arne Martin Klausen (Ed.) *Olympic Games as Performance and Public Event.* New York, Oxford: Berghahn Books, pp. 173–194.

Sakharov, Andrei. 1991. *Mein Leben.* Munich: Piper.

Sakurai, Tetsuo. 1993. *Shisô toshite no 60-nendai* [*The 60s as Ideology*]. Tôkyô: Chikuma.

Samatas, Minas. 2007. Security and Surveillance in the Athens 2004 Olympics. *International Criminal Justice Review, 17*(3): 220–238.

Samatas, Minas. 2008. "From Thought-Control to the Traffic-Control: CCTV Politics of Expansion and Resistance in Post-Olympics Greece." In: Mathieu Deflem (Ed.) *Surveillance and Governance.* Bingley: Emerald, pp. 345–369.

Samatas, Minas. 2011. "Surveilling the 2004 Athens Olympics in the Aftermath of 9/11." In: Colin Bennett and Kevin Haggerty (Eds) *Security Games: Surveillance and Control at Mega-Events.* London: Routledge, pp. 55–71.

Sarantakes, Nicholas Evan. 2011. *Dropping the Torch: Jimmy Carter, the Olympic Boycott, and the Cold War.* New York: Cambridge University Press.

Sasaki-Uemura, Wesley. 2001. *Organizing the Spontaneous: Citizen Protest in Postwar Japan.* Honolulu, HI: University of Hawai'i Press.

Sassen, Saskia. 2008. *Territory, Authority, Rights: From Medieval to Global Assemblages.* Princeton: Princeton University Press.

Satterthwaite, Margaret L. 2006. Rendered Meaningless: Extraordinary Rendition and the Rule of Law. *New York University Public Law and Legal Theory Working Papers,* Paper 43.

Scheppele, Kim Lane. 2010. The International Standardization of National Security Law. *Journal of National Security Law and Policy, 4*: 437–453.

Schiller, Kay and Christopher Young. 2010. *The 1972 Munich Olympics and the Making of the Modern Germany.* Berkley: University of California Press.

Schnell, Scott. 1995. Ritual as an Instrument of Political Resistance in Rural Japan. *Journal of Anthropological Research, 51*: 301–328.

Seidensticker, Edward. 1990. *Tokyo Rising: The City Since the Great Earthquake.* New York: Knopf.

Senn, Alfred E. 1999. *Power, Politics, and the Olympic Games: A History of the Power Brokers, Events and Controversies that Shaped the Games.* Champaign, IL: Human Kinetics.

Shelley, Louise. 1984. "Urbanization and Crime: The Soviet Experience." In: Henry W. Morton and Robert C. Stuart (Eds) *The Contemporary Soviet City.* New York: Sharp, pp. 113–126.

Shue, Vivienne. 2004. "Legitimacy Crisis in China?" In: Peter Hays Gries and Stanley Rosen (Eds) *State and Society in 21st-century China: Crisis, Contention, and Legitimation.* New York: Routledge Curzon.

Silk, Michael L., David L. Andrews and C. L. Cole (Eds.) 2005. *Sport and Corporate Nationalisms.* Oxford, New York: Berg.

Simmel, George. 1971. *George Simmel on Individuality and Social Forms.* Donald Levine (Ed.).

Singer, Peter W. 2003. *Corporate Warriors: The Rise of the Privatized Military Industry.* Ithaca: Cornell University Press.

Sleiman, Mark and Randy Lippert. 2010. Downtown Ambassadors, Police Relations and "Clean and Safe" Security. *Policing and Society: An International Journal of Research and Policy, 20*(3): 316–335.

Sloan, Elinor C. 2012. *Modern Military Strategy: An Introduction.* London and New York: Routledge.

Spicer, Tim. 1999. *An Unorthodox Soldier.* Edinburgh: Mainstream Publishing Company Ltd.

Spiro, Joanna. 2001. The Testimony of Fantasy in Georges Perec's *W ou le souvenir d'enfance. Yale Journal of Criticism, 14*(1): 115–154.

St. John, Graham (Ed.). 2008. *Victor Turner and Contemporary Cultural Performance.* New York, Oxford: Berghahn Books.

Stanger, Allison. 2009. *One Nation Under Contract: The Outsourcing of American Power and the Future of Foreign Policy*. New Haven: Yale.

Stoppani, Teresa. 2012. The Architecture of the Disaster. *Space and Culture, 15*(2): 135–150.

Stuart, Robert C. 1984. "The Sources of Soviet Urban Growth." In: Henry W. Morton and Robert C. Stuart (Eds) *The Contemporary Soviet City*. Armonk, New York: Sharp, pp. 25–42.

Tagsold, Christian. 2002. *Die Inszenierung der kulturellen Identität in Japan: Das Beispiel der Olympischen Spiele Tokyo 1964*. München: Iudicium.

Tagsold, Christian. 2007. "The Tôkyô Olympics as a Token of Renationalization." In: Andreas Niehaus and Max Seinsch (Eds) *Olympic Japan: Ideals and Realities of (Inter) nationalism*. Würzburg: Ergon-Verlag, pp. 111–129.

Tagsold, Christian. 2009. The 1964 Tokyo Olympics as Political Games. *Asia-Pacific Journal, 23*(3).

Taibo II, Paco Ignacio. 2004. *'68*. New York: Seven Stories Press.

Takagi, Masayuki. 1985. *Zengakuren to zenkyôtô [The All-Japan Federation of Student Self-Government Associations and the Council of All Student's Federation of Joint Fight]*. Tôkyô: Kôdansha.

Teetzel, Sarah. 2011. Rules and Reform: Eligibility, Gender Differences, and the Olympic Games. *Sport in Society: Cultures, Commerce, Media, Politics, 14*(3): 386–398.

Tenorio-Trillo, Mauricio. 1996. *Mexico at the World's Fairs: Crafting a Modern Nation*. Berkeley: University of California Press.

Thomas, Martin. 2007. *Empires of Intelligence: Security Services and Colonial Disorder after 1914*. University of California Press.

Tilly, Charles. 2001. "Welcome to the Seventeenth Century." In: Paul DiMaggio (Ed.) *The Twenty-First Century Firm: Changing Economic Organization in International Perspective*. Princeton: Princeton University Press, pp. 200–209.

Toohey, Kristine. 2008. Terrorism, Sport and Public Policy in the Risk Society. *Sport in Society, 11*(4): 429–442.

Toohey, Kristine and A. J. Veal. 2007. *The Olympic Games. A Social Science Perspective*, 2nd ed. Oxfordshire: CAB International.

Torpey, John. 2000. *The Invention of the Passport. Surveillance, Citizenship and the State*. Cambridge: Cambridge University Press.

Tremlett, Giles. 2006. *Ghosts of Spain: Travels Through a Country's Hidden Past*. London: Faber and Faber.

Trevizo, Dolores. 2006. Between Zapata and Che: A Comparison of Social Movement Success and Failure in Mexico. *Social Science History 30*(2 Summer): 197–229.

Tsoukala, Anastassia. 2006. The Security Issue at the 2004 Olympics. *European Journal for Sport and Society, 3*(1): 43–54.

Tsoukala, Anastassia. 2008. "Defining Terrorism in the Post-September 11th Era." In: Didier Bigo and Anastassia Tsoukala (Eds) *Terror, Insecurity and Liberty*. London: Routledge, pp. 49–99.

Tsoukala, Anastassia. 2009a. *Football Hooliganism in Europe. Security and Civil Liberties in the Balance*. Basingstoke: Palgrave Macmillan.

Tsoukala, Anastassia. 2009b. "Terrorist Threat, Freedom, and Politics in Europe." In: Patricia Noxolo and Jef Huysmans (Eds) *Security and Insecurity: Community, Citizenship and the "War on Terror."* Basingstoke: Palgrave Macmillan, pp. 71–88.

Tsoukala, Anastassia. 2010. "Risk-Focused Security Policies and Human Rights: The Impossible Symbiosis." In: Mark Salter (Ed.) *Mapping Transatlantic Security Relations*. London: Routledge, pp. 41–59.

Tsurumi, Shunsuke. 1991. *Sengo nihon no taishûka-shi [Japan's History of Massification in the Post-War Era]*. Tôkyô: Iwanami shoten.

Urry, John. 2003. *Global Complexity*. Malden, MA: Polity.

van Toorn, Tai. 2008. The Rules of the Road: New Media, Street Art, and Crime. *WRECK: Graduate Journal of Art History, Visual Art and Theory*, 2(1).

Vanolo, Alberto. 2008. The Image of the Creative City: Some Reflections on Urban Branding in Torino. *Cities*, 25(6): 370–382.

Vanolo, Alberto. 2015. The Image of the Creative City: Eight Years Later: Turin, Urban Branding and the Econcomic Crisis Taboo. *Cities*, 46: 1–7.

Virilio, Paul. 2007. *The Original Accident*. Translated by Julie Rose. Polity.

Vlastos, Stephen (Ed.). 1998. *Mirror of Modernity: Invented Traditions of Modern Japan*. Berkeley: University of California Press.

Wæver, Ole. 1995. "Securitization and Desecuritization." In: Ronnie Lipschutz (Ed.) *On Security*. New York: Columbia University Press, pp. 46–86.

Wagner-Pacifici, Robin. 2010. Theorizing the Restlessness of Events. *American Journal of Sociology*, 115(5): 1351–1386.

Walby, Sylvia. 1999. The New Regulatory State: The Social Powers of the European Union. *British Journal of Sociology*, 50: 118–140.

Weber, Max. 1964. *Theory of Social and Economic Organization*. New York: Free Press.

Williamson, Oliver E. 1975. *Markets and Hierarchies: Analysis and Antitrust Implications*. New York: The Free Press.

Williamson, Oliver E. 1985. *The Economic Institutions of Capitalism*. New York: The Free Press.

Wise, Mark and Richard Gibb. 1993. *Single Market to Social Europe: The European Community in the 1990s*. London: Longman.

Witherspoon, Kevin. 2008. *Before the Eyes of the World: Mexico and the 1968 Olympic Games*. DeKalb: Northern Illinois University Press.

Worrall, James. 2000. *My Olympic Journey: Sixty Years with Canadian Sport and the Olympic Games*. Toronto: Canadian Olympic Association.

Yamauchi, Toshihiro. 1976. Tennô no guntai: Sengo kenpôshi ni okeru mondai [The Emperor's Army: Problems in the Post-War History of the Constitution]. *Hôritsu jihô*, 4: 104–114.

Yttergren, Leif and Hans Bolling (Eds). 2012. *The 1912 Stockholm Olympics: Essays on the Competitions, the People, the City*. Jefferson, North Carolina: McFarland & Company, Inc.

Young, David. 1987. The Origins of the Modern Olympics: A New Version. *International Journal of the History of Sports*, 4(3): 271–300.

Yu, Ying, Francisco Klauser, and Gerald Chan. 2009. Governing Security at the 2008 Beijing Olympics. *International Journal of the History of Sport*, 26(3): 309–405.

Zedner, Lucia. 2009. *Security*. London: Routledge

Zimbalist, Andrew. 2015. *Circus Maximus: The Economic Gamble Behind Hosting the Olympics and the World Cup*. Washington, D. C.: The Brookings Institution Press.

Zolov, Eric. 2001. "Discovering a Land 'Mysterious and Obvious': The Renarrativizing of Postrevolutionary Mexico." In: Joseph Gilbert, Anne Rubenstein, and Eric Zolov (Eds) *Fragments of a Golden Age: the Politics and Culture of Mexico since 1940*. Durham, NC: Duke University Press, pp. 234–272.

Zolov, Eric. 2004. "Showcasing the 'Land of Tomorrow': Mexico and the 1968 Olympics." *The Americas*, 61(2 October): 159–188.

Zubok, Vladislav. 2009. *Zhivago's Children. The Last Russian Intelligentsia*. Cambridge: Belknap Press of Harvard University Press.

Index

420   *Index*

Printed and bound by CPI Group (UK) Ltd, Croydon, CR0 4YY